Major Problems in
American Women's History

MAJOR PROBLEMS IN AMERICAN HISTORY SERIES

GENERAL EDITOR

THOMAS G. PATERSON

Major Problems in
American Women's History

DOCUMENTS AND ESSAYS

FOURTH EDITION

EDITED BY

MARY BETH NORTON

CORNELL UNIVERSITY

RUTH M. ALEXANDER

COLORADO STATE UNIVERSITY

HOUGHTON MIFFLIN COMPANY
Boston   New York

For Grael and Lia
and
for Genny Nicole and Natalie

Publisher: Charles Hartford
Senior Consulting Editor: Jean Woy
Senior Development Editor: Jeffrey Greene
Project Editor: Aimee Chevrette
Editorial Assistant: Katherine Leahey
Senior Art and Design Coordinator: Jill Haber Atkins
Cover Design Manager: Anne S. Katzeff
Composition Buyer: Chuck Dutton
Manufacturing Manager: Karen Banks Fawcett
Senior Marketing Manager: Katherine Bates
Marketing Assistant: Lauren Bussard

Cover image: Smithsonian American Art Museum, Washington, DC / Art Resource, NY

Printed in the U.S.A.

Library of Congress Control Number: 2006928407

ISBN-13: 978-0-618-71918-1
ISBN-10: 0-618-71918-0

456789-DOC-10 09

Contents

CHAPTER 6

Women's Activism in the Early Republic

Page 140

CHAPTER 7

African American Women and Slavery

Page 175

C H A P T E R   8
White Women in the Civil War Crisis
Page 201

C H A P T E R   9
Women in the Trans-Mississippi Frontier West
Page 231

CHAPTER 10
Women's Work and Work Cultures in Modern America, 1890–1920s
Page 260

CHAPTER 11
The "New Woman" in Public Life and Politics, 1900–1930
Page 293

CHAPTER 15
Second-Wave Feminism in America, 1960–1990
Page 446

CHAPTER 16
Women, Social Change, and Reaction from the 1990s to the New Millennium
Page 501

Preface

Early in the twenty-first century, women from all backgrounds in the United States face daunting challenges that history can help to illuminate. Even though a majority of U.S. college students are female, on average college-educated women still have lower incomes than their male counterparts, and few women head major businesses, law firms, or large universities. At all levels of employment, female wage-workers— now constituting a large majority of all adult women—have lower earnings as a group than do comparably situated men. In the current economic climate, most households need two incomes to survive financially, so relatively few married women can afford to leave the labor force, even if they have very young children. Significant numbers of divorced and never-married mothers must raise and support their children largely alone. Thus, adult women at all economic levels confront the difficulties of balancing family and employment responsibilities. The rising number of female immigrants, both documented and undocumented, compounds such problems. Foreign-born women earn less than their native-born counterparts and are considerably more likely than foreign-born men to live in poverty.

Studying American women's history helps us to understand such trends and to recognize which aspects of these developments are new and which are more familiar, albeit in altered form. For example, the late nineteenth century also witnessed high levels of immigration and high levels of labor-force participation by household members other than adult men—although at that time the additional workers were children rather than adult women. In the early decades of the twentieth century, women from upper- and middle-class families attended colleges in proportions that subsequently fell dramatically and were not reached again until the 1970s. Political controversies involving reproduction—such as the debates over sex education, birth control, and abortion that seemingly date from the Supreme Court's famous *Roe v. Wade* decision (1973)—also have historical roots; Americans first began arguing about these subjects more than 150 years ago. Only in relatively recent years has the development of women's history brought to light the details about such aspects of the American past.

American women's history has been a subject of serious scholarly inquiry for about four decades. Until the mid-1960s, the study of history was dominated by men who showed little interest in studying the history of the other sex. That pattern changed dramatically when two interrelated developments had an enormous impact on the practice of history in the United States. First, the modern feminist movement erupted in the general turmoil of the sixties, and women pressed for equality with men in all areas of life. Second, appreciable numbers of women began to enter the historical profession, partly as a result of the new employment opportunities that had become available to them.

The demonstrations, riots, and iconoclastic atmosphere of the 1960s and 1970s helped to create a revolution in the way history was studied, bringing to the fore questions about ordinary people, their families, and their work lives in what has come to be called "the new social history." By the mid-1970s an increasing number of books and articles on women's experiences, most of them written by young female historians, began to appear in print. Graduate and undergraduate women could now study the history of their own sex in a formal educational setting, and men could learn the history of women just as women had long studied the history of men.

Today the field of American women's history is a lively one, characterized by disparate approaches to the subject and full of fervent debates, the most central of which we highlight in this fourth edition. Today's women's historians have gone beyond their roots in the new social history to study women using different methodologies and in a variety of contexts. Most recently, cultural history and an attention to language and categorization, commonly called "the linguistic turn," have achieved greater prominence in the field, as have studies that attempt to integrate women's history with the better-known history of men in such contexts as politics and law. Moreover, some scholars have now begun to study the history of gender, examining both women and men and how their lives, roles, and experiences differ because of their sexual identities. Yet most scholars still focus primarily on women, as do the essays in this volume.

For this fourth edition, we continue to emphasize multicultural diversity in women's experiences, an emphasis that brings into sharp focus the differences and similarities in women's experiences along lines of race and class. In addition, we have made significant changes in the contents of the volume. Throughout this edition, we have worked to include contributions from younger historians—such as Leslie Alexander, Virginia Bouvier, Daniel E. Bender, Megan Taylor Shockley, Alicia Chávez, and Wendy Kline, whose scholarship reveals the future direction of the field. One such historian, Kate Haulman, has contributed an essay written especially for this edition that provides an overview of the field. Chapter Two now focuses exclusively on Native American women. A new Chapter Three highlights recent work on witchcraft accusations. Chapter Four now includes Carole Shammas's classic essay on enslaved women's work in colonial Virginia, with related documents drawn from the records of George Washington and Landon Carter, and covers women's labor in California's Spanish missions. Chapter Six, on women's organizations in the antebellum years, is now more broadly cast, with an excerpt from Anne Boylan's important new comprehensive survey of the subject. Chapter Seven focuses exclusively on antebellum black women, both free and slave.

Material on sexuality, marriage, and women's bodies has been integrated into the appropriate historical periods instead of constituting a separate chapter. For example, Chapter Eleven, on the "new woman" of the early-twentieth century, now includes documents and essays on women reformers' calls for change in laws and cultural perceptions regarding prostitution and contraception. New documents and essays covering the late nineteenth century to the present day examine the history of women in the United States from a variety of ethnic, racial, socioeconomic, and immigrant backgrounds. Chapter Nine now includes Deena J. Gonzáles's essay about Gertrudis Barceló, an influential woman in nineteenth-century Santa Fe. A revised Chapter Ten includes an essay by Daniel E. Bender on Eastern European immigrant women who encountered persistent sexual harassment as garment workers in early-twentieth century sweatshops and factories. Chapter Twelve, on women in the Great Depression and the New Deal, has been revised to include Elaine Abelson's essay on women and homelessness. A new essay by Megan Taylor Shockley in Chapter Thirteen revises our understanding of African American women's resistance to racial discrimination in World War II industrial workplaces.

The last two chapters are completely reorganized. Chapter Fifteen now focuses on the multiple meanings of women's activism from the 1960s through the 1980s and includes new essays by Alicia Chávez and Wendy Kline about Latina activists and the feminist health movement. Chapter Sixteen covers American women since 1990. New documents in the chapter highlight the experiences of immigrant women, Chicanas, and "third-wave" feminists in contemporary America. This chapter also includes a new essay by Barbara Epstein about the persistence of "feminist consciousness" in a society that lacks a mass movement of women for gender equality.

The essays and documents in *Major Problems in American Women's History,* like those that appear in other books in this series, are intended to introduce students to a wide range of current scholarly approaches to key issues in the field. The book focuses on interpretive dialogues—that is, subjects on which historians disagree, either in their conclusions or in their emphases. In either case, the historians are engaging in perhaps their most important professional function: learning from and challenging each other's viewpoints in order to arrive at a better, more complete, and more accurate understanding of the past.

Each chapter opens with a brief introduction. There follows a selection of pertinent documents giving voice to participants in the issue explored by the chapter. Two or three essays then examine the subject from different viewpoints or approaches. Headnotes, setting the readings in historical and interpretive perspective, introduce each chapter's documents and essays sections. All writings are aimed at allowing students to reach their own conclusions. Each chapter ends with suggestions for further reading for students who would like to do additional research. Sources for all documents and essays are also provided.

Instructors and students who want to continue their study of women's history are encouraged to join organizations and subscribe to journals specializing in this subject area. The most important organizations promoting women's history in the United States are regional: the Western Association of Women Historians (http://www.wawh.org/), the Southern Association for Women Historians (http://www.h-net.org/~sawh/), the Berkshire Conference of Women Historians (http://www.berksconference.org/), and Women and Gender Historians of the Midwest (http://department.monm.edu/wghom/Default.htm). The most important American journal is the *Journal of Women's History,* published by Johns Hopkins University Press (http://www.press.jhu.edu/).

We are grateful to the scholars who reviewed the third edition and offered helpful suggestions for this revision: Amy Sue Bix, Iowa State University; Joyce Hanson, California State University, San Bernardino; Gwen Kay, SUNY Oswego; Rebecca Mead, Northern Michigan University; and Amy Richter, Clark University.

We also thank the many readers and users who helped us with the previous editions: Cara Anzilotti, Gail Bederman, Kathleen C. Berkeley, Joan Jacobs Brumberg, Jane Caplan, Patricia Cline Cohen, Sarah Deutsch, Nancy M. Forestell, Jane Hunter,

Carol F. Karlsen, Susan Estabrook Kennedy, Molly Ladd-Taylor, Ann J. Lane, Carolyn Lawes, Heather Munro Prescott, Sarah Stage, Pamela Tyler, Laurel Ulrich, and Nancy C. Unger.

For help in locating and copying documents and essays for this edition, the authors thank Karen Thomas, Suzy Denvir, and Jeremy Gatz-Miller. Ruth Alexander acknowledges financial assistance from the History Department at Colorado State University; Mary Beth Norton received aid from the Return Jonathan Meigs III Fund at Cornell University. Finally, we are grateful for the editorial assistance offered by Thomas G. Paterson, the general editor of the Major Problems in American History series; Jean Woy, Senior Consulting Editor; and Terri Wise, Development Editor.

M.B.N.
R.M.A.

*Major Problems in
American Women's History*

Approaches to American Women's History

As the field of women's history has matured in the United States in the past four decades, scholars' emphases have changed significantly. Initially concerned with rescuing from undeserved obscurity those women who had played a leadership role in the American past, historians later moved on to investigating women's lives in the "private sphere," to broadening the definition of "politics" to encompass many aspects of women's "public" activities, to examining the experiences of ordinary working women (both free and enslaved), and, more recently, to considering the implications of the development of the conceptual category "woman" in and of itself. Throughout, they have kept women—a previously ignored component of the population—at the center of their inquiry, even when they have added a consideration of men and masculinity to their studies, thus creating the new field of gender history.

Historians today confront a series of important issues when they set out to write "women's" history. Initially they have to define which women they are studying, because past scholarship has clearly demonstrated that women's lives differed dramatically, most obviously because of their race, ethnic, or class background, but for other reasons as well (for example, their level of education or their sexual orientation). Then historians have to develop useful analytical questions in order to go beyond the mere retrieval of information, however intrinsically interesting that information might seem to be. And finally they have to place the women they are studying in the appropriate historical contexts, for abstracting women's experiences from particular times and places can lead to ahistorical misunderstandings. While accomplishing all these tasks, they must also remain mindful of key historiographical and theoretical concerns that they address both implicitly and explicitly in their works.

ESSAYS

The four essays reprinted here provide an introduction to contemporary thinking about women's history in the United States. Kate Haulman, who teaches at Ohio State University, wrote especially for this volume a brief survey of the development of American women's history, or its *historiography*. She addresses the important issue

1

of definitions: what exactly does "American women's history" mean? The next essay, by a German historian, Gisela Bock, critically examines the dichotomous approaches that, in her view, have too often dominated women's historians' debates on key interpretive issues. Antonia I. Casteñeda, a professor at the University of California, Santa Barbara, approaches the writing of western history from the perspective of a woman of color, arguing that historians have to be sensitive to the diversity of ethnicities, cultures, and races in the American west in order to recapture the experience of all the region's women. Finally, Leslie Alexander, a historian at Ohio State, critiques standard feminist accounts of black women's history, contending that for African American women their identity as both black and female can be a source of strength. In doing so, she challenges the more common approach, which regards the combination of gender identity and racial minority status as representing a dual oppression. Together, the essays raise a key question: is it possible to take the same approach to writing a comprehensive history of all of America's women, or must historians employ different categories of analysis for different groups while simultaneously avoiding dichotomous thinking?

Defining "American Women's History"

KATE HAULMAN

One major problem facing scholars of American women's history is defining what the study of women's history is, and why anyone undertakes it. From the field's inception, practitioners of women's history have been remarkably reflective, creating a theory and a history of women's history alongside its practice. In the space of a generation, women's history has expanded from a politically-informed outgrowth of social history, with its inclusion of people other than "Great Men" in historical narratives, into a field with the power to alter the histories of women, men, and the societies they inhabit. But, like all histories, the interpretations—both of women's history scholarship and the story of the rise of women's history—shift according to the needs of the present. What, then, from the vantage point of the early twenty-first century, is this thing called "American Women's History," and what is its purpose? What has it accomplished, and what does it continue to do for its practitioners, readers, and the society from which it emerges? These questions can best be answered in two ways: by surveying the history of women's history and then examining the field's defining terms. Such an approach reveals that the project of "American" "Women's" "History" has implications for issues of social justice that arise from questioning the field's defining terms and yet extend beyond them.

In 1975, Gerda Lerner charted an early history of women's history that remains the standard narrative. As she recounted, scholars initially sought out "notable women," or "women worthies," to study, exceptional individuals who nonetheless remained largely invisible within traditional histories. The standards by which they were judged "exceptional" and thus worthy of scholarly attention—often their wealth, proximity to "notable" men, and in some instances the women's own accomplishments—were limiting and limited to figures such as physicist and Nobel

---

Prize winner Marie Curie or first lady Eleanor Roosevelt. These criteria for deter-mining who and what merited historical study persisted in slightly altered form into a "contribution" phase of women's history. This approach incorporated more than just the Marie Curies of the world into the study of the past through consideration of their "contributions" to events such as war efforts and political movements. Think of Clara Barton, founder of the Red Cross, and the nurses who served Union troops during the American Civil War. Yet, circumscribed as it was by conventional ways of selecting and defining historically important topics, contributionist work, like a focus on women worthies, remained women's history on "male" terms. Curie merited study because she revolutionized the male-dominated realm of physics, while Barton was significant because she founded a national organization. Both highly visible women received recognition and praise in their own times for their "exceptional" accomplishments. Yet their experiences by no means represented the majority of women's lives.

With the advent of new social history came a widening of history's lens, lead-ing to a seismic shift in what constituted women's history. Social history sprung in part from the equal rights movements of the mid-twentieth century. Its practitioners looked to recover usable pasts, stories such as the history of African American ac-tivism or of Native American cultural resistance that might ground current political and social struggles. Writers of social history adopted sociological models, and created demographic, methodological, and conceptual changes in the practice of his-tory. First, scholars began to consider more people—indeed, all people—worthy of historical examination and analysis, striving to recover the experiences of large swaths of the human population who had remained voiceless and invisible in existing histories. Historians chronicled the lives of factory workers in the American north-east and slaves in the antebellum South, to cite just two examples, bringing such communities to light. In addition, people from various social backgrounds were writ-ing history. Out of the impulse toward and reality of greater inclusion arose the need to examine different source materials—census data, probate records, artifacts—that might yield information about lives formerly unseen and uninterpreted by historians. Researchers dug into recently-recognized historical evidence with new questions, or found that making sense of those documents required fresh queries. For instance, what kinds of material possessions did working-class New Yorkers own, and how did the stuff of life contribute to class identity? These revolutions in the subjects and conductors of research, in source materials, and in historical questions proceeded almost simultaneously and reinforced each another.

The concerns and methods of social history helped to revolutionize the practice of women's history, which in turn altered the larger discipline. As scholars looked for "ordinary" women in the historical record, they realized that the old parameters, the old ways of doing history would not suffice. The sources revealed lives and experiences that demanded to be understood on their own terms, not merely in re-lation to the ostensible "big events" of history such as wars and elections. Perhaps ironically, as the Women's Movement of the 1960s and 1970s fought for inclusion and equal opportunity within bastions of male power such as the government and the workplace, scholars of women's history were illuminating separate "female worlds" of work and play that had existed and functioned in some distinction from masculine spaces and institutions. As Carroll Smith-Rosenberg demonstrated in her 1975 article "The Female World of Love and Ritual," a study of middle-class white women in Victorian America, women were often most profoundly connected to one another, spinning gold out of the straw of exclusion. They created rich, supportive social networks that seemed to exist apart from the eyes and influence of men. The "bonds of womanhood," argued historian Nancy Cott in her influential book of the same name, confined women to a domestic realm of home and family, but also knit them together. These were politically galvanizing stories for a generation of scholars and activists creating a women's movement grounded in female communities.

Indeed, the intersecting political and scholarly women's movements strove to raise women's consciousness of themselves *as women* by exposing the institutional, material, and cultural forces that produced long-standing oppression, as well as the opportunities (however circumscribed) that arose from being female at various times and places. The data and interpretations that emerged from social history and women's history complicated existing overarching narratives by presenting alternate stories, chronologies, and periodizations. History textbooks and courses, particularly the large surveys of United States history and western civilization, were typically organized by wars and battles, the rise and fall of empires, and political events such as elections or treaties. But perhaps other perspectives produced different ways of understanding change over time. Perhaps the most significant dividing point in a two-part survey course in U.S. history was not the Civil War but the shift in an industrializing nation to separate "spheres" of home and work, with their gender-bound associations; or the first women's rights convention held at Seneca Falls, New York in 1848; or the passage of the Fourteenth Amendment in 1869 with its inclusion of the word "male" into the Constitution, explicitly making men subject to due process of law and thus implicitly excluding women. By centering a new group of historical actors and their experiences, scholars created histories that both stood apart from and revised existing ways of understanding the past.

Yet the social history phase of women's history that flowered during the 1970s and 1980s presented several limitations, out of which grew the next phase of women's history in the 1990s. First, scholars tended to assess the female worlds they had uncovered, such as the "private" space of middle-class domestic life, apart from men and their ostensible "public" realms. Although a necessary step in claiming a place for women in history irrespective of their relationships to men, such a focus may have distorted, rather than illuminated, the reality of women's lives. Were not many of the participants in the "female world of love and ritual," married to men? Furthermore, did women not leave their homes to enter the "public" arena? And what of salons, mixed-sex gatherings in which women directed conversation on topics intellectual, cultural, and political in their own homes? As Lerner's essay suggested, one way forward was to assess male and female cultures, insofar as they existed independently, in intersection. But would such integration look like the results of a recipe that instructed scholars to "add women and stir"? Would this kind of inclusion keep women marginalized both in historical narratives and contemporary life, ever apart and "different," never part of the main story?

Second, like the women's movement itself, early women's history tended to focus on white, middle- and upper-class women in western or "developed" nations, treating their experiences as normative and using their lives to represent those of all women. This problem of privilege and exclusion could not be solved through mere inclusion in accordance with a "multicultural" or "diversity" model. Such incorporation was perhaps a necessary first step, but one that quickly revealed the limits of representational politics and scholarship. In much the same ways in which practitioners of women's history knew that the revision of traditional histories was not possible through "adding women," scholars studying women who had remained outside the bounds of women's history did not hope simply to add "women of color" or "working-class women" to the mix. To truly alter textbook narratives, a conceptual shift was required, one that resulted from both limitations of women's history as social history as well as a third presumption that underpinned its practice: namely, the category "woman" itself was implicitly assumed to be a given, an unalterable biological, and therefore social and cultural, reality.

But scholars began to consider that perhaps "woman" was no more constant and unchanging across time and place than were gender roles, which vary widely from society to society. Cultures define "man" and "woman" through encouraging or prohibiting activities that they regard as one and not the other, creating a dichotomy and thus giving meaning to the terms the actions perform—knitting as "woman's" work versus carpentry as "man's," to use one example. If a "man" knits is he still a "man"? And is knitting still "woman's" work?

Attention to the power of language to shape and give meaning to human experience provided ways to shake off some of the constraints of women's history as social history. Joan Wallach Scott's 1988 essay "Gender: A Useful Category of Analysis" called for the consideration of "woman," "female," and "feminine" as concepts shaped by the societies in which they existed, rather than static realities. If "woman" was a construction, albeit one that produced social and cultural experiences for those who inhabited the category, then other kinds of identity were also created rather than preexisting and unchanging. Most critically for the cause of gender studies, scholars began to consider "man" or "male" as a topic of inquiry, not the assumed and normal standard against which all other forms of identity were measured. Heeding Lerner's call to analyze male and female cultures, masculinity and femininity, in relationship to one another required making men visible *as men.* Putting women at the center of historical inquiry made understanding gender roles and relationships paramount. Such a focus in turn allowed for the incorporation of men as gendered subjects of history. This examination of sex/gender categories led to the questioning of other binaries, such as public and private, nature and culture, long thought to correspond to "male" and "female" in essential ways.

Yet the move to gender history, however rooted in women's history, had its detractors. Some felt that it compromised a feminist political project based on the identity of "woman" as a rights-bearing individual within the nation, and thus undermined "women" as a coherent political action group. If there was no "woman," per se, then who were the people who called for change on the basis of their positions as "women"? If a person's identity, either as a woman or a Native American or so forth was not stable, how could identity-driven politics succeed? Similar questions plagued other nationally-based rights movements that intersected with scholarly pursuits. Was the cause of civil rights in the United States best served by assuming the existence of "black" actors within history, or by the notion of racial identity as constantly created and in flux? Indeed, were these either/or propositions?

Two problems characterized these debates: first, scholars working in a particular field too often considered the making of their own terms of identity and inquiry apart from others. Thus, much like its predecessor, gender history might look normatively white while the history of race, for example, remained normatively male. Second, they often failed to appreciate the political uses of integrating analyses of topics such as land use with analyses of language and anthropological approaches to social practices. For instance, the development of chattel slavery in seventeenth-century Virginia resulted in part from the collision of English, Native American, and African cultures. In particular, different gender systems with respect to agricultural labor, done by men in English tradition and by women in African and Native American cultures, intersected with Anglo-Virginians' need for that very form of labor to cultivate tobacco. The convergence of cultural difference and economic necessity resulted in a definition of womanhood that separated African from English women on the basis of their labor and allowed for the transition to race-based slavery.

Ideally, the linguistic and cultural "turns" within the discipline of history, fueled largely by the methods and theories of literature and anthropology, counteract both of these forms of blindness by insisting on the relationship among socioeconomic hierarchy, linguistic systems, and cultural practices, and by regarding identities as multiple. In this way, gender history can generate broad social critiques without surrendering a focus on people's lives. A woman who self-identified as Chinese American in mid-twentieth-century California was not Chinese American four days out of the week and a woman the other three—she was always both. In addition she inhabited or expressed a certain sexual orientation, occupation, and class position, among other things, all as relational as her gender identity, shifting in response to situation, circumstance, and her own actions. What were the larger contexts— nation, neighborhood, family—in which she located herself, through which she identified? The upshot of such an approach is this: if gender is created rather than assumed, fluid rather than fixed, then so too is race, ethnicity, health, age, work, social status, sexuality, and so on. Only through such an approach can women's and gender history, or any scholarly field, truly comprehend the differences as well as the commonalities among people's experiences. This is not mere inclusion or "diversity" for its own sake, but rather a way to make sense of how people have understood, worked within, and attempted to expand the limits of the human in various societies, and with what consequences.

In order to consider the consequences of doing "American Women's History," scholars must ponder the meaning of that phrase. All three of its parts present thorny conceptual issues. At first blush "American" seems the most uncomplicated, referring to a particular area of the world in which women have lived. Yet "American" is perhaps the most problematic and hotly contested, for it is all too often a substitute for "United States," bespeaking a kind of scholarly occupation of conceptual territory that has frequently mirrored political and economic imperialism in the western hemisphere. This text is often used in courses covering "American" or "United States" women's history. Does your institution offer a similar class focusing on Mexico or Brazil? Uncritically considering "American" to be synonymous with "U.S." and its nationalist narratives allows the "developed" world to colonize women's history. Yet, for the purposes of this anthology, "American" refers also to the period and place before nation making, in which various powers and groups of men and women competed for power. Such lessons from the study of the colonial period have powerful post-colonial repercussions. Women's historians have used the lens of gender to examine politics and policies within the American nation-state, as well as the very concept, formation, and nature of the nation. But they must also consider the influence of American gender ways on America's role in international movements such as globalization and trans-national feminism.

Lest these ways of using and questioning the term "American" seem too removed from people's experiences, it must be remembered that human lives lie at the heart of women's history. "American" is a category of identity like any other, one that people claim, create, or resist at various moments for various reasons. The young women who worked in New England's textile mills in the early nineteenth century viewed themselves as "American" in particular ways; Cherokee women petitioning against removal used "American" differently. The women who wrote "Talented Tenth" African American literature around the turn of the twentieth century defined "American" identity as well, whereas the women agitating for suffrage during World War I claimed American-ness in still different ways. Many socialist women—and men—rejected the label entirely. In order to write "American" women's history, scholars must ask what meaning and uses the term had for women in the past, and why.

The meaning of the term "Women's" is equally important to question. Most of the essays in this volume do not hold "woman" fixed, but rather consider its making in context and in relationship to other concepts that are nevertheless lived and experienced. The "Women's" in "American Women's History" has come to stand for scholarship on women and gender, neither of which can truly exist without the other, yet remains an important means of insisting on the centering of bodies and voices denoted to be "female" in various societies. Gender, or the assignment of roles and behaviors grounded in ideas of sexual difference, is perhaps the longest-standing and most fundamental means of generating concepts of "natural" differences among people, and creating the hierarchies that often result. It is gender that fills the terms "man" and "woman" or "male" and "female" with meaning. Who has defined the category "woman" and how? Who has claimed the identity "woman" and why? What are the consequences of identifying, or being positioned as a "woman," in intersection with other identities? How have women and the societies they helped create dealt with these issues in the past?

Which brings us, at last, to "History." History is not the past but rather the study of the past, and much ink has been spilled over its meaning and purpose. Methodologically, women's and gender history have borrowed fruitfully from other disciplines in ways that focus the intersection of ideas, institutions and practices, discourses and experiences. Its scholars are always recovering and reinventing the field, throwing off march-of-progress narratives for stories more complex, historically accurate, and of greatest contemporary use. There remains much room for the consciousness-raising mission of early women's history, in which stories about women in the past are told in order to ground and galvanize political action. Greater attention to women's history has the power to frame current debates about justice and human equality in far more productive terms and to inform women's decisions about work, family, finances, relationships, and more, helping people solve the problems of daily life. As for the major problems within the field of women's history, they are ever shifting; this is what makes the field so vibrant. But history of any stripe can only receive its due when its practitioners define not only for themselves but for a wide audience why they do what they do. The challenge is to constantly reassess the presumptions and practices that comprise "American Women's History," to rewrite women's history and the field's history not merely for its own sake, but in the service of confronting the greatest problem-turned-opportunity of all—creating a more just society.

Challenging Dichotomies in Women's History

GISELA BOCK

Women's history has come a long way. Some twenty years ago, Gerda Lerner wrote that "the striking fact about the historiography of women is the general neglect of the subject by historians." Historical scholarship was far from "objective" or "universal," because it was based on male experience, placed men at the centre and as a measure of all things human, thereby leaving out half of humankind. In the past two decades, the situation has changed considerably. In an enormous (and enormously growing) body of scholarship women have been rendered visible. They have been placed at the centre, and what women do, have to do, and want to do has been re-evaluated in view of social, political and cultural change, of an improvement in women's situations and, more generally, in terms of a change towards more freedom and justice. More precisely, what has been rendered historically visible by making women a subject of research was, in the first place, their subjection. In the second place, however, it was their subjectivity—because women are not only victims, but also actively shape their own lives, society and history.

Much of this research was carried out in the context of three conceptual or theoretical frameworks that have been used by many feminist scholars, particularly historians, in the past two decades and which will be outlined in the first section of this paper. These frameworks point to three dichotomies in traditional thought on gender relations, and all of them have been not only used, but also profoundly challenged. The second section will illustrate three further dichotomies which, in the development of modern women's history, have emerged more recently and which presently seem to dominate and direct women's studies. . . .

1. Nature versus culture.   It was mainly in the United States in the early 1970s that the relation of the sexes was discussed in terms of the relation, or rather dichotomy, between "nature and nurture" or "nature and culture." Men and their activities had been seen as culture and of cultural value, whereas women and their activities had been seen as natural, outside of history and society, always the same and therefore not worthy of scholarly, political or theoretical interest and inquiry. Moreover, it was the relations between the sexes, and most particularly their relations of power and subjection, that had been attributed to nature. "Nature," in this context,

Gisela Bock, "Challenging Dichotomies: Perspectives on Women's History," in *Writing Women's History: International Perspectives,* ed. Karen Offen et al. 1991, pp. 1–12, 15–17. Reprinted by permission of Gisela Bock.

most often meant sexuality between men and women, women's bodies and their capacity for pregnancy and motherhood. Fatherhood, however, was usually seen not as natural but as "social." Female scholars challenged this traditional dichotomy. They argued that what "nature" really meant in this discourse was a devaluation of everything that women stood for, that "'nature' always has a social meaning," that both "nature" and "culture" meant different things at different times, in different places and to the different sexes, and that women's bodies and bodily capacities were not always and everywhere seen as disabilities, but also as a basis for certain kinds of informal power and public activities. The nature/culture dichotomy was recognised as a specific and perhaps specifically Western way of expressing the hierarchies between the sexes. The binary terms of this dichotomy only apparently refer to antagonistic and independent terms; but in fact, they refer to a hierarchy of social realities and cultural meanings, between strongly interdependent terms. In other words: no such nature without such culture, and no such culture without such nature. One of the linguistic results of such insights in women's history is that the term "nature" is now almost always placed in quotation marks. . . .

2. Work versus family.   A second theoretical framework for rendering women visible, and for dismantling their identification with the merely natural, unchanging and therefore uninteresting, was the issue of their distinctive patterns of work. The discussion around it had its origins more in the European than in the American context, particularly in Italy, Britain, Germany and France. What had been seen as nature was now seen as work: bearing, rearing and caring for children, looking after the breadwinner-husband and after other family members. To call this activity "work" meant to challenge the dichotomy "work and family" (because the family may mean work to women), but also "work and leisure" (because men's leisure may be women's work), and "working men and supported wives" (because wives support men through their work). It meant questioning the view that work is only that which is done for pay. Women have always worked, and unpaid work was and is women's work. Obviously, men's work is valued more highly than women's work. In theoretical and economic terms, it has been demonstrated that women's work was overlooked by male theoreticians of work and the economy and why this happened; accordingly the value or "productivity" of domestic work came to be discussed. . . .

The sexual division of labour was found to be not just a division, but a hierarchy of labour; and not just one of labour but, primarily, a sexual division of value and rewards. The lower value of women's work continues—through economic and cultural mediation—in employment outside the home. Here, where women have always worked, they earned only 50 per cent to 80 per cent of men's earnings in the nineteenth and twentieth centuries in western countries, with variations over time and space. . . .

The apparent dichotomy between "work and family," between men as workers and women as "non-workers," turns out to be one between paid and unpaid work, between underpaid and decently paid work, between the superior and inferior value of men's and women's work respectively. The underlying assumption of mutually exclusive superiority and inferiority seems to be another common feature of such gender-linked dichotomies. The challenge posed by women's studies to this opposition is obviously linked to political and economic challenges to pay women's as yet unpaid work, to raise their earnings in low-pay jobs, and to admit more women to well-paid professions. It has also led to some linguistic changes. Even though, in the English language, the terms "working women" and "working mothers" are still reserved for employed women only, and non-employed women are still often called "non-working," the terms "work and family" are now often replaced by "paid and unpaid work." . . .

3. Public versus private.   A third conceptual framework of women's history has been the relation between the public and the private, or the political and the personal, or the sphere of power and the domestic sphere. Traditional political theory has seen them, again, as a dichotomy of mutually exclusive terms, identified with women's "sphere" and men's "world." Women's studies have profoundly challenged this view, pointing out its inadequacy for understanding politics and society. The slogan "the personal is political" indicated that the issue of power is not confined to "high politics," but also appears in sexual relations. Men inhabit, and rule within both spheres, whereas women's proper place was seen to be only in the domestic sphere and in her subjection to father or husband. This means, on the one hand, the dichotomy is not one between two autonomous, symmetrical and equivalent spheres, but rather a complex relation between domination and subordination, between power and powerlessness. On the other hand, women's studies have shown that the public "world" was essentially based on the domestic "sphere." Male workers, male politicians and male scholars perform their tasks only because they are born, reared and cared for by women's labour. The boundaries between public and private shift significantly over time and cross-culturally, as in the historical transition between private charity and public assistance, in both of which women played important roles. . . .

Women's history has also discovered that what is perceived as "private" by some may be seen as "public" by others. The domestic tasks of bearing and rearing children, for instance, were proclaimed as being of public importance by many women in the early women's movement. They requested that it be re-evaluated, and many of them based their demand for equal political citizenship precisely on this vision of the "separate sphere," understood not as a dichotomy of mutually exclusive and hierarchical terms, but as a source of equal rights and responsibilities of the female sex in respect to civil society. On this basis, they did not so much challenge the sexual division of labour, as the sexual division of power. . . .

These three dichotomies seem to have some important characteristics in common. They are eminently gender-linked, and as such they have distant roots in European and western traditions of gender perception. They have been taken up and used as crucial conceptual frameworks in the newly emerging women's history of the past decades, and simultaneously their long-standing apparent validity for the perception of gender relations has been thoroughly challenged. This challenge concerned the analysis, historicisation and deconstruction of the character and meaning of these three dual categories, as well as the links between them, and it questioned the traditional assumption that these dichotomies were expressions—natural and necessary expressions—of sexual difference.

The question has been raised as to whether these dichotomies are just a few examples among many similar binary oppositions and dualistic modes of western thought in general, or whether their gender-linked character makes them very special. . . . But it seems that, whenever they are used for describing gender relations, they do not refer so much to separate, autonomous, independent, equivalent dual spheres, as to relations of hierarchy: hierarchies of spheres, meanings, values, of inferiority and superiority, of subordination and power; in other words, to relations where "culture" subjects "nature," the world of "work" reigns over that of the "family," the "political" dominates the "private." . . .

Somehow, ironically, the same process by which women became historically (and not only historically) visible through the critique of these contradictories has also led to a number of new dichotomies of which little or nothing was heard during the first phase of women's studies, and which later came to the fore within the context of feminist scholarship itself. In part, they are the result of past attempts to resolve the earlier binary modes with the help of new concepts and theoretical frameworks. It seems that future strategies for women's history lie precisely, and once more, in the possibility and necessity of challenging these newer dichotomies.

1. Sex versus gender.   The concept "gender" has been introduced into women's history and women's studies in the 1970s as a social, cultural, political and historical category, in order to express the insight that women's subordination, inferiority and powerlessness are not dictated by nature, but are social, cultural, political and historical constructions. Whereas "gender" had previously referred mainly to linguistic-grammatical constructions, it now became a major theoretical framework. One of the reasons for its success in replacing the word "sex" has been the insistence that the study of women does not only deal with sexuality, wifehood and motherhood, but with women in all walks of life. Women's studies do not only concern half of humankind, but all of it, because it is not only women who are gendered beings, but also men who are therefore far from representing universal humanity. Consequently, "men's history" and "men's studies" which analyse men as "men" have emerged. The concept of "gender" radicalised and universalized the efforts to make women visible, and the insight that gender is a basic, though flexible structure of society meant that women's and gender studies concern, in principle, any field or object of historical (and non-historical) scholarship.

But the new terminology has also brought to the fore major problems. They result from the fact that the concept of gender has been introduced in the form of a dichotomy. It distinguishes categorically between gender and sex, "sex" to be understood as "biological" and "gender" as "social" or cultural, and both are seen as combined in a "sex/gender system" where "raw biological sex" is somehow transformed into "social gender." The dichotomous structure of the pair had been evident since the late 1950s when, even before being taken up by feminist scholarship, it came to be theorised by male scholars who studied intersexuals and transsexuals. But this dichotomy between the "biological" and the "social" does not resolve but only restates the old nature versus culture quarrel. Again, it relegates the dimension of women's body, sexuality, motherhood and physiological sexual difference to a supposedly pre-social sphere, and it resolves even less the question of precisely what part of women's experience and activity is "biological" and what part "social" or "cultural." . . .

In this situation, it is not the concept of gender that should be challenged—as some feminist historians seem to prefer at present—but the linguistic and theoretical dichotomy of sex and gender. Particularly in history, the humanities and social sciences, it might be challenged through using "gender" in a comprehensive sense which may include both the physiological and the cultural dimension, and using "sex" in the same sense as "gender," thus leaving space for continuities instead of polarities of meaning.

2. Equality versus difference.   The problems of the sex/gender dichotomy are closely related to those of another dichotomy with which we are faced today in a new way and in an international debate which has taken on different shapes and phases in different countries: that of "equality versus difference." Women's studies have largely relied on the concept of "sexual" or "gender equality" as an analytical tool, and physiological "difference" has been played down as insignificant because it has so often been used to justify discriminatory treatment of women. In this perspective, it has been demanded that women be treated in the same way as men, as if they were men, and that new laws and reforms be formulated in gender-neutral terms . . . , thus eliminating sexual difference and rendering masculinity and femininity politically irrelevant. Other feminist scholars, however, argue that burning issues such as rape, abortion or wife-battering cannot be dealt with adequately in gender-neutral terms; that female "difference," physiological as well as social, should not be erased but recognised, in historical, philosophical and legal terms; that it has never had a chance to develop autonomous political and cultural forms other than in social niches and in opposition to dominant cultures; that emphasis should be laid on a critical evaluation of men's distinctive needs and activities and that women's distinctive needs and activities should be valued, thus opening alternatives both to female inferiority and to women's assimilation to men. . . .

Some scholars tend to believe that the dichotomy "equality versus difference" is simply a false dichotomy, more the result of misunderstandings than of insight. But others insist on the mutually exclusive character of the relation between "equality" and "difference," and therefore on the necessity of an either/or choice. The historian Joan Hoff-Wilson urges that a decision be made, particularly by feminist leaders, between either "equality between the sexes based on prevailing masculine societal norms" or "justice between the sexes based on a recognition of equal, but different socialised patterns of behavior." On the other hand, the historian Joan Scott considers this to be "an impossible choice," and she questions precisely the dichotomy itself. I also believe that it is unacceptable, among other reasons because both the "difference dilemma" ("difference" being used, overtly or implicitly, to confirm women's inferiority in relation to men) and the "equality dilemma" ("equality" being used, overtly or implicitly, to erase gender difference in view of women's assimilation to male societal norms) are far from being sufficiently explored. Such an exploration should be put on the agenda for future women's history. Why is it, for instance, that "equality" and "justice" seem to complement each other in the case of men, but be opposed to each other in the case of women? Why is it that "difference" is only attributed to one half of humankind and not to the other? Why is it that "equality" is so intimately bound up with "fraternity," but not with sisterhood, since the French Revolution but also in earlier political thought?

Again the only way forward seems to be to challenge the dichotomy itself, and to do so by analysing and dismantling the sexist construction of difference as well as of equality. . . .

3. Integration versus autonomy.   An analogous argument may be appropriate in regard to the problems of the "integration" or "autonomy" of women's studies in respect to scholarship at large, and of women in respect to academic institutions. Despite the expansion of women's studies, and even though it is now occasionally admitted as a "sub-disciplinary specialisation," its impact on and integration in the academic disciplines have remained minimal, and what has been called "mainstreaming" is still far from being implemented, even though there are important differences here as to countries and disciplines. . . .

Clearly, women's studies need to be recognised as an integral part of scholarship at large. But such "mainstreaming" may also risk being drawn into a dynamic that makes women invisible again. There are now a number of cases where "gender history" is being opposed, in a dichotomous way, to "women's history," and where chairs in "women's history" are strongly opposed, but chairs in "gender history" are welcome. As an institutional problem, the latter situation may be dealt with according to institutional circumstances, but the theoretical problem remains, largely due to a specific definition of "gender" which excludes sexual "difference," meaning women, by classifying it as "biological" and therefore as socially and historically irrelevant. In such a view, the radical promise of gender history as an extension of women's history risks being subverted by the reduction of the history of women, once again, to a mere appendix of an allegedly more "generic" gender history. Again, women are not considered to be an equally universal subject as are other, and male-centred subjects.

Therefore, women's history also requires autonomy from male-dominated scholarship, in institutional and particularly in intellectual terms, in order to develop its full potential. But "autonomy," another virtue central to the heritage of the Renaissance and the Enlightenment, also needs to be redefined. In practice, the difficult question is to recognize the fine line, which is also a profound divide, between autonomy and segregation, the ghetto in which women's studies often find themselves. It seems that the problem "autonomy versus integration" cannot be adequately dealt with through terminological distinctions, between women's history, feminist history, and gender history. . . .

Challenging dichotomies seems to be a major issue on the scholarly as well as the political agenda of women's and gender history, and of women's studies more broadly. The act of challenging requires, of course, further study of the precise character of the opposing categories, of the particularities and dynamics of the dichotomous relationship, and of the form and character of the challenge itself.

As to the nature of gender-based dichotomies, there is obviously a significant difference between the first set of three which have been mentioned in the earlier section of this paper, and the latter set of three. This difference reflects, among other things, the increasingly complex character of the categories under which gender relations are being considered and studied. The dichotomies nature/culture, paid/unpaid work, public/private were constructed in alignment with a fixed divide between women and men, the ostensibly internally homogeneous categories on each side of which pointing either to women or to men. In the case of sex/gender, equality/difference, integration/autonomy, however, both (apparently) opposing terms refer to both sexes. We are therefore not dealing just with relations between the sexes, but with relations between relational categories; and not just with (apparent) contradictories between women and men, but with opposing or apparently opposing conceptualisations and practices of gender relations. Hence, women's studies and the search for new visions of gender has led us—despite, or rather because of sometimes profoundly different approaches—to at least one common ground: gender issues are issues which concern complex human relations, relations both between the sexes and within the sexes.

And what could or should be the character of the challenge? It requires continuous work on the dismantling, historicisation, and deconstruction of the apparently given meanings of the various categories. I believe that it also implies the rejection of mutually exclusive hierarchies, and especially of either/or solutions, in favour of as-well-as solutions. . . . In the case of the two latter dilemmas, we may particularly need to challenge their mutual exclusiveness and claim "equality in difference" and "difference in equality," "autonomy in integration" and "integration in autonomy." For both of them one might object, and it has been objected, that women cannot have their cake and eat it too. But for too long, women have baked the cake and taken only the smallest slice to eat for themselves.

Women of Color and the Rewriting of Western History

ANTONIA I. CASTAÑEDA

The academic discourse on the historiography of women in the West still does not accept that studying and writing the history of racial ethnic people as well as of women in the United States are avowedly political acts. Yet the political and intellectual roots of the contemporary historical study of women in the West were sown in the political struggles of the late 1960s and 1970s—in the case of white women, in the women's liberation movements; in the case of women of color, in the national third-world liberation movements. These movements were at times related, but their political and intellectual origins, commitments, and ideologies were markedly different.

The women's liberation movement in the United States focused specifically on gender oppression. Never of one mind or one ideology, the women's movement was nevertheless fundamentally rooted in a middle-class political liberalism that subscribed to including the excluded as long as they fit within the existing norms. Its origins, identification, and praxis sprang from the suffragist movement of the mid-nineteenth century—a movement that never reconciled its origins in abolitionism with an abiding belief in white racial superiority.

The study of women began with the political struggles of the women's movements of the 1960s and 1970s and with the feminist theories and scholarship that grew from them. The women's movement was a middle-class, white women's movement, and until very recently, the historians who have researched and written the history of women in the West have been principally white women. Many of them participated in the women's movement or are members of the generation of scholars who struggled to found women's studies programs and departments in western colleges and universities. Most feminist scholars write the history not of women, but of white women in the West.

In contrast, most women scholars of color who research and write the history of women of color look not to the women's liberation movement, but to third-world liberation movements. These movements focused on the race and class oppression of African Americans, Chicanos, Native Americans, Puerto Ricans, and Asian Americans in the U.S. and identified with global struggles of third-world peoples for economic and political freedom. They found their historical and cultural origins in indigenous, native worlds that antedated European imperialism, and they began to reclaim those origins, which had been devalued and suppressed in Euro-American institutions and society. These national movements interpreted the exploitation and oppression of third-world peoples in the United States as an extension of the historical, global colonial, and neocolonial relationships that tied Europe and subsequently the United States to third-world countries. Drawing upon theories of dependency and, in some cases, interpreting their reality in the United States as internal colonialism, these movements had a transnational identification and praxis. Although different ideologies, including cultural nationalism, prevailed, most national liberation movements supported a Marxist or neo-marxist perspective that focused on class and racial oppression but ignored issues of patriarchy and gender oppression, gay and lesbian oppression, and the intersection of gender, race, sexuality, and class.

Women scholars of color, however, also struggled against the internal gender oppression of their own families, organizations, and communities and against a historical sexual exploitation rooted in the intersection of their gender with their race and class. This consciousness distinguished their gender oppression markedly from that of white women and distinguished their racial and class oppression markedly from that of men of color. It also differentiated the feminist ideologies of women of color from those of white women.

Individually and collectively, in conferences, presentations, and published works, feminists of color challenged male-dominated ethnic studies departments that ignored gender and sexuality and women's studies departments that ignored race and class. In the case of the latter, they were highly critical of the assumptions, the universalizing tendencies, and the lack of consciousness about the dynamics of power and privilege rooted in race and class that informed white feminist scholarship. . . . Although few in number, they began to recover the voices, histories, cultures, literatures, and experiences of women of color in the United States and to teach courses on women of color. . . .

The issue of diversity was . . . a reality for indigenous peoples in the Americas long before the arrival of Europeans. Although racial diversity in the West may be a relatively recent phenomenon (some two and four hundred years old in California and New Mexico, respectively), cultural diversity is not. Before the Spanish arrived in 1769, California was one of the most densely populated and culturally and linguistically diverse areas of the continent north of México. Precontact indigenous societies throughout the Americas included a broad spectrum of social structures ranging from the matrilineal and matrilocal societies of the Navajo and Western Apache to egalitarian, foraging bands in California to highly stratified, hierarchically organized social orders in central Mexico and Peru.

Recognizing and according significance to cultural diversity are important for two reasons. First, . . . [i]ndigenous cultural diversity was not unique to the West, and its decline in other regions of the country, the South and Southeast for example, was due precisely to the impact of European and Euro-American expansion and colonization. Moreover, although the diversity among indigenous groups declined, the importation of Africans from different parts of the continent added new elements of cultural, as well as racial, diversity to nonwestern regions. Diversity in the American West, then, merely reflects a pattern in place long before the arrival of Europeans, and the change in the composition of diverse groups across time—the decline of some groups and the addition of others—is a function of the political and economic developments occurring in a particular region.

Second, the women's gender experiences and definitions were as diverse as the cultures from which they came. Women apprehended knowledge and acted within their universe according to their culture and its particular economic and socio-politico-religious organization. Understanding the nature of gender systems and experiences before contact is critical to understanding how those experiences changed with conquest and colonialism and why women responded and acted the way they did in intercultural settings and relationships. It is also critical to understanding how they maintained, adapted, and transformed their own cultural forms while resisting, adopting, adapting, and affecting those of other groups. . . .

While feminist scholars are beginning to examine race and miscegenation within a multicultural framework, most continue to ignore the complexities of multiple racial and cultural mixtures in the United States and to avoid examining how the prevailing construction of race has been applied differently to different racial ethnic peoples across time and space. Mexicans (both native and foreign born), for example, were included in the 1920 U.S. federal manuscript census as part of the white population. In 1930, however, the U.S. Bureau of the Census classified them as nonwhite and set up "Mexican" as a race unto itself. Since Mexicans have been officially classified both as white and nonwhite, antimiscegenation laws sometimes applied to them and sometimes did not. Nevertheless, as one early study of the Mexican American community concluded, irrespective of the official racial classification, intermarriage with Mexicans was disparaged, and "the Anglo member of an intermarrying couple . . . is classified as a 'Mexican' by the American community."

Theories about the social construction of race do not yet examine or account for these kinds of complexities. Nor does the significance of interracial marriage and mixing among peoples of color, or the *mestizaje* of the Mexican population, form part of how the social construction of race and studies of miscegenation are conceptualized for nineteenth- or twentieth-century North American society. Acutely aware that the new theories remain constructed and defined by the same "hegemonic voices," scholars of color have vigorously critiqued the "rush to theory" that ignores, excludes, or does not comprehend the realities of people of color and, in this case, women of color. . . .

Generalizations about women of color perpetuate pernicious stereotypes. Native American, Chicana, African-American, and Asian American scholars have identified two dichotomous images of women of color in the literature—"good" and "bad." . . . Within this dichotomy, "good" women of color are light-skinned, civilized (Christian), and virgins. They are "good" because they give aid, or sacrifice themselves, so that white men may live; white men marry them. "Bad" women are dark-skinned, savage (non-Christian), and whores; white men do not marry them. . . .

During the first stages of contact and conquest, marriage to a Native American or a Mexican woman of a particular family or class had significant economic and political value. These marriages were often the vehicle by which Euro-American men gained access to land or other economic resources as well as to political and military alliances. This was not the case with African American or Asian women in the nineteenth-century West. As enslaved or contract workers, African American and Asian women had neither economic nor political value as marriage partners. The miscegenation laws, which criminalized marriage to people of African descent, were later extended to Asians.

Consequently, stereotypes of African and Asian women center almost exclusively on the pejorative "bad/whore." This image simultaneously sexualizes women and impugns their sexuality. The implicit sociopolitical message is clear: women of color are immoral because their peoples, races, and nations are immoral. Whereas the pejorative stereotype of African American and Asian women is rooted in sexuality, the positive stereotype, when it appears at all, is rooted in work and servitude. "Good" African American and Asian women serve their owners, or former owners, well. They do not run away, join or lead revolts, learn to read or write, or cause trouble. . . .

Especially important to historical scholarship on women of color in the United States, including the west, is the work of third-world feminists and other third-world scholars and writers who employ critical theory, postmodern anthropology, and poststructuralist literary criticism to analyze how the colonizer represented African, Native Americans, mestiza, and Asian women. Analyzing women and the female body as a metaphor for conquest, these scholars interpret the white colonizers' appropriation of the native woman—by representing her as sexually available to the colonizer and as oppressed within her own culture—to be pivotal to the ideology and the political agenda of colonialism. . . .

These scholars not only examine the centrality of sex-gender to the politics of colonialism but also focus on the relations of power both among cultures and within cultures. They view scholarship and the production of knowledge as a political and discursive practice—it has a purpose and is ideological. Within this broad framework, third-world feminists reexamine, reconstruct, and re-present native women within their own cultures as well as responding to colonialism. In doing so, they interrogate their own traditions from within. They call into question traditions, conventions, and contemporary relations of power and offer searching critiques of their own societies and historical conditioning. . . .

In focusing on women of color as historical subjects in the nineteenth-century Euro-American West, and employing gender, race, class, culture, and sexuality as categories of analysis within the context of colonization, newer studies, principally by women historians of color, are reexamining old sources, discovering new sources, using new methodologies, and challenging earlier interpretations of women in general. They are also refuting previous interpretations of women of color in particular. These scholars, states historian Deena González, have found it necessary first to "deconstruct the racialized and sexualized history of women of color in order to reconstruct it."

Their examinations reveal important commonalities and differences based on historical presence and on gender and its intersection with race, sexuality, culture, and class. These new findings form a critical new basis for reconceptualizing and reinterpreting not only women's and racial ethnic history, but the labor, economic, political, immigration, cultural, and social history of the West as well.

They have sketched some of the broad themes that are of importance to women of color, including sexual and other physical, as well as psychological, violence within the context of the politics of expansionism; devaluation of their sexuality by Euro-American society; discrimination based on race, culture, and class; resistance to oppression; use as labor (enslaved, contract, and wage); the *mestizaje* within Mexican communities as well as intermarriage and racial-cultural mixing among people of color; settlement; family; religion; and community building. Other themes, such as accommodation and adaptation to the Euro-American presence in their homeland; intermarriage with Euro-Americans; immigration; deportation; and the experience of slavery and freedom from bondage in the West, are more specific to one group or another.

Drawing upon new, interdisciplinary methodologies and frameworks defined in the scholarly studies of third-world women, these studies examine and analyze women of color within their own cultures; in particular, they examine how these women responded to the alien, hostile, often violent society of the nineteenth-century American West. These studies focus on women's agency and on how women of color use their own culture and knowledge to sustain them, how they subvert and/or change the environment, and how they adopt or create new cultural forms. Further, these studies explore the multiple contradictions of women's lives in colonialism. They explore both the hegemonic and counterhegemonic strategies, roles, and activities that women, depending on their position in society, developed and employed in both the historical and contemporary period. Women of all races, classes, and cultures are active subjects, not passive objects or victims of the historical process. . . .

Historians, including feminist historians and other feminist scholars, must examine their assumptions as well as their racial, class, and gender positions as they redefine historical and other categories of analysis. The structures of colonialism are the historical legacy of the United States and, as such, inform the profession of history and the production of historical scholarship as much as they do any other human relationship and endeavor. If western history is to be decolonized, historians must be conscious of their power and ideology within the structures of colonialism, and conscious as well of the ways in which historical scholarship has helped to sustain and reproduce those structures. The study of women of color requires us to reexamine, challenge, and change those structures. Only then will we decolonize western history.

Rethinking the Position of Black Women in American Women's History

LESLIE M. ALEXANDER

Perhaps the most significant ideological influence on early women's history was the feminist movement, which sought to overthrow male domination, patriarchy, and gender discrimination. . . . Specifically within the field of history, feminist thought advocated for a woman-centered approach, and argued that there was a common sisterhood among women. The creation of new feminist paradigms was tremendously useful in liberating White women from scholarly neglect and oversight, and therefore a debt of gratitude is owed to the scholars who blazed the trail and took intellectual risks to create this field.

Despite the importance of these early contributions, however, I believe that the most significant progress has been made since the 1980s, after Black scholars raised critiques regarding the "implicit racism" in women's history that systematically overlooked how race and class functioned in the lives of women of color. . . . At this moment in the development of women's history, we must be willing to look deeply at our approaches and evaluate their effectiveness. In my opinion, the scramble to incorporate race into the narrative, while critically important, was often clumsy, awkward, and strained. The problem is twofold; first, although feminism is a useful paradigm for White women, the attempt to force Black women into the same interpretive model is not applicable, and has prevented full understanding of Black women's lives. The deeper, yet interconnected, issue is that despite vast improvements in our intellectual approaches, women's historians have failed to respond adequately to the critiques launched by Black scholars nearly two decades ago.

In order to understand the current state of Black women in women's history, it is necessary to review the historiographical trends. Following the pattern of Black history and White women's history, the study of Black women initially employed a contributionist model. . . .

By the 1980s, Black scholars issued a new challenge, one that forced historians to move beyond the contributionist model. This movement demanded a broader understanding of the role of race and class in the lives of women of color and urged women's studies (and the women's movement) to become more expansive in their interpretations. . . . [T]he frustration among Black scholars stemmed from the conflation of "woman" with "white woman." This approach, they argued, not only rendered Black women invisible, but also suggested that all women's experiences could be understood exclusively through the lens of whiteness and White women's struggles. While the problem of exclusion received the majority of scholarly attention, Black scholars launched an additional critique which opposed the popular notion that there could be a "homogenous womanhood." Despite serious problems with racism within the movement, feminists had traditionally relied upon the notion

Leslie M. Alexander, "The Challenge of Race: Rethinking the Position of Black Women in the Field of Women's History," *Journal of Women's History* 16, no. 4 (2004): 50–60. Copyright © Journal of Women's History. Reprinted with permission of Johns Hopkins University Press.

of a common sisterhood among all women, both politically and intellectually. Yet women of color maintained that such a perspective eliminated the possibility that there could be multiple definitions and meaning of womanhood. The reality, Black scholars argued, was that race and class created a chasm that made a singular, unified womanhood impossible.

Faced with the need to reassess their approach, women's scholars clambered to incorporate race and class into their analysis, yet despite their best efforts, a fundamental flaw remained. Unable to release the notion of a single womanhood, they only addressed part of the original challenge. While scholars dealt with the first criticism (that "woman" and "white woman" were not synonymous), they did not fully engage the second issue of homogeneity. The result was the emergence of studies that sought to incorporate race into women's history by focusing exclusively on oppression. In particular, they struggled to understand how race exacerbated gender discrimination. Perhaps not understanding that Black women were not asking simply for an acknowledgement of their additional suffering, women's historians relied on the "dual oppression" analysis to explain Black women's experiences. This theory argued that in a White patriarchal society, both race and gender prevented the empowerment of women of color, and created simultaneous layers of subjugation. When class and sexual orientation were added to the discussion, it led to interpretations of triple and quadruple oppressions. Of course, as with contributionism, this understanding of multiple oppressions was certainly useful in its time; however, it ultimately failed to explore the full meaning and function of race.

I argue that the challenge for women's history today is to understand fully how race functions in Black women's lives. Early studies of race and gender failed to recognize that race does not only operate as an additional oppressive force but it also forms the foundation of how Black women live their daily lives, and what kinds of liberation strategies they embrace. Black scholars in the 1980s were trying to make this point when they attacked the concept of a homogenous womanhood. And this, of course, is the issue that most women's historians have yet to grasp: race is not simply about oppression; in reality, race influences culture, community, and political worldview. . . . Yet the recognition that Black and White women are culturally different opens a Pandora's box that many women's historians have understandably wanted to avoid. In particular, we must ask, what specifically are the cultural differences between women and how does the reality of race influence those differences? What effect do they have on women's lives and, perhaps the most important for our purposes, how do they affect the field of women's history?

Not surprisingly, women's historians have been reluctant to address these questions because the answers strike at the core of women's history. In order to explore Black women's lives, they have to confront differences between and among women and reject the notion of homogeneity. In particular, they have to look deeply at how race and culture undermined the possibility of a singular womanhood. What they have discovered to this point seems frightening: Black cultural distinctiveness contradicts the use of feminist interpretive models because these paradigms do not generally fit with Black women's experiences. The concern, of course, is that acknowledging the shortcomings of feminism will undermine everything that women scholars and activists have fought for. Yet the incompatibility of traditional feminism with the Black experience has been undeniable. . . .

Within Black culture, the concept of family, community, and kinship makes it impossible to remove Black women (or the study of Black women) from the context of the entire Black community. As a result, approaches such as feminism, which focus exclusively on gender, do not serve as useful models of interpretation for Black women because they seek to extract Black women from their community. . . . As a result, the stipulations of feminism that require a "gender first" policy have not felt applicable to Black women, who often view racial empowerment as equally, if not more, important than female empowerment. . . . Race, gender, and community are inextricably linked and any effort to analyze Black women solely in terms of gender will fail. Simply put, you cannot divorce Black women from the community; for if you do not understand the Black community you will not understand the Black woman.

It is important to note that Black women's reluctance to espouse traditional feminism does not mean that Black women are not concerned with sexism and gender equality, politically or intellectually. On the contrary, there is widespread acknowledgement of the fact that sexism and patriarchy are real problems in Black women's lives. Yet the inescapable reality is that while some Black female academics have embraced various forms of feminism, the vast majority of Black women have alternative liberation strategies, which are deeply rooted in their racial identity. . . . Assuming, then, that Black women are concerned about gender equality, but do not unilaterally embrace feminism, what are the ramifications for Black women's history?

Perhaps this question can be answered, at least in part, by looking at how gender is dealt with in the study of Black women. Since feminism is often not the primary mode of interpretation in Black women's scholarship, issues of gender are usually couched in larger discussions about race. . . . [U]nlike general women's history, books centered on Black women's subjects tended to focus mainly on race and women's organizations. This is not simply coincidence. . . . [R]ace and community, including community organizations, remain the most compelling issues in Black women's lives, and therefore are the focus of most historical studies dealing with Black women's experiences. Recent biographies on Black women also support this notion—in particular, studies on Ella Baker, Fannie Lou Hamer, and the women in the Montgomery bus boycott movement reveal that the activism and experiences of Black women must be studied in the context of the entire Black community. These studies prove that although Black women's experiences may be gendered, they are shaped most compellingly by their role as members of the Black community. As a result, Black women's history is fundamentally different, both in content and in focus, from White women's history.

Given the profound differences between Black and White women, it would be natural to wonder what the ramifications are for women's history; particularly because Black women's cultural orientation creates a unique challenge, both politically and intellectually. For women's history and women's studies, Black women's tendency to resist feminism and to embrace identification with the Black community raises and important question about the position of Black women within the academic field. . . .

I argue that it is possible for Black women to have a place in women's history; however, it will require some dramatic changes in the field. I also believe that women's history is gradually moving in the right direction. Over the past decade,

scholars and activists have slowly rejected the notion of homogeneity and are recognizing that women are not a monolithic group. Perhaps more important, Black
women scholars have immeasurably enriched the field with studies chronicling the
lives and experiences of Black women. Yet the problem remained of how to bring
race into the core of women's history. In 1995, Evelyn Brooks Higginbotham made a
crucial breakthrough when she challenged feminist scholars to rethink their approach
to the study of race. She argued that race operated as a "metalanguage," which required historians to understand the "powerful and all-encompassing effect" that
race has on the "construction and representation of other social and power relations,
namely, gender, class, and sexuality." Her analysis was transformative because it
forced race into the center of the discussion and urged women's historians to consider how race shaped gender. . . .

Despite my enthusiasm about these recent developments, I believe there are a
series of critical issues that must be addressed before the field of women's history
can respond adequately to Black women's experiences. The first challenge is largely
methodological and reveals my concern that Black women's voices are slowly van-
ishing from historical studies. This trend is likely due to the fact that Black women's
experiences have increasingly been used to understand the structure of American
society and the systemic nature of racism and sexism. While such studies are undoubtedly important, there is a compelling need to study Black women in their own
right. We must resist the temptation to use Black women solely as comparative
models through which we can explain other phenomena; we must also explore the
activities and contributions of Black women as members of the Black community.
In order to understand the influence of race and gender, historians must be willing
to ask important questions: how did Black women live their daily lives? How did
they view themselves, and their role in the Black community? What did they believe,
and what was their worldview? What liberation strategies did they embrace and
why? The only way to answer these questions is for all women's historians to use
the strategy employed by Black scholars: bring Black women's voices into the core
of analysis. The challenge remains for us to analyze Black women through their
own eyes rather than through the lens of whiteness and oppression.

The final two issues we must address are deeply interconnected, and return us to
the criticisms initiated in the 1980s regarding feminism and racial difference. First,
we need to reconcile the contradiction between Black women's experiences, and the
scholarly attachment to feminism. The question women's historians must now ask
themselves is, does a study have to be written using feminist tools and approaches in
order to be part of the field? It is understandable if the answer is "yes," but it is important to recognize the consequences of such a decision. Most troubling is that there
is no place for the study of Black women in a framework that demands a "gender
first" policy. In reality, the convergence of race, culture, and community makes it
impossible to privilege gender, either intellectually or politically, over race. Women's
historians must come to terms with that reality; otherwise they will continue to mis-
understand Black women's lives, both historically and contemporarily. In addition,
the insistence upon feminism as the primary methodological approach limits the
possibilities of what the field can become because it perpetuates the myth that this
model is applicable to all women. In truth, feminism is just one manifestation of
womanhood and there are many alternative expressions of women's experiences.

The need to acknowledge the multiplicity of women's experiences leads to my final point: we must become truly willing to explore difference. I believe that although most contemporary scholars no longer advocate for homogeneity, they remain reluctant to explore how the reality of race influences Black women's lives. Despite the creation of new methodologies and modes of interpretation, most women's historians have failed to comprehend how race shapes Black women's consciousness and worldview. Race and culture are still the most compelling issues that mold Black women's lives, and we must be willing to examine how these issues make their lives fundamentally different. Instead, many scholars have become fearful of difference. . . .

If women's historians are willing to delve into the differences among women, they will discover that there are rich layers of depth and intricacy that can enrich our understanding of women's experiences. Rather than lose a gender analysis, we will uncover the range of existing womanhoods. . . . Race, culture, community, class, sexual orientation—all of these factors influence and act upon women's lives in ways that we are just beginning to explore. We must not be afraid to grapple with diversity, difference, and complexity for only by dealing with these issues can we truly understand women's lives holistically.

FURTHER READING

Amott, Teresa, and Julie Matthaei. *Race, Gender, and Work: A Multicultural Economic History of Women in the United States* (1996).

Cott, Nancy, et al. "Considering the State of U.S. Women's History," *Journal of Women's History* 15, no. 1 (2003): 145–182.

Des Jardins, Julie. *Women and the Historical Enterprise in America: Gender, Race, and the Politics of Memory, 1880–1945* (2003).

DuBois, Ellen, and Vicki Ruiz, eds. *Unequal Sisters: A Multicultural Reader in American Women's History* (3d ed., 2000).

Evans, Sara. *Born for Liberty* (1997).

Freedman, Estelle. *No Turning Back: The History of Feminism and the Future of Women* (2002).

Giddings, Paula. *When and Where I Enter: The Impact of Black Women on Race and Sex in America* (1984).

Higginbotham, Evelyn Brooks. "African-American Women's History and the Metalanguage of Race," *Signs* 17 (1991–1992): 254–274.

Hine, Darlene Clark, et al., eds. *"We Specialize in the Wholly Impossible": A Reader in Black Women's History* (1995).

Kerber, Linda. "Separate Spheres, Female Worlds, Women's Place: The Rhetoric of Women's History," *Journal of American History* 75 (1988–1989): 3–39.

Lerner, Gerda. *The Majority Finds Its Past* (1979).

Melosh, Barbara, ed. *Gender and American History Since 1890* (1993).

Riley, Denise. *"Am I That Name?" Feminism and the Category of "Women" in History* (1988).

Scott, Anne Firor. *Making the Invisible Woman Visible* (1984).

Scott, Joan W. *Gender and the Politics of History* (1988).

Smith, Bonnie G. *The Gender of History: Men, Women, and Historical Practice* (1998).

Thurner, Manuela. "Subject to Change: Theories and Paradigms of U.S. Feminist History," *Journal of Women's History* 9, no. 2 (1997): 122–146.

Woloch, Nancy. *Women and the American Experience* (1984).

Zinsser, Judith P. *Feminism and History: A Glass Half Full* (1993).

CHAPTER
2

Native American Women

Some of the most important recent scholarship on the history of early American women has focused on women in indigenous communities. Studying women's roles in native societies is difficult, for North American Indians in the pre-contact period did not have written languages. Therefore they left primarily archaeological evidence of their lives. And literate arrivals among the Europeans, many of whom wrote lengthy descriptions of the peoples they encountered, did not necessarily produce trustworthy written accounts of native life. For one thing, the European observers saw Indian societies through biased eyes, assessing their customs through the lens of European practices and religious beliefs. For another, those observers—almost exclusively male—tended to devote more attention to men than to women, and when they wrote about women they often did so in ways that distorted female roles. Any historian in the field, therefore, must keep in mind the fundamental bias in her sources.

Two related questions in particular have concerned many historians: What was the standing of women in American Indian societies? Did the arrival of Europeans affect that status in significant ways? Some have argued that Indian women suffered a loss of position relative to their menfolk after European contact, because the invaders sought to impose their notions of proper gender roles on Indian societies. Others have contended, to the contrary, that the presence of European traders and settlers in North America instead offered women new opportunities for political and economic leadership in their own communities. No consensus has yet been achieved, and it may well be that European contact affected different Indian societies in different ways.

◈ D O C U M E N T S

The documents in this chapter offer differing perspectives on the lives of women in a variety of Indian societies in seventeenth- and eighteenth-century North America. In Document 1, the French explorer Samuel de Champlain, one of the first Europeans to spend a considerable amount of time living among American Indians, describes the Huron families he observed in the Great Lakes region of North America in 1616.

More than a century later, during the early decades of English settlement in Georgia, an Anglo-Creek woman named Mary Musgrove served as an important intermediary between the Indians and the settlers. Document 2 is a letter she addressed to James Oglethorpe, founder of the colony, in 1734, describing current relationships with the Choctaws. Thirteen years later (Document 3), she petitioned an English officer for compensation for her many services to Georgia. Document 4 again presents a European man's description of an Indian community; in this instance, the Moravian missionary John Heckewelder comments sympathetically on the lives of the Delaware Indians he is attempting to convert to Christianity. Finally, in Document 5, John Tanner, a former Ottawa captive, in an 1830s memoir, writes about Net-no-kwa, the Indian woman who raised him as his foster mother in the 1790s. What is the range of women's roles described in the documents? Are some accounts more trustworthy than others? Why?

1. The French Explorer Samuel de Champlain Describes the Lives of Huron Women and Men in the Great Lakes Region, 1616

These people are of a rather merry disposition, although there are many of them who have a gloomy and saturnine expression. They are well-formed and proportioned in body, some of the men being very strong and robust. And there are also women and girls who are very beautiful and attractive in figure, coloring (although it is olive) and in features, all in proportion; and their breasts hang down hardly at all, unless they are old. Some of them are very powerful and of extraordinary height. They have almost all the care of the house and the work; for they till the ground, plant the Indian corn, lay up wood for the winter, beat the hemp and spin it, make fishing-nets from the thread, catch fish, and do other necessary things. They also harvest their corn, store it, prepare it to eat, and attend to their household affairs. Moreover, they follow their husbands from place to place in the fields, where they serve as mules for carrying the baggage.

As to the men, they do nothing but hunt for deer and other animals, catch fish, make cabins and go to war. When they have done these things they go to other tribes, to whom they have access, and whom they know, to trade and exchange what they have for what they have not. When they come back they do not stir from the feasts and dances which they make for one another, and when these are over they go to sleep, which is the best employment of all.

They have a sort of marriage among them, which is like this: when a girl is 11, 12, 13, 14 or 15 years old, she will have several suitors, according to her good graces, who will woo her and ask the consent of her father and her mother, although often the girls do not accept their consent. Those who are the best and most discreet submit to their wishes. This lover, or suitor, gives the girl some necklaces, chains and bracelets of wampum. If the girl finds the suitor agreeable, she accepts this present. This done,

The Voyages and Explorations of Samuel de Champlain (1604–1616). Narrated by Himself. . . (New York: A. S. Barnes & Co, 1906, and reprinted. Dartmouth, NS: Brook House Press, 2000) 2: 186, 188, 193.

he comes to sleep with her three or four nights without saying a word, when they gather the fruit of their affections. And it often happens that after having spent a week or a fortnight together, if they cannot agree, she will quit her suitor, who forfeits his necklaces and other gifts made by him. Frustrated in his hope, he will seek another woman, and she another suitor; and thus they continue until a satisfactory union is made. There are many girls who pass their entire youth thus with several husbands, who are not alone in the enjoyment of the creature, married though they are; for, when night comes, the young women run from one cabin to another, as do the young men, on their part, visiting any girls they please. They do so without violence, however, referring the whole matter to the wish of the woman. The husband will do the same thing to a woman neighbor, without there being any jealousy among them on that account, or, in any case, very little; and they incur no ill-repute or insult for it, for it is the custom of the country.

When the women have children, the preceding husbands return to them, to show them the friendship and affection that they had borne them in the past, saying that it is more than that of any other man, and that the child who is to be born is his and of his begetting. Another will tell her the same thing; and so it is at the choice and option of the woman to take and accept him who pleases her most. Having gained by her loves a great deal of wampum, she remains with him without leaving him any more; or, if she leaves him, it must be for some important reason, other than impotence, for he is on trial. Nevertheless, while she is with this husband she does not cease to indulge herself freely; yet she keeps herself at home and busy always with the household, making a good appearance. The result is that children that they have together cannot be sure of being legitimate. They have a custom, however, which provides against this risk that they may never succeed to their property, by constituting the children of their sisters, whom they know to have been born of them, their heirs and successors. . . .

With regard to their housekeeping and living, each one lives on what he can get from fishing and from the harvest in as much land as is needed. They clear it with great difficulty, as they have no proper tools for the purpose. They strip the trees of all their branches, which they burn at their base, in order to kill them. They clean up the ground between the trees, then plant their corn at distances of a pace, putting about ten grains in each place; and so they continue until they have enough for three or four years' provision, for fear lest some bad year, barren and unfruitful, should come upon them.

If any girl marries in winter, each woman and girl is expected to carry to the bride a load of wood for her provision; for each household is furnished with what is necessary, inasmuch as she could not do it alone, and also that she may have time enough to attend to other things which are in time and season.

Their government is as follows: the elders and principal men assemble in council, where they decide and propose all that is necessary for the affairs of the village. This is done by vote of the majority, or by the advice of certain ones among them who are esteemed to be of excellent judgment. Such advice so given is scrupulously followed. They have no particular chiefs who command with absolute authority, but they show respect to the oldest and bravest, who are called captains. . . .

2. Mary Musgrove Assists the Georgians in Dealing with the Choctaws, 1734

Savannah, July 17, 1734

Honoured Sir

I make bold to acquaint You that Thomas Jones is returned from the Choctaws and according to your Honours Desire he has brought the Choctaws down and they have received great favours from Col. Bull and Mr. Causton and all the rest of the Colony, and a great deal of Respect shewed them which they are wonderfully pleased at. And when they came down Mr. Jones brought with him some of the Heads of the Tallooposes which is called the Upper Creeks; The Dog King of Uphalais Chauaway by name went with Mr. Jones up to the Choctaws to make peace, and he is mighty glad that he and Mr. Jones did persuade them to come down which is more than ever Carolina could do to get them down before. And the Choctaws are so glad that some white People whom they called their Masters had taken such Care of them as to send for them and they was very glad of the opportunity to come for they lived very poor before and now they are in good hopes to live as well as the other Indians do, for they had nor have no Trade with the French and their Skins lye by them and rot. When Mr. Thomas Jones came to them at first there was thirty Towns only that had the notice. Before Mr. Jones came away all they gave their Consents for their Coming, but Notice was still sent on farther. And they say that they like the English better than the French, and that they will stand by the English as long as they have one left alive. There was some of the Caupahauches and the Hulbaumors came with them. The Choctaws are all amazed to see the Creeks drink as they do, and they think the Creeks are saucy to the white People. The Choctaw King thinks they are obliged to the white People and thinks they cannot do enough for the white People especially the English. And since they have been here there has not one of them been disguised in Liquor or any ways saucy upon any Account. They have been here 21 Days for Mr. Causton thought it proper to send for Col. Bull and that was the Reason of their being Detained so long here. Governor Johnson has sent for them to come to Carolina but Thomas Jones was not willing they should go to Carolina for fear of disobliging your Honour, and as he was sent for them for the Colony he did not Care they should go any where else. You Honour's Name is spread very much amongst them and they say that when your Honour comes back to Georgia they will be bound to raise a thousand or two at your Honour's Command if desired, and they design to leave the French entirely and then they will come down and pay their Respects to You, and to Governor Johnson if your Honour desires they should go to Carolina but not without your Honour's Consent. Mr. Thomas Jones does insist of the Trade amongst the Choctaws as your Honour did promise him, and the Choctaws have so very great Respect and Value for Mr. Jones that they had rather have him to trade among them than any body else because he ventured his Life to bring them down to the English.

Colonial Records of Georgia, 20: 63–64. This document can also be found in John T. Juricek, ed., *Georgia Treaties 1733–1763*, vol. 11 of *Early American Indian Documents: Treaties and Laws, 1607–1789* (Frederick, Md.: University Publications of America, 1989), 38–39.

3. Mary Musgrove Seeks Aid from Georgia in Return for Past Service and Losses, 1747

August 10, 1747

TO The Honourable Lieutenant Collonel Alexander Heron Commander in Chief of his Majestys Forces in the Province of Georgia the Memorial and Representation of Mary Bosomworth of the Said Province.

HUMBLY SHEWETH.

That your Memorialist was born at the Cowetaw Town on the Oakmulgee River which is a Branch of the Alatamaha and the Chief Town of the Creek Indian Nation.

That She is by Descent on the Mothers Side, (who was Sister to the Old Emperor) of the Same Blood of the Present Mico's and Chief's now in that Nation, and by their Laws, and the Voice of the Whole Nation is esteemed their Rightfull and Natural Princess.

That her Ancesstors, Tho under the Appellation of Savages, or Barbarions, were a brave and free born people, who never owed Allegiance, to or Acknowledged the sovereignty of any Crowned Head whatever, but have always maintained their own Possessions and Independency, Against all Opposers by Warr, at the Expence of their Blood; as they Can shew by the many Troophies of Victory, and Relicts of their Enimies slain in Defence of their Natural Rights.

That they have entered into Several Treaties of Peace, Friendship and Commerce, with Persons properly impowered, in behalf of the Crown of Great Britain.

That they Have made Concessions of Several Portions of Land, (their Natural Right by Ancient Possession) in behalf of his Majesty; and have for several Years past on their parts, Strictly and faithfully Observed the Treaty of Friendship and Alliance entered into with the Honourable Major General Oglethorpe in behalf of his Brittannick Majesty. And have on all Occasions been ready to fight Against his Majestys Enimies which they Have very much Annoyed.

That both the french and Spaniards well know by Dear Experience how terrible they are to their Enemies in War. They are so highly Sensible of the Vast Importance of the Friendship and Alliance of the Creek Nation to the British Interest; (and the only Barrier to hinder them from gaining the utmost of their Wishes upon the Continent of America) That they Have for some time past, and are at this Juncture, Labouring by all the Artifices Imaginable to seduce that Nation from their Alliance with his Majestys Subjects, which will certainly be a great Addition and Increase of Territory Strength and Power to his Majestys Enimies; and the Dangerous Consequence May be the Utmost Hazard of the safety of his Majestys Southern Frontiers Carolina and Georgia.

That your Memorialist hath by her Intrest since the First Settlement of the Colony of Georgia for the Space of 14 Years continued that Important Nation Steady and Steadfast in their Friendship and Alliance with his Majestys subjects at the Expence of her own private Fortune to the Utter Ruin of her self and Famely as will evidently Appear by a plain Narrative of Incontestable Matters of Fact. . . .

Colonial Records of Georgia, 36: 256–273. This document can also be found in John T. Juricek, ed., *Georgia Treaties 1733–1763,* vol. 11 of *Early American Indian Documents: Treaties and Laws, 1607–1789* (Frederick, Md.: University Publications of America, 1989), 140–147.

THAT whereas His Majesty in the Preamble of his Royal Charter to the Honourable the Trustees for Establishing the Colony of the Georgia, bearing Date the 9th Day of June 1732 has been graciously pleased to Declare that the Intention of the Settlement of the Said Colony was partly as a Protection to his Majestys Subjects of South Carolina, whose Southern Frontiers continued unsettled and Lay exposed to the frequent Ravages of Enimy Indians etc. which Signal Instance of his Majestys peculiar Care for the Protection of that Province, is Most gratefully Acknowledged by a Memorial sent to his Majesty from the Governor and Council of the Said Province Dated the 9th April 1734.

And whereas his Majestys Gracious Intentions in the Settlement of the Colony of Georgia, have been so far Answered; that no out Settlements have been cutt off; Boats taken; nor men killed; since that time (which used before frequently to happen,) your Memorialist therefore humbly hopes that upon a Representation of her Case to his Majestys Governor and Council of the Province of South Carolina; How far his Majestys Subjects of that Province have been enabled to Improve the southern parts of that Province (which Before Lay Waste) by your Memorialist's Interest in Continuing the Indians in friendship and Alliance with his Majestys Subjects: THAT, That Government would be induced to make her some Restitution for her past services and Losses sustained in his Majestys service as she is Now indebted several Considerable sums of Money to Merchants in Charles Town, and Other Persons in south Carolina: and Destitute of Credit to Carry on her Affairs (which takes away the Very Means of her having it in her Power to Do Justice to her Creditors in that Province) and Whatever the Government shall think her Worthy off, she Desires may be Applyed to that end.

AND Lastly your Memorialist cannot Help repeating with an equal Mixture of a Real Grief of Heart, and Indignation; that her Injuries and Oppressions have been such, as she believes; have been scarce paralleled under a British Government. Language is too Weak to Represent her present Deplorable Case; She at present Labours under every sence of Injury; and Circumstances of Distress; Destitute of even the Common Necessaries of Life, being Insulted, Abused, contemned and Dispised by those ungratefull People who are indebted to her for the Blessings they Injoy.

The Only Returns she has met with for her past Services, Generosity, and Maternal Affection (she has at all times shewn for the whole Colony) has been injust Loads of Infamy and Reproach; Branded and Stigmatized with the Odious Name of Traytor, for Making any Pretentions to those Rights she is Justly entitled to by the Laws of God and Nature (as her ancestors were the Natural born Heirs Sole Owners and Proprietors of every Foot of Land which is now his Majestys Colony of Georgia,) tho she has in Vain made Application for a Grant from the Crown, and is Desireous and Willing to hold What Posesions she is there entitled to by the Laws of Nature and Nations, as a Subject of great Britain.

It is with the greatest Reluctancy, that your Memorialist is Drove to the Necessity to declare; That the Collony of Georgia was settled by her Interest with the Creek Indians: that it has in a Great Measure been supported by it, (as she can make Appear by Authentick Letters and Testimonies,) and that she has at this Day Interest enough to command a Thousand fighting men to stand in the face of his Majestys Enemies; and to Countermine every intended Design of both the french and spaniards in alienating the Creeks Nation of Indians from the British Interest; If

Suitable Encouragements are given her, to prevent her being Drove to the Necessity of Flying to her Indian Friends for Bread which will Greatly Confirm the Jealousies and uneasinesses which his Majesty's Enimies have so Industriously fomented and Spirited up Amongst them. . . .

THAT Whereas your Memorialist is highly sensible that its not in your Power to Redress her Grievances, and of the Great Difficulties you Labour under at this Juncture, in not being allowed any fund for continuing the Creek Indians in Friendship and Alliance with his Majestys Subjects and how far his Majestys service and Interest may Suffer thereby, she therefore Humbly begs that you would be Pleased to Lay this Memorial before his Grace the Duke of Newcastle one of His Majestys Principal Secretarys of State for His Graces Consideration with this Assurance, that if the Government should think proper to allow a Certain Sum per Annum to be applyed for maintaning his Majestys Peace and Authority Amongst the Indians that she on her Part would engage by her Interest Amongst them, to Doe every Duty that ever was Done by Rangers etc. in Georgia which have Cost the Government so many Thoussands, of Pounds, and With the Regiment under your Honours Command, and her Interest with the Creek Indians she believes that every Foot of his Majestys Possessions, and this Important Frontier could be maintained Against all his Majestys Enimies.

All Which is Humbly Submitted to your Consideration by your Memorialist this 10th Day August 1747.

4. The Moravian Missionary John Heckewelder Observes Delaware Indian Families in the Mid-Eighteenth Century

There are many persons who believe, from the labour that they see the Indian women perform, that they are in a manner treated as slaves. These labours, indeed, are hard, compared with the tasks that are imposed upon females in civilised society; but they are no more than their fair share, under every consideration and due allowance, of the hardships attendant on savage life. Therefore they are not only voluntarily, but cheerfully submitted to; and as women are not obliged to live with their husbands any longer than suits their pleasure or convenience, it cannot be supposed that they would submit to be loaded with unjust or unequal burdens.

Marriages among the Indians are not, as with us, contracted for life; it is understood on both sides that the parties are not to live together any longer than they shall be pleased with each other. The husband may put away his wife whenever he pleases, and the woman may in like manner abandon her husband. Therefore the connexion is not attended with any vows, promises, or ceremonies of any kind. An Indian takes a wife as it were on trial, determined, however, in his own mind not to forsake her if she behaves well, and particularly if he has children by her. The woman, sensible of this, does on her part every thing in her power to please her husband, particularly if he is a good hunter or trapper, capable of maintaining her by his skill and industry, and protecting her by his strength and courage.

John Heckewelder, *History, Manners, and Customs of the Indian Nations Who Once Inhabited Pennsylvania and the Neighboring States* (1819), 154–161.

When a marriage takes place, the duties and labours incumbent on each party are well known to both. It is understood that the husband is to build a house for them to dwell in, to find the necessary implements of husbandry, as axes, hoes, &c., to provide a canoe, and also dishes, bowls, and other necessary vessels for house-keeping. The woman generally has a kettle or two, and some other articles of kitchen furniture, which she brings with her. The husband, as master of the family, considers himself bound to support it by his bodily exertions, as hunting, trapping, &c.; the woman, as his *help-mate,* takes upon herself the labours of the field, and is far from considering them as more important than those to which her husband is subjected, being well satisfied that with his gun and traps he can maintain a family in any place where game is to be found; nor do they think it any hardship imposed upon them; for they themselves say, that while their field labour employs them at most six weeks in the year, that of the men continues the whole year round.

When a couple is newly married, the husband (without saying a single word upon the subject) takes considerable pains to please his wife, and by repeated proofs of his skill and abilities in the art of hunting, to make her sensible that she can be happy with him, and that she will never want while they live together. At break of day he will be off with his gun, and often by breakfast time return home with a deer, turkey, or some other game. He endeavours to make it appear that it is in his power to bring provisions home whenever he pleases, and his wife, proud of having such a good hunter for her husband, does her utmost to serve and make herself agreeable to him.

The work of the women is not hard or difficult. They are both able and willing to do it, and always perform it with cheerfulness. Mothers teach their daughters those duties which common sense would otherwise point out to them when grown up. Within doors, their labour is very trifling; there is seldom more than one pot or kettle to attend to. There is no scrubbing of the house, and but little to wash, and that not often. Their principal occupations are to cut and fetch in the fire wood, till the ground, sow and reap the grain, and pound the corn in mortars for the pottage, and to make bread which they bake in the ashes. When going on a journey, or to hunting camps with their husbands, if they have no horses, they carry a pack on their backs which often appears heavier than it really it; it generally consists of a blanket, a dressed deer skin for mocksens, a few articles of kitchen furniture, as a kettle, bowl, or dish, with spoons, and some bread, corn, salt, &c., for their nourishment. I have never known an Indian woman complain of the hardship of carrying this burden, which serves for their own comfort and support as well as of their husbands.

The tilling of the ground at home, getting of the fire wood, and pounding of corn in mortars, is frequently done by female parties, much in the manner of those husking, quilting, and other *frolics* (as they are called), which are so common in some parts of the United States, particularly to the eastward. The labour is thus quickly and easily performed; when it is over, and sometimes in intervals, they sit down to enjoy themselves by feasting on some good victuals, prepared for them by the person or family for whom they work, and which the man has taken care to provide before hand from the woods; for this is considered a principal part of the business, as there are generally more or less of the females assembled who have not, perhaps for a long time, tasted a morsel of meat, being either widows, or orphans, or otherwise in straitened circumstances. Even the chat which passes during their joint labours is highly diverting to them, and so they seek to be employed in this way as long as they can, by going round to all those in the village who have ground to till.

When the harvest is in, which generally happens by the end of September, the women have little else to do than to prepare the daily victuals, and get fire wood, until the latter end of February or beginning of March, as the season is more or less backward, when they go to their sugar camps, where they extract sugar from the maple tree. The men having built or repaired their temporary cabin, and made all the troughs of various sizes, the women commence making sugar, while the men are looking out for meat, at this time generally fat bears, which are still in their winter quarters. When at home, they will occasionally assist their wives in gathering the sap, and watch the kettles in their absence, that the syrup may not boil over. . . .

After all, the fatigue of the women is by no means to be compared to that of the men. Their hard and difficult employments are periodical and of short duration, while their husband's labours are constant and severe in the extreme. Were a man to take upon himself a part of his wife's duty, in addition to his own, he must necessarily sink under the load, and of course his family must suffer with him. On his exertions as a hunter, their existence depends. . . .

The husband generally leaves the skins and peltry which he has procured by hunting to the care of his wife, who sells or barters them away to the best advantage for such necessaries as are wanted in the family; not forgetting to supply her husband with what he stands in need of, who, when he receives it from her hands never fails to return her thanks in the kindest manner. If debts had been previously contracted, either by the woman, or by her and her husband jointly, or if a horse should be wanted, as much is laid aside as will be sufficient to pay the debts or purchase the horse.

When a woman has got in her harvest of corn, it is considered as belonging to her husband, who, if he has suffering friends, may give them as much of it as he pleases, without consulting his wife, or being afraid of her being displeased; for she is in the firm belief that he is able to procure that article whenever it is wanted. The sugar which she makes of out of the maple tree is also considered as belonging to her husband. . . .

The more a man does for his wife the more he is esteemed, particularly by the women, who will say: "This man surely loves his wife." Some men at their leisure hours make bowls and ladles, which, when finished, are at their wives' disposal.

If a sick or pregnant woman longs for any article of food, be it what it may, and however difficult to be procured, the husband immediately sets out to endeavour to get it. I have known a man to go forty or fifty miles for a mess of cranberries to satisfy his wife's longing. . . .

It very seldom happens that a man condescends to quarrel with his wife, or abuse her, though she has given him just cause. In such a case the man, without replying, or saying a single word, will take his gun and go into the woods, and remain there a week or perhaps a fortnight, living on the meat he has killed, before he returns home again; well knowing that he cannot inflict a greater punishment on his wife for her conduct to him than by absenting himself for a while; for she is not only kept in suspense, uncertain whether he will return again, but is soon reported as a bad and quarrelsome woman. . . .

Marriages are proposed and concluded in different ways. The parents on both sides, having observed an attachment between two young persons, negotiate for them. This generally commences from the house where the bridegroom lives, whose mother is the negotiatrix for him, and begins her duties by taking a good leg of venison, or bear's meat, or something else of the same kind, to the house where the bride dwells, not forgetting to mention, that her son has killed it: in return for this the mother of the bride, if she otherwise approves of the match, which she well understands by the presents to be intended, will prepare a good dish of victuals, the produce of the labour of *woman,* such as beans, Indian corn, or the like, and then taking it to the house where the bridegroom lives, will say, "This is the produce of my daughter's field; and she also prepared it." If afterwards the mothers of the parties are enabled to tell the good news to each other, that the young people have pronounced that which was sent them *very good,* the bargain is struck. . . . The friendship between the two families daily increasing, they do their domestic and field work jointly, and when the young people have agreed to live together, the parents supply them with necessaries, such as a kettle, dishes or bowls, and also what is required for the kitchen, and with axes, hoes, &c. to work in the field.

5. The Captive John Tanner in 1830 Recalls His Foster Mother, Net-no-kwa, an Ottawa, in the 1790s

I had been about two years at Sau-ge-nong, when a great council was called by the British agents at Mackinac. This council was attended by the Sioux, the Winnebagoes, the Menomonees, and many remote tribes, as well as by the Ojibbeways, Ottawwaws, etc. When old Manito-o-geezhik returned from this council, I soon learned that he had met there his kinswoman, Net-no-kwa, who, notwithstanding her sex, was then regarded as principal chief of the Ottawwaws. This woman had lost her son, of about my age, by death; and having heard of me, she wished to purchase me to supply his place. My old Indian mother, the Otter woman, when she heard of this, protested vehemently against it. I heard her say, "My son has been dead once, and has been restored to me; I cannot lose him again." But these remonstrances had little influence, when Net-no-kwa arrived with considerable whiskey, and other presents. She brought to the lodge first a ten gallon keg of whiskey, blankets, tobacco, and other articles of great value. She was perfectly acquainted with the dispositions of those with whom she had to negotiate. Objections were made to the exchange until the contents of the keg had circulated for some time; then an additional keg, and a few more presents completed the bargain, and I was transferred to Net-no-kwa. This woman, who was then advanced in years, was of a more pleasing aspect than my former mother. She took me by the hand after she had completed the negotiation with my former possessors, and led me to her own lodge which stood near. Here I soon found I was to be treated more indulgently than I had been. She gave me plenty of food, put good clothes upon me, and told me to go and play with her own sons. . . .

In the following spring, Net-no-kwa, as usual, went to Mackinac. She always carried a flag in her canoe, and I was told, that whenever she came to Mackinac she was saluted by a gun from the fort. I was now thirteen years old, or in my thirteenth

A Narrative of the Captivity and Adventures of John Tanner . . . During Thirty Years Residence Among the Indians in the Interior of North America (1830), 15, 19, 27, 31, 86–87, 94–95.

year. . . . I have never met with an Indian, either man or woman, who had so much authority as Net-no-kwa. She could accomplish whatever she pleased, either with the traders or the Indians; probably, in some measure, because she never attempted to do any thing which was not right and just. . . .

In the fall of the year, we arrived at the Lake of Dirty Water, called by the whites Lake Winnepeg. . . . We stopped at a place called Prairie Portage. . . . The Indians gave Wa-me-gon-a-biew [his foster brother] and myself a little creek where were plenty of beaver and on which they said none but ourselves should hunt. My mother gave me three traps, and instructed me how to set them by the aid of a string tied around the spring, as I was not yet able to set them with my hands as the Indians did. I set my three traps, and on the following morning found beavers in two of them. Being unable to take them out myself, I carried home the beavers and traps, one at a time, on my back, and had the old woman to assist me. She was, as usual, highly gratified and delighted at my success. She had always been kind to me, often taking my side when the Indians would attempt to ridicule or annoy me. We remained in this place about three months, in which time we were as well provided for as any of the band; for if our own game was not sufficient, we were sure to be supplied by some of our friends as long as any thing could be killed. . . .

[Several years later, at a fur trader's,] I had the presence of mind to purchase some of the most needful articles for the winter, such as blankets and ammunition, as soon as we met him. After we had completed our trade, the old woman took ten fine beaver skins, and presented them to the trader. In return for this accustomed present, she was in the habit of receiving every year a chief's dress and ornaments, and a ten gallon keg of spirits, but when the trader sent for her to deliver his present, she was too drunk to stand. In this emergency, it was necessary for me to go and receive the articles. I had been drinking something, and was not entirely sober. I put on the chief's coat and ornaments, and taking the keg on my shoulder, carried it home to our lodge, placed it on one end, and knocked out the head with an axe. "I am not," said I, "one of those chiefs who draw liquor out of a small hole in a cask, let all those who are thirsty come and drink;" but I took the precaution to hide away a small keg full, and some in a kettle, probably in all three gallons. The old woman then came in with three kettles, and in about five minutes the keg was emptied. This was the second time that I had joined the Indians in drinking, and now I was guilty of much greater excess than before. I visited my hidden keg frequently, and remained intoxicated two days. . . .

About this time, old Net-no-kwa began to wake from her long continued drunkenness. She called me to her, and asked me whether I had received the chief's dress, and the keg of rum. She was unwilling to believe that I had suffered all the contents of the keg to be expended without reserving some for her. When she came to be assured not only that this was the case, but that I had been drunk for two days, she reproached me severely, censuring me not only for ingratitude to her, but for being such a beast as to be drunk. The Indians hearing her, told her she had no right to complain of me for doing as she herself had taught me, and by way of pacifying her, they soon contributed rum enough to make her once more completely drunk. . . .

Wa-me-gon-a-biew, after remaining with me four days, went to look for Wa-ge-tote, but without telling me any thing of his business. In a few days he returned, and told me that he had been to see Wa-ge-tote on account of his daughter that had been so often offered to me, and wished to know if I had any intention to marry her. I told him I had not, and that I was very willing to afford him any aid in my power in furtherance of his design. He wished me to return with him, probably that I might remove any impression the old people might have, that I would marry the girl, and accompany him in bringing her home. I assented without reflection, to this proposal and as we were about making our preparations to start, I perceived from Net-no-kwa's countenance, though she said nothing, that the course we were taking displeased her. I then recollected that it was not the business of young men to bring home their wives, and I told Wa-me-gon-a-biew that we should be ridiculed by all the people if we persisted in our design. "Here," said I, "is our mother, whose business it is to find wives for us when we want them, and she will bring them, and show them our places in the lodge whenever it is right she should do so." The old woman was manifestly pleased with what I said, and expressed her willingness to go immediately and bring home the daughter of Wa-ge-tote. She went accordingly, and it so happened that when she returned bringing the girl, Wa-me-gon-a-biew and myself were sitting inside the lodge. It appeared that neither Wa-me-gon-a-biew, nor the old woman, had been at the pains to give her any very particular information, for when she came in, she was evidently at a loss to know which of the young men before her had chosen her for a wife. Net-no-kwa perceiving her embarrassment, told her to sit down near Wa-me-gon-a-biew, for him it was whom she was to consider her husband. After a few days, he took her home to his other wife, with home she lived in harmony.

E S S A Y S

Michele Gillespie, who teaches at Wake Forest University, in 1997 published a biographical account of the role of the remarkable Anglo-Creek woman Mary Musgrove, who for several decades worked as an intermediary between Georgia settlers and her Creek relatives. Two years later, Bruce White, an independent scholar, looked at the roles of Ojibwa women in the fur trade. Although Creek and Ojibwa societies differed in fundamental ways, both authors stress the importance of their subjects' responsibilities in their communities.

Mary Musgrove and the Sexual Politics of Race and Gender in Georgia

MICHELE GILLESPIE

Early Saturday evening on August 12, 1749 the white residents of Savannah learned that several dozen Lower Creek warriors and their chiefs, accompanied by Mary Musgrove, her third husband Reverend Thomas Bosomworth, and his brother Abraham, were nearing town. "Alarmed by the beat of the drum" and fearing an Indian

---

Michele Gillespie, "The Sexual Politics of Race and Gender: Mary Musgrove and the Georgia Trustees," in Catherine Clinton and Michele Gillespie, eds., *The Devil's Lane: Sex and Race in the Early South* (New York: Oxford University Press, 1997), 187–201. Copyright © 1996 by Catherine Clinton and Michele Gillespie. Used by permission of Oxford University Press, Inc.

attack, the residents called out the militia, who prepared to fire on the visitors as they approached the Upper Square. The colony's leaders wisely chose this moment to intervene, inviting the chiefs and Reverend Bosomworth to engage in wine and talk rather than combat. Mary Musgrove, once the most respected arbiter of Anglo-Creek relations in the colony, was excluded from this session.

As James Oglethorpe's princip[al] interpreter between 1733 and 1743, negotiator for many thorny problems between the Creeks and the white colonists, and the most popular Indian trader south of Augusta, Mary Musgrove, the adult daughter of a Tuckabachee Creek woman and a white Carolina trader, was insulted at her exclusion. So great was her anger at the white leaders' blatant snub and her concern that her authority over both the Lower Creeks and the English settlers had been sabotaged, that after several hours of waiting, she entered the meeting room unbidden and proceeded to berate the leaders and their "white town" for the successive abuses she and the Creek people had endured at their hands. The white men responded to her outburst by treating the nearly fifty-year-old woman like a child, admonishing her "to go home, go to Bed and not expose herself." To the astonishment of all in attendance, Musgrove not only refused to leave but rebuked those present for not recognizing her status as leader of the Creek Nation. The Creeks in the room, she stated, were "her People." She added that all who resided on Creek lands, including the English settlers, were subject to her sovereignty.

Mary Musgrove found herself in these circumstances because she was the progeny of an interracial sexual relationship between a Creek woman and an English man. Such interracial unions aided the exchange of cultures that hastened both English colonization and Native American acculturation in southeastern North America in the eighteenth century. No wonder then that some English authorities sanctioned interracial marriage between Native American women and Englishmen. Through these unions, colonizers sought more than the fostering of peaceful relations with Native Americans—they sought their conquest. History and myth have linked famous Native American women from Pocahontas to Sacagawea to virtually every so-called successful encounter, from the European point of view, between Europeans and Native Americans in the New World. But the scores of anonymous Native American women who engaged in sexual liaisons with European men, and the children these liaisons produced, acted as mediators between these two cultures and played an equally significant and enduring role in colonial history. . . .

Unlike native peoples to the north, the southeastern indigenous groups had adapted their reduced populations, political organizations and cultural practices in response to the Spanish presence over several generations of time and prior to settlement by the English in Carolina. Thus English merchants and their traders, eager to procure furs and deerskins from these Indians, discovered in the late seventeenth century that the native peoples of the southeast were already familiar with Europeans, their ways, and their goods. This familiarity, along with native customs that sanctioned premarital intercourse and exogamous marriage, made sexual relationships and marriages between Native American women and white traders acceptable practice in most southeastern native societies in the late seventeenth and early eighteenth centuries.

Although acceptable practice, neither sex or marriage between Native American women and European men ensured that Native American women's subsequent lives, or the lives of their children, would be ordinary by Native American standards.

Instead, these women and their bicultural children were forced to assume the mantle of "cultural broker." Caught between two worlds, they found themselves occupying the contested terrain between distinctly different cultures. Both of these worlds, moreover, anticipated not only that cultural brokers understood the differences that separated them, but could "broker" some measure of understanding between them.

Despite their significance to the history of British settlement in the colonial southeast, the voices of these women and their progeny are virtually absent from the historical record with a few exceptions—almost always "half-breed" sons such as Alexander McGillivray of the Creeks and John Ross of the Cherokees who came to assume important leadership positions in their societies in the last half of the eighteenth and early nineteenth centuries. Mary Musgrove, however, the daughter of an interracial union herself, achieved significant standing among both the white settlers and the Lower Creeks in the first half of the eighteenth century. Though she is probably the most frequently cited woman in the history of colonial Georgia, Mary Musgrove remains an enigmatic figure. She has alternately been celebrated for her critical role as Oglethorpe's interpreter, vilified by those who view as extortion her demand for prime coastal lands given her by the Lower Creeks, and pitied by those who see her as the unwitting dupe of her conniving husbands and their grandiose schemes.

While very few extant records document Musgrove's own words, the texts that describe her prove as revealing as those she penned herself. These documents indicate that Musgrove's status as a "mixed-blood" woman proved useful, at least at times, as she moved back and forth across two different cultures for some five decades. The privileges Musgrove garnered as well as the drawbacks she endured by virtue of her perceived racial and gendered status, however, were not unique to her alone. We simply know more about Musgrove because her life experiences and their impact on the colonial enterprise assured their inclusion in the official record. Musgrove was exceptional in that she wielded substantial power as a cultural broker for the settlers and the Lower Creeks alike during the first two decades of white settlement in Georgia. Yet her circumstances, because they are relatively well documented, can also help us begin to understand how scores of other women in colonial Georgia, also the daughters of intercultural unions, negotiated the same changing boundaries of race, gender, sex, and culture. . . .

Mary Musgrove carefully cultivated her identity in response to the racial and gendered boundaries she encountered in the colonial culture of Georgia. As a "subjugated body," her choices were shaped by each successive phase of English settlement. Like all bicultural women, her body literally and figuratively linked these two distinct societies. Musgrove's life, then, can be used to exemplify the process of colonization and the importance of shifting racial and gendered boundaries in that process. Through Musgrove's experiences we see how and on what terms the English colonizers dominated and excluded from the increasingly hierarchical world they were constructing those individuals and social groups who proved most threatening to the establishment of their authority.

Little about Mary Musgrove's youth can be fully documented since original accounts about her and by her differ greatly. She was probably born between 1700 and 1708 to a Lower Creek woman and a South Carolina trader who lived together in the Creek town of Tuckabachee, near the Chatahoochee River. Though many historians dispute her version of her lineage, she claimed late in life that her mother was the sister of two important Creek leaders, Brim and his brother and successor Chigelli, thereby entitling her to call herself "Princess Coosaponakeesa." Musgrove also related that, at the age of seven, she "was brought Down by her Father from the Indian Nation, to Pomponne in South Carolina; There baptized, Educated and bred up in the principles of Christianity." She returned to her Creek town shortly after the Yamasees and their allies attacked the Carolina frontier in the Yamasee War of 1715, living with her relatives for as many as ten years before marrying Johnny Musgrove.

Johnny Musgrove was also the child of an interracial liaison. His mother was either a Tuckesaw or Apalachicola Creek woman, whose identity is unrecorded; his father, John Musgrove, was a wealthy South Carolina planter. Mary and Johnny probably married in 1725 and lived in South Carolina for seven years before moving to the Yamacraw settlement in 1732, near the future site of Savannah. The Yamacraws, perhaps a hundred in number, were a mixed group of Creeks and Yamasees who had settled on this coastal site only a few years before Oglethorpe's arrival. The Musgroves had been invited to establish a trading post at this settlement at the request of the Governor of Carolina and Tomomichichi, the Yamacraw leader.

By the 1720s, Creek leaders had concluded that the best strategy for contending with the influx of European colonizers was to maintain respectful but removed relations with all three: the Spanish, French, and English. But from the vantage point of the English, relations with the Creeks needed to be far more cordial if the colony of Carolina and the proposed colony of Georgia were to succeed. The Musgroves came to the aid of the English by negotiating peaceful relations between the settlers and the Creeks and Yamacraws. Shortly after the official founding of Georgia in 1732, Mary Musgrove quickly became Oglethorpe's favorite interpreter, helping him secure two treaties and two land cessions before his final departure from Georgia in 1743. . . .

Because Mary Musgrove was especially influential with the Creeks, due as much to her savvy as her alleged royal relations, Oglethorpe took great advantage of her willingness to aid him. When war with the Spanish loomed on the horizon, Musgrove successfully urged the Creeks to stand by the English, much to Oglethorpe's relief. Worried about the colony's weak borders, Oglethorpe subsequently convinced the Musgroves to establish a trading establishment sixty miles up the Altamaha River, where Mary Musgrove could watch the Spanish and monitor Creek loyalties. Oglethorpe consistently relied on Mary Musgrove as translator, fact gatherer and mediator during almost all his negotiations with the Creek leaders during his decade in Georgia. Nor did Mary Musgrove's influence falter with the death of her husband in 1735.

Shortly after John Musgrove's demise, Mary wed Jacob Matthews, her former indentured servant and the current commander of twenty rangers stationed at her Altamaha trading house, Mount Venture. She continued to assist Oglethorpe, who secured a substantial land cession from the Creeks in 1737–1738 with her aid. Although some Savannah residents felt she had married beneath her—while Matthews was an Englishman, he was also her former servant—no one could contest her continued influence with Oglethorpe and the Creeks and the benefits this relationship reaped for the colonists.

In the fall of 1738, the leaders of four Lower Creek towns invited Oglethorpe to meet them, with Mary Musgrove acting as interpreter. At this meeting the chiefs informed Oglethorpe that they were bestowing on Mary Musgrove some 300 prime coastal acres south of Savannah (on the old Yamacraw tract). A surprised Oglethorpe found himself forced to acknowledge this exchange, though he had no legal right under English law to approve it. Yet by witnessing this event, Oglethorpe had in fact sanctioned it, at least in the eyes of the Creek leaders and Mary Musgrove. All three parties clearly understood that for Oglethorpe to challenge Musgrove's right to this land would threaten far more than his relationship with his trusted interpreter; it would threaten the hitherto cordial relationship between the Creeks and the English, since the Creeks had bestowed gifts of land to the English under similar circumstances. Oglethorpe's unfortunate but calculated presence at this event would not only cost him much of his credibility with the other trustees but would generate a host of problems for the colonists in years to come.

Respect for Oglethorpe's leadership skills waned from this date forward. Two years later, England's war with Spain and the tensions between the Cherokees and the Creeks that ensued meant that relations between the Creeks and the English were at their weakest in nearly a decade. Oglethorpe's increasing ineffectualness compelled the Georgia Trustees to assess his negotiations in a more critical light. One of their first decisions was to condemn his spending habits, which had included many gifts for the Native Americans, and to take over the financial reins of the colony for themselves. This action had serious repercussions for Creek relations; Mary Musgrove and her new husband Jacob Matthews now had far fewer presents to dispense at their trading post, which exacerbated bad will between the Creeks and the English. Meanwhile Mary Musgrove, because she had been providing food and supplies to needy colonists and Creeks alike and had frequently been forced to leave her store unattended to assist Oglethorpe, lost money and business.

Despite her legitimate disgruntlement with the English leaders, Musgrove continued to act as an intermediary for Oglethorpe. Yet the new colonial government refused to pay not only for the costs encumbered by hosting Creeks, Yamacraws, and traders at her trading post but for her services as interpreter as well. The leaders also refused to recognize her stake in the coastal property awarded her by the Creeks. Still, the colony's leaders did not want to alienate her completely, for she remained an influential ally and diplomat. The trustees, therefore, chose to stall her request for legal recognition of her lands by initiating a Trustee's Grant that required lengthy legal procedures on the other side of the Atlantic.

In June 1742, Jacob Matthews died, which compelled Musgrove to leave their home, the Mount Venture post on the Altamaha. Most of the Creeks who had settled with her in the area departed as well. In their absence, the Spanish and their new allies the Yamacraws destroyed the place, straining Musgrove's declining resources even more. Then in the spring of 1743, Oglethorpe was ordered to depart the colony just as relations between the Creeks and the English soured anew in the wake of England's successful repulsion of the Spanish. Before leaving Georgia, Oglethorpe gave Musgrove 100 pounds and a diamond ring from his own hand as payment for her services and the losses she suffered at Mount Venture. He also promised her an annual salary of 100 pounds.

Despite these gifts, Oglethorpe left Mary Musgrove in a precarious situation. The leadership that had replaced him encouraged further deterioration of Creek-English relations. The new governor would honor neither the gift-giving traditions that had smoothed these relations in the past nor the concessions Oglethorpe had reached with the Creeks in 1738–1739. Meanwhile, Musgrove's appeals to the colony for legal recognition of her Yamacraw tract lands were denied.

Especially vulnerable at this time of her life given her reduced resources, Oglethorpe's departure, and her widowed status, Mary Musgrove chose to marry a third time to Thomas Bosomworth, an Anglican minister in the town of Savannah. The two had met during a boat voyage in June 1743 and were wed shortly thereafter. Bosomworth retained his title as minister but moved with Mary to her plantation where the two of them renewed her battle for legal right to the Yamacraw tract. Over the next four years, the trustees summarily rejected Musgrove's successive requests despite the passionate memorials she and her husband penned. . . .

War in Europe . . . ended in 1748. The peace treaty that ensued vanquished fear of Spanish invasion in Georgia. At the same time, some two thousand settlers, largely self-sufficient landholders, now resided in the colony which was experiencing slow but steady economic growth. These changing diplomatic and economic realities turned the historic relationship between the Creeks and the colonists on its head. Previously courted by the English, the Creeks suddenly found themselves scrambling for their suitor's favor. The tensions between the Creeks, Mary Musgrove and the colony that accompanied this transformation culminated in the fateful visit of Mary Musgrove, her husband Thomas Bosomworth, and several dozen Creek men to Savannah on a steamy summer evening in 1749.

Once the arbiter for all significant Anglo-Creek discussions, Mary Musgrove was pointedly excluded by white leaders from the session that followed the delegation's arrival. Distraught at the larger significance of this action, she broke into the meeting without invitation to deliver her extraordinary speech before the Creek chiefs and the colonial leaders. An unsympathetic white male eyewitness described Mary Musgrove's entrance and words as follows:

> [She] rushed into the Room, in the most violent and outrageous manner, that a Woman spirited up with Liquor, Drunk with passion, and disappointed in her Views could be guilty of. . . . She then, if possible, grew more outrageous, and in the most insulting manner declared, She was Empress of the Upper and Lower Creeks, Yea, went so far in her imaginary Sovereignty, as to call herself King, and that she should command every Man in these Nations to follow her, and We should soon know it our cost. It is needless to repeat, the threatening and irritating language used by this woman, indicating both her and [her] husband's wicked designs.

The white male officials present responded to Mary Bosomworth's impassioned speech by putting her under temporary custody. They were convinced that she was out of her mind or at the very least in a drunken rage. While we can never truly know her actual state, it seems likely that her accusers were attempting to justify their punitive actions against her by identifying her behavior as flagrantly inappropriate in accordance with their expectations about racial and gendered behavior. By labeling her either crazy or "just another drunken Indian," the colonial authorities could dismiss the deeper meanings behind her actions. Although too little evidence exists to assess Mary Musgrove's condition, it seems highly likely that she was both sane and sober and that her speech was a heroic act to preserve her authority in a society that was shifting the terms of colonization and settlement to suit itself.

Thomas Bosomworth himself was clearly aware that his wife's relationship to the colonists had been dramatically altered by her speech and her subsequent imprisonment. He responded to this turn of events by asserting his authority as a white man and a husband within this marriage. The day after his wife's impromptu oration, he publicly apologized to the colony's leaders for her behavior, stating that henceforth he would speak on behalf of the couple and that any and all utterances made by his wife should be ignored. Mary Musgrove herself later claimed that from that day forward she was "no longer countenanced by the White People," despite her significant record of diplomacy and trade that had contributed so enormously to the colony's successful venture.

Mary Musgrove's verbal assault on the officials was a desperate measure by a desperate woman. She had come to understand that the colony no longer appreciated either her skillful negotiations with the Creeks or her right to lay claim to lands she had earned. She also had come to recognize that the role she had carved out for herself as Christian helpmeet to the colonists was no longer tenable.

By renouncing the colonial leaders and their "white Town," by reclaiming her Creek identity, Mary Musgrove not only lost the respect of the white male European leaders but was subsequently silenced by them. It did not help her cause that she had chosen such an inappropriate way for a woman in this society, particularly a Christian woman born of a Creek mother, to convey her anger. In the eyes of the colony's stewards, she had transformed herself overnight, reduced to the status of outcast and heathen. Even her spouse understood the implications of her debacle when he publicly declared himself her spokesman. While Mary Musgrove and her third husband would continue to seek legal right to the Creek lands awarded her for another decade, eventually securing a compromise deal that allowed her to claim St. Catherine's Island as her own, along with the money made from the public sale of Ossabaw and Sapelo Islands, she never regained her former status as cultural broker to the colony.

This denouement should not be too surprising. Mary Musgrove's speech in essence had denigrated every Anglo-American premise on which the white leaders had erected their colony and on which she had allegedly acted, with the understandable effect of turning the entire white colony against her. Although Mary Musgrove had supposedly been negotiating on behalf of the colonial leaders' best interests for years, her speech indicated that her allegiance now clearly lay with the Creeks. She had turned her back in a most deliberate and spectacular fashion on the white officials who believed she had embraced them as her own. Despite the serious consequences of her actions, one suspects that after years of negotiating the sexual, racial, and gendered boundaries of the Anglo-American male world as a woman of "mixed blood," she breathed a long sigh of relief at being able to shed the conflicting identities she had carefully negotiated for so long. . . .

Oglethorpe and his men had not considered Mary Musgrove a particularly worthy woman on making her acquaintance in 1732. Knowing little of her background, they used English notions about fashion and status as well as race and gender to mark her among the lower sort in social rank, observing that "she appeared to be in mean and low circumstances, being only cloathed with a red stround petticoat and

Osnabrig Shift." Yet Mary Musgrove soon earned their respect despite their initial assessment, proving her worth to Oglethorpe and the colony as a whole. These Englishmen discovered that the social codes embedded in notions of gender and race as well as dress and behavior, which structured their views of both Old World and New, were far from accurate in the early days of English settlement in Georgia.

Over time Mary Musgrove's authority as a cultural mediator was legitimated in English eyes more by her status as a good Christian helpmeet than by her rough attire or Creek background. Thus, while an earlier generation of historians pinned Musgrove's willingness to remarry so quickly following on the deaths of her husbands on her lusty nature, an assumption with unsavory undertones about status and sexual desire, another interpretation is well worth considering. Musgrove may have known that prolonged widowhood would have made her vulnerable to scandal as a single woman on a remote frontier working with men of all races. Marriage, especially to an Englishman, offered her reputation some measure of protection, especially since the institution was sanctified by the Church. Taken in that light, Musgrove may have held her third and final marriage to the minister Thomas Bosomworth as the most significant. In a society in which she remained in most ways an outsider, marriage to someone as venerable as a minister raised her social standing and protected her reputation. Widowed white women were legally permitted to retain their property in colonial Georgia, and Mary Musgrove was one of the largest women landholders in a colony where land afforded its owners status and independence as well as subsistence. Yet Musgrove may have chosen not to remain single, despite her relative wealth and influence, because of her marginal status as a mixed-blood woman.

Although Musgrove spent most of her adult life as a married woman, she bore children only with her first husband and none of them lived to adulthood. Yet she knew the significance that the English settlers tied to their prescribed gender roles. Childless by the 1740s, she publically upheld maternal feelings and used the term "Maternal Affection" to describe her relationship with "the Infant Colony" of Georgia. Musgrove's claim to be the Mother of the Colony, despite its grandiosity, remained grounded in Christian notions about a woman's special calling. Musgrove used this metaphor in her memorial to the trustees in 1747 since its meaning was understood by the white leaders. Through it she inferred that she was not a greedy powermonger, bent on shaping the colony to her will, but a Christian woman fulfilling her female duty as best she could. . . .

The complexities and contradictions that surrounded Mary Musgrove throughout her life were manifold. The daughter of a white father and a Creek mother, raised among whites, and the recipient of a Christian education, she aided both the Creeks and the English settlers as an interpreter and a trader, accruing substantial property, servants, and slaves throughout the 1730s and early 1740s. As the colonial leaders perceived that Musgrove's usefulness to the maturing colony was on the wane, however, and as Musgrove sought formal recognition of the lands the Creeks had bestowed on her, the English authorities who dealt with Musgrove reassessed her value to the colony. As they did so, they also reconceptualized her racial and gendered identity to suit their changing needs. Musgrove's influence with the Lower Creeks, along with her knowledge of English and Creek cultures, had made her an invaluable ally to the Georgia Trustees during the earliest stages of settlement. Her careful negotiations had in fact assured the relative success of the colonial venture. But by 1749 she was forced to contend with a new series of ordeals and confrontations at the hands of the latest colonial government. These challenges to her authority reflected the leadership's lowered opinion of her value to the Georgia colony. Colonial leaders had shifted the terms, demanding that she adhere to their conceptions of race and gender difference in order to diminish her authority and power. Henceforth she would be expected to observe a whole new set of boundaries to fit into their world.

Certainly Mary Musgrove was a product of, as well as a contributor to, the evolution of the triracial cultural encounter in Georgia and therefore defies easy analysis. After all, the limited nature of the sources makes it difficult to determine with absolute certainty where her allegiances really lay and how they changed over time. Nor can it be determined precisely how the shifting boundaries of race, class, gender, and sex in early Georgia influenced the kinds of choices she made, though again the sources seem suggestive. Was Mary Musgrove struggling to survive the personal circumstance of the cultural encounter? Or was she struggling for more power and influence given her special authority and status? The latter seems far more likely.

At the very least, Mary Musgrove clearly understood the cultural differences that separated the Creeks and the English. Moreover, she used that knowledge to wage a fierce contest, to triumph, however briefly, in this new society. Her life story demonstrates that colonial mix in Georgia was far more complicated than any simple depiction of violent conquest. Mary Musgrove's words, actions, and authority defy any essentialist interpretations that hinge on the good Indian woman's loss of status and respect in the evil Christian world of the white colonialists. Far more complex interactions were at play here.

Gender Roles in the Ojibwa Fur Trade

BRUCE M. WHITE

In 1904, Kagige Pinasi (John Pinesi), an Ojibwa (Anishinaabe)–French man living at Fort William on the north shore of Lake Superior, told the anthropologist William Jones a story about a young woman who married a beaver. With blackened face she went to fast for a long time during a vision quest. She saw a person in human form who spoke to her. He asked her to come live with him. She did and eventually agreed to marry him. She was well provided with food and clothing and soon gave birth to four children.

She soon noticed something very odd that led her to realize for the first time that she had married a beaver. From time to time the woman's husband or children would leave with a human being who appeared outside their house. "And back home would they always return again. All sorts of things would they fetch—kettles and bowls, knives, tobacco, and all the things that are used when a beaver is eaten; such was what they brought. Continually they were adding to their great wealth." They would go to where the person lived and the person would kill the beavers. Yet

Bruce M. White, "The Woman Who Married a Beaver: Trade Patterns and Gender Roles in the Ojibwa Fur Trade," *Ethnohistory* 46, no. 1 (Winter 1999). Copyright © by the American Society of Ethnohistory. All rights reserved. Used by permission of the publisher.

the beavers were never really killed. They would come back home again with the clothes and tobacco that people gave them. The beavers were very fond of the people and would visit them often. The woman herself was forbidden to go by her husband, but this is what she heard.

Eventually the woman's husband died and she returned to live with human beings. She lived a long time after that and often told the story of what happened while she lived with the beavers. She always told people that they should never speak ill of a beaver or they would never be able to kill any: "If any one regards a beaver with too much contempt, speaking ill of it, one simply [will] not [be able to] kill it. Just the same as the feelings of one who is disliked, so is the feeling of the beaver. And he who never speaks ill of a beaver is very much loved by it; in the same way as people often love one another, so is one held in the mind of the beaver, particularly lucky then is one at killing beavers." . . .

A primary purpose of such accounts is educational. Ojibwa elders told stories like this, usually in winter, to teach young people about the world while entertaining them. As such, these narratives are also a useful way for outsiders to learn about the people's worldview and understand their view of their history. . . .

. . . [T]his story is, like all Ojibwa stories, interesting on many levels. It instructs young people, especially girls, on the importance of the vision quest, the means through which an Ojibwa person obtained a relationship with powerful beings who would be helpful to her and could chart a unique course for her life. Further, it is a basic description of and commentary on the cooperative arrangements that many Ojibwa people believed existed between different kinds of beings in the world. Ojibwa people who hunted, fished, or gathered plants had to be aware of their reciprocal obligations with the natural world and give back something to the animals, fish, or plants from which they harvested. In taking small plants in the woods, or bark from the trees, people often left a gift of tobacco. After a bear was killed, they held an elaborate ceremony of thanks and gave presents to the bear. The beaver story shows that reciprocity was necessary to keep the system operating. Without gifts and respect, animals would no be so helpful to humans. They would hold themselves back and not allow themselves to be used by people. Without gifts and respect, the system would cease to function.

Ojibwa people also applied the principle of reciprocity to their dealings with people, including non-Indians. In their earliest interactions with the French and the British, the Ojibwa made use of the same gifts, ceremonies, and words that they used in dealing with animals, plants, and other beings. The logic of approaching Europeans in this way was solid; interaction with Europeans was important because of the valuable technology Europeans brought with them. Reciprocity was necessary to keep the system operating. Without gifts and respect, Europeans would not be so helpful to Indian people. They would withhold their technology from Indian people. Without gifts and respect, the system would cease to function.

Dealing with animals differed, of course, from dealing with Europeans. The Ojibwa quickly worked out a variety of strategies that were specific to the newcomers. For example, they gave different things. The story of the woman who married the beaver describes a reverse fur trade. In the European fur trade, Indian people gave furs in return for tools, kettles, and tobacco, but this story tells of a relationship in which people gave tools, kettles, and tobacco to beavers in return for the animals' furs.

There is yet another striking feature of the story: it delineates an intermediary role for women in the interaction between people and animals, suggesting a role for women in the interaction between the Ojibwa and Europeans. This story is not an origin tale. It does not describe the beginnings of the reciprocal arrangement between people and animals. For the people in the story, the relationship was a well-established, functioning system. Yet the story explains the system and how it works through the experiences of a woman. . . . Women, it would appear, have power to cross boundaries, explaining one world to another, in this case through a marriage relationship. This power had implications for the workings of the fur trade. . . .

From the seventeenth century on, the fur trade was important to the Ojibwa, who had a continuing, though variable, interest in obtaining European merchandise to use in their daily lives, in hunting, cooking, and religious ceremonies. Trade goods offered material benefits, increased status, and much more. But from the beginning, traders accommodated Ojibwa demand by bringing a rich assortment of goods, including cloth, blankets, utensils, tools, silver jewelry, thread, and beads. In return, traders needed more from the Ojibwa than furs. They also needed a rich variety of products that only women could provide. All these factors meant that both Ojibwa men and women had a variety of roles to play and methods of exerting power and influence over the trade process.

The major role of women in the fur trade was not evident in the earliest years of French-Ojibwa interaction, when canoe-loads of people from the western Great Lakes went east to Montreal to trade their furs with the French. It may be that women were involved in these expeditions, although most accounts suggest that the participants were mainly men. Later, however, when the location of trade shifted to native villages . . . women became crucial to the trade.

In the context of the trading post and the village, Ojibwa men and women had distinct and often different relationships with traders. The fur trade was never simply an exchange of furs for trade goods. It included a variety of other kinds of transactions. Traders needed to get food from native people; without it, they could not survive the winter in the western Great Lakes. They simply could not bring in or collect enough food to feed themselves, while at the same time carrying on the fur business. At the same time, . . . traders needed a variety of native-manufactured supplies. The multifaceted nature of this trade meant that native people interacted with traders in many ways.

The varied interactions of Ojibwa men and women with traders were manifested in the complex set of trade patterns that made up a complete trading year. In the eighteenth century, a trading year in a Southwestern Ojibwa community would begin with the arrival in the fall of the trader with a new supply of goods. Once established in a fort or trading house, he gathered members of the community and gave and received ceremonial gifts. Goods such as clothing and utensils designed to help the Ojibwa survive the winter were then given out on credit, and customers went on their fall and winter hunts. The trader often purchased supplies of wild rice for his own survival and in some cases hired a hunter and his family to provide him with meat during the winter. Later, the trader or his men might visit native families to collect the furs they produced. Similarly, native people might revisit the trading post bringing in furs. In such circumstances, there could be further gifts and further credit. At the end of the trading year in the spring, before the trader's departure, certain goods were traded in direct exchanges and there might be concluding gifts and ceremonies.

Gift, barter, and credit transactions were differentiated in a variety of ways. One means of differentiation was simply the way in which both parties spoke about them. Both traders and customers gave speeches in which they explained what they expected of their relationship as a whole and what they expected of any particular transaction. The temporal and seasonal context was also important. Gifts began the trading year, cemented other exchanges, and ended the year. Credit was largely given in the fall. Direct exchanges of furs for merchandise took place in late winter or in the spring.

Another means of differentiating these various transactions was in the trade goods and native products. Evidence suggests the existence of spheres of exchange, or categories of trade goods subject to different rules and procedures. For example, cloth goods and alcohol were defined and treated in strikingly different ways in the trade context. Alcohol, whether brandy, high wines, or rum, had some obvious culturally defined characteristics in the fur trade as well as native-European diplomacy. Among traders in the Lake Superior region in the late eighteenth and early nineteenth centuries, alcohol in the form of rum or brandy was chiefly given to native people in two kinds of transactions: as gifts and in exchange for food. The trading ceremonies at the beginning and end of the year, and on the repayment of debts, usually featured gifts of alcohol. The food on which the trader depended, such as wild rice, game, and maple sugar, was often obtained with liquor. By contrast, cloth, clothing, and blankets were mainly exchanged in the context of credit/debt transactions or in direct exchange for furs and possibly for supplies. Thus, contrary to the usual picture of the fur trade, the bulk of furs received by traders were not actually obtained in barter. Rather, they were received as repayment for credit granted in the fall, in the form of cloth, tools, and utensils.

Trade transactions were not only differentiated by time and type of trade merchandise, but also by gender. . . .

Men appear to have been the most frequent participants in trade ceremonies, as they were in other kinds of non–trade-related diplomacy. Leading men in the community gave speeches and sometimes, especially at the beginning of the trading year, presented gifts of furs or food. In return, they were given gifts of liquor, which they appear to have shared with men and women alike. It was also on such occasions that leading men were presented with chief's coats and other symbols of their role in the trade and in the community. Sometimes they were "made chiefs," that is, given status by the trader that they did not actually have in the community. It should be noted that the skillful leader—one who understood the need of leaders to give things away in order to increase their own status in the community—often gave away the clothing and other symbols of power given them by traders. Such gifts may have gone to women as well as men. In any case, trade ceremonies also involved more general gifts to men and women in the community. . . .

It is usually asserted that men were the primary traders of furs. This is hard to document, given the fact that few furs were actually traded directly. Instead, as noted, they were exchanged in credit/debt transactions. Traders seldom listed the goods they gave out on credit or even to whom credit was given, though usually traders recorded debts in the names of men. It is impossible to know whether women or men chose the goods given out in this fashion. It could be argued that even if the credit was granted to the hunters or trappers who were expected to produce the furs, this does not preclude the possibility that women were involved in the choice of goods or that men discussed with their wives what the wives or children needed for the winter. . . .

As for the repayment of the debts during the winter, a variety of people could be involved, including the hunter or trapper, his children, and his wives or female relations. Often the trader would be notified that a particular group of trappers had produced some furs. He would then send off his men to pick them up. Subsequently, the hunter or other members of the family would be given a gift of alcohol in some form, which would, again, be shared among men and women. It should also be noted that there were occasions when women traded furs directly. While men were the primary hunters and trappers in Ojibwa communities, women processed the furs, a fact that would have given them greater authority in deciding what would happen to the furs, as well as the opportunity to trade them.

The occasional role of women in bartering furs was part of a larger role in bartering. Food was an important part of women's trade. They supplied wild rice and maple sugar, both of which were mainstays for the trader. As noted, the characteristic return for such items of food was liquor. However, there were exceptions to this pattern. For example, food was sometimes traded for a variety of trade goods other than liquor, especially in times of scarcity. . . .

Wild rice was important not only as a trade item to be consumed by traders while living in an Ojibwa village near the Great Lakes, but also as an important way to feed brigades traveling further west. . . .

Canoes—the product of both men's and women's labor—were often traded by women and were a useful way to obtain a full range of trade goods. . . .

Considering their role in trading a wide variety of food and supplies, it may be that women were more often involved in direct trade than men. . . .

Beyond these opportunities for women to trade their own products for a wide range of goods, some women took part in the ceremonial trading roles of giving and receiving gifts and getting credit, the more typical role of men. A prime example was Netnokwa, the Ottawa mother of the adopted white captive, John Tanner, who lived with her family among Ojibwa west of the Red River around 1800. On the occasion of trading with one trader, according to Tanner, Netnokwa "took ten fine beaver skins, and presented them to the trader. In return for this accustomed present, she was in the habit of receiving every year a chief's dress and ornaments, and a ten gallon keg of spirits." Around the time described in the narrative, Charles Chaboillez, a North West Company trader, stated that on arriving in the region of the Red River, he exchanged presents with and gave credit to the "Old Courte Oreille [Ottawa] & Two Sons." This was clearly a reference to Netnokwa, Tanner, and Tanner's adopted brother. Later, Chaboillez stated that he gave her a present of rum and tobacco, "to encourage her to return" with furs and other products, a suggestion of her primary role in trading. How typical Netnokwa was of other women in the community in which she lived is not clear. . . .

There were various explanations for Netnokwa's participation in trade rituals more frequently undertaken by men. For one thing, when she and her family were coming west several years before, Netnokwa's husband had died. Death or illness of a husband and other emergencies appear to have been important reasons for women to undertake activities that were normally the work of men, as it would have been for men to undertake the work of women on occasion. . . .

In the case of Netnokwa, however, her transcendence of usual gender roles was evident even before her husband's death. As an older woman who had been married to a younger husband with two other wives, Netnokwa was, according to Tanner, considered to be the head of the household, even before his adopted father's death. Tanner stated that Netnokwa was seventeen years older than her husband, was an accomplished trader, and was owner of most of the family's wealth. Tanner said, perhaps exaggerating, that she was "notwithstanding her sex, . . . regarded as principal chief of the Ottawwaws," and that "whenever she came to Mackinac, she was saluted by a gun from the fort." Perhaps most significant of all—in terms of Ojibwa and Ottawa culture—Netnokwa was, as described by Tanner, a person of strong spirituality, and she used her power to aid her sons in hunting.

Dreams and visions were often cited as providing authorization for Ojibwa men and women to transcend the gendered division of labor. Despite the tendency of scholars to analyze gender roles based on material factors, including participation in the fur trade, power in an Ojibwa community was never purely material, and even material power was usually seen as having a nonmaterial basis. . . .

Thus, despite the existence of a well-understood division of labor, described as rigid in many generalized descriptions of the Ojibwa, the more recent ethnographic evidence suggests that the Ojibwa gave cultural acceptance to those who violated the usual gender roles, and who demonstrated competence brought about by spiritual aid. Such cultural acceptance suggests that for many Ojibwa, creative, dynamic women forging a unique course were seen as having a beneficial effect on their communities. This is also evident in a major aspect of the role of women in the fur trade, their role as the wives of traders. . . .

Among the Ojibwa, marriage was defined by the decision of two parties, sometimes through the intercession of parents or other relations, to sleep, live, and carry on their day-to-day lives together. Although the event was not marked by the ceremonies with which Europeans were familiar, it could involve ceremonial exchanges of gifts. From the point of view of the native community, marriages between traders and native women could help achieve the important aim of ensuring a steady supply of merchandise. Ties of affection could increase the likelihood that a trader would return to the community in future years and that he might be more generous with gifts and in the rates exacted for direct exchange. . . .

For fur traders, their wives or the wives of their employees could prove to be useful socially and economically. The evidence suggests that leading traders often married the daughters of Ojibwa leaders, although it is sometimes hard to say which came first. In marrying a leader's daughter, a trader gained a powerful ally among his Indian customers. Since the authority of a leader was in part the result of extended kin ties, the trader may have formed ties with a large number of people. The leader's influence over kin and nonkin alike depended also on his persuasive oratory. Thus, through marriage, the trader gained an alliance with a man of demonstrated ability to influence his fellows. The father-in-law could become, in a sense, an economic agent for the trader, useful in persuading the people to be friends and clients. . . .

The implication of some accounts of marriages arranged by traders and the parents of native women is that women were passive objects like the furs, food, and merchandise exchanged in the fur trade. . . . [I]t is open to question whether this was the case with most such marriages. To be effective in achieving the purposes native communities might envision for such marriages, women could not be passive. They had to exert influence and be active communicators of information. Further, there is evidence that marriages were not simply arranged by male and female elders in communities. Rather they were embraced by many women themselves as a way of achieving useful purposes for themselves and for the communities in which they lived. . . .

The fur trade is sometimes seen simply as an exchange that took place between men of European and native cultures. However, an examination of the trade among the Ojibwa of Lake Superior shows that women and men both participated in the trade. They also had different opportunities, different expectations, and different roles to play. As acknowledged by traders in their gift giving and trade, men and women sought a different assortment of trade goods. Women also played an important role in providing the resources that were their responsibility in native life: wild rice, maple sugar, and a variety of vital supplies necessary for the function of trade. While most women did not usually participate in trade ceremonies or receive credit from traders, they were able to trade the products of their labor for goods they needed. Finally, women also could serve as a vital link between their communities and European traders by marrying traders. Such marriages could ensure a steady supply of merchandise for a community by providing an incentive for traders to return to the communities from which their wives came and, possibly, by increasing their generosity toward their wives' relations. Although such marriages were encouraged and often arranged by men, women were not mere object to be exchanged. The value of such marriages to a native community could only be achieved if women exercised influence on the trader and served to increase the flow of information and merchandise in both directions. . . .

The extent to which Ojibwa women's power and status in their own communities may have changed since contact with Europeans remains to be demonstrated. A major problem with describing the course of changes in Ojibwa society in the last four hundred years is the difficulty of reconstructing Ojibwa gender relations in the era prior to European contact using only documents that result from that contact. Analysis of the changes in Ojibwa society in the era of the fur trade also requires care, especially if it is based on documents that interpret Ojibwa gender from a European point of view of how men and women should live their lives.

FURTHER READING

Anderson, Karen. *Chain Her by One Foot: The Subjugation of Native Women in Seventeenth-Century New France* (1991).

Barr, Juliana. "A Diplomacy of Gender: Rituals of First Contact in the 'Land of the Tejas,'" *William and Mary Quarterly* 61 (2004): 393–434.

Bragdon, Kathleen. "Gender as a Social Category in Native Southern New England," *Ethnohistory* 43 (1996): 573–592.

Brooks, James F. "'This Evil Extends Especially . . . to the Feminine Sex': Negotiating Captivity in the New Mexico Borderlands," *Feminist Studies* 22 (1996): 279–310.

Demos, John. *The Unredeemed Captive: A Family Story from Early America* (1994).

Devens, Carol. *Countering Colonization: Native American Women and Great Lakes Missions* (1992).

Fickes, Michael. "'They Could Not Endure That Yoke': The Captivity of Pequot Women and Children after the War of 1637," *New England Quarterly* 73 (2000): 58–81.

Gutiérrez, Ramón. *When Jesus Came, the Corn Mothers Went Away: Marriage, Sexuality, and Power in New Mexico, 1500–1846* (1991).

Merritt, Jane. "Cultural Encounters Along a Gender Frontier: Mahican, Delaware, and German Women in Eighteenth-Century Pennsylvania," *Pennsylvania History* 67 (2000): 503–532.

Namias, June. *White Captives: Gender and Ethnicity on the American Frontier* (1993).

Pesantubbee, Michelene. *Choctaw Women in a Chaotic World: The Clash of Cultures in the Colonial Southeast* (2005).

Plane, Ann Marie. *Colonial Intimacies: Indian Marriage in Early New England* (2000).

Rountree, Helen. "Powhatan Indian Women: The People Captain John Smith Barely Saw," *Ethnohistory* 45 (1998): 1–29.

Smith, Susan Sleeper. *Indian Women and French Men: Rethinking Cultural Encounter in the Western Great Lakes* (2001).

Townsend, Camilla. *Pocahontas and the Powhatan Dilemma* (2004).

CHAPTER
3

Witches and Their Accusers in Seventeenth-Century New England

The study of witchcraft has fascinated historians of early modern women in both Europe and America. Indeed, in recent years a great deal of scholarly attention has been devoted to the era of the witch-hunts, from the sixteenth century through the late seventeenth century. What sorts of women were accused as witches? Why were they accused? Who were their accusers? Many books and articles have examined such questions, without reaching consensus except on some very basic points, such as the fact that most of the accused were women rather than men, and that they tended to be middle-aged or older.

In early America, most of the known witchcraft prosecutions occurred in New England, but historians disagree about why that was so. Some contend that New England's Puritan beliefs led the settlers to fear women's sinfulness and potential alliance with the devil, whereas others argue that witchcraft accusations were primarily generated in small, close-knit, rural communities, like those that dotted the New England landscape. Another disagreement, which is reflected in the essays selected for this chapter, represents a difference of opinion about the appropriate emphasis in studies of witchcraft: should historians of women focus on the female accused (as has been the most common approach) or on female accusers?

 D O C U M E N T S

In seventeenth-century America, witchcraft prosecutions often began with gossip, and sometimes accused people could prevent formal charges from being filed against them by first suing the gossipers for slander. Under then-prevailing law, all that plaintiffs in such cases had to prove was that the defendants had uttered the words in question. Yet, as Document 1 shows, if the gossip was widely believed, that tactic did not always work. Elizabeth Godman, a reputed witch in the New Haven colony, sued those slandering her as a witch in 1653, but, as Document 2 reveals, she still faced trial for witchcraft two years later. Document 3, an excerpt from Cotton Mather's *Wonders of the Invisible World* (1693), details the 1692 trial of Bridget Bishop of Salem Town, who fit all the stereo-types of witch beliefs in the period. Document 4, by contrast, presents the accusations of a group of girls and young women (also in 1692) against the Reverend George Burroughs, the only New England minister ever charged with, and convicted of, witchcraft.

1. Elizabeth Godman Sues Her Neighbors for Accusing Her of Being a Witch, 1653

The Examination of Elizabeth Godman, May 21ᵗʰ, 1653

Elizabeth Godman made complainte of Mr. Goodyeare, Mris. Goodyeare, Mr. Hooke, Mris. Hooke, Mris. Bishop, Mris. Atwater, Hanah & Elizabeth Lamberton, and Mary Miles, Mris. Atwaters maide, that they have suspected her for a witch; she was now asked what she had against Mr. Hooke and Mris. Hooke; she said she heard they had something against her aboute their soone. Mr. Hooke said hee was not wᵗhout feares, and hee had reasons for it; first he said it wrought suspition in his minde be-cause shee was shut out at Mr. Atwaters upon suspition, and hee was troubled in his sleepe aboute witches when his boye, was sicke, wᶜh was in a verey strang manner, and hee looked upon her as a mallitious one, and prepared to that mischiefe, and she would be often speaking aboute witches and rather justifye them then condemne them; she said why doe they provoake them, why doe they not let them come into the church. Another time she was speaking of witches wᵗhout any occasion given her, and said if they accused her for a witch she would have them to the governor, she would trounce them. . . .

Mr. Hooke further said, that he hath heard that they that are adicted that way would hardly be kept away from yᵉ houses where they doe mischeife, and so it was wᵗh her when his boy was sicke, she would not be kept away from him, nor gott away when she was there, and one time Mris. Hooke bid her goe away, and thrust her from yᵉ boye, but she turned againe and said she would looke on him. Mris. Goodyeare said that one time she questioned wᵗh Elizabeth Godman aboute yᵉ boyes sickness, and said what thinke you of him, is he not strangly handled, she replyed, what, doe you thinke hee is bewitched; Mris. Goodyeare said nay I will keepe my thoughts to myselfe, but in time God will discover. . . .

Mr. Hooke further said, that when Mr. Bishop was married, Mris. Godman came to his house much troubled, so as he thought it might be from some affection to him, and he asked her, she said yes; now it is suspitious that so soone as they were contracted Mris. Byshop fell into verey strang fitts wᶜh hath continewed at times ever since, and much suspition there is that she hath bine the cause of the loss of Mris. Byshops children, for she could tell when Mris. Bishop was to be brought to bedd, and hath given out that she kills her children wᵗh longing, because she longs for every thing she sees, wᶜh Mris. Bishop denies. . . .

From Franklin B. Dexter, ed., *Ancient Town Records: New Haven Town Records, 1649–1684* (New Haven: New Haven Colony Historical Society, 1917, 1919) 1:249–252, 256–257.

June 16, 1653

Goodwife Thorp complained that M^ris. Godman came to her house and asked to buy some chickens, she said she had none to sell, M^ris. Godman said will you give them all, so she went away, and she thought then that if this woman was naught as folkes suspect, may be she will smite my chickens, and quickly after one chicken dyed, and she remembred she had heard if they were bewitched they would consume w^thin, and she opened it and it was consumed in ye gisard to water & wormes. . . .

Court of Magistrates, New Haven, August 4, 1653

M^ris. Elizabeth Godman accused goodwife Larremore that one time when she saw her come in at goodman Whitnels she said so soone as she saw her she thought of a witch. Goodwife Larremore said that one time she had spoken to that purpose at M^r. Hookes, and her ground was because M^r. Davenport aboute that time had occasion in his ministry to speake of witches, and showed that a froward discontented frame of spirit was a subject fitt for ye Devill to worke upon in that way, and she looked upon M^rs. Godman to be of such a frame of spirit, but for saying so at goodman Whitnels she denyes it. M^ris. Godman said, goodman Whitnels maid can testify it. The maid was send, and when she came she said she heard M^ris. Godman and good-wife Larremore a talking, and she thinks she heard goodwife Larremore say she thought of a witch in ye Bay when she see M^ris. Godman. . . .

   M^ris. Godman was told she hath warned to the court divers psons, viz^d: M^r. Goodyeare, M^ris. Goodyeare, M^r. Hooke, M^ris. Hooke, M^ris. Atwater, Hanah & Elizabeth Lamberton, goodwife Larremore, goodwife Thorpe, &c., and was asked what she hath to charge them w^th, she said they had given our speeches that made folkes thinke she was a witch, and first she charged M^ris. Atwater to be ye cause of all . . . and she further said that M^ris. Atwater had said that she thought she was a witch and that Hobbamocke [the devil] was her husband, but could prove nothing. . . . After sundrie of the passages in ye wrighting [the record of her examination] were read, she was asked if these things did not give just ground of suspicion to all that heard them that she was a witch. She confessed they did, but said if she spake such things as is in M^r. Hookes relation she was not herselfe. . . . Beside what is in the paper, M^ris. Godman was remembred of a passage spoken of at the governo^rs aboute M^r. Goodyeares falling into a swonding fitt after hee had spoken something one night in the exposition of a chapter, wch she (being present) liked not but said it was against her, and as soone as M^r. Goodyeare had done duties she flung out of the roome in a discontented way and cast a fierce looke upon M^r. Goodyeare as she went out, and imediately M^r. Goodyeare (thought well before) fell into a swond, and beside her notorious lying in this buisnes, for being asked how she came to know this, she said she was present, yet M^r. Goodyeare, M^ris. Goodyeare, Hanah and Elizabeth Lamberton all affirme she was not in ye roome but gone up into the chamber.

   After the agitation of these things the court declared to M^ris. Godman, as their judgment and sentence in this case, that she hath unjustly called heither the severall persons before named, being she can prove nothing against them, and that her cariage doth justly render her suspitious of witchcraft, wch she herselfe in so many words confesseth, therefore the court wisheth her to looke to her carriage hereafter, for it further proofe come, these passages will not be forgotten, and therefore gave her charge not to goe in an offensive way to folkes houses in a rayling manner as it seemes she hath done, but that she keepe her place and medle wth her owne buisnes.

2. Elizabeth Godman Is Tried for Witchcraft, 1655

New Haven Town Court, August 7, 1655

Elizabeth Godman was called before the Court, and told that she lies under suspition for witchcraft, as she knowes, the grounds of which were examined in a former Court, and by herselfe confessed to be just grounds of suspition, wch passages were now read, and to these some more are since added, wch are now to be declared: . . .

Goodwife Thorpe informed the Court that concerning something aboute chickens she had formerly declared, wch was now read, after wch she one time had some speech wth M^ris. Evance aboute this woman, and through the weakness of her faith she began to doubt that may be she would hurt her cowes, and that day one of her cowes fell sick in the herd, so as the keeper said he thought she would have dyed, but at night when she came into the yard was well and continewed so, but would never give milk nor bring calfe after that; therfore they bought another cow, that they might have some breed, but that cast calfe also; . . . then she thought ther was some thing more then ordinary in it, and could not but thinke that she was bewitched. . . . Aboute a weeke after, she went by M^r. Goodyeares, and there was Eliza: Godman pulling cherries in ye streete; she said, how doth Goody Thorpe? I am behoulden to Goody Thorpe above all the weomen in the Towne: she would have had me to the gallowes for a few chickens; and gnashed and grinned wth her teeth in a strang manner, wch she confesseth was true, but owned nothing about ye cowes. . . .

Allen Ball informed the Court that one time Eliza Godman came to his house and asked his wife for some butter-milke; she refused, and bid her be gone, she cared not for her company: she replyed, what, you will save it for your piggs, but it will doe them no good; and after this his piggs all but one dyed, one after another, but the cause he knowes not. . . .

These things being declared, the Court told Elizabeth Godman that they have considered them wth her former miscariages, and see cause to Order that she be committed to prison, ther to abide the Courts pleasure, but because the matter is of weight, and the crime whereof she is suspected capitall, therefore she is to answer it at the Court of Magistrats in October next.

Court of Magistrates, New Haven, October 17, 1655

Elizabeth Godman was called before the court and told that upon grounds formerly declared, wch stand upon record, she by her owne confession remaines under suspition for witchcraft, and one more is now added, and that is, that one time this last summer, comeing to M^r. Hookes to beg some beare, was at first denyed, but after,

From Charles J. Hoadley, ed., *Records of the Colony or Jurisdiction of New Haven, 1653 to the Union* (Hartford: Case, Lockwood, 1858) 2:29–36, 151–152.

she was offered some by his daughter which stood ready drawne, but she refused it and would have some newly drawne, wch she had, yet went away in a muttering discontented manner, and after this, that night, though the beare was good and fresh, yet the next morning was hott, soure and ill tasted, yea so hott as the barrell was warme w^thout side, and when they opened the bung it steemed forth; they brewed againe and it was so also, and so continewed foure or five times, one after another. . . .

[T]he court declared unto her that though the evidenc is not sufficient as yet to take away her life, yet the suspitions are cleere and many, wch she cannot by all the meanes she hath used, free herselfe from, therefore she must forbeare from goeing from house to house to give offenc, and cary it orderly in the family where she is, wch if she doe not, she will cause the court to comitt her to prison againe, & that she doe now presently upon her freedom give securitie for her good behaviour; and she did now before the court ingage fifty pound of her estate that is in M^r. Goodyeares hand, for her good behaviour, wch is further to be cleered next court, when M^r. Goodyeare is at home.

3. Bridget Bishop Is Convicted of Witchcraft, 1692

II. The trial of Bridget Bishop: alias, Oliver, at the Court of Oyer and Terminer held at Salem, June 2, 1692.

I. She was indicted for bewitching of several persons in the neighborhood, the indictment being drawn up, according to the form in such cases usual. And pleading, not guilty, there were brought in several persons, who had long undergone many kinds of miseries, which were preternaturally inflicted, and generally ascribed unto a horrible witchcraft. There was little occasion to prove the witchcraft; it being evident and notorious to all beholders. Now to fix the witchcraft on the prisoner at the bar, the first thing used was, the testimony of the bewitched; whereof, several testified, that the shape of the prisoner did oftentimes very grievously pinch them, choke them, bite them, and afflict them; urging them to write their names in a book, which the said specter called, ours. . . . Others of them did also testify, that the said shape, did in her threats, brag to them, that she had been the death of sundry persons then by her named; that she had ridden a man, then likewise named. Another testified, the apparition of ghosts unto the specter of Bishop crying out, you murdered us! About the truth whereof, there was in the matter of fact, but too much suspicion.

II. It was testified, that at the examination of the prisoner, before the magistrates, the bewitched were extremely tortured. If she did but cast her eyes on them, they were presently struck down; and this in such a manner as there could be no collusion in the business. But upon the touch of her hand upon them, when they lay in their swoons, they would immediately revive; and not upon the touch of anyone's else. Moreover, upon some special actions of her body, as the shaking of her head, or the turning of her eyes, they presently and painfully fell into the like postures. And many of the like accidents now fell out, while she was at the bar. . . .

Cotton Mather, *Wonders of the Invisible World* (1692).

IV. One Deliverance Hobbs, who had confessed her being a witch, was now tormented by the specters, for her confession. And she now testified, that this Bishop, tempted her to sign the book again, and to deny what she had confessed. She affirmed, that it was the shape of this prisoner, which whipped her with iron rods, to compel her thereunto. And she affirmed, that this Bishop was at a general meeting of the witches, in a field at Salem Village and there partook of a diabolical sacrament, in bread and wine then administered!

V. To render it further unquestionable, that the prisoner at the bar, was the person truly charged in *this* witchcraft, there were produced many evidences of *other* witchcrafts, by her perpetrated. . . .

VI. Samuel Gray, testified, that about fourteen years ago, he waked in a night, and saw the room where he lay, full of light; and that he then saw plainly a woman between the cradle, and the bedside, which looked upon him. He rose, and it vanished; though he found the doors all fast. Looking out at the entry door, he saw the same woman, in the same garb again; and said, *In God's name, what do you come for?* He went to bed, and had the same woman again assaulting him. The child in the cradle gave a great screech, and the woman disappeared. It was long before the child could be quieted; and though it were a very likely thriving child, yet from this time it pined away, and after divers months died in a sad condition. He knew not Bishop, nor her name; but when he saw her after this, he knew by her countenance, and apparel, and all circumstances, that it was the apparition of this Bishop, which had thus troubled him. . . .

IX. Samuel Shattuck testified, that in the year 1680, this Bridget Bishop, often came to his house upon such frivolous and foolish errands, that they suspected she came indeed with a purpose of mischief. Presently whereupon his eldest child, which was of as promising health and sense, as any child of its age, began to droop exceedingly; and the oftener that Bishop came to the house, the worse grew the child. . . . [W]hen she paid him a piece of money, the purse and money were unaccountably conveyed out of a locked box, and never seen more. The child was immediately hereupon taken with terrible fits, whereof his friends thought he would have died: indeed he did almost nothing but cry and sleep for several months together: and at length his understanding was utterly taken away. . . . About seventeen or eighteen years after, there came a stranger to Shattuck's house, who seeing the child, said, *This poor child is bewitched; and you have a neighbor living not far off, who is a witch.* He added, *Your neighbor has had a falling out with your wife; and she said in her heart, your wife is a proud woman, and she would bring down her pride in this child:* He then remembered, that Bishop had parted from his wife in muttering and menacing terms, a little before the child was taken ill. . . .

X. John Louder testified, that upon some little controversy with Bishop about her fowls, going well to bed, he did awake in the night by moonlight, and did see clearly the likeness of this woman grievously oppressing him; in which miserable condition she held him unable to help himself, till near day. He told Bishop of this; but she denied it, and threatened him, very much. Quickly after this, being at home on a Lord's day, with the doors shut about him, he saw a black pig approach him; at which he going to kick, it vanished away. . . .

XII. To crown all, John Bly, and William Bly, testified, that being employed by Bridget Bishop, to help take down the cellar wall, of the old house, wherein she formerly lived, they did in holes of the said old wall, find several poppets, made up of rags, and hog's bristles, with headless pins in them, the points being outward. Whereof she could now give no account unto the court, that was reasonable or tolerable.

XIII. One thing that made against the prisoner was, her being evidently convicted of gross lying, in the court, several times, while she was making her plea. But besides this, a jury of women, found a preternatural teat upon her body; but upon a second search, within three or four hours, there was no such thing to be seen. There was also an account of other people whom this woman had afflicted. And there might have been many more, if they had been, inquired for. But there was no need of them.

XIV. There was one very strange thing more, with which the court was newly entertained. As this woman was under a guard, passing by the great and spacious meetinghouse of Salem, she gave a look towards the house. And immediately a demon invisibly entering the meetinghouse, tore down a part of it; so that though there were no person to be seen there, yet the people at the noise running in, found a board, which was strongly fastened with several nails, transported unto another quarter of the house.

4. The "Casco Girls" (Susannah Sheldon, Mercy Lewis, and Abigail Hobbs) Accuse George Burroughs, 1692

[May 9, 1692]

The Complaint of Susannah Shelden against mr burroos which brought a book tomee and told mee if i would not set my hand too if hee would tear mee to peesses i told him i would not then hee told mee hee would starve me to death then the next morning he told mee hee could not starve mee. to death, but hee would choake me that my vittals should doe me but litl good then he told mee his name was borros which had preached at the vliage the last night hee Came to mee and asked mee whether i would goe to the village to morrow to witnes against him i asked him if hee was exsamened then hee told hee was then i told him i would goe then hee told mee hee would kil mee beefoar morning then he apeared to mee at the hous of nathanniel ingolson and told mee hee had been the death of three children at the eastward and had kiled two of his wifes the first hee smouthered and the second he choaked and killed tow of his own children

Abigail Hobbs Examination att Salem Prison May. 12. 1692—

Q. Did Mr Burroughs bring you any of the poppets of his wives to stick pinns into?

An. I do not Remember that he did.

Q. Did he of any of his Children, or of the Eastward Souldres[?]
A. No.

Q. Have you known of any that have been killed by witchcraft[?]

_____
Salem Witchcraft Records, Essex County, Mass., Phillips Library, Peabody Essex Museum. This document can also be found in Paul Boyer and Stephen Nissenbaum, eds., *Salem Witchcraft Papers* (New York, 1977).

A. No. No–Body. . . .

Q. [W]ere they Strangers to you, that Burrougs would have you afflict?

A. Yes[.]

Q. [A]nd were they afflicted accordingly?

A. Yes.

Q. [C]ant you name Some of them?

A. No I cannot Remember them[.]

Q. [W]here did they Live?

A. [A]tt the Eastward [in Maine]. . . .

Q. [W]as their any thing brought to you like them?

An. [Y]es.

Q. [W]hat did you stick into them?

A. Thorns.

Q. [D]id some of them dy?

A. Yes. one of them was Mary Laurence [that dyed.]

[*Q.* Where] did you stick the thorns?

A. I do not know[.]

Q. [W]as it about the middle of her body?

A. Yes and I stuck it right in.

Q. [W]hat provoked you, had she displeased you?

A. Yes by some words she spoke of mee.

Q. [W]ho brought the image to you?

A. It was Mr Burroughs.

Q. How did he bring itt to you?

A. In his own person Bodily.

Q. [W]here did he bring it to you?

A. Abroad a little way of from o'r house.

Q. [A]nd what did he say to you then?

A. He told me He was angry with that family.

Q. How many years Since was it?

A. Before this Indian Warr.

Q. How did you know mr. Burroughs was a Witch?

A. I dont know. She owned againe She had made two Covenants with the Devil, first for two years, and after that for four years, and She Confesseth herslef to have been a Witch these Six years. . . .

Q. And who brought those Poppets to you?

A. Mr Burroughs.

Q. [W]hat did you stick into them?

A. Pinns, and he gave them to mee.

Q. Did you keep those Poppets?

A. No, he carryed them away with him.

Q. [W]as he there himselfe with you in Bodily person?

A. [Y]es, and So he was, when he appeared to tempt mee to set my hand to the Book, he then appeared in person, and I felt his hand att the Same time[.]

Q. [W]ere they men, Women or Children you killed?

A. They were both Boys and Girls.

Q. Was you angry with them yourself?

A. Yes, tho I dont know why now.

Q. Did you know mr Burroughs's Wife?

A. Yes.

Q. Did you know of any poppits prickd to kill her?

A. No I dont[.]

Q. Have you seen several Witches at the Eastward[?]

A. Yes, But I dont know who they were.

1st June 1692

Abigaile Hobbs then confessed before John Hathorn & Jonathan corwin Esq'rs That at the generall meeting of the Witches in the feild near Mr Parrisse's house she saw Mr George Burroughs, Sarah Good Sara Osborne Bridgett Bishop als. Olliver & Giles Cory, two or three nights agone, Mr Burrough came & sat at the window & told her he would terribly afflict her for saying so much ag't him & then pinched her, deliverance Hobbs then saw s'd Burroughs & he would have tempted her to sett her hand to the book & almost shooke her to pieces because she would not doe it,

Mary Warren Testifyeth that when she was in prison in Salem about a fortnight agone Mr George Burroughs . . . came to this depon't & Mr Burroughs had a trumpett & sounded it, & they would have had this depon't to have gone up with them to a feast at Mr parrisses. . . .

[August 3, 1692]

the deposition of Mircy Lewes who testifieth and saith that one the 7'th of may 1692 att evening I saw the apperishtion of Mr. George Burroughs whom i very well knew which did greviously tortor me and urged me to writ in his Book and then he brought to me a new fashon book which he did not use to bring and tould me I might writ in that book: for that was a book that was in his studdy when I lived with them: but I tould him I did not beleve him for I had been often in his studdy but I never saw that book their: but he tould me that he had severall books in his studdy which I never saw in his studdy and he could raise the divell: and now had bewicthed Mr. Sheppards daughter and I asked him how he could goe to be wicth hir now he was keept at Salem: and he tould me that the divell was his sarvant and he sent him in his shapp to doe it then he againe tortored me most dreadfully and threatened to kill me for he said I should not witnes against him also he tould me that he had made Abigaill Hoobs: a wicth and severall more then againe he did most dreadfully tortor me as if he would have racked me all to peaces and urged me to writ in his book or elce he would kill me but I tould him I hoped my life was not in the power of his hand and that I would not writ tho he did kill me: the next night he tould me I should not see his Two wifes if he could help it because I should not witnes agast him this 9'th may mr Burroughs caried me up to an exceeding high mountain and shewed me all the kingdoms of the earth and tould me that he would give them all to me if I would writ in his book and if I would not he would thro me down and brake my neck: but I tould him they ware non of his to give and I would not writ if he throde me down on 100 pichforks: also on the 9'th may being the time of his examination mr. George Burroughs did most dreadfully torment me: and also several times sence

In 1982, John Putnam Demos, a professor at Yale University, examined all the witchcraft cases in New England other than the prosecutions in Salem in 1692 in order to learn the characteristics of accused witches. He summarized his findings and reveals what he regards as the crucial aspects of women's lives that could lead them to be suspected of dealings with the devil. More than two decades later, Mary Beth Norton, who teaches at Cornell University, took a different approach in her study of the Salem crisis. Instead of focusing on the accused (in her case, a prominent man, not a woman), she asked: Who were the accusers? Why did they choose to charge *this* man with witchcraft? She argues implicitly that witchcraft accusations cannot be understood without knowing the motivations of accusers. On which group—accusers or accused—should historians place their emphasis?

The Characteristics of Accused Witches

JOHN PUTNAM DEMOS

To investigate the witches as a biographical type is no easy task. With rare exceptions the record of their experience is scattered and fragmentary. Much of the surviving evidence derives from their various trial proceedings; in short, we can visualize them quite fully as *suspects,* but only here and there in other aspects of their lives. We lack, most especially, a chance to approach them directly, to hear their side of their own story. Most of what we do hear comes to us second- or third-hand, and from obviously hostile sources.

It is hard enough simply to count their number. Indeed, it is impossible to compile a complete roster of all those involved. We shall be dealing in what follows with 114 individual suspects. Of these people 81 were subject to some form of legal action for their supposed witchcraft, i.e., "examination" by magistrates and/or full-fledged prosecution. Another 15 were not, so far as we know, formally accused in court; however, their status as suspects is apparent from actions—for slander—which they themselves initiated. A final group of 18 (some not identified by name) are mentioned elsewhere in writings from the period.

Yet these figures certainly *under*-represent the total of witchcraft suspects in seventeenth-century New England. The court records are riddled with gaps and defects; it is possible, even probable, that important cases have been entirely lost from sight. . . .

But if our list of 114 is only the tip, its substantive and structural features still merit investigation. There is no reason to imagine any considerable difference between the known witches and their unknown counterparts. The former are presented here, as a group, in their leading biographical characteristics. . . .

John Putnam Demos, abridged from *Entertaining Satan: Witchcraft and the Culture of Early New England,* 57–94. Copyright © 1983 by Oxford University Press, Inc. Reprinted by permission of Oxford University Press, Inc.

Sex

There was no intrinsic reason why one sex should have been more heavily represented among New England witches than the other. The prevailing definitions of witchcraft—the performance of *maleficium* and "familiarity with the Devil"—made no apparent distinctions as to gender. Yet the predominance of women among those actually accused is a historical commonplace—and is confirmed by the present findings.

Females outnumbered males by a ratio of roughly 4:1. These proportions obtained, with some minor variations, across both time and space. Furthermore, they likely *under*state the association of women and witchcraft, as can be seen from a closer look at the males accused. Of the twenty-two men on the list, eleven were accused together with a woman. Nine of these were husbands of female witches, the other two were religious associates (*protégés* of the notorious Anne Hutchinson). There is good reason to think that in most, if not all, such cases the woman was the primary suspect, with the man becoming implicated through a literal process of guilt by association. Indeed this pattern conformed to a widely prevalent assumption that the transmission of witchcraft would follow the lines of family or close friendship. (There were at least two instances when a woman-witch joined in the charges against her own husband.) . . .

An easy hypothesis—perhaps too easy—would make of witchcraft a single plank in a platform of "sexist" oppression. Presumably, the threat of being charged as a witch might serve to constrain the behavior of women. Those who asserted themselves too openly or forcibly could expect a summons to court, and risked incurring the ultimate sanction of death itself. Hence the dominance of *men* would be underscored in both symbolic and practical terms. Male dominance was, of course, an assumed principle in traditional society—including the society of early New England. Men controlled political life; they alone could vote and hold public office. Men were also leaders in religion, as pastors and elders of local congregations. Men owned the bulk of personal property (though women had some rights and protections). Furthermore, the values of the culture affirmed the "headship" of men in marital and family relations and their greater "wisdom" in everyday affairs. Certainly, then, the uneven distribution of witchcraft accusations and their special bearing on the lives of women were consistent with sex-roles generally.

But was there *more* to this than simple consistency? Did the larger matrix of social relations enclose some dynamic principle that would energize actual "witch-hunting" so as to hold women down? On this the evidence—at least from early New England—seems doubtful. There is little sign of generalized (or "structural") conflict between the sexes. Male dominance of public affairs was scarcely an issue, and in private life there was considerable scope for female initiative. Considered overall, the relations of men and women were less constrained by differences of role and status than would be the case for most later generations of Americans. It is true that many of the suspects displayed qualities of assertiveness and aggressiveness beyond what the culture deemed proper. But these displays were not directed at men as such; often enough the targets were other women. Moreover, no single line in the extant materials raises the issue of sex-defined patterns of authority. Thus, if witches were at some level protesters against male oppression, they themselves seem to have

Coverture

been unconscious of the fact. As much could be said of the accusers, in the (putative) impulse to dominate. . . .

And one final point in this connection: a large portion of witchcraft charges were brought against women *by* other women. Thus, if the fear of witchcraft expressed a deep strain of misogyny, it was something in which both sexes shared. It was also something in which other cultures have quite generally shared. . . .

Age

How old were the accused? At what age did their careers as suspected witches begin? These questions are difficult to answer with precision, in many individual cases; but it is possible to create an aggregate picture by analyzing a broad sample of age-estimates. . . .

The results converge on one time of life in particular: what we would call "midlife," or simply "middle age." The years of the forties and fifties account for the great mass of accused witches, whether considered at the time of prosecution (67 percent) or of earliest known suspicion (82 percent). It seems necessary to emphasize these figures in order to counteract the now familiar stereotype which makes witches out to be old. In fact, they were not old, either by their standards or by ours. (One victim, in her fits, was asked pointedly about the age of her spectral tormentors, and "she answered neither old nor young.") Contrary (once again) to currently prevalent understandings, the New Englanders construed the chronology of aging in terms not very different from our own. Their laws, their prescriptive writings, and their personal behavior expressed a common belief that old age begins at sixty. All but a handful of the witches were younger than this. Indeed, substantial majorities of both the groups considered above were age fifty or less (72 percent of the general sample, and 78 percent of the "major suspects"). . . .

One can scarcely avoid asking *why* this should have been so. What, for a start, was the meaning of midlife in that time and that cultural context? One point seems immediately apparent: midlife was *not* seen as one of several stages in a fully rounded "life-cycle." Early Americans spoke easily and frequently of "childhood," "youth," and "old age"—but not of "middle age." The term and (presumably) the concept, so familiar to us today, had little place in the lives of our forebears centuries ago. Instead of constituting a stage, midlife meant simply manhood (or womanhood) itself. Here was a *general* standard, against which childhood and youth, on the one side, and old age, on the other, were measured as deviations. Early life was preparatory; later life brought decline. The key element in midlife—as defined, for example, by the Puritan poet Anne Bradstreet—was the exercise of power, the use of fully developed capacity. The danger was *mis*use of power, the besetting sin an excess of "vaulting ambition." In fact, these conventions gave an accurate reflection of experience and behavior. In the average life the years from forty to sixty enclosed a high point of wealth, of prestige, of responsibility for self and others. This pattern can be demonstrated most clearly for *men* in midlife (from tax-lists, inventories, records of office-holding, and the like); but it must have obtained for women as well. A middle-aged woman was likely, for one thing, to have a full complement of children in her care and under her personal authority. The numbers involved could well reach eight or ten, and in some families there would be additional dependents—servants, apprentices, other children "bound out" in conditions of fosterage. With female dependents the authority of the "mistress" was particularly extensive; significantly, it appeared as an issue in at least one of the witchcraft cases. Listen to the words of Mercy Short, "in her fits" and addressing her spectral tormentors:

> What's that? Must the younger women, do ye say, hearken to the elder? They must be another sort of elder women than you then! They must not be elder witches, I am sure. Pray, do you for once hearken to me!

Beyond the cultural insistence that others "hearken" to her, a woman in midlife would enjoy considerable prestige in her village or neighborhood. She was likely by this time to be a church member—and, if her husband was well to do, to have a front-row seat in the meeting-house. Indeed, her status reflected her husband's quite generally, and his was probably higher than at any time previous. The point, in sum, is this. Midlife was associated, in theory and in fact, with power over others. Witchcraft was a special (albeit malign) instance of power over others. Ergo: most accused witches were themselves persons in midlife.

If this seems a bit too simple, there are indeed some additional—and complicating—factors. The accused were not, on the whole, well positioned socially. Their personal access to power and authority was, if anything, below the average for their age-group. They can therefore be viewed as representative of midlife status only in a very generalized sense. Perhaps it was the discrepancy between midlife norms and their own individual circumstances that made them seem plausible as suspects. Perhaps a middle-aged person who was poorly situated (relative to peers) could be presumed to want "power"—and, in some cases, to seek it by any means that came to hand.

To suggest this is to acknowledge elements of *dis*advantage—of deficit and loss—in generating suspicions of witchcraft. And one more such element must be mentioned, at least speculatively. Most of the accused were middle-aged women; as such they were subject to the menopausal "change of life." The old phrase sounds quaint and slightly off-key to modern ears, but in traditional society menopause brought more—at least more tangible—change than is the usual case nowadays. Its effects embraced biology, psychology, and social position, in roughly equal measure. This process will need further, and fuller, consideration in relation to the putative victims of witchcraft; for the moment we simply underscore its meaning as loss of function. The generative "power" of most women was by midlife visibly manifest in a houseful of children; yet, that same power came suddenly to an end. There was a gap here between one mode of experience and another—past versus present—an additional kind of unsettling discrepancy. Was it, then, coincidental that witches appeared to direct their malice especially toward infants and very young children? . . .

Background

The most severe of all the deficiencies in the source materials relate to the early life of the witches. In what circumstances did they grow up? Was there something distinctive about their various families of origin? Were they orphaned, sent out into servitude, subject to illness, raised by disabled or insensitive parents, to any extent beyond the average for their cultural peers? Unfortunately, the material to answer such questions is not extant. . . .

Other elements of "background" deserve investigation. Were the witches anomalous in their ethnic and/or religious heritage? On this the evidence is clearer, and it supports a negative answer overall. . . . [T]he witches seem to have been of solidly English stock and mostly "Puritan" religion. . . .

Marriage and Child-Bearing

But what of the families in which witches lived as adults, the families they helped to create as spouses and parents? The results on this point seem generally unremarkable: there are no clear departures from the pattern of the culture at large. The portion of widows (10 percent) looks normal for the age-group most centrally involved, given the prevailing demographic regime. The never-married (another 10 percent) include those few young men who virtually courted suspicion and also the several children of witches accused by "association." . . .

In sum, most witches were married persons (with spouses still living) when brought under suspicion. Most, indeed, had been married only once. Four were definitely, and two probably, in a second marriage; one had been married (also widowed) twice previously. Perhaps a few others belong in the previously married group, assuming some lost evidence; however, this would not alter the total picture. Again, the witches seem little different in their marital situation from their cultural peers.

As part of their marriages the accused would, of course, expect to bear and rear children. But in this their actual experience may have differed somewhat from the norm. The pertinent data (vital records, genealogies, and the like) are flawed at many points, and conclusions must be qualified accordingly. Still, with that understood, we may ponder the following. It appears that nearly one in six of the witches was childless—twice the rate that obtained in the population at large. Moreover, those who *did* bear children may have experienced lower-than-normal fecundity (and/or success in raising children to adulthood). In numerous cases (23 out of 62) the procedure of family reconstitution yields but one or two clearly identifiable offspring. Meanwhile, relatively few cases (7 of 62) can be associated with large complements of children, i.e., six or more per family. Fuller evidence would surely change these figures, reducing the former and raising the latter; but it would take a quite massive shift to bring the witches into line with the child-bearing and child-rearing norms of the time.

Connections between witchcraft and children emerge at many points in the extant record: children thought to have been made ill, or murdered, by witchcraft; mothers apparently bewitched while bearing or nursing children; witches alleged to suckle "imps" (in implicit parody of normal maternal function); witches observed to take a special (and suspicious) interest in other people's children; witches found to be predominantly of menopausal age and status; and so on. Thus the witches' own child-bearing (and child-rearing) is a matter of considerable interest. And if they were indeed relatively ill-favored and unsuccessful in this respect, their liability to witch-charges becomes, by so much, easier to understand.

Family Relationships

There is another, quite different way in which the witches may have been atypical. Briefly summarized, their domestic experience was often marred by trouble and conflict. Sometimes the witch and her (his) spouse squared off as antagonists. Jane Collins was brought to court not only for witchcraft but also for "railing" at her husband and calling him "gurley-gutted Devil." Bridget Oliver and her husband Thomas were tried, convicted, and punished for "fighting with each other," a decade before Bridget's first trial for witchcraft. (A neighbor deposed that he had "several times been called . . . to hear their complaints one of the other, and . . . further [that] she saw Goodwife Oliver's face at one time bloody and at other times black and blue, . . . and [Goodman] Oliver complained that his wife had given him several blows.") The witchcraft trials of Mary and Hugh Parsons called forth much testimony as to their marital difficulties. . . .

This material cannot meaningfully be quantified; in too many cases the surviving evidence does not extend to any part of the suspect's domestic experience. But what does survive seems striking, if only by way of "impressionism." Harmony in human relations was a touchstone of value for early New Englanders, and nowhere more so than in families. A "peaceable" household was seen as the foundation of all social order. Hence domestic disharmony would invite unfavorable notice from neighbors and peers. A woman from Dorchester, Massachusetts, called to court in a lawsuit filed by her son, expressed the underlying issue with candor and clarity: "it is no small trouble of mind to me that there should be such recording up [of] family weaknesses, to the dishonor of God and grief of one another, and I had rather go many paces backward to cover shame than one inch forward to discover any." Yet the lives of witches—we are speculating—were often crossed with "family weaknesses." And perhaps these belonged to the matrix of factors in which particular suspicions originated.

Such weaknesses may have held other significance as well. . . . Conflict with spouse, siblings, children had the effect of neutralizing one's natural allies and defenders, if not of turning them outright into adversaries. The *absence* of family was also a form of weakness. Widowhood may not by itself have invited suspicions of witchcraft; yet where suspicions formed on other grounds, it could become a serious disadvantage. Case materials from the trials of the widows Godman (New Haven), Holman (Cambridge), Hale (Boston), and Glover (Boston) implicitly underscore their vulnerable position.

The experience of Anne Hibbens (Boston) is particularly suggestive this way. Mrs. Hibbens had arrived in New England with her husband William in the early 1630s. Almost at once William established himself as an important and exemplary member of the community: a merchant, a magistrate, a member of the Court of Assistants. But Anne made a different impression. In 1640 she suffered admonition, then excommunication, from the Boston church; a still-extant transcript of the proceedings reveals most vividly her troubled relations with neighbors and peers. In 1656 she was tried in criminal court—and convicted—and executed—for witchcraft. The long interval between these two dates invites attention; and there is a third date to notice as well, 1654, when William Hibbens died. It seems likely, in short, that William's influence served for many years to shield her from the full force of her neighbor's animosity. But with his passing she was finally, and mortally, exposed.

Crime

Witchcraft was itself a crime, and witches were criminals of a special sort. Were they also criminals of other—more ordinary—sorts? Were they as a group disproportionately represented within the ranks of all defendants in court proceedings? Was there possibly some implicit affinity between witchcraft and other categories of crime?

Again the extant records do not yield fully adequate information. Some 41 of the accused can be definitely associated with other (and prior) criminal proceedings; the remaining 73 *cannot* be so associated. The difficulty is that many in the latter group can scarcely be traced at all beyond their alleged involvement with witchcraft. Still the total of 41 offenders is a considerable number, which serves to establish a minimum "crime rate"—of 36 percent—for the witches as a whole. Clearly, moreover, this is only a minimum. To concentrate on witches for whom there is some evidence of *ongoing* experience is to reduce the "at risk" population to no more than 65. (The latter, in short, for a sub-sample among the accused whose offences might plausibly have left some trace in the records; the rest are biographical phantoms in a more complete sense.) This adjustment yields an alternative rate (of offenders/witches) of some 63 percent.

The two figures, 36 and 63 percent, may be viewed as lower and upper bounds for the actual rate, and their midpoint as a "best guess" response to the central question. In short approximately one half of the people accused of practicing witchcraft were also charged with the commission of other crimes. But was this a notably large fraction, in relation to the community at large? Unfortunately, there are no fully developed studies of criminal behavior in early America to provide firm standards of comparison, only scattershot impressions and partial analyses of two specific communities included in the current investigation. The latter may be summarized in a sentence. The overall "crime rate"—defined as a percentage of the total population charged with committing crimes at some point in a lifetime—was on the order of 10 to 20 percent.* Thus, even allowing for the possibility of substantial error, the link between witchcraft and other crime does look strong.

There is more to ask about the other crime, particularly about its substantive range and distribution. Taken altogether, the witches accounted for fifty-two separate actions at court (apart from the witchcraft itself). . . . Crimes of assaultive speech and theft are dramatically highlighted here. Together they account for 61 percent of all charges pressed against the witches, as opposed to 35 percent for the larger sample. Moreover, the fact that accused witches were predominantly female suggests a refinement in the sample population. If men were excluded—if, in short, the comparison involves witches versus *women* offenders generally—then the disparity becomes even larger, 61 percent and 27 percent.

Are there reasons why persons previously charged with theft and/or assaultive speech might be found, to a disproportionate extent, in the ranks of accused witches? Was there something which these two categories of offense shared (so to say) with

---

*The rate for *women only* was much lower, perhaps in the vicinity of 5 percent. And this may be a better "control group" for present purposes, since most witches were female. If so, the disparity between witch-behavior and prevailing norms appears even more pronounced.

witchcraft? Such questions point to the meaning of witchcraft in the minds of its supposed (or potential) victims. But consider what is common to crimes of theft and assaultive speech themselves. The element of loss, of undue and unfair taking away, seems patent in the former case, but it is—or was for early New Englanders—equally central to the latter one as well. Slander, for example, meant the loss of good name, of "face," of reputation, and thus was a matter of utmost importance. (The evidence against one alleged slanderer, who would later be charged as a witch, was summarized as follows: "She hath *taken away* their [i.e., the plaintiffs'] names and credits . . . which is *as precious as life itself.*" [Emphasis added.]) "Filthy speeches" was a somewhat looser designation, but in most specific instances it described a similar threat. Even "lying"—a third category of crime, notably salient for witches—can be joined to this line of interpretation. A lie was, in a sense, a theft of truth, and seemed especially dangerous when directed toward other persons.

In sum, each of these crimes carried the inner meaning of theft. And so did witchcraft. Theft of property, theft of health (and sometimes of life), theft of competence, theft of will, theft of self: such was *maleficium,* the habitual activity of witches.

Occupations

"Jane Hawkins, of Boston, midwife . . ." "Isabel Babson, of Gloucester, midwife . . ." "Wayborough Gatchell, of Marblehead, midwife . . ."; here was a special *woman's* occupation. That midwife and witch were sometimes (often?) the same person has long been supposed by historians; hence the evidence, for individual cases, deserves a most careful review. In fact, only two people in the entire suspect-group can be plausibly associated with the regular practice of midwifery. Otherwise the witches were not midwives, at least in a formal sense. It is clear, moreover, that scores of midwives carried out their duties, in many towns and through many years, without ever being touched by imputations of witchcraft.

However, this does not entirely dispose of the issue at hand. Witchcraft charges often did revolve in a special way around episodes of childbirth, and some of the accused were thought to have shown inordinate (and sinister) interest in the fate of the very young. Thus, for example, Eunice Cole of Hampton aroused suspicion by trying to intrude at the childbed (later deathbed) of her alleged victims. Others among the accused pressed medicines and advice on expectant or newly delivered mothers, or, alternatively, sought to take from the same quarter. Some may have displayed special skills in attending at childbirth, even without being recognized officially as midwives. . . . Perhaps, at bottom, there was a link of antipathy: the midwife *versus* the witch, life-giving and life-taking, opposite faces of the same coin.

Recent scholarship of English witchcraft has spotlighted the activities of so-called "cunning folk." These were local practitioners of magic who specialized in finding lost property, foretelling the future, and (most especially) treating illness. Usually they sided with moral order and justice; often enough their diagnoses served to "discover" witchcraft as the cause of particular sufferings. Yet their powers were mysterious and frightening: charms, incantations, herbal potions, a kind of second sight—all in exotic combination. Inevitably, it seemed, some of them would be tempted to apply such powers in the cause of evil. Thus they might move from the role of "discoverer" to that of suspect—in short, from witch-doctor to witch.

Were there also "cunning folk" among the transplanted Englishmen of North America? The extant evidence seems, at first sight, to yield a negative answer. There is little sign that individual persons achieved (or wanted) a public reputation of this sort, as was plainly the case in the mother country. . . .

And yet, while "cunning folk" did not present themselves as such, some of their ways (and character) may have survived in at least attenuated forms. For within the ranks of witches were several—perhaps many—women of singular aptitude for "healing." Not "physicians," not midwives, and not (publicly) identified by the pejorative term "cunning," they nonetheless proffered their services in the treatment of personal illness. For example: the widow Hale of Boston (twice a target of witchcraft proceedings) ran a kind of lodging-house where sick persons came for rest and "nursing." Anna Edmunds of Lynn (presented for witchcraft in 1673) was known locally as a "doctor woman"; references to her practice span at least two decades. . . . A woman of Boston, not identified but suspected in the "affliction" of Margaret Rule, "had frequently cured very painful hurts by muttering over them certain charms." . . .

What this and other evidence does make clear is a key association: between efforts of curing, on the one hand, and the "black arts" of witchcraft, on the other. Opposite though they seemed in formal terms, in practice they were (sometimes) tightly linked. "Power" in either direction could be suddenly reversed. We cannot discover how many New England women may have tried their hand at doctoring, but we know that some who did so brought down on themselves a terrible suspicion. Among the various occupations of premodern society this one was particularly full of hope—and of peril.

Social Position

There is a long-standing, and reasonably well attested, view of early America that makes the settlers solidly middle-class. To be sure, the notion of "class" is somewhat misleading when applied to the seventeenth century; "status" would be a better term in context. But "middle" does seem the right sort of qualifier. The movement of people from England to America included few from either the lowest or the highest ranks of traditional society—few, that is, from among the laboring poor (or the truly destitute) and fewer still from the nobility and upper gentry. Yet, with that understood, one cannot fail to notice how the middle range became itself divided and graded by lines of preference. The "planting" of New England yielded its own array of leaders and followers, of more and less fortunate citizens. Social distinction remained important, vitally so, to the orderly life of communities. . . .

The sorting attempted here posits three broad social groups—"high" (I), "middle" (II), and "low" (III)—of roughly equal size. Of course, all such categories are a matter of contrivance, conforming to no specific historical reality; but they do help to arrange the material for analysis.

Within our working roster of accused witches, some eighty-six can be classified according to this scheme. (For the other twenty-eight there is too little evidence to permit a judgement.) A substantial majority can be assigned directly to one or another of the basic rank-groups. Eighteen more occupy marginal positions (i.e., *between* groups), while seven seem distinctive in their mobility (up or down) and are on that account held for a separate category. . . . Witches were recruited, to a greatly disproportionate extent, among the most humble, least powerful of New

England's citizens. As a matter of statistical probabilities, persons at the bottom of the sorting-scale were many times more likely to be accused and prosecuted that their counterparts at the top. Moreover, when the results of such accusation are figured in, the difference looks stronger still. Among all the suspects in categories I, I/II, and II, only one was a *convicted* witch. (And of the remainder, few, if any, were seriously threatened by the actions taken against them.) The accused in categories II/II and III present quite another picture. Indeed they account for all convictions save the one above noted, and for the great bulk of completed trials.

Finally, the "mobile" group deserves special consideration. Five of them started life in a top-category position and ended near the bottom (e.g., Rachel Clinton). Two experienced equivalent change but in the opposite direction. None was convicted; all but one, however, were subject to full-scale prosecution. (Moreover, five were tried more than once.) In short, the mobile group, while not numerous, included people whose "witchcraft" was taken very seriously. To interpret this finding is difficult, without comparable information about the population at large. But there is the suggestion here of a significant relationship: between life-change and witchcraft, between mobility and lurking danger. Perhaps mobility seemed a threat to traditional values and order. And if so, it may well have been personally threatening to the individuals involved. As they rose or fell, moving en route past their more stable peers, they must at the least have seemed conspicuous. But perhaps they seemed *suspect* as well. To mark them as witches would, then, be a way of defending society itself.

Character

With the witches' sex, age, personal background, family life, propensity to crime, occupations, and social position all accounted for (as best we can manage), there yet remains one category which may be the most important of all. What were these people like—as people? What range of motive, of style, and of behavior would they typically exhibit? Can the scattered artifacts of their separate careers be made to yield a composite portrait, a model, so to speak, of witch-character? . . .

Witchcraft was *defined* in reference to conflict; and most charges of witchcraft grew out of specific episodes of conflict. Hence it should not be surprising that the suspects, as individuals, were notably active that way. . . .

What follows is a motley assemblage of taunts, threats, and curses attributed to one or another suspect: . . .

> She [Goodwife Jane Walford] said I had better have done it; that my sorrow was great already, and it should be greater—for I was going a great journey, but should never come there.

> She [Elizabeth Godman] said, "How doth Goody Thorp? I am beholden to Goody Thorp above all the women in the town; she would have had me to the gallows for a few chickens."

> Mercy Disborough told him that she would make him as bare as a bird's tail.

> Then said he [Hugh Parsons], "If you will not abate it [i.e., a certain debt in corn] it shall be but as lent. It shall do you no good. It shall be but as wild fire in your house, and as a moth in your clothes." And these threatening speeches he uttered with much anger.

> Goodwife Cole said that if this deponent's calves did eat any of her grass, she wished it might poison or choke them. . . .

Some suspects appeared to favor witchcraft and its alleged practitioners. Elizabeth Godman "would be often speaking about witches . . . without any occasion . . . and [would] rather justify them than condemn them"; indeed, "she said, 'why do they provoke them? why do they not let them come into the church?' " When her neighbor, Mrs. Goodyear, expressed confidence that God would ultimately "discover" and punish witches, "for I never knew a witch to die in their bed," Mrs. Godman disagreed. "You mistake," she said, "for a great many die and go to the grave in an orderly way." Hugh Parsons was suspected of holding similar views. According to his wife he could "not abide that anything should be spoken against witches." . . .

Some of these statements and postures serve to raise a further question. Was the impulse to provoke others through leading references to witchcraft a manifestation of some larger characterological disturbance? Here, indeed, is the germ of an odd supposition, that witches have usually been deranged persons, insane or at least deeply eccentric. For New England the situation was largely otherwise. . . .

Conclusion

From this long and somewhat tortuous exercise in prosopography a rough composite finally emerges. To recapitulate, the typical witch:

1. was female.
2. was of middle age (i.e., between forty and sixty years old).
3. was of English (and "Puritan") background.
4. was married, but was more likely (than the general population) to have few children—or none at all.
5. was frequently involved in trouble and conflict with other family members.
6. had been accused, on some previous occasion, of committing crimes—most especially theft, slander, or other forms of assaultive speech.
7. was more likely (than the general population) to have professed and practiced a medical vocation, i.e., "doctoring" on a local, quite informal basis.
8. was of relatively low social position.
9. was abrasive in style, contentious in character—and stubbornly resilient in the face of adversity.

The Accusers of George Burroughs

MARY BETH NORTON

On April 19, 1692, Abigail Hobbs, a fourteen-year-old girl from Topsfield, Massachusetts, became the third person that spring to confess to being a witch. Questioned in the Salem Village meetinghouse by John Hathorne and Jonathan Corwin, the Salem Town magistrates, she declared that the devil had recruited her into his ranks in Maine about four years earlier, after meeting her in the woods near her house at Falmouth on Casco Bay. In return for Satan's promise of "fine things," she had

Mary Beth Norton, "The Accusers of George Burroughs" published as "George Burroughs and the Girls from Casco: The Maine Roots of Salem Witchcraft." Reprinted from *Maine History* 40 (Winter 2001–2002).

signed a covenant to serve him for several years. The devil had then ordered her to afflict people, and she had done so, attacking a little Salem Village girl, Ann Putnam, and Mercy Lewis, a servant in the Putnam household.

The following evening, Ann Putnam, probably the most active of the so-called "afflicted girls" of Salem Village, had a remarkable vision of "the Apperishtion of a Minister," at which, she said, "she was greviously affrighted and cried out oh dread-full: dreadfull here is a minister com: what are Ministers wicthes to"? The specter tortured the twelve-year-old Ann while she carried on a dialogue with him. "It was a dreadfull thing," she told the apparition, "that he which was a Minister that should teach children to feare God should com to perswad poor creatures to give their souls to the divill." After repeatedly refusing to tell her who he was, the specter finally revealed his identity:

> presently he tould me that his name was George Burroughs and that he had had three wives: and that he had bewitched the Two first of them of death: and that he kiled . . . Mr Lawsons child because he went to the eastward with Sir Edmon and preached soe: to the souldiers and that he had bewicthed a grate many souldiers to death at the eastword, when Sir Edmon was their. and that he had made Abigail Hobbs a wicth and: severall wicthes more.

The roots of Ann Putnam's 1692 vision of a spectral George Burroughs lay not in Salem Village, the small community which has been the primary (or in some cases the only) focus of scholarship on the witchcraft crisis of 1692. Rather, the apparition had its origins in events that had taken place more than one hundred miles to the north, in the much-fought-over soil of Casco Bay, Maine—once home to George Burroughs and Abigail Hobbs, and birthplace and long-time residence of the Put-nams' afflicted servant, Mercy Lewis. Moreover, a settlement just a few miles south of Falmouth, Black Point (Scarborough), where Burroughs had also ministered, pro-duced another accuser who chimed in later that spring, Susannah Sheldon. Although their centrality has not previously been recognized, the three young women I have herein dubbed "the girls from Casco"—Abigail Hobbs, Mercy Lewis, and Susannah Sheldon—and George Burroughs, their former pastor and the man they accused of being a witch, played crucial roles in the 1692 crisis.

Only after April 20 did what had been an unusual though not wholly unprece-dented witchcraft episode (with fourteen accused prior to that date) explode into the burgeoning crisis that it quickly became. Within a week after the accusation of George Burroughs, fifteen more suspects had been accused; within a month, another forty had been named and jailed. By early November, over 140 New Eng-landers [had] been formally charged, and many more had been identified as witches, at least in popular gossip. What had happened to cause this incredible outburst of accusations of witchcraft, and what was its connection to Maine and specifically to the Casco Bay region?

To understand the origins of Salem witchcraft, it is first necessary to review the history of New England's early northeastern frontier, where all four of the subjects of this article had lived for much of their lives, and where they had known each other long before their encounters in Salem courtrooms.

By the late 1660s, English settlers had established fur-trading posts, fishing stations, and farming communities of varying sizes from Pemaquid in the north to the Piscataqua River in the south. . . .

Although the region was inhabited only by about 3,600 English people, its scattered settlements flourished before the mid-1670s. Exports of peltry, fish, and timber from the "eastward"—that is, Maine and New Hampshire—fueled the Massachusetts economy, providing the colony's major source of income. . . .

The Wabanaki who also inhabited the region were most commonly identified by the name of the river valleys in which their villages were located: Sacos, Androscoggins, Kennebecs, Penobscots, and so forth. Such villages consisted of multiple groups of family bands organized around older men and their wives, children, and other relatives. The villages were simultaneously intertwined and autonomous; no single Wabanaki chief sachem ruled the whole, but sachems of the different villages were related to one another by blood or marriage, and they often cooperated in both peace and war. By the final quarter of the seventeenth century, the Wabanaki had become heavily reliant on the manufactured items they obtained by trading furs to the Europeans (French as well as English) who had moved into their territory. Vital as that commerce was to both peoples—for the settlers in the region needed the income they earned by selling furs in Europe as much as the Indians needed guns and knives—the fur trade nevertheless was a source of constant friction, for each side regularly suspected the other of cheating.

The presence of French settlers and Catholic priests in the region northeast of Penobscot Bay complicated such commercial relationships, for English and French traders competed for the same pelts and moose hides. From the mid-1620s on, l'Acadie (as the French called the area) or Nova Scotia (as the English referred to it) changed hands repeatedly as the two nations struggled for preeminence along the northeast coast. . . .

Yet in all likelihood war would not have erupted in the region had it not been for the armed struggle between Indians and Anglo-Americans that broke out in southern New England in June 1675, when the Wampanoag King Philip (Metacom) led his forces in a series of attacks on settlements in Plymouth Colony, Rhode Island, and Massachusetts Bay. The Wabanaki, who would have preferred to remain neutral in King Philip's War, found themselves pulled inexorably into the conflict by the demands of the opposing forces. . . .

King Philip's War (or, as it was known in the region, the First Indian War) began in Maine in September 1675; through that fall, Indian assaults on Anglo farms and towns intensified, with the fort at Black Point a particular focal point for conflict. A tentative truce negotiated in December did not hold, and the Indians once again launched attacks on settlements in the area starting in August 1676. In October, the Wabanaki successfully captured Black Point fort. Anglo settlers fled the region en masse, abandoning Maine north of Wells to the Wabanaki. Even when the Indians abandoned their Black Point prize and the English subsequently reoccupied it, they did not return to their homes. The Casco Bay area continued to be contested throughout 1677. Finally, in April 1678 the Treaty of Casco nominally ended the war.

Over the next decade and especially in 1680 and thereafter, Maine was slowly resettled. By 1688, old timber mills had been rebuilt and new ones constructed on rivers up and down the coast, especially near Casco Bay; farms had been restocked with cattle; and the major settlements—Falmouth, Black Point, Saco, and Pemaquid—had been reoccupied. Yet everyone was nervous, for some new settlements were encroaching on Wabanaki land. Consequently, militia leaders in Maine overreacted when reports reached them in mid-August 1688 that several settlers had been killed in western Massachusetts. They seized twenty Wabanaki, many of them women and children, evidently planning to use them as hostages. But instead of preventing a war, they started one, for the Wabanaki engaged in retaliatory kidnappings, eventually killing several of their captives. That winter, Sir Edmund Andros, governor of the Dominion of New England (into which Massachusetts had been administratively incorporated), led an ineffective expedition to Pemaquid against the Indians.

But Andros was overthrown in the Glorious Revolution in April 1689 soon after his return to Boston, and the result was catastrophic for the frontier communities. The local men who thereafter took charge of the colony did not want to expend scarce resources defending the northern settlements, instructing frontier dwellers to defend themselves. Seizing the initiative, the Wabanaki launched a series of attacks on communities in both Maine and New Hampshire. . . .

Four moments during the two destructive Indian wars were of particular significance for George Burroughs and his eventual accusers, the three girls from Casco: October 10–11, 1675; August 11, 1676; September 21, 1689; and May 16–20, 1690. On the first of these, the Wabanaki attacked outposts near Black Point, the home of Susannah Sheldon; on the other three, they assaulted the town of Falmouth, the home of Mercy Lewis and George Burroughs and sometime residence of Abigail Hobbs.

October 10–11, 1675. "When the Indeans came first it was on a Lords day in the morning," Eleanor Barge recalled. . . . [T]he Indians "went to dunstone & fell upon Left. Alger, & the Dunston people." . . . [S]he personally asked Captain Joshua Scottow, commander of the Black Point garrison, to send some men to help the people at Dunstan, including Lt. Arthur Alger and his brother Andrew. But Captain Scottow replied, "there should not a man goe of[f] the Necke, for sayd Mr Scottow, they had warening enough & lyberty Enough [to have escaped] they & Arther Alger too . . . if they perish they perish." . . .

Among the alarmed people in the Black Point garrison that day were William Sheldon, his wife Rebecca, and their little daughter Susannah, who would then have been under two years old. Rebecca Scadlock Sheldon must have been particularly terrified by the news of the attack on Dunstan, for her sister Anne was married to Arthur Alger. Rebecca and her husband were surely dissatisfied with Captain Scottow's refusal to aid the outlying settlement and with his decision instead merely to dispatch a messenger to Saco to ask for assistance from that larger town. In the event, help arrived too late. Andrew Alger died in the assault on Dunstan on October 11, and Arthur Alger was fatally wounded at the same time. Brought with other injured men to Black Point after the battle, Arthur died at William Sheldon's garrison on October 14. The young Susannah must have witnessed both her uncle Arthur's death agonies and her aunt's and mother's consequent grief. In the 1680s, when her family returned to Black Point after having lived elsewhere between 1676 and 1681, she must also have heard her parents frequently denigrate their nemesis Joshua Scottow. Because Scottow seems to have been the prime mover in an attempt to persuade George Burroughs to leave his pastorate at Falmouth and relocate permanently to Black Point during the mid-to-late 1680s, the Sheldon family would have regarded the clergyman as Scottow's ally.

August 11, 1676. When the Indians assaulted Falmouth for the first time, Mercy Lewis was a three-year-old toddler, living with her parents and surrounded by her father's extended family. Her grandfather George Lewis had brought his wife and three children to Maine from England by 1640; four more children—including her father Philip—were born in America. All her father's siblings had land, spouses, and children on Casco Bay. But early in the morning of August 11, the Wabanaki attacked. . . .

Mercy's parents managed to escape with her to an island in the bay, along with their minister George Burroughs and others, but her father's siblings were hard hit. . . . Her paternal grandparents also numbered among the slain. Many of her cousins were killed or captured. . . . Mercy and her parents probably moved temporarily to Salem Town. . . . By 1683, though, they had returned to Maine [to] rebuild their lives in Casco Bay. She was then ten years old.

The Reverend George Burroughs, who also survived that attack on Falmouth, was twenty-three in 1676. Born in Virginia but raised in Roxbury, Massachusetts, he attended Harvard as a member of the class of 1670. In 1674 he moved his new wife and baby from Roxbury to Casco. In the wake of the August 11, 1676 assault, the Burroughs family retreated to Essex County, specifically to Salisbury, where the young clergyman assisted the aged local pastor, the Reverend John Wheelwright, and possibly hoped to be able to take over the congregation upon Wheelwright's death. Conflict in the church rendered that outcome impossible, and so he began to look elsewhere. At about the same time, Salem Village ousted its first minister, and in late 1680 the community recruited Burroughs to fill the vacancy. but the clergyman's tenure in Essex County was both brief and unpleasant. By the summer of 1682, dissatisfied Villagers were refusing to pay his salary. In early March 1683, Burroughs moved his family back to the recently reoccupied Falmouth, which was protected by Fort Loyal, newly constructed to help defend the region.

September 21, 1689. Before the Wabanaki attacked Falmouth in the Second Indian War, the colonists received a timely warning of the impending assault. Boston authorities thus had time to reinforce Ft. Loyal with a sizable contingent of militiamen under the command of Colonel Benjamin Church. Sylvanus Davis, the fort's commander, later reported "a fierce fight" lasting about six hours on September 21, in which the New Englanders "forced them to Retreate & Judge many of them to bee slaine . . . there was Grate firings on Both sides." The English lost eleven soldiers killed and ten wounded, some of whom died later. How many townspeople were among the casualties went unrecorded; they might have included Mercy Lewis's parents (her father is last known to have been alive in April 1689). But the Reverend George Burroughs again survived the attack; on September 22 Church declared himself "well Satisfied with" Burroughs, who had been "present with us yesterday in the fight."

In the aftermath of the battle, the by-then orphaned Mercy Lewis seems to have moved in with George Burroughs as his servant. How long she lived with her minister's family is unknown, but it was probably no more than a few months. When Burroughs, seeking a safer place to live, moved south to Wells some time during the winter of 1689–1690, Mercy appears to have gone to Beverly, Massachusetts, again as a servant. After about nine months there, she moved on to Salem Village, where her recently married sister lived, and where she was hired out to the Putnams. Even before Mercy arrived in Salem Village, William Sheldon had moved his family there from Black Point. They left Maine soon after the Second War began and had settled in the Village by November 1688.

May 16–20, 1690. Thus none of these former residents of the Casco region was present when the Wabanaki launched their third and most devastating attack on Falmouth in mid-May 1690. After a siege of five days, with almost all of its male defenders dead or wounded, Ft. Loyal surrendered to a combined force of French and Indians. Promises of quarter were not fulfilled, and most of the 200 or so survivors were slaughtered on the spot, with a few being carried off into captivity by the Wabanaki. Among the dead and captured were three more of Mercy Lewis's relatives. Black Point and all other settlements north of Wells were quickly abandoned once more.

What of Abigail Hobbs, the third "Casco girl"? Her family seems to have been present in Falmouth during only the third of these attacks, that of September 1689. The Hobbs clan did not move to Maine until after 1682; probably Abigail's father, William (who was perhaps born in New Hampshire) was one of a number of settlers lured to the reoccupied town by dreams of new prosperity on the frontier. Abigail's statements to the judges in 1692 indicated that she almost certainly lived in the town center, close to Mercy Lewis's home and not far from Burroughs's household. Surely the three eventual participants in the witch trials saw each other frequently, perhaps even on a daily basis, in the tiny community. In Falmouth in 1688, when Abigail said she first became a witch, her pastor Burroughs was in his mid thirties, while she herself was about 11 and Mercy about 16. Just to the south, in Black Point, where Burroughs occasionally preached, Susannah Sheldon was then approximately 14 years old.

It is now appropriate to return to Ann Putnam's vision of April 20, 1692. Other than its accusation that Burroughs had killed his first two wives (he wed his third in Wells in 1691), which is a charge beyond the scope of this article, its three major (interrelated) themes revolved around his conduct in Maine. The first accused him of killing "Mr Lawsons child because he went to the eastward with Sir Edmon and preached soe: to the souldiers," the second, of bewitching "a grate many souldiers to death at the eastword, when Sir Edmon was their"; the third, of recruiting Abigail Hobbs as a witch. That last should need no further explication beyond noting that Ann's charge, offered a day after Abigail had confessed to malefic activity, created the logical link between the Maine minister and the Maine witch. Abigail Hobbs had not yet accused Burroughs of enlisting her in the devil's ranks, but instead had described a direct encounter with Satan himself. In another confession offered about three weeks later, though, she joined Ann Putnam in indicating that Burroughs had approached her in Falmouth to ask her to practice witchcraft.

Ann's first two charges underscored Mercy Lewis's influence on the impressionable young girl, for Mercy was the only person in Ann's life who had lived "at the eastward" while Sir Edmund Andros was the governor of the Dominion of New England. (I can easily imagine the two sharing a bed in the Putnam household, and Mercy after dark filling Ann's head full of tales of the frontier and the war.) As was already noted briefly in the summary above, the events specifically referred to in the vision took place during the winter of 1688–1689, when Andros personally led a troop of militiamen into Wabanaki territory, attempting to quell the violence that had erupted in late August 1688. Andros later proclaimed his expedition a success, but colonists generally regarded it as a failure because Andros's men failed ever to engage the enemy directly. The "Mr. Lawson" of Ann's vision was the Reverend Deodat

Lawson, Burroughs's immediate successor as minister in Salem Village, who had served as the chaplain to Andros's troops that winter after he left the Village. Lawson's first wife and child both died at about that time (evidently during his absence), and others too later repeated Ann's charge that Burroughs had bewitched them.

But why would Ann Putnam—that is, Mercy Lewis—think to charge Burroughs with killing his successor's child because Lawson had been hired as chaplain to Andros's men? In September 1689 Benjamin Church alluded to a possible reason for Burroughs's purported malefic act. In his remarks on the minister, he commented that Burroughs "had thoughts of removeing" from Falmouth because "his present maintainance from this Town by reason of thier poverty, is not enough for his livelihood." So, Church declared, "I shall Encourage him to Stay promissing him an allowance from the publique Treasury for what Servis he shall do for the Army."

That observation suggests a motive for Burroughs's possible anger about Lawson's employment with Andros: perhaps he had wanted the job himself. It is easy to speculate that Burroughs expressed his jealousy or frustration about Lawson's chaplaincy in the hearing of Mercy Lewis when she lived in his household. She then later passed that on to Ann Putnam, who consciously or unconsciously (more likely the latter) incorporated the information into her spectral vision of the minister.

Burroughs's specter also told Ann that "he had bewicthed a grate many souldiers to death at the eastword, when Sir Edmon was their." The malevolent killing of soldiers in Maine during Andros's campaign could have had only one purpose: assisting the Wabanaki in their war against God's people. But why would Burroughs do that? And why would that treachery help to reveal his identity as a witch?

New Englanders had long thought of Native Americans as devil-worshippers. North America had been "the *Devil's* territories," Cotton Mather later wrote, before the Christian English settlers had arrived. That George Burroughs had indeed spectrally allied himself to Satan and the Wabanaki could well have appeared likely to anyone who contemplated his uncanny ability to survive the attacks on Casco in August 1676 and September 1689, followed by his remarkably prescient decision to leave Falmouth sometime in the winter of 1689–90, mere months before the town fell to the Wabanaki in May 1690. And the "anyone" in that sentence was not, of course, just *anyone*—it was a very specific *someone,* Mercy Lewis, whose large extended family had essentially been wiped out in the same devastating attacks from which Burroughs had so stunningly escaped unscathed.

He was, therefore, a witch. Mercy Lewis knew it because of her experiences on the northeastern frontier, and she, Ann Putnam, Abigail Hobbs, Susannah Sheldon, and others said it. At the clergyman's formal examination by the two Salem magistrates and two members of the colony's council on May 9, 1692, Mercy and Susannah took an active role in the proceedings, with Susannah describing how Burroughs's specter had appeared to her the day before to confess killing not only his wives but also two of his own children and "three children at the eastward." Susannah also mentioned "the soldiers," but what she said has unfortunately been lost. For her part, Mercy described an encounter with the minister's apparition two days earlier. Burroughs's specter "did grievously tortor me and urged me to writ in his Book," Mercy reported, and continued:

> Then he brought to me a new fashon book which he did not use to bring and tould me I might writ in that book: for that was a book that was in his studdy

when I lived with them: but I tould him I did not beleve him for I had been often in his studdy but I never saw that book their: but he tould me that he had severall books in his studdy which I never saw in his studdy and he could raise the divell: . . . also he tould me that he had made Abigaill Hoobs: a wicth and severall more.

When George Burroughs was tried in August, Mercy and probably Susannah joined other witnesses in accusing the clergyman of witchcraft. Before the grand jury on August 3, Mercy repeated under oath what she had said informally in May. Moreover, after Elizar Keyser, a resident of Salem Town, testified that Burroughs had bewitched his house after he had had an unsettling encounter with the imprisoned suspect in early May, Mercy eagerly interjected a confirmation: "Mr. Borroughs: told her: that he made lights: in Mr Keyzers chumny." At the trial two days later Abigail Hobbs surely added her accusing voice to those of the other Casco girls. Because she had confessed to being a witch, Abigail was not allowed to swear to the truth of her testimony, and so no written record of her words survives. But she must have been one of the eight confessors Cotton Mather noted as having appeared against Burroughs. And in that capacity she in all likelihood formally repeated to the court what she had revealed in a confession on May 12. Although she said she did not know whether the malefic clergyman had bewitched "the Eastward Souldres," Abigail indicated that Burroughs had brought her the devil's book to sign and that he had ordered her to afflict a number of residents of Falmouth, especially young people and members of families with which he had quarreled. In one case, "Before this Indian Warr," he had used her as an intermediary to bewitch the daughter of one of his enemies.

Although other witnesses also testified against Burroughs at his trial (including many who had known him in Maine), it was the Casco girls—Abigail Hobbs, then Mercy Lewis (initially through her surrogate Ann Putnam) and Susannah Sheldon—who had first pointed the authorities' attention toward the former minister of Salem Village and, more significantly, of Falmouth. A witch conspiracy of the extent that seemed to be operating in Essex County in 1692 needed a leader, and Burroughs fit the bill perfectly. Stereotypical female witches could hardly serve that function; why would the devil turn to an elderly, querulous widow to direct his forces? But a frontier clergyman who had briefly served the parish in Salem Village could easily link the malevolent forces of the visible and the invisible worlds, doing the devil's bidding in both. He would bewitch the soldiers sent against Satan's Wabanaki allies while simultaneously "encouraging" his English followers, whom he summoned to devilish sacraments "with the sound of a diabolical trumpet." At those satanic communions he predicted (recalled Deodat Lawson, who attended his predecessor's trial and recorded the content of the confessions repeated there) that "they should certainly prevail."

In the end, what prevailed was not the witches but rather the Casco girls' accusations of their former minister. They made him—a man who had, evidently through diabolical means, escaped unscathed from the war that had destroyed the lives and properties of so many members of their families—what his descendants later termed "the Head & Ringleader of all the Supposed Witches in the Land." And in doing so they also were the chief instigators of the widespread crisis referred to today by just one word: *Salem.*

✦ FURTHER READING

Briggs, Robin. *Witches & Neighbors: The Social and Cultural Context of European Witch-craft* (1996).

Demos, John Putnam. *Entertaining Satan: Witchcraft and the Culture of Early New England* (1982).

Gaskill, Malcolm. *Witchfinders: A Seventeenth-Century English Tragedy* (2005).

Godbeer, Richard. *The Devil's Dominion: Magic and Religion in Early New England* (1992).

Gragg, Larry. *The Salem Witch Crisis* (1992).

Hall, David, ed. *Witch-Hunting in Seventeenth-Century New England* (1999).

Hoffer, Peter. *The Devil's Disciples: Makers of the Salem Witchcraft Trials* (1996).

Karlsen, Carol. *The Devil in the Shape of a Woman: Witchcraft in Colonial New England* (1987).

Levack, Brian P. *The Witch-Hunt in Early Modern Europe* (2006).

Norton, Mary Beth. *In the Devil's Snare: The Salem Witchcraft Crisis of 1692* (2002).

Reis, Elizabeth. *Damned Women: Sinners and Witches in Puritan New England* (1997).

Rosenthal, Bernard. *Salem Story: Reading the Witch Trials of 1692* (1993).

Weisman, Richard. *Witchcraft, Magic, and Religion in 17th Century Massachusetts* (1984).

CHAPTER
4

The Economic Roles of
Early American Women

In the early days of American women's history, scholars assumed that from the beginnings of settlement colonial women of European descent primarily assisted their
husbands on the farm or engaged in spinning and weaving to produce the family's
clothing. Women, the narrative ran, worked as parts of a household economy and
were respected for their economic contributions to the family's welfare, achieving
near equality with men as a result. Echoing early twentieth-century authors who
compiled advertisements from newspapers, some historians also contended that in
colonial cities such women freely participated in many artisanal and other occupations closed to them after the nation industrialized.

 After several historians challenged that rosy picture, which is sometimes known
as the "golden age" theory of colonial women's history, others set out to uncover
the true parameters of women's labor in Early America; further, they included the
work of female African slaves and Native American servants in their purview. What
they found has both refined and rendered more complex what once seemed obvious.
In addition to unpaid labor in the home (encompassing such tasks as caring for
children and cooking for families, either their own or their masters'), women did
engage in paid labor, but only of particular sorts. Furthermore, their activities
changed over time and showed considerable regional difference. The documents
and essays in this chapter explore the range—and the limitations—of women's
employment in pre-industrial America.

DOCUMENTS

Document 1 consists of selected entries from the diary of the Philadelphia Quaker
Elizabeth Sandwith Drinker over a nearly forty-year period, from 1758 to 1794. Before
her marriage to the merchant Henry Drinker in 1761, when she was twenty-six, the
young woman kept a list of the needlework projects she had completed, occasionally
writing as well about other tasks in which she engaged. After 1761, she more commonly writes about the labor of other women she encountered; many of them came
to her house to work for her in various capacities. Document 2 is excerpted from the

diary of the irascible Virginia slaveholder Landon Carter, who complains constantly about his bondswomen. Documents 3 and 4, both taken from George Washington's diaries, are more matter-of-fact. In Document 3, Washington took the time in February 1786 to list all his slaves individually; in Document 4, extracted from entries written from 1786 through 1788, he details the work assignments of his enslaved field hands. Document 5 is the recollections of an old woman, Eulalia Perez, who worked in a Spanish mission in California in the early nineteenth century. Together, these documents highlight the differences and similarities of women's labor in the various regions that would become the United States.

1. Elizabeth Sandwith Drinker, a Wealthy Philadelphian, Describes Her Work and That of Other Women, 1758–1794

Work done in part of the Years: 175[7,] 1758: 1759: 1760.

Work'd a Irish stitch Pocket Book for Catn. Morgan.

A Double Pocket Book in Irish Stitch for Peggy Parr.

A Irish stich Purse Pincushon for Ditto.

Plated a Watch String for Saml. Wharton.

A Watch String for John Hunt.

Knit a round Pincushon for R. Drinker.

Knit a round Pincushon for R. Coleman. . . .

Crown'd a Boys cap, for R. Rawle.

Help'd to make Baby Cloaths, for Betty Smith at Point.

Work'd a Irishstitch Tea Kittle holder for M. Parr.

Work'd a large silk Needle Book, in several stitches, for self.

A pair of silk Sleve-strings for Ditto.

A pair of Irishstitch Garters for Ditto. . . .

Novr. the 1. 1758. Finish'd a pair of White Wosted Stockings for self.

Finish'd 7 shifts for self.

Finish'd Kniting a pair of blue yarn Stockings, for Susey Georges youngest Child.

Finish'd Kniting a pair of White wosted Stockings for Polly. . . .

1759 Plated 2 Horse-Whip-strings for B. Moode.

July the 19 Plated a Watch-string for Henry Drinker.

Augt. the 31: 1759: Finish'd Kniting a pair of fine thread Stockings for Self.

Septr. the 14 Finish'd 2 Tea Kittle-Holders, in Irish Stitch for. . . .

May the 9. 1760 Finish'd working a Screen, in Irishstitch Flowers.

May the 21, Finish'd Knitting a pair of thread Stockings for self. . . .

Decemr. the 31. Finish'd knitting a pair white thread Stockings for self.

1761. Janry. the 2. Plated a Watch-string for Henry Drinker.

Janry. the 8, Finish'd Knitting a pair of Silk Mittins for Self. . . .

27 [April 1759] Went in the Afternoon with M Parr, to M. Burrows and R[ebecca] Steels, and several other Shops; she came home and drank Tea with us. . . .

13 [July 1759] went to R Steels to buy Silk. . . .

Diary of Elizabeth Drinker, Historical Society of Pennsylvania. This document can also be found in Elaine Forman Crane, ed., *The Diary of Elizabeth Drinker* (Boston: Northeastern University Press, 1991), 3 vols.

14 Stay'd at home all Day; Nancy Mitchell, call'd in the After-noon to Borrow a Pocket-Book, for a Patren. . . .

12 [February 1760] Peggy, Polly & Self, busy kniting. . . .

6 [October 1760] Becky Rawle, and Caty Howel, spent this Afternoon with us—up stairs helping to Quilt. . . .

[She marries Henry Drinker, 1761.]

7 [September 1762] Sister and self very busy Ironing &c. . . .

26 [August 1763] put a Gown skirt in the Frame, to Quilt this Afternoon. . . .

30 Sister and self finish'd my Quilt this Afternoon. . . .

1 [July 1765] Phebe Morris . . . came to fit a Body Linning for me. . . .

15 Phebe Morris here this Afternoon fitting a Gown for me, Molly Worrel with Sitgreaves's Baby who she Nurses, were also here. . . .

1 December [1766] Sally Gardner came to live with us, at 2/6 p Week. . . .

22 June 1771 George Baker drove up Polly Campbell, whome I have hir'd this day to tind my little Henry. . . .

13 [July 1771] Dr. D. says I must wean my little Henry or get a nurse for him, either seems hard—but I must submitt. . . .

18 agree'd with [Sally Oats] to take my Sweet little Henry to Nurse. . . .

29 [August 1771] we set forward to David Levans 18 Miles from Reding, a Tavern in Manatawny, to this place we got about Dusk. . . . This Evening our Landlady, a dirty old Dutch Woman, refused Changing very dirty, for Clean Sheets, tho after much intreaty, she pretend'd to comply, but to our mortification found she had taken the same sheets, sprinkled them, then Iron'd and hung 'em by the fire and placed them again on the Bed; so that we were necessitated to use our cloaks &c & this Night slepp'd without sheets.—with the assistance of our two Servants cooking, we sup'd pretty Well and slep'd better than we had any Reason to expect, all in one Room. . . .

30 from this place to the Widdow Albrights at Macungee we proceeded about 8 miles, and then Breakfasted tolerably for a Dutch House. . . .

29 [September 1771] [on a second journey] about Dusk we got to the Widdow Jemmisons, here sup'd and lodg'd. . . .

23 January 1779 our Maid Elizabeth, has been in Bed all day, with the ague and Fiver, Sister is very much taken up in the Kitchen, having none but little John to help, Molly Brookhouse occasionly. . . .

20 [February 1779] Wid. Rusel [here] to measure the Girls for Stays. . . .

28 June [1779] I took Molly [her daughter] to School to Betsy Devonshire. . . .

9 [August 1779] we have had no Maid Servant for some weeks past but Molly Brookhouse who comes before dinner and goes away in the afternoon. . . .

10 [February 1780] I dismist my maid Caty Paterson this afternoon, on her return home after 2 or 3 days frolicking, our old maid Molly Hensel is to Supply her place tomorrow. . . .

23 [August 1784] a little before 7 before I was up, S Heartshorn sent for me;—she was deliver'd about 8 of a fine Girl,—who they call Susanna; I breakfasted there, came home about 9. . . .

30 [May 1792] Betsy Fordham at work here. . . .

19 [November 1793] Caty Mullen here to day, in great trouble; she came over from Irland a poor widdow, when her 2 Sons were small, she work'd industreously

for their and her own maintannance, put them apprentice, took great care of them during that term, they have been some years free, and have work'd at their trades with reputation; she hop'd that they would be her support in the decline of Life, but how uncertain are all human prospects? they were both taken this fall with the prevailing desease [yellow fever], and died, one the day after the other, the poor mother 'tho very ill at the same time surviv'd them, and may be truly call'd a 'lone woman. . . .

11 April [1794] S S[wett] spent the day try'd on a gown for me. . . .

26 Betsy Fordham left us this afternoon, she has been near 2 weeks at work for us. . . .

20 October [1794] S Swett fitted a mantua gown on me, which I had provided [ordered] in the Summer, she is so kind to do what little I want in that way for me, I beleive I never had a gown better made in my life, and she is now within about seven weeks of 73 years of age, to work so neatly at such an age is the cause of my making the memorandum.

2. Landon Carter Complains About His Female Slaves, 1771–1773

[July 9, 1771]

I find the [slaves at] Fork will not finish the field they are in this day as I expected. The pretence is Nanny was sick one day, when they all had worked half a day in that field before they went into it 4 days ago. But even with overseers this is a constant excuse, if any one person, the most trifling hand, is ill but a day or a piece of a day, it generally excuses the loss of a whole day's work of the gang. . . . The reason is everybody is lazy and careless enough to want an excuse and Catch at anything.

I went to see my cow pen ground and I find that missing and much injured by the horses. I ordered Sukey to make up the hills and set in the double plants at her peril. . . .

[August 10, 1771]

Mary, Mcginnis' daughter, at best from a whimsical mother has been hitherto a sound healthy wench, though full of Hysteric frights when ever anything ailed her. I remember once she sat crying as if somebody had whipped her for a trifling belly ache. And 3 weeks agoe she cryed herself into fits because she was sick at the Stomach, and about 10 days agoe A pain in her shoulders gave her more fits. I had her up here and by evacuations joined with nervines She was grown quite well; and of her own accord went out to work this morning; but by 9 o'clock a little fever brought her to her tears and she is as bad as ever. She has a Sister and brother exactly the same; any little complaint fills them with the Apprehensions of death. Nay, the old jade, the mother, cannot have a finger ach but the hole plantations hears her roar.

Jack P. Greene, ed., *The Diary of Colonel Landon Carter of Sabine Hall, 1752–1778* (University Press of Virginia, 1965) 2:588–589; 609–610, 672–673, 733, 742, 755.

As to this wench, nothing so odd. She has a full pulse, though too quick but yet soft which indicates she cannot want bleeding, and her looks are those of perfect health. . . . Perhaps she may be breeding; but that she will not confess; and as to every natural complaint, I am given to understand she is quite well. It would possibly be barbarity, but I apprehend there is some trick in all this. . . .

[April 22, 1772]

Billy Beale tells me the cowkeeper, Sicely, neglected her cattle yesterday and let a cow go into the mire below the barn swamp where she perished. I cannot tell what to do with these sordid creatures. The wench is kept to do nothing else but constantly to follow the cattle. But I suppose, tired with such a constant employment, though a very easy one, she looks herself to sleep and so this injury happened; for Beale says it was really a fine cow. I have ordered the wench to be tyed up and severely slashed to keep her care if possible; but I am afraid it will not be long enough remembered. It seems this is the first of that kind which we have lost up here this year. . . .

[September 25, 1772]

There is nothing so absurd as the generality of negroes are. If in the beginning of cutting tobacco without watching they will cut all before them, and now, when there is danger of losing the tobacco by the frost, should it happen, they will not cut plants really ripe because they may be thicker just as if there was time to let it stand longer. My Jades at the Fork would not cut half this they might have done yesterday, because they thought it would be thicker; however I set them in today and made them cut every good plant. . . .

[November 21, 1772]

Mcginnis's Jamy's foot, a good whipping and a stout vomit has at last cured him; for I saw his fevers the affect of these fall intermittants, and by proceeding that way he is got about. And so has Mr. Will's joints got clear of their pains by giving a revulsion by his back.

 Mrs. Dairy Mary is also cured the same way of her invisible pain in her hip. The mother and sister fell on Beale when he went to apply my Prescription; but by the stumps of the switches they got also cured of their rebellious impudence. . . .

[June 5, 1773]

I find it is almost impossible to make a negro do his work well. No orders can engage it, no encouragement persuade it, nor no Punishment oblige it. It was but on friday several were whipped for leaving the weeds in the middle of the corn rows, and yesterday I would indulge the weakness of some of the wenches. I put them to weeding the light ground Corn expressly ordering them to work from side to side the whole row and yet today I saw that not one had done so, but the whole is to be done over again.

3. George Washington Lists His Slaves, 1786

[February 18, 1786]

Took a list to day of all my Negroes which are as follows at Mount Vernon and the plantations around it—viz.—

HOME HOUSE.

Will	Val de Chambre	1
Frank *Austin	} Waiters in the House	2
Herculus Nathan	} Cooks	2
Giles *Joe Paris—boy	} Drivers, & Stablers	3
*Doll *Jenny	} almost past Service	2
*Betty *Lame Alice *Charlotte	} Sempstresses	3
*Sall *Caroline	} House Maids	2
Sall Brass *Dolly	} Washers	2
*Alce Myrtilla *Kitty Winny	} Spinners	4
	old & almost blind	
*Schomberg	past labour	1
Frank Cook Jack	} Stock keeper old Jobber	2
Gunner Boatswain Sam Anthony *Tom Davis *Will *Joe	} Labourers	7
Jack	Waggoner	1
*Simms	Carter	1
Bristol	Gardener	1
Isaac James Sambo *Tom Nokes	} Carpenters	4
Natt George	} Smiths	2
*Peter–lame	Knitter	1
	grown	41

Diaries of George Washington, Library of Congress Manuscript Division. This document can also be found in Donald Jackson and Dorothy Twohig, eds., *The Diaries of George Washington* (University Press of Virginia, 1978) 4:277–279.

CHILDREN HOUSE

*Oney	Betty's	12 yrs. old	
*Delphy	Ditto	6 do.	2
*Anna	little Alice's	13 do.	
*Christopher	Do.	11 do.	
*Judy	Do.	7 do.	
*Vina	Do.	5 do.	4
*Sinah	Kitty's	14 do.	
*Mima	Ditto	12 do.	
*Ally	Ditto	10 do.	
*Lucy	Ditto	8 do.	
*Grace	Ditto	6 do.	
*Letty	Ditto	4 do.	
*Nancy	Ditto	2 do.	7
*Richmond	Lame Alce	9 do.	
*Evey	Do.	2 do.	
*Delia	Do.	3 mo.	3
Lilly	Myrtilla's	11 yrs. old	
Ben	Ditto	8 do.	
Harry	Do.	3 do.	
Boatswain	Do.	6 do.	
Lally	Do.	3 mo.	5
*Cyrus	Sall's	11 do.	1
*Timothy	Charlottes	1 do.	1
*Wilson	Caroline	1 do.	1
*Moll	{ Mr. Custis's Estate		2
*Peter	{		
		In all	67

MILL

Ben	Miller	1
Jack		
Tom	Cowpers	3
Davy		
	In all	4

RIVER PLANTN.

*Davy	Overseer	1
*Breechy		
Nat		
Ned		
Essex		
Bath		
*Johny	Labourg. Men	10
Adam	dead	
*Will		
Robin		
*Ben		
*Molly	Overseers Wife	1

Ruth
*Dolly
Peg
Daphne
Murria
*Agnus
Suck
Sucky
Judy–M   } labourg. Women   17
Judy–F
*Hannah
*Cornelia
*Lidia
*Esther
Cloe
*Fanny
*Alice

grown   29

CHILDREN

Will	Mill Judy's	—— 13 yrs. old	1
*Joe	Hannahs	—— 12 Do.	1
Ben	Peg's	10 Do.	
Penny	Ditto	—— 8 Do.	2
Joe	Daphne's	8 do.	
Moses	Ditto	6 do.	
Lucy	Ditto	4 do.	
Daphne	Ditto	—— 1 do.	4
*Ned	Lidia's	7 do.	
*Peter	Ditto	5 do.	
*Phoebe	Ditto	—— 3 do.	3
Cynthia	Suckey's	6 do.	
Daniel	Ditto	—— 4 do.	2
*James	Ferry Doll's	8 do.	1
*Bett	Neck Doll's	7 do.	
*Natt	Ditto	4 do.	
*Dolly	Ditto	3 do.	
*Jack	Ditty	—— 1 do.	4
Rose	Suck-Bass	12 do.	1
*Milly	House Sall's	7 do.	1
*Billy	Do. Charlottes	4 do.	1
*Hukey	Agnus's	1 do.	1
*Ambrose	Cornelia's	1 month	1

In all   52

[Washington also listed 38 slaves at Dogue Run, including 10 men, 11 women, and 17 children; 30 slaves at Ferry plantation, of whom 5 were men, 10 were women, and 15 were children; and 25 at Muddy Hole, comprising 5 men, 9 women, and 11 children. He designated all of the adults as "labouring" except for two male overseers, one at Dogue Run and one at Muddy Hole; and two women at Dogue Run.

One of the latter is labeled "old" and the other as "overseers wife." Of these additional bondspeople, 46 had asterisks beside their names.]

N.B. Those marked with asterisks are Dower Negroes [slaves belonging to Martha Custis before her marriage to Washington].

4. George Washington Assigns Work to His Slaves, 1786–1788

[June 1786]

Monday 19th . . .

Rid to Muddy hole, Dogue run, and Ferry Plantations; and to the Meadows (where people were at Work) at the two latter.

Finding my Corn was in danger of being lost by Grass & weeds, I stopped Brickmaking, and sent Gunner, Boatswain, Anthony, and Myrtilla to assist at Dogue run in weeding it.

The grass at the Ferry being forwarder, and better than that at Dogue Run, where the Scythmen began last to cut, I removed them (tho' the grass was not half down) to the former place. 4 Cutters at work. . . .

[July 1786]

Wednesday 5th   I set out about sun rising, & taking my harvest fields at Muddy hole & the ferry in my way, got home to breakfast.

Found that my harvest had commenced as I directed, at Muddy hole & in the Neck on Monday last—with 6 Cradlers at the first—to wit, Isaac, Cowper Tom, Ben overseer Will, Adam, & Dogue run Jack who tho' newly entered, made a very good hand; and gave hopes of being an excellent Cradler. That Joe (Postilian) had taken the place of Sambo at the Ferry since Monday last, & the harvest there proceeded under the cutting of Caesar, Boatswain, & him. That in the Neck 6 cradles were constantly employed, & sometimes 7—viz. James, (who having cut himself in the meadow could not work constantly)—Davy, Overseer who having other matters to attend to, could not stick to it; Sambo, Essex, George (black smith) Will, Ned; and Tom Davis who had never cut before, and made rather an awkward hand of it. Tom Nokes was also there, but he cut only now & then, at other times shocking, repairing rakes &ca. That the gangs at Dogue Run & Muddy hole were united, & were assisted by Anthony, Myrtilla & Dolshy from the home house—That besides Tom Davis Ben from the Mill had gone into the Neck and that Sall brass (when not washing) & Majr. Washingtons Tom were assisting the ferry people—That Cowpers Jack & Da[v]ly with some small boys & girls (wch. had never been taken out before) were assisting the Farmer in making Hay after two white men who had been hired to cut grass. . . .

Diaries of George Washington, Library of Congress Manuscript Division. This document can also be found in Donald Jackson and Dorothy Twohig, eds., *The Diaries of George Washington* (University Press of Virginia, 1978) 4:349; 5:3–4, 91, 209, 225, 348, 349.

[January 1787]

Monday 8th . . .

Rid to all the Plantations. Finished cleaning and grubbing the New Meadow at the Ferry. Old Will & the Women at Fren[ch's] were grubbing and clearing away for the Plows in the field (No. 1) on the Road. At Dogue run they were plowing & filling gullies—In the Neck clearing the ground from Corn Stalks before the Plows and the Muddy hole people employed as usual in the New ground front of the home house. . . .

[October 27 1787]

At the Ferry set 3 plows to work. Put the girl Eby to one of them. . . .

[December 6, 1787] . . .

Rid to all the Plantations. . . .

At Dogue run 5 plows were at work. Moll, with the old dray Mare, & another Mare bot. for me by Mr. Muse ware set to this business. The other hands were cleaning Oats & threshing Pease.

At Frenchs two Plows were at Work—the other hands cleaning Oats.

At the Ferry 3 plows were at work in field No. 2. The other hands after finishing cleaning the tailings, Pease, & Beans were employed in getting the Cedar Berries. The quantity of Sound Pease *only* amounted to 3½ Bushls. and the Beans to 1¼ Bushls. 54 Pumpkins were sent from this place to the Mansion Ho. for the Cows.

Taking up Turnips, at Dogue by the small gang from the Mann. House. Three men from Do. cutting broom straw for litter. . . .

[June 1788] . . .

Tuesday 24th . . .

Rid to all the Plantations.

In the Neck—the ground being too wet to plow in the Corn ground, those & the harrow which were there, were obliged to quit and return to the Pease ground—the rest working as usual. About 10 Oclock the Hoe people finished weeding & transplanting Carrots, and all (except Ben who was left to Sow Pease, as the ground could be prepared—Lydia for the purpose of Milking, & Will because he was unable to walk and all 3 the weed the Pease in hills) came to the New ground at the Mansn. House.

At Muddy hole, the Hoes were in the New grd. and the Plows at French's.

At Dogue run all the Plows (the two being returned from Frenchs) were plowing the Corn and the Hoes weeding it.

At Frenchs the same work as yesterday—but a plow was ordered to open furrows for Potatoes & the People to go about Planting of them tomorrow.

At the Ferry—One Plow opening furrows for Potatoes—the others weeding Corn. The Hoe people planting Potatoes after an Interval, occasioned by the continual rains and very wet ground of 16 days. . . .

5. Eulalia Pérez Recalls Her Work in a Mission in Spanish California in the Early Nineteenth Century, 1877

I, Eulalia Pérez, was born in the Presidio of Loreto in Baja California.

My father's name was Diego Pérez, and he was employed in the Navy Department of said presidio; my mother's name was Antonia Rosalia Cota. Both were pure white.

I do not remember the date of my birth, but I do know that I was fifteen years old when I married Miguel Antonio Guillén, a soldier of the garrison at Loreto Presidio. . . . I lived eight years in San Diego with my husband, who continued his service in the garrison of the presidio, and I attended women in childbirth. . . .

After being in San Diego eight years, we came to the Mission of San Gabriel, where my husband had been serving in the guard. . . .

. . . When we arrived here Father José Sánchez lodged me and my family temporarily in a small house until work could be found for me. There I was with my five daughters—my son Isidoro Guillén was taken into service as a soldier in the mission guard. . . .

The priests wanted to help me out because I was a widow burdened with a family. . . . Because of . . . this, employment was provided for me at the mission. At first they assigned me two Indians so that I could show them how to cook, the one named Tomás and the other called "The Gentile." I taught them so well that I had the satisfaction of seeing them turn out to be very good cooks, perhaps the best in all this part of the country.

After this, the missionaries conferred among themselves and agreed to hand over the mission keys to me. . . . The duties of the housekeeper were many. In the first place, every day she handed out the rations for the mess hut. To do this she had to count the unmarried women, bachelors, day-laborers, vaqueros—both those with saddles and those who rode bareback. Besides that, she had to hand out daily rations to the heads of households. In short, she was responsible for the distribution of supplies to the Indian population and to the missionaries' kitchen. She was in charge of the key to the clothing storehouse where materials were given out for dresses for the unmarried and married women and children. Then she also had to take care of cutting and making clothes for the men.

Furthermore, she was in charge of cutting and making the vaqueros' outfits, from head to foot—that is, for the vaqueros who rode in saddles. Those who rode bareback received nothing more than their cotton blanket and loin-cloth, while those who rode in saddles were dressed the same way as the Spanish-speaking inhabitants; that is, they were given shirt, vest, jacket, trousers, hat, cowboy boots, shoes and spurs; and a saddle, bridle and lariat for the horse. . . .

Besides this, I had to attend to the soap-house, which was very large, to the wine-presses, and to the olive-crushers that produced oil, which I worked in myself. . . . When it was necessary, some of my daughters did what I could not find

Eulalia Pérez, "An Old Woman Remebers," in Harold Augenbaum and Marguerite Fernandez Olmos, eds., *The Latino Reader: An American Literary Tradition from 1542 to the Present* (Boston: Houghton Mifflin, 1997), 71–80.

the time to do. Generally, the one who was always at my side was my daughter María del Rosario.

After all my daughters were married—the last one was Rita, about 1832 or 1833—Father Sánchez undertook to persuade me to marry First Lieutenant Juan Mariné, a Spaniard from Catalonia, a widower with family who had served in the artillery. I did not want to get married, but the father told me that Mariné was a very good man—as, in fact, he turned out to be—besides, he had some money, although he never turned his cash-box over to me. I gave in to the father's wishes because I did not have the heart to deny him anything when he had been father and mother to me and to all my family.

I served as housekeeper of the mission for twelve or fourteen years, until about two years after the death of Father José Sánchez, which occurred in this same mission. . . .

In the Mission of San Gabriel there was a large number of neophytes. The married ones lived on their rancherías with their small children. There were two divisions for the unmarried ones: one for the women, called the nunnery, and another for the men. They brought girls from the ages of seven, eight or nine years to the nunnery, and they were brought up there. They left to get married. They were under the care of a mother in the nunnery, an Indian. During the time I was at the mission this matron was named Polonia—they called her "Mother Superior." The alcalde was in charge of the unmarried men's division. Every night both divisions were locked up, the keys were delivered to me, and I handed them over to the missionaries. . . .

In the morning the girls were let out. First they went to Father Zalvidea's Mass, for he spoke the Indian language; afterwards they went to the mess hut to have breakfast, which sometimes consisted of corn gruel with chocolate, and on holidays with sweets and bread. On other days, ordinarily they had boiled barley and beans and meat. After eating breakfast each girl began the task that had been assigned to her beforehand—sometimes it was at the looms, or unloading, or sewing, or whatever there was to be done. . . .

The Indians were taught the various jobs for which they showed an aptitude. Others worked in the fields, or took care of the horses, cattle, etc. Still others were carters, oxherds, etc.

At the mission, coarse cloth, serapes, and blankets were woven, and saddles, bridles, boots, shoes, and similar things were made. There was a soap-house, and a big carpenter shop as well as a small one, where those who were just beginning to learn carpentry worked; when they had mastered enough they were transferred to the big shop.

Wine and oil, bricks and adobe bricks were also made. Chocolate was manufactured from cocoa, brought in from the outside; and sweets were made. Many of these sweets, made by my own hands, were sent to Spain by Father Sánchez.

There was a teacher in every department, an instructed Indian who was Christianized. A white man headed the looms, but when the Indians were finally skilled, he withdrew. . . .

The Indians also were taught to pray. A few of the more intelligent ones were taught to read and write. Father Zalvidea taught the Indians to pray in their Indian tongue; some Indians learned music and played instruments and sang at Mass. The sextons and pages who helped with Mass were Indians of the mission. . . .

◈ *E S S A Y S*

About twenty years ago, Carole Shammas, who teaches at the University of Southern California, studied the labor performed by enslaved women on Virginia plantations and traced its evolution from the late seventeenth to the late eighteenth century, focusing primarily on occupations linked to the household. In 2000, Karin Wulf of William and Mary published the second essay, examining women's occupations in late eighteenth-century Philadelphia. Urban women, she found, had unique opportunities to earn money largely denied to their rural counterparts. The following year, Virginia Marie Bouvier, a Senior Program Officer in the Grants and Fellowships Program at the United States Institute of Peace in Washington, D.C., looked closely at the work lives of the Hispanic and Indian women who lived in California's Spanish missions in the late eighteenth and early nineteenth centuries. The three essays demonstrate the range of occupations that historians (perhaps too neatly) designate as "women's work."

The Work of Enslaved Women on Virginia Plantations

CAROLE SHAMMAS

One of the most distinctive features of the New World plantation system was the way it utilized the female labor force. On plantations a much higher proportion of women regularly engaged in field work than was usually the case in early modern Western society. This diversion of female labor away from more traditional employment ob-viously affected the living standards of both blacks and whites because it meant cer-tain household goods and services were not produced. Despite this fact, studies of slave labor patterns generally turn out to be examinations of male work only. . . .

Scarcity of sources accounts for some of this neglect, and those few historians who have tried to assess quantitatively the occupations of slave women are usually very tentative about their conclusions. According to the "educated guess" of one ex-pert on Afro-American culture, 5–10% of female slaves in 18th century Maryland engaged in non-field work. [Economic historians of the antebellum South estimate between 20 and 25% of enslaved women worked in non-agricultural pursuits.] . . . The most systematic examination of work assignments by gender is for an early 19th century Virginia estate where one-third of the females performed non-field labor. . . .

Even more of a mystery is the breakdown of occupations among non-field women workers. The employment could be truly domestic—cooking, childcare, cleaning—or it could have been housewifery activity—dairying, poultry raising, cloth and clothing manufacture, etc. The former category of household work would lead to the enhancement of the white domestic environment while the latter implies a diversification of the plantation economy and/or an emphasis on self-sufficiency. Either would indicate a shift in a plantation community's priorities.

Virginia, where slavery in the United States originated, is a good place to study long-term changes in slave women's work. It is possible there to begin in the 17th century when the Tidewater was a major tobacco growing area and trace the labor

Carole Shammas, published as "Black Women's Work and the Evolution of Plantation Society in Vir-ginia," in *Labor History* 26, no. 1 (Winter 1985), 6–28. Reprinted by permission of the author.

patterns of black women from that point to the early nineteenth century when production of the staple had sharply fallen off. At the time of the Deep South's cotton
boom, much of the Chesapeake plantation economy was in a mature, if not decayed,
state. While the transformation in work was obviously linked to changes in the plantation economy, the exact nature of the connection has never been examined. . . . The
author of nearly every early Virginia document is a white man and consequently the
sources are not particularly helpful in illuminating the way Afro-American women
altered their own work situation. The evidence produced by these male record keepers, however, can answer such questions as when female slaves replaced indentured
servants on plantations, how widespread ownership of women slaves became, and
whether the kind of work black women performed changed appreciably over the
two-century period. These subjects seem of sufficient importance to justify taking
what records are available and attempting a reconstruction of employment trends.

Throughout most of the 17th century, the Virginia labor force consisted primarily
of white indentured servants, but during the last two decades the situation began
changing rapidly. Much recent research on the colonial Chesapeake has dealt with
this conversion from indentured to slave labor. . . . [P]lanters still relied mainly on
indentured servants in the 1660–74 period but had clearly switched over to slaves
by the 1720s. At the time of the Revolution, not only did the bound work force continue to be overwhelming[ly] black but possession of such labor had become very
widespread. . . .

It is, of course, one thing to show that white families increasingly used female
slave labor and quite another to establish what type of work they performed. Occasionally one comes across a will, such as that of William Fitzhugh, where a house
slave his wife favored was to "be exempted from working in the Ground," but generally all black females from the age of 10 to 50 were at risk to be drafted into the field
to produce the staple. White families, however, could not live by tobacco alone and
consequently some of these black women had to be siphoned off into more traditional
women's work.

Before we proceed further, it might be wise to discuss briefly what Anglo-
American society in the early modern period understood as women's work. English
women commonly engaged in field labor but this work was not regarded as their primary responsibility in farming. Basically, the labor viewed as peculiar to their gender
can be divided into two categories: (1) domestic work—childcare, meal preparation,
the cleaning and maintenance of apparel and the house; (2) housewifery work—
dairying, tending poultry and hogs, vegetable gardening, candle and soap making,
cloth and clothing manufacturing. Generally, domestic chores were those connected
with personal services for family members while housewifery involved the production of goods for the family and/or the market. This categorization is not free of
problems of course. Sewing, for example, could be to mend apparel rather than to
manufacture a garment. Moreover, it should be clear that the common household
drudge would often have both domestic and housewifery tasks to perform. . . .

In 17th century plantation colonies, it has been suggested, the shortage of
females—whether free, indentured, or slave—and the profitability of the staple
[tobacco] altered female work patterns. Planters coped with the lack of women not by
channelling them regardless of color into traditional women's work but by keeping

demand for domestic services low and eliminating all but the most essential house-wifery tasks. The relatively high price of . . . tobacco made it desirable in the short term to buy products on the market or do without altogether and keep as many women as possible in the field. Planters' wives could do the essential duties—childcare, cook-ing, washing—for their own households and for those of single men. Gradually, as the settlements grew older, it is believed housewifery increased. The Revolution gave an additional boost to household production, so that by the end of the 18th cen-tury, plantation societies had a reputation for being the most self-sufficient. How exactly the shift to more household production affected black women's work though, is not clear. . . .

[In the] 17th century Virginians had the cows and pigs necessary to furnish milk and meat, but the poultry and processing equipment to produce those mainstays of good housewifery, eggs, butter, and cheese, were almost totally lacking. Nor could very many families have been engaged in brewing or spinning. . . .

One hundred years later, housewifery stocks in Virginia had increased. . . . Spinning had become practically universal in the colony by 1774. . . . Virginians, lacking a textile industry, relied upon homespun cloth for household purposes and slave apparel when imports were unavailable. It appears that the increase in spinning occurred gradually from the early 18th century on and cannot be attributed solely to the Revolutionary War. . . .

How much did female slave labor contribute to housewifery output? Most slaves in both the Tidewater and Piedmont areas of Virginia lived on estates with fewer than 10 slaves until the second third of the 18th century. After that point, slave communi-ties grew larger and more blacks resided in settlements of 10 to 20 people. Holdings of this size were either the home plantation of smaller planters or quarters owned by rich planters and supervised by overseers. . . .

Evidence from quarter lists and yearly agreements made between planters and overseers indicate that one or two female slaves might be used for household pur-poses, most frequently a "girl." If they allowed an overseer to use a slave for this purpose, the planters often hoped for some additional housewifery benefit. . . .

Planters, apparently, tried to limit household service on their quarters as much as possible and confine that work that had to be performed to female slaves unfit for field service. Thomas Jefferson, for example, directed that his overseers' contacts must not allow them "to keep a woman out of the crop for waiting on them" nor could other than "Superannuated women" or "children till 10 years" serve as nurses for mothers in the field. Out of the 144 slaves that Jefferson kept on six quarters (excluding Monticello) in 1774, he identified only two women over the age of 16 as being engaged in an occu-pation other than working the ground, and one of them, Betty Hemmings, had been his deceased father-in-law's mistress. Those plantation lists that give occupations on quar-ters suggest that Jefferson's practice was the usual one. . . . When the wife of one of Landon Carter's overseers invited him to dinner, all the sweet tempered old gent could notice was that she acted "the part of a fine Lady in all her towering apparell" and that she had "at least two maids besides her own girl to get the dinner and wait upon her." "I had rather seen the diligent, industrious woman," he maintained. In other words, he wanted her to do all the work herself. The one characteristic that clearly marked off a lady from a woman or a gentleman from a man was the possession of a personal ser-vant, and the large planters resented when their employees used slaves in that manner.

If the smaller plantations operated in a similar way to the quarters staffed by overseers, then it appears the average planter's wife had at most two female servants to do domestic and housewifery tasks for the "family" of whites and blacks, and these slaves would probably be very young. Comparing housewifery utensils with ownership of female slaves in the 1774 inventory sample, I found that those who possessed one or two female slaves more often had a spinning wheel than those having none. With cheese and butter equipment, though, it took three to five female slaves to make a difference, and with poultry, female slave ownership, if anything, seemed negatively related, lending credence to the contemporary statements about slave women being the "chicken merchants." Black women would sell poultry to white families for extra money and consequently planters' wives would not bother raising the birds.

From the evidence available, it appears that the young slave girl who served in the household would have her hands full with domestic drudgery—laundry, scullion work, and infant care—and have little time for increasing housewifery output. Age is of some consequence here also. . . . All in all, it would have to be said that in those households where most white and black Virginians lived, 18th century planters gradually increased household activities but resisted making a full commitment to them.

The large home plantations where groups of 40 or more slaves dwelled were a special case, and we have relatively ample records for at least the top tier of them. Male travel accounts, diaries, and letterbooks, in addition to business papers, illuminate the daily life of the 10–15% of the colony's slaves who lived on these establishments.

Any reader of accounts written by visitors to Virginia at the end of the colonial period knows that observers found planters, their wives, and children amazingly indolent and their slaves incredibly hardworking. . . .

One suspects Virginians such as William Byrd II and Landon Carter would have violently disagreed with these visitors' assessments, at least those that pertained to the men of fortune. In their diaries, the white master never experienced a moment's peace due to the slothful, thievish nature of his slaves, who had to be watched every moment. The visitor accounts and planter diaries, however, share one characteristic: both leave the impression that an army of house servants swarmed around the planter's family in the "Great House." It is something of a surprise, then, to examine the few slave lists of large plantations that remain and note the size and disposition of the staff. . . .

Prior to 1760, under 15% of working females on these large estates and the quarters attached to them were occupied in house service, while in the latter part of the 18th century the percentage increased to around a quarter and circa 1800 reached one third or more. For women, the greatest jumps occurred in the non-domestic area—housewifery, just as for men the increases came primarily in trades. After 1760 Tidewater planters obviously moved to increase the home production of consumer goods on their estates.

Three factors probably contributed to this shift. First, of course, was the break with the British Empire and the concomitant disruption in trade that made more local manufacture, especially that of low quality apparel, imperative. Second, the evolution of a native born population with larger numbers of young and old than were found in earlier generations when the African born pre-dominated resulted in an increased proportion of slaves physically unfit for field work. Third, the declining vitality of the Virginia tobacco business reduced the need for field labor. Planters transferred some of this workforce to other field pursuits, namely the cultivating of corn and wheat, but a larger portion of men and women than has perhaps been previously assumed went into craftwork. By this time, many of the major Chesapeake planting families derived a considerable amount of income from rents and financial assets, so they did not have to depend so heavily on profits from agricultural output. . . .

[It] is important to remember that while in the later years a third or more of the women belonging to large slaveowners performed household work, two thirds did not do the work Anglo-American society traditionally assigned to females. . . . [Instead, they did] daily gang work of the tobacco plantation.

What were the main characteristics of that minority of slave women who did household work? Let us look at domestic labor first. . . . At the big house, planters usually employed prime age adult women in two occupations, cook and washerwoman. . . . The cook prepared the breakfasts and dinners. Visitors' comments about light or non-existent suppers on most plantations imply that the kitchen closed down after the mid-day meal. The gradual development of a distinctive Southern cooking tradition is well-known and clearly connected to the black female servants. Less well-known to posterity but much celebrated by 18th century visitors to Virginia was the laundry. Sounding rather like a soap commercial, John Harrower, a Scottish indentured servant, wrote back to his wife that "they wash here the whitest that ever I seed for they first Boyle all the cloaths with soap, and then wash them, and I may put on clean linen every day if I please." . . . Seldom is more than one woman identified on the plantation lists as a washerwoman, although sometimes in addition an ironer is named. Their small daughters also may have helped. Judging from the above remarks, all probably worked quite hard.

The personal servants, nurses, and general household drudges who brought in water, carried out chamber pots, made beds and so forth, were frequently girls. Their duties centered around the person rather than the house itself. This relative lack of attention to house maintenance characterized traditional domestic service and was only beginning to change. These girls usually stayed in the house or in the very room where the white woman or child to whom they were assigned slept. What happened to them when they became adults is unclear. . . .

Planter families rarely conferred the title of housekeeper on a black female servant. I have come across only one example of a slave being so designated. Instead they hired a white indentured servant or local woman to handle these duties, which often included being in charge of the keys to the stores of provisions. If the family did not employ a housekeeper, they might retain a white nurse to provide milk and/or childcare. The relations between these white women servants and their employers were seldom harmonious and in most cases one side or the other abruptly terminated the association. Apparently white women did not find domestic service in the slave South appealing. . . .

Where . . . increased use of female slaves on the large colonial plantations did occur was in the housewifery area, particularly textile production. . . .

[T]he British commercial system did not encourage plantation self-sufficiency nor full scale housewifery. Slaveowners purchased the bulk of the commodities they distributed among their workforce rather than manufacturing them at home. They imported cloth, stockings, and shoes from the Mother Country, and white seam-stresses or tailors were frequently hired to cut out and sew garments. The growth in the textile staff at most plantations, then, proceeded at a leisurely pace until the conflict with Great Britain speeded up the process. In the early 1760s, before he set up a full scale manufactory, George Washington had a spinner and a seamstress at Mount Vernon, and Landon Carter had three spinners and a weaver. . . . To solve the weaver shortage, planters employed female slaves though it was an occupation that in England had become the preserve of white men. . . .

Plantation societies such as the one founded in Colonial Virginia were largely the creation of white men and reflected their priorities. Relatively few indentured ser-vants were female and any planter who wanted a female staff larger than one or two would have to buy slaves. . . . We always knew the black household possessed the barest minimum in the way of amenities. That the black woman's contribution to white domesticity and housewifery was so thinly spread is more surprising because Virginians used the home in preference to public spaces more extensively than al-most any other early modern community. During much of the colonial period white life on the quarters was still totally organized around production of [tobacco]. Those in the "Great Houses," the showplaces of the society, lived in what one observer termed a "tawdry luxury." . . .

The typical 18th century servant was not a Mammy figure but a young girl. She worked as household drudge out on a quarter or a small plantation, where she tended children, cooked, washed linens, and milked cows. If she lived at the "Great House" she might be a personal servant or, as became increasingly common as the 18th century progressed, a spinner. When she grew older and married, she might not stay in the house because it seems that only a few positions, mainly cook and washerwoman, regularly were held by adult women in their prime years. Conse-quently when a slave woman was most likely to be bearing and nursing children, she also was most likely to be assigned to the fields. Women, whether white or black, have shared one similarity when it has come to work. Their occupations have been mainly determined by their stage of life or marital status not their expe-rience or training. The two occupations most identified with the Mammy stereo-type, housekeeper and nurse, were actually those jobs the planter family most often sought white women to fill. Nor did "cleaning lady" accurately define many colo-nial female house slaves; close attention to home care had only just begun and rural Virginia did not lead the movement. . . .

A major change in the plantation situation I have just described seems to have occurred in the later 18th century with a noticeable rise in housewifery activities. . . . Specific information about slave women's occupations only exists for the larger plantations. The sources indicate that after 1760 the non-field contingent of the female as well as the male workforce grew until it constituted a third or more of all slave labor. The increases for women came in the housewifery area. Smaller planta-tions, of course, would probably not have maintained these elaborate craft establish-ments. Still, if we take into consideration the proliferation of towns and the additions to the free black population, it is conceivable that as early as 1800 an upper South state such as Virginia would have 20–25% of its black women in non-field work.

Women's Work in Colonial Philadelphia

KARIN WULF

Even in a city as large as Philadelphia, with a transient population and a seaport buzzing with daily arrivals and departures, dense webs of relationships underlay urban neighborhoods. Thus, when John Barker, the constable of Philadelphia's High Street Ward, set out to enumerate the residents of his district in 1775, he encountered familiar faces and families of long residence. Among the householders he greeted while making these rounds was the widow Rachel Draper, a tavernkeeper. Rachel Draper had lived in High Street Ward for over twenty years by the time Barker came to make his Constable's Return. Her husband, James, a tailor who had earned a modest living, had died relatively young. . . . Rachel Draper was the sole executor of her husband's estate, a common phenomenon among Philadelphia's lower sort. The larger and more complex an estate was, the less likely it was that the widow was named as the sole executor, or even as a co-executor. After administering the settlement of her husband's estate, Rachel Draper set about making a living for herself and her two young daughters. She held onto the house, but her financial status was precarious. She was considered too poor and too burdened by the costs of supporting her young children to pay any taxes.

Like many others among Philadelphia's working poor, Draper used a variety of economic strategies to meet her family's needs. She was granted successive city licenses to operate a "dram shop," or small tavern, probably right in her home on Chancery Lane. She was a tavernkeeper from at least 1767 through 1773, and perhaps for much longer. To help with the annual rent of £14 on a house and lot that served as both residence and place of business, Draper took in boarders: Jacob Potts was boarding there in 1770, and Thomas Draper, no doubt a relation, was boarding there in 1775.

By 1775 Rachel Draper had lived in her neighborhood for at least two decades, the last twelve years of which she had headed her household. Although clearly economically marginal, Draper was in some ways a success story. She never fell into the transiency that marked the lives of so many among Philadelphia's laboring population. She not only kept her family fed and clothed, but she also made sure that her two daughters received an education. . . .

Rachel Draper's circumstances as a working, unmarried woman were far from unique. She lived and worked alongside such women as upholsterer Elizabeth Lawrence, tavernkeeper Susannah Harditch, and tallow chandler Ann Wishart. Each of these women was a neighbor of Draper's and a resident of long tenure. Each had extensive ties to the community. These women, and others like them, helped to shape urban community and urban culture in the eighteenth-century city. As independent women, they could act legally and economically in ways that their married sisters, bound by coverture, could not. Although historians have emphasized the importance of all women in creating social networks, unmarried women not only

Karin Wulf, reprinted from *Not All Wives: Women of Colonial Philadelphia* (Ithaca, N.Y.: Cornell University Press, 2000), 119–121, 130–148. Copyright © 1999 by Cornell University. Used by permission of the publisher, Cornell University Press.

maintained existing ties of kinship and friendship but also created community ties that facilitated their independence. They exchanged credit and debt, rented property to and from their neighbors, served drinks, bought and sold goods, and engaged in friendly, practical, or even hostile conversation. Neighbors often worshipped together. Some were related by blood or marriage. Unmarried women were central actors in the creation and maintenance of the economic, religious, familial, and broadly political networks of association that defined urban life. . . .

Women's work was vital to Philadelphia's economy, but the extent and range of this work has been particularly hard to uncover. Scholars who study the occupational structure of early American cities have had to rely on sources that mask the work of women and other economically marginal groups, including laboring men, servants, and slaves. . . . The city was dependent on goods and services provided by laboring men and women. But the remaining inventories of merchants' goods, the records of indenture, and even tax records that nominally recorded occupations paid little attention to recording women's work in any systematic way. Thus sources have in some measure "hidden" women's work.

In addition, eighteenth-century culture was ambivalent about the meaning of women's work in general and about the economic contributions of domestic work in particular. *Present for an Apprentice: or, a Sure Guide to Gain both Esteem and Estate* circulated widely in the Anglo-American world. In Philadelphia, Benjamin Franklin printed the fourth edition of this book of advice for young, working men embarking on life's journey in 1749. The author cautioned that young men of the laboring sort should consider marriage an expense, rather than a financial gain. . . . Of the economic benefit of women's labor, there was no mention.

Although some source materials reflect the eighteenth-century elision of the significance of women's economic contributions, it is clear that women's work was both ubiquitous and necessary. A common assumption is that widows, who were the majority of unmarried women, were reliant on their inheritances. A husband's estate formed the bulk of a widow's wealth, and thus her own economic condition was utterly dependent on the state of his estate at his death and then on the provisions of his will. There are two problems with this assumption. The first is that it portrays widows as peculiarly financially dependent. In fact, economic interdependence, not independence, was the rule in this period. Men as well as women relied on inheritance and on transfers of wealth rather than strictly on accumulation through income. If anything, women aided men in this respect; the laws of coverture guaranteed men access to any property their wives possessed at marriage and gave them rights to their wives' earnings during the marriage. Men from George Washington to the famously "self-made" Benjamin Franklin prospered through the legally mandated transfer of wealth. The second problem with assuming that inheritance was widows' sole source of income is that it casts women as only passive recipients of wealth, rather than generators of wealth. A widow's inheritance, after all, was the product of her own as well as her husband's capital and labor. In addition, many widows who inherited subsequently increased their holdings through investment or through income-producing occupations.

The urban economy gave women more options for producing income or supplementing their capital than did strictly agricultural regions. Although widowhood often meant a difficult economic predicament, some female entrepreneurs flowered financially after they were widowed. Their experiences suggest that, as for men, familial, friendship, and economic connections helped them establish small businesses. Born in 1707, Hannah Breintnall was a little like Deborah Franklin. Mrs. Franklin often kept shop and accounts for her husband, but while Benjamin Franklin lived a long life during which Deborah was the distinctly subordinate partner in his ventures, Hannah Breintnall's husband died, leaving her to make her own way financially. She took up the most common occupations for female entrepreneurs: keeping a shop and tavern. . . .

Hannah Breintnall was not unusual. She married, bore children, became widowed, managed businesses and finances, and provided for her family. The typical picture of the colonial entrepreneur and provider assumes his masculine gender. But many women like Hannah Breintnall, some more and some less successfully, acted independently to support themselves and their families. Widows could rarely afford to be passive guardians of their portion of a husband's estate, and many did not remarry. It was clear to many widows that they would have to take on the financial responsibility of their own and their family's care.

Women who never married—even those from middling or wealthy families—often had to generate more wealth than they inherited because fathers most often passed real property to sons but gave cash or other personalty, often in the form of marriage settlements, to daughters. Spinsters' work was usually directly related to their lack of inherited resources and their need to support themselves. . . .

Women's occupational opportunities were more restricted than men's for several reasons. Women were less likely to get specialized training in a craft or skill than were men. Female servants, for example, usually were trained only in "housewifery." Strictly limited access to capital prevented most women from creating businesses on their own, with the exception of some retail establishments headed by wealthier women. Widows of tradesmen were sometimes able to continue in their husbands' work, but other women had a hard time entering trades. Perhaps most importantly, the close association of domestic labor with women made it difficult for them to do other kinds of work, simply because whatever the size or economic status of their household, they were responsible for child care and housework. This labor, which was so critical to the functioning of the household economy, left women little time and energy to apply to another occupation. Thus, women who needed income—that is, the majority of married women as well as the vast majority of unmarried women—looked to work that could be fitted around other obligations and used their domestic skills.

Women's work in the eighteenth-century city can be divided into two broad categories: gender-specific work, primarily domestic labor, and nongender-specific work that both men and women performed. Shopkeeping and other mercantile activity, trades, and unskilled labor were all primarily male preserves in which some women could find employment. A degree of gender segregation appeared, however, even within such occupations as retailing or artisanal work.

Among gender-segregated occupations, domestic service was the most significant and visible source of employment for women. Cleaning houses; growing, butchering, preserving, and cooking food; making, repairing, and laundering clothes; caring for children—all of these were tasks that kept women moving in and out of the house and at close quarters with their neighbors. For poorer families, it was deemed both more appropriate and more economical for women to perform such tasks themselves at home. The work required long hours and a strong back. Water for laundry and cooking had to be fetched from a pump. Although urban women did not have to go very far to get water, they still had to haul many gallons a day. Caring for apprentices, servants and slaves, or boarders was also part of women's domestic labor in families of tradesmen or artisans. Even for merchants or others whose work brought income to the family without requiring extensive household labor, the value and extent of domestic labor was enormous.

Female servants performed a large portion of this work. In colonial American cities, as in Europe, domestic service was an increasingly important part of the changing urban economy and reflected the growth of middling classes. In the American South, where domestic work was performed largely by enslaved women, white servants were rare. In the North, however, particularly in mid-Atlantic cities, a variant of the European pattern prevailed. Domestic household servants were not simply the preserve of the rich and titled but became a critical part of the household economy of the middling classes. Whereas in a merchant's home servants would perform purely household tasks, in the home of an artisan a "maid of all work" would lend a hand in the workshop, then contribute to the household tasks of cooking, cleaning, and sewing. . . .

Servants could be either indentured or hired for a day, a week, or a year. Female indentured servants came primarily from three groups. The first were adult women who signed indentures before departing Europe or upon arrival in America in order to pay for their passage. . . . The second type of indentured women were poor girls bound out by the city or by their parents. Indentures could provide some training as well as bed and board. . . . A third category of indentures was made privately, apprenticing girls and boys to specific trades. It is not possible to estimate the size and character of this population, although more boys than girls were trained for trades. Families also sent children to relatives' households in exchange for their care and training in a marketable skill. . . .

Work that was seen as feminine was often linked to domestic skills, specifically to providing care and personal services for others. Chief among these were nursing, midwifery, and mortuary work. Nursing seems to have been a specialized skill, but it also commingled with midwifery and laying out the dead. In an era when doctors were just beginning to acquire formal training, medicine was often administered by lay persons. Nurses were not simply women who happened to care for the sick, however. They were addressed as "Nurse," and some specialized in infant care, others in infectious diseases. . . . Despite increasing use of schooled physicians, midwives seem to have found regular, constant employment. . . . Even women who, later in the century, chose to have doctors rather than midwives deliver their babies hired nurses for their newborns. Breastfeeding was a matter of choice for elite women. . . . Wet-nursing supplied poorer households with some extra income, perhaps at a critical moment when a woman was prevented from income-earning activities by virtue of recent childbirth. . . .

Women's responsibility for attending the dead was both social custom and economic opportunity. Women regularly stayed with women friends who were either sick or in labor, and with friends' children who were sick. Once a person had died, however, professional services were engaged. Some women, like Precilla Cowley, both nursed the ill and prepared the dead body for burial, while other women provided specialized mortuary and funerary services. . . .

. . . [W]omen and men had differential employment opportunities, with more skilled work available primarily to men, and . . . women were paid from one-quarter to one-half of the wages that men could command for similar work. In urban areas, the greater demand for more specialized skills and trades benefited males more than females, especially because domestic service was women's primary employment. But it appears that when specialized work was called for, wage differentials shrank so that women earned perhaps one-half to two-thirds of the wages that men commanded. . . .

Unmarried women faced economic pressures particular to their situation. They needed to work, but remunerative employment was scarce. A handful of cases of bawdy house brought before the Philadelphia Mayor's Court in the 1760s and 1770s attest to the unsurprising existence of prostitution in the seaport, but prostitution must have been a last resort. Reported instances of prostitution among poor women increased sharply only after the Revolution.

Domestic service did have some economic advantages, in particular the security of room and board. Unmarried female domestic servants who lived with their employers were provided with food and sometimes with clothing. A regular annual salary of £10 might have compared favorably, at least in economic terms, with the situation of a mistress of a laboring household.

Retailing goods or food and drink provided the next largest group of occupations for women after domestic service. Women accounted for perhaps as many as half of all retailers in the eighteenth-century city, although women's retailing was generally conducted on a smaller scale than men's and was less likely to be combined with wholesaling. . . . Over the eighteenth century, retailing became an increasingly viable economic option for women. Retailing increased in importance as imported consumer goods washed over the colonies, a process that intensified at mid-century. . . . This increase in the availability and variety of consumer goods prompted the elaboration of retail establishments, and of the activity of shopping itself. . . .

Women were well positioned to take advantage of both the retailing and the consumption of goods. Provisioning the household (or "marketing") was long thought to be a feminine responsibility, but the new dynamics of class and status competition were specifically gendered. . . . Both men and women shopped, but the increasing attention of retail advertisements to their female clientele and to items of female apparel testifies both to women's importance as consumers and to the importance of feminine attire to class aspirations. As retailers, women could tap the very market they helped comprise. Female shopkeepers among the middling or elite whose customers came from the same networks of association could help determine fashions. . . .

Retailing varied widely. At the lower end of the scale, hucksters purchased cast-off, second-quality, damaged, or otherwise less desirable merchandise, which they then hawked through the streets. Peddlers who moved from the city out into the countryside with imported or finished goods were regulated and licensed, and were almost exclusively male. Hucksters who carried goods through the city were usually female. Hucksters could acquire goods for their baskets from a variety of sources. Fresh food was brought into the city from the hinterlands on market days, when the city's famously extensive markets could be overwhelmed with meat, cheese, butter, and produce, along with homespun cloth and other hand-made goods. Any goods left by the end of the day, unsold or of inferior quality, were sold to hucksters, who might make a tiny profit by reselling them. Walking outward from the city center, hucksters might find customers among those who could not get to the market—for example, housewives confined at home who had no servants to make their purchases, and laboring families for whom a trip to the market for first-quality fresh goods were a rare luxury. One step up from hucksters were those women who operated tiny shops within a corner of a room, sometimes buying only small lots of goods to sell at a time. . . .

A handful of elite women shopkeepers operating during the third quarter of the eighteenth century, including Mary Coates, Magdalena Devine, Elizabeth Paschall, and Mary and Rebecca Steel, were very prosperous and carried extensive inventory. For these women, as for many successful male entrepreneurs, economic, social, kinship, and religious circles all overlapped; shopkeeping mixed easily with their other social obligations. They shopped in each others' stores, bought wholesale goods together, and circulated within the same group of friends. Coates, Paschall, and Rebecca Steel bought goods together at vendue for sale in their respective shops. They purchased goods from each other when these items were not available from their own inventories, or when one happened on a better wholesale price. . . .

Opportunities in tavernkeeping also increased as the city grew. A few gathering spots, such as the London Coffee House on Market Street, catered to a new clientele of merchants who wanted not just to exchange business talk but to engage in the whole realm of discussions that were beginning to constitute public discourse. The only women welcomed there were servers. Most taverns, however, remained gathering spots for neighbors or work-fellows, providing modest provisions and drink at a low price. For many women like Rachel Draper, tavernkeeping was a reasonably good prospect. . . . In some areas of the city there were as many or more female as male publicans. Tavernkeeping could also be combined with shopkeeping in a single establishment, which may have made it especially appealing to women.

A few women worked in the specialized trades supported by the urban economy, especially after mid-century. Most probably had husbands or fathers who had worked in these trades and perhaps already established workshops that they could assume. Among those who made their living supplying the many seaport industries, Sarah Jewell continued the ropewalk her husband had founded, making ropes and rigging so necessary for shipbuilding, while Hannah Beales continued her father's fishnet-making business. No guilds kept women in Philadelphia from pursuing trades, as they did in early modern Europe, but the complications of acquiring apprentices and gaining master status were enough to discourage most women. Informal pressure from loose organizations of artisans may also have had a hand in discouraging women's participation in such trades.

Almost all urban women worked either within or outside the home, and most probably worked for pay. Economic connections that women made while working could be a critical outgrowth of other relationships, particularly among family members, but the formation of economic networks was also a fundamental opportunity provided by neighborhood. . . . Women, like men, accessed credit and debt networks by exercising familial and economic resources, including personal relationships. Because women had much less access to trans-Atlantic credit, however, wholesale merchant work was an unlikely pursuit, whereas local credit networks such as those employed by small retailers were much more readily available. . . .

By forming economic connections and networks, work also became an important source of personal and community identity. Although not all workers identified with their work, many did, especially those whose work enmeshed them in networks of obligation and association. Contributing to the association of work and identity was the way that work became bound up with the community's needs and one's place in the community.

Women's Work in California's Spanish Missions

VIRGINIA MARIE BOUVIER

Between 1769 and 1823, Spanish friars established a chain of twenty-one missions, each a day's journey from the next, along 650 miles of Pacific coastline from San Diego in the south to Sonoma in the north. . . .

Built like a military fortress, the main mission building generally formed a quadrangle with adobe walls six to eight feet thick. Its various compartments could be individually locked from the outside to provide both protection and control of the residents therein. A separate guardhouse with its own kitchen usually housed the five or six soldiers who were required to accompany the priests on their search for potential Indian converts and escapees. A palisade of wall often enclosed the main mission quadrangle, its separate buildings, and sometimes the adjoining rancherías of thatched huts, adobe houses, or long barracks, where the married neophytes and their families lived.

One of the first structures to be built was often the *monjerío,* the separate dormitory where neophyte girls and single or widowed neophyte women slept under lock and key. Until they reached adolescence, usually sometime after age eleven and sometimes at an earlier age, young Indian girls lived with their Christianized Indian parents in the nearby rancherías. When they reached adolescence (presumably when they began menstruating), the girls were brought to monjeríos, ostensibly to "safeguard their virginity and help them to prepare for Christian marriage." The girls left the mission compound only after they were married, when they returned to the rancherías with their husbands. The Indian men at the missions were sometimes housed in separate quarters called *jayuntes,* where they were only occasionally kept under lock and key.

Roles and experiences at each mission varied over time and were circumscribed by gender, religion, ethnicity, age, and marital status. The missions offered both opportunities and constraints for the women who came to Alta California from Mexico and Baja California. The role of the female newcomers to Alta California was initially an ideological one. Christian women—both Indians and Hispanics—would

Adapted from *Women and the Conquest of California, 1542–1840* by Virginia M. Bouvier, pp. 80–89 and 104–107. Copyright © 2001 The Arizona Board of Regents. Reprinted by permission of the University of Arizona Press. Footnotes available in the original text.

be role models for the neophytes at the Alta California missions. They were to accul-
turate women to both Christian and Hispanic ways, theoretically instilling in the neophyte population European habits of personal hygiene. As early as 1774, Father Font
noted that the young women at San Luis Obispo mission had been taught to sew "and
to keep clean; and they already do so very nicely, as if they were little Spaniards." . . .

The Hispanic acculturation of the Indians included the deliberate inculcation of
a European work ethic. . . . Such values were seen as essential to the priests' mission
and were imposed in part through a rigorous work regimen.

The priests and women from Baja California and Mexico trained the neophyte
girls in a number of practical tasks, such as sewing and weaving, designed to cultivate
industriousness and to prepare the girls for Christian marriages. The single or widowed
females at the monjerío carded, cleaned, and spun wool. They also wove and sewed.
Those who were married lived at the rancherías with their families, attending to domestic duties. At the monjeríos, the girls were taught to be useful subjects and wives. . . .

Religious and cultural considerations were more important than ethnicity for the
task of acculturation. Although there was some fluidity between Hispanic and Indian
women in terms of their labor, a definite hierarchy of responsibility put the priests
squarely in charge, followed by Hispanic women (when they were available) who
oversaw other Christianized Indian women, who oversaw Indian neophytes. Older
Indian women, as well as Hispanic and Baja California women, served as teachers
and role models for the new female converts. At the San Luis Obispo mission, the
wives of the soldiers sometimes served as guards at the monjeríos. At the San Diego
mission, older Indian women watched over the female neophytes. These indigenous
supervisors reported directly to the priest, without a Hispanic intermediary.

Eulalia Pérez, a self-described daughter of "pure white" parents from Baja
California, served as the *llavera,* or housekeeper, of the San Gabriel mission. Pérez
recalled than an Indian woman named Polonia, whom the girls called "Mother
Superior," was in charge of securing the girls in the monjerío. At the Santa Barbara
mission, Angustias de la Guerra Ord, the daughter of the Spanish *comandante* at
the nearby presidio, recalled that the female overseers were "ever so ladylike." The
Santa Barbara mission priests entrusted neither the Indian nor the Hispanic women
with the keys, however. The nunnery at Santa Barbara mission, Ord noted, had three
locks and three keys, which were held by the prelate, the *alcalde mayor,* and the cor-
poral of the mission guard. Without the consent of the three officials, no one could
enter the monjerío.

At the monjeríos, these Christianized (and usually Hispanicized) Indian women
taught female neophytes the ways of Hispanic culture and played a pivotal role in the
ideological conversion of their peers. The priests relied on Christianized Indian
women to bring female newcomers into the fold and to socialize them in the ways
of mission life. . . .

Female labor was not limited to social acculturation but served a socioeconomic
role as well—a role that expanded with the growing prosperity of the mission enterprise. The testimonies of Eulalia Pérez and Apolinaria Lorenzana, obtained as part of
an oral history project conducted in the 1870s at the behest of Hubert H. Bancroft,
shed some light on the changing roles and relationships of Baja California and Mexican women at the California missions. Lorenzana and Pérez amply documented the
contribution that women made in the supervision, teaching, and execution of basic

household tasks such as cooking, cleaning, sewing, caring for the sick, laundering, and managing the daily affairs of the missions. Such tasks were monumental when one considers that a single mission household might include hundreds of neophytes.

Four-year-old Apolinaria Lorenzana arrived with her mother in Alta California from Mexico City in 1800. Shortly thereafter, her mother remarried and returned to Mexico, leaving Apolinaria a virtual orphan. She was taken in by Lieutenant José Raimundo Carrillo and Doña Tomasa Lugo in Santa Barbara, and when Carrillo was promoted to captain of the San Diego presidio, she accompanied them there. Lorenzana had learned catechism and to read at a very young age, and she taught herself to write when she got to California. . . . After a few years, she moved in with Sergeant Mercado and Doña Josefa Sal. After the sergeant died, his widow opened a girls' school. Because Josefa's time was consumed with running her large estate, Apolinaria was given virtually exclusive custody of the school, where she taught girls reading, catechism, and sewing.

A few years later, she was brought to the mission, where she served as the nurse for the newly constructed mission hospital. As in other places and times, frontier priests in colonial California sometimes discouraged women from engaging in the healing arts. Although Apolinaria Lorenzana was put in charge of the patients in the mission hospital, the priests tried to limit her activities to administrative duties. She managed to exercise her skills as a *curandera* nonetheless. She narrated proudly that she took care of the sick people "even though Father Sánchez had told me not to do it myself, but to have it done, and only to be present so that the servant girls would do it well." Despite the priest's objections, she noted, "I always, as best I could, gave a hand, and attended to the sick." Her friend María Ignacia Amador also knew how to cure sick people and was described by Pérez as a "good curandera."

Faced with a shortage of doctors and medical supplies on the frontier, Hispanic women frequently engaged in such healing activities (sometimes learned from indigenous healers). Apolinaria Lorenzana and Eulalia Pérez both engaged in midwifery, assisting in childbirth for both the indigenous and the Hispanic communities. . . .

Women were often given roles as supervisors and teachers at the missions. Pérez emphasized that her responsibilities included supervising men as well as women. She oversaw the men involved in making soap, working the wine presses, and producing olive oil, and she directed the Indian servant who delivered food and supplies to the troops and servants. Lorenzana was responsible for stocking the mission from the cargo ships. She used to take servants with her on board to receive those items that were needed at the mission, and she was authorized to add to the list the priests had given her any additional items she deemed to be useful. Although Lorenzana never married and had no children, she served as a baptismal and confirmation sponsor to some 200 *ahijados,* or godchildren, of all backgrounds. She taught the Indian girls at the San Diego mission to sew, and she personally supervised the making and laundering of the church vestments. She wrote, "Everything was done under my direction and care. I took care not only of making clothing for the church, but saw that the Indian girls laundered it as well." In the 1840s, Lorenzana was the beneficiary of two land grants from the Mexican government; she later bought a third. In the wake of the Mexican-American War, Lorenzana lost her land to speculators.

Eulalia Pérez was married to Miguel Antonio Guillén, a soldier from the Loreto presidio in Baja California, where she gave birth to three sons (two of whom died) and a daughter. When her husband was reassigned to Alto California, she accompanied him to his new post at the San Diego presidio. There she served as a midwife for eight years, and she complained that she was unable to leave the presidio to visit relatives because her husband refused to accompany her and the presidio commander would not let her leave, owing to the shortage of midwives in the area. After her husband was transferred to serve as a guard at the San Gabriel mission, the family moved north. When her husband died, Pérez returned to San Diego, where she lived temporarily with Lieutenant Santiago Argüello and his family at their home, the only house in the area. Three years later, her son took a job as a mission guard at San Gabriel mission, and Pérez and her five daughters relocated there.

Because she was a widow "burdened with a family," Pérez recalled, "the priests wanted to help me out." The priests originally hired her in 1821 to teach the Indians at the San Gabriel mission (male and female alike) to cook. In the course of more than a decade there, Pérez assumed increasing responsibility for the supervision and administration of the mission. After one year, she was promoted to llavera and assumed responsibility for distributing the rations of food and clothing to the neophytes. At San Gabriel mission, the population grew from 1,201 in 1810 to 1,636 in 1820, and it then declined to 1,320 neophytes by the close of 1832. With 26,342 cattle, sheep, goats, hogs, horses, and mules, its corral in 1832 was second only to that of San Luis Rey mission; the agricultural production of San Gabriel surpassed that of every other mission. Pérez and her five daughters were responsible for cutting and sewing the clothing for the neophyte *vaqueros* who rounded up the livestock. When her daughters were unable to fulfill the clothing needs of the mission, they would ask the priest to contract other women from the nearby pueblo of Los Angeles to assist them.

Many of the women working and living at the missions felt a certain loyalty toward the priests. Pérez was so grateful for their assistance that she found it difficult to reject their counsel, even when it involved making decisions about marriage. When one of the San Gabriel priests urged her to remarry, she confessed that she had no desire to do so, but she "acceded to the father's wishes because I didn't have the heart to deny him anything when Father Sánchez had been like a father and a mother to me and to my family."

Women from Baja California and Mexico taught the Indians how to cook, and they assisted in the preparation of lemonade for the Indian workers and delicacies such as chocolate paste and preserves for the missionaries. Culinary skills were rather rare in the San Gabriel region. Eulalia Pérez recounted that when she arrived at the mission, only two other women in that part of California knew how to cook—María Luisa Cota, the wife of mayordomo Claudio López, and María Ignacia Amador, the wife of soldier Francisco Javier Alvarado. Pérez trained two Indians to cook for the missionaries' kitchen and distributed the daily food rations to the mission Indians. . . .

Despite the opportunities open to women on the frontier, there were still limitations on their activities. In an interview in 1874, eighty-one-year-old Dorotea Valdez, whose father had been one of the first settlers of San Diego and who was born in Monterey, referred to these limitations when she noted that because she was a woman, she "was denied the privilege of mixing in politics or in business." At the missions, women were further limited by ecclesiastical concerns about impropriety.

Church authorities in New Spain advised the Also California priests to limit their contact with women at the missions. . . .

Missionary priests believed that the mission would provide protection for Indian girls within the mission's walls, and they extolled the benefits of missionization for the female indigenous population. The Spaniards' assumptions derived in part from their gender ideology and its conflict with the ideologies of indigenous groups. The priests believed that the mission offered women an easier regime of labor than that experienced in pre-mission days. They were quick to underscore what they saw as the inequities of the pre-mission division of labor for women. Father Gerónimo Boscana noted, "It was the duty of the women to gather the seeds, prepare them for cooking, and perform all the meanest offices as well as the most laborious, whilst their lazy husbands were either at play or asleep. Frequently, they would receive ill-treatment in return." This contrast between the hardworking "squaw" and her lazy husband formed part of a rhetoric that suggested that women were better off at the missions.

Father President Fermín Francisco de Lasuén agreed that the indigenous division of labor was unfair to women, and he noted the abuse given to the indigenous wives by their spouses. He observed, "In their native state they [the women] are slaves to the men, obliged to maintain them with the sweat of their brow. They are ill-treated," he wrote, "trampled on by them even to the point of death if, on returning to their huts after spending the entire night in raids or in dancing, the entire morning in play, and the entire evening in sleeping they find that the women have made no provision for food for them." Conditions were better for women at the missions, according to Lasuén, who pointed out that the women "never object or show any dislike for the work we assign."

In the pre-mission period, California Indians had seldom engaged in subsistence agriculture, and then only in the extreme southwest. For most indigenous men and women of Alta California, sedentary agriculture at the missions and the lifestyle it entailed represented a marked departure. . . . In pre-mission days, women in most California tribes had primary responsibility for the collection of foodstuffs. They gathered acorns, roots, seeds, berries, and grasshoppers. They shelled the acorns, dried them, and ground them into flour for bread. The acorn permeated indigenous societies and provided the inhabitants of Alta California with their principal sustenance before the mission period. Its value extended beyond the merely nutritional. The year was measured from "acorn to acorn," or from "seed to seed." The northern Ohlone Indians at San José mission distinguished the seasons of the year by the rotations of the moon, the rains, the weather, and the ripening of the acorn seeds. Spring was marked by the appearance of flowers; summer was when the grasses became dry and the seeds matured; fall was discernible because wild geese and ducks appeared and the acorns ripened; and winter was recognized because of the rainfall. In pre-mission days, women made no pottery but crafted baskets so tightly woven that they could be used to boil water for cooking. They continued their basketry work at the missions.

Missionization disrupted indigenous survival patterns and transformed some aspects of gender roles. At the missions, the acorn was no longer a mainstay of the indigenous diet, although the failure of agricultural efforts in the early mission years provided some Indians with opportunities to supplement their mission diet with wild foods. As food production at the missions became more efficient and changed the ecological patterns of the land, some of the priests restricted the opportunities for neophytes to engage in their pre-mission patterns of food gathering, hunting, and fishing. The shift in patterns of food production may have affected female status as the acorn shifted to a less prominent place on the menu than it had held in pre-mission days.

Indigenous women at the missions nonetheless continued to be involved in aspects of childbearing and child rearing, food production, cooking, basket making, clothing production, and retrieval of water and wood, albeit on a greater scale and in a more systematic and controlled way than before. The women no longer controlled their own labor but were directed by others and subject to punishment if they did not comply. . . .

Just as priests cited the natives' inequitable gender roles and mistreatment of women in order to justify bringing indigenous women to the missions, so gender ideologies guided their enclosure of women in the monjeríos. The institution of the monjerío responded in part to Spanish ideas about gender and honor. Confinement of female neophytes was purported to assist the priests' efforts to regulate sexual relations between male and female Indians and to protect the women from abuse by Spanish-Mexican soldiers. . . .

The walls of the monjerío, like the walls of other mission structures, were virtually impenetrable blocks of silence that hid the experiences of female neophytes. Church codes of silence converged with another code of silence on the part of the Indians, who were seldom in a position to reveal the abuse they experienced at the hands of the mission system. Lack of faith in the justice system of the Spanish priests, along with linguistic, cultural, and gender barriers, encouraged such reticence. . . .

Gender ideologies provided the justifications for bringing women to the missions and the blueprint for their roles once they got there. Christianized Hispanic women worked to support the administration and functioning of the mission system and to cultivate European habits of hygiene and industry among the indigenous population. Soldiers, priests, and Indian men brought indigenous women to the missions by force. Sometimes women came of their own free will. Once at the missions, Christianized Indian women tutored newcomers in the ways of Hispanics. . . .

◈ *F U R T H E R   R E A D I N G*

Cleary, Patricia. " 'She Will Be in the Shop': Women's Sphere of Trade in Eighteenth-Century Philadelphia and New York," *Pennsylvania Magazine of History and Biography* 119 (1995): 181–202.

Goldin, Claudia. "The Economic Status of Women in the Early Republic," *Journal of Interdisciplinary History* 16 (1985–1986): 375–404.

Hood, Adrienne. "The Gender Division of Labor in the Production of Textiles in Eighteenth-Century Pennsylvania (Rethinking the New England Model)," *Journal of Social History* 26, no. 3 (March 1994): 537–561.

Lewis, Johanna. "Women Artisans in Backcountry North Carolina, 1753–1790," *North Carolina Historical Review* 68 (1991): 214–236.

Main, Gloria. "Gender, Work, and Wages in Colonial New England," *William and Mary Quarterly,* 3d ser., 51 (1994): 39–66.

Morgan, Jennifer. *Laboring Women: Reproduction and Gender in New World Slavery* (2004).

Nash, Gary B. "The Failure of Female Factory Labor in Colonial Boston," *Labor History* 20 (1979): 165–188.

Norton, Mary Beth. *Founding Mothers & Fathers: Gendered Power and the Forming of American Society* (1996).

——. " 'The Ablest Midwife That Wee Knowe in the Land': Mistress Alice Tilly and the Women of Boston and Dorchester, 1649–1650," *William and Mary Quarterly,* 3d ser., 55 (1998): 105–134.

Salinger, Sharon. " 'Send No More Women': Female Servants in Eighteenth-Century Philadelphia," *Pennsylvania Magazine of History and Biography* 107 (1983): 29–48.

Tannenbaum, Rebecca. *The Healer's Calling: Women and Medicine in Early New England* (2002).

Ulrich, Laurel Thatcher. "Wheels, Looms, and the Gender Division of Labor in Eighteenth-Century New England," *William and Mary Quarterly,* 3d ser., 55 (1998): 3–38.

CHAPTER
5

The Impact of the

American Revolution

In many ways, the American Revolution changed the course of history for the residents of what had been Britain's mainland North American colonies. In 1774, the settlers were colonials—subjects of a monarchy based thousands of miles across the Atlantic and participants in a traditional political system. Less than a decade later, these successful revolutionaries, now Americans, were the founders of an independent republic and the first colonists in history to win their freedom and establish their own nation.

Such dramatic events, it could be argued, impinged primarily on men, not women. After all, men alone fought in the armies, voted in the new republic's elections, drafted state and national constitutions, and served in legislative bodies. Women traditionally did not take part in formal politics; the public world was defined essentially as men's arena. Indeed, most of the earliest historians of women, those who lived and worked in the period between the late nineteenth century and the 1970s, ignored the Revolution because it seemed to have had little effect on America's female inhabitants. To point out the obvious, the postwar period brought no clear advances in women's rights or noticeable changes in women's daily lives. Yet did that mean that the struggle for independence had no impact at all on North American women? And did it have different effects on white, black, and Indian women? Those questions have recently attracted the attention of several historians.

◈ D O C U M E N T S

In March 1776, recognizing that the American colonies, which had already been at war with Britain for nearly a year, would soon declare independence, Abigail Adams wrote to her congressman husband John, in Philadelphia, reminding him to "remember the ladies" in the nation's "new code of laws." She thus initiated the first known exchange in American history on the subject of women's rights. The Adamses' comments on the matter, and her subsequent letter to her close friend Mercy Otis Warren, make up Document 1. Document 2 is a 1778 letter from merchants at Fort Niagara to Daniel Claus, a British officer, which describes the opinions and actions of the influential Iroquois matron

Molly Brant. The following year, in Document 3, Claus informs his superior, General Frederick Haldimand, of Molly Brant's importance. Document 4 dates from 1780: after the Americans had suffered one of their worst defeats of the war at Charleston, South Carolina, a Pennsylvanian named Esther DeBerdt Reed published a broadside, "The Sentiments of an American Woman," proposing a nationwide ladies association to contribute to the welfare of the troops. A laconic description of what happened to the slaves from Thomas Jefferson's plantations who ran off to join the invading British forces in 1781 constitutes Document 5. In Document 6, dated many years after the Revolution, Sarah Osborn, who had traveled with her husband and the American army, recalls those experiences as she applies for a government pension in 1837.

1. Abigail Adams, John Adams, and Mercy Otis Warren Discuss "Remembering the Ladies," 1776

Abigail Adams to John Adams

Braintree March 31 1776

I long to hear that you have declared an independancy—and by the way in the new Code of Laws which I suppose it will be necessary for you to make I desire you would Remember the Ladies, and be more generous and favourable to them than your ancestors. Do not put such unlimited power in the hands of the Husbands. Remember all Men would be tyrants if they could. If perticuliar care and attention is not paid to the Laidies we are determined to foment a Rebellion, and will not hold ourselves bound by any Laws in which we have no voice, or Representation.

That your Sex are Naturally Tyrannical is a Truth so thoroughly established as to admit of no dispute, but such of you as wish to be happy willingly give up the harsh title of Master for the more tender and endearing one of Friend. Why then, not put it out of the power of the vicious and the Lawless to use us with cruelty and indignity with impunity. Men of Sense in all Ages abhor those customs which treat us only as the vassals of your Sex. Regard us then as Beings placed by providence under your protection and in immitation of the Supreem Being make use of that power only for our happiness.

John Adams to Abigail Adams

Ap. 14. 1776

As to Declarations of Independency, be patient. Read our Privateering Laws, and our Commercial Laws. What signifies a Word.

As to your extraordinary Code of Laws, I cannot but laugh. We have been told that our Struggle has loosened the bands of Government every where. That Children and Apprentices were disobedient—that schools and Colledges were grown turbulent—that Indians slighted their Guardians and Negroes grew insolent to their

---

Adams Papers and Warren-Adams Papers, Massachusetts Historical Society, Boston, Mass. This document can also be found in L. H. Butterfield, et al., eds., *Adams Family Correspondence* (Harvard University Press, 1963) vol. 1.

Masters. But your Letter was the first Intimation that another Tribe more numerous and powerful than all the rest were grown discontented.—This is rather too coarse a Compliment but you are so saucy, I wont blot it out.

Depend upon it, We know better than to repeal our Masculine systems. Altho they are in full Force, you know they are little more than Theory. We dare not exert our Power in its full Latitude. We are obliged to go fair, and softly, and in Practice you know We are the subjects. We have only the Name of Masters, and rather than give up this, which would compleatly subject Us to the Despotism of the Peticoat, I hope General Washington, and all our brave Heroes would fight. I am sure every good Politician would plot, as long as he would against Despotism, Empire, Monarchy, Aristocracy, Oligarchy, or Ochlocracy—A fine Story indeed. I begin to think the Ministry as deep as they are wicked. After stirring up Tories, Landjobbers, Trimmers, Bigots, Canadians, Indians, Negroes, Hanoverians, Hessians, Russians, Irish Roman Catholicks, Scotch Renegadoes, at last they have stimulated the   to demand new Priviledges and threaten to rebell.

Abigail Adams to Mercy Otis Warren

Braintree April 27 1776

He is very sausy to me in return for a List of Female Grievances which I transmitted to him. I think I will get you to join me in a petition to Congress. I thought it was very probable our wise Statesmen would erect a New Government and form a new code of Laws. I ventured to speak a word in behalf of our Sex, who are rather hardly dealt with by the Laws of England which gives such unlimitted power to the Husband to use his wife Ill.

I requested that our Legislators would consider our case and as all Men of Delicacy and Sentiment are averse to Excercising the power they possess, yet as there is a natural propensity in Humane Nature to domination, I thought the most generous plan was to put it out of the power of the Arbitary and tyranick to injure us with impunity by Establishing some Laws in our favour upon just and Liberal principals.

I believe I even threatned fomenting a Rebellion in case we were not considered, and assured him we would not hold ourselves bound by any Laws in which we had neither a voice, nor representation.

In return he tells me he cannot but Laugh at My Extrodonary Code of Laws. That he had heard their Struggle had loosned the bands of Goverment, that children and apprentices were dissabedient, that Schools and Colledges were grown turbulant, that Indians slighted their Guardians, and Negroes grew insolent to their Masters. But my Letter was the first intimation that another Tribe more numerous and powerfull than all the rest were grown discontented. This is rather too coarse a complement, he adds, but that I am so sausy he wont blot it out.

So I have help'd the Sex abundantly, but I will tell him I have only been making trial of the Disintresstedness of his Virtue, and when weigh'd in the balance have found it wanting.

It would be bad policy to grant us greater power say they since under all the disadvantages we Labour we have the assendancy over their Hearts

And charm by accepting, by submitting sway.

Abigail Adams to John Adams

B[raintre]e May 7 1776

I can not say that I think you very generous to the Ladies, for whilst you are pro-claiming peace and good will to Men, Emancipating all nations, you insist upon re-taining an absolute power over Wives. But you must remember that Arbitrary power is like most other things which are very hard, very liable to be broken—and notwithstanding all your wise Laws and Maxims we have it in our power not only to free our selves but to subdue our Masters, and without violence throw both your natural and legal authority at our feet—

> "Charm by accepting, by submitting sway
> Yet have our Humour most when we obey."

2. Taylor & Duffin Report Molly Brant's Opinions and Actions, 1778

Niagara, 26 Octobr. 1778

Sir

It is about Sixteen days ago since Mr. Taylor arriv'd here. Miss Molly [Brant] being then in the Indian Towns, we postponed writing to you untill her return, which was daily expected, but it was 10 days after before she arrived. The little Trunk was delivered to her immediately. Her brother Mr. Joseph Brant was about 35 Miles above *Aughquago* when she heard of him last. He has been on the Frontiers since the beginning of May last: trying to make his Way through to the British Army with a pretty Considerable Party of Whites (which joined him there) and Indians, and though he has destroyed a great part of these back Settlements: it is told of him that he & his Party has Shewn dispositions of Humanity to Women & Children & Persons not found in Arms. . . . Miss Molly says he has now thoughts of penetrating through to the Army at New York, with only three or four with him: as he finds it impracti-cable with the whole of his Party, which he does not think Strong enough to force their way, and with three, or four he may March by back Roads, & in the Night. Miss Molly however thinks the risk is too great, so Wishes, & is not without hopes; that he may come in here, & if he does She Imagines he will go down to Canada to see his Excellcy. General Haldimand, & you. . . .

We paid Miss Molly £25 Halifax Currcy. agreable to his Excellcy. General Haldimands desire to Mr. Taylor, when in Montreal this fall. She desires you will thank his Excellency for her, and if the Season was not so far spent She wou'd have gone down to Canada to thank him herself. She is mightily pleased with his Exellcy's notice of her. . . .

Miss Molly told Mr. Taylor that the Indians often ask her what is the reason that Colo. Claus did not come to Niagara. If it were not for the Service She thinks She

---

Taylor & Duffin to Daniel Claus, 26 October 1778, British Library, Add. MSS. 21774, ff. 9–10. This document can also be found in Maryly B. Penrose, comp. *Indian Affairs Papers: American Revolution* (Franklin Park, N.J.: Liberty Bell Associates, 1981), 167–168.

can be of here: in advising & conversing with the Indians: She wou'd go down to Canada with her Family. She desires Mr. Taylor to inform you the Manner She lives here is pretty expensive to her: being obliged to keep, in a manner, open house for all those Indians that have any weight in the 6 Nations confederacy. We have told her we will not see her in want. We conclude in Haste

Sir

Your Most Obd. Hble. Servts.

Taylor & Duffin

[To] Daniel Claus Esqr.

3. Daniel Claus Assesses Molly Brant's Influence, 1779

Montreal 30th. Aug. 1779

Sir . . .

As soon as Molly heard of my arrival she paid me a Visit and gave me a full Detail of her Adventures & Misfortunes since the Rebellion but in particular in fall 1777 after our Retreat from Fort Stanwix when she was robbed of every thing by the Rebels & their Indns. for giving Intelligence of their Motions by wch they were surprised & defeated when She was obliged to leave her home & flee for her & childrens safety to the 5 Nats. wherein she was assisted by her Brother Joseph and proceeded to take Assylum among the five Nations every one of which pressed her stay among them but she fixed upon Cayouga as the Center & having distant Relations there by whom she was kindly recevd. After Genl. Burgoynes Affair she found them in general very fickle & wavering in particular the head Man of the Senecas called *Cayengwaraghton* with whom she had a long Conversation in Council reminding him of the great friendship wch. subsisted between him & the late Sr. William whose Memory she never mentions without Tears, wch strikes Indns. greatly and to whom she often heard him declare & engage to live & die a firm Friend to the King of Engld. And his Friends with other striking Arguements wch. had such an Effect upon that Chief & the rest of the 5 Nations Sachems present that they promised her faithfully to keep up to the Engagements to her late friend for she is in reality considered & deemed by them as his Relict & one word from her goes farther with them than a thousd. from any White Man with out Exception who in general must purchase their Interest & Influence at a high rate. After Majr. Butlers Return from Montreal in fall 1777 hearing she was at Cayouga he sent her repeated and very pressing encouraging Messages to reside at Niagara wch. she at first did not know how to comply wth. being so well taken care of by her friends till at last she brought it abt. so as they could her leaving them not take amiss & parted in friendship. Her departure from Niagara now was greatly regreted by all the Indns. that heard of it and would be more so when the Campaign was over & they all be acquainted wth it as she is their only confident to whom they communicating every thing of Importance & desiring her

Daniel Claus to Frederick Haldimand, 30 August 1779, Public Archives of Canada, MG 19, Fl, vol 2: 131–133. This document can also be found in Maryly B. Penrose, comp. *Indian Affairs Papers: American Revolution* (Franklin Park, N.J.: Liberty Bell Associates, 1981), 232–234.

Advice & she prevented many at mischief & much more so than in her Brother Joseph whose present Zeal & Activity occasioned rather Envy & Jealousy with for his last Excursion was greatly damped on that Accot. having had near 300 Indns. ready to join him wch. on his setting off was brot. abt. to be stopped & counter-manded, and he obligded to set out but with a small number. Molly seems to me not to be well contented with her present Situation having left her old Mother brother Relations & Acquaintances among the five Nation who she regrets & they will miss her on Accot. of her friendly conversation & Advice.

[Daniel Claus]

4. The Patriot Esther DeBerdt Reed Describes the "Sentiments of an American Woman," 1780

On the commencement of actual war, the Women of America manifested a firm reso-lution to contribute as much as could depend on them, to the deliverance of their country. Animated by the purest patriotism, they are sensible of sorrow at this day, in not offering more than barren wishes for the success of so glorious a Revolution. They aspire to render themselves more really useful; and this sentiment is universal from the north to the south of the Thirteen United States. Our ambition is kindled by the fame of those heroines of antiquity, who have rendered their sex illustrious, and have proved to the universe, that, if the weakness of our Constitution, if opin-ion and manners did not forbid us to march to glory by the same paths as the Men, we should at least equal, and sometimes surpass them in our love for the public good. I glory in all that which my sex has done great and commendable. I call to mind with enthusiasm and with admiration, all those acts of courage, of constancy and patriotism, which history has transmitted to us: The people favoured by Heaven, preserved from destruction by the virtues, the zeal and the revolution of Deborah, of Judith, of Esther! The fortitude of the mother of the Macchabees, in giving up her sons to die before her eyes: Rome saved from the fury of a victorious enemy by the efforts of Volumnia, and other Roman Ladies: So many famous sieges where the Women have been seen forgetting the weakness of their sex, building new walls, dig-ging trenches with their feeble hands, furnishing arms to their defenders, they them-selves darting the missile weapons on the enemy, resigning the ornaments of their apparel, and their fortune, to fill the public treasury, and to hasten the deliverance of their country; burying themselves under its ruins; throwing themselves into the flames rather than submit to the disgrace of humiliation before a proud enemy.

   Born for liberty, disdaining to bear the irons of a tyrannic Government, we as-sociate ourselves to the grandeur of those Sovereigns, cherished and revered, who have held with so much splendour the scepter of the greatest States, The Batildas, the Elizabeths, the Maries, the Catharines, who have extended the empire of liberty, and contented to reign by sweetness and justice, have broken the chains of slavery, forged by tyrants in the times of ignorance and barbarity. The Spanish Women, do they not make, at this moment, the most patriotic sacrifices, to encrease the means

A broadside. Historical Society of Pennsylvania, Philadelphia.

of victory in the hands of their Sovereign. He is a friend to the French Nation. They are our allies. We call to mind, doubly interested, that it was a French Maid who kindled up amongst her fellow-citizens, the flame of patriotism buried under long misfortunes: It was the Maid of Orleans who drove from the kingdom of France the ancestors of those same British, whose odious yoke we have just shaken off; and whom it is necessary that we drive from this Continent.

But I must limit myself to the recollection of this small number of atchievements. Who knows if persons disposed to censure, and sometimes too severely with regard to us, may not disapprove our appearing acquainted even with the actions of which our sex boasts? We are at least certain, that he cannot be a good citizen who will not applaud our efforts for the relief of the armies which defend our lives, our possessions, our liberty? The situation of our soldiery has been represented to me; the evils inseparable from war, and the firm and generous spirit which has enabled them to support these. But it has been said, that they may apprehend, that, in the course of a long war, the view of their distresses may be lost, and their services be forgotten. Forgotten! never; I can answer in the name of all my sex. Brave Americans, your disinterestedness, your courage, and your constancy will always be dear to America, as long as she shall preserve her virtue.

We know that at a distance from the theatre of war, if we enjoy any tranquility, it is the fruit of your watchings, your labours, your dangers. If I live happy in the midst of my family; if my husband cultivates his field, and reaps his harvest in peace; if, surrounded with my children, I myself nourish the youngest, and press it to my bosom, without being affraid of seeing myself separated from it, by a ferocious enemy; if the house in which we dwell; if our barns, our orchards are safe at the present time from the hands of those incendiaries, it is to you that we owe it. And shall we hesitate to evidence to you our gratitude? Shall we hesitate to wear a cloathing more simple; hair dressed less elegant, while at the price of this small privation, we shall deserve your benedictions, Who, amongst us, will not renounce with the highest pleasure, those vain ornaments, when she shall consider that the valiant defenders of America will be able to draw some advantage from the money which she may have laid out in these, that they will be better defended from the rigours of the seasons, that after their painful toils, they will receive some extraordinary and unexpected relief; that these presents will perhaps be valued by them at a greater price, when they will have it in their power to say: *This is the offering of the Ladies.* The time is arrived to display the same sentiments which animated us at the beginning of the Revolution, when we renounced the use of teas, however agreeable to our taste, rather than receive them from our persecutors; when we made it appear to them that we placed former necessaries in the rank of superfluities, when our liberty was interested; when our republican and laborious hands spun the flax, prepared the linen intended for the use of our soldiers; when exiles and fugitives we supported with courage all the evils which are the concomitants of war. Let us not lose a moment; let us be engaged to offer the homage of our gratitude at the altar of military valour, and you, our brave deliverers, while mercenary slaves combat to cause you to share with them, the irons with which they are loaded, receive with a free hand our offering, the purest which can be presented to your virtue,

BY AN AMERICAN WOMAN
[Esther DeBerdt Reed]

5. Thomas Jefferson's Slaves Join the British, 1781

DEATHS ETC.

1781.	Hannibal. Patty Sam. Sally. Nanny Fanny Prince Nancy	} fled to the enemy & died.

Elkhill

Flora. (Black Sall's) Quomina (Black Sall's) }	joined enemy & died.
Black Sall Jame. (Bl. Sall's Joe. (Sue's.) }	joined enemy, returned & died

Cumbl^d.	Lucy [erasure] [erasure] Sam.	} joined enemy.
Elk-hill Shadwell.	Jenny [erasure] Harry	

Monticello.   Barnaby. run away.
            returned & died.

Elkhill.	York. Isabel. Jack Hanah's child. Phoebe's child	} caught small pox from enemy & died.

[note Judy & Nat of Elkhill, Will & Robin of Shadwell joined the enemy, but came back again & lived. so did Isabel, Hannibal's daughter. aftwds given to A.S. Jefferson.]

Elk-hill	Branford sue. Sue's daur.	} caught the camp fever from the negroes who returned: & died
Monticello Elk-hill	Old Jenny Phoebe (Sue's) Nanny (Tom's) } 1782	

6. Sarah Osborn, a Camp Follower, Recalls the Revolution, 1837

That she was married to Aaron Osborn, who was a soldier during the Revolutionary War. That her first aquaintance with said Osborn commenced in Albany, in the state of New York, during the hard winter of 1780. That deponent then resided at the house of one John Willis, a blacksmith in said city. That said Osborn came

Edwin M. Betts, ed., *Thomas Jefferson's Farm Book* (Princeton, N.J.: Princeton University Press, 1953), 29.

Revolutionary War Pension Files, National Archives. This document can also be found in John Dann, ed., *The Revolution Remembered* (Chicago: University of Chicago Press, 1980), 241–246.

down there from Fort Stanwix and went to work at the business of blacksmithing for said Willis and continued working at intervals for a period of perhaps two months. Said Osborn then informed deponent that he had first enlisted at Goshen in Orange County, New York. That he had been in the service for three years, deponent thinks, about one year of that time at Fort Stanwix, and that his time was out. And, under an assurance that he would go to Goshen with her, she married him at the house of said Willis during the time he was there as above mentioned, to wit, in January 1780. . . .

That after deponent had married said Osborn, he informed her that he was returned during the war, and that he desired deponent to go with him. Deponent declined until she was informed by Captain Gregg that her husband should be put on the commissary guard, and that she should have the means of conveyance either in a wagon or on horseback. That deponent then in the same winter season in sleighs accompanied her husband and the forces under command of Captain Gregg on the east side of the Hudson river to Fishkill, then crossed the river and went down to West Point. . . .

Deponent further says that she and her husband remained at West Point till the departure of the army for the South, a term of perhaps one year and a half, but she cannot be positive as to the length of time. While at West Point, deponent lived at Lieutenant Foot's, who kept a boardinghouse. Deponent was employed in washing and sewing for the soldiers. Her said husband was employed about the camp. . . .

When the army were about to leave West Point and go south, they crossed over the river to Robinson's Farms and remained there for a length of time to induce the belief, as deponent understood, that they were going to take up quarters there, whereas they recrossed the river in the nighttime into the Jerseys and traveled all night in a direct course for Philadelphia. Deponent was part of the time on horseback and part of the time in a wagon. Deponent's said husband was still serving as one of the commissary's guard. . . .

They continued their march to Philadelphia, deponent on horseback through the streets, and arrived at a place towards the Schuylkill where the British had burnt some houses, where they encamped for the afternoon and night. Being out of bread, deponent was employed in baking the afternoon and evening. Deponent recollects no females but Sergeant Lamberson's and Lieutenant Forman's wives and a colored woman by the name of Letta. The Quaker ladies who came round urged deponent to stay, but her husband said, "No, he could not leave her behind." Accordingly, next day they continued their march from day to day till they arrived at Baltimore, where deponent and her said husband and the forces under command of General Clinton. Captain Gregg, and several other officers, all of whom she does not recollect, embarked on board a vessel and sailed down the Chesapeake. There were several vessels along, and deponent was in the foremost. . . . They continued sail until they had got up the St. James River as far as the tide would carry them, about twelve miles from the mouth, and then landed, and the tide being spent, they had a fine time catching sea lobsters, which they ate.

They, however, marched immediately for a place called Williamsburg, as she thinks, deponent alternately on horseback and on foot. There arrived, they remained two days till the army all came in by land and then marched for Yorktown, or Little York as it was then called. The York troops were posted at the right, the Connecticut troops next, and the French to the left. In about one day or less than a day, they reached the place of encampment about one mile from Yorktown. Deponent was on foot and the other females above named and her said husband still on the commissary's guard. Deponent's attention was arrested by the appearance of a large plain between them and Yorktown and an entrenchment thrown up. She also saw a number of dead Negroes lying round their encampment, whom she understood the British had driven out of the town and left to starve, or were first starved and then thrown out. Deponent took her stand just back of the American tents, say about a mile from the town, and busied herself washing, mending, and cooking for the soldiers, in which she was assisted by the other females; some men washed their own clothing. She heard the roar of the artillery for a number of days, and the last night the Americans threw up entrenchments, it was a misty, foggy night, rather wet but not rainy. Every soldier threw up for himself, as she understood, and she afterwards saw and went into the entrenchments. Deponent's said husband was there throwing up entrenchments, and deponent cooked and carried in beef, and bread, and coffee (in a gallon pot) to the soldiers in the entrenchment.

On one occasion when deponent was thus employed carrying in provisions, she met General Washington, who asked her if she "was not afraid of the cannonballs?"

She replied, "No, the bullets would not cheat the gallows," that "It would not do for the men to fight and starve too."

They dug entrenchments nearer and nearer to Yorktown every night or two till the last. While digging that, the enemy fired very heavy till about nine o'clock next morning, then stopped, and the drums from the enemy beat excessively. . . .

All at once the officers hurrahed and swung their hats, and deponent asked them, "What is the matter now?"

One of them replied, "Are not you soldier enough to know what it means?"

Deponent replied, "No."

They then replied, "The British have surrendered."

Deponent, having provisions ready, carried the same down to the entrenchments that morning, and four of the soldiers whom she was in the habit of cooking for ate their breakfasts.

Deponent stood on one side of the road and the American officers upon the other side when the British officers came out of the town and rode up to the American officers and delivered up [their swords, which the deponent] thinks were returned again, and the British officers rode right on before the army, who marched out beating and playing a melancholy tune, their drums covered with black handkerchiefs and their fifes with black ribbands tied around them, into an old field and there grounded their arms and then returned into town again to await their destiny. . . .

On going into town, she noticed two dead Negroes lying by the market house. She had the curiosity to go into a large building that stood nearby, and there she noticed the cupboards smashed to pieces and china dishes and other ware strewed around upon the floor, and among the rest a pewter cover to a hot basin that had a handle on it. She picked it up, supposing it to belong to the British, but the governor came in and claimed it as his, but said he would have the name of giving it away as it was the last one of twelve that he could see, and accordingly presented it to deponent, and she afterwards brought it home with her to Orange County and sold it for old pewter, which she has a hundred times regretted.

In the 1970s, wondering if the Revolution had changed the lives of American women in any way, Mary Beth Norton of Cornell University read hundreds of women's and men's letters and diaries from the period of the war. In her 1980 book, *Liberty's Daughters,* from which the first essay is excerpted, she contends that the Revolution was, to a limited extent, "liberating" for white women and for some black men and women as well. Jacqueline Jones, who teaches history at Brandeis University, focuses her attention exclusively on enslaved women, concluding to the contrary that for them the revolution had decidedly mixed results. James Taylor Carson, of Queen's University in Ontario, examines the role of one prominent Iroquois woman, Molly Brant, demonstrating that the Revolutionary War gave her new opportunities to exercise her considerable talents for diplomacy and what would today be termed "networking."

The Positive Impact of the American Revolution on White Women

MARY BETH NORTON

Women could hardly have remained aloof from the events of the 1760s and early 1770s even had they so desired, for, like male Americans, they witnessed the escalating violence of the prerevolutionary decade. Into their letters and diary entries—which had previously been devoted exclusively to private affairs—crept descriptions of Stamp Act riots and "Rejoicings" at the law's repeal, accounts of solemn fast-day observances, and reports of crowd actions aimed at silencing dissidents. The young Boston shopkeeper Betsy Cuming, for instance, was visiting a sick friend one day in 1769 when she heard "a voilint Skreeming Kill him Kill him" and looked out the window to see John Mein, a printer whose publications had enraged the radicals, being chased by a large crowd armed with sticks and guns. Later that evening Betsy watched "ful a thousand Man & boys" dragging around the city "a Kart [on which] a Man was Exibited as . . . in a Gore of Blod." At first Betsy believed Mein had been caught, but she then learned that the victim was an unfortunate customs informer who had fallen into the crowd's hands after Mein made a successful escape.

Betsy herself confronted an angry group of Bostonians only a few weeks later. She and her sister Anne had just unpacked a new shipment of English goods when "the Comitey wated" on them, accusing them of violating the nonimportation agreement. "I told them we have never antred into eney agreement not to import for it was verry trifling owr Business," Betsy explained to her friend and financial backer Elizabeth Murray Smith. She charged the committeemen with trying "to inger two industrious Girls who ware Striving in an honest way to Git there Bread," resolutely ignoring their threat to publish her name in the newspaper as an enemy to America. In the end, Betsy and Anne discovered, the publicity "Spirits up our Friends to Purchess from us," and they informed Mrs. Smith that they ended the year with "mor custom then before."

Mary Beth Norton, excerpts from Chapters 6 and 7 of *Liberty's Daughters: The Revolutionary Experience of American Women,* (HarperCollins, 1980), pp. 156–169 and 212–227. Reprinted by permission of the author.

Despite their bravado the Cuming sisters had learned an important political lesson: persons with their conservative beliefs were no longer welcome in Massachusetts. As a result, they emigrated to Nova Scotia when the British army evacuated Boston in 1776. Patriot women, too, learned lessons of partisanship. Instead of being the targets of crowds, they actively participated in them. They marched in ritual processions, harassed female loyalists, and, during the war, seized essential supplies from merchants whom they believed to be monopolistic hoarders. In addition, when they prepared food for militia musters and, in the early days of September 1774—when the New England militia gathered in Cambridge in response to a false rumor that British troops were mounting an attack on the populace—they were reported by one observer to have "surpassed the Men for Eagerness & Spirit in the Defense of Liberty by Arms." As he rode along the road to Boston, he recounted later, he saw "at every house Women & Children making Cartridges, running Bullets, making Wallets, baking Biscuit, crying & bemoaning & at the same time animating their Husbands & Sons to fight for their Liberties, tho' not knowing whether they should ever see them again."

The activism of female patriots found particular expression in their support of the colonial boycott of tea and other items taxed by the Townshend Act of 1767. Male leaders recognized that they needed women's cooperation to ensure that Americans would comply with the request to forgo the use of tea and luxury goods until the act was repealed. Accordingly, newspaper essays urged women to participate in the boycott, and American editors frequently praised those females who refused to drink foreign Bohea tea, substituting instead coffee or local herbal teas. . . .

In a marked departure from the tradition of feminine noninvolvement in public affairs, women occasionally formalized their agreements not to purchase or consume imported tea. Most notably, the *Boston Evening Post* reported in February 1770 that more than three hundred "Mistresses of Families" had promised to "totally abstain" from the use of tea, "Sickness excepted." Their statement showed that they understood the meaning of their acts: the women spoke of their desire to "save this abused Country from Ruin and Slavery" at a time when their "invaluable Rights and Privileges are attacked in an unconstitutional and most alarming Manner." In the South, groups of women went even further by associating themselves generally with non-importation policies, not confining their attention to the tea issue alone. The meeting satirized in the famous British cartoon of the so-called Edenton Ladies' Tea Party fell into this category. The agreement signed in October 1774 by fifty-one female North Carolinians—among them two sisters and a cousin of Hannah Johnston Iredell—did not mention tea. Instead, the women declared their "sincere adherence" to the resolves of the provincial congress and proclaimed it their "duty" to do "every thing as far as lies in our power" to support the "publick good."

This apparently simple statement had unprecedented implications. The Edenton women were not only asserting their right to acquiesce in political measures, but they were also taking upon themselves a "duty" to work for the common good. Never before had female Americans formally shouldered the responsibility of a public role, never before had they claimed a voice—even a compliant one—in public policy. Accordingly, the Edenton statement marked an important turning point in American women's political perceptions, signaling the start of a process through which they would eventually come to regard themselves as participants in the polity rather than as females with purely private concerns.

Yet the North Carolina meeting and the change it embodied aroused amusement among men. The same tongue-in-cheek attitude evident in the satirical drawing of the grotesque "Ladies" was voiced by the Englishman Arthur Iredell in a letter to his emigrant brother James. He had read about the Edenton agreement in the newspapers, Arthur wrote, inquiring whether his sister-in-law Hannah's relatives were involved in the protest. "Is there a Female Congress at Edenton too?" he continued. "I hope not," for "Ladies . . . have ever, since the Amazonian Era, been esteemed the most formidable Enemies." If they choose to attack men, "each wound They give is Mortal. . . . The more we strive to conquer them, the more are Conquerd!"

Iredell thus transformed a serious political gesture that must have been full of meaning for the participants into an occasion for a traditional reference to women's covert power over men. Like many of his male contemporaries, he dismissed the first stirrings of political awareness among American women as a joke, refusing to recognize the ways in which their concept of their role was changing. In an Englishman, such blindness was understandable, but the similar failure of perception among American men must be attributed to a resolute insistence that females remain in their proper place. The male leaders of the boycott movement needed feminine cooperation, but they wanted to set the limits of women's activism. They did not expect, or approve, signs of feminine autonomy.

Nowhere was this made clearer than in a well-known exchange between Abigail and John Adams. . . . Abigail asked her husband in March 1776 to ensure that the new nation's legal code included protection for wives against the "Naturally Tyrannical" tendencies of their spouses. In reply John declared, "I cannot but laugh" at "your extraordinary Code of Laws." Falling back upon the same cliché employed by Arthur Iredell, he commented, "[O]ur Masculine systems . . . are little more than Theory. . . . In Practice you know We are the subjects. We have only the Name of Masters." Adams, like Iredell, failed to come to terms with the implications of the issues raised by the growing interests in politics among colonial women. He could deal with his wife's display of independent thought only by refusing to take it seriously.

American men's inability to perceive the alterations that were occurring in their womenfolk's self-conceptions was undoubtedly heightened by the superficially conventional character of feminine contributions to the protest movement. Women participating in the boycott simply made different decisions about what items to purchase and consume; they did not move beyond the boundaries of the feminine sphere. Likewise, when colonial leaders began to emphasize the importance of producing homespun as a substitute for English cloth, they did not ask women to take on an "unfeminine" task: quite the contrary, for spinning was the very role symbolic of femininity itself. But once the context had changed, so too did women's understanding of the meaning of their traditional tasks. . . .

The first months of 1769 brought an explosion in the newspaper coverage of women's activities, especially in New England. Stories about spinning bees, which had been both rare and relegated to back pages, suddenly became numerous and prominently featured. The *Boston Evening Post,* which carried only one previous account of female domestic industry, printed twenty-eight articles on the subject between May and December 1769, and devoted most of its front page on May 29 to an enumeration of these examples of female patriotism. The editor prefaced his extensive treatment of women's endeavors with an enthusiastic assessment of their significance: "[T]he industry and frugality of American ladies must exalt their character in the Eyes of the World and serve to show how greatly they are contributing to bring about the political salvation of a whole Continent."

It is impossible to know whether the increased coverage of spinning bees in 1769 indicated that women's activities expanded at precisely that time, or whether the more lengthy, detailed, and numerous stories merely represented the printers' new interest in such efforts. But one fact is unquestionable: the ritualized gatherings attended by women often termed Daughters of Liberty carried vital symbolic meaning both to the participants and to the editors who reported their accomplishments.

The meetings, or at least the descriptions of them, fell into a uniform pattern. Early in the morning, a group of eminently respectable young ladies (sometimes as many as one hundred, but normally twenty to forty), all of them dressed in homespun, would meet at the home of the local minister. There they would spend the day at their wheels, all the while engaging in enlightening conversation. When they stopped to eat, they had "American produce prepared which was more agreeable to them than any foreign Dainties and Delicacies," and, of course, they drank local herbal tea. At nightfall, they would present their output to the clergyman, who might then deliver a sermon on an appropriate theme. For example, the Reverend Jedidiah Jewell, of Rowley, Massachusetts, preached from Romans 12:2, "Not slothful in business, fervent in spirit, serving the Lord," and the Reverend John Cleaveland of Ipswich told the seventy-seven spinners gathered at his house, "[T]he women might recover to this country the full and free enjoyment of all our rights, properties and privileges (which is more than the men have been able to do)" by consuming only American produce and manufacturing their own clothes.

The entire community became involved in the women's activities. Large numbers of spectators—Ezra Stiles estimated that six hundred persons watched the bee held at his house in 1769—encouraged the spinners in their work, supplied them with appropriate American foodstuffs, and sometimes provided entertainment. The occasional adoption of a match format, in which the women competed against each other in quality and quantity, must have further spurred their industry. And they must have glorified in being the center of attention, if only for the day. In reporting a Long Island spinning bee, the *Boston Evening Post* captured the spirit of the occasion with an expression of hope that "the ladies, while they vie with each other in skill and industry in their profitable employment, may vie with the men in contributing to the preservation and prosperity of their country and equally share in the honor of it."

"Equally share in the honor of it": the idea must have been exceedingly attractive to any eighteenth-century American woman raised in an environment that had previously devalued both her and her domestic sphere. Those involved in the home manufacture movement therefore took great pride in their newfound status, demonstrating that fact unequivocally when satirical essayists cast aspersions on their character.

Late in 1767, "Mr. Squibo" of Boston joked that the spinners were so patriotic they consumed only "New-England Rum . . . the principal and almost only manufacture of this country." Shortly thereafter, "A Young American" hinted that women discussed only "such triffling subjects as Dress, Scandal and Detraction" during their spinning bees. Three female Bostonians responded angrily to both letters, which they declared had "scandalously insulted" American women. Denying that gossip engrossed their thoughts or that rum filled their glasses, they pronounced themselves so committed to the patriot cause that they would even endure the unmerited ridicule of "the little wits and foplings of the present day" in order to continue their efforts. "Inferior in abusive sarcasm, in personal invective, in low wit, we glory to be," they concluded; "but inferior in veracity, honesty, sincerity, love of virtue, of liberty and of our country, we would not willingly be to any." Significantly, the Bostonians made a special point of noting that women had been "addressed as persons of consequence, in the present economical regulations." They thereby revealed the novelty and importance of that designation in their own minds. Having become established as "persons of consequence" in American society, women would not relinquish that position without a fight.

The formal spinning groups had a value more symbolic than real. They do not seem to have met regularly, and in most cases their output appears to have been donated to the clergyman for his personal use. The women might not even have consistently called themselves Daughters of Liberty, for many newspaper accounts did not employ that phrase at all. But if the actual production of homespun did not motivate the meetings, they were nonetheless purposeful. The public attention focused on organized spinning bees helped to dramatize the pleas for industry and frugality in colonial households, making a political statement comparable to men's ostentatious wearing of homespun on public occasions during the same years. The spinning bees were ideological showcases: they were intended to convince American women that they could render essential contributions to the struggle against Britain, and to encourage them to engage in increased cloth production in the privacy of their own homes. Sometimes the newspaper accounts made this instructional function quite explicit. The fact that many of the participants came from "as *good families* as any in town," one editor remarked, showed that "it was no longer a disgrace for one of our fair sex to be catched at a spinning wheel." . . .

Wives of ardent patriots and loyalists alike were left alone for varying lengths of time while their spouses served in the army or, in the case of loyalists, took refuge behind the British lines. Although women could stay with their soldier husbands and earn their own keep by serving as army cooks, nurses, or laundresses, most did not find this an attractive alternative. Life in the military camps was hard, and army commanders, while recognizing that female laborers did essential work, tended to regard them as a hindrance rather than as asset. Only in rare cases—such as the time when the laundresses attached to General Anthony Wayne's regiment staged a strike in order to ensure that they would be adequately paid—were camp followers able to ameliorate their living and working conditions. Consequently, most women who joined the army probably did so from necessity, lacking any other means of support during their husbands' absence.

At least, though, patriot women had a choice. For the most part, loyalists were not so fortunate. From the day they and their spouses revealed their loyalty to the Crown, their fate was sealed. Like other eighteenth-century women, their lives had focused on their homes, but because of their political beliefs they lost not only those homes but also most of their possessions, and they had to flee to alien lands as well. Understandably, they often had difficulty coping with their problems. Only those women who had had some experience beyond the household prior to the war were able to manage their affairs in exile in England, Canada, or the West Indies with more than a modicum of success.

Female loyalists' claims petitions are particularly notable because the women frequently commented on their lack of a network of friends and relatives. The laments convey a sense of an entire familiar world that had been irretrievably lost. Many women submitted claims after the deadline, each giving a similar reason in her request for special consideration: there had been "no person to advise her how to proceed," she "was destitute of advice and Assistance," or "she had nobody to advise with & that she did not know how to do it." Even when some of a woman loyalist's friends were also exiles her situation was little better; as one southerner pointed out to the claims commission, "[T]hose Friends and Acquaintances to whom under other circumstances she could look up to for comfort and Assistance are equally involved in the Calamities which overwhelm" her. . . .

The importance of friendship networks and a familiar environment for women left alone is further confirmed when the focus shifts from widowed loyalists to the patriots who called themselves temporary widows—those women whose husbands had joined the American army. In contrast to the distressed, disconsolate refugee loyalists, who often complained of their inability to deal effectively with their difficulties, patriot women who managed the family property in the absence of their menfolk tended to find the experience a positive one. Although they had to shoulder a myriad of new responsibilities, they did so within a well-known and fully understood context: that of their own households. Accordingly, aided by friends and relatives, they gained a new sense of confidence in themselves and their abilities as they learned to handle aspects of the family affairs that had previously fallen solely within their husbands' purview. And the men, in turn, developed a new appreciation of their wives' contributions to the family's welfare. . . .

Patriot men found it difficult to avoid service in the militia or the Continental Army. They accordingly had to leave their wives behind to take charge of their affairs for months or years at a time. Most sets of wartime correspondence that survive today come from the families of officers or congressmen—in other words, from those patriots of some wealth or prominence who also tended to experience the longest separations—but the scattered evidence available for couples of lesser standing suggests that the same process was at work in poor, middling, and well-to-do households alike. As the months and years passed, women became more expert in their handling of business matters and their husbands simultaneously more accustomed to relying on their judgment.

A standard pattern emerges from the sequences of letters, some of which will shortly be examined in greater detail. Initially, the absent husband instructed his wife to depend upon male friends and relatives for advice and assistance. In 1776, for example, Edward Hand, a Pennsylvania officer, told his wife, Kitty, to have one neighbor invest money for her and to ask another to estimate the value of two horses he had sent home for sale. Women, for their part, hesitated to venture into new areas. "In some particulars I have been really puzzled how to act," a South Carolinian informed her spouse, a private soldier; and in 1777 Esther Reed, asking Joseph whether she should plant some flax, explained, "[A]s I am not famous for making good Bargains in things out of my Sphere I shall put it off as long as possible, in hopes you may be at home before it is too late."

But as time went on, women learned more about the family's finances while at the same time their husbands' knowledge became increasingly outdated and remote. Accordingly, whereas men's letters early in the war were filled with specific orders, later correspondence typically contained statements like these: "I Can't give any Other Directions About Home more than what I have Done but must Leave all to your good Management" (1779); "Apply [the money] to such as you think proper" (1780); draw on a neighbor for "any Sums you may choose, for providing things necessary & comfortable for yourself & the little Folks & Family for the approaching Season, in doing which I am sure you will use the greatest discretion" (1779). By the same token, women's letters showed their increasing familiarity with business and their willingness to act independently of their husbands' directions. . . .

The diary of the Philadelphian Sally Logan Fisher provides an especially illuminating example of this process. Thomas Fisher was among the Quakers arrested and sent into exile in Virginia by the patriots just prior to the British conquest of Philadelphia in September 1777. Then nearly eight months pregnant with her daughter Hannah, Sally at first found "this fiery triall" almost more than she could bear. Nine days after the men had been forcibly carried off, she commented, "I feel forlorn & desolate, & the World appears like a dreary Desart, almost without any visible protecting Hand to gaurd us from the ravenous Wolves & Lions that prowl about for prey." Sally became so depressed that she failed to write in her diary for several weeks, and when she resumed her daily entries in mid-October she observed, "[N]o future Days however calm & tranquil they may prove, can ever make me forget my misery at this time."

Soon thereafter, though, Mrs. Fisher became too busy to be able to allow herself the luxury of debilitating depression. A long entry on November 1 reflected her changed role in its detailed attention to household financial affairs and at the same time signaled the end of her period of incapacitating despair. "I have to think & provide every thing for my Family, at a time when it is so difficult to provide anything, at almost any price, & cares of many kinds to engage my attention," she wrote revealingly. After Hannah's birth six days later Sally remarked, "[I have] been enabled to bear up thro' every triall & difficulty far beyond what I could have expected." Although in succeeding months she continued to lament Tommy's absence, her later reflections differed significantly from her first reaction to her situation. Instead of dwelling upon her despondency, Sally wrote of "the fond, the delightfull Hope" that her husband would return to love her as before. "Oh my beloved, how Ardently, how tenderly how Affectionately, I feel myself thine," she effused in February 1778, describing "the anxiety I feel for thee, the longing desire to be with thee, & the impatience I feel to tell thee I am all thy own"—but not indicating any sense of an inability to cope with problems in his absence. When Tommy returned in late April 1778, she welcomed him gladly, but she did not revert completely to her former role of ignorance about monetary matters. Her diary subsequently noted several consultations with him about household finances, a subject they had not discussed before his exile.

Although Mary Bartlett, the wife of a New Hampshire congressman, left no similar record of her feelings about her husband's extended stays in Philadelphia during the war, she nevertheless subtly disclosed the fact that her role had undergone a comparable change. When Josiah Bartlett first went to Congress in the fall of 1775, he told Mary he hoped she would have "no Great trouble about my out Door affairs," and he continued to write to her about "my farming Business." In 1776 she accepted his terminology, reporting on "Your farming business," but during Josiah's second stint in Congress in 1778 that phrase became "our farming business" in her letters. No longer was the farm simply "his": she had now invested too much effort in it for that. The distinction between male and female spheres she had once accepted without question had been blurred by her own experience.

Although Josiah Bartlett's persistent use of "my farm" implies that he did not recognize the way in which his wife's role had altered, other patriot men separated from their spouses for long periods revealed changing attitudes toward their womenfolk in their correspondence. The differences are especially apparent in the case of a New Englander, Timothy Pickering, because he began with a severely limited conception of his wife's capability. . . .

Pickering adopted a patronizing tone in his early letters to his wife, Rebecca White. In November 1775, before their marriage, he told her he wanted to "instruct" her and went on to quote the same poem other Americans cited in discussions of children's education: "'Tis a 'Delightful task to rear the tender thought, / To teach the fair idea how to shoot.'" Like a father teaching a daughter, he encouraged her to write to him, saying, "[F]requent writing will improve your hand." Unremarkably, Pickering's condescension continued during the early years of their marriage, after he had joined the Continental Army's quartermaster corps. When he sent home a lame horse in June 1777, he told her to consult male friends "for advice and direction" in caring for it, then apologized for asking her to undertake a task that was "entirely out of [her] sphere." Even his praise contained an evident patronizing note. "Your conduct in domestic affairs gives me the highest satisfaction," he told her in July 1778, spoiling it by adding, "even if you had done wrong I could not find fault; because I know in every action you aim at the best good of our little family: and knowing this: it would be cruel and unreasonable to blame you." In other words, he was telling her she would be judged on the basis of her intentions, not her actual performance, because he feared she could not meet the higher standard.

For the Pickerings matters changed in October 1780 after Rebecca acted as Timothy's agent in a complex arrangement for the repayment of a debt. "I am very glad you made me fully acquainted with it," she told him. "It is a satisfaction to me to pa[r]take of any thing that gives you Concern. I know my Dear you would make me happy in telling me any thing that had a tendency to make you so." After the successful resolution of the debt problem and her verbalization of her desire to assist him with their financial affairs, Timothy began to rely more heavily upon her. When the family rented a farm in 1782, she ably shouldered the responsibility for managing it despite her fears of "not being acquainted with farming business." Five years later, after they had moved to the frontier community of Wilkes-Barre, Pennsylvania, and Timothy's post required him to be in Philadelphia, she not only supervised the building of their new house but also oversaw the harvest, all the while nursing their newest baby. Timothy continued to apologize for the burdens he was placing on her (as well he should have), but he no longer mentioned her "sphere." Rebecca Pickering, like Mary Bartlett before her, began to speak in her letters of "our business" and "our crops." Timothy had already revealed his new attitude as early as August 1783: "This war which has so often & long separated us, has taught me how to value you," he told her then. . . .

The war dissolved some of the distinctions between masculine and feminine traits. Women who would previously have risked criticism if they abandoned their "natural" feminine timidity now found themselves praised for doing just that. The line between male and female behavior, once apparently so impenetrable, became less well defined. It by no means disappeared, but requisite adjustments to wartime conditions brought a new recognition of the fact that traditional sex roles did not provide adequate guidelines for conduct under all circumstances. When Betsy Ambler Brent looked back on her youth from the perspective of 1810, she observed, "[N]ecessity taught us to use exertions which our girls of the present day know nothing of. We Were forced to industry to appear genteely, to study Manners to supply the place of Education, and to endeavor by amiable and agreeable conduct to make amends for the loss of fortune."

The realization that they had been equally affected by the war led some women to expect equal treatment thereafter and, on occasion, to apply to their own circumstances the general principles promulgated by the revolutionaries. "I have Don as much to Carrey on the warr as meney that Sett Now at ye healm of government & No Notice taken of me," complained the New Jersey widow Rachel Wells as she protested to the Continental Congress in 1786 about a technicality that deprived her of interest payments on the money she had invested in state bonds during the war. "If she did not fight She throw in all her mite which brought ye Sogers food & Clothing & Let them have Blankets," she explained, asking only for the "justice" due her. "Others gits their Intrust & why then a poor old widow be put of[f]?" Mrs. Wells asked. "Now gentelmen is this Liberty?"

Mary Willing Byrd's social standing was much higher than that of Rachel Wells, but she advanced a similar argument when she contended in 1781 that Virginia had treated her unfairly. She claimed the right to redress of grievances "as a female, as the parent of eight children, as a virtuous citizen, as a friend to my Country, and as a person, who never violated the laws of her Country." Byrd's recital of her qualifications was peculiarly feminine in its attention to her sex and her role as a parent (no man would have included such items on a list describing himself), but it was also sexless in its references to her patriotism and her character as a "virtuous citizen." In developing the implications of the latter term, Byrd arrived at her most important point. "I have paid my taxes and have not been Personally, or Virtually represented," she observed. "My property is taken from me and I have no redress."

The echoes of revolutionary ideology were deliberate. Mary Byrd wanted the men she addressed to think about the issue of her status as a woman, and she adopted the revolutionaries' own language in order to make her point. The same tactic was employed by Abigail Adams in her most famous exchange with her husband.

In March 1776, after admonishing John to "Remember the Ladies" and to offer them legal protection from "the unlimited power" of their husbands, Abigail issued a warning in terms that John must have found exceedingly familiar. "If perticular care and attention is not paid to the Laidies," Abigail declared, "we are determined to foment a Rebelion, and will not hold ourselves bound by any Laws in which we have no voice, or Representation." On one level, she was speaking tongue-in-cheek; she did not mean her husband to take the threat seriously. Yet she chose to make a significant observation about women's inferior legal status by putting a standard argument to new use and by applying to the position of women striking phraseology previously employed only in the male world of politics. Like Mary Willing Byrd, Abigail Adams thus demonstrated an unusual sensitivity to the possible egalitarian resonances of revolutionary ideology and showed an awareness of implications that seem to have escaped the notice of American men.

The Mixed Legacy of the American Revolution for Black Women

JACQUELINE JONES

For the historian, race, as a socially defined category of human relationships, should constitute a central consideration in exploring the self-evident truths of this country's past. More specifically, during the era of the American Revolution, the status of all black women differed in fundamental ways from the status of all white women. Together, slave women and men endured the agony of bondage, and together blacks, both enslaved and free, struggled to form families that eventually served as the foundation of a distinctive Afro-American culture. The military conflict between loyalists and rebels intensified physical hardship among blacks, while the ensuing social and economic turmoil afforded some of their race the opportunities for a basic kind of freedom that white women and men—for all their rhetoric about the evils of tyranny—already enjoyed. Therefore, any discussion of the war's impact on American women must first highlight racial factors before dealing with issues related to class, regional, ethnic, and religious diversity in the late eighteenth-century population.

Yet within the confines of the slave system, and within the boundaries of their own households and communities, black women shouldered burdens that set them apart from their menfolk. In the period from 1750 to 1800, the nature and extent of these burdens varied according to whether a woman was African- or American-born; whether she lived in the North or South, in a town or rural area; whether she toiled in the swampy South Carolina lowcountry or on a Virginia wheat farm. This is not to suggest that black women suffered more than black men under the oppressive weight of the racial caste system, only that gender considerations played a significant role in shaping the task assignments parceled out to blacks by slaveholders, and in shaping the way blacks structured relationships among themselves. . . .

The ordeal of black women as wives, mothers, and workers encapsulates all the ironies and tensions that marked the history of slavery during the era of the American Revolution. In their efforts to create and preserve a viable family life, these women sought to balance caution and daring, fear and hope, as they reacted to the peculiar matrix of individual circumstances. Regardless of their work and family status in Boston, on a small farm in Pennsylvania, on George Washington's plantation, or in the South Carolina lowcountry, they saw freedom through the prism of family life. Consequently they perceived this revolutionary idea in ways fundamentally different

---

Jacqueline Jones, "Race, Sex, and Self-Evident Truths: The Status of Slave Women During the Era of the American Revolution," in Ira Berlin, et al., eds. *Women in the Age of the American Revolution* (Charlottesville, Va., 1989). Reprinted with permission of the University of Virginia Press.

from the white men who tried to claim the War for Independence as their own, and from the white women who remained so awkwardly suspended between their racial prerogatives on the one hand and gender and class liabilities on the other. Caught in the crossfire of sexual and racial oppression, black women contributed to the definition of liberation in these turbulent times. Indeed, through their modest everyday struggles, these wives and mothers offered a vision of freedom that was, by virtue of its consistency and fairness, more enduring than the one articulated so eloquently by the Founding Fathers. . . .

The political unrest and wartime devastation that marked the Revolutionary era brought into focus all the contradictions implicit in the emerging democratic republic of slaveholders and their allies. Masters found themselves confronted by their own demands for liberty and reacted accordingly, either by manumitting their slaves or by fighting ever more tenaciously to enforce black subordination. These conflicting impulses among the white elite helped to shape the experiences of black women during this period of upheaval, but so too did the economic transformations wrought by armed conflict and incipient nation-building. For their part, slaves seized the initiative whenever an opportune moment presented itself and fought their own battles for self-determination as field hands, refugees, and liberators of their own kin. Finally, black women's family responsibilities as wives and mothers remained constant even as the Revolution gave their productive abilities a new political significance. . . .

For the bulk of slave women located on southern plantations, the war entailed both physical suffering and great latitude for personal action. Forced to make do with less in the way of food, clothing, and other basic supplies, white southerners considered the daily needs of their slaves to be a low priority (especially after 1778, when fighting engulfed the region). At least some whites fulfilled the prediction of the patriot who railed against runaway slave men seeking protection from the British: "The aged, the infirm, the women and children, are still to remain the property of the masters, masters who will be provoked to severity, should part of their slaves desert them." Untold numbers of slave women felt the wrath of "an enraged and injured people" desperate to keep the upper hand at home as well as on the battlefield.

The women who remained with their masters gave whites cause enough for alarm. Thomas Pinckney's depleted South Carolina plantation consisted primarily of mothers and children in 1779, but they proved no more tractable than the male slaves who had already deserted; according to the white man, the slave women "pay no attention" to the overseer. Residing on another estate, Pinckney's mother commiserated with him, noting that she had lost control over her servants, "for they all do now as they please everywhere." As the war raged near her North Carolina estate in 1781, another mistress complained bitterly about the insolent Sarah: "She never came near me till after repeated messages yesterday to come and Iron a few clothes. . . . She made shift to creep here and then was very impudent." Such recalcitrance could provoke some whites to violence, others to reluctant indulgence. A Baltimore slaveholder urged his overseer not to upset the slave Ruth, or "she will run off, for she is an arch bitch."

Slaveholders might try to brutalize, cajole, or bribe black women into submission, but they could not escape the fact that they needed every available worker. The estimated 55,000 slaves who absconded, and many others pressed into service by the colonists and British alike, left some areas of the South bereft of field hands and thus devastated by food shortages. Planters who sought to institute a system of household cloth production reserved the positions of spinners and weavers for black women and girls, a sexual division of labor shaped in part by the now critical lack of male laborers. The rebels were not about to let gender considerations interfere with their exploitation of black labor in this time of crisis, and southern states often sought to buy, hire, or impress slaves of both sexes for use on public works projects. For example, in 1780 the Board of Trade of Virginia purchased twenty-six blacks (among them three women) to work in its tanneries, ironworks, boatyards, and army hospitals. The intense demand for unskilled labor during the war, exacerbated by a temporary halt in the foreign slave trade, endangered the well-being of free blacks, as well as slave women. In 1778 Ann Driggus of North Carolina suffered a beating at the hands of two men who then kidnapped four of her children in order to sell them.

Increased demands on their productive energies, combined with the confusion produced by wartime, prompted slave women to seek safety with the enemies of their master, whether rebel or loyalist. According to Gerald W. Mullin and other historians, family ties assumed even greater significance as a source of motivation among runaways, compared to the colonial period, perhaps reflecting more favorable conditions for flight and for beginning a new life elsewhere with kinfolk. Moreover, Mary Beth Norton has suggested that "although a majority of runaways were male, women apparently sought freedom in greater numbers [that is, proportion] during the war than in peacetime." Evidence from scattered sources reveals that up to a third of all wartime refugees were female, compared to the 10 percent or so of runaways listed in colonial newspapers who were female. Panic-stricken, patriot law-enforcement officials condemned to hard labor, executed, or sold to the West Indies those women and men who failed in their bid for freedom.

Benjamin Quarles has estimated that 5,000 black men served in the patriot armed forces, including the Continental army and navy, and state militias. This figure includes slaves who deserted their loyalist owners to fight with the rebels, and free blacks (almost all in the North) who volunteered for duty. But a far larger number of blacks perceived their best interests to lie with the British, a conviction no doubt encouraged early on by Virginia's royal governor Lord Dunmore, who in 1775 promised to liberate all the slaves of patriots who joined his army. As a slaveholder, Dunmore promoted policies that reflected the opportunistic attitude of the British toward blacks in general; they were considered worthy of decent treatment only insofar as they furthered the king's cause as soldiers, manual laborers, or insurgents who deprived the colonists of much needed labor. According to Sylvia Frey, British authorities showed little inclination to offer refuge to the slaves of loyalists. Dunmore himself refused sanctuary to runaways whom he could not readily use in his current military campaigns.

As might be expected, few slave women found a haven behind British lines. Army camps along the coast of Virginia were crowded and disease-ridden, with black people of both sexes and all ages suffering from exposure, hunger, and smallpox. The grisly image of a child seeking nourishment from the breast of its dead mother on Gwynne Island in 1776 conveys the bitter reality of black life—and death—in refugee camps. The image itself is also a reminder of the unique forms of oppression that impelled slave women to flee their owners' plantations and the lack of concern for their plight among officials on either side of the conflict. Few white women had cause to risk so much during the war. . . .

The black people evacuated with British troops after the war faced an uncertain future indeed. At least 15,000 black women and men left the country aboard British ships that sailed from Savannah, Charleston, and New York; some were self-defined loyalists, others served loyalist masters, and still others hoped to benefit from British efforts to deprive their conquerors of personal property. The wide range of experiences that awaited individual women—a lifetime of slavery in the West Indies; a struggle to survive in the fledgling British colony of Sierra Leone; or a new beginning of health, safety, and freedom in Nova Scotia—mirrored the crosscurrents of hardship and liberation that characterized the status of slave women during the Revolutionary War.

Thus the black fight for independence proceeded apace, whenever formerly compliant slave women suddenly turned "sassy" and defiant or abandoned their master's household, either to cast their lot with the British or slip as self-freed persons into the anonymity of urban life. A more formal (though no less difficult) route to freedom lay through the state courts and legislatures and through the efforts of free blacks to buy and then emancipate their own kin. . . .

Within three decades of the war's end, all of the northern states had provided for emancipation, although some enacted gradual provisions that left thousands of blacks in slavery for years to come. For example, according to New York's law of 1799, the daughters born to slave women after that date were to be bound (like indentured servants or apprentices) to the mother's master for twenty-five years, sons for twenty-eight years. . . . Two points are relevant to this issue: first, the most far-reaching antislavery legislation was enacted by northerners, who had the least to lose financially from their altruism; and second, the burden of transition from a slave to free black population fell most heavily on mothers whose offspring perpetuated the system of bondage. . . .

Regardless of how they obtained their freedom, black women shared common goals: to consolidate family members, keep their households intact, and provide for the material welfare of dependents. . . . Many newly freed blacks (and runaways) from the upper South and rural areas migrated to northern towns. This movement gradually produced an unbalanced urban sex ratio in favor of women (the reverse of the colonial pattern), probably because single women found it easier to support a family in the city than on the countryside. . . . Although they might now labor for wages, the vast majority continued to perform the same services they had for whites under slavery—cooking, washing clothes, cleaning, serving, and tending white children. The fact of freedom did not affect the racial caste system as it related to the social division of labor.

In the 1780s and 1790s, free and slave women together actively participated in the creation of an "institutional core" for Afro-American life—the formation of churches, schools, and benevolent societies separate and distinct from those of whites, blending an African heritage with American political realities. Although several historians have described in detail the emergence of black organized religion after the war, the role of women in that story remains untold. . . .

During these years the exhilaration of freedom experienced by some black women contrasted mightily with the plight of many more who remained condemned to slavery. . . . Masters fully appreciated a self-replenishing labor force, but their efforts each year to grow as much cotton as humanly possible worked to the detriment of childbearing females. Most white men did not fully comprehend the connection between overwork and high miscarriage and infant mortality rates; the result was untold pain and grief for slave mothers. As the institution of bondage renewed itself, so too did the drive for hegemony among ambitious men on the make as well as among the sons of Revolutionary-era slaveholders—a drive that held sacred the tenet of private property(no matter what its form) and eventually provoked a war far bloodier than the rebellion of 1776. While their free sisters kept alive the spirit of Afro-American community autonomy, black mothers and wives in the Cotton South would continue to eat the bitter fruit borne of a white man's political and economic revolution.

Molly Brant's War

JAMES TAYLOR CARSON

In the fall of 1777, on the heels of English General John Burgoyne's disastrous defeat at Saratoga, the pro-English chiefs of the Iroquois confederacy began to question their alliance with the Crown. The Mohawk, Oneida, Onondaga, Cayuga, Seneca, and Tuscarora nations of the New York and southern Canada made up the Iroquois confederacy, and several of their leaders met to consider the situation. A Cayuga chief, Cayengwaraghton, denounced the English and urged the others to reconsider their loyalty as well. Molly Brant, a Mohawk woman, spoke and reminded the chief of his long-standing ties to the English. Tears rolled from her eyes as she recounted the close friendship between the Iroquois and King George, and she urged the assembled men to fulfill their obligations to the Crown as military allies. In the end the council affirmed its support for the English war effort, but the outcome of the meeting meant more than the reaffirmation of a long-standing alliance. When Molly Brant challenged the Cayuga leader, she moved beyond the traditional rights and privileges the Iroquois associated with women and claimed for herself powers traditionally exercised by male chiefs.

Both men and women had power in Iroquois society, but they derived their powers from different sources and displayed them in different arenas. Women's power rested on their importance as farmers and as mothers. Mothers and daughters had custody of the land, and they contributed the corn, beans, and squash that they grew to the subsistence of their households and villages. Men moved in the forests that lay beyond the fields and villages, and they supplemented the bounty of the women's gardens with meat procured by the hunt. The complementary economic relationships between women and men, however, extended far beyond their different contributions to their people's diet. Male chiefs governed the villages and the larger confederacy, but in order to build a powerful consensus behind their leadership, they redistributed foodstuffs and trade goods. Such a system made the men beholden to the women for one of the most important currencies of chiefly

leadership—food—which enabled them to hold feasts, help those in need, and promote community spirit. Once chiefs established broad networks of support through
distribution and other evidence of leadership, they were free to negotiate matters
of diplomacy and to convene the preside over council talks. Even at these levels of
government, however, female councillors held a powerful voice that the men could
not discount. In politics as in economics, Iroquois men and women enjoyed particular rights and prerogatives, but for the whole to function, the two halves had to
be in agreement.

Beyond the community granary and the council house, women like Molly Brant
controlled other expressions of power and authority. In kinship, for example, the
Iroquois traced descent exclusively through the female line, so children belonged
to their mother's clan and had no blood relationship to their father's clan. Clans
formed the basis of Iroquois society. Clans bound children to many people, rather
than merely their birth parents and siblings. Iroquois women, for example, did not
distinguish between their own sons and daughters and those of their sisters. Children
of the same clan and generation regarded their biological mother, her sisters, and
all clan women of their mother's generation to be their mothers. Extended families
connected by women lived together in longhouses where they shared communal
living spaces. The heads of these households were the clan mothers, usually older
women so honored for their wisdom and industry, who sought to foster the family's
influence and power. These matrilineal clans performed many of the functions Europeans associated with government. When an individual was killed, for example, the
clan exacted revenge in order to redress the imbalance created by the death. If a clan
member perished in war, clan mothers harangued male warriors to avenge the loss.
By the same token, women might block a declaration of war for fear of the danger
war posed for their kinfolk. Mothers also increased their clan's influence and prestige by arranging marriages for their children with desirable partners and by using
their political clout to invest relatives with political and ceremonial titles that were
inherited through the clan line. Clan mothers chose chiefs, and, if those chiefs failed
to meet expectations, these same powerful women deposed them. Only men, however, actually served as chiefs. Men controlled redistribution, went to war, and negotiated with foreigners. They could do none of these things, however, without women
and the essential kin ties women provided.

Few European officials understood the dynamics of Iroquois society like Molly
Brant's future husband, William Johnson, an expatriate Irishman who served the
Crown as superintendent of northern Indian affairs. He cultivated his closest ties with
Canajoharie, the most important Mohawk town located in what is today upstate New
York, and its most powerful chiefs, the brothers Abraham and Hendrick. An astute
student of Native politics, Johnson realized that the Mohawks associated status and
legitimacy with kinship. In 1752, after his first wife, Catherine Weissenberg, died,
Johnson engaged Caroline Hendrick, Abraham's daughter and Molly Brant's aunt, as
his "housekeeper," a relationship that the Iroquois considered marriage. The kin relationship that bound Abraham and Hendrick to Johnson after the marriage symboli-
cally brought the English nation under the roof of the longhouse since men lived with
their wives. . . .

The bonds that linked Johnson to the Mohawks took on added significance when
in 1756 the Seven Years' War, a conflict known in United States history as the French

and Indian War, erupted between England and France across the globe. Johnson entreated the Mohawks to enter the war on the side of the English. . . . The Mohawk alliance worked well for the English, but the deaths of Hendrick in 1755 and Caroline in 1759 imperiled the superintendent's diplomatic efforts. . . .

The Brants were not only a prominent Mohawk family but they also had begun adopting some European practices. Molly's parents, Peter and Margaret, practiced Iroquois Christianity, a Catholicism that retained many vestiges of Iroquois practices and beliefs. Several years after Molly's birth in Canajoharie in 1736, they moved to the Ohio River Valley, where their son Joseph was born. Peter died, and when the family returned to Canajoharie, Margaret married Brant Canagaraduncka. Molly and Joseph, who had no surname at this point, took their new stepfather's first name as their family name. The Brants were a prominent and prosperous family. A traveler who visited their homestead in 1750 remarked that they inhabited a two-story, European-style house filled with "middle class" furnishings. . . .

Only through another marriage could Johnson hope to achieve some sort of reciprocal partnership with the Brants. During his stay with the family in April 1759 Johnson probably caught his first glimpse of Molly. That same year she took up residence in his home. While vicious rumors about Johnson and his propensity for Mohawk wives circulated in London, the marriage pleased the Brants and Johnson. The couple ultimately had nine children, an unusually large number of children for an Iroquois woman. These children made Molly the head of her own substantial Mohawk lineage as well as consort to the most powerful representative of the Crown in Iroquois country.

The new relationship between the Brants and Johnson benefited both parties. The Crown won invaluable military and political support in its struggles with France and other Indian nations while the Brants received access to goods and favors that augmented their status accordingly. . . . Molly Brant used her position to advance the interests of her family. She was particularly solicitous of her younger brother Joseph. . . .

Although William Johnson recognized the importance of having a Mohawk wife, he refused to countenance women's considerable political influence in councils. . . . During a visit to Canajoharie in 1763, Johnson met with a council of thirty-six men and thirty-three "principal women." The issue at stake was land, and the Mohawks refused to cede any. Johnson tried to limit the talks to the assembled men, but the Mohawk men demurred. One sachem asserted that the women were "the Truest Owners being the persons who labour on the Lands, and therefore are esteemed in that light." Granted the authority to make the final decision on the proposed cession, the women refused to agree to it. Johnson was frustrated, and he attempted to have them excluded form further council discussions. . . . Molly Brant's role in her husband's diplomatic efforts is unclear. Nowhere does her voice appear in the minutes of the various councils Johnson held, but in a chance encounter with a traveler in the 1780s, she recounted that "she often persuaded the obstinate chiefs into compliance with proposals" during her years with Sir William. There is no evidence, however, that she joined his attempts to subvert the power of women. . . .

In 1774 William Johnson died, and Molly Brant moved back to Canajoharie with their eight surviving children. She used the money her husband left her in his will and perhaps the funds and goods he bequeathed to their children to set up a household from which she distributed trade goods among her people. Extending hospitality was an important custom of Iroquois women, but Molly Brant expanded the practice until it began to resemble redistribution, a prerogative of male chiefs. Opening her home to the Mohawks enabled her to achieve the prestige and influence that came with the control of goods, but she had lost for the time being the potential diplomatic and political power that came from being married to a high-ranking English official.

The Revolutionary War, however, gave Molly Brant the opportunity to exploit her association with William Johnson and, consequently, to increase her family's power and influence among the Iroquois and within the British Empire. At the same time, she enhanced her own power. While her younger brother, Joseph Brant, used his connection to Johnson to win accolades on the battlefield, her diplomatic efforts behind the frontlines made her an even more important asset to England's war effort. At the outbreak of hostilities, she began gathering vital intelligence for the English army from her home in Canajoharie. In one case, she relayed to the high command information that rebel forces were moving on nearby Fort Stanwix. Her warning enabled the English to marshal a small force that ambushed the American column at Oriskany on 6 October 1777. After the victory, Loyalist Indians ransacked the homes of pro-American Oneidas, burning houses, destroying crops, and killing livestock. The Oneidas recognized Brant's role in the attack and singled her out for revenge.

After the Patriot Oneidas looted and burned her house, Molly Brant fled to the Cayugas where her kinfolk gave her shelter. Far from cowed by the destruction of her home, she became an even more outspoken Loyalist. An opportunity to make public her support for the Crown came in 1777 at the meeting where she confronted Cayengwaraghton. She wept before the council at the mention of Johnson's name, and was, one observer wrote, "considered . . . by them as his relict." By casting herself as her husband's "relict," Molly Brant established a claim to political authority that lay outside of the normal sphere of Iroquois women's power. Iroquois women derived status from their own accomplishments and from their clans, not from their husbands, but Molly Brant used the English conception of spousal relationships to assert greater authority among the Iroquois. She was, however, far from a Loyalist pawn. Although she used her status as Johnson's widow to legitimate her own exercise of power, she nevertheless sought to restore Mohawk land and sovereignty. "I hope," she wrote to a friend in 1778, "the time is very near when we shall all return to our habitations on the Mohawk River."

From Cayuga, Molly Brant moved to the English outpost at Niagara where she continued to broker military information. She was most interested in the actions of her brother, who had assumed command of a party of Loyalist Mohawks and colonists. On one occasion, fearful of Joseph's safety, she tried to block his ambitious plan to take his men and link up with the English army of New York. In exchange for monetary payments, Molly Brant also dispatched reports of American troop movements and descriptions of Native attitudes. Because of her close association with the military high command, she had easy access to English money, friendship, and favors. . . .

Molly Brant constantly insisted that the manner in which she needed to live at Niagara was "pretty expensive," which irritated colonial officials who believed their payments to her were more than fair. The cost of her lifestyle, however, did not reflect any extravagance on her part but instead revealed the very real costs of building a network of support based on the redistribution of goods. During her stay at Niagara, she was, one English officer observed, "obliged to keep, in a manner, open house for all those Indians that have any weight in the 6 Nations Confederacy." Perfectly willing to facilitate this redistribution in order to reap political rewards, her imperial benefactors told her that they would "not see her in want," and they supplied her with goods. Such official support enabled Molly Brant to achieve both political and diplomatic authority through redistribution, which enabled her to exercise chiefly power in wartime Iroquoia. Whereas Joseph's battlefield exploits incited "Envy & Jealousy" among the Crown's Native levies and diminished his prestige, military men considered Molly to represent an important pan-Indian consensus that respected her leadership and supported the Crown.

Molly Brant, however, worried that her residence at Niagara was undermining her influence among the Mohawks because it put her out of touch with affairs among her own people. She wanted to return to her homeland where formerly she had sat at the head of a "society of Six Nations matrons," the council of clan mothers. Aware that the Iroquois might attribute her absence from her home to fear, she made preparations to depart for Canajoharie. She had good reason to regret her distance from her homeland since chiefs across the region were again reconsidering their alliance with the Crown. . . .

Unable to patch over differences between the English and the Indians, General Haldimand ordered Molly Brant from Niagara to Carleton Island where he hoped she might impose order and discipline on his disenchanted allies. The new mission precluded her return to Canajoharie, but she looked forward to rendering to the Crown what she considered to be her "little services." The Indian inhabitants of Niagara "greatly regretted" her departure.

Molly Brant identified jealousy between the chiefs and resentment against the English as the most important problems among Carleton Island's Native community. The chiefs who favored a continued alliance with the English felt that the chiefs who threatened to abandon the Crown received more presents for their disloyalty than they did for their constancy. Moreover, under Haldimand's orders the officers refused to permit the Indians to enter either the fort or its harbor facilities for fear of treachery. . . . The task of repairing the damage done by mutual mistrust fell to Molly Brant. After a few months' residence on the island she was able not only to patch up factional divisions among the Indians but also to restore a measure of faith between her community and the garrison. The same officer who deplored the Indians as "worthless" later informed his superior that "the Chiefs were careful to keep their people sober and satisfied, but their uncommon good behavior is in a great Measure to be ascribed to Miss Molly."

Aside from her work in the Native community on Carleton Island, Molly Brant continued to play a significant role in the war as an informant and diplomat. . . . Informed observers told Haldimand that Brant was not overstating her family's importance to the northern war effort. One officer went so far as to say that she had an influence "far superior to that of all their Chiefs put together."

Molly Brant's successful contribution to the English war effort further enhanced her authority among the Carleton Island Native community. Employing the chiefly strategies, particularly the distribution of goods, she first had implemented at Niagara allowed her to unite Loyalist Indians of several nations. From time to time she visited the island's stores and took whatever she wanted. . . . She even began to bring the military and Native communities together under her own roof. During the winter of 1780 Molly Brant held a ball for the soldiers and Indians in her home, which afforded her the opportunity to distribute gifts and supplies to the entire island community. . . .

Molly Brant remained on Carleton Island and passed the last two years of the war uneventfully. Just as the war gave her an opportunity for enhanced status and political power, the peace took it away because the end of the war marked the end of her tenure as a Loyalist chief. General Haldimand acknowledged her contribution to the war effort, and, more importantly, he recognized her efforts as a clan mother. In reward for her and her family's services, the Crown granted Molly Brant a pension of one hundred pounds annually for life. While her brother Joseph led a reconstituted Mohawk Nation on the Grand River reserve in western Upper Canada, Molly retired to a fine home overlooking the Cataraqui River in Kingston and, still mindful of her maternal duties, married five of her daughters to prominent Canadian gentlemen. Her sole surviving son, George, found employment in the British Indian department. Having fulfilled her family obligations, she became involved in the local Anglican church and passed away quietly in 1796.

Molly Brant's life provides an exception to the assumption that Native women's power and authority declined as a consequence of contact with Europeans. As an important daughter, wife, and clan mother she enjoyed the traditional privileges and prerogatives that the Iroquois associated with women. Had she accepted the possibilities and limitations of her gender and of her culture, her life would have differed little from the lives of other prominent Iroquois women of the eighteenth century. But Molly Brant used the traditions of her own culture as a base from which she could expand her power in a time of crisis. She seized opportunities presented by the Revolution to construct a new kind of power, and she transformed herself from Mohawk clan mother to Loyalist chief. Molly Brant appropriated the strategies of male leaders as well as those of clan mothers to build patronage networks that underwrote her political and diplomatic authority. In mastering the intricacies of chiefly leadership and Native factionalism, Brant also earned the grudging respect of the English high command. Finding and holding a middle ground between the two sides was impressive enough; translating it into real authority where none had existed before was nothing short of remarkable.

✦ *F U R T H E R   R E A D I N G*

Berkin, Carol. *Revolutionary Mothers: Women in the Struggle for America's Independence* (2005).

Buel, Richard, and Joy. *The Way of Duty: A Woman and Her Family in Revolutionary America* (1984).

Gelles, Edith. *Portia: The World of Abigail Adams* (1992).

Gundersen, Joan R. "Independence, Citizenship, and the American Revolution," *Signs* 13 (1987–1988): 59–77.

———. *To Be Useful to the World: Women in Eighteenth-Century America* (1996).

Hoffman, Ronald, and Peter Albert, eds. *Women in the Age of the American Revolution* (1989).

Kerber, Linda K. *Women of the Republic: Intellect and Ideology in Revolutionary America* (1980).

Klinghoffer, Judith, and Lois Elkins. " 'The Petticoat Electors': Women's Suffrage in New Jersey, 1776–1807," *Journal of the Early Republic* 12 (1992): 159–193.

Knott, Sarah. "Sensibility and the American War for Independence," *American Historical Review* 109 (2004): 19–40.

Lewis, Jan. "The Republican Wife: Virtue and Seduction in the Early Republic," *William and Mary Quarterly,* 3d ser., 44 (1987): 689–721.

Norton, Mary Beth. "Eighteenth-Century American Women in Peace and War: The Case of the Loyalists," *William and Mary Quarterly,* 3d ser., 33 (1976): 386–409.

Skemp, Sheila. *Judith Sargent Murray: A Brief Biography with Documents* (1998).

Stabile, Susan M. *Memory's Daughters: The Material Culture of Remembrance in Eighteenth-Century America* (2004).

Zagarri, Rosemarie. *A Woman's Dilemma: Mercy Otis Warren and the American Revolution* (1995).

———. "The Rights of Man and Woman in Post-Revolutionary America," *William and Mary Quarterly,* 3d ser., 55 (1998): 203–230.

C H A P T E R
6

Women's Activism in
the Early Republic

Before the modern field of women's history was launched in the late 1960s and early 1970s, one of the few aspects of women's past that attracted much scholarly attention was the study of women's role in politics generally and in the women's rights movement in particular. Early practitioners of the new style of women's history rejected such an emphasis, arguing that it privileged men's priorities over women's. Accordingly, they devoted their primary energies to delineating women's familial and domestic ("private") lives and distinguishing them from men's "public" responsibilities. With respect to the antebellum period, scholars explored and analyzed what has become known as the doctrine of "separate spheres"—the then-prevalent notion that women and men had different, mutually exclusive, but complementary roles in life.

Eventually, historians came to realize that the women who stressed their commitment to "domestic" ideals and "separate spheres" often did not practice what they preached; some of the most popular purveyors of such ideas, for example, were women who supported themselves and their families by writing novels or editing magazines, belying their words by their actions. Other antebellum women used "woman's special role" as an argument for the employment of female teachers or the establishment of reformist benevolent societies, both involving activity outside the household. Such functions, scholars soon recognized, necessarily brought antebellum women into the public realm, even when they denied that they were engaging in political activity.

Now historians are studying women's organizations of all types, examining their aims and actions, their membership, and their impact. The aim is to go beyond the women's rhetoric to reveal the actual nature of their enterprises.

◆ D O C U M E N T S

In the 1790s, women in American cities began to form benevolent associations, primarily to aid other women. The founder of the first such group, Mrs. Isabella Graham of New York, in April 1800 proudly addressed the members of her Society for the Relief of Poor Widows with Small Children; six years later, she addressed their daughters, who had volunteered to teach for the society (Document 1). Minutes of the 1837 meeting of one of the best-known organizations, the Boston Female Anti-Slavery Society, constitute

Document 2. In Document 3, published two years later, the Female Moral Reform Society cautioned mothers against allowing their children to engage in the "solitary vice" (masturbation). At Seneca Falls, New York, in 1848, the women's rights movement was formally launched with the adoption of the Declaration of Sentiments, reprinted as Document 4. When the participants in that convention were publicly criticized, two of its leaders, Elizabeth McClintock and Elizabeth Cady Stanton, vigorously defended their actions (Document 5). Yet their approach did not easily or quickly carry the day. As Document 6 shows, Sarah Josepha Hale, editor of the most important women's magazine, *Godey's Lady's Book,* rejected woman suffrage in 1852.

1. Mrs. Isabella Graham Addresses Members of the Society for the Relief of Poor Widows with Small Children, April 1800, and Their Daughters (Volunteer Teachers), April 1806

To the Society for the relief of poor widows with small children, in April, 1800

LADIES,

It is with pleasure we, your board, again meet this benevolent society. With pleasure we announce the success of the Institution—its funds, its usefulness, and its respectability increase. We have on the books two hundred and seventy-four annual subscribers, thirty-nine more than at last meeting.

The Treasurer has received three hundred and thirty dollars from ladies, in donations; and from gentlemen, six hundred and seventeen dollars, nearly double what they gave us last year. Your managers have expended eight hundred and twenty dollars since last meeting, not quite five months. Perhaps this may surprise you, but there was no avoiding it. Though the winter has been mild, and the price of wood moderate, the wants of the poor have been more pressing than in former years. We have on our books one hundred and forty-two widows, with four hundred and six children below twelve years of age, by far the greater part below six; besides many boys bound apprentices, for whom their mothers must wash, mend, and provide part clothing. Though the sum expended appears great, you will find, on calculation, that it is not quite six dollars to each family. Yet, by prudent management, giving it to them by little and little, and in necessaries, nourishing, yet cheap, it went further than twice the sum given in money, and at once. . . .

Most of our widows have to learn economy from necessity: in the days of their husbands they lived not only plentifully, but luxuriously. Every class of mechanics in New-York could live well and lay up for their families, were they frugal; but the reverse of this is the case—the evil is general, and, I fear, not to be cured. The change to their widows greatly aggravates their misery—well may they read their sin in their punishment, when meagre want overtakes them. But God forgives, and so ought we: *We,* who have so much to be forgiven, yet have our necessaries, our comforts, and even our luxuries spared. To us, our comfortable dwellings, cheerful fires, and

---

The Power of Faith: Exemplified in the Life and Writings of the Late Mrs. Isabella Graham, of New-York (New York: Kirk & Mercein, 1819), 292–295, 299–301.

convivial parties, give to winter its charms. Alas, for her! the new-made widow! to whom all these are lost for ever—to her, the approach of winter is as the approach of death. Accustomed to spread the board by a cheerful fire-side, to welcome the companion of her heart from the labours of the day; to bless and share the social meal, provided by his industry, drest with neatness and ingenuity, rendered savoury by health and appetite, and heightened in its relish by mutual love! . . . Alas! the change!—Husband, father, support, provider, gone for ever! . . .

Many such, dear Ladies, have eaten of your bread, been warmed from your wood-yard, clothed from your web—in sickness revived by your cordials, consoled and soothed by your Managers. Blessed office!—they are your agents, Ladies: they are also the agents of your God, by whose ministration he is the Father of the fatherless, the Husband of the widow, the stranger's shield and orphan's stay. Blessed indeed is he who considereth the poor—the Lord will deliver him in time of trouble—the Lord will preserve and keep him alive; he shall be blessed upon the earth; the Lord will strengthen him in the bed of languishing, and make all his bed in sickness. Yes, blessed they who consider the poor, who devise liberal things! But more blessed still, ye, who, like the good Samaritan, bind up their wounds, pour the oil and wine of consolation into their bursting hearts, bring them to your homes, and share their griefs with them—who are eyes to the blind, feet to the lame, and make the widow's heart to sing for joy! May the blessing of them who are ready to perish come upon you—may your persons be accepted in Christ; then shall a reward of grace accompany, and follow your labours of love. May you be blessed in your basket, and blessed in your store—blessed in your going out and blessed in your coming in—blessed in life—blessed in death; and, through Christ the purchaser, blessed with the inheritance of his Saints, through eternity.

On opening a School for poor children; addressed to the Teachers who volunteered their services.

MY DEAR YOUNG LADIES,

Every thing new becomes matter of speculation, and variety of opinion.

An association of ladies for the relief of destitute widows and orphans, was a new thing in this country. It was feeble in its origin; the jest of most, the ridicule of many, and it met the opposition of not a few. The men could not allow our sex the steadiness and perseverance necessary to establish such an undertaking. But God put *his* seal upon it; and under his fostering care, it has prospered beyond the most sanguine expectations of its propagators. Its fame is spread over the United States, and celebrated in foreign countries. It has been a precedent to many cities, who have followed the laudable example. This fame is not more brilliant than just. The hungry are fed, the naked are clothes, and shelter is provided for the outcasts; medicine and cordials for the sick, and the soothing voice of sympathy cheers the disconsolate. Who are the authors of all these blessings? Your mothers, ladies, the benevolent members of this, so justly famed Society. But, who are these children, that idly ramble through the streets, a prey to growing depravity and vicious example? hark! they *quarrel,* they *swear,* and such, no doubt, will *lie* and *steal.* And that group of dear little creatures, running about in the most imminent danger, apparently without protection: are they under the care of this, so justly famed Society? They are?—They are fed, they are clothes, their mother's fire-side is made warm for them; but no culture is provided for their minds, nor protection from baneful example. These will in time follow that of the older ones, and grow up the slaves of idleness, and vice, the certain road to ruin.

Alas! alas! and is there no help? no preventive? Yes there is! Behold the angelic band! hail, ye virtuous daughters! worthy of your virtuous mothers! come forward and tread in their steps! Snatch these little innocents from the whirling vortex; bring them to a place of safety; teach them to know their Father, God: tell them of their Saviour's love; lead them through the history of his life; mark to them the example he set, the precepts he recorded for their observance, and the promises for their comfort. And by teaching them to read, enable them to retrace all your instructions, when their eyes see you no more.

My dear young ladies, the sacrifice you have made to virtue, shall most assuredly meet its reward: but, like your mothers, you will experience much painful banter, you will be styled school-madams. Let it pass—suffer it quietly; when your scheme begins to ripen, and the fruits appear, who shall be able to withhold their praise? Only be steadfast, draw not back, and justify the prophecies of many.

A great general, in ancient times, in search of glory, landed his troops on the hostile coast, and then burnt all his ships: it behooved them to conquer or die. You have, ladies, already embarked in this design; there is no remaining neuter now; your name and undertaking are in every mouth; you must press forward and justify your cause; and justified it shall be, if you persevere: it cannot be otherwise. The benevolence you contemplate, is as superior to that already in circulation, as the interest of the soul is to that of the body; and it is your own; the very scheme originated in a young mind in this company. The Society were contemplating mercenary agents; schools for pay, and one is already established.

But this labour of love! who could have hoped for it? A Society of *young ladies,* in rank, the first in the city, in the very bloom of life, and full of its prospects, engaged in those pleasures and amusements, which generally engross the mind, and shut out every idea unconnected with self, coming forward and offering—what? not their purses, that were *trash:* but, their own personal services to instruct the ignorant, and become the saviours of many of their sex. It is indeed a new thing, and more strange in this age of dissipation, than that institution from which it sprung. O may this too become the darling of Providence! may God put his seal upon this also! may he bless and prosper you in this undertaking! bless you, and make you a blessing!

2. The Anti-Slavery Convention of American Women Meets in New York City, May 1837

Wednesday, May 10

The Convention was called to order at 3 o'clock, P.M.

A portion of the Scriptures was read, and prayer offered. . . .

Lydia M.Child offered the following resolution:

RESOLVED, That a thorough investigation of the anti-slavery cause, in all its various aspects and tendencies, has confirmed us in the belief that it is the cause of God, who created

---

Dorothy Sterling, ed., *Turning the World Upside Down: The Anti-Slavery Convention of American Women* (Feminist Press, 1987), 10–20.

mankind free, and of Christ, who died to redeem them from every yoke. Consequently it is the duty of every human being to labor to preserve, and to restore to all who are deprived of it, God's gift of freedom; thus showing love and gratitude to the Great Redeemer by treading in his steps.

Mary L. Cox, of Germantown, Pa., spoke in favor of the resolution, and on the necessity of treading in the Redeemer's steps. She expressed her thankfulness that all sectarian feeling had been swept away by the strong current of abolition philanthropy.

The resolution was adopted.

Lydia M. Child offered the following resolution:

RESOLVED, That while we rejoice in any mitigation of cruelty in the treatment of our brethren and sisters held as slaves, we will bear in mind that the great question is not one of treatment, but of *principle;* hence, that no compromise can be made on the score of kind usage, while man is held as the property of man.

S. M. Grimké spoke in favor of the resolution, and remarked that the essential sin of slavery consisted in reducing man to a brute.

The resolution was adopted.

On motion of A. E. Grimké the following resolutions were adopted:

RESOLVED, That we regard the combination of interest which exists between the North and the South, in their political, commercial, and domestic relations, as the true, but hidden cause of the unprincipled and violent efforts which have been made, (at the North, but made in vain,) to smother free discussion, impugn the motives, and traduce the characters of abolitionists.

RESOLVED, That we regard the legalized practice of surrendering fugitive slaves to their southern task-masters, as utterly at variance with the principles of liberty *professed* by us—"the freest nation in the world"—and a daring infringement of the divine commands, "Thou shalt *not* deliver unto his master, the servant that is escaped from his master unto thee."—"Hide the outcast, betray *not* him that wandereth. Let my outcast well with thee, be thou a covert to them from the face of the spoiler."

RESOLVED, That the right of petition is natural and inalienable, derived immediately from God, and guaranteed by the Constitution of the United States, and that we regard every effort in Congress to abridge this sacred right, whether it be exercised by man or woman, the bond or the free, as a high-handed usurpation of power, and an attempt to strike a death-blow at the freedom of the people. And therefore that it is the duty of every woman in the United States, whether northerner or southerner, annually to petition Congress with the faith of an Esther, and the untiring perseverance of the importunate widow, for the immediate abolition of slavery in the District of Columbia and the Territory of Florida, and the extermination of the inter-state slave-trade.

On motion of S. M. Grimké the following resolution was adopted:

RESOLVED, That we regard those northern men and women, who marry southern slave-holders, either at the South or the North, as identifying themselves with a system which desecrates the marriage relation among a large portion of the white inhabitants of the southern states, and utterly destroys it among the victims of their oppression.

The movers of the previous resolutions, sustained them by some remarks. . . .

S. M. Grimké offered the following resolution:

RESOLVED, That whereas God has commanded us to "prove all things and hold fast that which is good,"—therefore, to yield the right, or exercise of free discussion to the demands of avarice, ambition, or worldly policy, would involve us in disobedience to the laws of Jehovah, and that as moral and responsible beings, the women of America are solemnly called upon by the spirit of the age and the signs of the times, fully to discuss the subject of slavery, that they may be prepared to meet the approaching exigency, and be qualified to act as women, and as Christians, on this all-important subject.

The resolution was supported by the mover, A. E. Grimké, and Lucretia Mott. A. E. Grimké offered the following resolution:

RESOLVED, That as certain rights and duties are common to all moral beings, the time has come for woman to move in that sphere which Providence has assigned her, and no longer remain satisfied in the circumscribed limits with which corrupt custom and a perverted application of Scripture have encircled her; therefore that it is the duty of woman, and the province of woman, to plead the cause of the oppressed in our land, and to do all that she can by her voice, and her pen, and her purse, and the influence of her example, to overthrow the horrible system of American slavery.

The resolution was sustained by the mover, and by Lucretia Mott. Amendments were offered by Mary Grew, and Mrs. A. L. Cox, which called forth an animated and interesting debate respecting the rights and duties of women. The resolution was finally adopted, without amendments, though *not unanimously*.

Adjourned to Thursday morning, 10 o'clock.

Thursday Afternoon, May 11

Convention was called to order at 3 o'clock, P. M.

Reading of the Scriptures by the President, and prayer by A. E. Grimké.

The minutes of the last meeting were read and approved. . . .

L. M. Child in consideration of the wishes of some members, who were opposed to the adoption of the resolution on the province of women, moved that the same be reconsidered. The motion was seconded by A. W. Weston, but after discussion was lost.

On motion of Mrs. A. L. Cox, seconded by Rebecca B. Spring,

RESOLVED, that there is no class of women to whom the anti-slavery cause makes so direct and powerful an appeal as to *mothers;* and that they are solemnly urged by all the blessings of their own and their children's freedom, and by all the contrasted bitterness of the slave-mother's condition, to lift up their hearts to God on behalf of the captive, as often as they pour them out over their own children in a joy with which "no stranger may intermeddle"; and that they are equally bound to guard with jealous care the minds of their children from the ruining influences of the spirit of pro-slavery and prejudice, let those influences come in what name, or through what connexions they may. . . .

On motion of A. E. Grimké

RESOLVED, That as most of the merchants and editors of our large cities have done every thing they could to close the door of access at the South against abolition doctrines by vilifying the characters and misrepresenting the motives of abolitionists, who have stood forth as the advocates of the oppressed American, whether bond or free; so we as their wives, mothers, sisters, and daughters, are resolved to do all that we can to open that door, by vindicating their characters from the aspersions which have been cast upon them, and to stand side by side with them in the great struggle between right and wrong, freedom and despotism, justice and oppression, Christian equality and American prejudice.

On motion of Martha Storrs,

RESOLVED, That as the northern churches are united to the sectarian slaveholding churches by the bonds of church government, or Christian fellowship, they are solemnly called upon to rebuke their brethren and not suffer sin upon them: And that it is the duty of women to send up memorials to the different ecclesiastical bodies to which they belong, praying them to declare slavery a sin, which ought to be immediately repented of lest the curse of Almighty God fall upon their churches for refusing, as Meroz did, to come up, "to the help of the Lord against the mighty."

A. W. Weston offered the following resolution, viz.:

RESOLVED, That we feel bound solemnly to protest against the principles of the American Colonization Society, as anti-Republican and anti-Christian, that we believe them to have had a most sorrowful influence in removing the chains of the slave by recognizing him as the property of his master, and in strengthening the unreasonable and unholy prejudice against our oppressed brethren and sisters, by declaring them "almost too debased to be reached by the heavenly light," that to the slave, the Society offers exile or bondage; to the free man, persecution or banishment, and that we view it as an expatriation Society.

This resolution elicited much expression of opinion, and some touching appeals from the colored members of the Convention. The resolution was adopted.
On motion of A. E. Grimké,

RESOLVED, That this Convention do firmly believe that the existence of an unnatural prejudice against our colored population, is one of the chief pillars of American slavery—therefore, that the more we mingle with our oppressed brethren and sisters, the more deeply are we convinced of the sinfulness of that anti-Christian prejudice which is crushing them to the earth in our nominally Free States—sealing up the fountains of knowledge from their panting spirits, and driving them into infidelity, and that we deem it a solemn duty for every woman to pray to be delivered from such an unholy feeling, and to act out the principles of Christian equality by associating with them as though the color of the skin was of no more consequence than that of the hair, or the eyes.

On motion of Lucretia Mott,

RESOLVED, That the support of the iniquitous system of slavery at the South is dependent on the co-operation of the North, by commerce and manufactures, as well as by the consumption of its products—therefore that, despising the gain of oppression we recommend to our friends, by a candid and prayerful examination of the subject, to ascertain if it be not a duty to cleanse our hands from this unrighteous participation, by no longer indulging in the luxuries which come through this polluted channel; and in the supply of the necessary articles of food and clothing, & c., that we "provide things honest in the sight of all men," by giving the preference to goods which come through requited labor.

On motion of A. E. Grimké, . . .

RESOLVED, That it is the duty of abolitionists to do all they can to establish and sustain day, evening, and Sabbath schools irrespective of color; and likewise to visit the schools in which colored pupils are taught, to encourage them in the acquisition of knowledge, and strengthen the teachers in their labor of love.

RESOLVED, That we view with heartfelt commendation the noble stand which Oberlin Collegiate Institute has taken with regard to prejudice; and that it is with peculiar satisfaction we have learned that our oppressed sisters may find at least one seminary in our republican despotism where they may enjoy the benefits of a liberal education. . . .

3. The American Female Moral Reform Society Warns Mothers About the "Solitary Vice," 1839

BELOVED SISTERS,

Will you permit an associated band, most of whom share responsibilities similar to your own, and know with yourselves the deep yearnings of maternal love, to call your attention, for a few moments, to a forbidding, but most important subject. Be assured that nothing but the fixed conviction that it is a subject affecting the temporal and eternal well-being of the young immortals committed to your care, would induce us to commend it to your consideration through the Press. We refer to a species of licentiousness from which neither age nor sex is exempt; a vice that has done its work of ruin, physical, mental, and moral, when no eye but that of Omniscience could behold it, a vice that has been practised in ten thousand instances, without a correct knowledge of its consequences, or its guilt, until it has paved the way for the most revolting excesses in crime. . . .

Recently it has pleased, our Heavenly Father to bring before our minds a flood of light, by which we have been solemnly convinced, that in nine cases out of ten, "solitary vice" [masturbation] is the first cause of social licentiousness, and the foundation and hidden source of the present corrupt state of society. . . .

The dangers to which all classes of the rising generation are exposed, are great beyond expression, they are dangers, too, that may stain the soul with guilt, and yet elude the vigilance of the most watchful parent, unless obviated *from the cradle,* by proper training and correct instruction. . . .

"A pupil in a select school, a child but ten years of age, confessed to her teacher, that she had been guilty of the sin alluded to for years, although she had never been taught it, and knew not that any one living practised it but herself. Her mind was fast sinking, she was wholly unable to reckon even small sums. This child had been religiously educated, but she was reared where the table was made a snare. Rich and high seasoned food, and abundance of dainties were given her, bathing was neglected, and a precocious development of the passions, and their consequent indulgence, was, in this case, the result."

"A child, under 12 years of age, whose morals in every respect had been carefully guarded, and who had never, except in one instance, been exposed, to the influence of an evil associate; on being questioned by her mother, confessed with tears that the sin had been taught her by the suspected individual."

"A son of a highly respectable physician, under three years of age, with no teacher but depraved instinct, had become so addicted to this pernicious habit, that

A Tract to Mothers by the Board of the American Female M.R. Society, New York, 1839.

the mother was obliged to provide a close night dress, and watch his waking hours with unceasing care." . . .

"A theological student, of superior mind and high attainments, deservedly beloved by numerous friends, and eminently fitted to be the centre of attraction in the highest circles of refinement, became a subject of this debasing vice. Presently his health failed, and abused reason deserted his throne. He was carried from the seminary to his friends, a maniac, and after lingering a few days, was ushered into the presence of his Judge."

A physician, who has long had an extensive practice in this city, confidently affirms that most of the young men in feeble health, who go south, to escape or re-cover from consumption, are the victims of this body and soul-destroying sin.

4. The Seneca Falls Convention Issues a "Declaration of Sentiments," 1848

When, in the course of human events, it becomes necessary for one portion of the family of man to assume among the people of the earth a position different from that which they have hitherto occupied, but one to which the laws of nature and of nature's God entitle them, a decent respect to the opinions of mankind requires that they should declare the causes that impel them to such a course.

We hold these truths to be self-evident: that all men and women are created equal; that they are endowed by their Creator with certain inalienable rights; that among these are life, liberty, and the pursuit of happiness; that to secure these rights governments are instituted, deriving their just powers from the consent of the governed. Whenever any form of government becomes destructive of these ends, it is the right of those who suffer from it to refuse allegiance to it, and to insist upon the institution of a new government, laying its foundation on such principles, and organizing its powers in such form, as to them shall seem most likely to effect their safety and happiness. Prudence, indeed, will dictate that governments long established should not be changed for light and transient causes; and accordingly all experience hath shown that mankind are more disposed to suffer, while evils are sufferable, than to right themselves by abolishing the forms to which they were accustomed. But when a long train of abuses and usurpations, pursuing invariably the same object evinces a design to reduce them under absolute despotism, it is their duty to throw off such government, and to provide new guards for their future security. Such has been the patient sufferance of the women under this government, and such is now the necessity which constraints them to demand the equal situation to which they are entitled.

The history of mankind is a history of repeated injuries and usurpations on the part of man toward woman, having in direct object the establishment of an absolute tyranny over her. To prove this, let facts be submitted to a candid world.

He has never permitted her to exercise her inalienable right to the elective franchise.

He has compelled her to submit to laws, in the formation of which she had no voice.

He has withheld from her rights which are given to the most ignorant and degraded men—both natives and foreigners.

Having deprived her of this first right of a citizen, the elective franchise, thereby leaving her without representation in the halls of legislation, he had oppressed her on all sides.

He has made her, if married, in the eye of the law, civilly dead.

He has taken from her all right in property, even to the wages she earns.

He has made her, morally, an irresponsible being, as she can commit many crimes with impunity, provided they be done in the presence of her husband. In the covenant of marriage, she is compelled to promise obedience to her husband, he becoming, to all intents and purposes, her master—the law giving him power to deprive her of her liberty, and to administer chastisement.

He has so framed the laws of divorce, as to what shall be the proper causes, and in case of separation, to whom the guardianship of the children shall be given, as to be wholly regardless of the happiness of women—the law, in all cases, going upon a false supposition of the supremacy of man, and giving all power into his hands.

After depriving her of all rights as a married woman, if single, and the owner of property, he has taxed her to support a government which recognizes her only when her property can be made profitable to it.

He has monopolized nearly all the profitable employments, and from those she is permitted to follow, she received but a scanty remuneration. He closes against her all the avenues to wealth and distinction which he considers most honorable to himself. As a teacher of theology, medicine, or law, she is not known.

He has denied her the facilities for obtaining a thorough eduction, all colleges being closed against her.

He allows her in Church, as well as State, but a subordinate position, claiming Apostolic authority for her exclusion from the ministry, and, with some exceptions, from any public participation in the affairs of the Church.

He has created a false public sentiment by giving to the world a different code of morals for men and women, by which moral delinquencies which exclude women from society, are not only tolerated, but deemed of little account in man.

He has usurped the prerogative of Jehovah himself, claiming it as his right to assign for her a sphere of action, when that belongs to her conscience and to her God.

He has endeavored, in every way that he could, to destroy her confidence in her own powers, to lessen her self-respect, and to make her willing to lead a dependent and abject life.

Now, in view of this entire disfranchisement of one-half the people of this country, their social and religious degradation—in view of the unjust laws above mentioned, and because women do feel themselves aggrieved, oppressed, and fraudulently deprived of their most sacred rights, we insist that they have immediate admission to all the rights and privileges which belong to them as citizens of the United States.

In entering upon the great work before us, we anticipate no small amount of misconception, misrepresentation, and ridicule; but we shall use every instrumentality within our power to effect our object. We shall employ agents, circulate tracts, petition the State and National legislatures, and endeavor to enlist the pulpit and the press in our behalf. We hope this Convention will be followed by a series of Conventions embracing every part of the country.

5. Elizabeth McClintock and Elizabeth Cady Stanton Defend the Seneca Falls Women's Rights Convention, 1848

For the National Reformer.

Woman's Rights.

Messrs. Editors:—As you announce Mr. Sulley, (the author of the article headed "Woman's Rights Convention," published in your paper of last week) as a man who seeks to know the truth, and one who will do justice to any subject he examines, and as he declares himself to be a great lover of his race, and one who has thought deeply on the subject of human improvement, I humbly ask *him* what are these other means to which he refers, by which the present social, civil and religious condition of woman can be improved. It is evident, aside from his own assertion, that Mr. Sulley has thought much on this subject, for he says, "I am not one of those who think that no improvement can be made in the condition of woman, even in this favored land." He is interested, too, in our movement, and has been kind enough to tell us what means will not effect what we desire. He says those recommended and presented by the convention will not do. He thinks legislative action cannot alter the laws of nature. Does Mr. Sulley assume that our present degradation is in accordance with the laws of God? Mr. Sulley having been announced as a lover of truth, we rejoiced in the belief that at length we had found one opponent who would meet us in fair argument, one who though not agreeing with us fully in our measures, was yet sufficiently interested in this subject to give us some plan by which the elevation of woman might be effected. But alas! we have the same old story over again—ridicule, ridicule, ridicule. We have hints of great arguments that could be produced—profound philosophy, fully convincing and satisfactory to all thinking minds, but he gives us nothing tangible, not even the end of the tail of any of these truths, by which could we get a fair hold, we might draw out all the rest. Mr. Sulley thinks our convention was a mere pompous outward show; because, forsooth, we could not give on the spot, a panacea for all the ills of life—because we could not answer Mr. Sulley's silly questions in a manner to satisfy him, though the audience thought him fully answered. We did not assemble to discuss the details of social life—we did not propose to petition the legislature to make our husbands just, generous and courteous; no, we assembled to protest against an unjust form of government, existing without the consent of the governed; to declare our right to be free as man is free: to claim our right to the elective franchise, our right to be

Elizabeth McClintock and Elizabeth Cady Stanton, "Women's Rights," *Rochester National Reformer,* September 21, 1848. This document can also be found in Patricia Holland and Ann D. Gordon, eds., *The Papers of Elizabeth Cady Stanton and Susan B. Anthony* (Wilmington, Del.: Scholarly Resources, 1991).

represented in a government which we are taxed to support; to have such laws as give to man the right to chastise and imprison his wife, to take the wages which she earns—the property which she inherits, and in case of separation the children of her love; laws which make her the more dependant on his bounty: it was to protect against such disgraceful laws, and to have them, if possible, forever erased from our statute books, as a shame and reproach to a republican, christian people in the enlightened nineteenth century. We did not meet to decide home questions—to say who should be the ruling spirit, the presiding genius of every household—who should be the umpire to settle the many differences in domestic life. . . .

Mr. S. expressed a wish to quote the Bible on this subject, but found it would have no authority with us. We affirm that we believe in the Bible. We consider that Book to be the great charter of human rights, and we are willing, yes, desirous to go into the Bible argument on this subject, for its spirit is wholly with the side of Freedom. . . .

E. W. MCCLINTOCK,

E. C. STANTON.

6. Sarah Josepha Hale, Editor of *Godey's Lady's Book,* Praises Women's Indirect Political Influence, 1852

HOW AMERICAN WOMEN SHOULD VOTE.—"I control seven votes; why should I desire to cast one myself?" said a lady who, if women went to the polls, would be acknowledged as a leader. This lady is a devoted, beloved wife, a faithful, tender mother; she has six sons. She *knows* her influence is paramount over the minds she has carefully trained. She *feels* her interests are safe confided to those her affection has made happy. She *trusts* her country will be nobly served by those whom her example has taught to believe in goodness, therefore she is proud to vote by her proxies. This is the way American women should vote, namely, by influencing rightly the votes of men.

E S S A Y S

In 1998, Julie Roy Jeffrey, a professor at Goucher College, examined "ordinary" women who supported abolition. Who were these unknown women who enlisted in such a radical cause? She read the letters and diaries of hundreds of women in her attempt to find out. That same year, Nancy Isenberg (a historian at the University of Northern Iowa) argued that women's rights advocates correctly understood the intertwining of church and state in the antebellum years when they developed simultaneous challenges to the authority of both political institutions and Protestant churches. In 2002, Anne M. Boylan of the University of Delaware published a wide-ranging survey of the development of women's organizations of all sorts before 1840. How do the radical groups chronicled by Jeffrey and Isenberg fit into the patterns she describes?

Godey's Lady's Book 44 (April 1852), 293.

Ordinary Women in the Antislavery Movement

JULIE ROY JEFFREY

In 1847, William Lloyd Garrison's abolitionist newspaper, the *Liberator,* declared that "the Anti-Slavery cause cannot stop to estimate where the greatest indebtedness lies, but whenever the account is made up, there can be no doubt that the efforts and sacrifices of the WOMEN, who helped it, will hold a most honorable and conspicuous position." Garrison's certainty that participants in the great crusade would ultimately recognize the contributions of women to abolitionism was not shared by his son. While acknowledging the importance of women to the movement to free the slave, William Lloyd Garrison Jr. seems to have accepted the fact of abolitionist women's historical invisibility when he referred to that "great army of silent workers, unknown to fame, and yet without whom the generals were powerless."

Scholars studying the most important reform movement before the Civil War have also tended until quite recently to overlook the army of silent workers. Although historians have offered differing interpretations of the significance of abolitionism, the motives and achievements of its leaders, and the relationship of abolitionism to historical processes and events, they have traditionally focused on male leaders and male activities like third-party politics. While the birth of women's history helped to remedy the neglect of abolitionist women, attention tended to center on the small number of radical women who became feminists. The majority of women who shied away from feminism still remained in the shadows. . . .

Frederick Douglass, who had ample reason to acknowledge the important role black and white abolitionist women played in sustaining his own activities, tried to describe why women were important to abolitionism. He pointed to the "skill, industry, patience and perseverance" shown at "every trial hour," the willingness to "do the work which in large degree supplied the sinews of war," and the "deep moral convictions" that helped to give abolitionism its character. As Douglass knew, it was white middle-class and some black women who did much of the day-to-day work of reform. For more than three decades, they raised money, created and distributed propaganda, circulated and signed petitions, and lobbied legislators. During the 1840s and 1850s, they helped to keep the moral content of abolitionism alive when a diluted political form of antislavery emerged.

Women formed the backbone of the movement, and without their involvement, as William Lloyd Garrison Jr. recognized, the leaders would have been powerless. Observers acknowledged at the time that individual women and women's groups often sustained abolitionism when men became dispirited. In 1850, a resident of Portland, Maine, admitted the "mortifying" fact that, in a period of darkness and discouragement, men had allowed the antislavery society to die, while the women of the Portland Anti-Slavery Sewing Society had "kept up their meetings" and work for the cause. The same year, when the English abolitionist lecturer George Thompson visited Salem, Massachusetts, he noted the advances abolitionism had made since his earlier visit in 1835: "A few faithful women," members of the Salem Female Anti-Slavery Society, had been "scattering anti-slavery seed," for fifteen difficult years and had changed "almost the entire sentiment" of the community. Women, Thompson knew, did not play a peripheral role in abolitionism but a central one.

Abolitionism was never a popular cause before the Civil War. Although it is impossible to know how many people either supported or worked for immediate emancipation between 1830 and 1865, one historian has estimated that, out of a population of over 20 million in 1860, only around 20,000, or 1 percent of all American men and women, were abolitionists. Not only was the reform unpopular, but it also generated hostility and even violence, as George Thompson learned when mobs accosted him during his first American tour in the 1830s. Women abolitionists belonged to a minority movement that many Americans distrusted and even despised.

Despite the "social ostracism, persecution, slander, [and] insult" that Rhode Island abolitionist Elizabeth Chace recalled abolitionist women encountering, evidence suggests that some, like Elizabeth herself and those women belonging to the Portland and Salem female societies, maintained their interest over long periods of time. Others, including members of Rochester's Female Anti-Slavery Society, took up and then abandoned abolitionism, and then sometimes became interested again years later. Although public hostility, lack of progress, and dissension among abolitionists caused attrition, more continuous interest in the cause may have existed than it is possible to document. At the end of the 1830s, disagreements within abolitionist ranks over the place of women in antislavery organizations, the relationship of abolitionism to other reforms, and the advisability of pursuing antislavery through politics rather than through moral suasion led to noisy and rancorous divisions that some scholars have suggested reduced women's involvement in antislavery. Most abolitionist women disagreed with Garrisonian radicalism, to be sure, but they did not necessarily reject the necessity of working for immediate emancipation. Dover, New Hampshire, women reorganized their antislavery society as a non-Garrisonian sewing society in 1840 and kept up associational records for decades, but more informal groupings like church sewing circles usually left no written evidence of their involvement at all. Letters written by abolitionist women of one faction often bemoaned the fact that they were almost alone in their support for the cause even as they acknowledged that other women in their communities were pursuing antislavery in secular or church societies. The emphasis on division, then, possibly obscures the extent of female commitment.

The collapse of a unified national antislavery effort in 1840 actually created a variety of individual and collective opportunities to work for the slave and encouraged different styles of activism. As Nancy Hewitt has shown in her study of Rochester, middle-class women from different social, economic, and religious backgrounds did not approach reform in similar ways.

While women differed in their expression of abolitionism over the decades, common convictions undergirded their activities. They agreed that slavery was a sin that, as women, they had a moral and religious duty to eradicate. Despite the scope of the change they were seeking, they were confident that, in the end, their cause would triumph, that moral activism would be efficacious. What might happen to former slaves once slavery had ended was not a question that troubled most of them. Yet they were not indifferent to racism that permeated American life in both the North and South. Although few women were interested in racial equality as understood in the late twentieth century, they did believe that abolitionists should work to improve the situation of free blacks in the North. The 1835 constitution for the first female antislavery organization in Dover, New Hampshire, like those of many other societies, proclaimed the importance of elevating the character and condition of blacks, correcting the "wicked prejudices" of the majority of northern whites, and striving for civil and religious equality.

Some groups and individuals, however, stressed certain of these ideas more than others. Black abolitionists, aware of the serious problems in their communities, became far more interested in improving the status of free blacks than most white abolitionists, and they felt the demands of moral duty far less keenly than the demands of racial responsibility. The egalitarian tradition of the Society of Friends led Quaker women abolitionists to minimize the idea of women's particular responsibility for moral causes that evangelical women stressed so strongly. But substantial ideological agreements undergirded abolitionist women's activism. . . .

[F]emale activism changed over time as abolitionism responded to outside events and internal realities. In the 1830s, for example, most abolitionist women expected that the church would support and further their cause. They joined secular antislavery societies and used them as their base for work like petitioning. When the reluctance of church leaders to take a stand against slavery became clear in the 1840s, however, strategies to expose and pressure Protestant denominations became more central, and the locus for activity often changed. For the abolitionists who established individual abolitionist congregations, the church became the main institutional home for antislavery work. . . .

Despite the changing rhythms of activism as time passed, women from different abolitionist camps relied on similar tactics to pursue their goals. Securing financial support for abolitionist work consumed countless hours and energy. Although women devised numerous ways to collect money, one of their most successful measures was the antislavery fair. When the black women of New York State who determined to raise money for the *Impartial Citizen,* a black Liberty Party newspaper, decided to hold a fair, they were in good company. Women from all camps of abolitionism mounted fairs and bazaars. While a major purpose of the fair was to generate income, fair managers also used the occasion as an opportunity to make powerful symbolic statements about the nature of their cause and to connect abolitionists to one another. They relied upon fairs as a means of energizing and linking local antislavery groups and individuals who produced the goods to be sold at the fair.

Despite disagreements on issues like the relevance of political action to abolitionism, abolitionist women undertook similar projects, ranging from collecting signatures on petitions to sewing. Although the greatest petitioning effort of the antebellum period occurred in the 1830s, women mounted petition drives throughout the 1840s and 1850s, culminating in a spectacular campaign during the Civil War. The work of creating and circulating antislavery propaganda and sponsoring lectures, as the Salem Female Anti-Slavery Society did for so many years, was also ubiquitous.

Sewing for fairs, fugitives, poor northern blacks, or for freedpeople during the war united abolitionist women of all stripes. The modest and tangible character of such work helped keep women involved in abolitionism. One Georgetown, Massachusetts, woman explained that the humble sewing circle had the power to "augment our numbers and cause a more punctual attendance." The exposure that members had to abolitionist conversation and literature during meetings meant that antislavery's "influence may be diffused into all the families where our members reside and thus the whole community be *abolitionised.*" While she may have overestimated the impact of the local sewing circle, the concrete tasks women undertook seem to have kept many of them attached to the cause for long periods of time. That women had something tangible in which to root their loyalty may be one reason that women, not men, constituted the great silent army of abolitionism. Continuing and often humble labors bound women together and provided milestones on the way to a distant goal. . . .

Most of the women who wrote the letters and diaries I read and who left the few surviving organizational records were busy women with substantial family and domestic commitments. Many came from modest backgrounds and did most of their own housework. Unmarried white women and married black women often also worked outside of the home. Written sources reveal some of the difficulties women experienced as they tried to mesh their abolitionist convictions with day-to-day responsibilities and suggest both the emotional costs and rewards involved in supporting the cause. They give brief but revealing glimpses of lives that are otherwise lost to the historical record. . . .

The tendency to classify some women abolitionists as radical and others as conservative, usually based upon their attitude toward feminism, misses an essential truth about abolitionism and the ways in which it led its adherents to transgress ideological norms. No matter what one's attitude might be toward women's rights, to embrace abolitionism was to embrace radicalism. The commitment to immediate emancipation challenged the political, economic, religious, and social status quo. It also became a challenge to gender arrangements. The latter challenge was ironic, for, with the exception of Quaker women, most women who adopted abolitionism did so because they accepted a gendered view of the world and women's unique religious and moral responsibilities. Their positive response to the call of duty, however, led them in unexpected directions. In the early 1830s, when the parameters of women's participation were unclear, the prevailing expectation was that white middle-class women would quietly pursue abolitionism in the privacy of their own homes. But it soon became apparent that the beleaguered movement needed more from women than home life would allow.

Abolitionist women, more directly than other women reformers who enjoyed greater community approval than did antislavery advocates, gradually and often in a piecemeal fashion, contested many of the norms that supposedly governed their behavior and woman's sphere. Moral commitments demanded public expressions. Abolitionists could neither be silent nor inconspicuous. The struggle against slavery led them to speak out in a variety of settings, ranging from their parlors to the public streets and meetinghouses. They confronted authority even when it claimed sacred prerogatives, and they broke the law when it was unjust. Even the women who formed church circles to sew for fugitive slaves and supply their settlements in

Canada were acting out their repudiation of the law of the land. The crisis in gender relations that some scholars have explored in terms of early feminism and the Civil War began as ordinary abolitionist women followed the dictates of duty. It affected not only women's relations with men but also their self-perception and self-image.

For women, whose sphere was supposedly private and domestic, in whom innate qualities of sympathy and intuition sufficed, abolitionism proved a demanding taskmaster. Home life proved to be an inadequate preparation for new responsibilities. To advocate immediate emancipation successfully, women had to learn to reason and to argue, to appeal to the mind as well as to the heart and emotions. Routine projects led them to transgress the usual norms for female behavior in public places and to participate alongside men in political events. While they did not vote, some assumed a more visible and meaningful political presence than the symbolic ceremonial role Mary Ryan describes in *Women in Public*. Indeed, some women went so far as to distribute third-party propaganda to voters. Their activities suggest that they understood that political activities encompassed far more than going to the polls. Far from being shielded from the vagaries of a market economy, their interest in raising money enmeshed them in the marketplace and the consumer economy. They acquired and used an array of managerial and financial skills. As time passed, they more frequently entered the public debate about slavery, and, when a second generation of abolitionists emerged, they felt an ease in their public identity as abolitionists that had been rare in the 1830s. . . .

In the decades during which abolitionists were active, a middle class, different from both the middling sort of the eighteenth century and the new industrial working class, was taking shape. Middle-class American men increasingly held nonmanual, "white collar" jobs that provided their families with the means for a respectable and genteel way of life. Because the process of class formation was incomplete and its membership and identity not yet set, there was room to contest class definitions and boundaries. The activities of abolitionist women defied emerging middle-class norms and helped to broaden the arena of action for white middle-class women, even though it did not lead most of them to feminism. The powerful conviction that women's moral duty demanded an abolitionist commitment limited the challenge to gender arrangements. Only a few women were willing to abandon woman's moral voice for feminist egalitarianism. . . .

Most of the women leaving a record of their involvement in abolitionism were white evangelical Protestant or Quaker women living in rural and small-town communities. . . . Several profiles suggest the nature of these ordinary women's lives and hint at the meaning abolitionism had for them.

Mary White (1778–1860), daughter of a minister, wife of a farmer and shopkeeper, and mother of ten children, lived in an old homestead, a "good specimen of New England domestic comfort," in Boylston, Massachusetts. Like most farm wives, she had varied responsibilities and chores, and her life was a busy one. Despite all her domestic commitments, she became active in antislavery in the mid-1830s. Mary joined a female antislavery society, circulated petitions, attended many antislavery lectures, and sewed for the Boston fair and for fugitives. In addition to her abolitionist activities, she also supported temperance and taught Sunday school. Her diary records the way in which she integrated her reformism into her day-to-day routine and shows the antislavery involvement of other members of her family and her community.

Lucy Colman was perhaps as much as forty years younger than Mary White and never enjoyed the settled life that Mary took for granted. One of her early memories was of her mother singing an antislavery song to her before her early death, when Lucy was only six. Lucy married twice and found herself a widow for the second time when she was not yet forty. Although her determination to work for emancipation predated the accidental death of her second husband, the work took on another meaning with her widowhood. Lucy became an antislavery lecturer during the 1850s, first earning her own expenses and salary as an agent of the Western Anti-Slavery Society of New York and then winning a paid position from the American Anti-Slavery Society. Primitive traveling conditions, frequently unsympathetic audiences, and constant self-denial made her tours through the Midwest taxing. "I never allowed myself the luxury of more than one meal a day, nor a fire in my room," she later recalled. Although eventually a young black woman shared speaking responsibilities, Lucy found life as an agent exhausting. When the war broke out, she left lecturing to become a teacher at a school for black children in Georgetown, New York. There, as she struggled to teach her students middle-class values, she concluded that "generations of the most debasing, abject slavery, is not productive of a high order of morals."

For decades, Frances Drake, probably the wife of Jonathan Drake, was a tireless worker for abolitionism in central Massachusetts. In the 1840s and 1850s, she organized local women to work for the great Boston fairs, gathered and sent greens to decorate the halls, and helped to plan and mount local fairs in Fitchburg and Worcester. She arranged for antislavery lectures and, in 1856, nursed Bernardo, a black boy, during his final illness. She regarded her nursing as a privilege, and, when Bernardo died, she acknowledged that it had been a "great . . . blessing . . . to me, to pillow his dying head on my bosom." An 1862 issue of the *Liberator* provides the last view of Frances in her role serving as secretary for an antislavery convention in Leominister, Massachusetts.

In Salem, New Jersey, Abigail Goodwin had kept her antislavery convictions alive for decades with little support from her immediate community. A Quaker and a friend of Esther Moore, first president of the Philadelphia Female Anti-Slavery Society, Abigail joined the society in its petition work during the 1830s. Determined to collect signatures and not to become discouraged, she found New Jersey weak in "the abolitionist faith." Local women did not even have enough enthusiasm "to form a society just yet." Twenty years later, Abigail, now a poor widow, again entered the historical record. A friend explained her new focus: "Giving to the colored people was a perfect *passion* with her." Abigail's correspondence with the Philadelphia Vigilance Committee reveals some of the details of this passion to assist fugitive slaves. Without the ability to dip into her own pocket for funds, Abigail either earned or solicited money to support her interests. In the 1860s she was still active, collecting dollars and clothing for contrabands. She died in 1867.

Like many abolitionists, Andrew and Sarah Ernst carried their commitments with them when they moved west in 1841. Originally from Boston, Sarah Otis Ernst was a strong Garrisonian. When she arrived in Cincinnati, she found that the city did not have one antislavery society, although African Americans had established the Educational Society for the Colored. Like many white abolitionists, Sarah was less interested in free blacks than in slaves and dismissed the Educational Society because it did "nothing at all for the slave." When political and Christian abolitionists became active in the city, she rejected their approaches as misguided. Yet, although she worked hard to generate a "new . . . spirit," she ultimately found it expedient to cooperate with other abolitionist groups. She made a major contribution to antislavery in the Midwest through her work for the Cincinnati fair and inclusive antislavery conventions. Her commitment had personal and familial costs. She found organizing the fair a "physical drudgery" and feared her work might be harmful to her newborn baby, whom she was nursing. "Sleepless nights and anxious distressed days are not calculated to give a healthy constitution to my baby," she worried. Moreover, the storage of fair items in her home disrupted domestic life and was contrary to her husband's "*wishes—his* pride." As Sarah discovered, stress was part and parcel of abolitionism.

Mary Still (1808–1889), an African American who left traces of her abolitionist activities, was the daughter of a former slave from Maryland and his fugitive wife. She grew up in New Jersey and, like four of her siblings, moved to Philadelphia. In the late 1840s, she kept a school for black children there and became involved in the life of Philadelphia's black community. As a member of the Female Union Publication Society of Philadelphia, an organization affiliated with the African Methodist Episcopal Church, she helped raise money for publications that contributed "to the improvement and elevation of our people." Her professional and organizational commitments, like her abolitionism, helped to establish her place in the city's black middle class. During the war, she volunteered to teach freed slaves. Heading south, she found her "heart . . . very sad" and realized that "I have desided hastily about going so far from home alone." Although the climate in South Carolina proved problematic for her health, the enthusiasm of her pupils lifted her spirits. She adapted so well to her important work that in 1869 she moved to another American Missionary Association school in Florida, where she remained until 1872.

The contributions of these and countless other women to abolitionism reveal the varied and important part they played in the most significant reform before the Civil War. Herbert Aptheker points out that abolitionism was the first major social movement to involve women in all aspects of the work. What he does not emphasize enough, however, is what many of the leaders realized: without women, abolitionism would have been far more marginal a movement for change than it was.

Women's Rights and the Politics of Church and State in Antebellum America

NANCY ISENBERG

In 1853 the editor of *Harper's Magazine* condemned "Woman's Rights—or the movement that goes by that name." No other movement was "so decidedly infidel," he claimed, opposed as it was to divine revelation, time-honored proprieties, and biblical authority. At stake was a fragile but socially vital alliance between church

Nancy Isenberg, "'Pillars in the Same Temple and Priests of the Same Worship': Woman's Rights and the Politics of Church and State in Antebellum America," *Journal of American History* 85 (June 1998): 98–122, 128. Reprinted by permission of the Organization of American Historians.

and state, because, the editor contended, the "Christian ecclesia" bound civil society together by preserving sexual differences. . . .

The editor's charges did not go unanswered. In three sequential articles— "Harper's Editor and the Women"—published in the *Lily,* the first significant period- ical to herald the woman's movement, the New York lawyer and woman's rights supporter Anson Bingham challenged what he claimed was an absurd view of the Christian ecclesia. The term itself, like the dispute in which it figured, linked the political and religious realms. Originally, the Greek work *ekklēsia* referred to an assembly of free citizens of a town. The early Christians borrowed it to name their religious assemblies, suggesting that the church constituted a social order. By the nineteenth century, Protestants had grown comfortable with the idea that the church and state had similar ways to legitimate masculine authority in public forums. Bingham thus rejected the contention that by "divine appointment" man acquired "domination" as his "prerogative," while woman acquired a place of "subordina- tion." If married couples commingled in the temple of the home, then man and woman likewise could establish a "co-equality in all that concerns their common interests" in the *res foras* or the life of the forum. . . .

A similar debate had occurred in 1848, in a public exchange of letters, published in newspapers in Seneca Falls and Rochester, New York, between a clergyman and Elizabeth Cady Stanton and Elizabeth McClintock. The dispute had been sparked by the first woman's rights convention, held in July, in Seneca Falls, in which Stanton and McClintock had assumed prominent public roles. In the aftermath of the Seneca Falls convention and during a meeting in Rochester the following month, Stanton and McClintock felt obliged to defend their gatherings against the combined charges of religious and political infidelity made by religious opponents—particularly Protestant ministers. They responded to a vociferous attack from a Seneca Falls minister who asserted that the existing government was "established by God" and that woman's rights mocked both Christianity and democracy. McClintock and Stanton claimed that woman's rights were founded on a religious liberty that rejected "fetters that bind the spirit of woman." They also called for ministers to engage in open and public debate on woman's rights. . . .

I argue that the church must be viewed as a political institution and that when scholarship treats religion as purely a moral activity, it obscures key historical developments. Religion involves not only moral values but also theories about caste hierarchy, ecclesiastical power, and disciplinary practices that define behav- ior and reinforce political ideologies. The debates between the *Harper's* editor and Bingham and between Stanton and McClintock and the local minister demon- strated that the church could not be reduced to a moral terrain separate and distinct from the *res foras* or the political sphere; on the contrary, the model of the church, or *ecclesia,* provided guidelines for gender relations appropriated by the state. An alliance between church and state, then, contributed significantly to cultural and legal perceptions of women's civil status. . . . Because nineteenth-century woman's rights advocates and their opponents used a political and legal vocabulary infused with religious meaning, modern distinctions between religious and private moral- ity, on the one hand, and political and public representation, on the other, distort our understanding of how religion shaped gendered notions of constitutional and political rights. . . .

Antebellum woman's rights activists believed that the older tradition of *ecclesia,* which celebrated religious liberty, had suffered as a result of what Antoinette Brown in 1851 saw as an "unholy alliance" between church and state. Public opinion required open debate and discussion, gatherings among equals. In 1843 Lucretia Mott urged that the "partition walls of prejudice" that divided men and women into different castes be surmounted. The "Christian ecclesia" had to return to its primitive, New Testament model of being "called forth," which antebellum reformers translated to mean being "called out" of conventional society. At the heart of this notion of the church was dissent—a critical posture that led many woman's rights activists to leave their churches, to form new religious organizations, or in the case of prominent activists such as Mott, to act as vocal critics and provocateurs within their well-established religious institutions. . . .

Recognition of the strong connection between church and state reveals the need for a reexamination of two themes important in women's history—the separation of private and public and the feminization or domestication of religion. . . .

Antebellum Americans conceived of public opinion and representation much as the adherents of classical and Enlightenment traditions did, highlighting speech as essential to defining a public gathering, equality as a forum of peers, and representation as based upon public appearance, presence, and the capacity to embody the views of the people. The same conceptions allowed politicians and constitutional interpreters to legitimize the restrictions placed on women's political and legal standing. As the New York jurist Elisha Hurlbut argued in his 1845 *Essays on Human Rights, and Their Political Guaranties,* women lacked the capacity for self-representation; women's exclusion from the polls was justified by the rule that women voted by proxy through male relatives. Similarly, although women had to appear before the court and stand trial, women did not exercise the right to judge others, as in jury service. From the beginning of the nineteenth century, jurors were "representatives" of the people, and women's exclusion from the jury box demonstrated that they were not considered the "peers" of men. Jurors were peers and "centinels and guardians of each other," language that reinforced the gendered assumptions about jury duty by comparing it to military service (sentinels) and legal guardianship. Consent and dissent—exercised by those able to voice public opinions and to renounce political decisions as equals in the halls of government—were fundamental rights denied women. At best, women had the right to petition, a right they had even before the American Revolution, or to request a hearing in the legislature. Such limitations, Mott remarked in 1849, made woman nothing more than a "cypher" in the state. . . .

[W]oman's rights activists eagerly and conscientiously applied the language of dissent to demand equal representation in both religious and political forums. In that language, two key terms of condemnation were *caste* and *sect.* Activists compared the clergy to "castes," groups whose authority came, not from current popular consent, but from inherited, vested privileges—especially the coveted monopoly over religious "truth" displayed through public speaking or preaching. Activists also challenged the existing church as a "sect," a narrow, exclusive, stultifying group. Their image of sect was revealed in the claim that the "ecclesiastical machinery" of most Protestant congregations had lost its public function as the embodiment of religious liberty and instead controlled the laity (and women, in particular) through rules, discipline, and creeds.

Woman's rights activists clearly believed that the antebellum debate over the Christian ecclesia was destined to shape representative democracy and American jurisprudence. Constitutional conventions and church secessions suggested that the 1840s were a time of political and ecclesiastical transformation. Activists argued that women's status as a "disabled caste" in the church or state constituted a violation of equal protection under the law, and they simultaneously promoted a revolutionary kind of public exchange between men and women that was premised on the ideal of "co-equal representation." By changing the public forum of the church, activists sought to enhance women's civil standing in government, thus reconstituting the meaning of representation for men and women in both religious and political assemblies.

Sacred Rights and Sectarian Wrongs

At the Seneca Falls convention on July 19–20, 1848, supporters gathered to discuss the "Social, Civil, and Religious condition of Woman." Most participants came from the town of Seneca Falls, New York, the neighboring village of Waterloo, and the nearby city of Rochester. Lucretia Mott, the only nationally known speaker at the meeting, acquired new notoriety as the "moving spirit of the occasion." The convention produced two major documents: a preamble and eleven resolutions, previously drafted and debated during the deliberations, and the Declaration of Sentiments, written a short time earlier by Elizabeth Cady Stanton, read and amended during the meeting.

In the Declaration of Sentiments, Stanton insisted that women should "have immediate admission to the rights and privileges which belong to them as citizens of the United States." Here Stanton imitated a strategy popular with antebellum legal reformers eager to revise state constitutions. They asserted that certain fundamental rights defined national citizenship and that states could not violate those basic inalienable rights. . . . In the Declaration of Sentiments Stanton also appealed to natural law, contending that women, contrary to their birthright, were "fraudulently deprived of their most scared rights." . . . [T]he burden of proof for women's exclusion from the rights and privileges of full citizenship now required a constitutional justification that explained this apparent disregard for the authority of natural law and the protection of women's "most sacred rights." . . .

Religion proved to be essential in helping women envision themselves as rights bearers, for the language of rights was closely intertwined with female activists' conception of religious liberty, accountability, and the exercise of conscience that, they believed, was necessary for forming public opinion. Consent had to be based on the "courthouse of conscience," as the members of the Worcester woman's rights convention were to proclaim in 1850, while dissent allowed women to demand the right to have rights, two exercises of liberty that antebellum woman's rights activists recognized as fundamental conditions for claiming and protecting sacred rights in the church and state. Conscience demanded respect for women's equality before God. . . .

Antebellum woman's rights advocates assumed that the church functioned as a bastion either of liberty or of censorship. The key issue was whether the church constituted a public forum. When ministers rewarded conformity and curbed public criticism and members kept silent for fear of reprisal, then . . . Christian liberty was sacrificed for church order and ecclesiastical rules were legitimated at the expense of the rights of the laity. As one reformer astutely noted in 1845, antebellum churches often sacrificed the life of the forum in the church to the ecclesiastical needs of the institution, especially when churches mobilized all their "ecclesiastical machinery" to make the "church itself into a state." To be a public forum, the church had to create an environment where members exercised consent and dissent, developing a critical perspective toward the abuses of state power. Absent such an environment, the greatest danger for the laity was spiritual paralysis or alienation, what McClintock and Stanton described as the "fetters that bind the spirit of woman."

This kind of criticism of the church resonated among reformers. In 1848, Gerrit Smith gave voice to what many antebellum dissenters believed, namely, that most churches or religious societies had been reduced to "the soul-shrivelling enclosures of a sect." The term "sect" and the political and denominational development identified as "sectarianism" reflected an intellectually and emotionally charged understanding concerning church-state relations. Having adapted the eighteenth century's contempt for political factionalism, critics were newly claiming that sectarianism resulted in the corruption of the public sphere through self-interested competition. The ambitious efforts of Protestant denominations for building the "evangelical empire" and factional struggles within churches over policy and creeds indicated to dissenters a dangerous climate. A vast expanse of sects vied for members, institutional power, and public influence. Sectarian churches were portrayed by dissenters as exclusive enclaves, preoccupied with theological squabbles and petty rivalries, that carefully circumscribed members within their "respective circles of theology." Antebellum dissenters gave sectarianism a modern meaning when they focused on the control of information and the closing of the American mind. . . .

The public nature of the church had a direct bearing on women's capacity for political action. Lucretia Mott echoed Smith's allusion when she described the "sectarian enclosure on woman's mind." Activists believed that sectarianism constrained women's knowledge, undermining and "dwarfing" women's mental capabilities by preempting their ability to make independent decisions. . . .

For antebellum dissenters, the solution to sectarianism was what they called a "free church" or "people-church." As in the Congregational Friends or the Religious Union of Associationists, membership was open to anyone in the community, and the goal was to attract men and women from a wide range of religious faiths to discuss moral and political questions. . . . These radical new assemblies all experimented with a more democratic church polity and blended the constitutional fiction of popular sovereignty or rule by the people with their notion of a religious public forum. . . .

Woman's rights advocates believed that the conception of a church as a "simple democracy" raised the question of whether women had an equal place in such assemblies. As Elizabeth Wilson, an orthodox Presbyterian turned dissenter and woman's rights supporter, asked in her comprehensive study, *A Scriptural View of Woman's Rights and Duties* (1849): "If women were collected together to hear the word of God, would they constitute a church?" Wilson's query went to the heart of the issue. Could women as "two or three gathered together" constitute a public assembly for worship?

The answer was "no" for most denominations because incorporation required that trustees and elders possess the legal status of property holders. . . . Wilson had her own explanation for the absence of all-woman churches. A church as a public body required the presence of men, which Wilson sardonically acknowledged. She wrote that for a typical congregation, the ideal church required a "fine" meeting-house and a male minister in the pulpit addressing a "large assembly of people ornamented with *beards.*" . . .

. . . Distinction and presence presupposed the marks of masculinity—the shared ornament of beards—which for Wilson connoted adulthood, civil standing, and, of course, manhood. The beard distinguished men from women; it also placed women in the same category as young male children incapable of self-representation, who had not yet achieved independence and public standing. In political parlance, women and children shared their status as dependents, which was why fathers and husbands represented their interests at the polls. Presence thus equated physical appearance with the capacity for representation and the symbolic marks of masculinity.

Antebellum activists saw that standing in the church and state was derived from the relationship forged between public appearance and investiture, in which the mas-culine coding of presence clothed men with certain rights and privileges. Women could not constitute a public assembly for worship, because, as Wilson implied, they lacked presence—the vested symbols of social and public power. Women also lacked the presence to stand in the place of another, particularly as the proxy for men. For antebellum Americans, the right of public representation meant the capacity to act as a peer of, and proxy for, the people. And as woman's rights advocates understood only too well, in the words of Abby Price, women were doomed to "stand without a temple," as long as they lacked the right of "co-equal representation."

Co-equality and Castes

In 1850, woman's rights activists decided to turn their convention at Salem, Ohio, into public theater by closing their proceedings to men. As a powerful symbolic gesture, the men were asked to retreat to the gallery, forced to watch the delibera-tions voicelessly. For the first time, women constituted the public assembly, debating and discussing resolutions, while the men were denied the right of public standing, assuming women's traditional role as silent spectators.

That year activists highlighted the theme of co-equality during the Salem and Worcester conventions, calling for women's "co-sovereignty" and shared administra-tion in the church and state. Abby Price cleverly used the word "co-equal" to redefine the "self-evident" phrase—*"life, liberty, and the pursuit of happiness"*—from the Declaration of Independence, and she, like Wilson and Mott, offered poignant bibli-cal interpretations using the creation story as a metaphor for the first covenant and social contract. Price, Wilson, and Mott all rejected the traditional biblical prescrip-tion of the ordained subordination of woman as the helpmeet of man, instead arguing that man and woman were created simultaneously as "co-equals." As Mott explained in her "Discourse on Woman," read at the Salem convention: "In the beginning, man and woman were created equal. 'Male and female created he them, and blessed them, and called their name Adam.' He gave dominion to both over the lower animals, but not to one over the other." By rewriting the social contract, woman's rights advocates did far more than argue for individual rights. Through co-equality, they carved a theoretical space for women within the imaginary script of the "original contract" in the state of nature, and they challenged the vested superiority of man—as the "first" and privileged creation of God—over all creatures, including woman. . . .

Co-equality was a counterpoint to what Paulina Wright Davis described as women's current political and legal status as a "disabled caste." In her presidential address at the 1850 national woman's rights convention held in Worcester, Davis called for the "emancipation of a class," predicated on the constitutional principle of equal protection and due process of the law. A year earlier she had observed that the sexual double standard flouted the principle of equality under the law. She had reason for concern. In 1849, Chief Justice Lemuel Shaw of Massachusetts reinforced the idea of unequal vested rights, ruling in *Roberts v. City of Boston* that men and women were not "legally clothed with the same civil and political powers." Shaw reaffirmed the argument that women and children were subject to "paternal consideration" but not vested with the same rights as adult men. He assumed that the courts acted as a surrogate father or guardian for legal dependents, an approach that mirrored the standard approach to female representation—proxy. As Davis understood, women's status as a "disabled caste" sealed their political disenfranchisement. The state divested women of political rights such as suffrage, because government had a prior obligation to protect the vote as a vested right of men.

Arguments about vested rights, the sexual order of creation, and public presence introduced by woman's rights activists contributed to the antebellum controversy over women's right to represent themselves in the church and the state. As activists realized, establishing a public presence was difficult for women, because distinction implied literally and figuratively commanding respect and the attention of a public audience. Drawing on an eighteenth-century critique of fashionable or aristocratic women, antebellum critics associated public women with "spectacles," that is, false women who treated the public domain as a stage, wore disguises, and, like actresses, recited lines rather than voicing their actual opinions. Women who commanded an audience inverted the order of creation, daring to preach or teach to men, as one minister argued at the New York woman's rights convention in 1853. By demanding "awe and reverence" from male spectators, women appeared "unnatural," and they were accused of imitating men, or arrogantly asserting their independence from the supervision of male guardians, husbands, or ministers. . . .

In the 1850s, "female politicians" and woman's rights activists were commonly lampooned in the newspapers either for stealing the breeches from duped husbands or pirating the petticoats of unsuspecting wives. Such images satirized apolitical men and public women as cross-dressing freaks and social misfits. The "battle for the pants" continued a much older motif of sexual inversion that had its origins during the Protestant Reformation in Germany. The power of its message persisted in attacks against those women seeking equality in "Christian, public, religious assemblies," as Elizabeth Wilson noted, who were labeled women "putting on the pantaloons." The fear of sexual confusion mimicked the more subtle reasoning used to restrict women's constitutional equality. Indeed, vested rights depended on political dress, and the idea of women "putting on the pants" indicated their unnatural attempts to usurp the civic power of male citizens.

Such charges surfaced in the *Harper's* editorial of 1853. The woman's rights movement was ridiculed for its "hybrid conventions," and the editor accused women of hiding behind their "Quaker bonnets." One particular bonnet—that of Lucretia Mott—probably inspired this angry harangue. During the previous decade, Mott had emerged as a highly visible public woman by traveling thousands of miles, attending hundreds of meetings, and speaking before large and small crowds on such topics as woman's rights, antislavery, sectarianism, peace reform, and land monopoly. She was considered the "principal speaker" at the Seneca Falls convention in 1848, and Mott either presided or gave keynote addresses at later conventions. . . .

To satisfy woman's rights advocates, the church had to eliminate all caste privileges, particularly the exclusive monopoly that men had over clerical offices, which elevated public speaking as the preeminent symbol of their vested authority. . . . Accordingly, the most telling sign of priestcraft for Mott was the "appropriation of the pulpit by one sex." Apostolic authority offered the most telling source of women's exclusion from teaching and preaching, borne in the biblical verse dictating that women remain silent in church and ask their husbands for instruction. Elizabeth Wilson summed up this credo by noting that ministers called for "woman always to be a learner" and "novice." Sarah Owen made a similar comment at the 1848 Rochester woman's rights convention, sarcastically remarking that priests and husbands shared the same faith that a woman's opinion must always echo their own.

Co-equality, then, required that the church create a public forum that vested men and women equally with the right to preach, that both encompassed and represented the opinions of the congregation. Dissenters promoted this idealized forum, encouraging a deliberative meeting of "so many different minds," where the public mind "presents itself without waiting to be re-presented." In this environment one was neither ruler nor ruled, men were not masters and women were certainly not novices, because there were "fewer orators, but more speakers; fewer speeches, but more talk; less spoken, but more said." By engaging in what Abby Price described as "an intercourse purified by a forgetfulness of sex," women and men could now recognize each other as co-equal sources of the truth. Indeed, men and women could view each other as two corresponding parts of the whole, each contributing a partial understanding of the truth. . . .

Antebellum feminists had seen the contradiction between abstract rights and the dominant political discourse that defined representation as a masculine enterprise. Gender was never peripheral to the meaning of representation; it was vital in explaining the masculine marks of presence and speech that remained crucial to a nineteenth-century understanding of the public forum. It was the "fetters of the law, both sacred and secular," as Antoinette Brown claimed, that had placed a "thorny crown" on the brow and a "leaden scepter" in the hands of woman. To untangle this unholy alliance between church and state, women had to be welcomed onto the same public platform as men and vested with the right of co-equal representation. As the president of the West Chester woman's rights convention, Mary Ann Johnson, declared in 1852, only then would the day arrive when "woman and her brother are pillars in the same temple and priests of the same worship."

Women's Organizations in New York and Boston

ANNE M. BOYLAN

Women's voluntary societies proliferated in the postrevolutionary years. As much as did men, American women helped create "the age of benevolent institutions" so striking to Noah Worcester in 1816, and so impressive to Alexis de Tocqueville in 1832. Some were little more than fund-raising agencies dedicated to a particular purpose—such as sending missionaries to convert nonbelievers—while others conducted far-flung charitable businesses that raised money, ran institutions such as orphanages or old age homes, lobbied politicians, and found foster homes for needy children. Still others devoted their energies to mutual aid and self-help, or to the eradication of specific social practices, such as prostitution. Many had nothing in common with others but the sex of their founders.

Paralleling the emergence and spread of these groups were important changes in women's social experiences and in ideologies about womanhood. The same decades that witnessed the development of the first permanent women's societies saw a major refiguring of the colonial gender system to accommodate the economic, political, and religious upheavals that accompanied and followed the American Revolution. The coincidence among these developments was not a mere temporal accident. After all, the earliest groups emerged in urban areas among Protestant women whose personal experience and social location provided both the motivation and the means to remake the traditional almsgiving woman into the modern organized benefactor. Moreover, the existence of collectively organized, publicly visible female benevolence quickly came to symbolize the new womanhood of the nineteenth century, and an individual's participation in associational endeavors came to be accepted and admired as evidence of her claims to "true womanhood." Only in the 1830s did some organized women—notably abolitionists—come under attack for their labors, and then only for their methods and goals, nor for organizational activity per se.

In both laboring and justifying their labors, the founders of women's organizations helped create and reproduce a gender system to fit the times. Although it remained hierarchical by sex, the new gender system incorporated democratic ideals, largely by defining women's secondary status within society as separate from and complementary to men's. Just as the primacy and political independence of the free male citizen would rest upon his control of property and dependents (wife, children, servants, or slaves), the authority of the democratic patriarch would devolve from his ability solely to represent the interests of the entire family unit in the public arenas of politics and law. By founding organizations and incorporating organizational work into new definitions of femininity, some women helped shape the new gender system and define the feminine sphere. At the same time, by setting limits on appropriately feminine activities, their labors created new distinctions among women themselves and new hierarchies of acceptable female behavior.

Anne M. Boylan, published as Chapter 1, "Patterns of Organization," *The Origins of Women's Activism: New York and Boston, 1797–1840* (Chapel Hill: University of North Carolina Press, 2002) 15–37.

Nineteenth-century gender ideology obscured these hierarchies of considering masculine and feminine "spheres" as equal, and by stressing women's common experiences as women. The concept of a unitary female nature rooted in biology served many useful functions in nineteenth-century society, including "contribut[ing] to many women's sense of power and autonomy . . . [and] to a process of middle-class self-definition." In embracing that notion, women activists shaped the new gender ideology while also justifying the extraordinary proliferation of woman-run organizations. New female social experiences, gender ideologies, and women's associations took root and blossomed together, their vines inextricably intertwined. In the process, the republican mother of the 1790s became the "true woman" and Christian mother of the 1830s, as femininity and religiosity came to be closely associated. The contradictory consequences that ensued from these new definitions of femininity can be seen in the differing experiences of women in different associations (as well as of their clients). For some, social experience and ideology blended seamlessly, offering personal validation and collective power. For others, especially those women whose racial, class, or religious identities made them ineligible for membership in the best-known and most prestigious organizations, ideology and experience could be confusingly at odds. Although they all gazed into the same ideological mirror, looking for the unitary "woman" of nineteenth-century lore, often the image became a fun-house reality fractured by the deep divisions of nineteenth-century urban life.

Examining the patterns of organization evident among various groups of women in New York and Boston over the decades from the 1790s to the 1840s enables us to see how the dominant antebelllum gender ideology evolved and to connect it to new practices in class relations. For as historians have frequently noted, in the nineteenth century, gender ideology and class definition were closely linked, and both found expression in the associations people joined. When we look at how different types of women's organizations came into being, created conditions for additional groups to form, institutionalized opportunities for organizational activity, formed networks or snapped linkages, and in general rooted associational activity deeply into women's "sphere," we can better understand both gender ideology and class formation in antebellum New York and Boston.

The First Wave, 1797–1806

Several patterns recurred independently in the two cities. The first pattern was temporal. Both cities witnessed an initial wave of organizing at the turn of the nineteenth century, followed by a cascade of activity during and after the War of 1812, then an ebb in the 1820s, followed by a new surge in the late 1820s and 1830s. . . . The latter surge contained within it smaller waves that broke separately, creating a succession of three organizational types: benevolent associations, which arrived first and remained the most numerous and ubiquitous throughout the era; mutual benefit or mutual aid societies, which arose in each city during the 1820s; and reform associations, which arrived in the 1830s.

Women in each city established the tradition of organized female benevolence in the 1790s; by 1840, both had an array of such groups. Devoted to improving the temporal and spiritual welfare of clients ranging from widows and orphans to ministerial students and prostitutes, such endeavors responded to concrete economic changes, especially in the conditions facing poor urban women and children. These efforts also reflected parallel alterations in well-off women's lives. Both "subjective necessity" and objective reality transformed individual charity into organized benevolence. Like their charitable forebears, members of benevolent associations assumed a vertical relationship between benefactor and client; unlike them, they employed a "rhetoric of female benevolence" that presupposed a uniform experience of womanhood. New York's Society for the Relief of Poor Widows with Small Children, initiated in 1797 with a singularly descriptive title, fit the genre. . . .

In creating formal associations with written constitutions, elected officers, fund-raising mechanisms, printed reports, and (sometimes) incorporated legal status, the founders of these societies cast conventional female charity into a new mold. Existing men's societies provided an accessible model, on which women drew freely, but the sources of their formalizing instincts were more numerous and diverse. One was certainly the revolutionary experience, when American women had first organized independently to pursue a collective public goal. Another was the Quaker tradition of women's meetings, which provided the proximate model for New York's Female Association. Still another was the long history of organized women's prayer meetings, which were well entrenched in evangelical practice by the 1790s. Yet a fourth was the experience of aiding men's groups; Isabella Graham had labored actively for the London and New York Missionary Societies, "gathering intelligence and endeavoring to collect money," before helping initiate the Society for the Relief of Poor Widows with Small Children, and the Orphan Asylum Society. But such specific precedents were less important than key alterations in northern urban women's experiences between the 1760s and the 1790s, including improved access to formal schooling, increased exposure to a new world of printed books and magazines, practical immersion in the rapidly changing commercial economy of the late eighteenth-century city, broader exposure to nonfamilial and noncongregational forms of religious proselytizing, and a new consciousness of gender as a way of organizing social experience. . . .

With extensive literary and epistolary contacts on both sides of the Atlantic, Graham represented yet another strain in the founders' experience. Like many of them, she regularly read English and Scottish publications; she also sent examples of American publications to her correspondents. But more than most, she was immersed in an evangelical religious world, one that fostered affiliation and outreach and worked against narrow sectarian parochialism. In this she resembled Bostonian Mary Webb, the twenty-one-year-old founder of the Female Missionary Society who by 1817 was corresponding with women in ninety-seven similar organizations. Whether evangelical or not, the founding generation inhabited a mental world increasingly constructed through printed materials circulating through national and transatlantic arteries. They also shared an understanding of gender—the experience of womanhood or manhood—that stressed common feminine experiences and common values. . . . In uniting as women (albeit as white, Protestant, and privileged women), both evangelical and nonevangelical founders harnessed new understandings of womanhood and new beliefs in the importance of shared feminine experience. . . .

The authority they sought was to be exercised primarily over other women and over children. The same economic and social changes that altered the founders' lives, opening new possibilities to them, simultaneously rendered many poorer women's lives more precarious and changed their relationship with their social "betters." The poor widow and her orphaned children, cast unprotected onto a cut-throat labor market, figured centrally in the founders' plans as the embodiments of an alternate fate. . . .

These early associations facilitated the formation of subsequent organizational waves by creating precedents and clearing paths that remained open for all successor groups. Leaders of both the New York Society for the Relief of Poor Widows with Small Children and the Boston Female Asylum, as pioneers in their cities, faced down criticisms that quickly evaporated. Seven years after helping found the New York group, Isabella Graham marveled at the change she had witnessed: initial "ridicule" and "opposition" had turned to approbation and fame. Whereas at first "the men could not allow our sex the steadiness and perseverance necessary to establish such an undertaking," she told the young women who operated the society's school, by 1804 God's "seal upon it" was evident in its prosperity. . . . Later societies might sometimes face severe obloquy, but whatever criticism came their way focused on their particular programs or activities, not their right to formal existence. Once settled, that question remained settled.

So too did issues surrounding organizations' legal status and financing techniques. Once the Society for the Relief of Poor Widows with Small Children had acquired corporate status under New York State law in 1802 and Boston's Female Asylum had done the same under Massachusetts law in 1803, future groups' right to incorporate was not challenged. . . . This occurred despite the ironic reality that, as several historians have underscored, corporate status granted the collective female body a range of legal rights that none of the wives within it could claim individually, including the right to own property, bring legal suits, indenture minor children, invest funds, and control wages. Whether incorporated or not, early societies drafted constitutions and by-laws and composed annual reports to supporters; when they published some or all such documents, they established their right of access to the public media. . . .

In developing fund-raising and financing techniques, too, early organizations smoothed the route for others. Women's first efforts to collect funds for public purposes dated to the Revolutionary War, when Philadelphian Esther De Berdt Reed instigated a campaign to provide monetary bonuses to soldiers in the Continental Army. The permanent organizations that followed the Revolution elaborated on techniques employed by Reed and her associates, including door-to-door solicitations and annual or lifetime membership subscriptions. The anniversary sermon delivered by a sympathetic and admiring clergyman was another existing technique; adapted from men's organizations, it proved a mainstay of women's fund-raising for generations. And selling clients products or access to their labor power was a popular practice derived from revolutionary-era poor-relief projects. In 1805, for example, the Society for the Relief of Poor Widows with Small Children sold client-made shirts at its store, while girls in the Boston Female Asylum labored on cash-producing sewing projects solicited from local families. Urban residents quickly got used to the sight of women soliciting donations in cash or in kind; when such solicitations proliferated or supported controversial activities, they might be annoyed or withhold contributions, but they would not challenge the womanliness of fund-raising.

Even the parish and antislavery fairs of the 1830s, which represented a new form of fund-raising because organization members sold the fruits of their own labor, along with donated goods, to the general public, nevertheless occupied, not terra nova, but a new section of older ground. Similarly, insuring an organization's permanence by financing it through a combination of annual fund-raising and judicious investment in income-producing bank stocks or United States treasury bonds reinforced the acceptability of woman-run institutions.

The Second Wave, 1812–1820

Societies founded during the second organizational wave drew upon and developed these precedents, sometimes quite directly, as individuals brought their experience to new organizational involvements. The continuities between the first and second surge were especially evident, however, in their concern for women and children. . . .

But change as well as continuity marked the second tide. Most striking was the surge in specifically religious societies run by Protestant women. Between 1814 and 1816, a Female Bible Society, Female Society for the Promotion of Christianity among the Jews, and Female Tract Society appeared on the Boston landscape. . . . In one year alone, 1816, New York's evangelical women created a Female Union Society for the Promotion of Sabbath Schools, Female Auxiliary Bible Society, and Female Missionary Society. In both cities, women formed congregation-based maternal associations and tract societies. . . .

[S]oliciting or accepting gifts of religious materials for circulation among charities' clients (not only Bibles but also evangelical books and tracts) became commonplace in the 1810s, within both old and new associations, as the number and visibility of Bible, tract and publication societies grew. . . .

To note this evangelical turn is not to suggest that all societies took it, or that those taking it had therefore displayed no interest in evangelical religion. The two existing nonevangelical associations—New York's Quaker Female Association and Boston's increasingly Unitarian Female Asylum—continued along their accustomed paths. . . . Within the other first-wave organizations, religion in general and evangelical religion in particular had provided powerful motivation for individual actions. . . . What was different in the 1810s was the increasingly tight package in which womanhood and evangelical associationalism came wrapped. The republican mother was becoming the true woman. . . .

Joining overtly evangelical organizations became a significant means whereby [women] signaled their religious commitments. In a way not possible in the 1790s, when republican and evangelical representations of womanhood were still separable, evangelical women in the 1810s combined religion and social action in collective, rather than individual ways. Affiliating with a missionary, Bible, or Sunday school society thus became an accepted and admired way to express one's faith, and root one's conversion experience in solid ground. In turn, associations enlarged the terrain of individual influence. . . .

Beyond collecting contributions, making clothing, or distributing tracts, subsidiary organizations served the important function of training and recruiting potential new members. Most were peopled with young women, often the single daughters of parent society leaders. . . . Formally organized with constitutions, lists of officers, and (sometimes) published annual reports, "juvenile" auxiliaries effectively propagated the ideals and practices of evangelical womanhood. . . .

As such definitions acquired shape and mass, and were disseminated through women's organizations, they revised and displaced nonevangelical republican ideals of womanhood. . . .

One result was that as evangelical women began to place themselves historically, they subtly distanced their organizations from that republican heritage, preferring instead a religious or domestic origin. . . . By the time these chroniclers summed up their organizations' past, the historical figures to whom they looked for models were less often the classical Roman matrons or Old Testament warrior women from whom many in the revolutionary generation had drawn inspiration. More frequently, they were the women of the scriptures; evangelical British writers such as Hannah More, whose publishing careers constituted "happy examples" of "silent preaching"; and the "eminently pious" American women whose memoirs increasingly crowded evangelical publishers' shelves. . . .

The Third Wave, 1823–1840

The third organizational wave coincided with significant changes in the religious and economic topography of each city. Especially in New York, evangelical revivals associated with the growth of Methodism and the preaching of the Presbyterian Charles Grandison Finney (who first came to New York City in 1827) transformed the features of evangelicalism and sparked new concern about social problems. In turn, these changes led to the formation of new women's associations. . . .

If the poor widow had been a figure of particular poignancy to members of first- and second-wave organizations, the working woman assumed that symbolic role in the 1820s and 1830s. In a rapidly changing economy characterized by large-scale migration of young women to new manufacturing jobs or servant positions, the white working woman seemed particularly vulnerable and in need of protection. . . . Two prostitution reform efforts—the Penitent Females Refuge Ladies' Auxiliary in Boston (1825) and the Female Benevolent Society in New York (1832)—sought religious and temporal redemption for young women, preferably "those whose departure from virtue has been the least aggravated, either in character or duration," this is, those not yet "hardened in vice." Both encouraged evangelical conversion as clear evidence of penitence; both offered domestic service as an alternative occupation.

Working women themselves had a different view of protection, as was suggested by the emergence of women's unions and mutual aid organizations during the same decades. . . .

The initiators of these endeavors were responding to the same economic and social conditions that were simultaneously shaping middle-class women's benevolence. Designed as forms of self-protection and self-insurance, mutual aid societies sought to allay some of the deepest fears of urban working women: the fear that illness would destroy their earning capacities, that burial in a potter's field would obliterate their very existence, that their motherless children would face a desolate, friendless future. In an economy in which the demand for female workers was high yet women's labor commanded extremely low wages, only those with some margin of disposable income could sequester the odd twenty-five or fifty cents against some future calamity. Still, the emergence of such organizations was an important indicator that working women were well aware of how vulnerable and unprotected the economies of the two cities rendered them. Their approach to protection was simply very different from that of middle-class women.

The growth of these societies also testified to changes in working-class women's consciousness of gender. Whereas existing mutual benefit groups offered assistance to women on the basis of their connection to men, in the form of widows' or survivors' benefits, their presumption of feminine dependence on a male breadwinner was increasingly at odds with the realities of urban existence. In forming their own societies, women exhibited an awareness that they faced different problems from the men of their class, and expressed their belief in the power of collective womanhood to address those problems. The particular popularity of such groups among free African American women, not only in Boston, where slavery had ended in 1783, but also in New York, where it remained a reality until 1827, reflected their lack of access to conventional notions of female dependency and male providership.

Commanding few resources, yet responding to desperate need in free black neighborhoods, black women's associations often blended mutual aid activities not only with benevolence but also with self-improvement, community service, and social reform. The African Dorcas Association, which held Wednesday sewing meetings at leaders' homes, and accounted carefully for all garments distributed, dispensed its bounty toward members' neighbors and friends and toward their children's schoolmates. Benevolence and mutual assistance shaded into each other as the women plied their needles. . . .

During the 1830s, self-help increasingly encompassed activities directed at ending slavery and aiding fugitive slaves. Women in church and literary societies added abolitionism to their lists, reasoning that by counteracting negative stereotypes of free blacks, they aided the cause of emancipation and promoted the welfare of all African Americans. . . .

It was just such reform activity by white women that sparked major controversy in the 1830s, as new, reform-oriented societies emerged in both cities. Their members' commitment to destroying important social institutions and practices such as slavery, prostitution, and liquor-dealing differentiated the Boston Female Anti-Slavery Society (1833), the New York Female Moral Reform Society (1834), and the like, from existing organizations. By abandoning or downplaying an emphasis on individual reformation, such groups instead stressed the need for radical changes in society. Antislavery societies in particular, with their demands for an immediate end to slavery, their commitment to racial equality (in principle if not always in practice), their integrated memberships, their claims of sisterly bonds with enslaved women, their adoption of highly visible political tactics, and their championing of white women's right to speak to mixed audiences, appeared so different from women's missionary or orphan societies that opponents reviled participants as "unsexed" and "amazons." Female Moral Reform Societies melded agitation against prostitution with rescue work for prostitutes. . . . [M]oral reformers courted publicity by starting their own newspapers and lobbying for laws to punish male seducers.

Using evangelical ideals of femininity, which two decades earlier had been instrumental in validating collective action, white women reformers challenged restrictions on the particular forms their actions took. Speaking in the language of evangelical femininity, the editor of the *Advocate of Moral Reform* reiterated the existing belief that women "have an important part to act in the renovation of a sin-ruined world," then went on to champion their right to advocate "the cause of moral reform" as well as that of Bible and tract distribution. Pointing to precedents—"women have organized associations, held meetings, published reports, appointed solicitors, . . . resolved themselves into committees, [and] even ascended the editorial chair"—she claimed the same privileges for female moral reformers. "If our sphere of action is limited to private life exclusively," she noted in 1837, "then we have long since left our own province and entered that of the other sex." The right to take "a personal responsibility in *all* that concerns the amelioration of the condition of man, and the good of society" was conferred "by God himself." Antislavery activists, too, claimed the mantle of divine sanction and pointed to the approbation that generally greeted "woman, stepping gracefully to the relief of infancy and suffering age," through benevolent associations.

Yet is was the very lack of such approbation for their work that elicited abolitionists' and moral reformers' comments. Even when they combined public agitation with stereotypically feminine fund-raising and charitable activity, they found the same religious ideals that energized them used against them. (Members of the Boston Female Anti-Slavery Society, for example, not only petitioned Congress for an end to slavery and sponsored public lectures by Angelina Grimké but also ran the Samaritan orphanage for black children and conducted fairs at which they sold their needlework and fancy imported trinkets.) This fracturing of religious and, specifically, evangelical ideals into warring concepts of womanhood reworked the gender ideology of the era by delineating acceptable from unacceptable female activism. Whereas in the 1810s, associational activity by itself marked the "true woman," in the 1830s women were judged worthy or unworthy according to membership in specific groups.

FURTHER READING

Alexander, Ruth M. " 'We Are Engaged as a Band of Sisters': Class and Domesticity in the Washingtonian Temperance Movement, 1840–1850," *Journal of American History* 75 (1988–1989): 763–785.

Boydston, Jeanne, et al. *The Limits of Sisterhood: The Beecher Sisters on Women's Rights and Woman's Sphere* (1988).

Cutter, Barbara. *Domestic Devils, Battlefield Angels: The Radicalism of American Womanhood, 1830–1865* (2004).

Davidson, Cathy N., and Jessamyn Hatcher, eds. *No More Separate Spheres!* (2002).

Dorsey, Bruce. *Reforming Men and Women: Gender in the Antebellum City* (2002).

DuBois, Ellen C. *Feminism and Suffrage: The Emergence of an Independent Women's Movement in America, 1848–1869* (1978).

Epstein, Barbara. *The Politics of Domesticity: Women, Evangelism, and Temperance in Nineteenth-Century America* (1980).

Ginzberg, Lori. *Women and the Work of Benevolence: Morality, Politics, and Class in the Nineteenth-Century United States* (1990).

Hansen, Debra G. *Strained Sisterhood: Gender and Class in the Boston Female Anti-Slavery Society* (1993).

Hewitt, Nancy. *Women's Activism and Social Change: Rochester, New York, 1822–1872* (1984).

Hoffert, Sylvia. *When Hens Crow: The Women's Rights Movement in Antebellum America* (1995).

Jeffrey, Julie Roy. "Permeable Boundaries: Abolitionist Women and Separate Spheres," *Journal of the Early Republic* 21 (2001): 79–93.

Matthews, Jean V. *Women's Struggle for Equality: The First Phase, 1828–1878* (1997).

McFadden, Margaret. *Golden Cables of Sympathy: The Transatlantic Sources of Nineteenth-Century Feminism* (2000).

Parsons, Elaine F. *Manhood Lost: Fallen Drunkards and Redeeming Women in the Nineteenth-Century United States* (2003).

Pierson, Michael D. *Free Hearts and Free Homes: Gender and American Antislavery Politics* (2003).

Salerno, Beth. *Sister Societies: Women's Antislavery Organizations in Antebellum America* (2005).

Wellman, Judith. *The Road to Seneca Falls: Elizabeth Cady Stanton and the First Woman's Rights Convention* (2004).

Yellin, Jean Fagan, and John C. Van Horne, eds. *The Abolitionist Sisterhood: Women's Political Culture in Antebellum America* (1994).

Yellin, Jean Fagan. *Women and Sisters: The Antislavery Feminists in American Culture* (1990).

CHAPTER

7

African American Women
and Slavery

*Historians once wrote about slavery as though only men were involved in per-
petuating and challenging that inhumane system. White men, after all, owned
the vast majority of slaves (because of married women's dependent legal status);
most prominent opponents of slavery, black and white, appeared to be men; and
men debated in state and national legislatures about maintaining or abolishing
the legal structures that sustained the system of perpetual bondage. Moreover, the
study of slaves themselves focused on men—their work, their day-to-day resistance,
their leadership of rebellions. Even slave families were examined primarily from a
male perspective; historians, for example, concerned themselves with such issues
as whether men were able to exert paternal or husbandly authority over their
wives and children in the absence of legal marriage and in light of masters' ability
to intrude on black family lives in various ways (such as separating or selling
family members).*

*All that has now changed dramatically, for women's historians have started
to investigate the many facets of women's involvement in the slave system. Many
new questions have come to the fore. How common was the sexual abuse of female
slaves by masters or their sons? How did enslaved women subsist within the slave
community and their own families? What were the roles of free black women, north
and south? How active were African American women in the abolitionist movement, and did their gender have a significant effect on them? The documents and
essays in this chapter address some of these important inquiries.*

◆ *D O C U M E N T S*

The documents in this chapter illustrate the varied ways in which African American
women, even those who were free, interacted with the slave system. In 1813, a Virginia
freedwoman, Lucinda, poignantly petitioned the legislature to allow her to be reenslaved
so she would not be separated from her husband (Document 1). In Document 2, "A Colored Woman" from Connecticut in 1839 asks other free African Americans to join her

in petitioning for the abolition of slavery in the District of Columbia. The Female Publication Society of Philadelphia, an organization of free black women, in 1861 wrote Document 3 to explain their decision to contribute to the support of racially uplifting publications. The documents section closes with two oral-history interviews from the 1930s: Rose Williams (Document 4) recounts her forced marriage to another slave in Texas; and Virginia Hayes Shepherd reminisces about her mother and a neighbor in Virginia (Document 5).

1. Lucinda, a Free Woman, Asks to Be Reenslaved, 1813

To the Legislature of the Commonwealth of Virginia,

The Petition of Lucinda, lately a slave belonging to Mary Matthews of King George county respectfully sheweth.

That the said Mary Matthews, by her last will and testament, among other things, emancipated all her slaves, and directed that they should be removed by her executor to some place where they could enjoy their freedom by the laws there in force. That all the slaves so emancipated (except your petitioner) were removed this year to the State of Tennessee; but your petitioner declined going with them, as she had a husband belonging to Capt. William H. Hooe in King George county, from whom the benefits and privileges to be derived from freedom, dear and flattering as they are, could not induce her to be separated: that, in consequence of this determination on her part, a year has elapsed since the death of her late mistress Mary Matthews, and your petitioner, is informed that the forfeiture of her freedom has taken place under the law prohibiting emancipated slaves from remaining in this State; and that the Overseers of the Poor might now proceed to sell her for the benefit of the Poor of the county: Your petitioner, still anxious to remain with her husband, for whom she has relinquished all the advantages of freedom, is apprehensive that, in case of a sale of her by the Overseers of the Poor, she may be purchased by some person, who will remove her to a place remote from the residence of her husband: to guard against such a heart rending circumstance, she would prefer, and hereby declares her consent, to become a slave to the owner of her husband, if your honorable body will permit it; and for that purpose she prays that you will pass a law vesting the title to her in the said William H. Hooe and directing that all proceedings on the part of the Overseers of the Poor for King George county to effect the sale of her may be perpetually staid;

And your petitioner will pray &c

Nov: 27th, 1813   *Lucinda*

Petition of Lucinda to the Legislature of the Commonwealth of Virginia, November 27, 1813, Library of Virginia, Richmond. This document can also be found in Appendix A of Loren Schweninger, "The Fragile Nature of Freedom: Free Women of Color in the U.S. South," *Beyond Bondage: Free Women of Color in the Americas,* ed. David Barry Gaspar and Darlene Clarke Hine (University of Illinois Press, 2004), 116–117.

2. "A Colored Woman" from Connecticut Implores Other Free Black Women to Sign Antislavery Petitions, 1839

Free women of Connecticut (for I speak not now to slaves, to the servile minions of pride, selfishness and prejudice), have you this fall signed the petitions in behalf of the dumb, and entreated *all* the women in your town to do the same? If you have not, I implore you to drop the work you have in your hand, or this paper, as soon as you shall have finished this article, and go to the work *now,* nor leave it till not one woman in your town shall have for excuse in the day of accounts, that she has not been *asked* to pray for the perishing.

Do you say you have so many family cares you cannot go? Thousands of your sisters may never hear the word *family* but to mock their desolation. But you must prepare your beloved children's *warm, winter clothing.* Look yonder. Do you not see that mother toiling with her *almost, or quite naked children, shivering in the keen blast?* Yet you cannot go, you must prepare the table for your family. The slave spends but little time in dressing her *"peck of corn per week."* Does your house need putting in order? Had you a house but *"fifteen feet by ten,"* furnished with a rough bench, a stool and a bunk, with a little straw and a blanket, and then, for cooking and table apparatus, a kettle, a spoon and a knife, it might not take you so long to set them in order. Why do you delay, and take up a book to read? Is it in derision of blighted intellect? Ah! throw it down in remembrance of the millions in whose bodies immortality has well neigh found a sepulchre. Do your precious babes demand your tender watchings, so that you cannot leave them? Hark! That shriek!! It proclaims the bursting of a heart, as the babe is torn from the frantic mother, and *sold for "five dollars the pound."* Still do you say "I have not time?" O! I pity you. You are yourself almost qualified to be a slave. Ay, *you are a slave*—a slave to hardness of heart. You have got a stone in your bosom; there is no flesh there; you are consumed in selfishness. Is this hard talk? How would *you* talk to *me,* were you allowed to speak, if I should wrap myself up in "my own concerns" and see your relatives and friends sold under the hammer, your clothing stripped from you, except, perhaps, a mere rag, your mind smothered to almost utter extinction, and then the defaced remnant of your former self driven before the gory lash, till, exhausted, you cannot finish your task, and are bound down, shamelessly exposed, and a cat hauled up and down your back to gratify the revenge of some lustful brute of an overseer. . . .

Women of Connecticut, I shall blush to acknowledge myself a woman, if women's souls have become so sear, so blighted, so shrunk to nonentity, as to neglect this labor of humanity. But I cannot think it will be neglected. I cannot think there will be a falling off in this important work.

Let us rouse ourselves and pour an overwhelming flood of rebuke upon those beings who claim to be men, agents of those who style themselves the "FREEST NATION ON THE EARTH," and use their freedom to say, . . . "For Four Hundred

---

"A Colored Woman," *Charter Oak* (Hartford, Ct.) November 1839. This document can also be found in C. Peter Ripley, et al., eds., *The Black Abolitionist Papers* (Chapel Hill: University of North Carolina Press, 1991) 3:326–327.

Dollars any human hyena may FATTEN ON THE BLOOD OF MEN, WOMEN AND CHILDREN, under the walls of our CAPITOL." Yes, worse still, they have made *robbery, adultery,* and murder, free game—ay, honorable sport—and he who holds the greatest number of trophies is deemed most noble. Up, my sisters, speak while there is time. Millions are perishing, victims of your delay.

A COLORED WOMAN

3. Mary Still, a Prominent Black Abolitionist, and Other Free Women in Philadelphia, Form the "Female Publication Society" to Promote the Moral Uplift of Free and Enslaved African Americans, 1861

Rev Elisha Weaver, Editor of the *Christian Recorder:*

Dear Brother:—The members of the Female Union Publication Society present to you a small donation ($20) to aid you in keeping the *Christian Recorder* in circulation. This we do with no ordinary degree of pleasure, as we are quite sure the high moral sentiments which it takes will prove an effectual means to the improvement and elevation of our people. There are thousands, this moment, of our helpless race, who are perishing from the want of moral and religious culture. The press has ever proved a powerful and an efficient means in producing a moral and religious element in a community. We therefore feel bound, as a society, to do all that we can to sustain you in your present position. The means which you have to work with are but limited, and your labor arduous, but your cause is most noble. Every week's issue may be regarded as so many sparks flying through the atmosphere, that will inevitably kindle ere long to a flame, and then our moral horizon will be lighted up with the glorious effects of its refulgent rays. Never was there a time in the history of our race, that required a more uncompromising and indefatigable effort to promote general literature than the present. A time when we, as an oppressed people, should rally to the standard, and concentrate an influence that will prove more than equivalent to the present state of ignorance, darkness, and spiritual wickedness. Come, friends of our common cause, let us be up and doing. These, truly, are perilous times, and they call for a concert of action. And then, there are four millions and a half of our countrymen who groan in abject slavery; they, too, call upon our sympathies. Humanity in general calls upon us. And He who holds the destiny of nations in his hand, is calling upon us. The issue of this political struggle, will decide an important question in our favor. The issue will clearly demonstrate the startling fact, that the people of color are to become citizens of these United States, and that the fields which they have reaped down without wages, will yet become the habitations for them and their children. It must be so. We can see it no other way. Then the thumb-screw, stock, and lash shall be felt and feared no more. But over them will wave majestically the banner of peace, liberty, and equal rights. The propriety of religious and moral publications was considered by many of us a matter of great importance. It was our earnest conviction,

---

The Christian Recorder, May 11, 1861. This document can also be found in *Black Abolitionist Papers,* microfilm, reel 13, frame 526.

that an effort like the present would help to sustain the object. We then called a meeting of our female friends, to take into consideration the propriety of forming a society, whose object should be to promote moral and religious publications, under the guidance and direction of the General Conference of the A. M. E. Church. It was thought best to form a society. It is now in existence, and bears the name of the Female Union Publication Society of Philadelphia. Its object is as above stated. Having all things in readiness, we laid it before our church, hoping to meet with their hearty co-operation. But like many other good efforts, it was sadly repulsed by the cold indifference manifested by the major part of the members. But, nothing daunted, we persevered, by asking the guidance of our Heavenly Father, who has promised to give wisdom to those who ask him and then patiently wait his answer. Our prayers have been graciously answered; and to-day finds that noble little band vigorously engaged in the dissemination of religion, morality, literature, and science. We humbly invite all who are friendly to this noble enterprise, to join with us.

MARY STILL,
On behalf of the Female Publication Society

4. Rose Williams Recalls Her Forced Marriage in the 1850s to Rufus, Another Slave

What I say am the facts. If I's one day old, I's way over ninety, and I's born in Bell County, right here in Texas, and am owned by Massa William Black. He owns Mammy and Pappy, too. Massa Black has a big plantation, but he has more niggers than he need for work on that place, 'cause he am a nigger trader. He trade and buy and sell all the time.

Massa Black am awful cruel, and he whip the colored folks and works 'em hard and feed 'em poorly. We-uns have for rations the corn meal and milk and 'lasses and some beans and peas and meat once a week. We-uns have to work in the field every day from daylight 'til dark, and on Sunday we-uns do us washing. Church? Shucks, we-uns don't know what that mean.

I has the correct memorandum of when the war start. Massa Black sold we-uns right then. Mammy and Pappy powerful glad to git sold, and they and I is put on the block with 'bout ten other niggers. When we-uns git to the trading block, there lots of white folks there what come to look us over. One man shows the interest in Pappy. Him named Hawkins. He talk to Pappy, and Pappy talk to him and say, "Them my woman and childs. Please buy all of us and have mercy on we-uns." Massa Hawkins say, "That gal am a likely-looking nigger; she am portly and strong. But three am more than I wants, I guesses."

The sale start, and 'fore long Pappy am put on the block. Massa Hawkins wins the bid for Pappy, and when Mammy am put on the block, he wins the bid for her. Then there am three or four other niggers sold before my times comes. Then Massa

Interview with Rose Williams, Federal Writers' Project, July 8, 1937. This document can also be found in George P. Rawick, et al., eds., *The American Slave: A Composite Autobiography,* supplement, series 2, vol 10: *Texas Narratives, Part 9* (Westport, Conn. Greenwood Press, 1979) 4117–4123.

Black calls me to the block, and the auction man say, "What am I offer for this portly, strong young wench. She's never been 'bused and will make the good breeder."

I wants to hear Massa Hawkins bid, but him say nothing. Two other men am bidding 'gainst each other, and I sure has the worriment. There am tears coming down my cheeks 'cause I's being sold to some man that would make separation from my mammy. One man bids $500, and the auction man ask, "Do I hear more? She am gwine at $500." Then someone say, "$525," and the auction man say, "She am sold for $525 to Massa Hawkins." Am I glad and 'cited! Why, I's quivering all over.

Massa Hawkins takes we-uns to his place, and it am a nice plantation. Lots better than Massa Black's. There is 'bout fifty niggers what is growed and lots of children. The first thing Massa do when we-uns gits home am give we-uns rations and a cabin. You must believe this nigger when I says them rations a feast for us. There plenty meat and tea and coffee and white flour. I's never tasted white flour and coffee, and Mammy fix some biscuits and coffee. Well, the biscuits was yum, yum, yum to me, but the coffee I doesn't like.

The quarters am pretty good. There am twelve cabins all made from logs and a table and some benches and bunks for sleeping and a fireplace for cooking and the heat. There am no floor, just the ground.

Massa Hawkins am good to he niggers and not force 'em work too hard. There am as much difference 'tween him and Old Massa Black in the way of treatment as 'twixt the Lord and the devil. Massa Hawkins 'lows he niggers have reasonable parties and go fishing, but we-uns am never tooken to church and has no books for larning. There am no education for the niggers.

There am one thing Massa Hawkins does to me what I can't shunt from my mind. I knows he don't do it for meanness, but I always holds it 'gainst him. What be done am force me to live with that nigger, Rufus, 'gainst my wants.

After I been at he place 'bout a year, the massa come to me and say, "You gwine live with Rufus in that cabin over yonder. Go fix it for living." I's 'bout sixteen year old and has no larning, and I's just ignomus child. I's thought that him mean for me to tend the cabin for Rufus and some other niggers. Well, that am start the pestigation for me.

I's took charge of the cabin after work am done and fixes supper. Now, I don't like that Rufus, 'cause he a bully. He am big and 'cause he so, he think everybody do what him say. We-uns has supper, then I goes here and there talking, till I's ready for sleep, and then I gits in the bunk. After I's in, that nigger come crawl in the bunk with me 'fore I knows it. I says, "What you means, you fool nigger?" He say for me to hush the mouth. "This am my bunk, too," he say.

"You's teched in the head. Git out," I's told him, and I puts the feet 'gainst him and give him a shove, and out he go on the floor 'fore he know what I's doing. That nigger jump up and he mad. He look like the wild bear. He starts for the bunk, and I jumps quick for the poker. It am 'bout three feet long, and when he comes at me I lets him have it over the head. Did that nigger stop in he tracks? I's say he did. He looks at me steady for a minute, and you could tell he thinking hard. Then he go and set on the bench and say, "Just wait. You thinks it am smart, but you am foolish in the head. They's gwine larn you something."

"Hush your big mouth and stay 'way from this nigger, that all I wants," I say, and just sets and hold that poker in the hand. He just sets, looking like the bull. There we-uns sets and sets for 'bout an hour, and then he go out, and I bars the door.

The next day I goes to the missy and tells her what Rufus wants, and Missy say that am the massa's wishes. She say, "You am the portly gal, and Rufus am the portly man. The massa wants you-uns for to bring forth portly children."

I's thinking 'bout what the missy say, but say to myself, "I's not gwine live with that Rufus." That night when him come in the cabin, I grabs the poker and sits on the bench and says, "Git 'way from me, nigger, 'fore I bust your brains out and stomp on them." He say nothing and git out.

The next day the massa call me and tell me, "Woman, I's pay big money for you, and I's done that for the cause I wants you to raise me childrens. I's put you to live with Rufus for that purpose. Now, if you doesn't want whipping at the stake, you do what I wants."

I thinks 'bout Massa buying me offen the block and saving me from being separated from my folks and 'bout being whipped at the stake. There it am. What am I's to do? So I 'cides to do as the massa wish, and so I yields. . . .

I never marries, 'cause one 'sperience am 'nough for this nigger. After what I does for the massa, I's never wants to truck with any man. The Lord forgive this colored woman, but he have to 'scuse me and look for some others for to 'plenish the earth.

5. Mrs. Virginia Hayes Shepherd Reminisces About Her Enslaved Mother and Diana, an Enslaved Neighbor, 1937

I was born in Churchland, Virginia December 21, 1856. My mother was a slave and my father—well the fact is so evident you can' dodge it. It's their stamp an' not ours; therefore I don't blush when I tell you this part of the story. Long before the war came, there weren't many professional people around, colored or white, so Doctor Harvey King came down from the North to be the physician in the community. My mother's master, John Granberry, hired Mommer out to work for the new doctor for periods of one year. At the end of the first year I was born—a white baby wid a slave mother. I don't know how you going to write that, but it's just the same true.

My Master John Granberry was a bachelor. His parents died and left him a large plantation and about 250 slaves. He was a pretty good master; never worked his slaves very hard. He allowed them to hire themselves out and when they come home he got what he could out of them. No, he never bothered to collect their wages himself. In fact, our master allowed his slaves so much freedom that we were called free niggers by slaves on other plantations.

Yes there were overseers on the place, but they weren't particularly mean. If some slave was defiant, he got a whipping and that ended [it]. . . .

At the beginning of the Civil War when I was about four or five years old my mother with her two children came to Portsmouth to live. She was hired out to cook at a hotel. By that time my mother was married and I had a little brother. He is now a superannuated minister in Philadelphia. I can remember well something that

"Mrs. Virginia Hayes Shepherd, Interview May 18, 1937," Library of Virginia, Richmond. This document can also be found in Charles Perdue, et al., eds., *Weevils in the Wheat: Interviews with Virginia Ex-Slaves* (Indiana University Press, 1980).

happened when I was about seven. I guess it was in 1863, . . . the sheriff came to the hotel where Mommer was working and called for her. Master had sent him. My mother, my brother and I were taken to the jail and locked up for safe keeping. Times were critical, but the confederates still had hope that they would win.

At this jail there were hundreds of other mothers and their children sleeping on the floor at night just waiting their turn to be sold South. Each day some were sold off. Mother prayed we'd be spared. Finally our old Master sent for us to come back home and that saved us. No, I didn't mind the jail. There were lots of little children there playing around. My mother cried a lot and I remember I was too young to realize how serious conditions were—so you see I have been locked up in jail. . . .

Diana was a black beauty if there ever was one. She had this thin silk skin, a sharp nose, thin lips, a perfect set of white teeth and beautiful long cole-black hair. Diana was dignity personified, the prettiest black woman I ever saw.

Diana was the house maid for the Gaskins and lived right in the house with the family. This girl was old master Gaskins Diana. He had his wife and children, but he just wanted his Diana in every sense of the world [word?]. He was really master of all he surveyed. He made demands on Diana just the same as if she had been his wife. Of course she fought him, but he wanted her and he had her. He use to send Diana to the barn to shell corn. Soon he would follow. He tried to cage her in the barn so she couldn't get out. Once she got away from him, went to the house and told her mistress how Gaskins treated her. The mistress sympathized with the girl, but couldn't help her, because she was afraid of her own husband. He would beat her if she tried to meddle. Indeed he would pull her hair out. Once when Diana was successful in fighting him off, he bundled her up, put her in a cart, and took her to Norfolk and put her on the auction block. But Diana was the sharpest black woman you ever saw. Before she was taken to town, she slipped around to one of the neighboring plantations and begged the master to buy her. He agreed. When she was put on the block the biggest bidder got her, and she went to live right back to the same neighborhood. Ole Gaskins was sore, but he couldn't do nothing about it. . . .

E S S A Y S

In 1990, historian Thelma Jennings of Middle Tennessee State University published a ground-breaking study based on reminiscences of sexual exploitation found in the narratives of former slaves collected by the Works Progress Administration in the 1930s. Even though the female storytellers were elderly and had experienced slavery primarily in their childhoods, they vividly describe the special sexual burdens suffered by enslaved women. In 1992 the University of Washington's Shirley J. Yee studied the small group of free-born black women who became prominent promoters of abolition through their public lectures and writings. What points did they stress, and what special hurdles did they have to surmount because they were both black and female? she asks. In 2004, Loren Schweninger, who teaches at the University of North Carolina, Greensboro, examined another small but important group of African American women: free blacks in the South, most of them emancipated slaves. Such women, Schweninger movingly demonstrates, often valued their loyalty to husbands and children above their own freedom.

The Sexual Exploitation of African American Slave Women

THELMA JENNINGS

Because they were slaves, African American women were affected by the rule of the patriarch in more ways and to a greater degree than the white women in the Big House. The size of the food allotment, brutal whippings, slave sales, and numerous other variables influenced the bondwoman's view of the patriarchy. Yet because she was a woman, her view, like that of the white woman, was also gender related. . . . This essay will, therefore, deal only with the bondwomen's perspective from the viewpoint of gender, using twentieth-century interviews with female ex-slaves who were at least twelve or thirteen years of age at the time of emancipation. Of the 514 women in this category, 205, or almost forty percent, made comments of this nature. Undoubtedly, the reluctance of ex-bondwomen to discuss such private matters, especially with white men and women, accounts for the fact that the number was not larger. A sample of fifty-eight male slave interviews in the same category was made for comparison; twenty-seven, or 46.55 percent, made gender-related comments. Likewise, a sample of contemporary testimony for both women and men was used. Compared to the Works Progress Administration narratives, contemporary testimony offers a great deal less evidence of sexual exploitation. The men outnumber the women even more than in the WPA narratives.

Female bondage was more severe than male bondage because these women had to bear children and cope with sexual abuse in addition to doing the work assigned to them, work that was often similar in type and quantity to that of male slaves. When it was profitable to exploit women as if they were men in the work force, slaveholders regarded female slaves, in effect, as genderless. But when they could be exploited in ways designed only for women, they were exclusively female—subordinate and unequal to all men. Bondwomen realized the white patriarch had the *power* to force them to mate with whomever he chose, to reproduce or suffer the consequences, to limit the time spent with their children, and even to sell them and their children.

From the beginning of adolescence, females were subject to their master's desire for them to reproduce because increasing the number of slaves meant profits to him. Intervention in the process of procreation, either through subtle or forceful means, became an integral part of the sexual exploitation of bondwomen. Numerous women testified that all owners wanted slaves to have a goodly number of children. . . .

Generally speaking, slaveowners dictated the rules governing slave unions. Whether the woman was allowed to mate with a man who chose her or had one forced upon her by the master was crucial. Phobe Henderson vowed that her master had nothing to do with bringing Phobe and her husband together. She guessed that God did it since they fell in love. . . .Though Rose Williams' master treated his slaves well, he forced Rose to live with an African American against her desires. She always held this against him. Rose's master told her to live with Rufus, a man she considered

Thelma Jennings, " 'Us Colored Women Had To Go Through A Plenty': Sexual Exploitation of African-American Slave Women," from *Journal of Women's History* I (1990), pp. 45–66. Reprinted by permission of Indiana University Press.

a bully. At first, Rose resisted and went to her mistress who explained the master's wishes. "Yous am de portly gal and Rufus am de portly man," Missus told Rose. "De massa wants 'you-uns for to bring forth portly chillen." Rose remained adamant until her master told her, "Woman, I'se pay big money for yous an' I'se done dat fo' de cause I'se wants yous to raise me chilluns. I'se put you to live wid Rufus fo' dat pu'pose. Now if yous don't want to be whupped at the stake, yous do w'at I'se want." After the war, Rose never married. "One 'sperience am 'nough fo' dis nigger," she explained. "Aftah w'at I'se do fo' de Marster, I'se never want any truck wid any man." . . .

Interference with sexual activities in such a direct manner as in the case of Rose and Rufus constituted slave breeding by some slaveowners. Considerable controversy exists among historians on the nature and extent of slave breeding. . . . [Most] discussions of slave breeding are strictly economic in focus—an increase in *quantity* for *profits*. No mention is made of *quality* or the improvement of the species; there is no hint at the practice of eugenics. In his quantitative analysis of the slave narratives, Paul Escott briefly discusses the interference of masters with the sexual activities of slaves. He enumerates several different types of slave breeding: rewards to good breeders or sale of barren women, directed pairings often between "fine and stout" individuals, the use of stock men, and the elimination of "runty" males as fathers. Most of these types of slave breeding represent a crude form of eugenics. Though Escott cites a few examples in such cases, he does not include an explicit discussion of the eugenics of slave breeding. . . .

When we turn our attention to the female interviewees in this study, we note that only twenty-five (4.86 percent) commented on slave breeding as outlined by Escott. However, six of the fifty-eight male interviewees (10.34 percent) in the sample made such comments. Only one slave (male) in the contemporary sample noted slave breeding. What is quite significant is that six of the twenty-five women and four of the six men made remarks that specifically indicated "eugenic manipulation." . . .

Some bondwomen revealed bitter resentment in very frank, pathetic terms. Katie Darling said her master would pick out "a po'tly man and a po'tly gal" and just "put 'em together because what he wanted was the stock." Slave weddings on Annie Row's place were compared to "de weddin' 'tween de cows and de bull" because "dey wants bigger niggers an' dey mates to suits demse'ves." In discussing the mating of men and women on her plantation, Polly Shine said "this never suited us much but we had to do just like our Masers made us, as we could not do any other way." Refusals would only result in whippings and "mean" treatment. . . .

Slave breeding made it very difficult for couples to establish stable family relationships. Describing the cruelty of her master, Louisa Everett said he mated slaves indiscriminately without any regard for family unions. If the master thought a certain man and woman might have strong, healthy offspring, he forced them to have sexual relations even though they were married to other slaves. In case either one showed any reluctance, the master would make the couple consummate this relation in his presence. . . . On Mary Ingram's plantation, the master made the decision on who could and could not get married. "Him select de po'tly and p'lific women, and de po'tly man, and use sich for de breeder an' de father ob de women's chilluns." The women selected were not allowed to marry and "de womens have nothin' to says 'bout de'rangement." . . .

One thing that distinguished a "good master" from a bad one in the slaves' eyes was his attitude toward marriage. It is impossible to determine how many couples had their marriage solemnized "officially" by a preacher or the master himself or how many simply jumped the broom. It is clear, however, that bondwomen who had a big wedding with a minister spoke with pride of the event. Lou Williams recalled, "I'se had a 'spectable weddin' 'cause Miss she say I was her nursemaid. De preacher he reads and I was all dressed up in white clothes and sech a supper we never had." Lou claimed she had the best white folks in the state of Maryland. Tempie Durham, dressed in white, was married on the front porch of the Big House by the black preacher of the plantation church. Tempie also spoke highly of her master and mistress. When interviewed in her early nineties, Nancy King related that she was married in a church two miles off the place by a white preacher. Her owners were "good" to their slaves and "didn' disfigure" them as some were known to do. These examples and others in the narratives indicate that a respectable wedding by a minister, black or white, definitely affected an ex-bondwoman's view of the patriarch, who often was described as a "good" master. . . .

Whether for black or white, the importance of prenatal care was not well understood; and, for both, childbirth was a dangerous procedure. Slaveowners faced a conflict of interests. They deplored the loss of time granted to a pregnant field worker, yet they faced the possibility of the loss of both mother and child if she were forced to work too long and too hard. The two objectives, immediate profits and long-term economic considerations, therefore, clashed at times. In their eagerness for profits, most slaveowners apparently agreed with the Mississippi planter who declared that "labor is conducive to health; a healthy woman will rear most children." Though they were aware to some extent that very hard work was not beneficial, they placed the blame for the loss of slave babies on their mothers, who were often accused of smothering their infants. Slaveowners also sometimes blamed the pregnant bondwomen for miscarriages that increased during the cotton boom years. . . .

Overseers and drivers were responsible for much of the physical abuse of pregnant women, but masters were also guilty at times. Without some explanation, such abuse is incomprehensible. The basic reason—immediate profits—that accounts for long hours of overwork also explains the use of violent methods to achieve a productive work force. Masters often suspected bondwomen of shamming and feigning illness. They became impatient with the slower work of pregnant women. In their eagerness for a bumper crop, they were determined to discipline pregnant women, as well as other workers, who failed to do the work expected of them. Undoubtedly, the patriarchal desire to show authority also accounts for some of the physical abuse. Moreover, there was unfortunately a trace of sadism in some slaveowners, as well as overseers and drivers, which was directed against the weaker members of the slave community—pregnant women, children, and the elderly. Thwarted in their desires to discipline a strong male, these slaveowners punished the pregnant women who fell behind with their work. Driven by impulse, masters in a fit of anger also punished pregnant women without ever thinking of the dangerous consequences for them and their unborn children. . . .

Given the pressure to reproduce for the master's profit at a time when childbirth was dangerous and children could be sold at the master's whim, we can readily understand why bondwomen would have reason to practice birth control and abortion and to induce miscarriages. Such practices may be seen as a form of passive resistance, depriving owners of what they demanded from bondwomen. . . . Forced by her master to marry a man she hated, Mary Gaffney at first refused to let him touch her, but he told the master who then whipped Mary. That night, then, she let her husband have his way. "Maser was going to raise him a lot more slaves, but still I cheated Maser." Mary had no babies, and her owner wondered what was wrong. She said she chewed cotton roots and was careful not to let her master catch her. After freedom, Mary had five children. Anna Lee claimed that female slaves had started chewing cotton roots to keep from having babies. If slavery had lasted much longer, there would have been only old ones left as "we had done quit breeding." Another Texas woman said women could cause a miscarriage by taking calomel, turpentine, and indigo. . . .

Soon after giving birth, most slave mothers usually had to trust the care of their babies to someone else in order to return to the fields. From that time on, the contact they had with their children during the day was limited by the rule of the patriarch who did not consider their maternal needs and feelings, his primary motive being profit. In most cases, an old slave woman took care of the babies and small children. Larger plantations had nurseries and hospitals; smaller places used an old slave woman's house. Young slave girls also cared for the children. The image of patriarchal society with happy, contented slaves dims when we read the words of Elvira Boles, who had to work very hard. "Don' evvy thing but split rails. I've cut timber—evvy thing a man could do." But she hated to leave her baby when working. "I'd leave mah baby cryin' in the yard and I'd be cryin', but I couldn't stay." As Louisa Everett pointed out, slave women had no time for their own children. Sometimes they were further deprived of what little time they did have by being forced to care for white children. Rachel Sullivan told her interviewer that as a young girl she took care of some black children while their mother served as wet nurse for a white woman. What this slave woman must have felt one can only imagine. . . .

In all probability, slave infants and children did receive fairly good physical care as measured by the standards of the time. After all, it was in the owners' best interests to see that they developed into strong, healthy adults to be used as workers and breeders or to be sold. It must be noted that knowledge of such things as diet, sanitation, and medical treatment was very limited. House flies, for example, were a menace to the whites as well as the slaves. Moreover, owners often seemed more concerned about unborn children than pregnant women. The former represented future investment. For the highest return, the labor of pregnant women and nursing mothers should, however, be utilized in the present, while they were making their contribution to the future. This also explains why owners were careful in regulating nursing periods.

Bondwomen were not only forced to live with males of their own race but were also forced to have sexual relations with white men. . . . Of the 514 female slaves selected for this study, sixty-three, or 12.26 percent commented on interracial sex. Twenty-two of this number (35 percent) were directly involved; that is, their fathers were white men and/or they had given birth to one or more mulatto children. The number was probably much higher. Escott has shown that the sex and race of the interviewer influenced the frequency of all ex-slaves' revelations concerning miscegenation. It is reasonable to believe that some freedwomen were reticent, except with a black woman interviewer. According to both white and black sources, *forced* interracial sex was much more frequent than slave breeding. In only one instance did an interviewee state that some bondwomen were not forced. She told her Fisk University interviewer that "all the colored women didn't have to have white men, some did it because they wanted to and some were forced. They had a horror of going to Mississippi and they would do anything to keep from it."

Regardless of the number involved, the freedwomen clearly indicate, as did white women, that crossing the racial barrier was a source of discontent. The difference, however, was that the bondwomen were the victims. Only slave breeding could compare with forced interracial sex in the extent of pain and humiliation they caused. Although male slaves were subjected to forced sex as stock men, in the case of miscegenation, only the bondwomen could be subjected to the white man's passion. . . .

Thirty-six of the interviewees who commented on miscegenation, or 57 percent, noted that the master himself was guilty of interracial sex. . . . Moreover, nine of the sixty-three interviewees who commented on interracial sex claimed the master or his son as father (14.28 percent). None treated their paternity as unusual. Alice Marshall explained that her mother was "a very light woman who never got beat" and was "kinda favorite wid de white folks." When asked about her father, Alice replied, "Well, I reckon I oughter not to tell dat, but it ain' my shame. 'Twas ole massa. . . . He's my father. Chile, dat was ev'y day happenin's in dem days." . . . The master-father of Amy Patterson ran a kind of agency through which he collected slaves and yearly sold them to dealers or hired them out to other people. He promised Amy's mother he would never sell their mulatto child, but later he decided to sell all his slaves and move to another place. At first he refused to sell his daughter, but he finally sold Amy to her mother's new master because of the grief of mother and daughter. Amy's stinging remark, disguised as a question, was "when a father can sell his own child, humiliate his own daughter by auctioning her on the slave block, what good could be expected where such practices were allowed?" . . .

How could a white father ignore his own flesh and blood and even sell his offspring? The first reason is the ideology of race. Children with even a drop of African blood were not considered members of the white family. Only offspring of a man with his white wife were family and legitimate heirs to carry on his name. Moreover, some white men did not feel responsible for the mulatto children they fathered since, according to their justification, the black, promiscuous Jezebel had initiated the sexual relationship. Sex and race were further intertwined with capital. Slave offspring could increase the labor force or add money to the master's pockets if he sold them. . . .

Female bondage was not only different from male bondage, it was more severe as a result of sexual exploitation. Twentieth-century interviews and contemporary autobiographies of black women narrate sexual abuse and sufferings "peculiarly their own." Male slave testimony confirms the bondwomen's perspective. Throughout the South, slaveowners required bondwomen to reproduce for their profit in addition to working as long and often as hard as male slaves. The master's attitude, often insensitive and cavalier, was deeply disturbing on such matters as choice of mates, marriage, pregnancy, and child care. Some bondwomen were even subjected to breeding. Moreover, they knew they could become victims of the white man's sexual desires any time. Anne Firor Scott has described the resulting "widespread discontent" among white women; bondwomen responded in different ways, depending on temperament and circumstances. Most acquiesced in an effort to prevent themselves or family members from being beaten or sold. Others reacted violently but with little success, which caused greater pain, such as whippings and sale. Many of them seethed with resentment and bitterness, which perhaps they passed on to their children. Undoubtedly, they experienced both mental anguish and physical pain as a result of the selfish desires of the white patriarch, but they just went "on hopin' that things" wouldn't "be that way always."

Free Black Women in the Abolitionist Movement

SHIRLEY J. YEE

For a number of black women, commitment to the movement for racial equality led to participation in activities that challenged nineteenth-century notions of acceptable behavior for women and blacks. When women wrote antislavery poetry and prose, spoke from public platforms, or signed and circulated petitions condemning slavery and northern racism, they defied customary codes of behavior. In the process, they, as individuals and as a group, reconstructed notions of respectability within the free black community regarding black female activism. . . .

With the exception of Sojourner Truth and Ellen Craft, many of the leading black women who engaged in public speaking and writing shared a common background. Margaretta Forten, Sarah Forten, Maria Miller Stewart, Frances Harper, Mary Ann Shadd Cary, and Sarah P. Remond had all been born into free black families in which they enjoyed some measure of economic privilege and formal education. Their background of education, relative economic comfort, and family activism set them apart from both slaves and the majority of free blacks. Their personal and professional connections with abolitionist friends, in addition to their own talents, undoubtedly helped them gain access to abolitionist newspapers and the public platform.

Public speaking and writing had long been acceptable ways for men to engage in intellectual self-expression, but not until the 1840s had women, white or black, begun in any numbers to break the custom barring them from such activities. . . . Proclaiming the evils of slavery and the possibility of racial equality, on the antislavery lecture circuit, was risky for anyone. Like abolitionist writers and editors, who faced the destruction of their presses and physical violence at the hands of anti-abolitionist mobs, antislavery lecturers risked their personal safety in their travels. Black women speakers, like other abolitionist men and women, were often at the mercy of hostile audiences who harassed them physically as well as verbally. . . . Violence on the lecture tours was an even greater threat for black women than for black men and white abolitionists. Physical and verbal attacks against black women activists could originate at any time or place from crowds motivated by three sources of hostility: anti-black feelings, anti-abolitionist sentiments, and hatred of "public" women. Unlike male abolitionists, women who spoke in public invited criticism from audiences who believed they had violated basic ideals of "proper" behavior for women.

Shirley J. Yee, "Breaking Customs," in *Black Women Abolitionists: A Study in Activism, 1828–1860* (Knoxville: University of Tennessee Press, 1992), 112–135. Reprinted by permission of the University of Tennessee Press.

Although black women enjoyed support from the men of their race for their writings and, eventually, for their speeches, they still found themselves bound by codes of proper behavior for women. As in the white community, social custom in the free black community still required women to act like "ladies." Black male leaders applauded black women speakers only so long as they did not criticize black men directly or assume a position of authority in gatherings where men were present. The period between 1830 and the 1860s was one in which female public speakers gradually gained acceptance from both abolitionist leaders and their audiences. . . .

Public speaking, more than any other abolitionist activity, seemed to spark the greatest conflict between the sexes. Public opinion was slow to accept female lecturers, regardless of race, because public speaking was an activity in which an individual assumed a role of authority long the domain of political leaders and a predominantly male clergy and forbidden to women by social and religious custom. Much of the criticism of women who spoke in public came from clergymen, who consistently condemned this form of activism as not only improper for respectable women but also in violation of St. Paul's biblical order for women to "keep silent." . . .

During the 1820s and 1830s, a number of influential black men also made strong objections to female lecturers. . . . Black male audiences were especially hostile when women speakers publicly criticized the behavior of black men. In 1831 in Boston, an audience of black men jeered and threw rotten tomatoes at Maria Miller Stewart when she delivered an address to black men that criticized them for failing to follow basic Christian principles of thrift, sobriety, and hard work. . . .

Abolitionists such as Frederick Douglass and Charles Lenox Remond, who gave wholehearted support to female lecturers, perceived the situation a bit differently. They put aside such notions of sex roles for the moment and saw these women as assets to the campaign to promote race pride, as well as a source of public opposition to slavery and racism. By the 1840s and 1850s, many male leaders argued that black women speakers . . . occupied an important place in the abolitionist movement. . . . The appeal to race pride, in particular, helped to justify black women's participation in public activities and made it more acceptable for black women than for white women to engage in non-traditional activities such as public speaking. Mary Ann Shadd Cary, for example, received praise from black colleagues for her speaking efforts. Her coeditors of the *Provincial Freeman* portrayed her in 1856 as a positive representative of the free black community: "Remember, that they [blacks] belong to a class denied all social and political rights, and after they had been listened to, will the people say they are inferior to ANY of the lecturers among white fellow citizens? O' why will the people not be just?"

The fact that many black female speakers delivered effective lectures also helped make them more acceptable to their audiences. Black and white observers could not deny that many of the black women who gained prominence as speakers were actually talented orators who often expressed ideas that intrigued their audiences. . . . Finally, the fact that black women speakers exuded "feminine qualities" when they spoke from the public platform undoubtedly helped make them more acceptable to their audiences. William Still once described Frances Harper as "gentle," as well as an "earnest, eloquent, and talented heroine." When Shadd Cary delivered an address at Elkhorn, Indiana, in 1856, one observer praised not only the content of her speech, but the manner of its delivery, which was termed "modest, and in strict keeping with the popular notions of the 'sphere of women.'" . . .

Both black and white women also challenged contemporary codes of appropriate behavior for women through the act of writing. White women writers found themselves limited primarily by gender expectations: they found a large, receptive audience only when they wrote on "feminine" subjects, such as female piety and domesticity, and only so long as they were not aggressive or political. Even within these bounds, however, the success of white women writers such as Catharine Maria Sedgewick and Lydia H. Sigourney led competition with male writers in the already crowded literary marketplace. To defend such obvious intrusion into a male domain, many white women writers felt obliged to argue that their writing would not lead them away from their homes and domestic duties.

Black women writers struggled not only with contemporary views on women's "sphere" but with barriers of race. For them, the act of writing challenged prevailing stereotypes of black female intellectual inferiority, even though they were following in a tradition first charted by writers such as Lucy Terry and Phillis Wheatley, who had established writing as a form of black female expression during the mid-eighteenth century. Between 1830 and 1865, Sarah Forten, Margaretta Forten, Frances Harper, and Mary Ann Shadd Cary all continued to write, within the context of protest.

Race prejudice usually prevented black women from getting their works published. Lucy Terry's poem, "Bar's Fight," for example, was not published until 1895, though it had been written in 1746. During the antebellum period, black women poets and essayists were able to publish their works only with the aid of prominent abolitionists, and they gained the most public attention when they wrote for abolitionist audiences. Lydia Maria Child, Garrison, and Still, for example, helped several black women writers publish collections of poetry and essays.

Readers often praised the women and their works as shining examples of black progress, which refuted racist stereotypes. . . . Mary Ann Shadd Cary, the first black female newspaper editor, also received praise for providing a vehicle for black voices and for expanding the role of black women in the movement. Shadd was well aware of the significance her position held for black women, and even congratulated herself for setting a precedent: "To colored women, we have a work—we have 'broken the Editorial ice' . . . for your class in America; so go on editing, as you are ready." H. T. Williams, a black male abolitionist, commended Shadd for breaking the gender barrier in publishing: "Although this routine of business for a female looks masculine, in the eyes of some, and is sneered at by the same class . . . yet it is creditable and praiseworthy, and never fails to produce a salutary effect. If Miss Shadd has gained any new plumes to her wreath, she is fully deserving of them, for her intrinsic value is not half known, nor appreciated by the people she has so faithfully served."

Several common themes emerge from Black women's oral and written work: the sexual exploitation of slave women by white men and the impact of slavery on slave mothers, the hope for creating an alliance between black and white women, and the need for black community improvement. An examination of their speeches and writings reveals the particular contribution they made to abolitionist thought and rhetoric. Sarah Forten, Frances Harper, Sarah Remond, and Sojourner Truth described the harshness of slavery; though only Truth had actually been a slave, even the free-born women related vivid descriptions of the black woman's experience under slavery. They probably gained their knowledge of slavery from contacts with fugitive slaves that can be traced to their families' involvement in the Underground Railroad and their connections with prominent abolitionists. In Sarah Forten's poem. "Grave of the Slave," she suggests that death might be preferable to life in bondage:

> Poor slave! shall we sorrow that death was thy friend!
> The last and the kindest that Heaven could send:—
> The grave to the weary is welcome and blest;
> And death to the captive is freedom and rest.

Harper, Remond, and Truth argued that slavery was especially difficult for slave mothers, who often saw their children sold away from them, and their writings examined the breakup of the slave family and the sexual exploitation of slave women. . . . By emphasizing the experience of motherhood, perhaps Harper and Truth hoped to appeal to white women and to create a common bond between all women abolitionists and slave women. Black women writers and speakers, when addressing the public, often promoted the idea of a cross-racial "sisterhood," even though they knew that racism existed openly within the movement as well as in society at large. The writings of Sarah Forten reflect this effort to emphasize the shared experiences of women of both races. . . .

Another topic of much concern to black women writers and speakers was the encouragement of free black men and women to participate in community-improvement activities. Not all audiences, of course, appreciated this advice, as Maria Stewart discovered more than twenty years earlier when she attempted to advise black men on "proper" conduct. Like other reformers of her generation, Stewart promoted middle-class values of thrift, sobriety, and hard work, and argued against gambling and dancing, which she believed undermined efforts to achieve black self-sufficiency: "I would implore our men, and especially our rising youth, to flee from the gambling board and the dance-hall; for we are poor, and have no money to throw away." Contemporary newspapers note that her advice met with hostility.

Stewart also argued that improved education in the free black community would help end racial prejudice by convincing whites of the "moral worth and intellectual improvement" of blacks. During the early 1830s, Stewart predicted that "prejudice would gradually diminish, and the whites would be compelled to say— Unloose those fetters! Though Black their skins as shades of night, Their hearts are—pure—their souls are white." Using widely accepted Christian imagery in her arguments, Stewart, like most thinkers of her time, referred to sin as black and righteousness as white.

Nearly a generation later, Frances Harper maintained that education in "virtue and morality" as well as in practical skills was necessary for improving the condition of free blacks and would result in their reception "as citizens, not worse than strangers." She added that material wealth among free blacks, though important for improving the community, entailed a special responsibility to the slave. In an essay submitted to the *Anglo-African Magazine* in May 1859, Harper urged blacks to use their time and money to support the movement to end slavery: "We have money among us, but how much of it is spent to bring deliverance to our captive brethren? Are our wealthiest men the most liberal sustainers of the Anti-slavery enterprise? Or does the bare fact of our having money, really help mould public opinion and reverse its sentiments?"

Although these writers and lecturers often received praise from black male abolitionists, social custom within the black community still required them to act like "respectable ladies." The career of Mary Ann Shadd and her tumultuous relationship with Henry Bibb suggests that as late as the 1850s such ideas prevailed, even when black male leadership supported female public activism. The feud between Shadd and Henry Bibb over "caste" schools and the Refugee Home Society contributed to Shadd's decision to establish her own abolitionist newspaper, symbolic of the rift between them. Her newspaper, the *Provincial Freeman,* published articles on a variety of subjects, including anti-colonization, emigration, slavery, self-help, and moral improvement. The project, however, was more than simply a vehicle for opposing the Bibbs; it was intended in part to open the way for black women who desired careers in editing and publishing. White abolitionist women, such as Elizabeth Chandler and Lydia Maria Child, already had broken the white gender barrier in newspaper editing. Shadd's claim that she had "broken the Editorial Ice" for the women of her race reveals that she clearly identified herself with her female readers, whom she urged to pursue careers in writing and publishing.

Shadd's plainspoken and direct style contrasted markedly with the eloquent poetry and prose of Sarah Forten and Frances Harper. Shadd never hesitated to criticize persons and institutions she considered harmful to herself, to the antislavery cause, or to the progress of the free black community. For example, she attacked churches in Canada and the United States for allegedly supporting slavery, arguing that the "American church is the pillar of American slavery." In 1856, she expressed disdain for Frederick Douglass in an article for the *Provincial Freeman:* "Having been permitted so long to remain in our tub, we would rather that the great Frederick Douglass, for whose public career we have the most profound pity, would stay out of our sunlight." In the same issue, she despaired that a number of leading white and black abolitionists (including, in her opinion, Douglass) could still support colonization. . . .

Black women abolitionists' use of the pen and the public platform to articulate their opinions demonstrated an individual independence and a willingness to challenge prevailing expectations of gender and race. The act of public speaking and writing among black women, by defying racist expectations of black docility and intellectual inferiority, led black male leaders as well as many white abolitionists to accept black women writers and speakers as symbols of black success and resistance. Unlike white women, they could be perceived as assets to both the black community and the abolitionist movement. Their writings and speeches, as explicit forms of black protest and self-expression, provided fuel for abolitionist propaganda even as they continued a tradition of writing established by black female authors a century earlier. For black women, public speaking gradually became socially acceptable, as long as they stopped short of direct criticism of black men or challenges to male authority.

Male and female abolitionists of both races had frequently used the petition as a way to protest slavery and race discrimination in the "nominally free states." They flooded Congress and their state legislatures with antislavery petitions throughout the antebellum period, demanding the end of slavery and race discrimination in the District of Columbia and the United States. The onslaught of petitions so incensed

southern congressmen that they succeeded in passing a gag rule, which, until its repeal in December 1844, tabled any discussion of slavery on the floor of the House.

For women and black men, however, the petition was more than an abolitionist
tactic. Political disfranchisement was a condition they shared until 1869, when the
passage of the Fifteenth Amendment left women as the only adult group without
the right to vote. Although anyone could circulate and sign a petition, this form of
political expression reflected their exclusion from the American political system. For
disfranchised groups—but not, of course, for white men, who had the right to vote—
the petition was the only legal means to make their voices heard and seek changes
in the law. In 1840, several white male abolitionists formed an antislavery political
party in hopes of overthrowing the "Slave Power" in Congress. For women and most
black men, who could not vote, the formation of political parties held little meaning.
A contributor to the *Colored American,* known only as "A Friend," expressed support
for women's involvement in petition drives: "I think as they are identified with us in
our sufferings. . . . [T]hey are the aggrieved with us, and being aggrieved with us certainly ought to have the right to petition also to have these grievances removed."

Many male observers considered women's participation in petitioning campaigns an improper intrusion into a traditionally male domain. One defender of
female petitioners described some of these criticisms: "The New York Sun is very
severe upon the 'Eastern women' who are getting up petitions against the admission of Texas [as a slave state], and thinks they had better be shaking bed ticks rather
than politics." Supporters of women petitioners combined ideas of women's "nature"
and patriotism as justification for participation in a political activity. . . . Supporters
also argued that these women were merely following in the patriotic traditions of
their foremothers in the War for Independence. . . .

Female antislavery societies and activist groups within the black community
provided black women with opportunities to participate in abolitionist petition drives.
Between 1834 and 1850, for example, the members of the Philadelphia Female Anti-
Slavery Society sent petitions to the state legislature of Pennsylvania and to Congress, demanding the end of slavery. To Congress, they wrote: "The undersigned
respectfully ask that you will . . . abolish everything in the Constitution or Laws of
the U.S. which in any manner sanctions or sustains slavery." In the society's 1836
annual report, members wrote of their commitment to petitioning:

> Since the year 1834, we have annually memorialized Congress, praying for the abolition
> of slavery in the District of Columbia and the Territories of the United States. We are fre-
> quently asked what good have petitions done: The full amount of good produced by them,
> is yet to be revealed. . . . We knew that our petitions were not ineffectual, when the wise men
> of the South, sent back to us the cry, "Impertinent intermeddlers! incorrect devils! &c."

Black women members of the society frequently served on committees to coordinate
petition drives in the Philadelphia area. Committee members drew up detailed maps
of the city and assigned individuals and groups of women to cover specific neighborhoods. In 1835, for example, Sarah Forten and Hetty Burr were the two black members appointed to a committee to "obtain signatures to a petition to Congress."

In Boston, members of the Female Anti-Slavery Society also signed and circulated petitions. In 1837, Maria Weston Chapman, representing the society, coordinated
women's petitions protesting the annexation of Texas as a slave state. In addition to

petitioning against slavery, members also circulated petitions protesting race discrimination against free blacks. Black and white abolitionists petitioned, in particular,
against discrimination on railroads, racial segregation in public schools, and the state
marriage law, which outlawed interracial marriages.

In 1839, black members Susan Paul, Eunice R. Davis, Lavinia Hilton, Chloe Lee,
Jane Putnam, and Julia Williams joined with the other "undersigned women of
Boston," in submitting a petition to the Massachusetts legislature denouncing the law
that forbade interracial marriage. This protest revealed a radical side to the predominantly white, middle-class group. It has been argued that the movement to abolish
the marriage law, which was repealed in 1843, was primarily the result of white
initiative, because blacks, recognizing the sensitivity of the issue, approached it
cautiously. Additional evidence, however, indicates that although the movement for
repeal had been a pet project for white abolitionists since the emergence of Garrison,
the black community may also have felt strongly; in February 1843, a group of
"Colored Citizens of Boston" met to draw up resolutions supporting *The Liberator,*
and denouncing the state marriage laws and race discrimination on railroads. The
group agreed to circulate these resolutions within the black community in Boston,
and antislavery-society member Eunice R. Davis was one of three black women
appointed to a committee to obtain signatures for the petitions. . . .

Although they failed to convince Congress to abolish slavery and prevent its extension into the territories of the Southwest, black and white petitioners did succeed
in obtaining repeal of some discriminatory laws on the state and local levels. For black
women, petitioning served as a way both to protest slavery and race discrimination
and to participate in a political system that excluded them from full citizenship on the
basis of race and sex.

Petitioning provided black women with their only opportunity to appear to
the state and federal governments for the end of slavery and race discrimination. Like
writing and speaking, it was a way to make their voices heard in a society in which
they, as blacks and as women, had been expected to keep silent. The public work that
many women performed for the sake of abolition, however, quickly raised questions
about the "proper" role of women in public reform. For black women abolitionists,
this "woman question" held important implications for the black abolitionist agenda,
because women's rights would, in some ways, directly contradict black goals for the
creation of a truly free community.

Free Women of Color in the South

LOREN SCHWENINGER

In 1813 Lucinda, a free woman of color; petitioned the Virginia General Assembly
for relief. Following her owner's death, she explained, she and a number of other
slaves had been manumitted by the owner's last will and testament. According to the
will, they were required to leave the state. Their owner knew that if they remained in

---

Loren Schweninger, "The Fragile Nature of Freedom: Free Women of Color in the U.S. South," in
David Barry Gaspar and Darlene Clark Hiue eds., *Beyond Bondage: Free Women of Color in the Americas*
(University of Illinois Press, 2004), 107–116. Copyright © 2004 by Board of Trustees of the University
of Illinois. Used with permission of the University of Illinois Press.

Virginia they would be returned to slavery under an 1806 statute that required freed slaves to emigrate from the state within a year or be reenslaved. "[A]ll the slaves so emancipated (except your petitioner) were removed this year to the State of Tennessee," Lucinda wrote, "but your petitioner declined going with them, as she had a husband belonging to Capt. William H. Hooe in King George county, from whom the benefits and privileges to be derived from freedom, dear and flattering as they are, could not induce her to be separated." The question for Lucinda was not whether she was willing to sacrifice her freedom for her "marriage" but rather who would become her new owner. She feared being sold to someone who might "remove her to a place remote from the residence of her husband." She therefore asked the Virginia General Assembly to allow her to become a slave of her husband's owner. . . .

Other free women of color in the U.S. South shared Lucinda's dilemma during the late eighteenth century and the first six decades of the nineteenth century. They, too, confronted increasingly hostile and restrictive laws and faced wrenching decisions about their families as they struggled against economic, political, and legal barriers. Laws varied from state to state, but by the 1820s most states in the Upper South required manumitted slaves to emigrate or face a return to slavery; most in the Lower South prohibited manumission altogether except by a special act of the legislature. Lawmakers also passed codes to restrict the movement of free blacks, prohibiting them from assembling with slaves and requiring them to carry proof of their status ("freedom papers") on their persons at all times. How free black women (in this essay a term used interchangeably with "free women of color") responded to these restrictions reveals a great deal about their tenuous status in southern society, the brittle nature of freedom, and how far some of them were willing to go in order to maintain the integrity of their families.

With a few exceptions, historians have neglected the plight of free women of color in the U.S. South. Although devoting substantial attention to slave women, including their work routines, family and household structure, relationships with whites, and other dimensions of slave life, scholars have not examined the women who attained freedom with the same intensity. This essay explores the difficulties free women of color confronted as they struggled as wives and mothers to preserve their family relationships. It does so by using a primary source that scholars have largely ignored: petitions to southern legislatures. Although relatively few in number, these legislative petitions articulate the values, attitudes, and mores of free black women, individually and collectively, as they lived out their lives a few steps away from being returned to bondage.

During the period from the American Revolution to the Civil War, free women of color occupied a unique place in southern society. They were manumitted in greater numbers than their male counterparts, they represented a larger portion of the free black population, and they controlled a significant percentage of the black wealth. Their freedom came more readily because white men who took slave women as sexual partners sometimes provided them with deeds of manumission. As a result, in most communities they outnumbered free men of color. That was especially true in towns and cities where free blacks tended to congregate. For a variety of reasons—selective manumission, high male morality, and large female slave populations—women dominated the urban free black population. By 1860, in towns and cities with 2,500 or more inhabitants, they constituted 57 percent of the free black population; in the largest cities with populations of ten thousand or more they constituted 58.5 percent.

In towns and cities, most free black women worked as laundresses, maids, seam-stresses, cooks, midwives, venders, and servants. In a few cases they managed small businesses, including hairdressing shops, confectioneries, bakeries, coffee houses, and boardinghouses. . . . Such enterprises, however, were unusual and tended to be more numerous in cities of the Lower South, especially New Orleans, where white men offered assistance to a few free black women. In most cities the vast majority of free black women found employment at the bottom of the economic ladder.

Despite their low occupational status, free women of color gradually acquired small amounts of property. During the early nineteenth century, when many among them had only recently emerged from slavery, the number who owned property re-mained tiny. Following 1830, however, the number of black female property-owners increased rapidly. In 1830 in Petersburg, Virginia, a typical small town in the Upper South, only seven black females owned lots (compared with sixteen black men); by 1860, the number of black women who owned real estate had risen to ninety-two, nearly 40 percent of the black realty-owners. As in others towns, most of their hold-ings were valued at only a few hundred dollars, but by the eve of the Civil War free black women owned 22 percent of the total wealth controlled by free blacks in the region. Although there were significant differences in average holdings between the Upper and Lower South, that large proportion pointed to the independent role of free women of color. It also suggested that some women controlled property for both themselves and their slave husbands.

Among the most difficult problems confronting free women of color was how to maintain their families. Women manumitted late in life, or who, as slaves, had started a family, or who married slave men, often found themselves confronting wrenching personal decisions regarding themselves and their loved ones. It is impossible to know exactly how many free black women faced such situations, but it is clear that a significant proportion of them remained closely tied to slaves and thus constantly faced possible separation from their spouses and/or children. It is true that in the Lower South small enclaves of prosperous free people of color intermarried and sep-arated themselves as much as possible from other free blacks and slaves. Many of them owned slaves for commercial purposes. But they were not the norm, even in the lower states. Free blacks and slaves came together in the workplace, in church, at social gatherings, and in marriage. Indeed, with the relatively small number of avail-able free black men, free women of color were often left with few alternatives except to "marry" slaves.

One way for free women of color to obtain marital stability was to purchase husbands out of slavery. Except in Georgia, there were no legal barriers to such a purchase. In most cases, however, costs were prohibitive, and even when enough money could be saved, or paid out over a period of years, the final transaction de-pended on the willingness of slave-owners to part with their property. And even when full payment was made, the owner could renege and sell the man if no legal agreement had been signed. Even if there were such an agreement, contracts between blacks and whites were sometimes not upheld in the courts.

If everything went smoothly, women then faced the problem of freeing their hus-bands by deed or legislative act. Doing so presented additional obstacles because state laws either made it difficult, at times virtually impossible, to manumit slaves or required freed slaves to emigrate. . . . During the 1790s Madelene St. Rigue of North Carolina arranged to purchase her husband, Major, from his owner, a man who lived in Edenton; she paid the final amount in 1801 and then petitioned the Assembly for his freedom. The General Assembly did not pass an act, but at the bottom of the docket page of her petition the word "granted" was written.

The ambiguous result of Madelene St. Rigue's petition symbolized the difficulties free women of color confronted in seeking redress from state legislatures. Those who were successful usually presented strong arguments about how they had saved to purchase loved ones over many years, or they showed that their husbands as slaves had always been industrious, hard-working, and obedient. Even then, depending on the political climate or the level of fear among whites concerning slave unrest, forcefully argued and well-reasoned petitions might be rejected. . . . [S]uccessful petitions occurred primarily during the late eighteenth and early nineteenth centuries. By the 1830s and 1840s, as sectional conflict intensified, it was highly unusual for free women of color to receive favorable consideration from state legislatures.

Most freedwomen, of course, did not possess the financial resources to purchase their husbands. If during the early nineteenth century it was very difficult to save the purchase price, as time passed it became virtually impossible. The price of a young male salve in 1800 ranged from $350 in Richmond to $500 in New Orleans; by 1837 the prices in those two cities rose to $900 and $1,300, respectively, and by 1856 to $1,300 and $1,500. Unable to buy their slave husbands, women who remained in a state longer than the law allowed following their emancipation petitioned legislatures to remain with them. . . .

It was not only husbands that free women of color sought to protect but also children. . . . In Virginia during the early 1800s, Jenny Parker, even as a slave, assisted her children in obtaining their freedom. When, as an old woman, she finally acquired her own freedom, one of her children owned real estate and had purchased two of Parker's other children. Most women who succeeded in freeing their children did so after many years of struggle.

When it was not feasible to manumit children, mothers made every effort to avoid separation. Sometimes that was not possible because owners refused to release children from bondage, or traded them to neighbors, or sold them to distant markets. Even when slave-owners were amenable to assisting mothers, restrictive laws made it difficult to remain with offspring. Texas free black Fanny McFarland was manumitted by the last will and testament of her owner in 1835 for "long and faithful services." She acquired some "little property," she said, but was required by law to leave the state. Her four children, however, were slaves. She had neither the means nor the time to purchase them out of bondage. Leaving them would be a fate worse than death she confessed. She simply could not bear the thought of spending the "few remaining days of her life" without her children.

Even when a mother and children obtained freedom, it was difficult to leave family members and friends. One Virginia woman explained that traveling to an unknown land, "in the midst of Strangers, cut off from the society & aid of relations & friends," would be unbearable. "Tis with anxious and trembling forebodings then that Your Petitioner presents herself before the Legislature," Elvira Jones of Richmond, Virginia, said in her 1823 petition, "to supplicate of their liberality and clemency, permission to herself and children to live and die in the Land of their nativity." She explained that she had purchased herself and her two children, Julie Ann and William. . . .

Only a small proportion of the women who sought to protect their families by petitioning legislatures succeeded. As the years passed, especially following the Denmark Vesey slave conspiracy in South Carolina in 1822 and the Nat Turner slave revolt in Virginia in 1831, petitioners confronted increasingly hostile anti-free black laws and attitudes. Most states passed new comprehensive slave codes, and many slave-owners argued that free blacks provided a bad example for slaves. . . .

As onerous as these attitudes and statutes were for free women of color, even more so was the determination of some whites to push them back into slavery. Indeed, many lived in constant fear that some "ill disposed person or persons" would return them to slavery. . . . They not only feared for themselves but also for their loved ones. What calamity could be worse, one mother agonized, than having children "taken up and sold." She could not think about it without terror in her heart. During the 1820s and 1830s, as slave prices rose in the Deep South, free black women in the upper states remained constantly on guard to fend off slave traders or kidnappers who might sell them as slaves to plantation owners in the lower Mississippi river valley. . . .

The contradictions in the lives of free women of color were perhaps nowhere more evident than in their relationships with whites. During the nineteenth century, South Carolina, Georgia, Florida, and Alabama enacted guardianship laws that required free blacks to obtain white guardians in much the same manner as parentless or propertied children would secure patrons to handle their legal affairs. No specific laws were passed in the upper states, but free blacks were often forced to secure white "protectors," people in the community who then would vouch for their good character. Free women of color who lived alone or with their children sometimes paid a heavy price for such "protection." They could be forced into an unwanted sexual relationship with their "protectors"; they could also be forced to work without pay to gain the good graces of a white family; and, whatever their feelings, they were obliged to act deferentially and humbly before whites. Free colored women fully realized that defiant or aggressive behavior might spell disaster.

Nonetheless, many free black women relied on whites to assist them in finding suitable employment and protect them in times of racial unrest. . . . In other cases, too, white men described free black women as honest, industrious, dependable, and loyal. . . . Similar "certificates" said that black women were orderly, submissive, and trustworthy. Such recommendations meant the difference between employment and joblessness, family unity and separation, and sustenance and impoverishment. . . .

Besides their efforts to assist their husbands and protect their children, free black women occasionally approached state legislatures about other matters, usually in unison with free black men. In 1825 a group of black women (and men) in Charleston, South Carolina, complained about a new tax placed on individuals who owned or rented houses "inhabited by negroes or persons of color" or who worked as mechanics (as did a number of free people of color in the city). The tax, $10 a year, was designed to help defray the cost of the municipal guard, which spent so much time seeking to control the black population. The women argued that the tax was unfair, unjust, and inequitable; it was tantamount to leveling a surcharge on black property owners and mechanics. . . . In another case of 1823, a group of free women of color in Richmond, Virginia, along with their husbands and others, petitioned the legislature for permission to erect a Baptist African Church. "It has been the misfortune of your petitioners to be excluded from the churches, meeting Houses and other places of public devotion which are used by white persons," they explained. As a result, they were "compelled to look to private Houses, where they are much crowded and where a portion of the Brethren are unable to hear or to partake of the worship which is going on." Thus, they sought to build their own church. They promised that its preachers would be fully acceptable to city fathers and that they would never hold night services. This fervent plea, like the request for tax relief in Charleston in 1825 . . . was ignored. Nonetheless, as these cases show, free women and men of color presented arguments to the highest legislative tribunals in South Carolina and Virginia during the 1820s and 1830s.

Free black women faced many obstacles in their attempts to seek legislative redress. Those who sat in judgment over their petitioners were often unsympathetic slaveholders. Indeed, a substantial number of legislators wished to expel free blacks from the South, "return" them to West Africa, or, during the 1850s, reduce them to slavery. The women also faced a legislative process that was cumbersome. Petitions were read to the house or senate, sent to committee, returned to the floor, and voted up or down; at any time the requests might be tabled, amended, or rejected. In addition, illiterate women were dependent on whites to articulate their views and formulate their arguments. Although that was sometimes ably done, at other times whites who offered assistance knew little about the law or how to plead a case. Thus, in the midst of a society in which many whites sought to stifle free black aspirations, free women of color presented their pleas nevertheless. It is little wonder, then, that they usually failed and that their pleas to secure "justice" for themselves and their loved ones went unheeded. It is surprising indeed that they continued to seek redress through state legislatures.

A few free women of color gave up the struggle and opted to return to slavery, a route that only a handful among the tens of thousands of free black women in the South chose. Most, unlike Lucinda in Virginia in 1813, did so on the eve of the Civil War, when some whites were arguing that all free people of color should be reenslaved. Fear, anxiety, economic hardship, and the suffering of children prompted most of them to seek out whites who would agree to become their owners. . . .

In some ways the pleas of free women of color were similar to those of free black men who tried to protect spouses, obtain freedom for family members, and remain within a state. Indeed, in a few cases, women joined with men to request some basic rights. Yet free women of color confronted particular burdens, especially with regard to protecting their children. Most of their petitions, like the ones by Lucinda in Virginia in 1813 and Lucy Andrews in South Carolina in 1858, were rejected, but the petitions themselves remain valuable documents because they reveal a great deal about the difficulties free women of color faced in seeking to maintain family stability in the midst of the oppositional forces of slave society. During the decades from the 1780s to the eve of the Civil War, free black women of the U.S. South struggled to sustain themselves and protect their husbands and children against onerous laws and the unsympathetic attitudes of most whites. That some would choose slavery over freedom rather than relinquish their ties with loved ones who remained in slavery bears witness to their deep commitment to family stability and to the fragile nature of freedom in the U.S. South.

◈ *F U R T H E R   R E A D I N G*

Bynum, Victoria. *Unruly Women: The Politics of Social and Sexual Control in the Old South* (1992).

Camp, Stephanie M. H. *Closer to Freedom: Enslaved Women and Everyday Resistance in the Plantation South* (2004).

Fox-Genovese, Elizabeth. *Within the Plantation Household: Black and White Women of the Old South* (1988).

Frankel, Noralee. *Freedom's Women: Black Women and Families in Civil War Era Mississippi* (2000).

Horton, James O. "Freedom's Yoke: Gender Conventions among Antebellum Free Blacks," *Feminist Studies* 12 (Spring 1986): 51–76.

Lebsock, Suzanne. *The Free Women of Petersburg: Status and Culture in a Southern Town, 1784–1860* (1984).

McMillen, Sally. *Southern Women: Black and White in the Old South* (1991).

Morton, Patricia, ed. *Discovering the Women in Slavery: Emancipating Perspectives on the American Past* (1996).

Perrin, Liese. "Resisting Reproduction: Reconsidering Slave Contraception in the Old South," *Journal of American Studies* 35 (2001): 255–274.

Schaefer, Judith K. " 'Open and Notorious Concubinage': The Emancipation of Slave Mistresses by Will and the Supreme Court in Antebellum Louisiana," *Louisiana History* 28 (1987): 165–182.

Schweninger, Loren. "Property Owning Free African-American Women in the South, 1800–1870," *Journal of Women's History* 1, no. 3 (1989–1990): 13–44.

Tate, Gayle T. *Unknown Tongues: Black Women's Political Activism in the Antebellum Era, 1830–1860* (2003).

Weiner, Marli. *Mistresses and Slaves: Plantation Women in South Carolina, 1830–1880* (1998).

White, Deborah Gray. *Arn't I a Woman? Female Slaves in the Plantation South* (1985).

Yellin, Jean Fagan, and John C. Van Horne, eds. *The Abolitionist Sisterhood: Women's Political Culture in Antebellum America* (1994).

CHAPTER
8

White Women in the

Civil War Crisis

In the United States, the Civil War is frequently described as a conflict of "brother against brother." Recent scholarship and the publication of many women's wartime diaries and letters in the last decade suggest that it might also be called a struggle of "sister against sister." Union and Confederate women recorded in their private and public writings their attachment to the causes of their respective sections and their contempt for each other.

After years of surprising neglect, the experience of women in the Civil War has finally become the subject of intense scholarly study. Historians have begun the process of exploring the impact of the war on the women of both sides, and they have found significant differences. Whereas wartime privations and the ultimate Confederate defeat helped to leave southern white women in conditions that emphasized resistance to change after the war, the Union victory and northern white women's pride in their role therein gave them confidence in their organizational abilities and inspired lasting patriotic sentiments. The differences were so profound that some have argued that the disparate impact of the war on northern and southern women was still evident as recently as the 1950s, prior to the development of the civil rights movement in the South.

◆ *D O C U M E N T S*

In 1862, a Confederate nurse, Ada Bacot, described in her diary her reactions to being asked to tend two wounded Yankee soldiers (Document 1). At almost the same time, Maria Daly, a New Yorker, recorded her observations on southern women and on her war-relief-worker friends; some selected journal entries comprise Document 2. The following year, Sarah Morgan, a resident of Louisiana, penned an entry in her diary "confessing herself a rebel" (Document 3). In the aftermath of the battle of Gettysburg (July 1863), the Quaker and Union nurse Cornelia Hancock wrote about the sufferings she saw around her in letters to female relatives (Document 4). When some northern men accused Union women of being less attached to their cause than their Confederate counterparts, Caroline Kirkland indignantly wrote and published Document 5, "A Few Words in Behalf of the Loyal Women of the United States" (1863). As the war drew to a close in 1865, Ella Gertrude Clanton Thomas, a Georgia slave mistress, contemplated Sherman's march to the sea, General William T. Sherman himself, and his wife (Document 6). Nearly four decades after the war began, in Document 7, Mary Livermore, a Union partisan, recalled with pride women's role in the first days of northern mobilization.

1. Ada Bacot, a Confederate Nurse, Comments on Two Wounded Yankees, 1862

Charlottesville
Monticello Hospital
Saturday Morning. June 14″ 62

It is oppressively warm, crouds of wounded & sick are coming in every hour, the streets are thronged with Soldiers, hurying to & frow. Officers of every rank below a Col. some sick & some wounded. Dr. Rembert & Mr. Jones have been busy dressing wounds all the morning. Two wounded Yankees were brought in & put on my lower ward[.] I would rather not have them & fear I will not have the patience to do for them, I cant help feeling pity for them, they are human beings. They are our enemys too, wounded & in our power. It will be hard to treat them as I do the other men but I know it is my duty. The heat is almost over powering.

(Night. My room) . . .

Eight more men came in tonight, they were sent to the Monticello, where they were put is a mistry for the house was crouded to overflow before. There are now 120 men staying there. The Yankee prisoners seem very comfortable since their wounds were dressed. The young men of our army who came in at the time were very severly wounded, they were taken to the same room when they arrived, but Dr. Rembert thought best to remove them. . . .

Charlottesville
Sunday afternoon. June 15.″ 62

Another warm morning, too busy to go to church. Mr. Alexander is still bright, but his wound is very dangerous. Dr. Rembert thinks it very doubtful if he recovers. It is almost impossible to keep him from talking. The men are very kind to the two yankees one of them is polite & grateful for any thing done for him the other is sulkey, says very little & pretends to sleep most of the time[.] I force myself to ask after their health once a day, & see that they get their food regularly. I have never inquired there names nor do I intend to.

Jean V. Berlin, ed., *A Confederate Nurse: The Diary of Ada W. Bacot, 1860–1863* (Columbia, S.C.: University of South Carolina Press, 1994), 125–126.

2. Maria Daly, a New Yorker, Criticizes Southern Women and Records the War Work of Her Acquaintances, 1862

June 26, 1862

In the paper this morning, there is an incendiary appeal of the women of New Orleans to the Southern soldiers, the burden of which is that they would rather be buried beneath the ruins of their homes than be left to the mercy of the barbarous Yankees—these barbarous creatures who have done nothing but feed their hungry and clothe their naked since they took their pestilent city. . . .

July 3, 1862

Mrs. Hilton told me that a lady who knew [A. T.] Stewart's head-man, Fairchild, walked up to him and asked him to look at her brooch. He said it seemed to be nothing very remarkable.

"No?" said she, "No? It is made from the skull of a Federal soldier!"

Now such a demon in female form as that, I think, should have been arrested. I lose all patience when I think of these demoniac Southern women, whose pride and arrogance have had so much to do with this fearful state of things. Southern ladies and gentlemen . . . are very agreeable people with very finished and courtly manners, but they are a class utterly unsuited and antagonistic to the principles of our government. We do not want a nobility here of any kind, except intellect; no millionaires with miles of territory belonging to them and an army of retainers. So they must go down, like the old feudal keeps, etc., which were very picturesque but dangerous from their strength to the public weal. . . .

August 14, 1862

Ellen Naudain, spending the evening here a few nights since, told us much about the hospitals where she attends two days in the week. She had been attending a sick soldier who told her that he and two brothers and their father had all enlisted the same day and that he was anxious to get well to rejoin them. She thinks the army very patriotic from what she has seen. . . .

September 13, 1862 . . .

Harriet Whetten stopped this morning, dear old soul, to see us. She has seen hard service this summer, and says that the rank and file of the army are splendid. She says little for the officers. The soldiers bear all with unmurmuring patience, but she is disgusted by the coldness and delay and want of feeling in the government officers. She related that the day after the last battle of Fair Oaks, the *Spalding* came near enough for them to go and try to feed some of the men on the battlefield. The cargo

Maria Daly, *Diary of a Union Lady,* ed. Harold E. Hammond (New York: Funk & Wagnalls, 1962), 155, 158–159, 164, 172–173.

was taken out and five hundred of the most badly wounded were to be taken aboard. Orders came to replace the cargo and move to Harrison's Landing (seven miles), where the poor fellows were left.

Harriet has met Arabella, who has been living, it seems, very comfortably at government expense at the hospital at Harrison's Landing near her husband's regiment. She has done nothing, comparatively, but lounge on a sofa, for the men told her that there had not been a lady near them to sit beside them a moment for ten days. The hospital, too, is small. Harriet was asked, although she was a stranger, for a night only to give out the linens whilst Mrs. Barlow was sprawling out on the couch. My instincts are right about her. Barlow, they say, is very cruel to his men. He may, however, be only a stern disciplinarian.

Whilst waiting for the return prisoners from Richmond, the rebel officers came on board, drank with Captain Harris and his officers, and to Harriet's disgust dined on board. After dinner, the Captain asked her if she would not give these men some tea. Harriet said she wished she had authority to say no, but she answered that she only distributed things to the sick. He must ask the quartermaster, who she was vexed to see give it. The rebels said it was $16 a pound, and it would be a great comfort. How contemptible to take it! I would not, it seems to me, have touched a leaf. Harriet said the utmost cordiality seemed to exist between them, and the surgeon said: "Our officers told all they knew. The rebels were not quite so bad."

Charles advised Harriet to leave the boat, as so much is said about the nurses who have gone. Some of the men say that they are closeted for hours with the surgeons in pantries and all kinds of disorders go on. The surgeons dislike, as a body, the Sisters of Charity because they are obliged to be respectful of them.

3. The Louisianian Sarah Morgan Proudly Proclaims Herself a Rebel, 1863

January 23, 1863

I confess my self a rebel, body and soul. *Confess?* I glory in it! Am proud of being one, would not forego the title for any other earthly one! Though none could regret the dismemberment of our old Union more than I did at the time, though I acknowledge that there never was a more unnecessary war than this in the beginning, yet once in earnest, from the secession of Louisiana I date my change of sentiment. I have never since then looked back; forward, forward! is the cry; and as the Federal States sink each day in more appalling folly and disgrace, I grow prouder still of my own country and rejoice that we can no longer be confounded with a nation which shows so little fortitude in calamity, so little magnanimity in its hour of triumph.

Yes! I am glad we are two distinct tribes! I am proud of my country; only wish I could fight in the ranks with our brave soldiers, to prove my enthusiasm; would think death, mutilation, glorious in such a cause; cry "war to all eternity before we submit!" But if I cant fight, being unfortunately a woman, which I now regret for

Charles East, ed., *The Civil War Diary of Sarah Morgan* (Athens: University of Georgia Press, 1991), 410–411.

the first time in my life, at least I can help in other ways. What fingers could do in knitting and sewing for them, I have done with the most intense delight; what words of encouragement and praise could accomplish, I have tried on more than one bold soldier boy, and not altogether in vain; I have lost my home and all its dear contents for our Southern Rights, have stood on its deserted hearth stone and looked at the ruin of all I loved without a murmur, almost glad of the sacrifice, if it would contribute its mite towards the salvation of the Confederacy. . . .

Well! I boast myself Rebel, sing Dixie, shout Southern Rights, pray for God's blessing on our cause, without ceasing, and would not live in this country if by any possible calamity we should be conquered; I am only a woman, and that is the way I feel.

4. A Union Nurse, Cornelia Hancock, Describes the Aftermath of the Battle of Gettysburg, 1863

Gettysburg, Pa. July 7th, 1863.

MY DEAR COUSIN

I am very tired tonight; have been on the field all day—went to the 3rd Division 2nd Army Corps. I suppose there are about five hundred wounded belonging to it. They have one patch of woods devoted to each army corps for a hospital. I being interested in the 2nd, because Will [her brother] had been in it, got into one of its ambulances, and went out at eight this morning and came back at six this evening. There are no words in the English language to express the sufferings I witnessed today. The men lie on the ground; their clothes have been cut off them to dress their wounds; they are half naked, having nothing but hard-tack to eat only as Sanitary Commissions, Christian Associations, and so forth give them. I was the first woman who reached the 2nd Corps after the three days fight at Gettysburg. I was in that Corps all day, not another woman within a half mile. . . . To give you some idea of the extent and numbers of the wounds, four surgeons, none of whom were idle fifteen minutes at a time, were busy all day amputating legs and arms. I gave to every man that had a leg or arm off a gill of wine, to every wounded in Third Division, one glass of lemonade, some bread and preserves and tobacco—as much as I am opposed to the latter, for they need it very much, they are so exhausted.

I feel very thankful that this was a successful battle; the spirit of the men is so high that many of the poor fellows said today, "What is an arm or leg to whipping Lee out of Penn." I would get on first rate if they would not ask me to write to their wives; *that* I cannot do without crying, which is not pleasant to either party. I do not mind the sight of blood, have seen limbs taken off and was not sick at all.

It is a very beautiful, rolling country here; under favorable circumstances I should think healthy, but now for five miles around, there is an awful smell of putrefaction. Women are needed here very badly, anyone who is willing to go to field hospitals. . . .

Henrietta Stratton Jaquette, ed., *Letters of a Civil War Nurse: Cornelia Hancock, 1863–1865* (University of Nebraska Press, 1998), 7–12.

Gettysburg—July 8th, 1863.

MY DEAR SISTER . . .

I feel assured I shall never feel horrified at anything that may happen to me hereafter. There is a great want of surgeons here; there are hundreds of brave fellows, who
have not had their wounds dressed since the battle. Brave is not the word; more, more
Christian fortitude never was witnessed than they exhibit, always say—"Help my
neighbor first he is worse." The Second Corps did the heaviest fighting, and, of
course, all who were badly wounded, were in the thickest of the fight, and, therefore,
we deal with the very best class of the men—that is the bravest. My name is particularly grateful to them because it is Hancock. General Hancock is very popular with
his men. The reason why they suffer more in this battle is because our army is victorious and marching *on* after Lee, leaving the wounded for citizens and a very few
surgeons. The citizens are stripped of everything they have, so you must see the
exhausting state of affairs. The Second Army Corps alone had two thousand men
wounded, this I had from the Surgeon's head quarters. . . . Get the Penn Relief to send
clothing here; there are many men without anything but a shirt lying in poor shelter
tents, calling on God to take them from this world of suffering; in fact the air is rent
with petitions to deliver them from their sufferings. . . .

The Christian Committee support us and when they get tired the Sanitary is on hand.
Uncle Sam is very rich, but very slow, and if it was not for the Sanitary, much suffering would ensue. We give the men toast and eggs for breakfast, beef tea at ten o'clock,
ham and bread for dinner, and jelly and bread for supper. Dried rusk would be nice if
they were only here. Old sheets we would give much for. Bandages are plenty but
sheets very scarce. We have plenty of woolen blankets now, in fact the hospital is
well supplied, but for about five days after the battle, the men had no blankets nor
scarce any shelter.

It took nearly five days for some three hundred surgeons to perform the amputa-
tions that occurred here, during which time the rebels lay in a dying condition without their wounds being dressed or scarcely any food. If the rebels did not get severely
punished for this battle, then I am no judge. We have but one rebel in our camp now;
he says he never fired his gun if he could help it, and, therefore, we treat him first
rate. One man died this morning. I fixed him up as nicely as the place will allow; he
will be buried this afternoon. We are becoming somewhat civilized here now and
the men are cared for well. . . .

I am black as an Indian and dirty as a pig and as well as I ever was in my life—
have a nice bunk and tent about twelve feet square. I have a bed that is made of four
crotch sticks and some sticks laid across and pine boughs laid on that with blankets
on top. It is equal to any mattress ever made. The tent is open at night and sometimes I have laid in the damp all night long, and got up all right in the morning.

The suffering we get used to and the nurses and doctors, stewards, etc., are very
jolly and sometimes we have a good time. It is very pleasant weather now. There is
all in getting to do what you *want* to do and I am doing that. . . .

There is no more impropriety in a *young* person being here provided they are
sensible than a sexagenarian. Most polite and obliging are all the soldiers to me. . . .

2nd Army Corps—3rd Division Hospital
near Gettysburg.
July 21st, 1863.

MY DEAR MOTHER

It is with trouble that I can find time and quiet enough to write to anyone. I have been sick but one day since I have been here, and then I went into a tent and was waited upon like a princess. I like to be here very much, am perfectly used to the suffering and the work just suits me; it is more superintending than real work, still the work is constant. I like being in the open air, sleep well and eat well. . . . The men are very polite to me and I get on remarkably well, but quiet is impossible to obtain at camp. . . .

I received, a few days ago, a Silver Medal worth twenty dollars. The inscription on one side is "Miss Cornelia Hancock, presented by the wounded soldiers 3rd Division 2nd Army Corps." On the other side is "Testimonial of regard for ministrations of mercy to the wounded soldiers at Gettysburg, Pa.—July 1863."

5. Caroline Kirkland Offers "a Few Words in Behalf of the Loyal Women of the United States," 1863

It has lately become the fashion to say that, with regard to their interest in the present most unhappy war, the women of the North have not equalled those of the South in patriotic interest, labors, and sacrifices. The first utterer of this opinion probably aimed at nothing more than a sensational paragraph; for had there been any more serious or earnest intent, some specifications would have been given, that those accused might have had either the opportunity to defend themselves, or valuable hints for their future guidance and incitement to duty. One writer says—and this is as distinct a form of the accusation as any we remember to have met with: "But for the courage and energy of the women of the South, we believe the Rebellion would not have survived to this time. Had the women of the North with like zeal addressed themselves to the work of encouraging a loyal and devoted spirit among us, the copperhead conspiracy in behalf of the enemy would have been strangled at its birth, and the rebels would have learned, long ago, the futility of expecting aid and comfort from such a source." . . .

The gist of all that has been said of our deficiency in the present crisis, so far as we understand it, is that we have not shown *passion* enough; that we have acted naturally, in short. . . .

It can hardly be expected that the great body of loyal women should quietly accept the derogatory comparison alluded to. . . . Soldiers! you can speak for us. Have we been indifferent to your wants and sufferings; have we chilled your noble devotion by our faint-hearted words; have our letters to you breathed a spirit of discontent and repining, or failed to hail your enthusiasm and give the full measure of praise and joy to your heroic achievements? You who have lately, in a time

---

Caroline Matilda Kirkland, *A Few Words in Behalf of the Loyal Women of the United States,* Loyal Publication Society, no. 10 (New York: Bryant and Co., 1863).

of need, spoken so nobly for your country and its government, to the confusion of blatant traitors, lift your voices once more, in behalf of the loyal women who await you at home! . . .

As to the "sacrifices" said to have been made by the women of the South, and which are insisted upon by their Northern sympathizers as proofs of heroic resolution, their merit must depend upon circumstances. It is no virtue to wear a coarse dress if you can obtain no other, or to live poorly when good living is too costly for your means. It is very probable that the sacrifices of the women have been greater than those of the men, if we exclude from the calculation the hardships which all soldiers in all wars must necessarily endure. But we cannot class such sacrifices with those voluntarily borne by our revolutionary mothers, for they suffered gladly in the cause of LIBERTY, while the women of the South have no higher incentive than the determination to uphold their husbands in the attempt to perpetuate SLAVERY. The sacrifices required by a war which the South voluntarily commenced should have been counted beforehand. A rebellion against just and lawful, kind and beneficent authority; a war which pretends to no high or holy motive, and can allege in its justification no public wrong or injury, can claim no general sympathy for the sufferings and sacrifices it compels a consenting people to bear, nor can sacrifices in a bad cause take the rank which belongs to those endured for a principle sanctioned alike by God and man. We know that women usually adopt the political views of their husbands, and we profess no surprise that Southern women should have done so. We see it among ourselves, and have felt it in the refusal of women whose husbands sympathize with the South to do anything for the country or the army in this crisis, but we must regret that their sacrifices should not have been made in a more worthy cause, and hope for their own sakes that they will never glory in them. To suffer for liberty is glorious; to deprive ourselves of the comforts and necessaries of life in behalf of slavery, can never be anything but ignominious, though human sympathy views with pity the sufferings of those so desperately mistaken.

It is true that we of the North have seen as yet little occasion for these personal sacrifices which, doubtless, press heavily upon our belligerent neighbors. Our industry has known no interruption, and our prosperity has been ample, so far as material things are concerned. We weep for our losses by this cruel war, but not for any lack experienced in the ordinary comforts of our firesides. . . .

[W]e advance no claim to *superiority* in zeal and devotedness, over the women of the South. It is to vindicate loyal women from a charge of *deficiency,* as compared with the other side, that we venture to speak. . . .

If we interpret aright the attempt to contrast us unfavorably with Southern women in devotion to the public service, the meaning is that *they* have sustained their men in fiery hate and contempt for their countrymen of the North, and done everything possible to incite and encourage them in the determination to found an empire, whose corner-stone should be human slavery. They, having seen slavery, felt it, known its horrors, suffered under its attendant evils, and learned, so far as they have learned Christianity, its incompatibility with God's benign law of love, have deliberately lent themselves and those dearer than life to them, to the perpetuation of so awful an evil, for the sake of an idea, however futile, of worldly prosperity! The separation of families, the lashing of women, brutal tortures of young girls from the most atrocious motives—all these and long list of crimes and outrages upon humanity, of which these are but specimens, excite no repugnance, it seems, in the minds of Southern women? They are willing to go on and on, and to uphold the whole abomination just as it is, and the reward for which they submit to this fearful self-degradation is the pleasure of a triumph over the hated "Yankees!" . . .

We are told of the sacrifices they have made in the cause of War—have they ever made a sacrifice in the cause of Truth? If all the women in the rebellious States who disapprove of slavery, and believe it to be an evil and a sin, had, as with one voice, re-monstrated against this war for its extension and perpetuity, instead of weakly allow-ing passion to influence them, without regard to principle or conscience, there would have been no war. If every Southern wife had done her whole duty by her husband, using the "still, small voice" to which God has given such power, in persuading him to listen to reason and duty, rather than to the trumpet-blare of a wicked and heartless ambition, what misery might have been saved! But not only failing to prevent, she has, so we are told, used all her power, and most successfully, to add fuel to the cruel flame, and to stifle, as far as possible, the whisper of conscience, which might at some happy moment have become audible.

6. Ella Gertrude Clanton Thomas Describes Conditions in the Confederacy and Criticizes Northern Women, 1865

Tuesday, January 3, 1865

Mr Thomas has gone up stairs and I have just finished reading an interesting letter giving an account of the movements of the state line troops during Sherman's march through Georgia. Alluding to the evacuation of Savannah he mentions that after our troops left the city he could hear the shrieks of women caused by the stragglers—the skullers of our army who had commenced to pillage and destroy. Some of them were shot by the citizens and others captured by the Yankees. "Wither are we drifting?" is the pertinent question asked by the Editor of the Charleston *Mercury* in commenting upon the increase of crime and lawlessness in that city—and this enquiry comes with startling energy from others when the time appears rapidly approaching when we have almost as much to dread from our own demoralized mob as from the public enemy. . . .

[I]n God's name what are we doing? Striving to defend ourselves against our brethren who would butcher us—annihilate us if they could—War is a terrible demon. It does not elevate—it debases. It does not lift heavenward—it crushes into the dust. I lose faith in humanity when I see such efforts to sink the nobler better part of man's nature in an effort to exterminate the white race at the South in order to elevate the Negro race to a position which I doubt their ability to fill—

The time will come when Southern women will be avenged—Let this war cease with the abolition of slavery and I wish for the women of the North no worse fate than will befall them. Their husbands already prepare for them the bitter cup of

Virginia Ingraham Burr, ed., *The Secret Eye: The Journal of Ella Gertrude Clanton Thomas* (Chapel Hill: University of North Carolina Press, 1990), 252–254.

humiliation which they will be compelled to drink to the dregs—General Kilpatrick spent a night in Waynesboro. [H]is headquarters were at Mrs Dr Carter's. He demanded that the best bed room in the house should be prepared for himself and a good looking mulatto girl whom he had traveling with him. A seat at the table was furnished her—The officers deferential in their manner to her while thus publicly insulting Mrs Carter in her own house. Lolling indolently in a rocking chair the girl awaits the entrance of the Gen. "What not retired yet Nellie?" is his salutation. "Not until your majesty returns" is her reply—Take *that scene* Mrs Kilpatrick as a reward for encouraging your husband to come amongst us. . . .

I don't know why it is but that man Sherman has interested me very much—perhaps it is upon the principle that all women admire successful courage and that Gen Sherman has proven himself to be a very brave man there can be no doubt. Our enemy as he is I can imagine that his wife loves him. A short time ago I read that his baby six months old had died—I could not be glad of it altho his men in their eager search after hidden treasure opened the graves of babys that had just been buried and left the coffins on the brink of the grave. At one time just after Sherman passed through Burke I wrote Mrs Sherman a letter which I intended having published under the head of Personal in one of the Richmond papers—I did not send it and now that I have read of the recent death of her baby I am glad that I did not. Woman's nature is the same the world over. She brooks no rival near the throne (except amongst the [illegible] that strange anamoly of nature). Northern women are colder in their temperature than our warm hearted children of the sun but I know that amongst the jubilee attendant upon her husband's "Christmas present" to Lincoln [Savannah] I could send Mrs Sherman "a New Year's gift" which would dim and make hollow and empty the mirth by which she is surrounded—I do feel very very sorry for her and will not send this letter if I could—

Mrs Gen Sherman—A few days since I read your husband's farewell telegram to you dated Atlanta. Will you believe it? *for a moment* I felt sorry for you. Forgetting who you were and for what purpose he was coming among us my heart went out in womanly sympathy for you. He bids you expect to hear from him only through rebel sources and urged by the same womanly intuition which prompted me to sympathise with you, I a rebel lady will give you some information with regard to Gen Sherman's movements. Last week your husband's army found me in the possession of wealth. Tonight our plantations are a scene of ruin and desolation. *You* bad him "God speed" on his fiendish errand, did you not? You thought it a gallant deed to come amongst us where by his own confession he expected to find "only the shadow of an army." A brave act to frighten women and children! desolate homes, violate the sanctity of firesides and cause the "widow and orphan to curse the Sherman for the cause" and this you did for what? to elevate the Negro race. Be satisfied Madam your wish has been accomplished. Enquire of Gen Sherman when next you see him who has been elevated to fill your place? You doubtless read with a smile of approbation of the delightfully fragrant ball at which he made his debut in Atlanta? Did he tell you of the Mulatto girl for whose safety he was so much concerned that she was returned to Nashville when he commenced his vandal march? This girl was spoken of by the Negroes whom you are willing to trust so implicitly as "Sherman's wife." Rest satisfied Mrs Sherman and quiet the apprehension of your Northern sisters with regard to the elevation of the Negros—Your husbands are amongst a coloured race whose reputation for morality has never been of the highest order—and these gallant cavaliers are most of them provided with "a companion du voyage"—As your brave husband considers a southern lady a fair object to wage war against and as I do not yet feel fully satisfied that there is no danger of a clutch from his heavy hand upon my shoulders, I will only add that intensely Southern woman as I am *I pity you.*

7. Mary Livermore Recalls Northern Women's Response to the Beginning of the Civil War, 1890

If men faltered not, and went gayly to death, that slavery might be exterminated, and that the United States might remain intact and undivided, women strengthened them by accepting the policy of the government uncomplainingly. When the telegraph recorded for the country, "defeat" instead of "victory," and for their beloved, "death" instead of "life," women continued to give the government their faith, and patiently worked and waited.

It is easy to understand how men catch the contagion of war, especially when they feel their quarrel to be just. One can comprehend how, fired with enthusiasm, and inspired by martial music, they march to the cannon's mouth, where the iron hail rains heaviest, and the ranks are mowed down like grain in harvest. But for women to send forth their husbands, sons, brothers and lovers to the fearful chances of the battle-field, knowing well the risks they run,—this involves exquisite suffering, and calls for another kind of heroism. This women did throughout the country, forcing their white lips to utter a cheerful "good-bye," when their hearts were nigh breaking with the fierce struggle.

The transition of the country from peace to the tumult and waste of war, was appalling and swift—but the regeneration of its women kept pace with it. They lopped off superfluities, retrenched in expenditures, became deaf to the calls of pleasure, and heeded not the mandates of fashion. The incoming patriotism of the hour swept them to the loftiest height of devotion, and they were eager to do, to bear, or to suffer, for the beloved country. The fetters of caste and conventionalism dropped at their feet, and they sat together, patrician and plebeian, Protestant and Catholic, and scraped lint, and rolled bandages, or made garments for the poorly clad soldiery.

An order was sent to Boston for five thousand shirts for the Massachusetts troops at the South. Every church in the city sent a delegation of needle-women to "Union Hall," heretofore used as a ballroom. The Catholic priests detailed five hundred sewing-girls to the pious work. Suburban towns rang the bells of the town hall to muster the seamstresses. The plebeian Irish Catholic of South Boston ran the sewing-machine, while the patrician Protestant of Beacon Street basted,—and the shirts were made at the rate of a thousand a day. On Thursday, Dorothea Dix sent an order for five hundred shirts for her hospital in Washington. On Friday, they were cut, made, and packed—and were sent on their way that night. Similar events were of constant occurrence in every other city. The zeal and devotion of women no more flagged through the war than did that of the army in the field. They rose to the height of every emergency, and through all discouragements and reverses maintained a

Mary A. R. Livermore, *My Story of the War* (A. D. Worthing and Co., 1890), 110–112, 120–122.

sympathetic unity between the soldiers and themselves, that gave to the former a marvellous heroism.

At a meeting in Washington during the war, called in the interest of the Sanitary Commission, President Lincoln said: "I am not accustomed to use the language of eulogy. I have never studied the art of paying compliments to women. But I must say that if all that has been said by orators and poets since the creation of the world in praise of women, was applied to the women of America, it would not do them justice for their conduct during this war. I will close by saying, God bless the women of America!" . . .

It is better to heal a wound than to make one. And it is to the honor of American women, not that they led hosts to the deadly charge, and battled amid contending armies, but that they confronted the horrid aspects of war with mighty love and earnestness. They kept up their own courage and that of their households. They became ministering angels to their countrymen who perilled health and life for the nation. They sent the love and impulses of home into the extended ranks of the army, through the unceasing correspondence they maintained with "the boys in blue." They planned largely, and toiled untiringly, and with steady persistence to the end, that the horrors of the battle-field might be mitigated, and the hospitals abound in needed comforts. The men at the front were sure of sympathy from the homes and knew that the women remembered them with sleepless interest. "This put heroic fibre into their souls," said Dr. Bellows, "and restored us our soldiers with their citizen hearts beating normally under their uniforms, as they dropped them off at the last drum-tap." . . .

So determined were the people that their citizen soldiers should be well cared for, that "Relief Societies" were frequently organized in the interest of regiments, as soon as they were mustered into the service. They proposed to follow the volunteers of their neighborhoods with their benefactions—"to provide them with home comforts when well, and with hospital supplies and nurses when wounded or sick." It would have been an admirable plan if it could have been carried out. But numerous difficulties and failures soon brought these methods into disrepute. The accumulation of perishable freight for the soldiers became fearful. It demanded instant transportation, and the managers of freight trains and expresses were in despair.

Women rifled their store-rooms and preserve-closets of canned fruits and pots of jam and marmalade, which they packed with clothing and blankets, books and stationery, photographs and "comfort-bags." Baggage cars were soon flooded with fermenting sweetmeats, and broken pots of jelly, that ought never to have been sent. Decaying fruit and vegetables, pastry and cake in a demoralized condition, badly canned meats and soups, whose fragrance was not that of "Araby the blest," were necessarily thrown away *en route.* And with them went the clothing and stationery saturated with the effervescing and putrefying compounds which they enfolded.

◈ E S S A Y S

The contrasting experiences of northern and southern white women during the Civil War are treated in two recent publications. LeeAnn Whites of the University of Missouri, Columbia, goes behind the fervent Confederate rhetoric to examine a region that was, she declares, "teetering on the edge of a critical racial and gender imbalance, pushed to the brink by changes in the sectional social and economic structure." Jeanie Attie, a historian at the C. W. Post campus of Long Island University, focuses on northern women's patriotism and involvement in the war effort. She concludes that the war offered them many new opportunities and raised their expectations about advances in the future.

Southern White Women and the Burdens of War

LEEANN WHITES

It was a cold winter's day and greenish ice flows clogged the turbulent river. Across its vast expanse, Eliza could see the far shore of Ohio and freedom. Behind her, coming ever closer, she could hear the baying dogs of the slavetrader, Haley. What could she do? On the one side was slavery and the certain loss of her child to the slavetrader. On the other was an impassable river and probable death. Looking down at her small son, Eliza knew only that she could not bear to lose him. And with one desperate burst of courage, she jumped onto the nearest ice flow. Scrambling and leaping from one teetering piece of ice to another, she struggled across the mighty Ohio and gained the far shore of freedom for herself and her child.

Laying down the collection of antislavery tracts she was reading, Harriet Beecher Stowe was deeply moved. In Eliza's desperate act of undaunted mother love, Stowe heard an almost irresistible call to action. She would tell the world Eliza's story, for herein lay the true sin of slavery—the way in which it thwarted and repressed the maternal bond, separating mother and child, brother and sister, husband and wife, eroding the emotional fabric of the black family in the name of the vested property rights of white slaveowners. The emergence of the family as a separate sphere in the North, freed from the sordid economic concerns of men, had constituted the domestic realm of the mother as a sphere in its own right, allowing her older sister, Catharine Beecher, to claim a new and boldly autonomous role for women as the moral arbiters of social life. Now Harriet Beecher Stowe would shine this newly emancipated light of the family and of the moral mother as the spokesperson of its interests upon what increasingly appeared to be a domestically retrograde southern slave system.

The rest is history. *Uncle Tom's Cabin,* the novel that Harriet Beecher Stowe wrote as if driven to it, swept the nation by storm to become the most popular novel of the entire century. Its claim for the domestic rights of slaves popularized the antislavery cause in the North in a manner that no abstract calls to the inherent equality of all mankind had ever succeeded in doing in the past. As Abraham Lincoln commented upon first meeting Harriet Beecher Stowe in the midst of the Civil War, "So you are the little woman who wrote the book that made this great war."

If, however, popular antislavery sentiment in the North, and the war that followed from it, was grounded upon a new understanding of the domestic rights of the family, and in particular in the expansion of the private and public authority of the mother as the bearer and rearer of life, then we must ask, what did this war of

LeeAnn Whites, "The Civil War as a Crisis in Gender," in Catherine Clinton and Nina Silber, eds., *Divided Houses: Gender and the Civil War* (New York: Oxford University Press, 1992), 3–9, 13–21. Copyright © 1992 by Catherine Clinton and Nina Silber. Used by permission of Oxford University Press, Inc.

domestic liberation mean for women of the South? How are we to understand the widespread support for the war among Confederate women, support for a War of Southern Independence that was understood by at least some of their northern sisters to be nothing less than the defense of the independence of Confederate men from the dictates of reproduction and the moral authority of motherhood? An independence that so subordinated the interests of reproduction and the family as a whole to the particular economic and productive interests of the individual planter that it gave him the right not only to own the child of some woman's heart and body but to dispose of it as *his* material interests would dictate.

While the readership of *Uncle Tom's Cabin* in the South was not as widespread as in the North, those who did read it were undoubtedly at least equally consumed by the critique of the southern slave household structure that it presented. Mary Boykin Chesnut, daughter of a prominent planter-class family and wife of a member of Jefferson Davis's staff, was haunted by the novel and returned to it time and again in her Civil War diary. She took particular umbrage at Stowe's claim for the moral superiority of northern women. "What self-denial," queried Chesnut, did northerners like Stowe practice while sitting in their "nice New England homes—clean, clear, sweet smelling?" She contrasted this picture of the northern household, pristine in its isolation, with the experience of her female relations, living in households enmeshed in the institution of slavery. These women of the planter elite were, according to Chesnut, educated in the same northern schools as their abolitionist critics. They read the same Bible and had the "same ideas of right and wrong," yet they were not so fortunate as to be safely ensconced in a separate familiar sphere dedicated to the domestic interests of their families alone. Instead they lived in "negro villages" where they struggled to "ameliorate the condition of these Africans in every particular."

> They set them the example of a perfect life—a life of utter self-abnegation. . . . Think of these holy New Englanders, forced to have a negro village walk through their houses whenever they saw fit. . . . [These women] have a swarm of blacks about them as children under their care—not as Mrs. Stowe paints them, but the hard, unpleasant, unromantic, undeveloped savage Africans. And they hate slavery worse than Mrs. Stowe.

Here the ultimate figure of domestic self-sacrifice and thus *the* "true woman" was not those abolitionist spokeswomen for the "cult of domesticity" and the family as a separate sphere, but rather the planter-class woman, who precisely *because* of the presence of slavery within the southern household was placed in a position to act as the mother of not only her own children but of her slave dependents as well. Of course, in Harriet Beecher's account, the most militant defender of motherhood was not in fact the northern abolitionist woman like herself, who risked only her good reputation in taking a public stance against slavery. Domesticity at its most insurgent was represented by those slave mothers, like Eliza, who in the very act of mothering their children could be called upon to subvert the institution of slavery itself. Chesnut's defense of the motherhood of the plantation mistress, on the other hand, spoke from within the confines of the institution of slavery. For it was the very same slave system that worked to deny Eliza her motherhood that gave Chesnut the basis for claiming it as the slave mistresses' own. Ownership in slaves not only made the planters the wealthiest men in the country through their appropriation of the productive labor of their slaves, but it also served to make their women into "ladies" by virtue of their own ability not only to "mother" their slaves but more fundamentally to appropriate their domestic labor. It was this ownership in slaves that empowered the white mistress, like Mary Boykin Chesnut, to define the slave woman not as a mother in her own right but as one of the many "children" under her own maternal care.

As slavery was an organic part of the southern household, it became organic to the slaveowners' very conception of themselves as men and as women, as mothers and as fathers. It both served to expand their own domestic claims as *individual* mothers and fathers, while it served to subordinate, literally to enslave, the sphere of reproduction and of domestic life as a whole to the class interests of this same planter elite. Ultimately the extent to which motherhood was rendered unfree within the southern slave system served to undermine the domestic position of even those women of the planter class who benefited from it most in class terms. For whatever power they gained for their own domestic position by having slave dependents, they lost by the manner in which slaveownership further empowered their own men. So while women of the planter class could claim to "mother" their slaves, at least some of their husbands were literally fathers of slaves. The outcome, concluded Chesnut, was often far more devastating than even Harriet Beecher Stowe envisioned, She recorded the conversation among one group of elite Confederate women. ". . . I knew the dissolute half of Legree well," asserted one of these women,

> He was high and mighty. But the kindest creature to his slaves—and the unfortunate results of his bad ways were not sold, had not to jump over ice blocks. They were kept in full view and provided for handsomely in his will. His wife and daughters in the might of their purity and innocence are supposed never to dream of what is as plain before their eyes as the sunlight, and they play their parts of unsuspecting angels to the letter.

"Southern women," wrote Ella Gertrude Clanton Thomas, in her antebellum journal, "are I believe all at heart abolitionists." When she made this claim, she in fact meant that all women of *her* class and race were abolitionists. Had she actually meant to refer to all southern women, her case would have been a stronger one. For to the extent that planter-class women were abolitionists, it was not in the first instance the consequence of their recognition of a common likeness among all women. It reflected instead their desire to be full-fledged members of their class, empowered like their men to dictate the cultural norms of their society. Planter-class women burned, admittedly in private or in the company of other women, at the power that the ownership of slaves gave their men to create a double standard of sexual behavior within the planter class itself. As Rebecca Latimer Felton, a Georgia planter-class woman, wrote in her memoirs many years after the war, for the "abuses" that made "mulattoes as common as blackberries," the planters deserved to have their entire system collapse.

> In this one particular slavery doomed itself. When white men put their own offspring in the kitchen and the cornfield and allowed them to be sold into bondage as slaves and degraded them as another man's slave, the retribution of wrath was hanging over this country and the South paid penance in four years of bloody war.

Hindsight is twenty-twenty, but where was this voice for the larger interests of southern motherhood in 1860? Jumping across ice flows? Not, certainly, coming from the likes of Rebecca Felton, who asserted in her memoirs that upon the outbreak of the Civil War, a war that she perceived to be a "battle to defend our rights in owner-ship of African slaves," there was "never a more loyal woman" than herself. "I could not," she wrote, "fight against my kindred." Besides, she concluded, she was "only a woman and nobody asked me for opinion." The political voice of domesticity was silenced even among these most powerful of southern women, if only by the force of their own class interests. For at bottom was the undeniable fact that the slave plan-tation economy promoted their own material well-being. Therefore, no matter how frustrated they may have been in their own efforts to claim an enlarged sphere of authority in relation to the men of their class, they could not ignore the benefits that their own position as members of this class, however subordinated, gave them. If only out of their concern for their own children, women of the planter class were forced to recognize that the same planter who "defied the marriage law of the state by keeping up two households on the same plantation," as Rebecca Latimer Felton wrote, was also, as Mary Chesnut concluded, "the fountain from whom all blessings flow." . . .

The mid-nineteenth-century South presents the picture of a society teetering on the edge of a critical racial and gender imbalance, pushed to the brink by changes in the sectional social and economic structure. The incredible demand generated for cotton by the industrial revolution taking place in Britain and in the North made cot-ton the King of plantation staple crops and made the planter King as well—a King empowered by the profitability of this crop to buy the reproductive capacity of ever larger numbers of slave women as well as to turn the domestic voice of the women of his own class to his own self-empowerment. Almost perversely, however, the very same industrial revolution which served to fuel the expansion of the patriarchal power of southern planter-class men also created the basis for the emergence of the family as a separate sphere in the North. Therefore while reproduction remained en-slaved within the plantation household economy and the voice of domestic politics was muted, it burst forth with equally dazzling clarity in the North. Northern feminist and abolitionist women formed organizations and petitioned for fundamental changes within households and in the society at large. Some of these women even claimed the right to demand a single sexual standard of behavior from their men. . . .

As the fiction of slave servility and childlike dependence upon the patriarchal planter dissolved in the crucible of war, it left only the subordination of southern white women—as the only dependents on whose loyalty the planter could continue to rely. As the racial and class basis for dependence slipped away, gender thus emerged as an ever more critical basis for the persistence of southern white men as "free men." Not surprisingly, Confederate men at the time and for years afterward have written in self-congratulatory tones of the loyalty that their women demonstrated during the conflict. Confederate women, we are repeatedly told, constituted the "very soul of the war," offering up that which they did possess, their domestic attachments to those nearest and dearest to them, for that which they as individuals could never hope to obtain, the liberties of free men. This was the discipline that the patriarchal slave system had reared them up to, to deny the interests of domesticity in the face of the interests of their class. Now, however, the necessity of placing class prerogatives over the interests of domestic life had come to their own families, rather than to those of their slaves. But they did not flinch. At least, not in public. . . .

Some historians have gone so far as to argue that the women of the Confederacy were even more intensely committed to the war than were their men, packing the galleries of secessionist congresses, hissing at the delegates who opposed secession and cheering on its advocates. One Selma belle was reputed to have broken off her engagement when her fiancé failed to enlist. She sent him a skirt and female undergarments with the message, "wear these or volunteer." A letter of one young woman to her local newspaper upon the outbreak of war certainly reflected an intense identification with the cause:

> You will pardon the liberty I have taken to address you, when I tell you that my great inclination to do so assails me so constantly that I can only find relief in writing to you. . . . My father and family have always been the strongest of Whigs, and of course not in favor of immediate secession; but as that has been the irrevocable act of the South I submit to it, and say "as goes Georgia, so go I." But at the same time I am conscious that that very act has increased our responsibilities tenfold. We have outwardly assumed the garb of independence and now let us walk in the path our state has chosen. And shall man tread it alone? . . . No, no a thousand times no.

Urging other Confederate women to join her in the cause, she suggested that they "hurl the destructive novel in the fire and turn our poodles out of doors, and convert our pianos into spinning wheels." Not only would this return to home manufacturing make a critical contribution to their male relation's pursuit of political autonomy, the drive for political independence would make Confederate women more independent as well. As she concluded, "I feel a new life within me, and my ambition aims at nothing higher than to become an ingenious, economical, industrious housekeeper, and an independent Southern woman."

The demands of the war effort offered Confederate women a rare opportunity. Through their contributions to the cause they could enter into the heart of the struggle and like their men define themselves as "independent" southern women. Women who were independent because their privatized domestic pursuits were now thrust onto the center stage of southern life were not in violation of their subordinated domestic status. Confederate women in their role as mothers found themselves in a particularly critical position. It was after all their children who were the very stuff of the war machine. If men, especially young men, were to participate in the war effort, women, especially their mothers, would have to acquiesce in their departure. As one newspaper noted, "The man who does not love his mother and yield to her influence is not the right stuff to make a patriot of, and has no business in a patriot army."

With such influence came a newfound responsibility for southern women. Letters in southern papers therefore urged women to consider the long-range impact the war might have on their sons. "Let them not, in future years . . . be forced in sadness of heart and reproaches of conscience, to say that in all this they took no part." Mothers should, according to this writer, consider with what "humiliation" sons would be forced to recognize that they were "unworthy of the liberty and home secured for them by the valor of others." Motherhood should exert a public and political presence.

Not only did the war serve to intensify the centrality of reproduction in southern society, it also gave public, political significance to the domestic manufacturing of women. For not only did the war demand the contribution of women's reproductive product, their children, but critical economic problems now revolved around essentially domestic questions of how the troops were to be clothed, fed, and nursed.

Cotton proved to be virtually useless in this regard as it could not be eaten, made poor shoes, coats and blankets, and could hardly be shot. Local newspapers urged planters to turn their production toward subsistence crops instead and promoted the public organization of women into local Ladies Aid Societies dedicated to organizing their previously privatized labor in order to more efficiently clothe, feed, and nurse the troops. . . .

While Confederate men may have gone to war in defense of what they perceived to be their prerogatives as free men and in rejection of the threatened domination of a "horde of agrarians, abolitionists and free lovers," the actual demands of fighting the war made them increasingly conscious of their own dependence upon women's love and labor. As a result the southern soldier had to recognize, if only unconsciously, the extent to which his manhood and independence was relational—a social construction built upon the foundation of women's service and love, out of the fabric of his women's "dependence." For the more the war called forth women's domestic labor into the public arena, making public those "small gifts of service," the more the war itself was transformed from a struggle of men in defense of their individual prerogatives into a battle for the "firesides of our noble countrywomen." Confederate women seized this opportunity to lay claim to an increased reciprocity in gender relations. As one woman wrote to the newspaper, ". . . Do impress upon the soldiers, that they are constantly in our thoughts, that we are *working* for them, while they are *fighting* for us—and that their wants shall be supplied, as long as there is a *woman* or a *dollar* in the 'Southern Confederacy.'"

Confederate women found that the war might support a newly independent stature on their part. As Rebecca Latimer Felton wrote, "Nobody chided me then as unwomanly, when I went into a crowd and waited on suffering men. No one said I was unladylike to climb into cattle cars and box cars to feed those who could not feed themselves." Nor did the press find Amy Clark to be "unwomanly" when it was discovered that not only had she enlisted with her husband, but after he was killed she fought on alone in the ranks as a common soldier. She was described as "heroic *and* self-sacrificing" (emphasis added). But then as Sarah Morgan recorded in her diary upon hiding a pistol and a carving knife on her person in order to defend herself against the invading Union soldiers in Baton Rouge, "Pshaw! There are *no* women here! We are *all* men!"

As their women became more independent and, hence, more "male," Confederate men increasingly had to recognize their own dependence upon women, whether in managing their households in their absence, outfitting them in the field, or nursing them when wounded. Such men, in fact, became increasingly feminized. The male world of the camps was enough in and of itself to make many men think longingly of their lost domestic comforts. As Will Deloney wrote home to his wife, "Don't imagine that I have forgotten you—for I think of nobody else—and if you could see the discomfort my life held now you would conclude I could never forget. . . ."

William Deloney was shot from his horse while leading a cavalry charge in the fall of 1863. He died a hero to the cause, but he was lost to his family. He left his wife, Rosa, with four young children to carry on as best she might. In a letter written shortly after his death, a cousin urged Rosa to "take care of yourself for your dear children. Who can fill a *Mother's* place?" Who indeed? Here was the expansion of the domestic autonomy of planter-class women with a vengeance, as impoverished widows. For those Confederate men like Frank Coker, who were so fortunate as to survive the war and return to their homes, being a father and a husband was also at once more and less than it was before the War. For despite his wife's clever management and hard efforts at retrenchment during the war, the Cokers' finances were in great disarray. The economy was devastated, their section was defeated, and their slaves were emancipated. Frank Coker was no longer the same "lord of creation" that he once was: no longer a veritable "fountain from whom all blessings flow."

The Cokers' economic loss was mirrored in their slaves' domestic gain. For the ultimate *structural* rebalancing of southern domestic relations began when the southern household was sheared apart with the emancipation of the slaves. As the freedmen departed en masse from the households of their ex-masters in search of members of their own families lost to them under slavery, they moved toward a new domestic integrity for *all* southern families. They established themselves as heads of their own households, fathers and husbands in their own right. As freedwomen turned their labor toward the needs of their own kin, withdrawing from the kitchens and the fields of the master class insofar as they were able, they laid claim to a common status with their white counterparts as wives and mothers. In so doing they began to carve out what might have become a common ground for a future unity among southern women.

At the time, however, this newfound integrity of the southern family structure and the increased gender commonality of all women that it portended presented itself to planter-class women not as a victory for their gender interests but rather as the defeat of their men and of their class. For if the war served to intensify Confederate women's commitment to their men's class interests, their defeat served to set that commitment in concrete. "It was as though," in the words of one southern newspaper editor, "the mighty oak" was "hit by lightning" and only the "clinging vine" now kept it erect. Planter-class women urged their men to take solace in their own family circle, a family circle which should be more valued for that which had been lost. "Your wives and children are around you," wrote one woman, "sharing your sorrows as well as your joys. Though you may not have as many luxuries as in former days, you still have enough to eat and wear and can repose in security."

A retreat to familial life could make the sting of defeat more palatable, but it could not erase the necessity of subordination for defeated Confederate men. The "proud Southron" wrote one planter-class woman, Susan Cornwall, must now learn to "obey those laws which neither you nor yours had any hand in framing and those men who you fought four long years to be free from." It was defeat at the hands of other men that would finally force these men to adopt a world view more like that of their dependents. For as both slaves and women of the planter class had recognized before the war, the way to accept such subordination to another man's will and yet retain some sense of self-respect was to acknowledge a master above the master— to believe that subordination on this earth was but a prelude to some ultimate self-realization in another. "Teach us Oh, Father," wrote Cornwall, "those lessons of patience and resignation which hitherto we have refused to learn and grant that once more we may lift our hearts to thee and cry *Our* father." . . .

This lesson of victory in defeat—the proper place and power of the virtuous sufferers—was the lesson that Harriet Beecher Stowe meant to convey in the closing scene of her novel, through the story of Uncle Tom's fateful struggle with his rapacious owner, Simon Legree. For Harriet Beecher Stowe, Simon Legree represented the potentially devastating consequences of a male domination untempered by a recognition of the domestic claims of either his own family or that of his slaves. Running away to sea as a young man and abandoning his poor mother to die of a broken heart, Legree had eventually ended up in the South. There he acquired a plantation and many slaves, but never a home and a loving wife. Living in domestic squalor, he sexually exploited his female slaves while he worked all his field hands to exhaustion. Uncle Tom in fact sacrificed his own life to protect one of the slave women on the plantation from Legree's sexual abuse.

In the character of Uncle Tom, Harriet Beecher Stowe presented what she considered to be the highest exemplar of moral social behavior among men; men who, motivated by a keen sense of their own humility, turned their energies to upholding the human rights of those who were even more subordinated in the world than themselves. From this feminized vantage point, the defeat of the Confederacy and the economic difficulties of the region that followed upon it were perhaps not an unmitigated loss. The possibility of some gain ensued from the expanded significance and integrity that domestic life achieved. By sacrificing his own life, Uncle Tom had succeeded in forcing Simon Legree to recognize some limits to his power to dominate others. For although Legree won the battle and killed Uncle Tom, he was forced to acknowledge that he had lost the war for his soul. Through the moral power of his ultimate sacrifice, Tom found a better home, one in which he would be freed from the defeats and oppression he had endured in this world. "I'm right in the door," he gasped with his final breath, "I've got the victory."

For one brief moment in the course of the war itself, as advancing Union forces intensified the erosion of slavery that was already occurring from within, it had appeared that the defeat of the Confederate war effort would underwrite the earthly victory of the enslaved southern black population. The land would be redistributed and freedmen would acquire their forty acres and a mule and thereby their status as "free men" as it had been constructed in the antebellum social order. At the same time, it appeared that the subordinated status of motherhood would also be at least mitigated as the abolition of slavery promised to ratify the increased public status and significance that domestic concerns had gained during the war. The collapse of the slave plantation household in war and reconstruction did indeed fundamentally limit the extent to which some men could define their own status as free men by the measure of the limits of freedom on others. It did set certain structural limits to the subordination of reproduction and the family to the interests of the market. Families could no longer be bought or sold. It did not, however, create the basis for racial or gender equality in this country. For although the planter class was defeated, it was not vanquished. They lost their ownership in slaves, but not their control of the land. As a result, the war left white southern men feeling like less than men. It left black men with a manhood that frequently continued to cost them their lives. It left white southern women clinging to what was left of white southern men's ability to provide, and, all too often, it left black southern women with no alternative but to work in some white woman's kitchen. All men were not created equal and few women found themselves even comparatively free.

Northern White Women and
the Mobilization for War

JEANIE ATTIE

On April 22, 1861, as southern troops shelled the federal base at Fort Sumter, igniting the American Civil War, Mary Livermore, an abolitionist and temperance lecturer, became swept up by the war fervor that suddenly engrossed Boston. For Livermore, those "never-to-be-forgotten days of Sumter's bombardment" were days of deep ambivalence, marked by apprehension about the possibility of a long and calamitous war but, at the same time, by elation about the prospect of slavery's demise. More than anything else, she remembered the exhilarating outbursts of patriotism and civic unity. On the following Sunday, pulpits in Boston "thundered with denunciations of the rebellion," recalled Livermore, who was surprised by the radical sermons offered by antislavery clergy. Amid this "blaze of belligerent excitement" came Lincoln's call for 75,000 troops to protect Washington and federal property; in what seemed like no time, recruiting offices opened in "every city, town, and village." In her memoir, Livermore wrote admiringly about military volunteers who were escorted through Boston by throngs of supporters. "Merchants and clerks rushed out from stores, bare-headed, saluting them as they passed. Windows were flung up; and women leaned out into the rain waving flags and handkerchiefs." By the time she returned to Chicago a few days later, Livermore was deeply impressed by the popular demonstrations that she had witnessed across the northern landscape; the "war spirit was rampant," she wrote, and "engrossed everybody."

Livermore's account echoed those of other northerners, who were astonished by the precipitous shift in public sentiment and the spirit of cohesiveness that characterized the first days and weeks of the war. In what became a familiar refrain among contemporaries, the North suddenly coalesced into a patriotic whole. Even in a society with a strong voluntarist tradition, and despite frequent evocations of comparable behavior during the Revolutionary War, the scope of civilian initiative during the Civil War seemed unprecedented. Given the contentious partisanship that had characterized the antebellum decades and the divisiveness generated by the secession of the southern states, the sudden disappearance of political differences elicited frequent comment. . . .

"It is easy to understand how men catch the contagion of war," Livermore conjectured; what required explanation was why women, "who send forth their husbands, sons, brothers and lovers to the fearful chances of the battle-field," were willing to endure such "exquisite suffering." The answer, she believed, lay in "another kind of patriotism," a love for their men and their country that diverged from male loyalties and masculine combativeness and provided women with a special strength to maintain "their own courage and that of their households."

Reprinted from Jeanie Attie, " 'We All Have Views Now': Tapping Female Patriotism," in *Patriotic Toil: Northern Women and the Civil War* (Ithaca, N.Y.: Cornell University Press, 1998), 19–47. Copyright © 1998 by Cornell University. Used by permission of the publisher, Cornell University Press.

Implicit in Livermore's commentary on female loyalty was not only the idea that men's patriotism was something ingrained but also the idea that women's support of the war represented a conscious decision to make unique sacrifices in defense of the nation. Many women took on soldier aid work out of concern for husbands, sons, and neighbors leaving for war. Others were propelled by the excitement and urgency that marked mobilization drives. Yet the war's appeal to northern women went deeper than personal attachments or susceptibility to popular passions. Although the ferment surrounding the outbreak of military conflict seemed to cut across all social categories, troop mobilization presented distinct opportunities for many northern women. In a nation with a weak central government and a long tradition of political obligations performed at the local level, the urgent need for civilian support furnished women, especially white women of the middle class, with an occasion for presenting themselves as skilled members of the polity whose contributions were essential to the government's defense, a chance to enact their political beliefs on terms that both they and men appreciated and held to be legitimate. In the emergency conditions generated by war, women welcomed the sudden expansion of the emotional and physical spaces in which they could perform their citizenship. Although the antebellum gender divisions of labor and power meant that women would not be able to dictate either the extent of their political contributions or the measure of their sacrifices, many women nonetheless perceived that the military crisis might erase some of the boundaries that separated them from male preserves of power. . . . .

Mary Livermore was struck by the ways in which the war created arenas for men and women to join together as a newly constituted public, which was sanctioned to support the military on the battlefield whatever the cost. When, at Boston's Faneuil Hall, men filed in military-like columns to answer Lincoln's first call for volunteers, Livermore observed that "men, women, and children seethed in a fervid excitement." Amid the seemingly universal approbation for combat, women felt free to vent a belligerency toward the Confederacy and a fondness for military regalia that contravened the bourgeois socialization of women. Maria Lydig Daly was surprised to hear upper-class New York City women "admiring swords, pistols, etc., and seeming to wish to hear of the death of Southerners." Many women coveted masculine emblems of militarism. In Skowhegan, Maine, one group of women appropriated local artillery to stage "a salute of thirty-four guns." And then there were the famous cases—estimated at a minimum of four hundred—of women who disguised themselves as men and joined the Union army.

But the historic identification of militarism with masculinity also pointed to the disadvantages women faced in enacting their politics. When the ultimate gesture of political obligation was military service, offering one's life for the preservation of the state, more than a few women chafed at the legal constraints imposed on their sex. As soon as the war began, Louisa May Alcott confided in her diary: "I long to be a man; but as I can't fight, I will content myself with working for those who can." Another woman who devoted herself to war relief work reasoned, "[F]or . . . what else can we women do, at such a time as this? We cannot fight ourselves, but we can help those who can."

Although legal and social codes prevented women from performing their loyalties in the same manner as men, war mobilization nonetheless presented women with ways of exploiting the very structures of gender inequality to demonstrate their politics and loyalties. In acts of production and self-denial, many women discovered distinctly feminine methods for increasing their visibility as members of the polity. "They lopped off superfluities, retrenched in expenditures, became deaf to the calls of pleasure, and heeded not the mandates of fashion," Livermore wrote of her middle-class peers. In the production of uniforms and supplies for departing soldiers, women applied their mastery of domestic arts to political uses. Through military rallies, village parades, charity bazaars, and the household production of patriotic artifacts, they devised creative means to express their inclusion in the national crisis, while simultaneously underscoring their identities as women.

The symbol women chose most often to signify their patriotism was the United States flag. This choice of symbol was not surprising; northerners everywhere embraced the flag as an expression of their loyalty to the Union. . . . "Love for the old flag became a passion," Livermore recalled, as women "crocheted it prettily in silk, and wore it as a decoration on their bonnets and in their bosoms." Household reproductions of the flag motif proliferated as women incorporated its design and colors in a variety of crafted items. . . . Along with declaring one's nationalism, the flag could also embody more particular political content. For Livermore, the flag came to represent her antislavery sentiments. . . .

In spite of the poignant emotions they voiced about the purposes of the war and the passion they displayed for political affairs, most northern women were depicted by the popular culture of the war years as personifying a special "female" patriotism. Though women believed they had responded to the war emergency as members of communities and citizens of a nation alongside men, their support of the military was frequently characterized as gender-specific behavior, the manifestation of an apolitical and charitable nature. Whether women expressed their patriotism through their domesticity or as a result of the gendered modes of thought that permeated mid-century American culture, wartime invocations of political cohesion went hand in hand with an intensely gendered nationalist rhetoric. Throughout the war, northern women worked in a context that cast their patriotism as reflecting "feminine" rather than universal political concerns.

The Civil War notion of female patriotism stressed the naturalness of female loyalty, implying that women engaged in mobilization drives and soldier relief out of moral instincts, not political reason. When northern women threw themselves into the war effort, male contemporaries had a readymade intellectual framework through which to comprehend such activities, and few were surprised or unduly impressed. In his account of northern war charity, the Sanitary Commission's chronicler noted that the "earliest movement that was made for army relief [was] begun, as it is hardly necessary to say, by the women of the country." What appeared, rhetorically, to be a single patriotism was, in fact, a dichotomous concept, calling men to patriotic obligation as citizens who offered services to the state through their own free will and summoning women as citizens who were guided by apolitical and irrepressible propensities.

Wartime references to women's distinct political nature were plentiful. In 1863, the conservative *Godey's Lady's Book and Magazine* intoned that, although women could not "grasp all the subjects relating to the world," it was unimportant, for "moral sense is superior to mental power." An 1862 article in *Arthur's Home Magazine* declared that while men dominated as statesmen, patriots, and conquerors, women were invisible but all-important heroines at home. Extolling the female heroism of "self-sacrifice [and] self-denial" the article explained that the "heroisms of the home" were in fact undertaken unconsciously. "They are *only natural.* They are nothing more than the spontaneous impulses and instincts of the heart. Those who perform them could do no less."

The idea of female patriotism repackaged domestic ideology for the war emergency, placing voluntarism and moral purity at the heart of women's political obligations to the state. Just as the antebellum ideology of separate spheres mystified the economic contributions of housework during the expansion of waged labor, so female patriotism veiled women's domestic labor in service to the Union with an aura of sentiment. Because the rhetoric of female patriotism was about love and not work, about sacrifices driven by nature rather than by calculation, women's wartime benevolence was assumed to be limitless. This dichotomous reading of patriotic loyalty elevated men's capacity to control women's unpaid domestic labor, moving from appropriating ownership of such labor in individual households to claiming authority over it for the nation. While men were never asked to perform labor for free, whether as soldiers or agents of benevolent organizations, women were expected to demonstrate their loyalty through donating labor.

One measure of the dominance of this gendered construction of northern patriotism was the effort many women made to distance themselves from it. As if to deflect the repercussions of their unequal access to military service and to question the double standard applied to their patriotic activities, women who wrote about the war frequently stressed the inherent parity of their political passions with those of men. In her autobiography, the feminist Elizabeth Cady Stanton made a point of noting that the "patriotism of woman shone forth as fervently and spontaneously as did that of man." . . .

The sense of possibility that attended women's voluntary support of the Union grew out of the particular conditions of northern mobilization, predicated on the voluntary enlistment of soldiers and the freely offered support of their communities. As a consequence of the customary American reliance on volunteer troops and citizen militia, and of the absence of mandatory conscription policies, the Union army was largely constructed through individual acts of voluntarism. Even after the federal government instituted conscription in 1863, the draft functioned primarily as an incentive to voluntarism (and the bounty systems functioned more as revenue-raising devices), rather than as compulsory means of raising troops. The numerous permissible exemptions to the draft and the prerogative, until the middle of 1864, to pay for substitutes greatly weakened the force of Union draft rules. Throughout the course of the war, the vast majority of men joined the Union forces as volunteers. . . .

In the context of a highly decentralized and voluntaristic mobilization of human and economic resources, middle-class women constituted a wellspring of needed labor and supplies. Anxious to convey loyalty to the Union cause and accustomed to handling the welfare needs of others, thousands of northern middle-class women reacted to the war emergency both by refocusing existing charitable organizations to meet the increased demands of military mobilization and by creating new societies devoted solely to the needs of soldiers.

Many of the initiatives undertaken by women during the first weeks of the war drew on the social networks they had developed in antebellum sewing groups, church associations, and moral reform societies. They also drew on women's extensive domestic skills. It is probable that nearly every nineteenth-century northern woman had some ability to sew and, at the outbreak of the war, most were still responsible for the production of their households' clothing. While the burgeoning textile industry increasingly relieved women from the spinning of yarn and manufacture of cloth, few could afford to rely solely on ready-made clothing. Indeed, most women were regularly occupied with the cutting, sewing, and repairing of clothing. Even genteel women, who could hire the services of seamstresses (and whose husbands and fathers purchased ready-made suits), were expected to be able to sew and do needlework. Women often sewed together, gathering to share each other's company while engaged in the time-consuming task of stitching personal garments. Farm women, with less available time, came together for quilting bees, combining their labor to produce large items, sharing techniques and camaraderie. In smaller towns and villages, women formed sewing circles and "Dorcas" societies, merging work and social interaction in quasi-institutional formats.

Though it was easy to modify the object of a local sewing group to serve the needs of mobilization, the war prompted women in many locales to create organizations specifically charged with aiding the federal war effort and, through a process of renaming, provided women with another means of making their patriotism visible to a larger public. The first recorded soldiers' aid society was constituted on April 15, 1861, in Bridgeport, Connecticut. In many cases, organized relief was instigated by the elite—"leading"—women in the community, such as those in Peekskill, New York, who arranged to receive contributions and prepare supplies before the first volunteers departed from town. The women of Rockdale, Pennsylvania, began war relief within days of the South's insurrection, soon extending their labors to the military hospital in nearby Philadelphia.

The historical record is inherently skewed to reflect the activities of those with the resources and self-consciousness to keep accounts of their doings, or those with sufficient social stature to merit attention in contemporary narratives and regional histories. But working-class women also participated in soldier relief work: some, like their propertied counterparts, as members of local aid societies, and others as laborers hired to work in improvised workshops to produce garments from materials purchased by wealthier neighbors. Mary Marsh reported that at Henry Ward Beecher's Brooklyn church "a dozen sewing machines [were] hard at work ever since Sumter," allowing the wealthier women to boast that they had accomplished "heaps of work." . . .

A few women sought more direct means of providing needed supplies and assistance to the men they gave up to the Union army. Learning of horrid camp conditions, a dearth of nursing services, and inadequate cooking, these women took it upon themselves to carry food and clothing directly to men at the warfront. For many, the line separating the war from the homefront was blurred by the improvisational means through which the army itself was constituted, as well as the realities of a civil war fought on familiar territory at close proximity. While most women paid only brief visits, a few remained at camp, some donning uniforms and traveling with their husbands to battle. The most famous military wife to join her husband at the front was Julia Grant. Coming at General Grant's request, Julia brought their children as well. . . .

As women in remote villages and small cities mobilized themselves to outfit troops and provide supplies, believing that their labors translated into real assistance to the war effort, stories began to surface that their energies were in fact producing an opposite effect. By rumor and hearsay, accounts of useless clothing, ill-fitting uniforms, spoiled food, and overstocked hospital supplies flowed from army camps and military hospitals back to the homefront. Despite the efforts of women who, according to Livermore, "rifled their store-rooms and preserve-closets of canned fruits and pots of jams" and packed all these together with clothing, blankets, and books, the results were dispiriting. "Baggage cars were soon flooded with fermenting sweetmeats, and broken pots of jelly. . . . Decaying fruit and vegetables, pastry and cake in a demoralized condition, badly canned meats and soups . . . were necessarily thrown away *en route*."

More than the cakes stood to become demoralized. Even before such reports surfaced, the prospect that women's labors for the army might be viewed as well-meaning but feeble attempts to augment military strength worried a group of professional and upper-class New York City women. Barely a week after the firing on Fort Sumter, these women anticipated the criticisms that would be leveled at female volunteers. The absence of some system of coordination threatened to efface the considerable labors northern women had undertaken. They concluded that the "uprising of the women of the land" was in need of "information, direction, and guidance." . . .

Only two weeks into the war, [Dr. Elizabeth] Blackwell announced . . . a review of the voluntary activities already under way on behalf of Union recruits. Blackwell invited women from many of New York's leading upper-class and Unitarian families, including Mrs. William Cullen Bryant, Mrs. Peter Cooper, and Mrs. George Schuyler and her daughter, Louisa Lee Schuyler. She also extended an invitation to the Unitarian minister Henry Whitney Bellows, who led the city's prominent All Soul's Church.

The meeting's organizers published a letter the next day in the New York newspapers addressed to the women of New York, "especially . . . those already engaged in preparing against the time of wounds and sickness in the Army." Signed by "Ninety-Two of the Most Respected Ladies," the announcement offered to coordinate the efforts of existing charities and soldiers' aid societies through one organization and warned women that their lack of direct communication with government authorities about the needs of the army would cause problems. Anticipating what indeed was about to happen, the letter predicted that women engaged in voluntary war relief "are liable to waste their enthusiasm, to overlook some claims and overdo others, while they give unnecessary trouble in official quarters." The plan emphasized the collaborative nature of the work; to avoid competition among voluntary associations, no single group would be elevated above any other. The chief goal was to facilitate and intensify what the meeting had identified as the two predominant forms of female war relief contributions: the donation of "labor, skill and money," and the "offer of personal service as nurses." Henceforth both activities would be managed by a single administrative structure. To consolidate the proposals and gain citywide support for the idea, the women's letter called for a second public meeting to be held the next day at Cooper Union.

On April 26, the Great Hall at Cooper Union was filled to capacity. On the platform, according to the *Tribune,* were the "wives and daughters of many of our most distinguished citizens." Among those who addressed the crowd of four thousand were Henry Bellows, Vice President Hannibal Hamlin, and a number of noted physicians. Before adjourning the meeting, a committee of women and men announced the formation of the Woman's Central Association of Relief. The new organization would meet the needs outlined the day before: "give organization and efficiency to the scattered efforts" already in progress; gather information on the wants of the army; establish relations with the Medical Staff of the army; create a central depot for hospital stores; and open a bureau for the examination and registration of nursing candidates. The women's association would be run with the voluntary labor of elite women, but it was to some degree a women's organization in name only. Its board of managers was composed of twelve women and twelve men, and was responsible for the selection of officers. Dr. Valentine Mott was named President and Rev. Henry Bellows Vice President of the Board of Management. Though men were given overriding authority, the association's structure provided a number of well-known, upperclass women with important positions as well. Two women, Mrs. Eliza L. Schuyler and Miss Ellen Collins, were included on the eight-member executive committee. Dr. Elizabeth Blackwell was made chair of the registration committee, which was charged with examining and registering women volunteering as nurses. Louisa Lee Schuyler was appointed corresponding secretary of the WCRA.

Of all the women appointed to the new association, none would have more influence than the young Louisa Lee Schuyler. The daughter of George Schuyler and Eliza Schuyler—one of the "Ninety-Two . . . Most Respected Ladies" and herself a well-known figure in New York's reform circles—Louisa Schuyler was a member of the Dutch Hudson Valley family that traced its lineage to Alexander Hamilton and Philip Schuyler. The Schuylers were also important members of Bellow's All Soul's Church. Then twenty-four years old, Louisa Schuyler was already active in one of the philanthropic enterprises that emerged in prewar New York City, working under the auspices of the Children's Aid Society as a sewing instructor in an industrial school for immigrant children. Louisa Schuyler's appointment as corresponding secretary accorded with her mother's view that the day-to-day running of the office was best left to the "younger ladies." Schuyler worked closely with Ellen Collins, herself a daughter of a wealthy New York merchant family that was prominent in New York philanthropic circles. At the outset of the war, Collins was thirty-two and like Schuyler, unmarried.

As the volume of women's voluntary work grew, Schuyler assumed an increasingly important role in the coordination of homefront relief to the army. Handling the correspondence between the WCRA headquarters and regional societies, she possessed a unique vantage point from which to observe female voluntarism and apprehend the homefront's approach to war relief. "She is certainly a most intelligent & energetic diligent young damsel," George Templeton Strong observed in his diary, "though not pretty at all," he felt compelled to add. . . .

Able to exploit an established network of women's organizations, the women who led the WCRA expected that these groups would be sufficient to meet the demands of warwork. The association promoted greater participation in war relief and pushed for a coordinated handling of supplies, but it refrained from dictating the ways in which localities were to organize themselves and from calling for the creation of new societies. Aware that thousands of women had already rededicated their prewar benevolent and church groups to warwork and that some had even created new aid societies, the WCRA felt confident that these organizations could meet the army's demands. The association emphasized providing accurate information about army needs and assuring the efficient transport of donations from the homefront to the warfront.

The strategy worked; in response to WCRA announcements, hundreds of women mobilized neighbors, collected donations, and forwarded them to the association's office at Cooper Union. For small-town and rural women, the initiative taken by elite urban women provided an example they were anxious to emulate. "On the same day of the monster meeting of ladies at the Cooper Institute in New York," the women of the Dorcas Society of Cornwall, New York, resolved to organize themselves into the Cornwall Soldiers Aid Society and work for the duration of the war. "The response made to our appeals is grand," wrote Louisa Lee Schuyler in August 1861, "and it is a privilege to know and feel the noble spirit that animates the women of the loyal states."

The preliminary work of the Woman's Central Relief Association revealed more than the potential for a mass voluntary participation for the war effort; it also hinted at the possibility of revising popular notions of female sacrifice. Suddenly, women were being flattered and appreciated by national institutions and men of power, who paid tribute to women's supposedly unique contributions and the vital part they played in supplementing the limited, and sometimes shoddy, provisions of the federal government. Here was a scenario in which unpaid female labor might be judged as expressing unqualified political commitment and producing real economic value. The exigencies of war would test the ability of the antebellum ideology of gender to dictate how women's labors were comprehended, whether they would be reviewed as mere emanations of female nature or as the results of human exertion and skill.

Historically, wars have offered the politically disadvantaged opportunities to contribute to the defense of the state in return for expanded rights. African Americans, both slave and free, understood the Civil War to represent just such possibilities; by sacrificing lives and livelihoods to protect the Union, people could "earn" political and civil rights. For women, wars likewise have presented occasions to demonstrate their right to political inclusion by means of economic and personal sacrifices. While women have supported wars for immediate reasons, including the assistance of local regiments and defense of the military cause, the quid-pro-quo formula invariably emerges at war's end. During the American Revolution, colonial women organized consumers' organizations, anti-tea leagues and soldier relief societies. But despite some agitation for their inclusion in the apportionment of political rights during the writing of the Constitution, there was no reciprocity. The gendering of republican concepts of public virtue and liberty positioned women not as active citizens but as mothers of citizens, who possessed the morality necessary for producing virtuous free male citizens but were unsuited for participation in the political realm.

The Civil War portended something different. As a result of decades of agitation for women's rights, the feminist critique of women's secondary status hovered over northern society as an unanswered challenge. Wartime expectations for gains in women's status drew not only on the woman's rights movement but also on the experiences of those women who tried to enact the gender compromise through reform work. . . . With war mobilization so dependent on voluntary civilian support, the time seemed ripe for translating women's assistance to the state into an exchange of support for full inclusion in the body politic. Though women's patriotic sentiments were cast as the natural expression of moral beings, the changing conditions of women's lives and the need for their contributions opened the way for a different reading of their wartime activities. Soon after the fighting began, a number of northerners suggested that this war might permanently alter women's status. The movement for woman's rights was effectively put on hold for the duration of the conflict, as feminists decided it was incumbent on them to demonstrate their loyalty to a state to which they were making bids for greater political access. But expressions of raised expectations came from sectors beyond the woman's rights camp. In fact, it is probable that the American Civil War was the first modern war in which masses of women participated with expectations that their homefront contributions would translate into expanded political rights.

From the outset of the military conflict, the question of political compensation for women's assistance was in the air, palpable, alluded to in public as well as in private statements, by men as well as women. The idea that the war offered women unusual opportunities for advancement was voiced across the political and cultural spectrum. Just as the larger society cohered politically in the face of disunion, so too northern women put aside differences over feminist demands for equality in order to advance the war. In all the expressions of raised expectations lay assumptions that women would make some sort of political gain as result of their wartime sacrifices.

◈ F U R T H E R   R E A D I N G

Blanton, DeAnne, and Lauren Cook. *They Fought Like Demons: Women Soldiers in the American Civil War* (2002).

Campbell, Edward, and Kym Rice, eds. *A Woman's War: Southern Women, Civil War, and the Confederate Legacy* (1997).

Clinton, Catherine. *Civil War Stories* (1998).

Edwards, Laura. *Scarlett Doesn't Live Here Any More: Southern Women in the Civil War Era* (2000).

Fahs, Alice. "The Feminized Civil War: Gender, Northern Popular Literature, and the Memory of the War, 1861–1900," *Journal of American History* 85 (1999): 1461–1494.

Faust, Drew Gilpin. *Mothers of Invention: Women of the Slaveholding South in the American Civil War* (1996).

Giesberg, Judith Ann. *Civil War Sisterhood: The U.S. Sanitary Commission and Women's Politics in Transition* (2000).

Hamand, Wendy F. "The Woman's National Loyal League: Feminist Abolitionists and the Civil War," *Civil War History* 35 (1989): 39–58.

Leonard, Elizabeth. *All the Daring of the Soldier: Women of the Civil War Armies* (1999).

———. *Yankee Women: Gender Battles in the Civil War* (1994).

Women in the Trans-Mississippi Frontier West

Historians of the American frontier used to focus their attention almost entirely on white male figures in western landscapes—explorers and trappers, cowboys and ranchers, miners and traders, railroad workers and corporate owners. Such is no longer the case. Historians now include Indian leaders and warriors, Spanish traders and priests, African American soldiers and Chinese laborers among the men whose historical experiences are critical to a full understanding of America's trans-Mississippi frontier. So too, women of diverse class and ethnic backgrounds are now important figures in historical studies of the American West.

By the nineteenth century, the American West was a place of discord and violence as male and female Anglos, Native Americans, Hispanics, and Asians competed—on highly unequal terms—for land, mineral resources, jobs, and cultural dominance. Disparate cultural communities struggled to co-exist in the "frontier" West as straightforward instances of Anglo "conquest" mixed with patterns of exploitation, dependency, negotiation, and exchange. In the multicultural American West, women's experience was shaped simultaneously by gender, ethnicity, and class. Thus, while thousands of nineteenth-century Indian women and girls witnessed the destruction of their traditional cultures and struggled to negotiate encounters with arrogant whites who believed them to be less than "true women," countless Anglo women of middle-class background experienced the loneliness and hardship that came with trying to transplant, in unfamiliar soil, the ideals and social practices of genteel eastern or midwestern communities. As this example suggests, the West was a place where women of diverse backgrounds encountered tragedy, deprivation, and a loss of status or identity. Yet it was also a place where women attempted both to retain cherished cultural traditions and to prosper amid persistent disadvantage and rapid change. How well did they succeed? What does the historical record tell us about the impact of continental migration and cross-cultural contact on the roles, status, and self-perceptions of Indian, Hispanic, Anglo, and Asian women in the nineteenth- and twentieth-century West? Under what circumstances did women of different racial or ethnic communities sustain injury or a diminution of social standing and power? And when were they able to advance their interests by nego-tiating across cultural or gender boundaries?

◈ D O C U M E N T S

Document 1 offers the observations of Susan Shelby McGoffin, the eighteen-year-old bride of a successful merchant, who traveled to New Mexico with her husband as the Mexican War began, and interacted with both Spanish and American residents of Santa Fe. In Document 2, an anonymous individual pens a letter to a small California newspaper, denouncing the rape of elderly Indian women in Tehama County by a party of United States soldiers who had been sent to that locale to protect white settlers. Document 3 provides examples of several "bills of sale" of Chinese women who "consented" to become prostitutes after they entered the United States in order to repay the individuals who funded their passage from Asia. In Document 4, a young Indian girl describes her eagerness to attend a white-run school for Indian children and the profound disorientation she felt once her journey to the school had begun. Document 5 describes the self-pity and desolation felt by Mrs. A. M. Green, a white native of Pennsylvania, on moving to Colorado's Union Colony with her ambitious young husband and two small children in 1870. In Document 6, Violet Cragg, an ex-slave and former army nurse, requests a pension from the federal government for her service during the Civil War. Cragg's request describes many of the hardships of her life as a black woman, including those encountered while working as a servant for army officers' families in Texas, New Mexico, and Kansas.

1. Susan Shelby Magoffin Describes
Her First Days in Santa Fe, 1846

August 31, 1846 . . .

This morning a Mexican lady, Dona Juliana, called to see me. She is a woman poor in the goods of this world, a great friend to the Americans and especially to the Magoffins whom she calls a *mui bien famile* [*muy buena familia*—very good family]. Though my knowledge of Spanish is quite limited we carried on conversation for half an hour alone, and whether correct or not she insists that I am a good scholar.

Tuesday September 1st.

Today has been passed pretty much as yesterday, in receiving the visits of my countrymen. Dr. Mesure called early, before I had pulled off my wrapper, to congratulate me on my good fortune in getting through the Raton without a fractured limb.

Mr. Houck called too. Brother James dined with us, and also supped on oyster-soup and champain. Like the rest of his brothers he is quite lively, and this evening he appeared unusually so, cracked jokes and spun yarns, laughed, drank &c. He thinks because I take the slow way of travelling and frequent detentions so coolly, that I am quite a phylosophic old woman, and will do to travel any place. He leaves tonight for the *Rio Bajo* settlements to prepare for Gen. Kearny's arrival; and from thence he

Stella M. Drumm, ed., *Down the Santa Fe Trail and into Mexico: The Diary of Susan Shelby Magoffin, 1846–1847*. Copyright © 1926, 1962 by Yale University Press. Reprinted by permission of Yale University Press.

goes to Chihuahua to prepare for us, at least he is to get a house & necessary articles for house-keeping as he did here.

Dona Juliana called again this P. M. to see *mi alma* who was out yesterday. I rather retired from the conversation, save a little which *mi alma* interpreted to her. She is a great rogue to win the respects, good wishes, and esteem of *la nina* [little child], as she flatteringly spoke of me to my good husband, who by the way took it all well. *"A que Don Manuel, la Senora es muy linda, muchachita, la nina! Y que es major, ella es muy afabla, muy placentera, muy buena."* [Ah! Don Manuel, the lady is very pretty, only a little girl, a child: And what is more, she is very affable, very pleasing, very good.] Of course I heard none of this. . . .

Thursday 3rd.

Una Senora [a lady] called to see me today, *mi alma* was in and interpreted for me, so my tongue was *vale nada* [no account]. Her name I do not know as yet, but her *lengua* [tongue] I do, for she kept in constant motion all the time of her visit, which lasted an hour and a half, very fashionable! She is a good old lady I dare say; speaks in favour of the foreigners, and without hesitation says Gen A[r]mijo is a *ladrón* [thief] and coward.

She has great confidence in her own knowledge of *the men,* as she speaks of those staple objects of Creation, and says she wishes we could understand each other sufficiently well that she might give me some advice respecting their snares! She could lesson me to the fullest limit, I'd venture to say.

We are having fine protection near us in case of danger; the soldiers have made an encampment on the common just opposite our house, and though we are situated rather "out of town," we have as much noise about us as those who reside in the center of the city.—We have constant rhumours that Gen. A[r]mijo has raised a large fource of some five or six thousand men, in the South, and is on his march to retake possession of his kingdom. The news has spread a panic among many of his former followers, and whole families are fleeing, lest on his return they should be considered as traitors and treated accordingly.

In other families there is mourning and lamentations, for friends they may never again see on earth. A day or two before Gen. Kearny arrived, A[r]mijo collected a fource of some three thousand men to go out and meet him, and even assembled them ready for a battle in the canon some twelve miles from town, but suddenly a trembling for his own personal safety seized his mind, and he dispersed his army, which if he had managed it properly could have entirely disabled the Gen's troops by blockading the road &c. and *fled himself!* While all these men, the citizens of Santa Fé and the adjacent villages, were assembled in the canon, and their families at home left entirely destitute of protection, the Nevijo [Navaho] Indians came upon them and carried off some twenty families. Since Gen. K.— arrived and has been so successful, they have petitioned him to make a treaty with them, which he will not consent to till they return their prisoners, which 'tis probable they will do thro' fear, as they deem the Gen. something almost superhuman since he has walked in so quietly and taken possession of the pallace of the great A[r]mijo, their former fear.

Friday 4th.

Mi alma has been away all day, and though entirely alone, I cannot say I have grown lonesome, for both my mind and body have been actively engaged.

I have my *housekeeping* to attend to now; and the opportunity for growing lonesome or sad in any way is rather poor. I've been teaching one of the Mexican servants his business how he is to do it &c., and though we have considered him one of the *numbskulls,* I have found him both willing and apt in learning. The great virtue of these servants is their ever pleasant faces; they never begin their work sullenly, and you may change it as often as you please or make them do it over, and over, and they continue in the same good humour, never mouthing and grumbling because they have too much to do, but remain perfectly submissive, and indeed it is a pleasure, when an underling is so faithful, to do them any little favour. Mine is a quiet little household, the servants are all doing their duty, the great bugbear to most house-keepers; and if I can do my duty so well as to gain *one* bright smile and sweet kiss, from my good, kind husband, on his return my joy will be complete for I trust my spiritual business has not been neglected. . . .

Sunday 6th.

I hope the first sabbath in the city of Santa Fé has been passed, so far as opportunities would admit, in a way deserving it. The morning was spent in reading the Bible and other pious books, and in serious reflections.

Though the sabbath, two gentlemen, Lieu. Warner & the aid de camp of our Gen. [called]; with the latter I had some conversation in regard to the neglect of this day by people generally, the traders and soldiers, especially, on the Plains; the advantage of a pious leader to the latter, and this called forth the information of the strict piety of Gen. Kearny an Episcopalian. This is truly fortunate, and increases doubly the already high esteem I have for that General.

Monday 7th. . . .

And today I've been constantly engaged, with my needle, market people, of whom I have gained some little information as to the names of different vegetables, prices &c.

What an everlasting noise these soldiers keep up—from early dawn till late at night they are blowing their trumpets, whooping like Indians, or making some unheard of sounds, *quite shocking to my delicate nerves.*

Tuesday 8th.

No one has called today! surely we are not to be deserted thus! I've sat alone a good part of the day, thinking of those at home; how I should like to step in unawares upon them, and give what I know would be an "agreeable surprise," and how I would like for *some* of them to see me now how very happy and contented I am, how I am delighted with this new country, its people, my new house, or rather my *first* house, *which 'twas supposed* I should not be capable of managing, and last of all what a good, attentive, and affectionate husband I was fortunate enough to choose, though "young and wholly inexperienced." . . .

Wednesday 9th.

Una Senora called this morning, and as usual when *mi alma is out.* I talked a good deal, she thinks I both speak and understand *bastante* [sufficiently] What an inquisitive, quick people they are! Every one must know if I have *una madre un padre, hermanos e hermanas* [a mother, father, brothers, and sisters], their names &c. They examine my work if I am engaged at any when they are in, and in an instant can tell me how it is done, though perhaps 'tis the first of the kind they have ever seen.

The market affords us fine *durasnos* [peaches] and delicious grapes, which though quite small are remarkably sweet and well flavoured; also good melons, the apples though, are inferior.

Thursday 10th.

A cool day this, such weather though as we have had for more than a week. The air is fine and healthy; indeed the only redeeming quality of this part of New Mexico is its perfectly pure atmosphere, not the damp unhealthy dews of the States. One can walk through the deep grass here, and his shoes will never show at any time, either late in the evening or at early dawn, the slightest moisture. We have occasionally a little thunder and slight sprinkle of rain, enough to settle the dust.

News is received that Gen. Kearny will be here by the 12th and that Col. Price, who has command of an other detachment of Malitia from the States, will be in soon, he is now within a few miles of the city. Lieut. Warner has waited on me this A. M. with an invitation to attend a Spanish ball given by the officers to the traders. As the only *traderess,* it would be offending in me after so polite a request, not to exhibit myself to the *managerie,* along with other bipeds of curiosity.

Friday 11th.

What did I write of last yesterday? The managerie, well, now for a little critical view of it. I went in of course somewhat prepared to see; as I have often heard of such a show, I knew in a measure what to look for. First the ballroom, the walls of which were hung and fancifully decorated with the "stripes and stars," was opened to my view—there were before me numerous objects of the biped species, dressed in the seven rain-bow colours variously contrasted, and in fashions adapted to the reign of King Henry VIII, or of the great queen Elizabeth, *my memory* cannot exactly tell me which, they were entirely enveloped, on the first view in a cloud of smoke, and while some were circling in a mazy dance others were seated around the room next the wall enjoying the scene before them, and quietly puffing, both males and females their little cigarritas a delicate cigar made with a very little tobacco rolled in a corn shuck or bit of paper. I had not been seated more than fifteen minutes before Maj. Soards an officer, a man of quick perception, irony, sarcasm, and wit, came up to me in true Mexican style, and with a polite, "Madam will you have a cigarita," drew from one pocket a *handfull of shucks and from an other a large horn of tobacco,* at once turning the whole thing to a burlesque.

Among the officers of the army I found some very agreeable, and all were very attentive to me. Liuts. Warner & Hammund, the principal managers of affairs did themselves credit in their interested and active movements to make the time pass agreeably to their visitors.

El Senor Vicario [the priest] was there to grace the gay halls with his priestly robes—he is a man rather short of statue, but that is made up in width, which not a little care for the stomach lends as assisting hand in completing the man. There was "Dona Tula" the principal *monte-bank keeper* in Santa Fé, a stately dame of a certain age, the possessor of a portion of that shrewd sense and fascinating manner necessary to allure the wayward, inexperienced youth to the hall of final ruin. There was Col. Donathan, a native of Ky. "as you will see by my *statue* Madam," leaving unknowing listeners to believe that state the mother of a giant tribe. There, too, circling giddily through the dance, Cpt M[oore] of [First] Dragoons; if necessary we can be sure of at least one person to testify to the "virtues or vices" of what has been graphically called "the ingredient." There in that corner sits a dark-eyed Senora with a human footstool; in other words with her servant under her feet—a custom I am told, when they attend a place of the kind to take a servant along and while sitting to use them as an article of furniture.

The music consisted of a gingling guitar, and violin with the occasional effort to chime in an almost unearthly voice. *Las Senoras y Senoritas* [the ladies and girls—young ladies] were dressed in silks, satins, ginghams & lawns, embroidered crape shawls, fine rabozos—and decked with various showy ornaments, such as hugh necklaces, countless rings, combs, bows of ribbands, red and other coloured handkerchiefs, and other fine *fancy* articles. This is a short sketch of a Mexican ball. Liuts Warner & Hammond called this evening to see how I *enjoyed* the dance (not that I joined [in] it myself).

Saturday 12th.

William arrived this morning, and oh, how provoked I am with him; he had letters for me and instead of bringing them left them in his trunk at the wagons. I may almost expect some of the express by the time they get here, the wagons have that ugly Raton to pass through, and to be broken all to pieces, and mended before they get here. Men are such provoking animals when they take it into their heads. I must be more expert in my Spanish, that I may receive the advice that la Senora [the lady—Mrs.] Ortis wishes to give me respecting them; how I shall *punish them for their misconduct,* spoil them for their good deeds, & other little fixings—

2. A Citizen Protests the Rape of Indian Women in California, 1862

Editor *Beacon:*—It is well known that there is, or has been, a body of soldiers in this county for several weeks past, for the avowed object of defending and protecting the citizens of the county against Indian depredations. . . .

Beacon (Red Bluff), October 9, 1862. This document can also be found in Robert Hezier, ed., *The Destruction of California Indians* (Santa Barbara, Calif.: Peregrine Smith, 1974), 281–283.

On Friday night a party of these soldiers visited the ranch of Col. Washington, and made themselves annoying to the Indians in the rancheria. This party was small, only three, as reported.

Saturday night, the 4th of October, 1862, was made memorable by the visit of a portion of this command, headed, aided and abetted by the commanding officer, Lieut. ———, (or some one assuming his title,) to the farm of Col. Washington, and to the rancheria of peaceful and domesticated Indians resident thereon. Not one of the soldiers, private or Lieutenant, (or pretended Lieutenant, if such he was,) called at the farm house, but rode by and entered the Indian rancheria, with demands for Indian women, for the purpose of prostitution! They were requested to leave and ordered off the place. They answered they would do as they pleased, as they had the power. They were then told that it was true they were the strongest, and no force at hand was sufficient to contend with them, and they were left in the Indian rancheria. Most of the young squaws in the rancheria had by this time ran off and concealed themselves, and were beyond the reach and brutal grasp of the ravishers. They, however, were to be satiated, and like brutes dragged the old, decrepit "tar-heads" forth, and as many as three of the soldiers, in rapid succession, had forced intercourse with old squaws. Such was the conduct of the portion of the command of Co. E, on the night of the 4th of October, 1862, who visited the Indian rancheria at the Old Mill Place, about 3 miles from N. L. headquarters.

It is but proper, after consulting with those who are acquainted with the outrage, to say that the Lieut. (or pretended Lieut., if such he was,) did not arrive at the scene of action until after the larger portion of his men were on the ground—But it is absolutely certain that he was there—that he put his horse in the stable to hay, and then prowled around and through the Indian rancherias in quest of some squaw. Whether he found a fit subject upon which to practice his virtuous and civilizing purposes, the writer is not informed. He, however, saddled up and left the scene of moral exploit about daylight.

In justice to decency, humanity and civilization, these brutes should be punished. It is due to the honor, the reputation, the chivalry of the army of the United States, that the insignia of rank and position should be torn from the person of the Lieutenant (if it was he who was there,) as an officer unworthy its trust and confidence.

3. Bills of Sale of Chinese Prostitutes, 1875–1876

An Agreement Paper by the Person Mee Yung

At this time there is a prostitute woman, Yut Kum, who has borrowed from Mee Yung $470. It is distinctly understood that there shall be no interest charged on the money and no wages paid for services. Yut Kum consents to prostitute her body to receive company to aid Mee Yung for the full time of four years. When the time is fully served, neither service nor money shall be longer required.

If Yut Kum should be sick fifteen days she shall make up one month. If she conceives, she shall serve one year more. If during the time any man wishes to redeem

Congressional Record, 43rd Congress, 2d session, March 1875, 3, pt. 3: 41.

her body, she shall make satisfactory arrangements with the mistress, Mee Yung. If Yut Kum should herself escape and be recovered, then her time shall never expire. Should the mistress become very wealthy and return to China with glory, then Yut Kum shall fulfill her time, serving another person.

This is a distinct agreement made face to face, both parties willingly consenting. But lest the words of the mouth should be without proof, the agreement-paper is executed and placed in her hands for proof. There are four great sicknesses against which Mee Yung is secured for one hundred days, namely, leprosy, epilepsy, conception, and "stone-woman," i.e., inability to have carnal intercourse with men. For any of these four diseases she may be returned within one hundred days.

Truly with her own hands Mee Yung hands over $470.

Tung Chee 12th year, 8th month, 14th day. The agreement is executed by Mee Yung.

Contract Between Ah Ho and Yee-Kwan

An agreement to assist the woman Ah Ho, because coming from China to San Francisco she became indebted to her mistress for passage. Ah Ho herself asks Mr. Yee-Kwan to advance for her $630, for which Ah Ho distinctly agrees to give her body to Mr. Yee for services as a prostitute for a term of four years.

There shall be no interest on the money. Ah Ho shall receive no wages. At the expiration of four years Ah Ho shall be her own master. Mr. Yee-Kwan shall not hinder or trouble her. If Ah Ho runs away before her time is out her mistress shall find her and return her, whatever expense is incurred in finding and returning her Ah Ho shall pay.

On this day of the agreement Ah Ho with her own hands has received from Mr. Yee-Kwan $630.

If Ah Ho shall be sick at any time for more than ten days she shall make up by an extra month of service for any ten days' sickness.

Now this agreement has proof. This paper received by Ah Ho is witness.

TUNG CHEE.

Twelfth year, ninth month, fourteen day.

An Agreement to Assist a Young Girl Named Loi Yau

Because she became indebted to her mistress for passage, food, &c., and has nothing to pay, she makes her body over to the women Sep Sam, to serve as a prostitute to make out the sum of $503. The money shall draw no interest, and Loi Yau shall receive no wages. Loi Yau shall serve four and a half years. On this day of agreement Loi Yau receives the sum of $503 in her own hands. When the time is out Loi Yau may be her own master, and no man shall trouble her. If she runs away before the time is out and any expense is incurred in catching, then Loi Yau must pay that expense. If she is sick fifteen days or more, she shall make up one month for every fifteen days. If Sep Sam should go back to China, then Loi Yau shall serve another

"Chinese Immigration," *Senate Report 689,* 44th Congress, 2d Session (serial 1734): 145, 146.

party till her time is out. If in such service she should be sick one hundred days or more, and cannot be cured, she may return to Sep Sam's place. For a proof of this agreement this paper.

LOI YAU.

Dated second day sixth month of the present year.

4. Zitkala-Ša Travels to the Land of the Big Red Apples, 1884

The first turning away from the easy, natural flow of my life occurred in an early spring. It was in my eighth year; in the month of March, I afterward learned. At this age I knew but one language, and that was my mother's native tongue.

From some of my playmates I heard that two paleface missionaries were in our village. They were from that class of white men who wore big hats and carried large hearts, they said. Running direct to my mother, I began to question her why these two strangers were among us. She told me, after I had teased much, that they had come to take away Indian boys and girls to the East. My mother did not seem to want me to talk about them. But in a day or two, I gleaned many wonderful stories from my playfellows concerning the strangers.

"Mother, my friend Judéwin is going home with the missionaries. She is going to a more beautiful country than ours; the palefaces told her so!" I said wistfully, wishing in my heart that I too might go.

Mother sat in a chair, and I was hanging on her knee. Within the last two seasons my big brother Dawée had returned from a three years' education in the East, and his coming back influenced my mother to take a farther step from her native way of living. First it was a change from the buffalo skin to the white man's canvas that covered our wigwam. Now she had given up her wigwam of slender poles, to live, a foreigner, in a home of clumsy logs.

"Yes, my child, several others besides Judéwin are going away with the palefaces. Your brother said the missionaries had inquired about his little sister," she said, watching my face very closely.

My heart thumped so hard against my breast, I wondered if she could hear it.

"Did he tell them to take me, mother?" I asked, fearing lest Dawée had forbidden the palefaces to see me, and that my hope of going to the Wonderland would be entirely blighted.

With a sad, slow smile, she answered: "There! I knew you were wishing to go, because Judéwin has filled your ears with the white man's lies. Don't believe a word they say! Their words are sweet, but, my child, their deeds are bitter. You will cry for me, but they will not even soothe you. Stay with me, my little one! Your brother Dawée says that going East, away from your mother, is too hard an experience for his baby sister."

Thus my mother discouraged my curiosity about the lands beyond our eastern horizon; for it was not yet an ambition for Letters that was stirring me. But on the following day the missionaries did come to our very house. I spied them coming up

---

Zitkala-Ša, *American Indian Stories* (1921; reprint, Lincoln: University of Nebraska Press, 1985), 39–45.

the footpath leading to our cottage. A third man was with them, but he was not my brother Dawée. It was another, a young interpreter, a paleface who had a smattering of the Indian language. I was ready to run out to meet them, but I did not dare to displease my mother. With great glee, I jumped up and down on our ground floor. I begged my mother to open the door, that they would be sure to come to us. Alas! They came, they saw, and they conquered!

Judéwin had told me of the great tree where grew red, red apples; and how we could reach out our hands and pick all the red apples we could eat. I had never seen apple trees. I had never tasted more than a dozen red apples in my life; and when I heard of the orchards of the East, I was eager to roam among them. The missionaries smiled into my eyes and patted my head. I wondered how mother could say such hard words against him.

"Mother, ask them if little girls may have all the red apples they want, when they go East," I whispered aloud, in my excitement.

The interpreter heard me, and answered: "Yes, little girl, the nice red apples are for those who pick them; and you will have a ride on the iron horse if you go with these good people."

I had never seen a train, and he knew it.

"Mother, I am going East! I like big red apples, and I want to ride on the iron horse! Mother, say yes!" I pleaded.

My mother said nothing. The missionaries waited in silence; and my eyes began to blur with tears, though I struggled to choke them back. The corners of my mouth twitched, and my mother saw me.

"I am not ready to give you any word," she said to them. "Tomorrow I shall send you my answer by my son."

With this they left us. Alone with my mother, I yielded to my tears, and cried aloud, shaking my head so as not to hear what she was saying to me. This was the first time I had ever been so unwilling to give up my own desire that I refused to hearken to my mother's voice.

There was a solemn silence in our home that night. Before I went to bed I begged the Great Spirit to make my mother willing I should go with the missionaries.

The next morning came, and my mother called me to her side. "My daughter, do you still persist in wishing to leave your mother?" she asked.

"Oh, mother, it is not that I wish to leave you, but I want to see the wonderful Eastern land," I answered.

My dear old aunt came to our house that morning, and I heard her say, "Let her try it."

I hoped that, as usual, my aunt was pleading on my side. My brother Dawée came for mother's decision. I dropped my play, and crept close to my aunt.

"Yes, Dawée, my daughter, though she does not understand what it all means, is anxious to go. She will need an education when she is grown, for then there will be fewer real Dakotas, and many more palefaces. This tearing her away, so young, from her mother is necessary, if I would have her an educated woman. The palefaces, who owe us a large debt for stolen lands, have begun to pay a tardy justice in offering some education to our children. But I know my daughter must suffer keenly in this experiment. For her sake, I dread to tell you my reply to the missionaries. Go, tell them that they may take my little daughter, and that the Great Spirit shall not fail to reward them according to their hearts."

Wrapped in my heavy blanket, I walked with my mother to the carriage that was soon to take us to the iron horse. I was happy. I met my playmates, who were also wearing their best thick blankets. We showed one another our new beaded moccasins, and the width of the belts that girdled our new dresses. Soon we were being drawn rapidly away by the white man's horses. When I saw the lonely figure of my mother vanish in the distance, a sense of regret settled heavily upon me. I felt suddenly weak, as if I might fall limp to the ground. I was in the hands of strangers whom my mother did not fully trust. I no longer felt free to be myself, or to voice my own feelings. The tears trickled down my cheeks, and I buried my face in the folds of my blanket. Now the first step, parting me from my mother, was taken, and all my belated tears availed nothing.

Having driven thirty miles to the ferryboat, we crossed the Missouri in the evening. Then riding again a few miles eastward, we stopped before a massive brick building. I looked at it in amazement, and with a vague misgiving, for in our village I had never seen so large a house. Trembling with fear and distrust of the palefaces, my teeth chattering from the chilly ride, I crept noiselessly in my soft moccasins along the narrow hall, keeping very close to the bare wall. I was as frightened and bewildered as the captured young of a wild creature.

5. Mrs. A. M. Green Gives an Account of Frontier Life in Colorado, 1887

Of the founder of this place I have nothing to say except that I regret the sad manner in which he came to his death, for I really believe he was a very pure minded man, and one who sought the good of his fellow beings. After securing several lots in the new town, we pitched our tent, which was almost daily blown to the ground. To say that I was homesick, discouraged and lonely, is but a faint description of my feelings.

It was one of those terrible gloomy days that I sat in my lonely tent with my baby, Frank, in my arms, who was crying from the effects produced by the sands of the American desert, while beside my knee stood my little Sisy, (as we called her) trying to comfort her brother by saying: "Don't cry, F'ankie, we is all going back to grandpa's pitty soon, ain't we, mamma?" Not receiving an immediate answer from me, she raised her eyes to mine, from which gushed a fountain of burning tears. "Don't cry, mamma," said she; "sing to F'ank like you always does, and he will stop crying." I obeyed the child's request. . . .

As I closed my song the curtain raised and my husband entered, sank wearily on a three-legged stool and took up our little five-year-old, placed her upon his tired knee and then addressed me thus: "Well, dear, how do you get along to-day? I see the tent hasn't blown down." I attempted to answer in the negative, but failed, the meaning of which he comprehended in a moment. Notwithstanding any vain attempts to conceal my emotion, he pressed to his sad heart the little charge which he held in his arms, saying in a low voice: "Darling little one, you and your poor

Mrs. A. M. Green, *Sixteen Years on the Great American Desert; or, the Trials and Triumphs of a Frontier Life* (Titusville, Pa.: Frank Truedell, Printer, 1887), 8–31. This document can also be found in Ruth Moynihan, Susan Armitage, and Christiane Fischer Dichamp, eds., *So Much to Be Done: Women Settlers on the Mining and Ranching Frontier* (Lincoln: University of Nebraska Press, 1990), 123–146.

mamma have hard times, don't you?" Then turning to me, he said: "Annie, I am very sorry for you. If I had compelled you to come to this country I could never forgive myself; as it is, I feel that you reflect on me." By this time I had regained my speech and endeavored with all my might, mind and strength to convince him to the contrary. Whether I succeeded or not I never knew, but I resolved there and then to cultivate a cheerful disposition, which I believe has prolonged my life, for, at the rate I was going into despair at that time, I could not have retained my reason six months' longer, and doubtless the brittle thread of life would have been snapped long ere this. O how thankful I am that I still live to love, work and care for those whom to me are dearer than life itself! If I have one wish above another in this world, it is that I may live a long and useful life. . . .

The 7th of July was Sabbath, and in those days I was usually found under the droppings of the sanctuary, for, though there was not a church in the town, we had regular services every Sabbath in the Union Colony Hall; but this morning I felt so depressed in spirits that I dispensed with going, and busied myself in writing to those for whom my heart panted continually. I had finished my third letter, closing up with a fervent prayer to Him whom I had been taught to believe would hear and answer the prayer of faith, for the preservation of my life, and also for those to whom I had been writing, until we should meet again (?) when the word *never, never,* sounded in my ear, and penetrated my aching heart with an arrow, the effect of which I feel to this day. At that moment my little girl approached me bearing in her hand the picture of her who loved me first and best on earth. I took it from the child, pressed it to my quivering lips, and cried: Oh, God, bereave me not of her! Until this time I had not ventured to open our album, but now that the ice was broken, I looked it through while tears gushed from my eyes. During this terrible emotion my husband returned from church, and again found me in tears and deep sorrow. This added pain to his already desponding heart. "Annie," said he, with a self-reproaching look, and in a pathetic tone which I shall never forget, "do you know you are killing me?" "I thought," he continued, "you had resolved to cultivate a more cheerful disposition; this will not do; it is cruel in the extreme for me to compel you to remain where you are so unhappy." My heart bounded for joy; and then, my pulse stood still to listen for the much longed for sentence,—we will go home; but, alas! it came in the singular number; "you must go home." "What!" I cried, "go without you, no, never," and I repeat those words to-day; and ever shall, so long as circumstances control my husband's freedom. Again I resolved to try and be cheerful, but, my resolution and promise were but to be broken in less than twenty-four hours. On this occasion the physician was summoned and my disease pronounced mountain fever, from which I recovered, after an illness of six weeks. During all my affliction I had answered each letter from home without intimating that I was out of health, until the shortness of my communications excited their attention, and they demanded an explanation, which I was obliged to give.

It was now August, but oh! how different from any one which I had ever witnessed. Not a tree, plant nor shrub on which to rest my weary eye, to break the monotony of the sand beds and cactus of the Great American Desert. My attention was often called to the grandeur of the snow capped Rocky Mountains, towering toward the skies; and although I sometimes feigned an appreciation of their beauty in order to coincide with my other half, who displayed much anxiety to have me

month before President Lincoln was assassinated. No, I did not have any husband either white or colored. I was 18 years old when my daughter was born and I was only about 16 when I came to St. Louis, Mo. The City of Alton was a hospital boat and there were twelve doctors on it. Dr. Edenton of Peoria, Ill., was one of the doctors on the boat and I knew him at Peoria, Ill. Dr. Abbey had two sons, Sidney and George. George was a captain in the Confederate army. Dr. Abbey's wife was living. I was known by the name Violet Evans when I was bought by Dr. Abbey and afterwards I was known as Violet Abbey. My father was Jefferson Williams and I took the name Williams after I was free. He died in Sacramento, Calif. My mother is dead too. I went to Sacramento to visit him once. That was about 1894. I never saw my mother after I was sold away from her. I have a sister two years and a half younger than I am, Mrs. Sarah Dorsey, who lives in Sacramento, I don't know her husband's first name. I never saw her from the time I was sold "down the river" until I saw her in 1894. My father said it was 37 years since he had seen me. I have no other brothers or sisters living. After I was at Fort Duncan, Texas, I worked for different families at Matamoras, Brownsville, and Ringgold Barracks, Texas, Camp Supply, Ind. Terr., and Dodge City, Kans. I went from Dodge City to Junction City, Kans., and was married to soldier at the latter place. Much of the time I worked as a laundress, doing the washing of a great many different people, and it is impossible for me to name persons with whom I was acquainted in all the different places I lived before my marriage. My memory is very poor since I became paralyzed on my left side seven years ago and I have a nervous trouble and my heart is weak. This high altitude affects my heart. I was never married, however, until I married the soldier. My daughter lived with me or near me until my marriage to soldier and her husband was a soldier in the same regiment as Allen Cragg. He is now retired and living in Santa Fe. He and my daughter can testify that soldier and I were not divorced. Jeremiah Brabham knew me at Dodge City, Kans., and he and Israel Murphy knew me at Junction City, Kans. They also knew us for seven or eight years in Los Angeles and Israel Murphy served with my husband in the 9th Cavalry. I had lovers and sweethearts during the period before I married Cragg, plenty of them, but I never had but one lawful husband. I never had a license to marry but one man and I was never married to but one man and that was Allen Cragg. I never knew nor heard nor had reason to believe that my husband was married before his marriage to me. He always claimed that he had never been married before and he enlisted as a single man in 1880 and in 1885 and his last discharge showed that he was a married man while the others did not show it. He was born in Kentucky and went into the army as a drummer boy during the war. I don't know where he grew up. He had a brother Clay who died, but I don't know of his having any brothers or sisters living. Israel Murphy served with him in the volunteer service and knew him long before his marriage and they served in the same troop in the 9th Cav. I worked for the U.S. Consul at Matamoras whose name was Wilson. I worked for a Mrs. Tuttle at Fort Duncan, Texas. I washed for a lot of soldiers and officers at Brownsville and Ringgold Barracks. I cannot give names. I worked for an old lady in Dodge City, Kans., who kept a restaurant, but I do not remember her name. I became acquainted with soldier only a short time before I married him. I am utterly unable to furnish any further data as to non-prior [sic] marriage of either myself or my husband, Allen Cragg. I have no photograph of soldier taken during the war or very soon after, but will furnish one taken with me after our marriage, or can furnish one taken in his soldier's uniform about 1889. The latter is the better likeness and I should like to have it returned to me after it has served its purpose. I have understood and thoroughly comprehended the questions asked and my answers are correctly recorded in this deposition which I have heard read. Soldier had a scar on his leg, but don't remember which leg from a gunshot wound received during his volunteer service. The wound was in the calf of the leg. There were no other marks or scars on his body as far as I know. I cannot write. I applied for a pension as an army nurse several years ago in Los Angeles and my claim was rejected because I did not serve six months. The contraband hospital was in ward 6 at Benton Barracks. I have no papers in my possession referring to said claim and I have forgotten the name of the attorney who filed the claim for me. He was an old soldier in Los Angeles and a regular pension attorney. I have heard the foregoing read, have understood the same, and am correctly recorded herein.

her

Violet "X" Cragg

mark

E S S A Y S

The essays that follow explore the complex interactions of Spanish-Mexican women and Chinese women with Anglo-Americans in the American West, looking both at the losses these women sustained and at their efforts to exert agency or turn hardship into opportunity. Judy Yung, University of California, Santa Cruz, Emerita, examines the serious abuse that Chinese women faced in late-nineteenth-century San Francisco, as well as the new opportunities and identities that began to open for them. Deena J. González, of Loyola Marymount University, Los Angeles, looks at the life and legend of Gertrudis Barceló, a Spanish-Mexican business woman in Santa Fe who found ways to profit from her interaction with Anglo conquerors.

Chinese Women in Nineteenth-Century San Francisco

JUDY YUNG

Few women were in the first wave of Chinese immigrants to America in the mid-nineteenth century. Driven overseas by conditions of poverty at home, young Chinese men—peasants from the Pearl River delta of Guangdong Province (close to the ports of Canton and Hong Kong)—immigrated to Gold Mountain in search of a better livelihood to support their families. . . . Like other immigrants coming to California at this time, Guangdong men intended to strike it rich and return home. Thus, although more than half of them were married, most did not bring their wives and families. . . . [B]ecause of the high costs and harsh living conditions in California, the additional investment required to obtain passage for two or more,

Judy Yung, excerpts from "Bound Feet: Chinese Women in the Nineteenth Century," chapter 1 in *Unbound Feet: A Social History of Chinese Women in San Francisco* (Berkeley and Los Angeles: University of California Press, 1995), 15–51. Copyright © 1995 Judy Yung. Reprinted by permission.

and the lack of job opportunities for women, it was cheaper and safer to keep the family in China and support it from across the sea. . . .

Although initially welcomed to California as valuable labor and investors in an expanding economy, Chinese immigrants quickly became the targets of white miners, workers, and politicians when the gold ran out and economic times turned sour. . . . Laws were also passed by the California legislature that denied Chinese basic civil rights, such as the right to immigrate, give testimony in court, be employed in public works, intermarry with whites, and own land. Negatively stereotyped as coolie labor, immoral and diseased heathens, and unassimilable aliens, the Chinese were driven out of the better-paying jobs in the mines, factories, fishing areas, and farmlands. They were generally not allowed to live outside Chinatown, and their children were barred from attending white schools. . . .

The most damaging blow to Chinese immigration and settlement proved to be the Chinese Exclusion Act of 1882, passed by a Congress under siege from white labor and politicians at the height of the anti-Chinese movement. The act suspended the immigration of Chinese laborers to the United States for ten years. It was renewed in 1892 for another ten years, and in 1904 extended indefinitely. The Exclusion Acts were strictly enforced until they were repealed in 1943. . . . Although the number of Chinese immigrants dropped sharply—only 92,411 entered during the Exclusion period (1882–1943), as compared to 258,210 prior to the 1882 act—Chinese immigration was not totally stopped. . . . Chinese immigrants who could pool enough money to become partners in import-export businesses were able to attain merchant status and so send for their wives and children. Many others who had merchant or U.S. citizenship status would falsely report a number of sons (rarely daughters) in China, thereby creating "paper son" slots that were then sold to fellow villagers who desired to immigrate. . . . Wives of laborers, although not specifically mentioned in the act, were barred by implication. . . .

The Exclusion Act severely limited the number of Chinese women who could come to America, keeping a crack open mainly for the privileged few—the wives and daughters of merchants. But in fact, rigorous enforcement of the act, along with the implementation of anti-Chinese measures regulating prostitution such as the Page Law of 1875, kept even those Chinese immigrant women with legitimate claims out of the country and made immigration to America an ordeal for any woman who tried to enter. Immigration officials apparently operated on the premise that every Chinese woman was seeking admission on false pretenses and that each was a potential prostitute until proven otherwise. Only women . . . who had bound feet and a modest demeanor were considered upper-class women with "moral integrity." . . .

A good number of the Chinese women who came to the United States in the nineteenth century—despite the social, economic, and political barriers—settled in San Francisco: 654, or 37 percent of all Chinese women in the country, lived in San Francisco in 1860; 2,136, or 47 percent, in 1900. But they were still grossly outnumbered by men, who on the average made up 95 percent of the total Chinese population during these years. . . . Most had either been sold into prostitution or domestic slavery, or they were coming to join their husbands. . . .

As in China, Chinese women stayed close to home and appeared as little as possible in public. Indeed, the predominantly male and relatively lawless society of mid-nineteenth-century San Francisco contributed to their sheltered existence. Moreover, the Chinese kinship system, which formed the buttress for patriarchal control in Chinatown, successfully kept them outside the power structure: only men could be members of the clan and district associations that governed Chinatown, or of the trade guilds and tongs (secret societies) that regulated both legal and illicit businesses. Footbinding, practiced only among the merchant wives, was not necessary to stop Chinese women in San Francisco from "wandering"; their physical and social mobility was effectively bound by patriarchal control within Chinatown and racism as well as sexism outside. . . .

Whereas the majority of white prostitutes came to San Francisco as independent professionals and worked for wages in brothels, Chinese prostitutes were almost always imported as unfree labor, indentured or enslaved. Most were kidnapped, lured, or purchased from poor parents by procurers in China for as little as $50 and then resold in America for as much as $1,000 in the 1870s. One young woman testified in 1892:

> I was kidnapped in China and brought over here [eighteen months ago]. The man who kidnapped me sold me for four hundred dollars to a San Francisco slave-dealer; and he sold me here for seventeen hundred dollars. I have been a brothel slave ever since. I saw the money paid down and am telling the truth. I was deceived by the promise I was going to marry a rich and good husband, or I should never have come here. . . .

A selected number of young women were sold to wealthy Chinese in San Francisco or outlying rural areas as concubines or mistresses and sequestered in comfortable quarters. As long as they continued to please their owners, they were pampered and well cared for. But if they failed to meet their masters' expectations, they could be returned to the auction block for resale. The remainder of the women either were sold to parlor houses that served well-to-do Chinese or white gentlemen or ended up in cribs catering to a racially mixed, poorer clientele.

Parlor houses were luxurious rooms on the upper floors of Chinatown establishments that were furnished with teakwood and bamboo, Chinese paintings, and cushions of embroidered silk. Here, anywhere between four and twenty-five Chinese courtesans, all richly dressed and perfumed, were made available to a select clientele. The "exotic" atmosphere, the relatively cheap rates, and the rumor that Chinese women had vaginas that ran "east-west" instead of "north-south" attracted many white patrons. . . .

In contrast, the cribs—considered the end of the line—were shacks no larger than twelve by fourteen feet, often facing a dimly lit alley, where prostitutes hawked their wares to poor laborers, teenage boys, sailors, and drunkards for as little as twenty-five cents. The cribs were sparsely furnished with a washbowl, a bamboo chair or two, and a hard bed covered with matting. The women took turns enticing customers through a wicket window with plaintive cries of "Two bittee lookee, flo bittee feelee, six bittee doee!" Harshly treated by both owners and customers and compelled to accept every man who sought their business, most women succumbed to venereal disease. Once hopelessly diseased, they were discarded on the street or locked in a room to die alone. Thus, Chinese prostitutes in San Francisco, exploited as they were for their bodies by men who had control over their fates and livelihoods, were the archetype of female bondage and degradation.

Various studies of the manuscript schedules of the U.S. population censuses indicate that a high percentage of the Chinese female population in San Francisco worked as prostitutes: from 85 to 97 percent in 1860; 71 to 72 percent in 1870; and 21 to 50 percent in 1880. There were reasons for these high percentages. . . . Chinese cultural values and American immigration policies that discouraged the immigration of women resulted in a skewed sex ratio that, when combined with anti-Chinese prejudice and antimiscegenation attitudes (institutionalized in 1880 when California's Civil Code was amended to prohibit the issuance of a marriage license to a white person and a "Negro, Mulatto, or Mongolian"), forced most Chinese immigrants to live a bachelor's existence. Stranded in America until they could save enough money to return home, both married and single Chinese men found it difficult to establish conjugal relations or find female companionship. Some married other women of color— black, Mexican, or Native American; a few cohabited with white women; but the majority sought sexual release in brothels. The demand for Chinese prostitutes by both Chinese and white men intersected with an available supply of young women sold into servitude by impoverished families in China. What resulted was the organized trafficking of Chinese women, which proved immensely profitable for the tongs that came to control the trade in San Francisco. . . .

As hopeless and pathetic as this picture of enslavement appeared, Chinese prostitutes found a number of escape avenues. As in China, they were sometimes redeemed and married, mostly to Chinese laborers who had saved enough money to afford a wife. A few successfully ran away with lovers despite the heavy bounty often placed on the man's head by the owner. Others escaped their sordid reality through insanity or suicide by swallowing raw opium or drowning themselves in the bay— an honorable act of protest and vengeance by Chinese cultural standards. But being in America accorded them additional avenues of resistance. A few went to the police for protection. Some women, like Mah Ah Wah and Yoke Qui, two women detained by the authorities upon arrival, were able to escape prostitution by refusing to accept bail, claiming that they had been imported for immoral purposes against their will. Both were remanded to China. . . .

The most viable option open to Chinese prostitutes was two Protestant mission homes that singled them out for rescue and rehabilitation beginning in the 1870s; for in their view, "Of all the darkened and enslaved ones, the Chinese woman's fate seems the most pitiful." Inspired by the Social Gospel Movement, missionary women were intent on establishing female moral authority in the American West and rescuing female victims of male abuse. They saw Chinese women as the ultimate symbol of female powerlessness, as exemplified in their domestic confinement, sexual exploitation, and treatment as chattel. Unable to work effectively among Chinatown bachelors and spurned by white prostitutes, they found their calling among Chinese prostitutes and *mui tsai*. In turn, some Chinese prostitutes, calculating their chances in an oppressive environment with few options for improvement, saw the mission homes as a way out of their problems. . . .

Many . . . Chinese women sought refuge at the Presbyterian Mission Home. . . . As superintendent of the home from 1877 to 1897, Margaret Culbertson devised the technique of rescue work, whereby brothels were raided with the assistance of the police whenever a Chinese girl or woman sent word for help. According to Donaldina Cameron, who succeeded Culbertson, approximately 1,500 girls were rescued in this way during the first thirty years of the home's existence. Because of the high value placed on prostitutes, owners went to great expense to recover their "property," hiring highbinders to retrieve the women or paying legal fees to file criminal charges against the women on trumped-up charges of larceny. Once rescued, the women often had to be guarded in the home and defended in court. As inmates, the women were subjected to strong doses of Christian doctrine and a regimented life of constant activity, the combination of which was meant to instill "virtue" in them. . . . Women were assigned household chores, taught Chinese and English, trained for industrial or domestic employment, and encouraged to work for wages either sewing in the Mission Home or serving as domestic workers outside the institution. Some—particularly those assigned to the home by the courts— resented the restrictions and austerity of the Mission Home and chose to return to their former status. Others opted to return to China. A significant number, however, agreed to marry Chinese Christians and begin life anew in America. . . .

Chinese women who sought help from the mission homes were neither powerless victims nor entirely free agents, but women who lived in a world with many constraints and few opportunities. Recognizing that the Mission Home offered them a chance to change their circumstances, they went there with their own hidden agendas. A number of entrants to the Presbyterian Mission Home between 1874 and 1880 were prostitutes who wanted the protection of home officials in order to marry suitors of their choice. Other women used the Mission Home as a temporary refuge from male abuse, to escape arranged marriages, or to gain leverage in a polygynous marriage. Although they were genuinely grateful for the services of the Mission Home, many did not convert to Christianity or end up mirroring the Victorian ideals of womanhood. Rather, . . . Chinese wives came to shape a new set of gender relations in their Chinese American marriages.

Not far from the reaches of prostitution were *mui tsai*—girls who were brought from China to work as domestic servants in affluent Chinese homes or brothels, or young daughters of prostitutes who worked in this capacity in brothels. Although John W. Stephens, in his study of the manuscript censuses, estimates that only 2 percent of Chinese women were listed as "young servants" in the 1870 census, their presence and role were more significant than that. The *mui tsai* system, a cultural carryover from China, was generally regarded by the Chinese as a form of charity for impoverished girls. The term itself comes from the Cantonese dialect and means "little sister." Under this age-old system, poor parents would sell a young daughter into domestic service, usually stipulating in a deed of sale that she be freed through marriage when she turned eighteen. Meanwhile, the girl received no wages for her labor, was not at liberty to leave of her own free will, and had no legal recourse for complaint should she be mistreated, raped, or forced into an unhappy marriage. . . . There was no guarantee that their contracts would be honored—that they would obtain freedom through marriage when they came of age. Indeed, depending on the family's economic situation, a *mui tsai* could be resold into prostitution for a handsome sum. . . . Nevertheless, like organized prostitution, the *mui tsai* system had all but vanished by the 1920s thanks to the efforts of missionary women and Chinese social reformers intent on modernizing Chinatown—this in a country, it should be noted, where slavery had been abolished in 1865 and contract labor in 1885.

Between 1870 and 1880, the percentage of Chinese women in San Francisco who were prostitutes had declined from 71 to 50 percent, while the percentage of women who were married had increased from approximately 8 to 49 percent, most likely owing to the enforcement of antiprostitution measures, the arrival of wives from China, and the marriage of ex-prostitutes to Chinese laborers. The number of wives continued to rise after the passage of the Chinese Exclusion Act of 1882, when merchant wives became the prime category of female immigrants from China. By the turn of the century, married women made up 62 percent of the Chinese female population in San Francisco.

Within the patriarchal structure of San Francisco Chinatown, immigrant wives occupied a higher status than *mui tsai* and prostitutes, but they too were considered the property of men and constrained to lead bound lives. Members of the merchant class, capitalizing on miners' and labor crews' need for provisions and services, were among the first Chinese to come to California. They were also the only Chinese who were allowed to and who could afford to bring their wives and families, or to establish second families in America. In the absence of the scholar-gentry class, which chose not to emigrate, the merchant class became the ruling elite in Chinatown, and their families formed the basis for the growth of the Chinese American population and the formation of the middle class.

Referred to as "small-foot" or "lily-feet" women in nineteenth-century writings because of their bound feet, most merchant wives led the cloistered life of genteel women. They generally had servants and did not need to work for wages or be burdened by the daily household chores of cooking, laundering, and cleaning. . . . At least one merchant wife in San Francisco Chinatown did not view her life . . . positively, though. "Poor me!" she told a white reporter. "In China I was shut up in the house since I was 10 years old, and only left my father's house to be shut up in my husband's house in this great country. For seventeen years I have been in this house without leaving it save on two evenings." To pass her time, she worshiped at the family altar, embroidered, looked after her son, played cards with her servant, or chatted with her Chinese neighbors. Periodically, her hairdresser would come to do her hair, or a female storyteller would come to entertain her. Her husband had also provided her with a European music box and a pet canary. Only through her husband, servant, hairdresser, and female neighbors was she able to maintain contact with the outside world.

Despite her wealth, she envied other women "who are richer than I, for they have big feet and can go everywhere, and every day have something new to fill their minds." This woman, however, as she was well aware, was still only a piece of property to her husband, always fearful of being sold "like cows" if her husband tired of her, or of having her son taken from her and sent back to China to the first wife. Also, as she herself pointed out, she had few avenues of escape. Chinatown was governed by the laws of China, and the Mission Home could provide her with only a temporary refuge. "I am too old for any man to desire in marriage, too helpless in the ways of making money to support myself, too used to the grand living my husband provides to be deprived of it."

In fact, however, such women of leisure were but a small proportion of immigrant wives in the late nineteenth century. Most wives were married to Chinese laborers who, having decided to settle in America, had saved enough money to send for a wife or to marry a local Chinese woman—most likely a former prostitute or American-born. As it was for other working-class immigrant women, life for this group of wives was marked by constant toil, with little time for leisure. Undoubtedly, they were the seamstresses, shirtmakers, washerwomen, gardeners, fisherwomen, storekeepers, and laborers listed in the manuscript census. Even those listed as "keeping house" most likely also worked for wages at home or took in boarders to supplement their husbands' low wages. In addition to their paid work, they were burdened with child care and domestic chores, which they had to perform in crowded housing arrangements. According to the San Francisco Health Officer's Report for 1869–70, "Their mode of living is the most abject in which it is possible for human beings to exist. The great majority of them live crowded together in rickety, filthy and dilapidated tenement houses like so many cattle." . . .

Like peasant women in China, working-class wives in San Francisco could freely go out to work, worship at the temple, or shop in the Chinatown stores that provided for all their needs. But they did not travel far from home or mingle with men. Even when they spent an occasional evening at the Chinese opera, they would sit in a separate section from the men. Nor did they linger long in the streets, so threatened were they by the possibility of racial and sexual assaults. . . . As it became more difficult to import Chinese prostitutes, Chinese women found themselves the targets of kidnappers, sometimes in broad daylight, to be sold into prostitution. During one week in February 1898, eight such kidnappings occurred. . . .

One of the advantages for women who immigrated to America was the chance to remove themselves from the rule of the tyrannical mother-in-law, the one position that allowed women in China any power. Not only was the daughter-in-law freed from serving her in-laws, but she was also freed of competition for her husband's attention and loyalty and given full control over managing the household. Because of the small number of Chinese women, wives in America were valued and accorded more respect by their men (although there were still incidences of wife abuse). In addition, most Chinese men, because of their low socioeconomic status, could not afford a concubine or mistress, much less a wife. Thus, having a wife was a status symbol to be jealously guarded. . . .

Wives were also more valued in America because they were essential helpmates in the family's daily struggle for socioeconomic survival. As it was for European immigrants, the family's interest was paramount, and all members worked for its survival and well-being. A Chinese wife's earnings from sewing, washing, or taking in boarders could mean the difference between having pork or just bean paste with rice for dinner, or between life and death for starving relatives back in China. It was also her duty to cook and prepare the Chinese meals and special foods for certain celebrations, to maintain the family altar, to make Chinese clothing and slippers for the family, to raise the children to be "proper Chinese," and to provide a refuge for the husband from the hostile world outside. Thus, even while the family was a site of oppression for Chinese women in terms of the heavy housework and child care responsibilities and possibly wife abuse, it was also a source of empowerment. Wives ran the household and raised the children; they also played an important role in the family economy and in maintaining Chinese culture and family life as a way of resisting cultural onslaughts from the outside.

As Protestant women gained a foothold in bringing Christianity, Western ideas, and contact with the outside world into Chinatown homes, Chinese wives became more aware of their bound lives. They also became an important link between the Chinese family and the larger society and an influential factor in the education and socialization of Chinese American children. Convinced that there was little hope of redeeming the Chinese unless the women were converted to Christianity and Americanized, missionary women visited Chinese homes regularly to give lessons on the Bible and American domestic and sanitary practices, often while the women worked—"one woman making paper gods, another overalls, another binding shoes." . . .

These visits won few converts, but some mothers were persuaded to educate their daughters and discontinue the practice of binding their feet, and a small number of women also began to venture out of the home to attend church functions. Abused wives also found their way to the mission homes. Records of the Presbyterian Mission Home indicate that a number of "runaway wives" came asking for help when they were threatened with being sold, subjected to beatings, or just unhappy with their husbands. In one case, Lan Lee, who had continually been beaten by her husband and threatened with murder, was assisted by the Presbyterian mission in winning a divorce on the grounds of extreme cruelty in 1893. Slowly, Chinese women were becoming aware of legal rights in America, rights that European women already knew how to take advantage of. . . .

Even at this early stage of their history, Chinese women were adapting to life in Gold Mountain with mixed results. Although most of them lived bound lives, remaining confined to the domestic sphere and subordinate to men, their important roles as producers (wage earners) and reproducers (childbearers as well as homemakers) in a predominantly male and pervasively racist land elevated their value as scarce commodities and essential helpmates to their men. Others, most notably prostitutes and *mui tsai,* suffered considerable abuse in America but found new options opened to them, through the assistance of missionary women and what legal rights were available to them at the time. Nonetheless, . . . it took the additional influence of Chinese nationalism and its inherent feminist ideology, combined with increased economic opportunities and the continued support of Protestant women, before Chinese immigrant women could become "new women" in the modern era of the twentieth century.

The Life and Legend of Gertrudis Barceló in Nineteenth-Century Santa Fe

DEENA J. GONZÁLEZ

In the summer of 1846, Doña Gertrudis Barceló stood at an important crossroad. Exempted from the hardships and tribulations endured by the women around her, Barceló had profited enormously from the "gringo" merchants and itinerant retailers who had arrived in Santa Fé after the conquest. The town's leading businesswoman, owner of a gambling house and saloon, and its most unusual character, Barceló exemplified an ingenious turnaround in the way she and others in her community began

Deena J. González, "Gertrudis Barceló: La Tules of Image and Reality," in *Latina Legacies: Identity, Biography, and Community.* Edited by Vicki L. Ruiz and Virginia Sanchez Korrol. (New York: Oxford University Press, 2005), pp. 39–58. Copyright © 2005 by Oxford University Press, Inc. Used by permission of Oxford University Press, Inc.

resolving the problem of the Euro-American, now lodged more firmly than ever in their midst. Barceló also epitomized the growing dilemma of dealing with newcomers whose culture and orientation differed from hers.

Since 1821, people like Barceló had seen traders enter their town and change it. But local shopkeepers and vendors had done more than observe the developing marketplace. They had forged ahead, establishing a partnership with the adventurers who brought manufactured items and textiles to Santa Fé while exporting the products of Nuevo México, including gold, silver, and equally valuable goods, such as Navajo blankets and handwoven rugs. . . .

Gertrudis Barceló was said to have controlled men and to have dabbled in local politics, but these insinuations do not form the core of her legend. Rather, reporters of her time, professional historians today, and novelists have debated her morals, arguing about her influence over political leaders and speculating about whether she was operating a brothel. These concerns are consistently revealed in early accounts of Barceló by writers and soldiers recalling their experiences in the "hinterlands" of northern Mexico. The negative images and anti-Mexican stereotypes in these works not only stigmatized Barceló but also helped legitimize the Euro-Americans' conquest of the region. Absorbed and reiterated by succeeding generations of professional historians and novelists, the legend of Barceló has obscured the complex reality of cultural accommodation and ongoing resistance.

Moreover, the legend evolving around Barceló affected the lives of other Spanish-Mexican women. Her supposed moral laxity and outrageous dress were generalized to include all the women of Santa Fé. Susan Shelby Magoffin, the first Euro-American woman to travel down the Santa Fé Trail, observed in 1846 that "These were dressed in the Mexican style; large sleeves, short waists, ruffled skirts, and no bustles—which latter looks exceedingly odd in this day of grass skirts and pillows. All danced and smoked cigarittos, from the old woman with false hair and teeth [Doña Tula], to the little child."

This was not the first account of La Tules, as Barceló was affectionately called (in reference either to her slimness or to her plumpness, because *tules* means "reed")[.] Josiah Gregg, a trader during the 1830s, said that La Tules was a woman of "loose habits," who "roamed" in Taos before she came to Santa Fé. In his widely read *Commerce of the Prairies,* Gregg linked local customs—smoking, gambling, and dancing—to social and moral disintegration. La Tules embodied, for him and others, the extent of Spanish-Mexican decadence. . . .

Josiah Gregg . . . first brought Barceló notoriety because his book described her as a loose woman. But Gregg also argued that money from gambling eventually helped elevate her moral character. A Protestant, and a doctor in failing health, Gregg respected only her gift—the one he understood best—for making money. During her lifetime, she became extraordinarily wealthy, and for that reason as well, Gregg and others would simultaneously admire and disdain her. . . .

Since the 1820s, Barceló had engaged in an extremely profitable enterprise. Gambling, dubbed by observers the national pastime, was ubiquitous, and by the mid-1830s nearly every traveler and merchant felt compelled to describe Barceló's contributions to the game. . . . By any account, Euro-Americans could understand what drove Barceló. Because they recognized in her their own hungry search for profit, they embellished their stories and, just as frequently, maligned her.

When Barceló died in 1852, she was worth over ten thousand dollars, a sum twice as high as most wealthy Spanish-Mexican men possessed and larger than the average worth of Euro-Americans in Santa Fé. Her properties were extensive: she owned the saloon, a long building with large rooms, and she had an even larger home not far from the plaza. She made enough money to give generously to the church and to her relatives, supporting families and adopting children. Military officers claimed that she entertained lavishly and frequently.

Dinners, dances, gambling, and assistance to the poverty-stricken elevated Barceló to a special place in New Mexican society, where she remained throughout her life. The community respected her since it tolerated atypical behavior in others and rarely seemed preoccupied with what Barceló represented. Even her scornful critics were struck by how well received and openly admired the woman with the "red hair and heavy jewelry" was among Santa Fe's "best society."

What was it about Nuevo México in the two decades before the war that allowed a woman like Barceló to step outside the accepted boundaries of normal or typical female behavior, make a huge sum of money, undergo excessive scrutiny, primarily by newcomers to Santa Fé, and yet be eulogized by her own people? Some answers lie within her Spanish-Mexican community, which, although beset by persisting problems, had flexibility and an inclination toward change. Others lie in the general position and treatment of women in that society.

Court records and other documents reveal that Santa Fé's women were expected to defer to men but did not, that they were bound by a code of honor and respectability but often manipulated it to their advantage, and that they were restrained by fathers and brothers from venturing too far out of family and household but frequently disobeyed them. One professional historian has argued that social codes in colonial New Mexican society, with their twin emphasis on honor and virtue, were primarily metaphors for expressing hierarchical relationships but also served to resolve conflict as much as to restrict women. . . .

Barceló's gambling and drinking violated the rigid codes that organized appropriate female behavior, but such behavior was not the key to her distinctiveness. Rather, her success as a businesswoman and gambler gave her a unique independence ordinarily denied women. Thus, the most hostile comments about her frequently came from Spanish-Mexican women. In particular, complaints filed against Barceló reveal the extent of other women's animosity, not men's, and were usually thinly disguised as aspersions on her honor. In 1835, Ana María Rendón remonstrated that Barceló and Lucius Thruston, a migrant from Kentucky, were cohabiting. In fact, Barceló's husband lived in the same house, indicating that Thruston was probably a boarder. Honor lay in the proof, and Barceló achieved both by defending herself and her husband as well. Another time, Barceló complained about a slanderous comment made by Josefa Tenório and was also exonerated. Spanish-Mexicans of Santa Fé remained a litigious people, and they waged battles on many fronts. The *alcalde* court (local court) prevailed as the best place to seek resolution. However, Catholic Spanish-Mexican *vecinos* were generally a forgiving people, especially where slander and gossip were involved. Barceló forgave Ana María Rendón's complaint when Rendón retracted it, and the records are filled with similar recantations in other cases.

At issue, then, were not Barceló's violations of gender and social codes—she had in part moved beyond that—but the others' violations of her good name and reputation. On one level, their hostility and outright distrust of Barceló were vendettas directed against a neighbor on the road to wealth and prestige. On another, women upheld the gender code (albeit with some trepidation) because, in complaining about Barceló, they defended themselves and their society. Even when she was fined for gambling, the amounts were so minuscule that they neither halted Barceló's gambling nor conveyed a forceful message about modifying social behavior.

Barceló, a married woman, would not have been able to step outside the boundaries of her society . . . if there were no disjunction between the idealized married life and the conditions that stood in the way of its realization—conditions such as taking in boarders or having children out of wedlock. Rallitas Washington, Barceló's grandniece born out of wedlock, as well as hundreds of other women whose mothers were unmarried, formed a decidedly heterodox, yet devoutly Catholic, community. In relationships as in personal behavior, these women's lack of conformity did not shake the conscience of a community as much as needle it. . . .

Barceló cleverly crossed social and sexual barriers to gamble, make money, buy property, and influence politicians, but she avoided marginality. She did not regard herself as a marginal woman, nor was she necessarily marginalized, except by Euro-Americans. She was unusual and she was mocked for it, but not by her own people. In fact, her life and legend are interesting precisely because, in the eyes of observers, she came to represent the worst in Spanish-Mexican culture while, as a Spanish-Mexican, she mastered the strategies and methods of the Americanizers. . . .

Translated into several languages, Gregg's *Commerce of the Prairies* was reprinted three times between 1844, when it first appeared, and 1857. Thousands of readers learned through him of the "certain female of very loose habits, known as La Tules." What Gregg and the others could not communicate to their audience was that La Tules was adaptable, and that, before their eyes, she had begun disproving their notion that Spanish-Mexicans were "lazy and indolent." . . .

Barceló was hardly the excessive woman the travelers depicted. Instead, she became pivotal in the achievement of their conquest. Worth thousands of dollars, supportive of the army, and friendly to accommodating politicians, Barceló was in the right place to win over Spanish-Mexicans for the intruders. Using business and political skills, she made the saloon the hub of the town's social and economic life, and at the hall she kept abreast of the latest political developments. Politicians and military officers alike went there seeking her opinion or involved her in their discussions about trade or the army. As adviser and confidante, she took on a role few other women could have filled. If she existed on the fringes of a society, it was because she chose to place herself there—a woman with enormous foresight who pushed against her own community's barriers and risked being labeled by the travelers a madam or a whore.

Such caricatures denied her contributions to the economy and the society. Had she not been a gambler, a keeper of a saloon, or a woman, she might have been praised for her industry and resourcefulness, traits that antebellum Euro-Americans valued in their own people. But from the point of view of the writers, the admirable qualities of a woman who lived by gambling and who was her own proprietor would have been lost on Protestant, middle-class readers. Furthermore, they could hardly imagine, let alone tolerate, the diversity Santa Fé exhibited. It became easier to reaffirm their guiding values and walk a literary tightrope by making La Tules a symbol of

Spanish-Mexican degeneracy or an outcast altogether. Barceló had exceeded their wildest expectations, and in their eyes she was an outlaw.

Yet the aspersions heaped on Barceló were not designed solely to obscure her personality and life or to make her activities legendary. They created an image that fit the Euro-Americans' preconceptions about Spanish-Mexicans. . . .

Racial slurs and derogatory comments about Mexicans appeared regularly in the *Congressional Record,* in newspapers, and, not coincidentally, in travel accounts. Speeches and statements consistently equated brown skin with promiscuity, immorality, and decay. Albert Pike, who arrived in New Mexico from New England in 1831, called the area around Santa Fé "bleak, black, and barren"; New Mexicans, he said, were "peculiarly blessed with ugliness." The chronicler of a military expedition of New Mexico in the 1840s, Frank Edwards, said that all Mexicans were "debased in all moral sense" and amounted to little more than "swarthy thieves and liars." The same judgments were made later, long after the war had ended, and reflect the persistence of the same thinking. . . .

These select references—and there are hundreds of other comments like them—depict a set of racist attitudes and ethnocentric beliefs from the Jacksonian period that carried into Santa Fé. Travelers thus mirrored the intrinsic values of a nation encroaching on Mexican territory and were fueled by the heightened fervor over destiny and superiority. . . .

To the Protestant mind, nothing short of the complete elimination of gambling would lift New Mexicans out of their servility and make them worthy of United States citizenship. The Jacksonian Americans wanted to replace gambling with industry and enterprise. To them, gambling stemmed from a fundamental lack of faith in the individual, and it was risky besides. Travelers called monte a game of chance; they said that it required no particular skills and brought undeserved wealth. By that logic, La Tules, a dealer par excellence, was not an entrepreneur; her wealth was undeserved because it sprang from "unbridled passions." Her gravest sin against Protestant ethics became not the unskilled nature of her trade or her undeserved success but her lack of restraint: her wealth was uncontrolled. Yet initial misgivings about Barceló and the games passed after many entertaining evenings at the gambling house. Once soldiers and others began going there, they lingered, and returned often. Deep-seated anti-Mexican feelings and moralistic judgments gave way to the profits that awaited them if they won at monte, or the pleasures to be savored each evening in Santa Fé even if they lost.

At the numerous tables that lined Barceló's establishment, men who could not speak Spanish and people who did not understand English learned a new language. Card games required the deciphering of gestures and facial expressions but did not depend on any verbal communication. Soldiers and travelers new to Santa Fé understood easily enough what was important at the gaming table. Over cards, the men and women exchanged gold or currency in a ritual that emblazoned their meetings with new intentions. Drinking, cursing, and smoking, the soldiers and others unloaded their money at the table; if Barceló profited, they lost. But the game was such a diversion for the lonely soldiers that they hardly seemed to mind. The stakes grew larger at every turn, and many dropped away from the table to stand at the bar. Barceló's saloon took care of those who did not gamble as well as those who lost. Sometimes a group of musicians arrived and began playing. Sometimes women—who, if not gambling, had been observing the scene—cleared a space in the long room, and dancing began.

Barceló did more than accommodate men by inviting them to gamble. She furthered their adjustment to Santa Fé by bringing them into a setting that required their presence and money. At the saloon, the men were introduced to Spanish-Mexican music, habits, and humor. They could judge the locals firsthand and could observe a community's values and habits through this single activity. After they had a few drinks, their initial fears and prejudices gradually yielded to the relaxed, sociable atmosphere of the gambling hall. . . .

Barceló was was not the only one practicing accommodation; it worked in two directions. Whether obeying the community's laws or breaking them, new men were adjusting to life away from home. Santa Fé modified the settling Euro-Americans, at times even the sojourning ones, and Barceló had begun to socialize them in the traditions of an older settlement. The people of the Dancing Ground continued their practice of accepting newcomers, particularly those who seemed able to tolerate, if not embrace, the community's religious and secular values.

At the same time, the conquering soldiers were armed, as the merchants Gregg and Webb were, with purpose and commitment. Military men brought plans and realized them: a fort above the town was begun the day after Kearny marched into Santa Fé. Soldiers built a two-story-high flagstaff, and the imposing structure on the plaza attracted visitors from the Dancing Ground who came supposedly to admire it, but probably also were there to assess the military's strength. What better symbol than a new garrison and an obtrusive monument rising high for all the people to notice? Soldiers hailed these crowning achievements as signs of blessings from God to a nation destined to control the hemisphere, but locals were not so pleased.

A new wave of resistance derailed Barceló's efforts to help resettle Euro-Americans in Santa Fé. Nevertheless, even after her death in 1852, Barceló's legend continued to indicate that her role extended beyond the immediate helping hand she had lent Euro-Americans. No documents written by her, except a will, have survived to tell whether she even recognized her accomplishment or if she read much into the assistance she had given the American cause. Her wealth would suggest that she might have harbored an understanding of her influential status in the process of colonization. One fact remains, whether she realized it or not: beginning with her, the accommodation of Euro-Americans proceeded on several levels. Barceló had inaugurated the first, at the gambling hall, and she set the stage as well for the second, when women began marrying the newcomers.

But as one retraces the original surrounding tensions—deriving from the steady and continuing presence of traders, merchants, and soldiers—and juxtaposes them against Barceló's achievement as an architect of a plan that reconciled the Euro-American to Santa Fé, the realities of displacement and encroachment must not be forgotten. Lieutenant Dyer reported problems as he observed them, and he commented a year after his arrival in Santa Fé: "Still it began to be apparent that the people generally were dissatisfied with the change." In January 1847, resisters in Taos caught and scalped Governor Charles Bent, leaving him to die. In the spring, a lieutenant who had been pursuing horse thieves was murdered, and forty-three Spanish-Mexicans were brought to Santa Fé to stand trial for the crime. In October of the same year, some months after several revolts had been suppressed and their instigators hanged, Dyer reported "a large meeting of citizens at the Palace," where speakers expressed "disaffection at the course of the commissioned officers."

Local dissatisfaction and political troubles had not subsided, in spite of Barceló's work. In the late 1840s, Navajos and Apaches stepped up their raids, and reports filtered in of surrounding mayhem. The garrisoned soldiers grew impatient and acted rashly, and Dyer reported that "a Mexican was unfortunately shot last night by the sentinel at my store house. Tonight we have a rumor that the Mexicans are to rise and attack us." The government in Santa Fé was being forced again to come to terms with each new case of racial and cultural conflict, because it was still charged with trying murders and treason, and it had now become the seat for initiating solutions. Problems no longer brewed outside; they had been brought home by accommodated Euro-Americans.

But Barceló should not be blamed here, as she has been by some, for so many problems. She symbolized the transformations plaguing her people. She symbolized as well how an older community had handled the arrival of men from a new, young nation still seeking to tap markets and find a route to the Pacific. Moreover, she exemplified contact and conflict between independent female Catholics and westering male Protestants. The political and social constraints within which she existed had not disappeared as a community contemplated what to do with the strangers among them.

The people of Santa Fé did not kill any newcomers as residents of Taos had. Surrounding the Dancing Ground, stories and legends of other people resisting Americanization were about to begin, and these no longer emphasized accommodation. Barceló was unusual in that way as well. She was of a particular time and a special place. The famed resister to American encroachment, Padre Antonio José Martínez of Taos, opposed (in his separatist plans and principles) all that Barceló had exemplified. A legend developed around him that stands in interesting contrast to La Tules's. . . .

Yet in giving herself to the conquest, but not the conquerors, [Barceló] survived and succeeded. She drew betting clients to her saloon; they played but lost; she gambled and won. In the end, the saloon that attracted conquerors released men who had been conquered.

◈ *F U R T H E R   R E A D I N G*

Armitage, Susan, and Betsy Jameson, eds. *The Women's West* (1987).

Babcock, Barbara, and Nancy J. Parezo. *Daughters of the Desert: Women Anthropologists and the Native American Southwest, 1880–1980: An Illustrated Catalogue* (1980).

Bouvier, Virginia M. *Women and the Conquest of California* (2001).

Brooks, James F. *Captives and Cousins: Slavery, Kinship, and Community in the Southwest Borderlands* (2002).

Butler, Anne M. *Daughters of Joy, Sisters of Mercy: Prostitutes in the American West, 1865–1890* (1985).

Casas, Maria Raquel. *"Married to a Daughter of the Land": Interethnic Marriages in California* (2005).

Chavez-Garcia, Miroslava. *Negotiating Conquest: Gender and Power in California, 1770s to 1880s* (2004).

Del Castillo, Adelaida R., ed. *Between Borders: Essays on Mexicana/Chicana History* (1990).

Fink Deborah. *Agrarian Women: Wives and Mothers in Rural Nebraska, 1880–1940* (1992).

Foote, Cheryl J. *Women of the New Mexico Frontier, 1846–1912* (1990).

Gonzalez, Deena J. *Refusing the Favor: The Spanish-Mexican Women of Santa Fe, 1820–1880* (1999).

Gutierrez, Ramón A. *When Jesus Came the Corn Mothers Went Away: Marriage, Sexuality, and Power in New Mexico, 1500–1846* (1991).

Haas, Lizbeth. *Conquests and Historical Identities in California, 1769–1936* (1995).

Hirata, Lucie Cheng. "Free, Indentured, Enslaved: Chinese Prostitutes in Nineteenth-Century America," *Signs* 5 (Autumn 1979): 3–29.

Hoffert, Sylvia D. "Childbearing on the Trans-Mississippi Frontier, 1830–1900," *Western Historical Quarterly* 22 (1991): 273–288.

Hune, Shirley, and Gail M. Nomura, eds. *Asian/Pacific Islander Women: A Historical Anthology* (2003).

Jensen, Joan M., and Darlis A. Miller. "The Gentle Tamers Revisited: New Approaches to the History of Women in the American West," *Pacific Historical Review* 49 (1980): 173–213.

Kolodny, Annette. *The Land Before Her: Fantasy and Experience of the American Frontiers, 1630–1860* (1984).

Ling, Huping. "Family and Marriage of Late-Nineteenth- and Early-Twentieth-Century Chinese Immigrant Women," *Journal of American Ethnic History* 19 (2000): 43–63.

Lomawaima, K. Tsianina. *They Called It Prairie Light: The Story of Chilocco Indian School* (1994).

Martin, Patricia Preciado. *Songs My Mother Sang to Me: An Oral History of Mexican-American Women* (1992).

Matsumoto, Valerie J., and Blake Allmendinger, eds. *Over the Edge: Remapping the American West* (1999).

Mihesuah, Devon A. *Cultivating the Rosebuds: The Education of Women at the Cherokee Female Seminary* (1993).

Milner II, Clyde A., ed. *A New Significance: Re-envisioning the History of the American West* (1996).

Nacy, Michele J. *Members of the Regiment: Army Officers' Wives on the Western Frontier, 1865–1890* (2000).

Osburn, Katherine M. B. " 'To Build up the Morals of the Tribe': Southern Ute Women's Sexual Behavior and the Office of Indian Affairs, 1895–1932," *Journal of Women's History* 9 (1997): 10–27.

Pascoe, Peggy. *Relations of Rescue: The Search for Moral Authority in the American West, 1874–1939* (1990).

Riley, Glenda. *Confronting Race: Women and Indians on the Frontier, 1815–1915* (2004).

———. *Taking Land, Breaking Land: Women Colonizing the American West and Kenya, 1840–1940* (2003).

Schlissel, Lillian, Vicki L. Ruiz and Janice Monk, eds. *Western Women: Their Land, Their Lives* (1988).

Van Kirk, Sylvia. *Many Tender Ties: Women in Fur Trade Society, 1670–1870* (1980).

Yohn, Susan. *A Contest of Faiths: Missionary Women and Pluralism in the American Southwest* (1995).

C H A P T E R
10

Women's Work and Work Cultures in Modern America, 1890–1920s

During the late nineteenth and early twentieth centuries, women became a significant presence in the American labor force, accounting for nearly 22 percent of all wage earners by 1930. Though they were as yet unwelcome in the majority of occupations and professions, millions of women found employment as factory operatives, retail clerks, and clerical workers. Women workers had not always been so conspicuous. For most of the nineteenth century, the labor force was overwhelmingly male and women were limited to a handful of occupations, the most common being live-in domestic service. In the decades after the Civil War, however, industrialization created millions of new jobs in manufacturing and commerce. Many jobs required only modest skills or strength and were highly repetitive; employers quickly hired single women to fill them, reasoning that "working girls" would suffer low wages and monotony with fewer complaints than men. To some extent, the employers' assumptions proved correct. Since women were usually ignored by unions, most could ill-afford to complain about their wages or conditions of work. Moreover, the majority planned to work only until they married and thought it not in their interest to pursue formal changes in the workplace. With great advantage accruing to employers, the industrial work force thus became highly sex segregated.

Women in the work force were also divided by ethnicity, class, and race. Working-class and European immigrant women flocked to factory positions, while middle-class women with a high-school or advanced education favored white-collar employment or tried to gain professional status in fields such as teaching, nursing, and social work that were also expanding in response to industrialization. A small number of educated and ambitious black, Hispanic, and Asian women also entered the so-called "feminized" professions or the world of business, but most women of African American, Mexican, and Asian heritage (married or single) filled the domestic service jobs abandoned by more fortunate women.

While historians recognize the disadvantages under which women labored in the early twentieth century, their attention has recently turned to evaluating what paid employment actually meant to women and the society around them. Did contemporary observers consider women's growing presence in the industrial, clerical, and professional sectors of the labor force a sign of meaningful and positive change in gender roles or social relations? How did wage work alter women's sense of self and their relations with family members and the wider community? Were women able to challenge or subvert disagreeable features of their work, even when they lacked the formal authority to do so? Finally, despite the intentions of their employers, did women discover in patterns of gender or racial segregation a foundation for workplace or professional solidarity?

D O C U M E N T S

In Document 1, Rose Cohen, a young Russian-Jewish immigrant, describes the exhaustion, exploitation, and loneliness she experienced in her first job in a New York City sweatshop in 1892. In Document 2, Fannie Barrier Williams comments on the employment difficulties facing black women, urging them to make the best of segregation and to treat domestic service as a field open to "unlimited improvement." In Document 3, Harriet Brunkhurst, writing for the *Ladies Home Journal* in 1910, speaks sympathetically of young women who encountered difficulties at home after they joined the work force. The *New York Times* describes in a 1911 article (Document 4) the tragic circumstances of the Triangle Factory Fire, which claimed the lives of scores of women workers. In Document 5, the Vice Commission of Chicago reports on working conditions that may have induced women to enter prostitution.

1. Rose Cohen Describes Her First Job in New York City, 1892

The next morning when I came into the shop at seven o'clock, I saw at once that all the people were there and working as steadily as if they had been at work a long while. I had just time to put away my coat and go over to the table, when the boss shouted gruffly, "Look here, girl, if you want to work here you better come in early. No office hours in my shop." . . .

From this hour a hard life began for me. He refused to employ me except by the week. He paid me three dollars and for this he hurried me from early until late. He gave me only two coats at a time to do. When I took them over and as he handed me the new work he would say quickly and sharply, "Hurry!" . . . I hurried but he was never satisfied. By looks and manner he made me feel that I was not doing enough. Late at night when the people would stand up and begin to fold their work away and I too would rise feeling stiff in every limb and thinking with dread of our cold empty little room and the uncooked rice, he would come over with still another coat.

"I need it the first thing in the morning," he would give as an excuse. I understood that he was taking advantage of me because I was a child. . . .

I did not soon complain to father. . . . But when I had been in the shop a few weeks I told him, "The boss is hurrying the life out of me." I know now that if I had

---

Rose Cohen, *Out of the Shadow: A Russian Jewish Girlhood on the Lower East Side* (1918; reprint, Ithaca, N.Y.: Cornell University Press, 1995), 112–114.

put it less strongly he would have paid more attention to it. Father hated to hear things put strongly. Besides he himself worked very hard. He never came home before eleven and he left at five in the morning.

He said to me now, "Work a little longer until you have more experience; then you can be independent."

"But if I did piece work, father, I would not have to hurry so. And I could go home earlier when the other people go."

Father explained further, "It pays him better to employ you by the week. Don't you see if you did piece work he would have to pay you as much as he pays a woman piece worker? But this way he gets almost as much work out of you for half the amount a woman is paid."

I myself did not want to leave the shop for fear of losing a day or even more perhaps in finding other work. To lose half a dollar meant that it would take so much longer before mother and the children would come. And now I wanted them more than ever before. I longed for my mother and a home where it would be light and warm and she would be waiting when we came from work. Because I longed for them so I lived much in imagination. For so I could have them near me. Often as the hour for going home drew near I would sit stitching and making believe that mother and the children were home waiting. On leaving the shop I would hasten along through the street keeping my eyes on the ground so as to shut out everything but what I wanted to see. I pictured myself walking into the house. There was a delicious warm smell of cooked food. Mother greeted me near the door and the children gathered about me shouting and trying to pull me down. Mother scolded them saying, "Let her take her coat off, see how cold her hands are!" But they paid no attention and pulled me down to them. Their little arms were about my neck, their warm faces against my cold cheeks and we went tumbling all over each other. Soon mother called, "Supper is ready." There was a scampering and a rush to the table, followed by a scraping of chairs and a clattering of dishes. Finally we were all seated. There was browned meat and potatoes for supper.

I used to keep this up until I turned the key in the door and opened it and stood facing the dark, cold, silent room.

2. Fannie Barrier Williams Describes the "Problem of Employment for Negro Women," 1903

It can be broadly said that colored women know how to work, and have done their full share of the paid and unpaid service rendered to the American people by the Negro race. This is a busy world; the world's work is large, complicated, and increasing. The demand for the competent in all kinds of work is never fully supplied. Woman is constantly receiving a larger share of the work to be done. The field for her skill, her endurance, her finer instincts and faithfulness is ever enlarging; and she has become impatient of limitations, except those imposed by her own physical condition. In this generalization, colored women, of course, are largely excepted.

Fannie Barber Williams, "The Problem of Employment for Negro Women," *Southern Workman* 32 (1903): 432–437.

For reasons too well understood here to be repeated, ours is a narrow sphere. While the kinds and grades of occupation open to all women of white complexion are almost beyond enumeration, those open to our women are few in number and mostly menial in quality. The girl who is white and capable is in demand in a thousand places. The capable Negro girl is usually not in demand. This is one of the stubborn facts of to-day. . . .

In the city of Chicago domestic service is the one occupation in which the demand for colored women exceeds the supply. In one employment office during the past year there were 1,500 applications for colored women and only 1,000 of this number were supplied. Girls of other nationalities do not seem to compete with colored women as domestics. It is probably safe to say that every colored woman who is in any way competent can find good employment. Her wages for general housework range from four to seven dollars per week, while a good cook receives from seven to ten dollars. Now what is the condition of this service? The two most important things are that the wages paid are higher than those given for the same grade of intelligence in any other calling; and that colored women can command almost a monopoly of this employment.

It might be safe to presume that as our women are so much in demand for this service they give perfect satisfaction. In considering that it is important to bear in mind that there are two kinds of colored women who perform domestic service:— First, there are those who take to the work naturally and whose training and habits make them perfectly satisfied with it; and second, those who have had more or less education and who are ambitious to do something in the line of "polite occupations." The women of the latter class do not take to domestic service very kindly. They do not enter the service with any pride. They feel compelled to do this work because they can find nothing else to do. They are always sensitive as to how they may be regarded by their associates and friends, and shrink from the term servant as something degrading "per se." . . .

It is of course an easy thing to condemn our young women who have been fairly educated and have had good home training, because they prefer idleness to domestic service, but I am rather inclined to think we must share in that condemnation. If our girls work for wages in a nice home, rather than in a factory or over a counter, they are ruthlessly scorned by their friends and acquaintances. Our young men, whose own occupations, by the way, will not always bear scrutiny, will also give them the cut direct, so that between the scorn of their associates and the petty tyranny of the housewife, the colored girls who enter domestic service are compelled to have more than ordinary strength of character.

But after all is said, I believe that it is largely in the power of the young woman herself to change and elevate the character of domestic service. She certainly cannot improve it by taking into it ignorance, contempt, and inefficiency. There is no reason why a woman of character, graciousness, and skill should not make her work as a domestic as respectable and as highly regarded as the work of the girl behind a department-store counter. For example, if by special training in domestic service, a girl can cook so well and do everything about a house so deftly and thoroughly that she will be called a real home helper and an invaluable assistant, it is in her power, with her intelligent grasp upon the possibilities of her position, to change the whole current of public opinion in its estimate of domestic service. . . .

When domestic service becomes a profession, as it surely will, by the proper training of those who follow it, what will be the condition of colored girls who would participate in its benefits? It is now time to prepare ourselves to answer this question. In my opinion, the training for this new profession should be elevated to the dignity and importance of the training in mathematics and grammar and other academic studies. Our girls must be made to feel that there is no stepping down when they become professional housekeepers. The relative dignity, respectability, and honor of this profession should first be taught in our schools. As it is now, the young woman in school or college knows that if she enters domestic service, she loses the relationships that she has formed. But schools of domestic science cannot do it all. The everyday man and woman who make society must change their foolish notions as to what is the polite thing for a young woman to do. The kind of stupidity that calls industrial education drudgery is the same kind of stupidity that looks upon the kitchen as a place for drudges. We must learn that the girl who cooks our meals and keeps our houses sweet and beautiful deserves just as high a place in our social economy as the girl who makes our gowns and hats, or the one who teaches our children. In what I have said on this particular phase of our industrial life, I do not wish to be understood as advocating the restriction of colored girls to house service, even when that service is elevated to the rank of a profession. My only plea is that we shall protect and respect our girls who honestly and intelligently enter this service, either from preference or necessity. . . .

There is still another consideration which suggests the importance to the colored people of taking the lead in helping to improve and elevate this service. Race prejudice is kept up and increased in thousands of instances by the incompetent and characterless women who are engaged in this work. While there are thousands of worthy and really noble women in domestic service who enjoy the confidence and affection of their employers, there is a large percentage of colored women who, by their general unworthiness, help to give the Negro race a bad name, for white people North and South are very apt to estimate the entire race from the standpoint of their own servant girls. When intelligence takes the place of ignorance, and good manners, efficiency, and self-respect take the place of shiftlessness and irresponsibility in American homes, one of the chief causes of race prejudice will be removed.

It should also be borne in mind that the colored girl who is trained in the arts of housekeeping is also better qualified for the high duties of wifehood and motherhood.

Let me say by the way of summary that I have dwelt mostly upon the opportunities of domestic service for the following reasons:—

1. It is the one field in which colored women meet with almost no opposition. It is ours almost by birthright.
2. The compensation for this service, in Northern communities at least, is higher than that paid for average clerkships in stores and offices.
3. The service is susceptible of almost unlimited improvement and elevation.
4. The nature of the work is largely what we make it.
5. White women of courage and large intelligence are lifting domestic service to a point where it will have the dignity of a profession, and colored women are in danger, through lack of foresight, of being relegated to the position of scrub women and dishwashers.

6. The colored girl who has no taste or talent for school teaching, dressmaking, or manicuring is in danger of being wasted in idleness, unless we can make domestic service worthy of her ambition and pride.

7. There can be no feature of our race problem more important than the saving of our young women; we can perhaps excuse their vanities, but idleness is the mildew on the garment of character.

8. Education has no value to human society unless it can add importance and respectability to the things we find to do.

9. Though all the factories and offices close their doors at our approach, this will be no calamity if we are strong enough to so transform the work we must do that it shall become an object of envy and emulation to those who now deny us their industrial fellowship.

3. Harriet Brunkhurst Laments the Home Problems of "Business Girls," 1910

That the girl who goes to business frequently faces home problems more difficult than those she meets in an office is a fact that comparatively few people recognize. The status of the girl in the home changes when she becomes a breadwinner, yet there are many homes where the new order not only is not accepted, but is also stoutly combated. Perhaps the main difficulty arises from the fact that although the girl is out in the world and may develop capabilities and breadth unattainable to the one whose life lies in a narrower groove, yet she is still a girl, shrinking, sensitive, possessed of all the whims, fancies and weaknesses that have marked her sex from the beginning of things.

The mother whose daughter goes to business, as do the husband and sons, finds it difficult to realize that anything is changed beyond the mere fact that the girl is away all day. When she returns she slips into her old place; not "all in a minute" can the mother bring herself to acknowledge that the daughter's position in the home is, in fact, precisely like that of her brother. If the mother is long in recognizing this so is the rest of the world. Meanwhile the daughter may be having a hard time.

A certain little woman whose daughter is the household provider has a grievance that seems to her almost insupportable. The daughter, Rose, is advertising manager in a big store; she has a private office, a stenographer, errand-boys and clerical workers to assist her; she employs no heavier implement than pen or scissors; her hours are from nine to five, six, seven—possibly ten at night, as the occasion may demand. She earns a comfortable salary, and she pays into the family exchequer whatever sum is necessary, with never a question as to where the money goes.

The mother is careful in her expenditure and an excellent housekeeper; she refuses to keep a maid because they have no room for her, but the rough work is done by outside hands. Her ideas of housekeeping demand rising at five-thirty A.M. She sleeps lightly, having a midday siesta, and she prefers to do her work in the early morning. She is ready for breakfast at six-thirty. There is no necessity for Rose

---

Slaters Mill, Pawtukett, RI

to breakfast before eight, but the mother begins each day with a complaint at the late breakfast hour. This point of difference, trivial in itself, causes continual irritation.

Rose, capable executive head of a big department though she is, simply cannot fight the matter to a finish. The same girl who calmly gives orders right and left, once the office is reached, chokes with tears and has not a word to say when the little mother, who does not know even the rudiments of business, tells her that she is indolent and selfish. Rose knows that she herself is right—that she must have recreation and rest; deprivation of her morning sleep might be serious to the point of a breakdown—and she must not be ill, for she is the breadwinner. It is the principle of the thing, the mother avers, and she means just the best in the world, of course. But there is only one right way, and that is her way.

This mother is overlooking some very pertinent facts, even excluding the unhappiness she causes her daughter. Rose is actually, by right of her earnings, the head of the house; yet the mother, who would yield without question to husband or son occupying the same position, debates Rose's every movement simply because she is a girl. Were Rose to take her courage in her own hands and face her mother it would avail nothing. So she accepts an unnecessary unhappiness simply because she can see no solution. If the mother could see things in their true light she would be appalled.

There is another mother whose daughter, Cecil, carries a similar burden in the home. The latter finds that many little economies are necessary in order to conduct the home liberally. With fingers as nimble as her brain she finds a woman's innumerable tasks about her wardrobe—lace to be mended, fresh ribbons needed, a stitch here and there that she may be immaculate and insure the longest possible service from her clothing. When Cecil returns from her work, however, she is too weary to attempt any sewing. If she is to remain bright and alert, hold her position and not become ill, she must have relaxation in the evening. She goes to the theater, opera, concerts, has friends to see her, or spends a quiet evening with a book. At nine in the morning she is at her desk, bright-eyed and with a clear brain.

That their support is absolutely dependent upon Cecil's remaining "fit" the mother knows; but that recreation is necessary to maintain the condition she cannot grasp. Consequently, when Cecil takes Sunday morning for the little fussy tasks about her wardrobe the mother sees only sheer perversity, to say nothing of incipient depravity, about it. And there is the incontrovertible fact that Cecil "has all her evenings free." Moreover the mother wails: "She never has time to do anything for me!" It does not occur to her that she is asking of Cecil, whose strength already is fully taxed, more than she would ask from a man. She is the type of woman who would say of her husband: "John is so tired when he returns from work!" That Cecil may be tired she never considers. . . .

One of the most difficult phases of the situation appears with the subject of housework. While going to business absolves the daughter, even as it does the husband and sons, it is a fact not so fully recognized as it might be. To the mother seven or eight hours of work followed by complete release appear so easy in comparison with her own lot that a few additional duties seem no more than fair. Moreover there is that family, its relations and friends, to make the contention should the mother take a different view of the matter.

Maud's mother, for instance, is criticised severely by her relatives for her careful fostering of her daughter's strength.

"It is perfectly ridiculous for you to iron Maud's shirtwaists," declared an elderly aunt. "She doesn't work half as hard as you do, and it wouldn't hurt her a bit to do her ironing in the evening. We used to do ours, and we were none the worse for it."

Maud's mother made no reply as she hung the sixth white blouse in a row with its mates. The years had gifted her with a sweet wisdom the other had not attained, and she knew well the futility of argument.

"I did my own fine ironing at home," she said afterward, "but there was never an afternoon or a morning when I could not go out if I chose. A task in the evening, unless it was for our pleasure, we never knew. Maud goes to the office in sun and in storm; she has never a day or an afternoon, except holidays, when she is free to do as she pleases. Days of headache or other slight indisposition, when I would have been on the sofa or comfortably in bed, she trudges bravely away. Often she is too tired even for recreation, to say nothing of work, when she returns in the evening."

"But six white shirtwaists!" exclaimed the listener.

"She works in an office where the furnishings are of mahogany, with rich rugs, polished brass and other things in harmony. How long could she hold her position were she to appear in a soiled blouse?"

Now that was only plain, practical good sense, clear-eyed recognition of pertinent facts; but astonishingly few people can boast it.

Mabel's mother, for example, takes a different and a more usual view of a similar situation. True, her work is far heavier than is that of Maud's mother, but Mabel works eight hours a day while Maud works seven. She is home in time to assist in preparing dinner, she helps with the dishes afterward, and there are innumerable little "odd jobs" that frequently keep her busy until nine o'clock. If she goes out there is a mad rush to finish the dinner work and be dressed sufficiently early. She does not go out very much, however, for she must rise at six-thirty, assist with the preparation of breakfast, and be at the office by eight-thirty o'clock.

That Mabel is fagged continually is inevitable. "I am so tired, Mother," she said once, when an additional bit of work was suggested.

"Aren't you ashamed to say that when you see how your mother works?" demanded the father.

Mabel did the required work with no further comment, although the tears smarted in her eyes, her heart ached with the injustice of the taunt, and her weary little body seemed ready to fail her. She could earn her own living, but she could not fight her own battles. . . .

The problems these girls face are delicate, whichever way they are viewed. Perhaps part of the trouble arises from non-recognition of arrival at "years of discretion." We are all of us individuals first, and members of a family afterward. The family fosters and develops, but it may hamper freedom as well. There must be dependence upon one another, there must be community of interests; but in the successful home there must also be a clearly-defined recognition of individual existence. The girl attains her "majority" when she goes to business, and the home must learn when to "let go." It is not a question of independence—a word often misapplied and misunderstood—but simply one of self-reliance, and acknowledgment of the girl's right to it.

4. The *New York Times* Reports on the Tragedy of the Triangle Factory Fire, 1911

Three stories of a ten-floor building at the corner of Greene Street and Washington Place were burned yesterday, and while the fire was going on 141 young men and women at least 125 of them mere girls were burned to death or killed by jumping to the pavement below.

The building was fireproof. It shows now hardly any signs of the disaster that overtook it. The walls are as good as ever so are the floors, nothing is the worse for the fire except the furniture and 141 of the 600 men and girls that were employed in its upper three stories.

Most of the victims were suffocated or burned to death within the building, but some who fought their way to the windows and leaped met death as surely, but perhaps more quickly, on the pavements below.

All Over in Half an Hour.

Nothing like it has been seen in New York since the burning of the General Slocum.* The fire was practically all over in half an hour. It was confined to three floors the eighth, ninth, and tenth of the building. But it was the most murderous fire that New York had seen in many years.

The victims who are now lying at the Morgue waiting for some one to identify them by a tooth or the remains of a burned shoe [are] mostly girls from 16 to 23 years of age. They were employed at making shirtwaist by the Triangle Waist Company, the principal owners of which are Isaac Harris and Max Blanck. Most of them could barely speak English. Many of them came from Brooklyn. Almost all were the main support of their hard-working families.

There is just one fire escape in the building. That one is an interior fire escape. In Greene Street, where the terrified unfortunates crowded before they began to make their mad leaps to death, the whole big front of the building is guiltless of one. Nor is there a fire escape in the back.

The building was fireproof and the owners had put their trust in that. In fact, after the flames had done their worst last night, the building hardly showed a sign. Only the stock within it and the girl employees were burned.

A heap of corpses lay on the sidewalk for more than an hour. The firemen were too busy dealing with the fire to pay any attention to people whom they supposed beyond their aid. When the excitement had subsided to such an extent that some of the firemen and policemen could pay attention to this mass of the supposedly dead they found about half way down in the pack a girl who was still breathing. She died two minutes after she was found.

The Triangle Waist Company was the only sufferer by the disaster. There are other concerns in the building, but it was Saturday and the other companies had let their people go home. . . .

The *New York Times*, March 26, 1911, p. 1.

*The General Slocum was an excursion ferry boat that caught fire on June 15, 1904. It was carrying over 1,300 pleasure goers from lower Manhattan to Long Island; 1,021 of the passengers perished in the accident.

Leaped Out of the Flames.

At 4:40 o'clock, nearly five hours after the employe[e]s in the rest of the building had gone home, the fire broke out. The one little fire escape in the interior was resorted to by [m]any of the doomed victims. Some of them escaped by running down the stairs, but in a moment or two this avenue was cut off by flame. The girls rushed to the windows and looked down at Greene Street, 100 feet below them. Then one poor, little creature jumped. There was a plate glass protection over part of the sidewalk, but she crashed through it, wrecking it and breaking her body into a thousand pieces.

Then they all began to drop. The crowd yelled "Don't jump!" but it was jump or be burned the proof of which is found in the fact that fifty burned bodies were taken from the ninth floor alone. . . .

Messrs. Harris and Blanck were in the building, but they escaped. They carried . . . Mr. Blanck's children and a governess, and they fled over the roofs. Their employe[e]s did not know the way, because they had been in the habit of using the two freight elevators, and one of these elevators was not in service when the fire broke out. . . .

First Avenue was lined with the usual curious east side crowd. Twenty-sixth Street was impassable. But in the Morgue they received the charred remnants with no more emotion than they ever display over anything.

Back in Greene Street there was another crowd. At midnight it had not decreased in the least. The police were holding it back to the fire lines, and discussing the tragedy in a tone which those seasoned witnesses of death seldom use.

"It's the worst thing I ever saw," said one old policeman.

Chief Croker said it was an outrage. He spoke bitterly of the way in which the Manufacturers' Association had called a meeting in Wall Street to take measures against his proposal for enforcing better methods of protection for employe[e]s in cases of fire. . . .

The Triangle Waist Company employed about 600 women and less than 100 men. One of the saddest features of the thing is the fact that they had almost finished for the day. In five minutes more, if the fire had started then, probably not a life would have been lost.

Last night District Attorney Whitman started an investigation not of this disaster alone but of the whole condition which makes it possible for a firetrap of such a kind to exist. Mr. Whitman's intention is to find out if the present laws cover such cases, and if they do not to frame laws that will. . . .

How the fire started no one knows. . . . The victims mostly Italians, Russians, Hungarians, and Germans were girls and men who had been employed by the firm of Harris & Blanck, owners of the Triangle Waist Company, after the strike in which the Jewish girls, formerly employed, had become unionized and had demanded better working conditions. The building had experienced four recent fires and had been reported by the Fire Department to the Building Department as unsafe in account of the insufficiency of its exits.

The building itself was of the most modern construction and classed as fireproof. What burned so quickly and disastrously for the victims were shirtwaists, hanging on lines above tiers of workers, sewing machines placed so closely together that there was hardly aisle room for the girls between them, and shirtwaist trimmings and cuttings which littered the floors above the eighth and ninth stories.

Girls had begun leaping from the eighth story windows before firemen arrived. The firemen had trouble bringing their apparatus into position because of the bodies which strewed the pavement and sidewalks. While more bodies crashed down among them, they worked with desperation to run their ladders into position and to spread firenets. . . .

Five girls who stood together at a window close the Greene Street corner held their place while a fire ladder was worked toward them, but which stopped at its full length two stories lower down. They leaped together, clinging to each other, with fire streaming back from their hair and dresses. They struck a glass sidewalk cover and it to the basement. There was no time to aid them. With water pouring in upon them from a dozen hose nozzles the bodies lay for two hours where they struck, as did the many others who leaped to their deaths.

One girl, who waved a handkerchief at the crowd, leaped from a window adjoining the New York University Building on the westward. Her dress caught on a wire, and the crowd watched her hang there till her dress burned free and she came toppling down.

All Would Soon Have Been Out.

Strewn about as the firemen worked, the bodies indicated clearly the preponderance of women workers. Here and there was a man, but almost always they were women. . . . Nearly all were dressed for the street. The fire had flashed through their workroom just as they were expecting the signal to leave the building. In ten minutes more all would have been out, as many had stopped work in advance of the signal and had started to put on their wraps.

What happened inside there were few who could tell with any definiteness. All that those escaped seemed to remember was that there was a flash of flames, leaping first among the girls in the southeast corner of the eighth floor and then suddenly over the entire room, spreading through the linens and cottons with which the girls were working. The girls on the ninth floor caught sight of the flames through the window up the stairway, and up the elevator shaft.

On the tenth floor they got them a moment later, but most of those on that floor escaped by rushing to the roof and then on to the roof of the New York University Building, with the assistance of 100 university students who had been dismissed from a tenth story classroom.

5. The Vice Commission of Chicago Reports on the Working Conditions in Department Stores that Lead Female Employees into Prostitution, 1911

As an introduction to the study of Department Stores it may be well to call particular attention to the fact that the present economic and insanitary conditions under which the girls employed in factories and department stores live and work, has an

The Vice Commission of Chicago, *The Social Evil of Chicago: A Study of Existing Conditions.* (Chicago: The Vice Commission of Chicago, Inc. 1911), 198–213.

effect on the nervous forces of the girl in such a way as to render her much more susceptible to prostitution.

This is true as a basis. The whole tendency of modern life, which places a greater strain on the nervous system of both men and women of all classes than has ever been placed at any time in the history of the civilized world, cannot but help, to a great extent, develop considerable eroticism. The sexual senses of the brain, as well as the seminal parts, are from the very nature of their natural functions, susceptible organisms and they will be the most readily influenced by modes of life, and highly speeded modern life must stimulate these organisms. . . .

The girl in the department store is confronted with certain temptations which are ever pressing harder upon her. The first of these is the procuress, the second the "cadet," and the third, the man directly over her, who may even be the manager or the proprietor himself.

But in spite of these temptations it is only fair to say that many of these girls never fall before these allurements. They work grimly on enduring and suffering to the end.

It has been established after exhaustive study that it is quite impossible for a working girl in any large city to live on less than eight dollars per week, yet employers of these department stores say that they pay on an average of from $6.00 to $7.00 per week.

This is all the girls are worth, they maintain, the law of supply and demand regulates all this.

And because the unskilled girl workers are a drug on the market the employer keeps piling up enormous profits and paying great dividends, sometimes extra dividends.

In writing upon this subject in Pearson's Magazine for February, 1911, at page 178, Richard Barry refers to a census taken last year by the Woman's Trade Union League of Chicago, which showed that "from 25 per cent. to 30 per cent. of the women employed in the department stores were not receiving sufficient money to enable them to procure the necessities of life."

And again, Mr. Barry calls attention to the work of a New York home for women, the matron of which is said to have declared that "16 per cent. of the girls who applied there for refuge, have entered a life of immorality in the greatest city in the country because of insufficient wages, which do not allow them to pay for food and lodging." . . .

Does it surprise one in the face of these conditions that many weak, tempted, nervously exhausted girls realizing the financial profits from the sale of their virtue enter upon what they believe for the moment to be the "easiest way," only to experience finally its sad consequence?

A former salesgirl in a department store was seen in a fashionable all-night restaurant. She said that four weeks previous she had been earning $8.00 per week. She enumerated different articles of clothing which she was wearing, and gave the prices of each, including her hat. The total amount came to over $200.00. Her eyes had been opened to her earning capacity in the "sporting" life by a man who laughed at her for wasting her good looks and physical charms behind a counter for a boss who was growing rich from her services, and the services of others like her.

A girl who had been employed as a misses' model in another department store at $10.00 per week also learned that she could easily become a "$5.00" girl, by frequenting a notorious dance hall. She had been in this hall two weeks when she remarked that the "graft" was so easy she was almost "ashamed to take the money," and "it beat the department store game all to hell." . . .

As pointed out above, the girl in the department store is subjected to certain temptations to which some yield, and from which many flee.

These temptations appear in the following guises:

I. The Procuress. The woman who appears before the girl's counter or in the waiting room and compliments her on her good looks and bewails with her the injustice which prevents her from having the beautiful clothes to which she is entitled and the good times, because of her youth and beauty. Too often the girl listens and accepts the "elegant" lady's invitation to come to her flat for dinner or to spend Sunday.

One of these women did so appear before a young girl and did invite her to her "beautiful flat," in fact she was continually asking other girls to do the same thing. But her flat was a disorderly house and her own daughter was one of the inmates. . . .

II. The "Cadet." This boy or man may be seen any evening near the employes' exit of department stores with the avowed purpose of making the acquaintance of some attractive girl and bearing her off in triumph to the restaurant and the theater. . . .

A young saleswoman, 19 years of age, in one of the department stores, formed the habit of going to cafes in the evening. One night she met a young man, and he persuaded her to live with him. Afterward she became acquainted with a rich man who gave her a great many presents. Finally, she gave up her position, and shared the rich man's gifts with her first lover. She continued to send money home to her mother, who lived in a small town, and thought her married. The girl eventually paid off a mortgage on her mother's home. . . .

III. Married Men. Married men are among the worst offenders against salesgirls, and use all sorts of methods to induce them to accept invitations to dine, or go to the theater. These men come to the counters while their wives are shopping, and thus enter into conversation with the girls. They are very bold and aggressive in their actions, and if the girls resent these attentions, some of these men actually report them to the floor walkers, claiming they neglected their business. In some cases these complaints have led to the discharge of the girls in the store.

IV. Men Employers. . . . A certain floor walker had been in the habit of taking girls out. He was continually harassing the girls who did not accept his invitation. A house detective finally succeeded in having him discharged. Some salesgirls will testify their downfall was caused by their employers, and they actually wore diamonds belonging to these employers. . . .

An employe of (X985b) store said she actually heard a superintendent ask a girl who had complained that she could not work for $6.00 per week, if this was the *only way* she had of earning money. She answered that it was. He then told her that the house could not pay her any more.

A man at (X985c), a large department store, had charge of inspectors. One day he went so far as to take one of the girls to his home when his wife was away. The girl got into trouble and he left the city. The firm cautioned all the employes not to speak of the incident. . . .

A matron at one of the large department stores once told a salesgirl she was foolish to work there, as she could make money easier in the "sporting life." About two weeks later this girl resigned, and was found by a detective from this store in a basement saloon on Madison street.

V. Voluntary.   One day a house detective in one of the stores actually heard several young cash girls relating their experience while out with men during the evening. They made such remarks as, "He opened a bottle for me," and "We had a swell time."

One salesgirl, 17 years of age, by the name of Sadie, was heard to remark in one of the stores that she wasn't going to work again, as she had "touched a guy last night for $50.00, and now I will have a swell hat." The man from whom she had stolen the money came to the store with an officer, and the girl was compelled to return the money. This man would not prosecute.

Several young salesgirls, who entered a life of professional prostitution, have done so on the plea that they could live on "easy street." One of these girls died, another married a doctor on the North Side. . . .

VI. Typical Cases. . . .   Rosie was seen in a dance hall at (X991) North Clark street. She works in the basement of one of the large department stores, and receives $6.00 per week. Out of this she pays $3.00 for her meals and $2.00 room rent, and 60 cents per week carfare. She "hustles" three nights every week, as a business proposition. She said that during these nights she could be found in the rear room of (X992) saloon at (X993) North Clark street. She is about 20 years of age. . . .

Mag was seen at the dance hall on North Clark street. She works in one of the large department stores at a salary of $5.00 per week. She has a furnished room on North Clark street. At one time she had a baby which died. She was "hustling" certain nights in the week, and claims she does it to help support herself. . . .

Violet . . . is about 18 years of age, and works in a department store at $6.00 per week. She has two steady friends, who take her out each week, and give her $2.00 a week. This brings her salary to $10.00 per week. They take her to a room downtown, but she would not give the name of the place. She lives at home with her parents, and when she goes out tells them she is going to a show with a girl friend. . . .

An inmate of a house of prostitution at (X1025) Dearborn street by the name of Paulette said that she was 22 years of age, but she looks much younger. She formerly lived in (X1026), Massachusetts, where she married at 17. After living with her husband two years, they had a misunderstanding and parted. She first came to Chicago to work in one of the department stores downtown in the shirt waist department, and received $7.00 per week. This sum was afterward reduced to $6.00. "I could not live on that," she said, "so I took up the sporting life, because it appealed to me. It was impossible to make a living where I was. And even while I was in the store I made money on the side. I was in the habit of taking men to hotels, one, two or three times a week, when I wasn't too tired. After I had been working two months, I left the position and entered the house."

Paulette, in speaking further of her experience in department stores, says: "One can't live downtown; that is no district for a girl to live in; she might as well be here.

If a girl in a store wears soiled clothing, they will tell her about it. You have to work in a department store for years and years and years before you get anything. While in the store," she continued, "I heard of a case of a good girl getting $6.00 a week. She asked for more money. She said she couldn't live on that. The man said, 'Can't you get somebody to keep you?'"

At the present time Paulette earns $17.00 to $23.00 above her expenses each week.

◈ E S S A Y S

Daniel E. Bender of the University of Toronto at Scarborough explores how sexual harassment in the garment industry harmed women workers while protecting masculine definitions of skill and authority; Bender explores as well wage-earning women's efforts, largely unsuccessful, to resist sexual harassment. Elizabeth Clark-Lewis of Howard University examines the experience of black women who moved from the rural South to become domestic workers in Washington, D.C., in the early twentieth century. Despite constraints imposed by race, gender, and class, Clark-Lewis finds that domestic workers discovered novel ways to enhance their autonomy.

Women Workers and Sexual Harassment in the Garment Industry

DANIEL E. BENDER

In the close quarters of the sweatshop, with the loud whirring of the sewing machines echoing in her ears, in the gloom of the tenement apartment-turned-garment work-shop, a young Eastern European Jewish immigrant named Pesha dropped her thimble. By the end of the day, Pesha, in tears, left the shop and her job. She had not been fired.

Pesha had not quit. Like many other recent immigrant workers in Progressive-Era industrial cities, Pesha had been loath to abandon her religious ethics. This made the cramped space of the tenement flat sweatshop an especially difficult place for Pesha to work. Her prayers, uttered before every meal, and her Orthodox dress drew the attention and ridicule of her less *frume* (pious) co-workers. They called her Pesha the *Rebbitsin* (Rabbi's Wife). But she was not married, which is why she was still working in the needle trades, and few married Jewish immigrant women worked for wages. She was a single woman working in a shop, surrounded by male workers. Even in the best of circumstances, it would have been difficult for Pesha to maintain the strict sexual segregation demanded by Orthodox tradition. She would surely have brushed up against the hands and bodies of her male co-workers.

But this was not the best of circumstances. Since she had first started working in the shop, Pesha faced jokes from male co-workers and unwanted touching from her boss. That is why she dropped her thimble. The boss had pinched her and, perhaps

Daniel E. Bender, "'Too Much of Distasteful Masculinity': Historicizing Sexual Harassment in the Garment Sweatshop and Factory," *Journal of Women's History* 15, no. 4 (Winter 2004): 91–116. Reprinted by permission of Indiana University Press.

because of her anger and discomfort, she dropped the thimble. The boss grabbed it and put it back on her finger. Then, things got worse. He recited the Hebrew blessing of marriage, *haray at mekudheshes lee b'tabat zu k'das Moshe v'Yisroel* ("with this ring, I wed thee according to the laws of Moses and Israel.") For Pesha, these were sacred words, not to be said in jest. Was it a real ring and was she now married?

Her male co-workers did not come to her rescue. For these men, this was a good joke, not a prime example of the exploitation of the sweatshop system. They unscrewed a light bulb and, in another tradition of the Jewish wedding service, they stomped on it—in place of a glass—and shouted *mazel tov* (congratulations).

Pesha ran from the shop and sought her rabbi who assured her that she was not, in fact, married. Still, the rabbi was angry and returned with Pesha to the shop where he berated her boss. The boss agreed that the joke had gone too far and he apologized.

Toward a History of Sexual Harassment

While she may have felt isolated in the small shop, Pesha was not alone in her confrontation with sexual harassment. The memoirs of female and male garment workers suggest that everything from "salacious bantering and indecent ribaldry" to sexual demands rendered the garment sweatshop a sexualized workplace. Sexual harassment was so prevalent and so visible in the sweatshop probably because the Progressive-Era garment industry was a mixed-sex industry, in which neither men nor women composed an overwhelming majority. In some trades, such as shirtwaistmaking, women were a majority of the workforce. By contrast, in cloakmaking, male workers were a majority. The American garment industry of the Progressive Era offers an opportunity to study the role of sexual harassment in the creation and maintenance of workplace-gendered hierarchies. . . .

Harassment did more than make sweatshop work uncomfortable for women. As Pesha's experience suggests, sexual harassment was central to the way male workers advanced and protected conceptions of sexual difference and then translated these conceptions into gendered hierarchies of skill and pay. Sexual harassment was an expression of power that helped male workers maintain associations of men's work with skill, even as the garment sweatshop that emerged in the 1880s gave way to larger factories after 1910. Still, as Pesha's efforts to get help from her rabbi indicate, women did seek to resist sexual harassment. Women's strategies of resistance changed with the rise of unions in the garment industry after the turn of the century, but, in general, women's resistance focused largely on the experience of harassment and rarely on its structural outcome. Pesha raised religious objections to harassment; in later years, women cast harassment as an affront to lady workers. . . .

Sexual harassment is, paradoxically, one of the most noted but least studied topics in American women's labor history. Although the first labor historians interested in women's working lives examined sexual harassment, they ironically tended to describe it as a non-historical phenomenon. Sexual harassment, defined by one historian as "unwanted pressure for sexual activity, [that] includes verbal innuendos and suggestive comments, leering, gestures, unwanted physical contact (touching, pinching, etc.), rape, and attempted rape," is cast as a constant of women's sex-integrated labors, from slavery to the present. Historians have documented the persistence of harassment in a range of paid workplaces: offices, textile factories, auto factories, canneries, homes where women worked as domestics, and sweatshops. However, despite the rich documentary evidence uncovered by these historians, sexual harassment is treated not as a subject of analysis in itself but as one of many challenges faced by women workers, "what might be defined today as sexual harassment." The use of today's legal languages to understand and give a name to different forms of sexual harassment removes them from the context of specific workplace systems of power. Instead of offering a gaze into the consolidation and protection of shop floor hierarchies, sexual harassment is treated as a "common experience" of working women. . . .

The work of scholars of women and slavery offers a different possible interpretation of workplace sex and sexual harassment. They suggest the centralilty of sexuality in the maintenance of gender hierarchies at work by tracing the importance of sexual abuse—rape or the threat of rape—in the propagation of the slave labor system. On the one hand, sexual abuse reinforced a legal system that made slave women (and men) the productive and reproductive property of male masters. On the other hand, the rape of female slaves strengthened representations of black women as "innately and immutably immoral" and denied the primacy, strength, and legitimacy of the slave family. . . . [S]uch representations of black women as immoral were resurrected after emancipation to provide justifications for the exclusion of African Americans from Southern factories. These images also shielded forem[e]n from criticism when they demanded "sexual favors from black women as the price of keeping their jobs." . . .

Such an analysis that stresses the role of sexuality in the maintenance of workplace power and control helps connect the study of sexual harassment to the history of skill, masculinity, and femininity. One of the most important insights of the recent cultural and gender turn in working-class history is the idea that social constructions of what it means to be a manly worker are integral to how skill is defined and how this definition helps maintain hierarchies of pay and prestige. Scholars have begun to trace the specific ways in which masculinity is constructed and explain the association of masculinity with particular visual and cultural signs, such as muscular bodies and family breadwinning. Such constructions of masculinity have protected otherwise artificial hierarchies of skill and pay, safeguarded men's monopolies over certain jobs, and served as a basis for workplace solidarity among male workers. And such hierarchies have, in turn, reinforced masculinity. So too have scholars suggested how changing constructions of masculinity as well as femininity have coded certain types of work as women's and men's work. The segmentation of work is not simply, as some scholars have argued, a macro-economic process encouraged and used by employers. It is also a process linked to the gendering of work.

Perhaps the most important recent insight into the study of the construction of gender at work for the study of sexual harassment is the notion that masculinity and femininity are continually reconstructed in response to changing relationships between men and women, shifting management strategies, and changing economic circumstances. The sexual harassment of women in garment sweatshops and, later, garment factories can be seen as an unequal form of interaction between men and women that helped lay out the terrain of gender difference and contestation in the garment factory; or . . . sexual harassment is "a tool or instrument of gender regulation." In the sweatshop, the gendering of work served to restrict women's access to skilled jobs and, at least initially, to organizing.

As women forced their way into garment unions in the 1910s, at the same time that the sweatshop gave way to larger factories, they used the structures of labor relations won by unions to confront the sexual harassment of bosses. . . . [F]or female garment workers, there was no legal term they could use to describe their abuse. . . . [P]opular culture, especially dime novels, helped working women articulate a form of ladyhood that cast harassment as morally wrong and punishable. However, it is unclear . . . how women found the institutional framework to advance their claims. An examination of harassment as a form of "gender regulation" reveals that women claimed to be "ladies" in the context of demands for a place in garment unions, which women increasingly saw as the best means to counteract sexual harassment. Thus, in their focus on unions, female sweatshop workers came to rely on gendered as well as classed languages about respect and ladyhood. Male garment workers generally supported women's efforts because this resistance to harassment cast it as a problem between women and bosses and as a question of respect, not skill. As a result, male workers, while supporting labor relations challenges to sexual harassment, recreated the heterosexual division of labor in unions while reinforcing hierarchies of skill at work.

However, the immigrant women who made up the bulk of the female garment workforce did not generally see themselves as the only victims of harassment. In fact, when talking about their harassment[,] garment workers often compared their fate to that of African American slaves. One garment worker in Kalamazoo described the abuse she faced as "the same insult the overseer offered the Negro girl before the war." They were, perhaps, suggesting that harassment was, at its heart, a question of power and dominance, and they seemed to wonder if the kind of harassment faced by Pesha and other women like her had reduced them to slaves. At the same time, women's recognition that abuse was, in some form, part of the history of women's labors in America allowed for the transmission of understandings of abuse and strategies of resistance from one group of workers to another, from immigrant to native-born women. In taking on an American labor discourse that compared the worst kind of exploitation to slavery, the first sweatshop workers were defining sexual harassment as a labor, not an ethnic, problem. Thus, Jewish and Italian garment workers in New York, Chicago, and Cleveland and native-born garment workers in Kalamazoo united in the same union, advanced similar definitions of harassment, and pursued similar strategies of resistance. Thus[,] sexual harassment in garment shops must be examined for what it reveals about specific and localized gendered systems of power as well as for the way garment workers of different ethnicities and in different working situations saw their harassment as something they shared with other working women. . . .

Sexual interaction in the garment workplace could be, in its most benign form, titillating, profitable, and exciting. It could . . . provide women the chance to meet men who would treat them to meals, gifts, and entertainment, which was, for women, a way of augmenting low wages. It also helped workers find a husband. Many female garment workers considered marriage the only means of escape from the sweatshop.

However, Pesha's ordeal also reveals that sexual interaction also worked to justify, create, and maintain boundaries between male and female workers. Harassment solidified and crystallized potentially flexible distinctions between men's and women's work. Sexual harassment was crucial in the definition and policing of the heterosexual division of labor at work. . . . The harassment of women garment workers by men transformed workplace heterosexuality into a sphere of power that, in some cases, blurred class contestations. The material effects of sexual harassment could potentially benefit management as well as male workers. The sexualization of the workplace was propagated not simply by bosses (as has often been argued), but also by male co-workers.

Sex and the Sweatshop, 1880–1909

The Jewish, and to a lesser extent Italian, immigrants who entered the industry in such cities as New York and Chicago beginning in the 1870s and 1880s did not inherit a stable sexual division of labor. Their struggle to determine who would control those jobs considered skilled is clearly visible. Religious codes about contact between men and women that were necessarily fractured in the close quarters of the sweatshop only heightened the tension. Harassment emerged, at least partially, out of this struggle. The arrival of Eastern European Jewish immigrant workers, who came to compose the majority of the garment workforce after 1880, signaled a massive transformation in the sexual division of labor in the garment industry. In the 1870s and early 1880s, when Eastern European Jewish immigrants began arriving in the United States, men dominated only a few garment crafts. Within the largely Irish and German workforce that, at the time, still populated the garment industry, men controlled only two of the principal trades. Both of these trades, custom tailoring and skilled cutting, were declining segments of the needle trades. In some trades such as cloakmaking, with the arrival of immigrants, women workers were in the minority. In other trades, shirtwaistmaking in particular, women remained in the majority. By the turn of the century, the garment sweatshop was a sexually divided workplace with men claiming the best paid, most skilled jobs. The garment industry came to feature a strict hierarchy of skills and crafts, despite the fact that few garment trades demanded much specialized knowledge or strength.

 The rising numbers of male garment workers helped foster a new sexual division of labor, hierarchies of skill and pay, and a shift from factory production to sweatshop production. In 1880, garment shops in New York averaged fifty workers; by 1890, they averaged only eight. Only after the turn of the century would the size of shops increase again, albeit slowly. At the same time, even in trades where they were still a minority, Jewish male workers solidified a monopoly over highly paid trades that men and women, bosses and workers, came to consider skilled or semi-skilled. Thus, by 1911, one report about cloakmaking noted that "there are very few women among the operators, none among the cutters, and hardly any among the pressers." Instead, women were employed in low paying, unskilled crafts such as "basting, finishing, and button-hole making." In other crafts, such as shirtwaistmaking, where women were more numerous, some were machine operators. However, the fact that few were cutters or pressers highlights the flexibility of definitions of skill and the persistence of gendered hierarchies in trades where men were in the minority. As a result, when female Italian immigrants began seeking jobs in the garment industry in the 1890s, they tended to find work primarily as finishers, the worst paying, least skilled jobs. A new sexual division of labor and definitions of skill had been forged in the course of a few decades.

Changes in technology, such as the introduction of the cutting knife, and changes in production, such as the team system, greatly simplified the cutting of cloth, broke down the manufacture of a garment into simple steps, and eliminated the need for well-paid artisans. While these changes helped restructure definitions of skill, they cannot fully explain the transformation in the sexual division of labor. Instead, it is clear that male workers, with the consent and collaboration of male bosses, somehow came to claim control over the sexual division of labor in different crafts. Crucial to immigrant men's control over the organization of the workplace was the gendering of the term "worker." Men came to claim the normative title of worker, often equating it with the family wage-earner. Especially for Jewish immigrants, if men's work was, ideally, family breadwinning, women's labor was transient. Women, men insisted, were only temporary workers, "shopgirls" who would leave work with marriage.

It was a measure of manly success for Jewish male workers to keep their wives out of the workplace. As one male immigrant recalled: "As soon as I was able to earn six to seven dollars a week, I did not let my wife go into a shop, but stay at home." Male workers relied on notions of women's work as temporary to suggest that men's work was most significant and deserving of the best pay. As one observer noted, "Jewish men . . . are not inclined to regard the work of women as worthy of serious attention."

However, translating gendered ideals about work—distinguishing men's work from women's—was a contested, sometimes even violent, process. Sometimes this conflict remained within families and couples. Thus, Fannie Shapiro, for example, reported that her "husband pestered" her until she quit her job. Often, this conflict over the strict segregation of tasks spilled over into a garment workplace characterized by divided loyalties. The immigrant sweatshop owner often relied on relatives, friends, and acquaintances from the old country for workers. Family and community ties potentially might also divide the workplace and threaten the sexual segregation of work. Indeed, in one shop, a boss hired a female relative as a pocketmaker, a well-paid, supposedly skilled trade claimed by men. Gendered notions of skill conflicted with family loyalties and Jewish male workers defended their control of certain trades with great ferocity. Male workers sabotaged the woman's work and smudged oil on her coat. Her acceptance of lower wages would not mollify the men. They eventually went on strike "with a warning to the boss that they would refuse to work as long as a woman ran a machine." . . .

Sexual harassment was a constant of the garment sweatshop and succeeded in dividing the workplace along lines of gender especially when it was propagated both by male workers and male bosses, often in tacit alliance. The sexual taunting of such women as Pesha was part of the way male workers and male bosses might, in the humor of the situation, forget or assuage the tension of daily conflicts. This was especially true in a workshop as cramped and crowded as the garment sweatshop, where the lines separating boss and worker were already unclear. Sweatshops, especially between 1880 and 1910 when Jewish and Italian immigration was highest, were generally very small and few had expensive equipment or electricity. One observer estimated that it took only fifty dollars to open a shop. As a result, an immigrant, who in the previous season was a wage worker, might now be a boss. And, depending on his fortunes, he might become a worker again the next year. In addition, most bosses would join their employees in sewing.

Thus, while the lines separating the boss from his workers had become blurred by the turn of the century, sexual harassment (re)established clear hierarchies, along the lines of gender, even more than along the lines of class. In the strike that followed the hiring of a female relative, male workers were asserting the primacy of gender. In this shop, kinship loyalties threatened the gendered division of labor. Elsewhere, the familiarity of the sweatshop united male workers and bosses. Sadie Frowne remembered that when both male workers and bosses "passed me they would touch my hair and talk about my eyes and my red cheeks and make jokes." Isaac Pomerance also recognized the sexualized atmosphere of the sweatshop as garment shop conversations were rife with "genito-urinary jokes." Working women, as in the case of Pesha, sometimes recalled male workers and bosses joining in elaborate sexual jokes and pranks. An experience related by the sweatshop worker and proletarian poet Morris Rosenfeld is exemplary. Rosenfeld described the harassment of Lily, who, like Pesha, was a religious Jewish immigrant. Although most men in the shop joined in, the "two boldest and freshest" men were Lipkin and Schwartz. Lipkin was the boss and Schwartz was the operator, a skilled position Rosenfeld pointed out, that made him the "star" of the shop. Through taunting Lily, the two men became "friends" and "companions." Lipkin even called Schwartz his "prime minister."

The distinction between harassment by male workers and male bosses was linked to the kinds of power they held over women. Bosses held an obvious form of power: the ability to withhold pay and work. In particular, bosses could demand sexual favors in return for pay or as the terms of keeping a desperately needed job. One woman recalled that her boss demanded she eat dinner and spend the night with him at a "swell hotel." Male workers, in contrast, generally held no such obvious power. They only claimed positions above women in the workplace hierarchy and, as a result, their abuse was less aggressively physical, consisting generally of jokes and taunts. Thus, Rosenfeld recalled that Lipkin pinched Lily while Schwartz made comments, for example, about the color of her underwear. Still, both men and women recognized that sexual harassment, whether as jokes or as demands for sex, reaffirmed unequal relations between men and women at the same time that they calmed tensions between men. One male worker, "Loony" Berger, claimed that tickling his female co-workers helped him overlook the daily indignities and trials he faced as a low-paid, overworked sweatshop laborer. Without tickling, he insisted, he would "become loony." More sympathetically, Sam Liptzin recognized that "there was no greater torments than to work in the midst" of men's "vulgarity." "Life in the sweat-shop was miserable enough for the men," he concluded, "but for the women it was a thousand times worse."

Collective resistance to harassment in the sweatshop was difficult, especially when harassment merged with the informal kinship and friendship ties of the workplace. In one famous strike, Jewish working women went on strike to protest the "laying on of the hands" of the boss, who explained that his pinching was "fatherly." Female workers insisted instead that they be treated as "orphans." However, the fact that the "Orphan Strike" is so widely cited points to its uniqueness. Most other examples of collective resistance to sexual harassment in the sweatshop were not as successful. More typical was the case of "A Shopgirl" who complained that fellow female workers were afraid "to be witness" against the "vulgar advances" of a male worker. Resisting individual sexual abuse was even more difficult. Most women either "bent their heads low over their work" and pretended not to hear or . . . quit their jobs. In effect, in quitting their jobs, bending their heads low over their work, or even striking over specific extreme examples of sexual abuse, women were leaving intact the hierarchies of skill and pay that harassment protected.

Paradoxically, as much as sexual harassment might smooth tensions between male workers and bosses and help keep workers like Berger sane, it also, through the terms it fastened to women's work, provided the justification for the exclusion of women workers from early efforts at unionization. Men reasoned that women were merely temporary workers and thus did not need the benefits of unionization. As one worker asked, "After working a few years, they get married and leave the shops. Why should we have them in the union and have to fight for them?" Thus, Rose Cohen remembered that when the male workers in her shop—the same ones who forced women to bend their heads low over their work—went on strike, she and the other "girls . . . sat down to work at once." And, like other gendered systems of power, men insisted that the meanings they ascribed to women workers were natural reflections of women's character. Because women workers were temporary, more wedded to the world outside the sweatshop, men concluded, "it is hopeless to expect women employees to be unionists."

After 1900, the size of shops was growing once again, spreading outside of New York and Chicago, and expanding its workforce beyond Jewish immigrants who monopolized the industry in the 1880s and 1890s. Antagonism between male workers and bosses increased. Male-led unionization in the garment industry gained momentum beginning first in New York and later in secondary industry centers including Philadelphia, Cleveland, Baltimore, Chicago, and Kalamazoo. Critical to this organizing was the founding of the International Ladies' Garment Workers' Union (ILGWU) in 1900, the most stable union yet in the garment industry. Female Jewish and Italian immigrants as well as native-born women soon came to demand a place in the ILGWU. No amount of resistance from Jewish male workers and unionists, who made up the bulk of the ILGWU's leadership and original rank-and-file, could keep them out. Unionization opened up a space, albeit circumscribed, for women to resist sexual harassment collectively and to share strategies of resistance across boundaries of ethnicity and religion.

Between 1909 and 1913, Jewish and, to a lesser extent, Italian immigrant workers and native-born female garment workers participated in a series of strikes. Despite the hesitancy and overt discouragement of male ILGWU leaders, the 1913 strike alone produced 50,000 new female union members. Although female unionists actually physically attacked their male leadership so that they could bargain effectively, these strikers won many of the same benefits—with the exclusion of pay equity—as did male cloakmakers in a 1910 strike. In particular, the Joint Board of Sanitary Control (JBSC), a powerful body supervising workplace conditions that was formed after the 1910 strike, now came to inspect shirtwaist and dress, as well as cloak shops.

Strikes were not limited to New York City or, even, to Eastern and Southern European immigrant women. The surge of women's organizing in New York catalyzed strikes of women workers in Philadelphia in 1909, Chicago in 1911, Cleveland in 1912, Kalamazoo in 1912, and Boston in 1913. Together, these strikes fundamentally altered the landscape of the national garment industry and the industry's unions. In fact, by 1920, women composed 75 percent of the ILGWU's membership. . . .

Respectability, Morality, and the Challenge to Harassment, 1909–1913

Beginning in the 1909 strike heralded as the famed "Uprising of the 20,000," female Jewish and Italian garment workers cited harassment as a justification for organizing and as a reason to join garment unions. But, this organizing, in the way that it defined harassment as morally wrong, left intact hierarchies of skill. The sexuality of the workplace was described publicly, not by women workers alone— . . . these women had little access to newspapers and rarely could speak at union meetings—but through their collaboration with middle- and upper-class members of the Women's Trade Union League (WTUL). WTUL members were the undisputed leaders of the strikes, even though, with the exception of such organizers as Leonora O'Reilly, Rose Schneiderman, and Pauline Newman, few had ever worked in the garment industry. However, their class position and unchallenged public respectability allowed them to act as bridges between female workers and reluctant male unionists and between workers and an otherwise unsympathetic press, judiciary, and city government. WTUL members and supporters provided day-to-day direction of the strikes and, most important, prepared strikers' publicity, including articles in the WTUL's own magazine, *Life and Labor,* mainstream magazines and newspapers, and in the socialist press.

At first, WTUL leaders seemed reluctant to cite sexual harassment as a justification for organizing. After all, given Progressive-Era understandings of sexuality, women, more than men, were likely to be blamed publicly for the sexualization of the workplace. Instead, they sought to replicate male unionists' complaints about low wages, abominable conditions, and management's refusal to recognize the union. As Dorothy Dix wrote in the New York *Evening Journal,* the 1909 strike was launched to "wrest fair pay and decent working conditions from oppressive employers." However, the sexuality of the workplace had followed female strikers to the picket lines. Garment manufacturers hired prostitutes to intimidate picketers and to cast doubt on the morality of female strikers who were so obviously occupying a public space. Almost in collaboration, unsympathetic judges suggested that they would prosecute strikers in much the same way as prostitutes. . . . At the same time, women workers, upon whose quotes WTUL leaders relied for publicity, often cited sexual harassment as a reason for their activism. For example, one worker told Leonora O'Reilly and Rose Schneiderman when they were preparing a publicity article that strikers hoped "to be treated like ladies, with the union behind us, they wouldn't dare use the same language with us."

WTUL leaders and working women seized upon this idea of ladyhood starting in the 1909 strike. They even seemed to connect poor and disrespectful treatment of "lady" workers in the courts and on the picket lines to the pinching and immoral demands of bosses and foremen. Thus, during the 1909 strike, one sympathetic article quoted a picketer complaining of having been jailed with "horrid women that came off the street." . . . In Kalamazoo, WTUL leaders transformed the picket line into a prayer meeting to contrast it with a workplace where "girl workers must use basins and towels polluted by sin-soaked prostitutes . . . and coarse jokes and foul insinuations are current in every quarter. . . ." Organizers and workers passed a resolution insisting that the goal of the strike "was the abolition of shocking economic, moral, and sanitary conditions . . . where innocent young [g]irls and women are working."

Although this language of respect and ladyhood did not fully give a name to sexual harassment, it did provide a vocabulary for women workers to complain about the workplace abuse through the publicity prepared by the WTUL. Thus, in New York, the WTUL member Rose Pastor Stokes reported that "there are foremen who insult and abuse girls beyond endurance." And, in Cleveland, the WTUL organizer Gertrude Barnum claimed to speak for the garment worker "Miss Krial" and other strikers in declaring that "no foreman of any shop should compel [any girl] to sacrifice her womanhood."

Most important, such publicity provided the justification for women to create and use an infrastructure of labor relations to counter harassment. The use of contracts and labor relations to challenge abuse began slowly in New York. Female workers turned to arbitration procedures, guaranteed by the Protocol of Peace, the agreement between the garment unions and manufacturers that governed labor relations throughout much of the New York needle trades, to complain about treatment at the hand of individual foremen. Women workers turned an arbitration board, designed initially to handle questions of pay and conditions, into a body to handle grievances around harassment. By the time female garment workers went on strike in Chicago in 1911, the WTUL was openly pointing to "industrial democracy" as a means of addressing the "tyranny of formen [sic]." . . .

Union "Manhood," 1913–1930

While it gave women workers a distinct and previously unavailable ability to challenge harassment, the language of respect, ladyhood, and morality was as limiting as it was liberating. In asserting that sexual abuse came from bosses and foremen alone and was a question of respect, women workers and WTUL organizers effectively ignored the abuse they suffered at the hands of male workers and, in the process, they tended to overlook the relationship between workplace power and sexual harassment. Female garment workers and the WTUL cast sexual harassment as primarily a class-based interaction between workers and bosses. It was gendered only insofar as it assaulted the morality of working-class "ladies." This contradictory approach not only ignored the benefit that male workers received as sexual harassment helped code certain trades as men's trades, but the language of ladyhood and respect also seemed to confirm ideas of sexual difference at work. . . .

By 1910, mechanized factories, housed in industrial loft buildings and employing dozens of workers, had largely replaced smaller sweatshops. As Rosenfeld noted in 1913, the relationship that Lipkin and Schwartz had forged through taunting Lily was now impossible: "The gulf between them has widened and deepened. They are now utter strangers." Few male workers could expect to become shop owners. In addition, unionization and industry-wide contracts further strengthened and formalized class distinctions. Thus, male workers were probably less inclined or able to use sexual abuse of women as a way of soothing relations with bosses and, in fact, as early as 1911, the ILGWU was reminding male workers that "the time has gone by when there was any chance of getting women out of trade."

However, while male workers may have lost the battle over women's right to join unions, they fought doggedly and largely successfully to reproduce the shop floor sexual division of labor within the union. Similarly, male leaders never sought to negotiate contracts that sought to open particular trades to women or to lower pay differentials between skilled men's trades and unskilled women's trades. Nor is there evidence that female activists demanded such contracts. As the garment industry was transformed once more in the years after 1910, social constructions of skill and gendered pay scales remained remarkably stable. For example, in 1902 and again in 1915, New York State inspectors found that women earned about half the wages of men. In addition, both studies revealed a strict sexual division of labor. As the segmenting of work benefited employers, it also offered benefits to men. Even as women composed the majority of the ILGWU rank and file, the skilled trades and the union's leadership, even on the local level, remained overwhelmingly male.

Male leaders continued throughout the 1920s to rely on binaries of men's and women's work to defend pay differentials. . . . Similarly, male leaders employed images of women workers as transients to justify women's subordinate union roles and to minimize women's complaints about their leadership. The worker and organizer Jennie Matyas recalled that the union's president Benjamin Schlesinger responded to critical female shirtwaistmakers by asking "what do you women know of the economics of an industry. . . . You'd better go home and have babies." . . .

Women in the union, Pauline Newman recalled, felt "swallowed up in a sea of masculinity." In much the same way, male workers had dominated shop floor life, so too did they monopolize union meetings. As one woman complained: "Men necessarily bring into the meetings too much distasteful masculinity." The masculinity of the sweatshop with its language of sexual harassment had found its way out of the sweatshop and into the union. . . .

The very fact that, long after harassment was defined as immoral, female unionists were complaining about the weighty masculinity of garment unions highlights the distinct discursive limitations of their strategies of resistance to harassment. In defining harassment as an insult to the self-respect of "girls," working women were able to build strong "networks of solidarity." But these networks, paradoxically, were born from the very gendered binaries that sexual harassment protected and maintained.

Community Life and Work Culture Among African American Domestic Workers in Washington, D.C.

ELIZABETH CLARK-LEWIS

When African-American women migrated from the rural South to the urban centers of the North to work as live-in servants, few imagined they were beginning an escape from restraints imposed by race, gender, and class. But escape they did, and this essay examines the transition of twenty-three such women as they moved beyond live-in household servitude to self-employment during the first three decades of this century. It also demonstrates that as their roles changed, they experienced a new freedom to exercise control over their own lives, and their perceptions about themselves and their relationships to others underwent a significant change. It is important to recognize, however, that these changes occurred within a restrictive cultural environment. . . .

When foreign immigration slowed to a trickle after World War I, an important source of new white servants was eliminated. Within the first two decades of the twentieth century, household work lost its importance as an occupation for white women. By contrast, the number of African-American female household workers *increased* by 43 percent. Nationally, during the 1900–1930 period, the southern exploitive system triumphed: African-American women were forced into a "servant caste."

Surveys of specific northern urban centers found that the sharp rise in the number of African-American household workers had three sources: the new, large-scale migration of African-Americans to urban centers outside the South; the fact that African-American women were twice as likely as white women to be employed; and discriminatory policies that barred African-American women from 86 percent of employment categories. By 1926 the predominance of African-American migrant women in household service in Washington, D.C., was well established. . . . In 1900, 54 percent of the employed African-American women in the District were working in domestic service; by 1930, that figure had risen to 78 percent.

Expanded employment opportunities lured a stream of migrants to the urban North, where they moved into segregated communities that coalesced around churches, schools, philanthropic institutions, and businesses. But because of anti-migrant biases in the established African-American communities, only rarely could the newcomers find work in businesses owned by African-Americans or in the segregated schools of the communities where they settled. Disproportionately young, female, and poorly educated, they found themselves in urban centers where the pattern of racial segregation combined with class and gender restrictions to limit the jobs available to them. In overwhelming numbers the female migrants became household workers. . . .

Fourteen of the twenty-three women I interviewed grew up on farms owned by their parents; nine lived on share-tenant farms. Nearly all were reared in extended family households consisting of mothers, fathers, grandparents, siblings, and other relatives. They were all born between 1884 and 1911. Each household included at least one former slave; thus every woman in the study vividly recalled hearing first-hand descriptions of the degrading conditions of slavery. Further, the women were able to cite beliefs held by those former slaves regarding patterns and practices that enabled slave families to survive under the harshest of circumstances.

Family support, according to all of the women interviewed, was a focal point of rural churches. In addition to religious instruction, churches provided the only mutual aid, educational, and recreational activities available to African-American families in the rural South. After the family, the church was the most important means of individual and community expression.

The education of all of the women in the study had been severely limited by the need to help support the family, which they recognized as their primary responsibility by the age of seven. They worked first on the family farm, caring for the youngest children and serving as apprentices to older girls and women. Each of the twenty-three women recalled her mother's leaving home for residential (live-in) employment in white households in the surrounding area and recognized that independently employed children were an important part of the family's survival strategy. "Like everybody, by eight years old I went in to work with Mama," said Bernice Reeder in discussing the short period of outside tutelage which preceded a girl's first employment as live-in servant to a white family. She was alone on her first job, "at just nine years old! I was so scared," she continued. "Nobody cared you were a child. . . . You was a worker to them." The economic constraints faced by African-Americans in the rural South in the late nineteenth and early twentieth centuries made such early labor an unavoidable and accepted part of family and community life. . . .

By the age of ten, the women in this study told me, they also had to show clearly that they had the maturity to take another step: to travel to Washington, D.C., where sisters and aunts who worked as live-in servants (and sent money home) needed support in the form of child care and housekeeping by younger family members. These girls made the journey north by train. None had ever been out of her home state before. Twenty were taken to the train station by a male relative; all left their places of birth in the early morning, traveled alone, and were met by other relatives upon arrival in Washington.

When sharing reminiscences of their northbound journey, the women always described the feeling of freedom they experienced. "When you got on the train," Velma Davis exclaimed, "you felt different! Seem like you'd been bound up, but now this train untied you. It's funny . . . like being untied and tickled at the same time!" The girls understood that their first obligation was to carry on the rural-based family survival strategy in the homes of kin who served Washington's white households as live-in workers. The only significant change in their lives, initially, was the move to the North. . . .

Urban kin gave support to the migrant in several ways, if we may judge from information provided by the women interviewed. They paid all of her travel expenses to Washington, helped her adjust to urban life, and found employment for her within twelve months. In all the cases studied, the women were hired where their kin had contacts; in twenty-one of twenty-three cases, the coresident kin acquired employment for the migrants in households where they themselves were currently living. The girls migrated originally to provide support only to their urban kin; once they themselves became employed, however (after an average of one year), they were expected to assume responsibility for meeting the needs of both the urban and rural segments of the family.

As newly hired live-in servants, these female migrants learned that their primary role was to serve the mistress of the house, not just to complete the assigned tasks—a departure from the way they had worked in southern households. In the South, these African-American household workers had received daily task assignments from the white male head of the household. Migrants stressed that in Washington they slowly learned a new employment reality. Through trial and error, and with the advice of the more experienced earlier migrants, they learned to act in response to the needs of the wife rather than the husband.

Each of the twenty-three women was dismayed to learn that uniforms were mandatory in the District of Columbia. The wearing of uniforms was perceived by all as the major difference between their servant *work* in the South and their servant *role* in Washington. For these women, the uniform objectified the live-in servant and determined her fate in the workplace. The home was the white mistress's stage and major realm of influence, and the uniform legitimized her power. Ophilia Simpson recalled that "them uniforms just seemed to make them know you was theirs. Some say you wore them to show different jobs you was doing. Time in grey. Other times serving in black. But mostly them things just showed you was always at their beck and call. Really that's all them things means!" . . .

Despite the fact that each woman (and her family in the rural South) desperately needed the income her labor generated, within seven years these women were actively trying to leave the "servant life." There were several aspects of live-in employment that they all disliked. The uniform formalized the serving of the family for long hours, which they could not control. The wife as the authority figure had little respect for their needs. Worse still, they were forced to live in small quarters completely isolated from the African-American community.

But it was the question of church participation that first stimulated more than half of those interviewed to seek a change. Not being able to attend regular services on Sundays and generally feeling left out of the continuing life of their churches became for these women a potent symbol of the restrictions of live-in labor. "Even working-out down home, you'd go to church," Costella Harris explained, bedridden at eighty-six after a lifetime of household employment in Georgetown. "Everybody did," she continued slowly. "Now, most came just to hear the Word. But some came to keep from being in a kitchen somewhere. . . . Church gave you six, not seven days of work. But up here you never saw inside any church on Sunday, living-in."

Painful as all these restrictions were, however, they were probably not sufficient by themselves to lead the women to reject live-in servant work. The *ability* to make the change emanated from the phenomenon known as "penny savers clubs." Twenty-one of the twenty-three women actively associated themselves with such mutual benefit associations, which sponsored social gatherings and provided sickness and death benefits to members. . . . Although rarely mentioned in the literature, the penny savers clubs served as a vital economic base for the female migrant. After an average of six years of saving, the women were able to develop the important economic leverage they needed to leave servant life.

The role of the church and of the penny savers clubs in first awakening the desire for change and then facilitating the process of that change cannot be overestimated. The clubs permitted the women, during the transition from live-in service to household day work, to maintain financial security for themselves and their kin in the rural South. No woman left live-in work until she had saved enough money to maintain herself and send money monthly to rural kin. . . . They sought to find a less circumscribed economic and employment environment without abandoning one of the original motivations for leaving their rural families—relief of the family's economic distress.

The women soon identified laundresses as critical figures in their search for autonomy. Laundresses served as role models: unlike the other staff members, they did not belittle the migrant woman's desire to gain household work on a nonresidential basis, and they alone knew the categories and rules related to operating within several households simultaneously. The laundress also brought information about households that were seeking the services of women on a live-out basis for one or two days a week. . . .

The women saw six major benefits to the shift from live-in servant to household day worker. First, as indicated by the language they used to describe their experiences, their work seemed more their own. They spoke of their earlier jobs in depersonalized language because they sought detachment from their employers and a buffer against the employers' insensitivity to them as workers and African-Americans. . . . Velma Davis recalled, "When I say 'my job,' I mean a job I got and I'd keep if they acted decent. 'They job' is for them; a job that you did and did, more and more—from one thing to another, early to late, and you worked!" . . .

Second, the previously isolated African-American women began to make contact with one another amid their newly flexible working conditions, encountering many others like themselves. The structure that had created social marginality among African-Americans in Washington was slowly being dismantled; the women's isolated and restrictive living circumstances were relegated to an oppressive past. . . .

Third, as the women changed jobs, they moved to rooms in boardinghouses and began to adopt a sharply different lifestyle. The other girls in the house where Velma Davis became a boarder "was all doing day-work, too," and "soon I was doing just about everything with them. I just liked being with these girls [who] was single, nice." After the move from live-in servant work, Velma Davis said that she did not see her family for long periods of time. She said that it was when she moved to the boardinghouse that she began to feel she had finally left home. . . .

Fourth, their places of work changed. Employers usually hired someone other than their former live-in servants to work as daily household employees. The women acknowledged this policy; thus, in communicating their new plans to their employers, they understood that future employment in that household would not be considered. . . .

Fifth, each woman indicated that turning to day work produced a subtle change in her relationship to the white women for whom she worked. Virginia Lacey described the new experience with an employer this way: "She'd meet you at the door, tell you how she wanted her house done, and she'd be gone. You did the work without her in the way, slowing you up. On a day job we all knew how to get everything done—but, in your own way. Having anybody around will make you work slower." . . .

Finally, all of the women stressed that as they moved out of live-in work, they shed their uniforms and other symbols of their identities as live-in servants. Each had felt locked into a narrow and constricted role by the need to wear uniforms of "black for this" and "gray for that." Discarding that badge of their station in life clearly disaffiliated them from their previous work. . . .

Virginia Lacey agreed: "I'd go to whatever house I'd have to be to work at. I change to my work clothes and then clean the house. . . . I never liked to be in the uniform. I guess serving in a uniform made you be back on staff. And you wasn't, so you'd just not want to wear that uniform." She paused for a moment, reflecting. "Wearing your own clothes—that's like you being your own boss! You was on your own job for a day and pay, then go home."

Some scholars and artists who are sensitive to the problems of domestic service have tended to view negatively the bags in which day workers carried their clothes. But these women took pride in the fact that they "carried work clothes" to their jobs; they felt that the bags were symbols of personal freedom and in that sense were positive. In fact, Marie Davis reported that workers often called them "freedom bags"; she observed, "When I got to carry clothes, I was finally working in what I wanted to. No black or gray uniforms or castoffs from the whites down home. I was proud to put my stuff in a bag at home. I guess I wanted to finally show I didn't wear a uniform. I wasn't a servant." . . .

A new identity was gained. Gone was the identity to which they were born or which had been ascribed to them; this new one they had *achieved* on their own, and their newly acquired friends and associates validated their achieved status. As Bernice Reeder explained, "Once you got some work by the day and got around people who did it, you'd see how you could get ahead, get better things. You'd see how to get more and more days, some party work, extra sewing, stuff like that." Velma Davis agreed: "When I started working days, other people [other household day workers] would show you how to get a few extra dollars. In this town you could make more money, and they'd sure show you how."

The women's transformed identities and modified employment modes led to several other changes in the African-American community. For one, the women's interest in the penny savers clubs waned. . . . Although the associations continued to exist . . . household day workers perceived them as institutions serving the needs of live-in servants. The day workers transferred their money to banks, in part because their new jobs gave them the opportunity to do so. As Eula Montgomery remarked, "I'd have used them [banks] earlier, but with that woman you never got time to go to a place like that. I know I didn't." Minnie Barnes verified this point: "I used a bank as a day worker because it was on my streetcar line home." . . .

The waning of the mutual benefit associations did not, however, mean the decline of support for rural kin. On the contrary, economic assistance typically increased after the transition to household day work. In speaking of the support she provided her relatives still living in the South, Velma Davis said, "I didn't miss a month. . . . That's why I got myself set before I left live-in. I never missed sending my share home." If anything, the women adhered even more strongly to their premigration beliefs concerning kinship obligations. . . .

The level of these women's participation in the African-American churches of Washington also changed significantly. Live-in servant work had greatly restricted their attendance and involvement in church activities. Velma Davis recalled, "Living in? You never dreamed of going to day service. Sundays, you'd be out of there [the live-in household], if you was good, by four or five." Regular participation in daytime church services was also an indication of status. "Big people, like government messengers, or people working in a colored business office, that's who'd be regular at Sunday day services," Eula Montgomery said. Individuals who worked in those types of jobs, she pointed out, had their Sundays free; they could also, therefore, "be on the church's special committees."

Live-in service had limited all aspects of interactions with other church members. Eula Montgomery went on: "If you lived in a room in the attic, how could you be in any of them clubs? You couldn't bring nobody over there. . . . You never got to be in a fellowship. That was for people who got off on Saturday and Sunday. They had a nice place to have people over to—not no kitchen." . . .

Regular church attendance, achieved through less confining employment, was accompanied by more leisure-time activity. A married couple could go to morning church services, and in summer they could go out for picnics, Dolethia Otis pointed out.

Participation in church and leisure activities was viewed, not surprisingly, as representative of the attainment of *better* work; according to Nellie Willoughby, a migrant from Virginia, "it showed you had work you didn't live at." It did not mean that these women did *easier* work. The point was that the work they did—even if more strenuous—permitted some previously unavailable free time. . . .

All of the women interviewed asserted that household day work was directly responsible for their ability to participate in the churches. The result of this change was wider church membership. Previously, working-class women had not been well represented in the African-American churches. "Most women down at Mason Street Baptist who were real active," said Helen Venable, "were educated good and had jobs like teaching. As people got more away from live-in you saw a lotta different people in all the things that church has. Then more and more people got in the church's clubs or work."

The growth of African-American churches in Washington, then, was a direct consequence of the steady influx of these working-class (former live-in) women. They strongly supported church expansion because their participation in the church activities further separated them from the stigma of servitude. . . .

Live-in servant work imposed countless burdens upon African-American female migrants to the District of Columbia before the Depression, yet "service-class" women developed and controlled philanthropic organizations that allowed them eventually to escape the boundaries of live-in servant employment. Although the African-American women quoted here remained in household service work all their lives, they restructured its salient features and created more freedom for themselves.

Reformers who rely only on archival records may view household service work as "a dead end." Scholars all too often see household workers as merely products of change, never as its causes; as objects of events, not as their subjects; as passive reactors, not as active forces in history. The words and lives of these women refute such views. Orra Fisher's response sums up best what the women expressed when asked about the progress and the success they have seen in their lives:

> I worked hard to serve God and to see that my three girls didn't have to serve nobody else like I did except God. I satisfied to know I came a long way. From a kitchen down home to a kitchen up here, and then able to earn money, but live with my children and grands. Now Jesus took me every step—that's real.
>
> But look at me, with more than I ever dreamed I'd have. And my three, with houses, and jobs. My girls in an office, and the baby—my son—over twenty years in the Army. I get full thinking about it. I had it bad, but look at them.

F U R T H E R   R E A D I N G

Benson, Susan Porter. *Counter Cultures: Saleswomen, Managers, and Customers in American Department Stores, 1890–1940* (1986).

Brown, Carrie. *Rosie's Mom: Forgotten Women Workers of the First World War* (2002).

Cobble, Dorothy Sue. *Dishing it Out: Waitresses and Their Unions in the Twentieth Century* (1991).

Cohen, Lizabeth. *Making a New Deal: Industrial Workers in Chicago, 1919–1939* (1990).

Cohen, Miriam. *Workshop to Office: Two Generations of Italian Women in New York City, 1900–1950* (1993).

Cooper, Patricia A. *Once a Cigar Maker: Men, Women, and Work Culture in American Cigar Factories, 1900–1919* (1987).

DeVault, Ileen A. *Sons and Daughters of Labor: Class and Clerical Work in Turn-of-the-Century Pittsburgh* (1990).

Dudden, Faye. *Serving Women: Household Service in Nineteenth-Century America* (1983).

Dye, Nancy Schrom. *As Equals and as Sisters: Feminism, the Labor Movement, and the Women's Trade Union League of New York* (1981).

Einsenstein, Sarah. *Give Us Bread But Give Us Roses* (1983).

Enstad, Nan. *Ladies of Labor, Girls of Adventure: Working Women, Popular Culture, and Labor Politics at the Turn of the Twentieth Century* (1999).

Ewen, Elizabeth. *Immigrant Women in the Land of Dollars: Life and Culture on the Lower East Side* (1985).

Faue, Elizabeth. *Community of Suffering and Struggle: Women, Men, and the Labor Movement in Minneapolis, 1915–1945* (1991).

Fine, Lisa. *The Souls of the Skyscraper: Female Clerical Workers in Chicago, 1870–1930* (1990).

Frank, Dana. *Purchasing Power: Consumer Organizing, Gender, and the Seattle Labor Movement, 1919–1929* (1994).

Fraundorf, Martha. "The Labor Force Participation of Turn-of-the-Century Married Women," *Journal of Economic History* 39 (1979): 401–418.

Gamber, Wendy. *The Female Economy: The Millinery and Dressmaking Trades, 1860–1930* (1997).

Garrison, Dee. *Apostles of Culture: The Public Librarian and American Society, 1876–1920* (1979).

Gilligan, Maureen Carroll. *Female Corporate Culture and the New South: Women in Business Between the World Wars* (1999).

Glenn, Evelyn Nakanno. *Issei, Nisei, War Bride: Three Generations of Japanese American Women in Domestic Service* (1986).

Glenn, Susan A. *Daughters of the Shtetl: Life and Labor in the Immigrant Generation* (1990).

Goldin, Claudia. "The Work and Wages of Single Women, 1870–1920," *Journal of Economic History* 40 (1980): 81–88.

Hall, Jacquelyn Dowd. "Disorderly Women: Gender and Labor Militancy in the Appalachian South," *Journal of American History* 73 (1987): 354–382.

Hareven, Tamara. *Family Time and Industrial Time* (1982).

Harris, Barbara. *Beyond Her Sphere: Women and the Professions in American History* (1978).

Hine, Darlene Clark. *Black Women in White: Racial Conflict and Cooperation in the Nursing Profession, 1890–1950* (1989).

Hummer, Patrice M. *The Decade of the Elusive Promise: Professional Women in the United States, 1920–1930* (1981).

Jensen, Joan, and Sue Davidson, eds. *A Needle, A Bobbin, A Strike* (1984).

Jones, Jacqueline. *Labor of Love, Labor of Sorrow: Black Women, Work, and the Family from Slavery to the Present* (1985).

Katzman, David. *Seven Days a Week: Women and Domestic Service in Industrializing America* (1978).

Kessler-Harris, Alice. *In Pursuit of Equity: Women, Men, and the Quest for Economic Citizenship in 20th-Century America* (2001).

———. *Out to Work: A History of Wage-Earning Women in the United States* (1982).

Lowry, Beverly. *Her Dream of Dreams: The Rise and Triumph of Madam C.J. Walker* (2003).

Meyerowitz, Joanne. *Women Adrift: Independent Wage Earners in Chicago, 1880–1930* (1988).

Moldow, Gloria. *Women Doctors in Gilded Age Washington: Race, Gender, and Professionalization* (1987).

Norwood, Stephen. *Labor's Flaming Youth: Telephone Operators and Worker Militancy, 1878–1923* (1990).

Orleck, Annelise. *Common Sense and a Little Fire: Women and Working-Class Politics in the United States, 1900–1965* (1995).

Peiss, Kathy. *Cheap Amusements: Working Women and Leisure in Turn-of-the-Century New York* (1986).

Reitano, Joanne. "Working Girls Unite," *American Quarterly* 36 (1984): 112–134.

Rose, Elizabeth. *A Mother's Job: The History of Day Care, 1890–1960* (1999).

Rossiter, Margaret W. *Women Scientists in America: Struggles and Strategies to 1940* (1982).

Rotella, Elyce. *From Home to Office: United States Women at Work, 1870–1930* (1981).

Ruiz, Vicki L. *From Out of the Shadows: Mexican Women in Twentieth-Century America* (1998).

Sawaya, Francesca. *Modern Women, Modern Work: Domesticity, Professionalism, and American Writing, 1890–1950* (2004).

Shakir, Evelyn. *Bint Arab: Arab and Arab American Women in the United States* (1997).

Shaw, Stephanie J. *What a Woman Ought to Be and to Do: Black Professional Women Workers During the Jim Crow Era* (1996).

Soloman, Barbara Miller. *In the Company of Educated Women* (1985).

Stricker, Frank. "Cookbooks and Lawbooks: The Hidden History of Career Women in Twentieth-Century America," *Journal of Social History* 10 (1976–1977): 1–19.

Strom, Sharon Hartmann. *Beyond the Typewriter: Gender, Class, and the Origins of Modern American Office Work, 1900–1930* (1992).

Tax, Meredith. *The Rising of the Women: Feminist Solidarity and Class Conflict, 1880–1917* (1981).

Walsh, Mary Roth. *Doctors Wanted: No Women Need Apply* (1977).

Wandersee, Winifred. *Women's Work and Family Values, 1920–1940* (1981).

CHAPTER
11

The "New Woman" in
Public Life and Politics,
1900–1930

In the early decades of the twentieth century, American women joined a myriad of women's organizations, thereby trying to expand opportunities for their sex, to remove obstacles to women's advancement, and to "uplift" the nation's culture, government, and politics. Often referred to as "new women," this generation of organized women became important players in Progressive reform at the local, state, and national levels, even as they sought to expand their own civil rights. Women's long campaign for suffrage was finally victorious when Congress ratified the nineteenth amendment to the Constitution in 1920. Other reform campaigns spearheaded by women produced a federal children's bureau, protective labor legislation, pure food and drug acts, juvenile courts, public kindergartens, city beautification projects, and a wide array of public health and social welfare programs for mothers and children.

Historians have found that organized women did not always act in concert; indeed, they were often divided by values, strategies, and differences in social background. For example, while black women's collective experience taught them that race and sex oppression must be challenged simultaneously, the majority of white women refused to participate in efforts to combat racist ideology, segregation, disenfranchisement, or lynching. Some women reformers hoped to carry a "maternalist" identity and ethic into civic life and public policy; others eschewed the constraints of maternalism. After suffrage was won, Florence Kelley and other advocates of women's protective labor legislation became entangled in a bitter debate with members of the National Woman's Party over the party's fight for an Equal Rights Amendment. And yet, though they experienced disunity and disagreement, organized women also struggled with a common problem: how to claim rights or authority in public life in the face of persistent discrimination and patterns of marginalization. Recent historical scholarship has sought to explain how and to what extent organized women tried to combine a belief in sexual difference with the pursuit of gender or racial equality. Conversely, in what circumstances did women downplay gender differences? And what were the benefits and limitations of their varied approaches to reform?

In Document 1, Mary Church Terrell, the president of the National Federation of Colored Women's Clubs, praises the reform efforts of organizations composed entirely of black women. In Document 2, Terrell calls on white women, especially those of the South, to join in the fight against lynching. The U.S. Supreme Court, in Document 3, upholds a maximum hours law for working women in Oregon, ruling that women workers are vulnerable to physical harm in the workplace and need state protections and regulations not needed by men. In Document 4, Margaret Dreier Robbins urges women, especially privileged members of the middle class, to consider the plight of young women wage earners and lend support to the goals of the Women's Trade Union League. Reformer Jane Addams applauds the development of a new social consciousness in response to the problem of prostitution in Document 5. Inez Haynes Irwin recounts in Document 6 how militant suffragists in the National Woman's Party challenged President Woodrow Wilson to support a federal suffrage amendment. In Document 7, published in 1922 in *The Nation* magazine, Elsie Hill of the National Woman's Party calls for the elimination of all legal distinctions between men and women. Florence Kelley of the National Consumers' League, presented a rejoinder to Hill (also included), arguing that the National Woman's Party misunderstood women's legal interests and seemed intent on undermining hard-won labor laws that protected and benefitted women wage-earners. The letters in Document 8 were written to birth control advocate Margaret Sanger, who published these missives and others like them, to document American husbands' and wives' desperate need for safe and legal contraception.

1. Mary Church Terrell Praises the Club Work of Colored Women, 1901

Should anyone ask me what special phase of the Negro's development makes me most hopeful of his ultimate triumph over present obstacles, I should answer unhesitatingly, it is the magnificent work the women are doing to regenerate and uplift the race. Though there are many things in the Negro's present condition to discourage him, he has some blessings for which to be thankful: not the least of these is the progress of our women in everything which makes for the culture of the individual and the elevation of the race.

For years, either banding themselves into small companies or struggling alone, colored women have worked with might and main to improve the condition of their people. The necessity of systematizing their efforts and working on a larger scale became apparent not many years ago, and they decided to unite their forces. Thus it happened that in the summer of 1896 the National Association of Colored Women was formed by the union of two large organizations, from which the advantage of concerted action had been learned. From its birth till the present time its growth has been steady. Interest in the purposes and plans of the National Association has spread so rapidly that it has already been represented in twenty-six states. Handicapped though its members have been, because they lacked both money and experience, their efforts have for the most part been crowned with success.

Mary Church Terrell, "Club Work of Colored Women," 1901. This document can also be found in *Southern Workman* 30 (1901): 435–438.

Kindergartens have been established by some of its organizations, from which encouraging reports have come. A sanitarium with a training school for nurses has been set on such a firm foundation by the Phyllis Wheatley Club of New Orleans, Louisiana, and has proved itself to be such a blessing to the entire community, that the municipal government of that Southern city has voted it an annual appropriation of several hundred dollars. By the members of the Tuskegee branch of the association the work of bringing the light of knowledge and the gospel of cleanliness to their poor benighted sisters on the plantations in Alabama has been conducted with signal success. Their efforts have thus far been confined to four estates, comprising thousands of acres of land, on which live hundreds of colored people yet in the darkness of ignorance and in the grip of sin, and living miles away from churches and schools.

Plans for aiding the indigent orphaned and aged have been projected, and in some instances have been carried into successful execution. One club in Memphis, Tenn., has purchased a large tract of land on which it intends to erect an Old Folks' Home, part of the money for which has already been raised. Splendid service has been rendered by the Illinois Federation of Colored Women's Clubs, through whose instrumentality schools have been visited, truant children looked after, parents and teachers urged to cooperate with each other, rescue and reform work engaged in, so as to reclaim unfortunate women and tempted girls, public institutions investigated, and garments cut, made and distributed to the needy poor.

Questions affecting our legal status as a race are sometimes agitated by our women. In Tennessee and Louisiana colored women have several times petitioned the legislature of their respective states to repeal the obnoxious Jim Crow car laws. . . .

Homes, more homes, better homes, purer homes, is the text upon which our sermons have been and will be preached. There has been a determined effort to have heart-to-heart talks with our women, that we may strike at the root of evils, many of which lie at the fireside. If the women of the dominant race, with all the centuries of education, culture and refinement back of them, with all the wealth of opportunity ever present with them, feel the need of a Mothers' Congress, that they may be enlightened upon the best methods of rearing their children and conducting their homes, how much more do our women, from whom shackles were stricken but yesterday, need information on the same vital subjects! And so the Association is working vigorously to establish mothers' congresses on a small scale, wherever our women can be reached.

From this brief and meagre account of the work which has been and is still being accomplished by colored women through the medium of clubs, it is easy to observe how earnest and effective have been our efforts to elevate the race. No people need ever despair whose women are fully aroused to the duties which rest upon them, and are willing to shoulder responsibilities which they alone can successfully assume. The scope of our endeavors is constantly widening. Into the various channels of generosity and beneficence the National Association is entering more and more every day.

Some of our women are urging their clubs to establish day nurseries, a charity of which there is an imperative need. The infants of wage earning mothers are frequently locked alone in a room from the time the mother leaves in the morning until she returns at night. Not long ago I read in a Southern newspaper that an infant thus locked alone in the room all day had cried itself to death. When one reflects on the slaughter of the innocents which is occurring with pitiless persistency every day, and thinks of the multitudes who are maimed for life or are rendered imbecile, because of the treatment received during their helpless infancy, it is evident that by establishing day nurseries colored women will render one of the greatest services possible to humanity and to the race. . . .

Nothing lies nearer the heart of colored women than the cause of the children. We feel keenly the need of kindergartens, and are putting forth earnest efforts to honey-comb this country with them from one extreme to the other. The more unfavorable the environments of children the more necessary is it that steps be taken to counter-act blameful influences upon innocent victims. How imperative is it then, that, as colored women, we inculcate correct principles and set good examples for our own youth, whose little feet will have so many thorny paths of prejudice, temptation and injustice to tread. . . .

And so, lifting as we climb, onward and upward we go, struggling, striving and hoping that the buds and blossoms of our desires will burst into glorious fruition ere long. With courage born of success achieved in the past, we look forward to a future large with promise and hope. Seeking no favors because of our color, nor patron-age because of our needs, we knock at the bar of Justice and ask for an equal chance.

2. Mary Church Terrell Describes Lynching from a Negro's Point of View, 1904

Before 1904 was three months old, thirty-one negroes had been lynched. Of this number, fifteen were murdered within one week in Arkansas, and one was shot to death in Springfield, Ohio, by a mob composed of men who did not take the trouble to wear masks. Hanging, shooting and burning black men, women and children in the United States have become so common that such occurrences create but little sensation and evoke but slight comment now. . . . In the discussion of this subject, four mistakes are commonly made.

In the first place, it is a great mistake to suppose that rape is the real cause of lynching in the South. Beginning with the Ku Klux Klan the negro has been con-stantly subjected to some form of organized violence ever since he became free. It is easy to prove that rape is simply the pretext and not the cause of lynching. Statistics show that, out of every 100 negroes who are lynched, from 75–85 are not even accused of this crime, and many who are accused of it are innocent. . . .

In the second place, it is a mistake to suppose that the negro's desire for social equality sustains any relation whatsoever to the crime of rape. . . . It is safe to assert that, among the negroes who have been guilty of ravishing white women, not one had been taught that he was the equal of white people or had ever heard of social equality. . . .

The third error on the subject of lynching consists of the widely circulated statement that the moral sensibilities of the best negroes in the United States are so stunted and dull, and the standard of morality among even the leaders of the race is

Mary Church Terrell, "Lynching from a Negro's Point of View," *North American Review* 178 (June 1904): 853–868. This document may also be found in Gerda Lerner, ed., *Black Women in White America: A Documentary History* (New York: Pantheon Books, 1972), 205–211.

so low, that they do not appreciate the enormity and heinousness of rape. . . . Only those who are densely ignorant of the standards and sentiments of the best negroes, or who wish wilfully to misrepresent and maliciously slander a race already resting under burdens greater than it can bear, would accuse its thousands of reputable men and women of sympathizing with rapists, either black or white, or of condoning their crime. . . .

What, then, is the cause of lynching? At the last analysis, it will be discovered that there are just two causes of lynching. In the first place, it is due to race hatred, the hatred of a stronger people toward a weaker who were once held as slaves. In the second place, it is due to the lawlessness so prevalent in the section where nine-tenths of the lynchings occur. . . .

Lynching is the aftermath of slavery. The white men who shoot negroes to death and flay them alive, and the white women who apply flaming torches to their oil-soaked bodies today, are the sons and daughters of women who had but little, if any, compassion on the race when it was enslaved. The men who lynch negroes today are, as a rule, the children of women who sat by their firesides happy and proud in the possession and affection of their own children, while they looked with unpitying eye and adamantine heart upon the anguish of slave mothers whose children had been sold away, when not overtaken by a sadder fate. . . . It is too much to expect, perhaps, that the children of women who for generations looked upon the hardships and the degradation of their sisters of a darker hue with few if any protests, should have mercy and compassion upon the children of that oppressed race now. But what a tremendous influence for law and order, and what a mighty foe to mob violence Southern white women might be, if they would arise in the purity and power of their womanhood to implore their fathers, husbands and sons no longer to stain their hands with the black man's blood!

3. The U.S. Supreme Court Upholds a Maximum Hours Law for Working Women in *Muller v. Oregon*, 1908

Messrs. William D. Fenton and Henry H. Gilfry for plaintiff in error.

Messrs. H. B. Adams, Louis Brandeis, John Manning, A. M. Crawford, and B. E. Haney for defendant in error.

Mr. Justice Brewer delivered the opinion of the court:

On February 19, 1903, the legislature of the state of Oregon passed an act (Session Laws 1903, p. 148) the first section of which is in these words:

"Sec. 1. That no female (shall) be employed in any mechanical establishment, or factory, or laundry in this state more than ten hours during any one day. The hours of work may be so arranged as to permit the employment of females at any time so that they shall not work more than ten hours during the twenty-four hours of any one day."

Sec. 3 made a violation of the provisions of the prior sections a misdemeanor subject to a fine of not less than $10 nor more than $25. One September 18, 1905, an

---

Muller v. Oregon, 208 U.S. 412 (1908).

information was filed in the circuit court of the state for the county of Multnomah, charging that the defendant "on the 4th day of September, A. D. 1905, in the county of Multnomah and state of Oregon, then and there being the owner of a laundry, known as the Grand Laundry, in the city of Portland, and the employer of females therein, did then and there unlawfully permit and suffer one Joe Haselbock, he, the said Joe Haselbock, then and there being an overseer, superintendent, and agent of said Curt Muller, in the said Grand Laundry, to require a female, to wit, one Mrs. E. Gotcher, to work more than ten hours in said laundry on said 4th day of September, A. D. 1905, contrary to the statutes in such cases made and provided, and against the peace and dignity of the state of Oregon."

A trial resulted in a verdict against the defendant, who was sentenced to pay a fine of $10. The supreme court of the state affirmed the conviction . . . whereupon the case was brought here on writ of error.

The single question is the constitutionality of the statute under which the defendant was convicted, so far as it affects the work of a female in a laundry. That it does not conflict with any provisions of the state Constitution is settled by the decision of the supreme court of the state. The contentions of the defendant, now plaintiff in error, are thus stated in his brief:

> "(1) Because the statute attempts to prevent persons sui juris from making their own contracts, and thus violates the provisions of the 14th Amendment as follows: 'No state shall make or enforce any law which shall abridge the privileges or immunities of citizens of the United States; nor shall any state deprive any person of life, liberty, or property, without due process of law; nor deny to any person within its jurisdiction the equal protection of the laws.'
>
> "(2) Because the statute does not apply equally to all persons similarly situated, and is class legislation.
>
> "(3) The statute is not a valid exercise of the police power. The kinds of work prescribed are not unlawful, nor are they declared to be immoral or dangerous to the public health; nor can such a law be sustained on the ground that it is designed to protect women on account of their sex. There is no necessary or reasonable connection between the limitation prescribed by the act and the public health, safety, or welfare."

It is the law of Oregon that women, whether married or single, have equal contractual and personal rights with men. . . .

It thus appears that, putting to one side the elective franchise, in the matter of personal and contractual rights they stand on the same plane as the other sex. Their rights in these respects can no more be infringed than the equal rights of their brothers. We held in *Lochner v. New York* . . . a law providing that no laborer shall be required or permitted to work in bakeries more than sixty hours in a week or ten hours in a day was not as to men a legitimate exercise of the police power of the state, but an unreasonable, unnecessary, and arbitrary interference with the right and liberty of the individual to contract in relation to his labor, and as such was in conflict with, and void under, the Federal Constitution. That decision is invoked by plaintiff in error as decisive of the question before us. But this assumes that the difference between the sexes does not justify a different rule respecting a restriction of the hours of labor. . . .

Constitutional questions, it is true, are not settled by even a consensus of present public opinion, for it is the peculiar value of a written constitution that it places in unchanging form limitations upon legislative action, and thus gives a permanence and stability to popular government which otherwise would be lacking. At the same time, when a question of fact is debated and debatable, and the extent to which a special constitutional limitation goes is affected by the truth in respect to that fact, a widespread and long continued belief concerning it is worthy of consideration. We take judicial cognizance of all matters of general knowledge.

It is undoubtedly true, as more than once declared by this court, that the general right to contract in relation to one's business is part of the liberty of the individual, protected by the 14th Amendment to the Federal Constitution; yet it is equally well settled that this liberty is not absolute and extending to all contracts, and that a state may, without conflicting with the provisions of the 14th Amendment, restrict in many respects the individual's power of contract. . . .

That woman's physical structure and the performance of maternal functions place her at a disadvantage in the struggle for subsistence is obvious. This is especially true when the burdens of motherhood are upon her. Even when they are not, by abundant testimony of the medical fraternity continuance for a long time on her feet at work, repeating this from day to day, tends to injurious effects upon the body, and, as healthy mothers are essential to vigorous offspring, the physical well-being of woman becomes an object of public interest and care in order to preserve the strength and vigor of the race.

Still again, history discloses the fact that woman has always been dependent upon man. He established his control at the outset by superior physical strength, and this control in various forms, with diminishing intensity, has continued to the present. As minors, thought not to the same extent, she has been looked upon in the courts as needing especial care that her rights may be preserved. Education was long denied her, and while now the doors of the schoolroom are opened and her opportunities for acquiring knowledge are great, yet even with that and the consequent increase of capacity for business affairs it is still true that in the struggle for subsistence she is not an equal competitor with her brother. Though limitations upon personal and contractual rights may be removed by legislation, there is that in her disposition and habits of life which will operate against a full assertion of those rights. She will still be where some legislation to protect her seems necessary to secure a real equality of right. Doubtless there are individual exceptions, and there are many respects in which she has an advantage over him; but looking at it from the viewpoint of the effort to maintain an independent position in life, she is not upon an equality. Differentiated by these matters from the other sex, she is properly placed in a class by herself, and legislation designed for her protection may be sustained, even when like legislation is not necessary for men, and could not be sustained. It is impossible to close one's eyes to the fact that she still looks to her brother and depends upon him. Even though all restrictions on political, personal, and contractual rights were taken away, and she stood, so far as statutes are concerned, upon an absolutely equal plane with him, it would still be true that she is so constituted that she will rest upon and look to him for protection; that her physical structure and a proper discharge of her maternal functions—having in view not merely her own health, but the well-being of the race—justify legislation to protect her from the greed as well as the passion of man. The limitations which this statute places upon her contractual powers, upon her right to agree with her employer as to the time she shall labor, are not imposed solely for her benefit, but also largely for the benefit of all. Many words cannot make this plainer. The two sexes differ in structure of body, in the functions to be per-formed by each, in the amount of physical strength, in the capacity for long continued labor, particularly when done standing, the influence of vigorous health upon the future well-being of the race, the self-reliance which enables one to assert full rights, and in the capacity to maintain the struggle for subsistence. This difference justifies a difference in legislation, and upholds that which is designed to compensate for some of the burdens which rest upon her.

We have not referred in this discussion to the denial of the elective franchise in the state of Oregon, for while that may disclose a lack of political equality in all things with her brother, that is not of itself decisive. The reason runs deeper, and rests in the inherent difference between the two sexes, and in the different functions in life which they perform.

For these reasons, and without questioning in any respect the decision in *Lochner v. New York,* we are of the opinion that it cannot be adjudged that the act in question is in conflict with the Federal Constitution, so far as it respects the work of a female in a laundry, and the judgment of the Supreme Court of Oregon is affirmed.

4. Margaret Dreier Robins Describes the Purposes of the Women's Trade Union League, 1909

What is the Women's Trade Union League?

This question is asked of me daily, and, I think, my friends, that I can answer it best by asking you some questions in turn:

Do you know that the average wage of the women workers of our country is less than $270.00 a year? Do you know that one-half of the six million working women in the United States are under twenty-one years of age, and that the conditions of work in many of the trades into which women have entered put such a strain upon the physical organization that a brief service precludes motherhood?

We have tried to tell you very simply in the following pages what some of these conditions are; and we believe that the more you study these conditions the more convinced you will become that they are destructive, not only of all physical strength, but also of all mental and spiritual development—destructive alike of all expression of ideals in the life of the individual and in the nation.

What is to be done?

Many things; but it will be readily understood that the most important factor in the industrial problem is the worker herself, and that the most significant fact about the woman worker is her youth.

We are forcing young girls of fourteen and sixteen years of age into the indus-trial struggle, and are demanding of them the knowledge and wisdom of trained ma-turity. If in her need for work whereby to earn her daily bread, and in her ignorance of the cost, a girl of fourteen underbids her fellow-worker, how is she to know that in so doing she is competing against her own home; and that, in the years to come, as wife and mother she must bear the heaviest burden of the lesser wage? How is she

National Women's Trade Union League, *Handbook, Convention at Chicago, September 27–October 2, 1909* (Chicago: National Women's Trade Union League, 1909).

to know that the division and sub-division of labor demands of her the joyless task of tending a machine; not only for today, but for tomorrow as well, and for all the succeeding tomorrows? Can you see her standing alone in the midst of her fellow-workers, alone and afraid, because she has discovered that even as she became the underbidder, so all may become "underbidders" or pace-makers? Where can she learn that "two are better than one, for if they fall the one will lift up his fellow"? Where can she find this fellowship?

Where, but in the great school of the Working People, the Trade Union, which is open to all and within the reach of all? In this school the members are taught that "An injury to one is the concern of all," and thus they enter into fellowship with one another, for they have found the way to work with each other and not against each other. Knowledge of the trade in all its aspects, judgment, decision, patience and fidelity are here called into action, for by seeking to establish trade agreements with her fellow-workers and with her employer, the duties and rights of each must be discussed, considered, and voted upon; and except in those states or cities where the initiative and referendum have been enacted into law I know of no training in democratic self-government and citizenship that equals the training received in the School of the Trade Union. As the personal needs become increasingly protected by collective action, thoughts are turned into new channels, energies are directed towards other tasks, and with a wider horizon educational and social issues command attention. The child has grown into the woman; the untutored girl has grown into the intelligent, capable, clear-sighted leader and citizen, and under her direction social progress is written into the laws of our country. This opportunity for learning, for development, for character-building, has been given to her in the Trade Union School—the open sesame to fellowship and service.

5. Jane Addams Applauds the "Beginnings of a New Conscience" Regarding the "Ancient Evil" of Prostitution, 1912

In every large city throughout the world thousands of women are so set aside as outcasts from decent society that it is considered an impropriety to speak the very word which designates them. Lecky calls this type of woman "the most mournful and the most awful figure in history": he says that "she remains, while creeds and civilizations rise and fall, the eternal sacrifice of humanity, blasted for the sins of the people." But evils so old that they are imbedded in man's earliest history have been known to sway before an enlightened public opinion and in the end to give way to a growing conscience, which regards them first as a moral affront and at length as an utter impossibility. Thus the generation just before us, our own fathers, uprooted the enormous upas of slavery, "the tree that was literally as old as the race of man," although slavery doubtless had its beginnings in the captives of man's earliest warfare, even as this existing evil thus originated.

Jane Addams, *A New Conscience and an Ancient Evil.* Introduction by Katherine Joslin. (Urbana and Chicago: University of Illinois Press, 2002). Originally published by New York: The MacMillan Company, 1912, pp. 3–8.

Those of us who think we discern the beginnings of a new conscience in regard to this twin of slavery, as old and outrageous as slavery itself and even more persistent, find a possible analogy between certain civic, philanthropic and educational efforts directed against the very existence of this social evil and similar organized efforts which preceded the overthrow of slavery in America. Thus, long before slavery was finally declared illegal, there were international regulations of its traffic, state and federal legislation concerning its extension, and many extra legal attempts to control its abuses; quite as we have the international regulations concerning the white slave traffic, the state and interstate legislation for its repression, and an extra legal power in connection with it so universally given to the municipal police that the possession of this power has become one of the great sources of corruption in every American city.

Before society was ready to proceed against the institution of slavery as such, groups of men and women by means of the underground railroad cherished and educated individual slaves; it is scarcely necessary to point out the similarity to the rescue homes and preventive associations which every great city contains.

It is always easy to overwork an analogy, and yet the economist who for years insisted that slave labor continually and arbitrarily limited the wages of free labor and was therefore a detriment to national wealth was a forerunner of the economist of to-day who points out the economic basis of the social evil, the connection between low wages and despair, between over-fatigue and the demand for reckless pleasure.

Before the American nation agreed to regard slavery as unjustifiable from the standpoint of public morality, an army of reformers, lecturers, and writers set forth its enormity in a never-ceasing flow of invective, of appeal, and of portrayal concerning the human cruelty to which the system lent itself. We can discern the scouts and outposts of a similar army advancing against this existing evil: the physicians and sanitarians who are committed to the task of ridding the race from contagious diseases, the teachers and lecturers who are appealing to the higher morality of thousands of young people; the growing literature, not only biological and didactic, but of a popular type more closely approaching "Uncle Tom's Cabin."

Throughout the agitation for the abolition of slavery in America, there were statesmen who gradually became convinced of the political and moral necessity of giving to the freedman the protection of the ballot. In this current agitation there are at least a few men and women who would extend a greater social and political freedom to all women if only because domestic control has proved so ineffectual.

Qualms

We may certainly take courage from the fact that our contemporaries are fired by social compassions and enthusiasms, to which even our immediate predecessors were indifferent. Such compunctions have ever manifested themselves in varying degrees of ardor through different groups in the same community. Thus among those who are newly aroused to action in regard to the social evil are many who would endeavor to regulate it and believe they can minimize its dangers, still larger numbers who would eliminate all trafficking of unwilling victims in connection with it, and yet others who believe that as a quasi-legal institution it may be absolutely abolished. Perhaps the analogy to the abolition of slavery is most striking in that these groups, in their varying points of view, are like those earlier associations which differed widely in regard to chattel slavery. Only the so-called extremists, in the first instance, stood for abolition and they were continually told that what they proposed was clearly impossible.

The legal and commercial obstacles, bulked large, were placed before them and it was confidently asserted that the blame for the historic existence of slavery lay deep within human nature itself. Yet gradually all of these associations reached the point of view of the abolitionist and before the war was over even the most lukewarm unionist saw no other solution of the nation's difficulty. Some such gradual conversion to the point of view of abolition is the experience of every society or group of people who seriously face the difficulties and complications of the social evil. Certainly all the national organizations—the National Vigilance Committee, the American Purity Federation, the Alliance for the Suppression and Prevention of the White Slave Traffic and many others—stand for the final abolition of commercialized vice. Local vice commissions, such as the able one recently appointed in Chicago, although composed of members of varying beliefs in regard to the possibility of control and regulation, united in the end in recommending a law enforcement looking towards final abolition. Even the most sceptical of Chicago citizens, after reading the fearless document, shared the hope of the commission that "the city, when aroused to the truth, would instantly rebel against the social evil in all its phases." . . . Few righteous causes have escaped baptism with blood; nevertheless, to paraphrase Lincoln's speech, if blood were exacted drop by drop in measure to the tears of anguished mothers and enslaved girls, the nation would still be obliged to go into the struggle.

Throughout this volume the phrase "social evil" is used to designate the sexual commerce permitted to exist in every large city, usually in a segregated district, wherein the chastity of women is bought and sold. . . . This volume does not deal with the probable future of prostitution. . . . It endeavors to present the contributory causes . . . and to state the indications, as I have seen them, of a new conscience with its many and varied manifestations. . . .

This ancient evil is indeed social in the sense of community responsibility and can only be understood and at length remedied when we face the fact and measure the resources which may at length be massed against it. Perhaps the most striking indication that our generation has become the bearer of a new moral consciousness in regard to the existence of commercialized vice is the fact that the mere contemplation of it throws the more sensitive men and women among our contemporaries into a state of indignant revolt. . . . [O]ne of the most obvious resources at our command . . . is the overwhelming pity and sense of protection which the recent revelations in the white slave traffic have aroused for the thousands of young girls, many of them still children, who are yearly sacrificed to the "sins of the people." All of this emotion ought to be made of value, for quite as a state of emotion is invariably the organic preparation for action, so it is certainly true that no profound spiritual transformation can take place without it.

After all, human progress is deeply indebted to a study of imperfections, and the counsels of despair, if not full of seasoned wisdom, are at least fertile in suggestion and a desperate spur to action. Sympathetic knowledge is the only way of approach to any human problem, and the line of least resistance into the jungle of human wretchedness must always be through that region which is mostly thoroughly explored, not only by the information of the statistician, but by sympathetic understanding. We are daily attaining the latter through such authors as Sudermann and Elsa Gerusalem, who have enabled their readers to comprehend the so-called "fallen" woman through a skilful portrayal of the reaction of experience upon personality. . . .

The treatment of this subject in American literature is at present in the pamphlet-eering stage, although an ever-increasing number of short stories and novels deal with it. On the other hand, the plays through which Bernard Shaw constantly places the truth before the public in England as Brieux is doing for the public in France, produce in the spectators a disquieting sense that society is involved in commer-cialized vice and must speedily find a way out. Such writing is like the roll of the drum which announces the approach of the troops ready for action.

Some of the writers who are performing this valiant service are related to those great artists who in every age enter into a long struggle with existing social condi-tions, until after many years they change the outlook upon life for at least a handful of their contemporaries. Their readers find themselves no longer mere bewildered spectators of a given social wrong, but have become conscious of their own hypocrisy in regard to it, and they realize that a veritable horror, simply because it was hidden, had come to seem to them inevitable and almost normal. . . .

Secure in the knowledge of evolutionary processes, we have learned to talk glibly of the obligations of race progress and of the possibility of racial degeneration. In this respect certainly we have a wider outlook than that possessed by our fathers, who so valiantly grappled with chattel slavery and secured its overthrow. May the new conscience gather force until men and women, acting under its sway, shall be constrained to eradicate this ancient evil!

6. Inez Haynes Irwin Recalls the Militance of Suffragists in the National Woman's Party, 1921

As a result of the first series of protest meetings, the Administration had yielded to the point of no longer interfering with the meetings at the Lafayette Monument. But as time went by and neither the Senate nor the President did anything about Suffrage, the National Woman's Party announced that a protest meeting would be held at the Lafayette Monument on September 16 at four o'clock. Immediately the President announced that he would receive a delegation of Southern and Western Democratic women that day at two.

The same day, September 16, as Maud Younger was coming back from the Capi-tol to Headquarters, Senator Overman of the Rules Committee came and sat by her in the car. In the course of his conversation, he remarked casually: "I don't think your bill is coming up this session."

That afternoon, Abby Scott Baker went to see Senator Jones of New Mexico, Chairman of the Suffrage Committee, to ask him to call a meeting of the Committee to bring Suffrage to the vote. Senator Jones refused. He said he would not bring up the Suffrage Amendment at this session in Congress.

When—still later—that delegation of Southern and Western Democratic women called on the President, he said to them:

> I am, as I think you know, heartily in sympathy with you. I have endeavored to assist you in every way in my power, and I shall continue to do so. I shall do all that I can to assist the passage of the Amendment by an early vote.

Inez Haynes Irwin, The Story of the Woman's Party. (New York: Harcourt Brace and Company, 1921. Reprint, New York: Kraus Reprint Company, 1971), 362–365.

This was the final touch.

The National Woman's Party hastily changed the type of its demonstration. Instead of holding a mere meeting of protest, they decided to burn the words which the President had said that very afternoon to the Southern and Western Democratic women. At four o'clock instead of two, forty women marched from Headquarters to the Lafayette Monument. They carried the famous banners:

HOW LONG MUST WOMEN WAIT FOR LIBERTY?

MR. PRESIDENT, WHAT WILL YOU DO FOR WOMAN SUFFRAGE?

At the Lafayette statue, Bertha Arnold delivered an appeal to Lafayette, written by Mrs. Richard Wainwright and beginning with the famous words of Pershing in France:

Lafayette, we are here!
We, the women of the United States, denied the liberty which you helped to gain, and for which we have asked in vain for sixty years, turn to you to plead for us.
Speak, Lafayette! Dead these hundred years but still living in the hearts of the American people. Speak again to plead for us, condemned like the bronze woman at your feet, to a silent appeal. She offers you a sword. Will you not use the sword of the spirit, mightier far than the sword she holds out to you?
Will you not ask the great leader of our democracy to look upon the failure of our beloved country to be in truth the place where every one is free and equal and entitled to a share in the government? Let that outstretched hand of yours pointing to the White House recall to him his words and promises, his trumpet call for all of us to see that the world is made safe for democracy.
As our army now in France spoke to you there, saying, "Here we are to help your country fight for liberty," will you not speak here and now for us, a little band with no army, no power but justice and right, no strength but in our Constitution and the Declaration of Independence, and win a great victory again in this country by giving us the opportunity we ask to be heard through the Susan B. Anthony Amendment?
Lafayette, we are here!

The police, having no orders to arrest the women, smiled and nodded. And while the crowd that had very quickly gathered applauded, Lucy Branham stepped forward. Beside her was Julia Emory, holding a flaming torch.

"We want action," Miss Branham stated simply, "not words." She took the torch from Julia Emory, held the words of the President's message of that afternoon in the flames. As it burned, she said:

The torch which I hold symbolizes the burning indignation of women who for a hundred years have been given words without action. In the spring our hopes were raised by words much like these from President Wilson, yet they were permitted to be followed by a filibuster against our Amendment on the part of the Democratic Senate leaders.
President Wilson still refuses any real support to the movement for the political freedom of women. . . .
We, therefore, take these empty words, spoken by President Wilson this afternoon, and consign them to the flames. . . .

Applause greeted these spirited words. As Jessie Hardy Mackaye started to speak, a man in the crowd handed her a twenty-dollar bill for the Woman's Party.

Others began passing money to her. The Suffragists were busy running through the crowd collecting it. The crowd continued to applaud and cheer.

Mrs. Mackaye said:

> Against the two-fold attitude on the part of the Senate toward democracy, I protest with all the power of my being. The same Congress and the same Administration that are appropriating billions of dollars and enlisting the services of millions of men to establish democracy in Europe, is at the same time refusing to do so common a piece of justice as to vote to submit the Woman Suffrage Amendment to the States.

This was the first time the President's words were burned.

The President's car drove up to the door during the progress of this demonstration, and President Wilson stepped in. But instead of going out at the usual gate, the driver turned the car about, so that he could make his exit elsewhere.

7. Elsie Hill and Florence Kelley Take Opposing Positions on a Proposed Woman's Equal Rights Bill, 1922

Elsie Hill Explains Why Women Should Have Full Legal Equality

The removal of all forms of the subjection of women is the purpose to which the National Woman's Party is dedicated. Its present campaign to remove the discriminations against women in the laws of the United States is but the beginning of its determined effort to secure the freedom of women, an integral part of the struggle for human liberty for which women are first of all responsible. Its interest lies in the final release of woman from the class of a dependent, subservient being to which early civilization committed her.

The laws of various States at present hold her in that class. They deny her a control of her children equal to the father's; they deny her, if married, the right to her own earnings; they punish her for offences for which men go unpunished; they exclude her from public office and from public institutions to the support of which her taxes contribute. These laws are not the creation of this age, but the fact that they are still tolerated on our statute books and that in some States their removal is vigorously resisted shows the hold of old traditions upon us. Since the passage of the Suffrage Amendment the incongruity of these laws, dating back many centuries, has become more than ever marked. . . .

The National Woman's Party believes that it is a vital social need to do away with these discriminations against women and is devoting its energies to that end. The removal of the discriminations and not the method by which they are removed is the thing upon which the Woman's Party insists. It has under consideration an amendment to the Federal Constitution which, if adopted, would remove them at one stroke, but it is at present endeavoring to secure their removal in the individual

---

Elsie Hill and Florence Kelley, "Should Women Be Equal Before the Law?" *The Nation,* April 12, 1922, 415–421.

States by a blanket bill, which is the most direct State method. For eighty-two years the piecemeal method has been tried, beginning with the married women's property act of 1839 in Mississippi, and no State, excepting Wisconsin, where the Woman's Party blanket bill was passed in June, 1921, has yet finished. . . .

The present program of the National Woman's Party is to introduce its Woman's Equal Rights Bill, or bills attaining the same purpose, in all State legislatures as they convene. It is building up in Washington a great headquarters from which this campaign can be conducted, and it is acting in the faith that the removal of these discriminations from our laws will benefit every group of women in the country, and through them all society.

Florence Kelley Explains Her Opposition to Full Legal Equality

"The removal of all forms of subjection of women is the purpose to which the National Woman's Party is dedicated."

A few years ago the Woman's Party counted disfranchisement the form of subjection which must first be removed. Today millions of American women, educated and uneducated, are kept from the polls in bold defiance of the Suffrage Amendment. Every form of subjection suffered by their white sisters they also suffer. Deprivation of the vote is theirs alone among native women. Because of this discrimination all other forms of subjection weigh a hundred fold more heavily upon them. In the family, in the effort to rent or to buy homes, as wage-earners, before the courts, in getting education for their children, in every relation of life, their burden is greater because they are victims of political inequality. How literally are colored readers to understand the words quoted above?

Sex is a biological fact. The political rights of citizens are not properly dependent upon sex, but social and domestic relations and industrial activities are. All modern-minded people desire that women should have full political equality and like opportunity in business and the professions. No enlightened person desires that they should be excluded from jury duty or denied the equal guardianship of children, or that unjust inheritance laws or discriminations against wives should be perpetuated.

The inescapable facts are, however, that men do not bear children, are freed from the burdens of maternity, and are not susceptible, in the same measures as women, to poisons now increasingly characteristic of certain industries, and to the universal poison of fatigue. These are differences so far reaching, so fundamental, that it is grotesque to ignore them. Women cannot be made men by act of the legislature or by amendment of the Federal Constitution. This is no matter of today or tomorrow. The inherent differences are permanent. Women will always need many laws different from those needed by men.

The effort to enact the blanket bill in defiance of all biological differences recklessly imperils the special laws for women as such, for wives, for mothers, and for wage-earners. . . .

Why should wage-earning women be thus forbidden to get laws for their own health and welfare and that of their unborn children? Why should they be made subject to the preferences of wage-earning men? Is not this of great and growing importance when the number of women wage-earners, already counted by millions, increases by leaps and bounds from one census to the next? And when the industries involving exposure to poisons are increasing faster than ever? And when the over-work of mothers is one recognized cause of the high infant death rate? And when the rise in the mortality of mothers in childbirth continues?

If there were no other way of promoting more perfect equality for women, an argument could perhaps be sustained for taking these risks. But why take them when every desirable measure attainable through the blanket bill can be enacted in the ordinary way? . . .

Is the National Woman's Party for or against protective measures for wage-earning women? Will it publicly state whether it is for or against the eight-hour day and minimum-wage commissions for women? Yes or No?

8. Margaret Sanger Publishes Letters Documenting American Wives' and Husbands' Urgent Need for Legal Birth Control, 1928

Number One

I had thought from my reading in magazines, etc., that after marriage the direct in-formation necessary to prevent too large a family would become mine "on demand." But to my amazement others older and supposedly wiser seem as ignorant as I. I was nearly twenty-five when we married and had I realized this condition I should have remained single a while longer. I was never very strong, and now as the mother of three children I feel my little strength slowly going and know that the demands of motherhood is the cause.

Already our doctor has warned me to take care of my health. Heart weak, liable to lung trouble. Since we lost our second child I would not object to one other but I would like better to be able to choose when.

After marriage I lived in the country on a farm and since I was from town *many neighbors thought I knew and appealed* to me. It was almost with tears I had to refuse to aid the poor creatures who seemed to think I knew because I was from town. Oh, you indeed know their despair! I too have seen it. A woman, the mother of nine children, appealed to me, but I was powerless to aid her. . . .

Number Two

I have a problem which to me and to those with whom I am concerned is very serious and in the full meaning of the word, vital. I shall try to be candid and brief in stating it knowing that with your great work you cannot afford to spend much time on any individual. I am thirty-three years of age. Have been married for ten years. We have an adopted child.

My wife has always been delicate and was some years ago severely injured in an accident and a doctor told me she could never bear children. Knowing that it

Margaret Sanger, *Motherhood in Bondage,* Foreword by Margaret Marsh (Columbus: Ohio State University Press, 2000), 298–299, 341–343, 347. Reprinted by permission of Ohio State University Press.

probably meant her death if conception took place I have refrained from sexual intercourse, for my wife's welfare is more to me than anything else.

Now I am not under- or over-sexed but am a healthy strong normal man. Yet the strain is very very hard not to live and have intercourse naturally. The intense desire always balked has ill mental and physical effects and I fear may lead to estrangement. But I need not dwell on this as you will understand it. I love my wife dearly and if she could only obey nature without the shadow of death as a penalty it would enable us to live normally and happily and do our work with mental faculties clear.

Number Three

I am thirty-four years old and am the mother of six children now and expect to become a mother again shortly. I dread the months to come very much as we haven't the means to hire help. I expect to do all my housework, take care of the children, do all the cooking and milk six cows, as I have done before, up to the day my baby is born. Being a mother, you know this is too much to expect of any woman. We live on a farm, but my husband is working at public work at the present time and don't have much time to work at home. I would not mind my work so much but about five years ago I had a very bad case of typhoid fever. I was bedfast for eight weeks. Had to have two trained nurses all the time. I was unconscious and had many hemorrhages the first few weeks of my sickness.

The worst thing of all is this: I love my husband as much as any woman could and it nearly breaks my heart when he is not affectionate to me or the children or when he says anything harsh. We get along good only for one thing. He says our family is already larger than it should be to take care of them right. I think too, that seven will be as many as I can care for properly.

He would rather stay away from me and not have intercourse at all rather than make the family larger. This don't please me for I know every time he doesn't come to me for a week or two he gets so contrary with me and children that there is no pleasure living in the house with him. I have never refused him his privilege once. He is very moderate in his passions. He has always been true to me and I to him and owing to my afflictions and desire to live happy with my husband.

I think Birth Control would be all right in our case. I love babies but I think we have had our share after we get the one we expect in a few months.

I am a Catholic and would not think of destroying a child after conception. Can you tell me of any sure way by which my husband and I can enjoy the privilege of married life without conception. It seems some people know how, but we don't. I know my life will be a torture if I cannot find a way of satisfying him without conceiving more children. He says this is our last and I know he means it and that he will keep away from me rather than conceive more. . . .

Number Four

In the first place, my husband and I started all wrong. We got married before we had enough money to keep house. We went to live with his folks where we still are and thought we could soon save enough to go by ourselves. Thirteen months after we were married our first baby was born, and in fifteen and a half months after our second baby came.

We love our baby girls dearly, but are so afraid of having more that we have had no intercourse since before the birth of the second child, three and one-half years ago tomorrow.

Although my husband says he is still faithful to me (and I have seen no indication that he isn't) naturally we are not very happy; we have a good many quarrels and he has told me a good many times that he could divorce me because of my refusing him. It is not that the sexual union is revolting to me, for it is not and has not been in a single instance, but I dread the expense of rearing more children and I am not very strong and everything worries me so. I cannot sleep nights through worrying about losing my husband and it makes me so cross and irritable and naturally I feel tired all the time. Can't you possibly help me?

☒ E S S A Y S

Kathryn Kish Sklar of Binghamton University compares the male-dominated American Association of Labor Legislation (AALL) and the (all-female) National Consumers' League (NCL). The NCL emphasized gender difference in seeking reforms beneficial to women and children and accomplished more than the AALL. Sklar is convinced that women were at the very center of the politics and policies that most characterize Progressive reform. Yale history professor Glenda Elizabeth Gilmore argues that by claiming a distinctly female moral authority and an identity as clients of the emerging welfare state, organized black women in North Carolina challenged the racism of the dominant culture. Specifically, they resisted the political disempowerment of blacks that Southern whites hoped to achieve by depriving black men of access to the ballot and political office, and they foiled plans by racist Southerners to reserve the benefits of progressivism solely for whites. Black women's subversion was masked by outward cooperation with whites, especially white women. Unable to claim full civil rights, they nonetheless gained limited social services for the black community.

Differences in the Political Cultures of Men and Women Reformers During the Progressive Era

KATHRYN KISH SKLAR

The single most important center of reform activity during the Progressive Era could be found at the Charities Building at Twenty-second Street and Fourth Avenue in New York City. Behind a four-story stately exterior, the structure's spacious offices and corridors housed the national headquarters of many leading reform organizations, including the National Child Labor Committee, the National Consumers' League (NCL), and the staffs of *Survey* and *Outlook,* prominent reform periodicals. There men and women reformers constantly interacted, occasionally worked together

---

as members of the same organization, but more often formed ad hoc coalitions across the boundaries of their gender-specific associations. "What's this bunch call itself today?" the editor of *Outlook* asked in March 1906, pausing by a meeting room filled with many familiar faces. The presence of Florence Kelley, head of the National Consumers' League and one of the era's most active coalition builders, may have prompted his affectionate gibe. Less well known in this New York setting was John R. Commons, who had come from the University of Wisconsin to introduce the newly founded American Association for Labor Legislation (AALL). The March 1906 meeting drew together men and women interested in joining the AALL's efforts.

If we had a snapshot of this gathering we might think that it depicted the growing equality of women and men reformers as they met on common ground to work toward shared goals. Yet if we take a longer view and compare the two chief organizations represented that day—the NCL and the AALL—we find a different story, one that locates more importance in their gender-specific differences than in their cross-gender similarities.

This essay explores those differences and what we can discover from them about the political consequences of the social construction of gender during a major watershed in American history between 1900 and 1920. . . . Fundamental social, political, and economic changes in American life between 1890 and 1930 laid the foundation for the modern nation that we know today, but these changes were anything but smooth. By 1890 massive immigration, rapid industrialization, and urbanization had generated the potential for widespread social disorder. Social relationships and values constructed in preindustrial America no longer met the needs of an increasingly diverse and stratified society. Pastoral landscape gave way to sprawling cities and towering smokestacks. Day laborers and an urban proletariat outnumbered the skilled artisans who previously had dominated working-class life. Great wealth accumulated in the hands of a few, their spacious mansions contrasting grotesquely with the crowded tenements of immigrant neighborhoods.

Native-born middle-class Americans benefited in many ways from the new entrepreneurial opportunities available within the expanding national economy. For example, they moved into the new white-collar jobs created by the managerial revolution that accompanied vertical economic integration, and they had access to a cornucopia of new consumer goods. But the same forces that enhanced middle-class life also threatened to topple middle-class dominance within American political and social institutions. Politically, they were displaced by urban bosses who drew much of their support from recent immigrants. Socially, their authority diminished when, due to the Catholic and Jewish identities of most "new" immigrants from Southern and Eastern Europe, Protestant churches and clergymen became less important arbiters of social and class relations. Clearly, a new America was emerging, but its connections with earlier patterns of life were unclear. Did the grinding poverty of vast numbers of working people imperil the comforts of middle-class life? What did the social classes owe one another? Was democracy compatible with capitalism? These questions grew in urgency during the 1890s, when struggles between capital and labor repeatedly erupted into bloody armed conflict, and a severe depression crippled the economy.

Out of this crucible a multitude of middle-class organizations emerged to address the nation's problems. Women's organizations were prominent among them.

"Progressive reform" (as this movement came to be called) developed three basic thrusts—economic, political, and social. Economic reform, expressed in the Sherman Antitrust Act of 1890, sought to protect the competitiveness of small economic units and curb the growing might of large ones. Political reform, seeking changes in governmental structures and the electoral process, tried to increase governmental responsibility and responsiveness by instituting innovations like the referendum, the recall of public officials, and the popular election of U.S. senators. Political reform also sought to rationalize governmental decision making by creating new administrative units, especially city managers, whose decisions were based more on scientifically based expertise and less on purely political considerations. Last, but not least, social reform expressed concern for the nation's social fabric by focusing on the quality of life among working people.

The efforts of middle-class women were concentrated in political and social reform, but their chief impact lay with the latter. Were working-class children attending schools? Or did their families' economic circumstances require them to work? Were wage-earning women and children exploited through long hours and low wages? Did working-class families have adequate food, housing, and health care? Middle-class women, better educated than ever before, posed and answered these questions through expertise acquired in women's organizations. . . .

My own work . . . emphasizes a "strong state–weak state" paradigm to explain the broad strokes of women's activism and sees class relations as a prominent theme. In this view, women's activism was greater when the state's activism was weaker, and crucial dimensions of women's success were achieved because gendered policies acted as a surrogate for class policies. . . .

To highlight the effects of class and the impact of American traditions of limited government on women's activism, this essay compares two organizations with very similar goals in neighboring niches in the pantheon of Progressive reform, the National Consumers' League and the American Association for Labor Legislation. . . . Both organizations were part of the remarkable surge of social reform in the Progressive Era that sought the passage and enforcement of laws promoting "the conservation of the human resources of the nation." Founded within a decade of one another, the NCL in 1898, the AALL in 1906, each was responding to the problematic qualities of industrial work in the context of the growing power of the American nation-state. Although both forged cross-class coalitions that embraced organized labor, the heart and soul of each was middle-class. Both claimed to speak for the welfare of the whole society, and to rise above "interest group" or "partisan" politics. Both maintained national offices with a paid staff, drew on professional expertise, lobbied for legislation, and forged coalitions with other reform organizations. While they chiefly worked at the state level, each also became involved in federal legislative campaigns. Their shared goal of creating nationwide minimum standards of labor legislation placed them among the progenitors of the American welfare state. These similarities meant that the two organizations frequently interacted and benefited from one another's activities.

More remarkably, perhaps, the two groups functioned relatively independently. By exploring their differences we learn about the gendered construction of American politics and public policies. This essay explores three dimensions of the differences between the National Consumers' League and the American Association for Labor

Legislation: the origins of the two groups, their organizational structures, and their legislative agendas. These differences show that an analysis of women's experience sheds new light on fundamental themes in American history, especially the process by which knowledge and power translated into expanded state responsibility.

The National Consumers' League came into being in 1898, when local consumer leagues in New York, Massachusetts, Pennsylvania, Illinois, Minnesota, New Jersey, and Wisconsin decided to form a national office to coordinate their efforts. The movement began in New York City in 1888 in response to protests by wage-earning women against sweatshop working conditions. Leonora O'Reilly, [who was] a shirt-maker, . . . and others "made an eloquent appeal for help and sympathy from the wealthy and educated women of New-York for their toiling and down-trodden sisters." . . . Two years later, when wage-earning and middle-class women met again to discuss women's working conditions, an organization emerged. Imitating a group formed in London a few months earlier wherein consumers compiled a register similar to the list of "fair houses" published by trade unions, they hoped to enlist "the sympathy and interest of the shopping public" in a "White List" of retail stores that "treated their employees fairly." . . .

With Florence Kelley's appointment as general secretary of the national league in 1899, the NCL assumed leadership of a burgeoning Consumers' League movement. Her early annual reports urged new forms of knowledge and power on league members as a by-product of persisting gender distinctions. "The one great industrial function of women has been that of the purchaser," Kelley wrote in 1899. "All the foods used in private families," as well as furniture, books, and clothing, are "prepared with the direct object in view of being sold to women." To be effective consumers, women had to be organized. "What housewife can detect, alone and unaided, injurious chemicals in her supplies of milk, bread, meat, home remedies?" Goods that women used to make themselves were now produced in unregulated shops and factories. . . . By uniting in the Consumers' League, Kelley promised, women could safeguard their families and at the same time could drive out of the marketplace articles produced under conditions "injurious to human life and health."

The NCL thus held out a dual hope of aiding both consumers and producers. This vital link between consumer and producer generated substantial social power for the NCL. It lent personal meaning to the commitment that members made to the organization and connected that meaning to the lives of working people. The NCL not only supplied its members with knowledge of the relationship between consumer and producer, it also sought to transform that knowledge into a moral force. Far from being passive purchasers, consumers actually constructed production, Kelley insisted. Daily choices "as to the bestowal of our means" determined how others "spend their time in making what we buy." Kelley and the NCL sought to politicize those choices by moralizing them: "It is *the* aim of the National Consumers' League to moralize this decision, to gather and make available information which may enable all to decide in the light of knowledge, and to appeal to the conscience, so that the decision when made shall be a righteous one." This old-fashioned word, "righteous," captured the league's stance as a moral arbiter anchored in an earlier era. . . .

[I]n the first five years of the league's existence, Florence Kelley devoted herself to building a grassroots movement of righteously knowledgeable consumers.

Between 1900 and 1907 she spent roughly a day on the road for every desk-bound day. Her efforts were rewarded by the spectacular expansion of NCL locals, both in number and location. The NCL's 1901 report mentioned thirty leagues in eleven states; by 1906 they numbered sixty-three in twenty states. . . . Local leagues sustained the national's existence, channeling money, ideas, and the support of other local organizations into the national office. At the same time locals served as vehicles for the implementation of the national's agenda at the state level. Most league members were white, urban, middle-class Protestants, but Jewish women held important positions of leadership. Catholic women became more visible after Cardinal James Gibbons of Baltimore consented to serve as a vice president of a Maryland league, and Bishop J. Regis Canevin of Pittsburgh encouraged members of that city's Ladies Catholic Benevolent Association to join. In 1903 the Massachusetts league undertook a systematic effort "to enlist the wives of farmers through the Farmers' Institutes, Granges, etc."

But "righteous" choices by a multitude of consumers were not in themselves strong enough to counter the economic and cultural forces against which they were arrayed. Women's knowledge could be translated into power only if women forced government to act. . . . The "Consumers' White Label," devised by Florence Kelley and adopted by the NCL as the chief activity during its first decade, became the tactic that wove together women's knowledge, women's power, and expanded state responsibility. It replaced the White List of stores with a strategy that sought to regulate the conditions under which goods were produced, not only the conditions under which they were sold. Both White List and White Label carefully avoided the appearance of blacklisting or secondary boycotts, which, as a tool tried by organized labor, the courts had declared illegal.

The NCL's White Label campaign focused on the manufacture of white muslin underwear. Seeking to affect the conditions under which these goods were produced throughout the country, the league awarded its White Label to manufacturers who shunned child labor and overtime work and abided by state factory regulations. By limiting its attention to "one narrow field of industry," the NCL shined an investigative spotlight on the production of garments that every middle-class consumer needed. . . .

The goods were intimate, but the goal was political. Throughout the Northeast, Midwest, and Pacific West, the White Label ineluctably carried middle-class women into the nitty-gritty of local factory conditions and law enforcement. Did the manufacturer subcontract to home workers in tenements? Were children employed? Was overtime required? Were working conditions safe and sanitary? Were state factory laws violated? How far below the standard set by the consumers' label were their own state laws? Even more technical questions arose when women's organizations came into contact with factory inspectors, bureaus of labor statistics, state legislatures, and courts. Should the state issue licenses for home workers? What was the relationship between illiteracy in child workers and the enforcement of effective child labor laws? . . . Questions recently quite alien to middle-class women held the interest of thousands of the most politically active among them. This was no small accomplishment. State leagues differed in the degree to which they worked with state officials, but wherever they existed they created new civic space in which women used their new knowledge and power to expand state responsibility.

To some degree the NCL's mobilization of middle-class women against the power of unregulated capitalism derived from Florence Kelley herself, . . . a warrior with formidable rhetorical and organizational skills. Yet Kelley's rage for social justice bore fruit because her vision of expanded state responsibility for the welfare of women and children took root within the ranks of "organized womanhood." Her chief means of carrying the NCL's vision to a larger constituency lay through the General Federation of Women's Clubs (GFWC). By 1900 the GFWC had grown to thirty-six state federations of 2,675 clubs with a membership of more than 115,000. At the GFWC biennial meeting that year in Milwaukee, Kelley and others introduced the federation to the work of the Consumers' League at a special evening program, and federation officers "asked the delegates to report favorably to their respective clubs and federations upon the work of the League." The results, Kelley said in 1901, "are still perceptible at our office in the form of invitations for speakers, requests for literature, and a vast increase in correspondence and in the demand for labeled goods in many diverse parts of the country."

Between 1900 and 1902 Kelley chaired the federation's standing committee on "The Industrial Problem as It Affects Women and Children." This committee and its state counterparts were expected "to influence and secure enforcement of labor ordinances and state laws." State federations were asked to "agitate for enforcement of laws, and for amendments to laws, if they were not up to the standard of the Massachusetts labor laws." . . . To individual clubs Kelley sent 2,000 copies of a circular offering a brief but cogent class-based explanation of "the industrial problem as it affects women and children." . . . Arguing that middle-class and working-class women were related to and affected by the same industrial process, one positively, one adversely, this analysis pricked the consciences of middle-class women about the material basis of their leisure and linked their destinies with working women and children. . . .

Where statewide Consumers' Leagues existed, they worked closely with state federations of women's clubs. . . . By 1903 both the National Congress of Mothers and the National American Woman Suffrage Association had created child labor committees, and Florence Kelley headed both. . . . Standing between capital and labor, a grassroots phalanx of consumers became thoroughly implicated in the conditions under which goods were produced.

Having built her constituency, Kelley in 1906 shifted away from the White Label into a campaign for the legal limitation of women's hours. . . . Throughout the industrializing world, reformers and trade unionists alike viewed shorter working hours as the key to the improvement of working-class standards of living; for trade unionists, shorter hours were second in importance only to the right to unionize. . . . Yet only a small, well-organized portion of the labor force, mostly skilled men, could achieve the benefits of shorter hours. Others, including most female and child workers and the vast majority of unskilled male workers, . . . endured twelve-hour, fourteen-hour, or even longer working days that imperiled their health and undercut their ability to rise above their impoverished circumstances. . . .

Despite the need that reformers saw for legislative regulation of hours or wages, such statutes were very difficult to achieve in the United States, primarily because American political institutions circumscribed the power of legislatures by investing courts with the power to rule legislative enactments unconstitutional. . . . [T]he harsh conditions of laissez-faire capitalism were preserved by political traditions that defended the freedom of employers to devise the terms on which they employed workers. Between 1900 and 1920 the National Consumers' League circumvented those traditions by invoking gender-specific justifications for legislation designed to benefit working women. The league and its supporters argued that gender-specific legislation was constitutional because it utilized the state's police powers to pre-serve health and morals. First, they asserted, since women workers tended to be young and unskilled and therefore did not have trade unions to represent them in negotiating better working conditions directly with their employers, they were unable to protect themselves, so it fell to the state to safeguard their health and morals through legislation. Second, they contended that because most women workers later became mothers, their injuries through overwork or low wages could produce birth defects or lead to prostitution, each of which affected the welfare of the whole com-munity and should be prevented through legislation. These arguments embodied nineteenth-century notions of gender differences, which women reformers like Kelley shared when it was pragmatically effective for them to do so, but just as easily evaded when it helped their cause. Most important, these assertions earned them the support of constituencies beyond the reach of their own organizations, including judges and working men.

Responding to such arguments, nineteen states passed some form of hours laws for women by 1906. That year the NCL successfully defended an Oregon ten-hour law for women before the state supreme court. After the U.S. Supreme Court upheld the Oregon statute in 1908, the NCL led a campaign that established hours laws for women in twenty-one more states by 1919. . . .

The American Association for Labor Legislation offers a compelling contrast to the NCL's rallying of middle-class women. AALL leaders treated knowledge as professional, not personal. They exercised power through the prestige of their posi-tion and expertise, not through numbers. And, rather than seeing government as a democratic extension of the popular will, the AALL viewed the state as a vehicle of enlightened administration. This set the association on a different political path from the NCL and made it a frustrating ally.

The AALL grew . . . under the leadership of John Commons, Richard Ely, and other economists. . . . From the start, the AALL was an elite group, "composed of experts and officials as well as public spirited citizens." Article III of the constitution limited membership to those who were "elected by the Executive Committee."

In contrast to the NCL's mass mobilization for direct consumer action, the AALL's mandate was grander but more vague: "the conservation of the human re-sources of the nation." But for what purpose? An early AALL statement answered this question by declaring its commitment to both labor and capital, to the "conser-vation of human resources in the mutual interest of employer and employee by non-partisan legislation." Ever "objective," the AALL viewed partisanship as its antithesis. Yet without a political constituency and the partisanship that came with it, the AALL had much greater difficulty than the NCL in forging an effective political agenda.

Whereas the NCL treated local branches as its main arteries of power, the AALL tolerated local branches only briefly. . . . By 1916, . . . they had all lapsed. . . .

The AALL, Commons concluded, "occupies the unique position of an organization to promote legislation by means of scientific investigation." Societies "equipped for the work of propaganda and political agitation . . . must necessarily look to us for the scientific basis that will make their agitation effective and keep it on solid ground." This "work of information" did not require local branches. . . .

Yet at the same time that the AALL cleared its decks for "the work of information," Andrews and Commons recognized the need to engage in more substantive activities and pursue its secondary mandate of recommending particular forms of legislation. . . . [T]he AALL placed compensation for workplace injuries at the top of its agenda. . . . In 1911 ten states passed some form of compensation, and by 1915 the number had grown to thirty-three. Yet the AALL experience with workmen's compensation differed in one crucial respect from the NCL's contemporaneous campaign to reduce hours and raise wages for working women. Although it claimed a leadership position by virtue of its "scientific" superiority, in fact the AALL often took second place to a group that sought to represent the joint interests of workers and employers, the National Civic Federation (NCF). Founded in 1900 to pursue arbitration and mediation between capital and labor, the NCF began working on workmen's compensation in 1908. By 1910 its Department on Compensation attracted the participation of 600 representative employers, attorneys, labor leaders, insurance experts, economists, state officials, and members of state compensation commissions. The NCF's model laws on workmen's compensation, although they often favored employers, became the chief focal point for discussion among state legislatures, employers, and representatives of organized labor because they were seen as efforts to combine the interests of labor and employers. For example, the NCF's model compensation law of 1914 was sent to all the affiliated bodies of the AFL and to 25,000 employers. The AALL lacked this reach into grassroots constituencies and failed to dominate the issue on the basis of scientific expertise alone. . . .

The AALL's ability to shape public policy was severely limited by its failure to form an effective relationship with organized labor—the most obvious group capable of serving as its grassroots equivalent to the NCL's women's organizations. Whereas trade union organizing was an important secondary or indirect goal of the NCL—for example, Kelley thought that shorter hours and higher wages would increase the number of women who joined trade unions, and she worked closely with the WTUL [Women's Trade Union League]—this was never the case with the AALL. "The active support of organized labor would probably tend to strengthen the work of your association," Morris Hillquit wrote Andrews in 1911, but Andrews explained to an AALL member in 1913, "while I am a firm believer in the necessity for trade unions, yet my conclusion is that the greatest permanent social gains have come and will continue to come from remedial legislation, slow and conservative as this movement sometimes appears and is." He expressed special concern for "the cause of the unskilled worker," which seemed "particularly hopeless" through organization. . . .

Knowledge, power, and expanding state responsibility meant different things to the NCL and the AALL and flowed in different channels. One practical effect of those differences can be seen in the relationship of each organization to the nation's first minimum wage campaign, 1909–17. . . .

Viewed by one advocate as "the keystone of the arch in labor legislation," minimum wage laws were integrally related to other reform efforts aimed at the working poor, especially to hours legislation, and antisweatshop measures. More explicitly intended as a means of redistributing wealth than any previous labor laws, minimum wage legislation expressed a new form of social justice that aimed to establish a floor beneath which wages could not fall. Reformers hoped that such a floor would end the downward spiral of wages wherein sweatshop employers paid low wages to workers, who then required support from relief or charity, thereby indirectly providing employers with subsidies that enabled them to lower wages further. . . .

As early as 1899 Kelley hoped "to include a requirement as to minimal wages" in the NCL's White Label, . . . but the path to an American equivalent did not seem clear until she and other Consumers' League leaders in 1908 attended the First International Conference of Consumers' Leagues, in Geneva, where they learned about the proposed British wage boards. Almost immediately on her return Kelley established her leadership in what became an enormously successful campaign. First she raided the languishing AALL branches for male supporters. . . . In 1911 Kelley organized a "special Committee on Minimum Wage Boards" in the NCL. . . .

Also in 1911 the Massachusetts Consumers' League, the Women's Trade Union League, the United Textile Workers, and the Massachusetts Association for Labor Legislation all lobbied for the creation of a state commission to investigate minimum wage legislation. But the power to shape the proposal fell to the NCL when Mary Dewson, a Consumers' League activist, was appointed the commission's secretary, and Elizabeth Glendower, one of the commission's five members and a close friend of Kelley, . . . funded much of the commission's work. The high point of the campaign occurred in 1913, when eight additional states passed minimum wage laws for women: California, Colorado, Minnesota, Nebraska, Oregon, Utah, Washington, and Wisconsin.

Relying on grassroots support from women's organizations, the NCL's leadership in this campaign was augmented by organized labor and conscientious employers who sought to eliminate unscrupulous competition. Although the NCL could not count on universal backing from women or men trade unionists, cooperation with the Women's Trade Union League and with many state federations of labor produced a much smoother alliance than the relationship the AALL had forged with the national American Federation of Labor. The political stance of organized labor varied from state to state, but whereas the AFL officially opposed wage legislation (arguing that the minimum could become the maximum), the NCL promoted minimum wage as an agent of both class and gender realignment. . . .

In some respects the wage campaign reinforced the gendered status quo. . . . Reformers had to squeeze their arguments through the only constitutional loophole through which the courts might sustain wage laws—that low wages affected the health and morals of (young) women and therefore were properly subject to intervention under the police powers of the state. . . .

During this arduous campaign Kelley received almost no help from the AALL. . . . [T]he AALL . . . opposed minimum wage legislation as premature. . . .

Until the passage of the Fair Labor Standards Act (FLSA) of 1938, all state minimum wage laws and many state laws regulating working hours in the United States applied only to women. Not until 1942, when the U.S. Supreme Court approved the constitutionality of the FLSA, did the eight-hour day and the minimum wage become part of the social contract for most American workers. The class-bridging activism of middle-class women forged the way with these fundamental reforms. . . .

[T]he activism of NCL members can best be seen as the culmination of nineteenth-century trends, many of which have not survived into the late twentieth century. Moral notions about public responsibility for the welfare of women and children rank high among these. Because they accentuated gender differences, today these notions seem outdated and ineffective. Yet as this comparison between the NCL and the AALL shows, through grassroots mobilization women's organizations succeeded in accomplishing reforms that male expertise and power could not initiate. Women did not reside at the margins of progressive social reform; they occupied its center.

The agency of women and the agency of men were shaped by the gendered definitions of their opportunities for political activism in the Progressive Era. Ultimately, this comparison suggests that no corner of American political life was unconnected to the system of gendered meanings that informed the ongoing process by which civic activity was molded. The more we understand about American women, the more we understand about American history.

Diplomats to the White Community: African American Women in Progressive-Era North Carolina

GLENDA ELIZABETH GILMORE

After disfranchisement, "the Negro," white supremacists were fond of saying, was removed from politics. But even as African American men lost their rights, the political underwent a transformation. As state and local governments began to provide social services, an embryonic welfare state emerged. Henceforth, securing teetertotters and playgrounds, fighting pellagra, or replacing a dusty neighborhood track with an oil-coated road would require political influence. Thus, at the same time that whites restricted the number of voters by excluding African Americans, the state created a new public role: that of the client who drew on its services. Contemporaries and historians named this paradoxical period the Progressive Era.

From the debris of disfranchisement, black women discovered fresh approaches to serving their communities and crafted new tactics designed to dull the blade of white supremacy. The result was a greater role for black women in the interracial public sphere. As long as they could vote, it was black men who had most often brokered official state power and made interracial political contacts. After disfranchisement, however, the political culture black women had created through thirty years of work in temperance organizations, Republican Party aid societies, and churches furnished both an ideological basis and an organizational structure from which black women could take on those tasks. After black men's banishment from politics, North Carolina's black women added a network of women's groups that crossed denominational—and later party—lines and took a multi-issue approach to civic action. In a nonpolitical guise, black women became the black community's diplomats to the white community.

In the first twenty years of the century, the state, counties, and municipalities began to intervene in affairs that had been private in the past. Now, government representatives killed rabid dogs and decided where traffic should stop. They forced bakers to put screens on their windows and made druggists stop selling morphine. They told parents when their children could work and when their children must go to school. As they regulated, they also dispensed. Public health departments were formed, welfare agencies turned charity into a science, and juvenile court systems began to separate youthful offenders of both sexes from seasoned criminals. Public education expanded exponentially and became increasingly uniform across the state. The intersection of government and individual expanded from the polling place to the street corner, from the party committee meeting to the sickbed.

Black women might not be voters, but they could be clients, and in that role they could become spokespeople for and motivators of black citizens. They could claim a distinctly female moral authority and pretend to eschew any political motivation. The deep camouflage of their leadership style—their womanhood—helped them remain invisible as they worked toward political ends. At the same time, they could deliver not votes but hands and hearts through community organization: willing workers in city cleanup campaigns, orderly children who complied with state educational requirements, and hookworm-infested people eager for treatment at public health fairs. . . .

In comparing black women's progressivism to white women's progressivism, one must be cautious at every turn because black and white women had vastly different relationships to power. To cite just one example, white middle-class women lobbied to obtain services *from* their husbands, brothers, and sons; black women lobbied to obtain services *for* their husbands, brothers, and sons.

Black women's task was to try to force those white women who plunged into welfare efforts to recognize class and gender similarities across racial lines. To that end, they surveyed progressive white women's welfare initiatives and political style and found that both afforded black women a chance to enter the political. They had two purposes in mind. First, they would try to hold a place for African Americans in the ever-lengthening queue forming to garner state services. Second, they would begin to clear a path for the return of African Americans to the ballot box. . . .

Given the expansion of the public sphere and whites' attempts to exclude African Americans from new state and municipal programs, black women's religious work took on new meaning. In the wake of disfranchisement, African American men and women turned to their churches for solace and for political advice. Yet many black men now feared the potentially explosive mixture of politics and religion in turbulent times. Ministers of all denominations began to circumscribe their own discourse and to monitor their flocks' debate. A Baptist minister declared that such "perilous times" made even "preaching of the pure gospel embarrassing, if not dangerous."

Using women's church organizations to press for community improvement incurred less risk than preaching inflammatory sermons on civil rights. . . . While white political leaders kept their eyes on black men's electoral political presence and absence, black women organized and plotted an attack just outside of their field of vision. They began by transforming church missionary societies into social service agencies. . . .

The tasks of black women's home missionary societies read like a Progressive Era primer. They organized mothers' clubs and community cleanup days. They built playgrounds and worked for public health and temperance. Marshaling arguments from the social purity and social hygiene movements, they spoke on sexual dangers outside of marriage. To achieve their goals, southern black women entered political space, appearing before local officials and interacting with white bureaucrats.

Even as they undertook this "peculiar work," black women knew that they must avoid charges of political interference. . . . Taking a lesson from the high price of black men's former public presence, capitalizing on the divisions among whites over the allocation of new services to African Americans, and concerned about gender politics among African Americans, black women reformers depended on not being seen at all by whites who would thwart their programs and not being seen as political by whites who would aid them. They used their invisibility to construct a web of social service and civic institutions that remained hidden from and therefore unthreatening to whites.

Women's organizations within religious bodies were not new, but they became more important, expanded, and reordered their priorities after disfranchisement. For example, the Women's Baptist Home Mission Convention of North Carolina began in 1884, primarily as an arm for evangelical work. At the turn of the century, the group employed [Sallie] Mial as a full-time missionary in the state. In this capacity, she organized local women's groups and founded Sunshine Bands and What-I-Can Circles for girls. Mial explained her work to the African American Baptist men this way: "We teach the women to love their husbands, to be better wives and mothers, to make the homes better." At the same time, church workers taught Baptist women lobbying and administrative skills. One woman remembered, "From this organization we learn[ed] what is meant to be united." Another observed, "Many of our women are being strengthened for the Master's use." Along the way, the organization began calling itself the Baptist State Educational Missionary Convention.

Making "the homes better" covered a wide range of community activities. Good homes rhetoric was, of course, promulgated by whites to justify white supremacy; southern educational reformers used depictions of debasement, for example, to justify industrial education. Black women could use this discourse for their own purposes, and they grasped the opportunity it gave them to bargain for the state services that were beginning to improve whites' lives but were denied to African Americans. As Margaret Murray Washington put it, "Where the homes of colored people are comfortable and clean, there is less disease, less sickness, less death, and less danger to others [that is, whites]." Good homes, however, required good government. "We are not likely to [build good homes] if we know that the pavements will be built just within a door of ours and suddenly stop," Washington warned. Turning from the ballot box to the home as the hope of the future was canny political strategy that meshed nicely with the new welfare role of the state, and it explicitly increased women's importance at a time when women across the nation campaigned to extend their influence through volunteer activities and the professionalization of social work.

The elevation of the home to the centerpiece of African American life sprang from several sources. Certainly it resonated with a nationwide Progressive Era movement for better homes, particularly among immigrant enclaves in crowded northern cities. But among North Carolina's African Americans, the movement's roots reached closer to home. Religious convictions that had inspired nineteenth-century black women who did church work continued to serve as moral imperatives to bring families to godly lives. African American women tried to eliminate grist for the white supremacy mill by abolishing the images of the immoral black woman and the barbaric black home. Moreover, now that voting required literacy, education was political, and it began at home. Able to tap into the larger context of rhetoric on better homes and the importance of literacy, black women expanded their roles, first in the church, then in the community as a whole. . . .

African American women's denominational groups created a vast network throughout the South, virtually invisible to whites. It is helpful to see the groups as cells through which information and ideas could pass quickly. The invisibility of black women's work suited them. They did not want to antagonize their husbands by making a power play within their denominations—the men in the church were already uneasy about their activities. They did not want to endanger their families by drawing attention to themselves. They did not want to risk interference from whites by being overtly political. Better to call social work "missionary work"; better to gather 100,000 Baptist women in a movement to produce good homes. If such activities resulted in organizing the community to lobby for better schools, swamp drainage, or tuberculosis control, no white could accuse them of meddling in politics.

From these bases, women forged interdenominational links. North Carolinian Anna Julia Cooper, by then living in Washington, D.C., was present at the creation of the National Association of Colored Women's Clubs in 1896. Delegates to that first meeting represented a wide range of women's denominational organizations, interdenominational unions such as the WCTU and the King's Daughters, and secular civic leagues. . . . North Carolina black women founded a statewide federation of clubs in 1909 and elected Marie Clinton president. . . .

Activist black women also met at frequent regional sociological conferences. The Progressive Era trend toward organization, discussion, and investigation blossomed in these huge confabulations. Mary Lynch went to the Negro Young People's Christian and Educational Congress in Atlanta in 1902, where she delivered the address, "The Woman's Part in the Battle against Drink." There she met Charlotte Hawkins, a young Boston student who had just moved to Sedalia, North Carolina, and banker Maggie L. Walker of Richmond. She also renewed ties with Lucy Thurman of the national WCTU and Josephine Silone-Yates, president of the National Association of Colored Women's Clubs. The Woman's Day theme was "No race can rise higher than its women."

As women were building vast voluntary networks, public school teaching was becoming an increasingly feminized profession. In 1902, the number of black women teachers and black men teachers was almost the same: 1,325 women and 1,190 men. The percentage of black women teachers exactly matched that of white women teachers: 52 percent. By 1919, 78 percent of black teachers were women, and 83 percent of the white teachers were women. . . . The increasing number of black women teachers was a result . . . of declining wages. In addition to driving black men from the profession, low wages contributed to a difference in the marital status of white and black women teachers. White women teachers were almost always single. Many black women teachers were married women who remained partially dependent upon their husbands' income. . . .

Even without their own progressive agenda, African American women teachers would have found schools to be an increasingly politicized setting. After 1900, the importance of literacy for voting and the movement toward industrial education commanded the attention of both the black and white community, and perennial battles over allocating taxes for education turned the black schoolhouse into a lightning rod, propelling female teachers into the political sphere, for better or for worse. . . .

The racial inequities of school funding have been well documented, but the efforts of black students and teachers to keep their schools from starving cannot be celebrated enough. Even in the best black schools, for example, the Charlotte graded school, there were few desks and "two and sometimes three small pupils sat crowded in a wide seat." The state gave so little—inadequate furniture, a meager library—but teachers made so little go so far. "There was much blackboard space in a room which was a good thing," Rose Leary Love recalled. "At the time, blackboards were not termed visual aids, but they really were the most important available ones." The teachers used them to explain lessons; the pupils used them in lieu of paper. In the state's eyes, African Americans were not training to be full citizens; they needed no civics classes, no maps, no copy of the Constitution, no charts on "How a Bill Becomes a Law." That left teachers on their own to define citizenship. Somehow they did. Teachers chose talented students to "draw the National Flag or the State Flag on the blackboard," Love remembered. "These flags were assigned a place of honor on the board and they became a permanent fixture in the room for the year. Pupils were careful not to erase the flags when they cleaned the blackboards." Despite whites' efforts to rob African Americans of their country, black teachers taught each day under the flag.

A centralized state bureaucracy grew to oversee the curriculum in African American schools. In 1905, Charles L. Coon, a white man who had recently been superintendent of Salisbury's schools and secretary of the General Education Board, accepted the newly created position of superintendent of the state colored normal schools. According to his boss, Coon's oversight would "send out into the counties each a larger number of negro teachers, equipped with the knowledge and the training, and filled with the right ideals necessary for the . . . most practical, sensible and useful education of the negro race." By putting African American normal schools under the control of a white man, the state hoped to produce teachers who embraced industrial education and to force the private African American normal schools out of business.

Ironically, state oversight created controversy rather than quelling it primarily because of Coon's independent personality. An amateur statistician who often challenged authority, Coon created a furor by proving that the state spent less on African American education than the taxes blacks paid in. In fact, Coon produced figures to prove that black tax dollars educated white children. Coon's boss, James Y. Joyner, distanced himself from Coon's argument and decried him to Josephus Daniels. But Aycock admitted that Coon spoke the truth. . . .

Whites quarreled a great deal more over funding black education than they did over its content, which white educators overwhelmingly agreed should be based on the Hampton model.* Very little industrial training could begin, however, without spending dollars on equipment and tools. Ironically, it proved more expensive to build a bookcase than to explain an algebra problem on a broken piece of slate. Outside help would be critical. As a few dollars began to trickle down, black women teachers learned to exploit whites' support of industrial education. The Negro State Teachers Association recognized in 1903 that "the industrial and manual idea . . . is a much felt need in our public and private schools, since the development of negro womanhood is one of its immediate results." At the same time that black women recognized the potential of industrial education to improve home life, they began to clamor for a greater voice in its administration. When officials from the Rockefeller-funded General Education Board and local white educators met with black teachers in 1913, Charlotte Hawkins Brown told the group flatly that since women made up the majority of rural teachers, industrial education would fail unless philanthropists and white educators listened more closely to black women's suggestions and rewarded them for their efforts. African American women's tilting of the industrial education ideology was slight but important. While paying lip service to the ideal of producing servants for white people, black women quietly turned the philosophy into a self-help endeavor and the public schools into institutions resembling social settlement houses. Cooking courses became not only vocational classes but also nutrition courses where students could eat hot meals. Sewing classes may have turned out some dressmakers and cobbling classes some cobblers, but they had the added advantage of clothing poor pupils so that they could attend school more regularly.

The Negro Rural School Fund, a philanthropy administered by the Rockefeller Foundation's General Education Board, gave the state's black women teachers the basic tools they needed to incorporate social work into the public school system. Begun in 1909 as the Anna T. Jeanes Fund, it paid more than half of the salary of one industrial supervising teacher on the county level. County boards of education paid the rest. The Jeanes supervisor traveled to all of the African American schools in a county, ostensibly to teach industrial education. In 1913, the General Education Board offered to pay the salary of a state supervisor of rural elementary schools in North Carolina to oversee the thirteen Jeanes teachers already in place and to expand the work to other counties. In naming the supervisor, the board had a hidden agenda: northern philanthropists did not trust southern state administrators to allocate and spend their grants wisely. They wanted a white man loyal to them in state government, a professional who could walk the tightwire of interracial relations, placating obstreperous legislators at the same time that he kept a keen eye on black industrial curricula. They found their man in Nathan C. Newbold, who had been superintendent of public schools in Washington, North Carolina. . . .

Nonconfrontational and optimistic, as state agent for the Negro Rural School Fund Newbold became an extraordinary voice for African American education. He quickly persuaded more county boards of education to fund half of a Jeanes

---

*The Hampton model was a type of school for blacks and Native Americans that emphasized industrial, manual, and agricultural education. Academic instruction was of secondary importance.

teacher's salary at the same time that he forged strong alliances with the incumbent Jeanes teachers. By the end of his first year, twenty-two counties employed Jeanes teachers, who found themselves in the often awkward position of having to report to both Newbold and the county superintendent. Newbold appointed a black woman, Annie Wealthy Holland, as his assistant. The Jeanes board's initial expenditure of $2,144 in the state in 1909 grew to $12,728 by 1921. . . .

Faced with local white administrators' neglect, Jeanes teachers had an enormous amount of responsibility. Sarah Delany, the Jeanes supervisor in Wake County, recalled, "I was just supposed to be in charge of domestic science, but they made me do the county superintendent's work. So, I ended up actually in charge of all the colored schools in Wake County, North Carolina, although they didn't pay me to do that or give me any credit." Delany, raised as a "child of privilege" on the Saint Augustine's College campus, stayed overnight with parents in rural areas, where she encountered not just a lack of indoor plumbing but a condition even more appalling to a citified house guest: no outhouse. Delany went to her pupils' homes to teach their parents how to "cook, clean, [and] eat properly," and when General Education Board officials visited North Carolina in 1913, she agreed to serve on the statewide committee to establish a cooking curriculum. She painted schoolrooms, taught children to bake cakes, raised money to improve buildings, and organized Parent Unions. Jeanes teachers also transformed their students into entrepreneurs. In 1915, their Home-Makers Clubs, Corn Clubs, and Pig Clubs involved over 4,000 boys and girls and 2,000 adults in 32 counties. The clubs were intended to teach farming, of course, but they also enabled poor rural African Americans to make money on their produce. The students raised more than $6,000 selling fruits and vegetables that year.

Jeanes teachers saw themselves as agents of progressivism, and they combined public health work with their visits to schools and homes. . . . Carrie Battle, the Jeanes supervisor in Edgecombe County, . . . visited the homes of pupils across the county to organize a Modern Health Crusade against tuberculosis in the schools. Moving from school to school with a set of scales, she would not weigh ill-groomed boys and girls, nor would she weigh anyone in a dirty schoolroom. She made the children promise to clean up the room, bathe, use individual drinking cups, and sleep with the windows open. . . . Soon Battle had established Modern Health Clubs in every school and a total of 4,029 children enrolled as Crusaders. Her work attracted attention from the white community, and she began to cooperate with the white Red Cross nurse to produce public health programs. Many of Battle's students had never been farther than ten miles from their homes. She brought the world to them through regularly scheduled visits of the "Moving Picture Car," a truck equipped with projection equipment used to screen films on health education.

Jeanes teachers also built schools across the state—schools for which the state took credit and of which the counties took possession. Weary of asking for their fair share of tax dollars, black communities simply built their own schools and gave them to the county. For example, in the academic year 1915–16, thirty-two black schools were built and thirty improved at a total cost of $29,000. African Americans contributed over $21,000 of the total: $15,293 in cash and the equivalent of $5,856 in labor. . . .

The next year, the Julius Rosenwald Committee, a Chicago-based philanthropy, appropriated $6,000 to stimulate public school building in rural areas of

North Carolina. Although this amount was a great deal less than African Americans were already raising annually to build their own schools, Rosenwald grants often embarrassed state and county officials into contributing funds for building black schools. . . .

The unique role of the Jeanes teacher points up the distinctiveness of southern progressivism and provides clues to the reasons for historians' difficulties in finding and understanding it. The Jeanes teacher had no counterpart in the North. She did social work on the fly, leaving neither permanent settlement houses nor case files behind through which one might capture her experience. She understood the latest public health measures and passed them along even in the most remote areas. She fought to obtain Rosenwald school money to build schools that were airy and modern, then turned them into clubhouses in the evenings. By establishing Parent Unions, she provided a new organizational center for black communities. She lobbied school boards and county commissions for supplies and support. And she accomplished all of this while trying to remain invisible to the white community at large. To locate the progressive South, one must not just visit New South booster Henry Grady in Atlanta but find as well a schoolroom full of cleanly scrubbed Modern Health Crusaders, lined up for hot cereal cooked by the older girls in Rosenwald kitchens, each Crusader clutching the jelly jar that served as his or her very own glass.

By 1910, African American women in the state realized the need to create a united front to lobby local governmental officials and to improve civic life. Connected on the state level through the North Carolina Association of Colored Women's Clubs, these organizations would have to bring together on the local level denominational women's groups, interface with public school programs, and marshal all of the experience and resources that women had acquired in the past decade. The Salisbury Colored Women's Civic League exemplifies such an organization. . . .

Women from all walks of life joined the Civic League. As Rose Aggrey's daughter recalled, "There wasn't poor and rich . . . not a rigid difference between people. The difference between people was those who had training and those who didn't." Her mother, an active Civic Leaguer, had a knack for getting "women of all backgrounds together." The league's rolls included the wife of an AME Zion bishop, a dressmaker, a teacher, a laundress, a domestic worker, and a woman "from the other side of town—not trained, whose husband was in trouble, but a fine Christian woman." Members embraced a wide range of religious denominations—Mrs. A. Croom was a Baptist minister's wife, Lizzie Crittendon an Episcopalian, Lucy Spaulding a Presbyterian, and Mary Lynch and Victoria Richardson members of the AME Zion Church—and they put the agendas of their women's missionary societies into action in the Civic League. . . .

Many of the Civic League's projects involved interaction with white women. In fact, the impetus for the league's formation appears to have been an interracial community cleanup day, a project initiated by white club women throughout the state. Whites had tried to organize cleanup efforts before 1913, but "the most vigorous urging failed to stir the Negroes to action." It was not until they recruited Lula Kelsey to meet with a white male civic leader that plans for a joint cleanup day went forward. White Salisbury citizens finally realized that they could not coerce civic action among African Americans and that "without a Negro leader it is probable that the movement would have been a flat failure." The city donated twelve barrels of lime, a disinfectant, and the Civic League supervised its distribution. The city's two African American doctors spoke to the women on sanitation and disease.

Cleanup days evoked images of African Americans in the traditional role of servants, but they also put white people to work at servants' tasks: raking yards, whitewashing fences, carting trash, and improving housing. This made them a perfect place for black women to launch interracial forays. Moreover, on cleanup days, the entire community expected white landlords to improve their rental houses in black neighborhoods. As segregation rigidified, even the most prosperous black families found it difficult to buy decent housing, and they often had to tolerate living in neglected white-owned rental housing at close quarters. In the absence of building standards and housing laws, community cleanup days focused white attention on slumlords while also organizing black neighbors around a positive self-help project.

As knowledge of disease transmission grew, whites initiated cleanup days to protect themselves from the peril they imagined they were in due to their poor black neighbors' lack of sanitary measures. Typhoid spread by flies and tuberculosis by uncleanliness, and both represented public health emergencies in the South in the 1910s. It is difficult to imagine just how prevalent and problematic flies were in urban areas with poor sanitation or how thoroughly they invaded homes before screening. In a sketch entitled, "You better eat before you read this," Eula Dunlap recalled that people sold the contents of their privies for fertilizer, and it was spread on fields and gardens, with dire consequences. The flies were so thick inside homes that if someone was sick in the summer, a family member had to fan constantly. Babies wore fly netting draped around them as they played outdoors in the summertime. The death rate during "fly season" soared dramatically in the black community and increased modestly in the white community. In reality, germs traveled to both communities, but better health care for whites limited their mortality rate.

The fly carried more than disease; it also carried the germ of interracial cooperation. Since flies knew nothing about the color line, they flew back and forth across it with no regard for class standing or race. As white interracialist Lily Hammond put it in her essay, "The Democracy of the Microbe," "The [white] club women came upon Christian principles of racial adjustment without realizing that they were dealing with racial problems at all. They simply started out with common sense as their guide and cleanliness as their goal." In order to eradicate flies, one had to pick up garbage and extend sanitary sewage treatment to both the white and the black community. Such a cause fit perfectly into African American women's better homes movement. . . .

These efforts, begun through voluntary club work, aided the institutionalization of charity after 1910. In the following decade, large cities in North Carolina established Associated Charities branches to formalize and coordinate social service casework. In cities that were large enough, as in Charlotte, African Americans formed auxiliaries of the Associated Charities, presided over by leading black club women. In Salisbury, the relationship was more informal, and Lula Kelsey became an unpaid social worker for the Associated Charities. The Civic League joined the Associated Charities in 1917. Soon Civic Leaguers passed out pledge cards for the Associated Charities' annual fund-raising campaign throughout the African American community. Thereafter, when a needy case came to the attention of the Civic League, they referred it to the Associated Charities. The Associated Charities used the league to determine whether a person seeking help really needed it and asked Kelsey to perform home studies on applicants. Kelsey's son recalled that whenever an African American came for help to the Associated Charities office, the white social worker there would telephone Lula Kelsey before she acted.

With disfranchisement, African American women became diplomats to the white community, and contact with white women represented a vital, though difficult, part of that mission. As white women gained more power in social service organizations and public education during the first two decades of the century, they began to exercise growing influence in the public sector. Contact between black and white women came about not because the two groups felt gender solidarity but because white women controlled the resources that black women needed to improve their communities. What interracial contact meant to white club women is more confusing, as it must have been to the white club women themselves. Just as their mothers had met educated, middle-class black women for the first time in the 1880s in the Woman's Christian Temperance Union, after the white supremacy campaign, many white club women got their first glimpse of organized African American women when they planned cleanup days together. Such meetings may have been the first time a white woman had ever spoken to [a] black woman who was not a servant. From these contacts, a handful of white and black women formed cooperative working partnerships to further mutual goals, as did Lula Kelsey and the white Association Charities social worker. But those partnerships were rare. To some, they represented a necessary step toward accomplishing their own civic goals; to others, they offered some fulfillment of religious imperatives. Beyond that, most white women probably did not give much thought to the meaning of their contacts with black women.

Yet however sporadic and confusing women's interracial contacts were, they represented a crack in the mortar of the foundation of white supremacy. White club women came to know more about the black community and its women leaders and became less pliant in the hands of male politicians who attempted to manipulate them to further the gendered rhetoric of white supremacy. The same process had taken place in the 1880s when white temperance women ignored the dire warnings of men and planned local-option campaigns together with black women. But imperialist rhetoric, scientific racism, the Democrats' white supremacy campaign, and women's lack of direct access to the political process had ended those contacts. This time, things would be different. This time, the local contacts between black and white club women had a chance to take root and grow.

In addition to fostering useful contact between women of both races, community cleanup work earned certain black women power within their neighborhoods and brought them into contact with city officials. The Civic League did not just hold cleanup days; it inspected homes afterward, counseled residents who did not follow sanitary practices, and reported them to the city if they did not comply with sanitary guidelines. The membership card of the Civic League required the bearer to pledge to "improve the sanitary condition of the home in which I live" and to use "lime to disinfect and whitewash." Upon presentation, the bearer of the card could claim one gallon of lime, "Given by City; distributed by COLORED WOMEN'S CIVIC LEAGUE." This public/private partnership across racial lines was a shaky one, but organized African American women quickly capitalized on it.

White men in local government came to know Lula Kelsey, Rose Aggrey, Mary Lynch, and the other leaguers as spokespeople for the black community—as women who could get things done. The women proceeded as if the city owed them a fair hearing in return for their civic work. Shortly after the first cleanup day, the league voted to send a representative to speak with the city administration about "helping with the cemetery," and by the next month, Lula Kelsey announced to the group that she had met with the mayor and he had "promised that it would be taken care of better in the future." . . .

The city lacked a public playground for its African American children, and the Civic League lobbied city officials to provide one. . . . Likewise, the women participated in "maternalist politics" by sponsoring "baby day," when mothers could bring their babies to a meeting for a doctor's advice. Civic League women centered much of their effort around the public schools. They held fairs and paper drives to raise money for the industrial department of the graded schools, and a teacher who was a member of the league organized a Junior Civic League at her school. The women visited the city jail regularly, ministered to a chain gang, and began an outreach program at the county home for the indigent.

By 1917, Salisbury's African American women had two mechanisms in place to gain a hearing before both private and public manifestations of the state. First, contacts with white club women provided entry into the growing private social welfare system. Since black club women had met the white club women involved in social service, the Civic League could join the Associated Charities and then use that membership to direct the flow of aid to the African American community. Second, with husbands and brothers virtually disfranchised, diplomatic women could go in their places to the mayor and county commissioners to lobby for city services and, once there, cast their mission in female-coded, and unthreatening, terms.

As much as southern whites plotted to reserve progressivism for themselves, and as much as they schemed to alter the ill-fitting northern version accordingly, they failed. African American women embraced southern white progressivism, reshaped it, and sent back a new model that included black power brokers and grass roots activists. Evidence of southern African American progressivism is not to be found in public laws, electoral politics, or the establishment of mothers' aid programs at the state level. It rarely appears in documents that white progressives, male or female, left behind. Since black men could not speak out in politics and black women did not want to be seen, it has remained invisible in virtually every discussion of southern progressivism. Nonetheless, southern black women initiated every progressive reform that southern white women initiated, a feat they accomplished without financial resources, without the civic protection of their husbands, and without publicity.

At the same time that black women used progressivism to reshape black life and race relations, an organizational approach slowly began to replace racial "paternalism." The black community in Salisbury would not listen to influential whites who told them to clean up their communities. Nothing happened until whites recognized black women leaders, met with them publicly, and gave them authority. Then the city was "completely transformed." Despite whites' extensive efforts to undermine black education by imposing a nineteenth-century version of industrial education, black women's progressive ideas made industrial education modern and useful by linking it to the sanitary science movement. Contacts between white and black women with progressive agendas set the groundwork for inclusion of African Americans in formal social service structures. Her desire to help solve civic problems gave Lula Kelsey the right to appear before city officials during a period when black men risked their lives if they registered to vote for those officials.

This is certainly not to argue that disfranchisement was a positive good or that African Americans were better off with limited social services than they would have been with full civil rights. It means that black women were given straw and they made bricks. Outward cooperation with an agenda designed to oppress them masked a subversive twist. Black women capitalized upon the new role of the state to capture a share of the meager resources and proceeded to effect real social change with tools designed to maintain the status quo.

FURTHER READING

Alexander, Ruth M. *The "Girl Problem": Female Sexual Delinquency in New York* (1995).

Antler, Joyce. "After College, What? New Graduates and the Family Claim," *American Quarterly* 32 (1980): 409–434.

Baker, Paula. "The Domestication of Politics: Women and American Political Society, 1780–1920," *American Historical Review* 89 (June 1984): 620–647.

Barker-Benfield, G. J. "Mother Emancipator: The Meaning of Jane Addams' Sickness and Cure," *Journal of Family History* 4 (1979): 395–420.

Becker, Susan D. *The Origins of the Equal Rights Amendment* (1981).

Blair, Karen. *The Torchbearers* (1994).

———. *The Clubwoman as Feminist: True Womanhood Redefined* (1980).

Blee, Kathleen, M. *Women of the Klan: Racism and Gender in the 1920s* (1991).

Chafe, William. *The Paradox of Change: American Women in the 20th Century* (1991).

Chen, Constance M. *"The Sex Side of Life": Mary Ware Dennett's Pioneering Battle for Birth Control and Sex Education* (1996).

Chesler, Ellen. *Woman of Valor: Margaret Sanger and the Birth Control Movement* (1992).

Conway, Jill K. "Women Reformers and American Culture, 1870–1930," *Journal of Social History* 5 (1971–1972): 164–177.

Cott, Nancy F. *The Grounding of Modern Feminism* (1987).

Davis, Allen. *American Heroine: The Life and Legend of Jane Addams* (1973).

———. *Spearheads for Reform: The Social Settlements and the Progressive Movement, 1890–1914* (1967).

Deutsch, Sarah. *Women and the City: Gender, Space, and Power in Boston, 1870–1940* (2000).

Drachman, Virginia G. *Sisters in Law: Women Lawyers in Modern American History* (2001).

DuBois, Ellen Carol. *Harriot Stanton Blatch and the Winning of Woman Suffrage* (1997).

Fitzpatrick, Ellen. *Endless Crusade: Women Social Scientists and Progressive Reform* (1990).

Frankel, Noralee, and Nancy S. Dye, eds. *Gender, Class, Race, and Reform in the Progressive Era* (1992).

Frankfort, Robert. *Collegiate Women: Domesticity and Career in Turn-of-the-Century America* (1977).

Freedman, Estelle B. *Maternal Justice: Miriam Van Waters and the Female Reform Tradition* (1996).

———. "Separatism as Strategy: Female Institution Building and American Feminism, 1870–1930," *Feminist Studies* 5 (1979): 512–529.

Giddings, Paula. *When and Where I Enter: The Impact of Black Women on Race and Sex in America* (1984).

Glenn, Susan A. *Female Spectacle: The Theatrical Roots of Modern Feminism* (2000).

Goodwin, Joanne. *Gender and the Politics of Welfare Reform: Mothers' Pensions in Chicago, 1911–1929* (1997).

Gordon, Linda. *The Great Arizona Orphan Abduction* (1999).

———."Black and White Visions of Welfare: Women's Welfare Activism, 1890–1945," *Journal of American History* 78 (September 1991): 559–590.

———. *Woman's Body, Woman's Right: A Social History of Birth Control in America* (1976).

Green, Elna. *Southern Strategies: Southern Women and the Woman Suffrage Question* (1997).

Hall, Jacquelyn Dowd. *Revolt Against Chivalry: Jessie Daniel Ames and the Women's Campaign Against Lynching* (1979).

Hayden, Dolores. *The Grand Domestic Revolution: A History of Feminist Design for American Homes, Neighborhoods, and Cities* (1981).

Hewitt, Nancy A. and Suzanne Lebsock, eds. *Visible Women: New Essays on American Activism* (1993).

Higginbotham, Evelyn Brooks. *Righteous Discontent: The Women's Movement in the Black Baptist Church* (1993).

Horowitz, Helen Lefkowtiz. *The Power and Passion of M. Cary Thomas* (1994).

Kennedy, Kathleen. *Disloyal Mothers and Scurrilous Citizens: Women and Subversion During World War I* (1999).

Koven, Seth, and Sonya Michel, eds. *Mothers of a New World: Maternalist Politics and the Origins of Welfare States* (1993).

Kraditor, Aileen. *Ideas of the Woman Suffrage Movement* (1981).

Kunzel, Regina G. *Fallen Women, Problem Girls: Unmarried Mothers and the Professionalization of Social Work, 1890–1945* (1993).

Ladd-Taylor, Molly. *Mother-Work: Women, Child Welfare, and the State, 1890–1930* (1994).

Lageman, Ellen. *A Generation of Women: Education in the Lives of Progressive Reformers* (1979).

Lasch-Quinn, Elizabeth. *Black Neighbors: Race and the Limits of Reform in the American Settlement House Movement, 1890–1945* (1993).

Lemons, J. Stanley. *The Woman Citizen: Social Feminism in the 1920s* (1973).

Lerner, Gerda. "Early Community Work of Black Club Women," *Journal of Negro History* 59 (1974): 158–167.

Lissak, Rivka Shpak. *Pluralism and Progressives: Hull House and the New Immigrants, 1890–1919* (1989).

Lunardini, Christine. *From Equal Suffrage to Equal Rights: Alice Paul and the National Woman's Party, 1913–1928* (1986).

Matthews, Jean V. *The Rise of the New Woman: The Women's Movement in America, 1870–1930* (2003).

Morgan, David. *Suffragists and Democrats* (1972).

Muncy, Robyn. *Creating a Female Dominion in American Reform, 1890–1935* (1991).

Newman, Louise Michele. *White Women's Rights: The Racial Origins of Feminism in the United States* (1999).

Nielsom, Kim E. *Un-American Womanhood: Antiradicalism, Antifeminism and the First Red Scare* (2001).

Odem, Mary E. *Delinquent Daughters: Protecting and Policing Female Adolescent Sexuality in the Untied States, 1885–1920* (1995).

Orleck, Annelise. *Common Sense and a Little Fire: Women and Working-Class Politics in the United States, 1900–1965* (1995).

Parker, Alison M. *Purifying America: Women, Cultural Reform, and Pro-Censorship Activism, 1873–1933* (1997).

Payne, Elizabeth Anne. *Reform, Labor, and Feminism: Margaret Drier Robins and the Women's Trade Union League* (1988).

Preito, Laura R. *At Home in the Studio: The Professionalization of Women Artists in America* (2001).

Rosen, Ruth. *The Lost Sisterhood: Prostitution in America, 1900–1918* (1982).

Rosenberg, Rosalind. *Beyond Separate Spheres: The Intellectual Roots of Modern Feminism* (1982).

Rothman, Sheila. *Woman's Proper Place* (1978).

Rousmaniere, John. "Cultural Hybrid in the Slums: The College Woman and the Settlement House, 1889–1914," *American Quarterly* 22 (1970): 45–66.

Ruiz, Vicki L. *From Out of the Shadows: Mexican Women in Twentieth-Century America* (1998).

Rupp, Lelia J. *Worlds of Women: The Making of an International Women's Movement* (1998).

Salem, Dorothy. *To Better Our World: Black Women in Organized Reform, 1890–1920* (1990).

Scharf, Lois, and Joan Jensen, eds. *Decades of Discontent: The Women's Movement, 1910–1940* (1983).

Scott, Anne Firor. *Natural Allies: Women's Associations in American History* (1992).

Sklar, Kathryn Kish. *Florence Kelley and the Nation's Work* (1995).

Skocpol, Theda. *Protecting Soldiers and Mothers: The Political Origins of Social Policy in the United States* (1992).

Taylor, Ula Yvette. *The Veiled Garvey: The Life and Times of Amy Jacques Garvey* (2002).

Terborg-Penn, Rosalyn. *African-American Women in the Struggle for the Vote, 1850–1920* (1998).

Tomes, Nancy. *The Gospel of Germs: Men, Women, and the Microbe in American Life* (1999).

Wheeler, Marjorie Spruill. *New Women of the New South: The Leaders of the Woman Suffrage Movement in the Southern States* (1993).

Wilson, Margaret Gibbons. *The American Woman in Transition: The Urban Influence, 1870–1920* (1979).

Wolfe, Allis R. "Women, Consumerism, and the National Consumer's League in the Progressive Era, 1900–1923," *Labor History* 16 (1975): 378–392.

Wortman, Marlene Stein. "Domesticating the Nineteenth-Century American City," *Prospects* 3 (1977): 531–572.

C H A P T E R
12

Women in America
During the Great Depression
and New Deal

In 1929 the United States descended into the worst economic crisis of its history, a
crisis that ruined thousands of businesses and left nearly one-quarter of the work force
unemployed by 1933. Hoping to restore the nation to prosperity, Franklin Delano
Roosevelt's administration intervened in unprecedented ways in society and the
economy: New Deal legislation created federal relief and jobs programs, boosted
unionization (and worker militancy), established social security and unemployment
funds, and mandated a federal minimum wage. Even though Roosevelt's New Deal
did not end the Great Depression, it did dramatically increase the regulatory and
social welfare obligations of the federal government, thereby altering the relationship
between American citizens and the state.

Historians have long debated the significance of the Great Depression and New
Deal for women, questioning whether the economic crisis of the 1930s and the policy
innovations that it produced caused Americans to affirm or forsake traditional gender
roles and expectations. Some facts are well known and oft-repeated. For example,
Americans in great number expressed heightened anxiety about women's presence
in the work force during the Great Depression and seem to have supported, at least
tacitly, decisions by federal agencies, state governments, school districts, and private
businesses to fire or deny employment to married women in hopes of creating job
opportunities for married men. In addition, Eleanor Roosevelt and a network of
liberal Democratic women became important figures in the New Deal bureaucracy,
influencing the development of policy and programs. Finally, the Great Depression
was primarily a crisis of consumption, not production, and policies of the 1930s
sought to enhance both the appeal of the marketplace and the purchasing power
of American consumers, most of whom were women.

But these simple facts raise more questions than they answer. How did women,
as individuals or in groups, try to define, protect, or advance their interests during
this decade of crisis and governmental reform? How did gender combine with race,
class, regional location, or other social markers to define women's experience and

relationship to the state in the 1930s? Did the Great Depression and New Deal alter in significant ways women's identity or vulnerabilities in the labor force, the family, the marketplace, or public life? How did the New Deal give legal or formal definition to women's interests, and how did women of different backgrounds profit or suffer from the programs and policies that were the result of New Deal reform agendas? The documents and essays in this chapter offer partial answers to these complex questions.

⊞ D O C U M E N T S

The *New York Times* reports in Document 1 on an alarming increase in the number of destitute and homeless women living on the streets of New York City. Ann Marie Low, a single college-educated white woman, kept a diary during the 1930s while she and her North Dakota family struggled to withstand both the Great Depression and the Dust Bowl. Excerpted in Document 2, Low's diary is a record of her feelings about lost job opportunities, family obligations, and marriage. Writing for *Harper's Monthly Magazine,* Dorothy Dunbar Bromley examines women's great need for reliable contraception in the 1930s and the obstacles they confronted in trying to obtain it (Document 3). In Document 4, Lydia Mendoza, the first star of Tejano music, recalls how her family confronted economic hardship and helped her launch a musical career during the Great Depression. In Document 5, Eleanor Roosevelt urges Americans to confront racial injustice, restore faith in the rule of law, and improve cooperation between white and black citizens. The First Lady applauds, in Document 6, the repeal of federal legislation that permitted employment discrimination against married women. In Document 7, a woman writer for the *Chinese Digest* in San Francisco exposes the racism of white club women in that city and thereby calls into question America's claim that it was one of the truly authentic democracies in a world beset by economic crisis and "race hatred." Writing for *The Daily Worker* in 1940, Louise Mitchell (Document 8) discloses the harsh conditions under which black women sought work in New York City during the Great Depression; as domestic servants they lacked job security and were ineligible for New Deal work benefits or entitlements.

1. The *New York Times* Reports, "Destitute Women on Increase Here," 1932

Many Are Cultured Girls

Salvation Army officials reported yesterday a large increase in the number of women seeking shelter in emerging lodging houses.

Major Florence Dean, superintendent of the Army's emergency lodging house for women in West Twenty-second Street, reported an increase of 50 percent in applicants in the last few months.

"This increase is serious enough in itself, but it becomes a major tragedy when it is realized that the greater part of this increase represents married women and women with children," she said.

"Another sad phase of the increased demand for aid is the fact that the type of women forced to apply for shelter has changed so greatly. When we originally opened this lodge two years ago the majority of women seeking help were of the laboring class—women who were trained to do nothing but factory work or to serve as domestics.

"This has all changed. Now we have women of the highest type, women who formerly had large incomes, school teachers, college graduates, highly trained office workers and girls who have been brought up in an atmosphere of luxury but now are forced to seek food, shelter and clothing from charity organizations.

"It is a terrible thing to contemplate what might happen to these girls and women if they could not secure shelter from the Army. And yet, we are told that funds for emergency relief are exhausted and that we must prepare to curtail activities. If we can't get the money to continue I suppose we will have to start turning these women out into the streets. Already we are not able to take in all of the women who come to us for help. We can't turn out those we already are helping."

2. Ann Marie Low Records Her Feelings About Life in the Dust Bowl, 1934

April 25, 1934, Wednesday

Last weekend was the worst dust storm we ever had. We've been having quite a bit of blowing dirt every year since the drouth started, not only here, but all over the Great Plains. Many days this spring the air is just full of dirt coming, literally, for hundreds of miles. It sifts into everything. After we wash the dishes and put them away, so much dust sifts into the cupboards we must wash them again before the next meal. Clothes in the closets are covered with dust.

Last weekend no one was taking an automobile out for fear of ruining the motor. I rode Roany to Frank's place to return a gear. To find my way I had to ride right beside the fence, scarcely able to see from one fence post to the next.

Newspapers say the deaths of many babies and old people are attributed to breathing in so much dirt.

May 7, 1934, Monday

The dirt is still blowing. Last weekend Bud and I helped with the cattle and had fun gathering weeds. Weeds give us greens for salad long before anything in the garden is ready. We use dandelions, lamb's quarter, and sheep sorrel. I like sheep sorrel best. Also, the leaves of sheep sorrel, pounded and boiled down to a paste, make a good salve.

Still no job. I'm trying to persuade Dad I should apply for rural school #3 out here where we went to school. I don't see a chance of getting a job in a high school when so many experienced teachers are out of work.

He argues that the pay is only $60.00 a month out here, while even in a grade school in town I might get $75.00. Extra expenses in town would probably eat up that extra $15.00. Miss Eston, the practice teaching supervisor, told me her salary has been cut to $75.00 after all the years she has been teaching in Jamestown. She wants to get married. School boards will not hire married women teachers in these hard times because they have husbands to support them. Her fiancé is the sole support of his widowed mother and can't support a wife, too. So she is just stuck in her job, hoping she won't get another salary cut because she can scarcely live on what she makes and dress the way she is expected to.

Dad argues the patrons always stir up so much trouble for a teacher at #3 some teachers have quit in mid-term. The teacher is also the janitor, so the hours are long.

I figure I can handle the work, kids, and patrons. My argument is that by teaching here I can work for my room and board at home, would not need new clothes, and so could send most of my pay to Ethel and Bud. . . .

May 21, 1934, Monday

Ethel has been having stomach trouble. Dad has been taking her to doctors though suspecting her trouble is the fact that she often goes on a diet that may affect her health. The local doctor said he thought it might be chronic appendicitis, so Mama took Ethel by train to Valley City last week to have a surgeon there remove her appendix.

Saturday Dad, Bud, and I planted an acre of potatoes. There was so much dirt in the air I couldn't see Bud only a few feet in front of me. Even the air in the house was just a haze. In the evening the wind died down, and Cap came to take me to the movie. We joked about how hard it is to get cleaned up enough to go anywhere. . . .

Sunday the dust wasn't so bad. Dad and I drove cattle to the Big Pasture. Then I churned butter and baked a ham, bread, and cookies for the men, as no telling when Mama will be back.

July 6, 1934, Friday

I am still herding cows, and it is awfully hot. Where they have eaten every weed and blade of grain. Bud is plowing so the ground will be softened to absorb rain (if it comes). He is very fed up and anxious to get away to school and fit himself for a job.

Poor Bud. He has worked so hard and saved so hard. He has done without nice clothes and never went to a dance or movie oftener than about once a year because he was saving every penny for college. He hoped his livestock would pay his way for four years. The price was so low he didn't sell any last year. This year they are worth less, and he absolutely must sell them because there is not enough feed for them and no money to buy feed. All the stock he has won't pay his way through one year of college. . . .

July 9, 1934, Monday

Saturday night Cap and I went to the movie, Claudette Colbert in *The Torch Singer.* Afterward he bought ice cream cones and we sat in the car in front of the store eating them. He brought up the subject of marriage. I reminded him that he promised, if I would go out with him occasionally, he would not mention marriage. I also pointed out the impossibility. He has to run the farm until Sonny is old enough and then will have nothing to start out on his own. I have to work until Ethel gets through college and can help Bud, at least two years. If she doesn't help Bud, we are looking at four years. Though I didn't mention it, in four years Cap will be thirty-six years old. Forget it.

He insisted he wants to get married now. Then I turned shrewish and said I'd seen him leave a dance last year with Joan. If he wants a wife, she would doubtless marry him.

He said he did take her home from a dance once, but there is absolutely nothing between him and Joan and I know it—I am all he wants and I know it.

"Let's not quarrel," I murmured. "Things will work out somehow."

He leaned back against the car seat, saying somberly, "Oh, how I wish it would rain."

The light from the store window was on his face. He is really a handsome man, with a John Barrymore profile and thick wavy auburn hair. Suddenly I seemed to see what his face will be someday—a tombstone on which is written the epitaph of dead dreams. I shivered.

"Oh, Sweetheart, you are cold and have no wrap. I'll take you home."

I didn't tell him I wasn't shivering from cold.

3. Dorothy Dunbar Bromley Comments on Birth Control and the Depression, 1934

"Nobody wanted Jimmy, but he was born anyhow." This caption appears, not on propaganda issued by the American Birth Control League, but on a flier recently distributed by the Cincinnati Committee on Maternal Health. The story told by Dr. Elizabeth Campbell, Chairman of the Medical Committee, is a graphic one. At the time Jimmy was born his father had been out of work for seventeen months, and the parents with five children were subsisting on a five dollars a week relief allowance. His mother, sick with worry before he came, did not want Jimmy. The community did not want him, as the city was already spending $350,000 on relief. Jimmy himself, had he had any say, could hardly have wanted to be born, for his short life meant only misery to him. His home was so cold that in four months time he died of pneumonia. His brief and painful life had cost the community a total of $130.02 for hospital, nursing, and medical care, for milk, for baby clothes, and for his burial. Was it fair to Jimmy to be born at this time? And was it fair to the community, which was already taking care of 21,380 families, that he should have been born?

Half of the women, Dr. Campbell says, who have applied during the past year to the Maternal Health Clinic of Cincinnati for contraceptive advice had unemployed husbands and all of them, for some good reason, feared the birth of another

Dorothy Dunbar Bromley, "Birth Control and the Depression," *Harper's Monthly Magazine* (October 1934): 563–574. Copyright 1934 by *Harper's Magazine*. All rights reserved. Reproduced from the October issue by special permission.

child. Dr. Campbell's arguments are frank and to the point. "Every child," she says, "has a right to be wanted. Hunger and fear cannot create a wholesome life for a baby. During this crisis the birth of those babies whose coming is a cause of dread, should be postponed until a better time, since the community cannot keep in health and decency the children that are here."

The situation in Cincinnati is no different from that in other cities. Proof is to be found in an economic health survey recently made by Milbank Memorial Foundation in co-operation with the United States Public Health Service, covering 8000 urban families in the lower-income groups living in ten different localities. Investigation showed that in 1932 there were 43 per cent more births in families without any employed workers than in families with one or more full-time workers. Families that were actually receiving relief had a birth rate 54 per cent higher than those not on relief. The study further showed that families who were poor in 1929 and continued in that condition in 1932 had the highest birth rate of all, while those who dropped below the $1200 a year level during the depression had a considerably higher birth rate than those with an income of from $1200 to $2000 a year. Summing up their conclusions, Messrs. Perrott and Sydenstricker, the authors of the study, say:

> Low social status, unemployment, and low income in 1932 went hand in hand with a high illness rate and increased malnutrition among children. It was in these same groups of families that a high birth rate prevailed. Whatever the broad implications of the findings may be, it is evident that a high birth rate during the depression prevailed in families which could least afford, from any point of view, to assume this added responsibility. . . .

The findings cited above are paralleled by another Milbank Fund study, recently made under the direction of the famous biologist, Dr. Raymond Pearl of Johns Hopkins University. This survey concerned contraceptive practices among 4945 hospitalized urban women of all classes, living in thirteen different States. The results showed, as was to be expected, that a much higher percentage of well-to-do and rich women were practicing birth control than poor white and colored women. But the study also showed, contrary to expectations, that the women of the well-to-do and rich classes who took no preventive measures were as fertile as the women of the poorer classes, colored women included. In other words, the failure on the part of the poorer classes to practice birth control appears alone to be responsible for their too rapid propagation.

Dr. Pearl had for many years questioned the social value of birth control. But his findings now lead him to the emphatic conclusion that "the national policy of prohibiting the free dissemination of accurate scientific information about birth control methods is adding definitely and measurably to the difficulty of the problems of poverty and unemployment with which our children and grandchildren will have to deal."

Dr. Pearl might have gone on to say that our national policy regarding birth control has added definitely and measurably to the enormous relief load which burdens the country to-day. It is as ironic as it is tragic that parents who cannot take care of the children they already have should have no choice but to bring more into the world. In one year's time—between October, 1932 and October, 1933 according to the Federal Unemployment Relief Census taken last October—there were as many as 233,822 children born to families who were receiving public relief. These families, 3,134,678 in number, also had 1,589,480 children from one to five years of age or, all told, 1,823,302 children under six years of age. . . .

The ill health and hardships so often suffered by members of over-large families are argument enough for birth control. As Margaret Sanger has said, "There can be no justification for violating the right of every married woman to decide when and how often she shall undertake the physical and far-reaching responsibilities of motherhood." The argument that large families among the indigent are an additional burden on the taxpayer is hardly a generous one. Yet it may have its effect on legislators and their constituents who have so far been unmoved by humane considerations.

Unfortunately there is no way of estimating the cost of relief for the million or more babies born during the depression to families that were living on public funds in October, 1933. The sum total of relief expenditures, however, is sufficiently appalling. For the year 1933 all forms of public relief reached approximately $800,000,000. For the same year combined public and private expenditures are estimated by the Monthly Bulletin on Social Statistics, published by the Children's Bureau, to have been three times as great in 120 cities as they were in 1929. . . .

The moral of these figures is that the comfortable and well-to-do can no longer remain indifferent to the fate of the indigent. We have reached the point that England reached in 1919. Families and individuals in want are admitted to be a charge on government, and it is not likely that even a reactionary administration, should one come into power, would dare to discontinue public relief so long as there is unemployment on a large scale. Given present-day conditions in industry and increasing technological unemployment, there appears slight possibility that the relief problem will disappear. . . .

The country has become birth-control-conscious. Economic conditions make family limitation in both the white-collar and the working class imperative. There can, therefore, be no turning back. It is only a question whether the setting up of clinics shall be left to lay organizations with limited facilities, and the wholesale distribution of doubtful products be further tolerated, or whether the medical profession will awaken to its clear duty. Mrs. Margaret Sanger and the American Birth Control League are ready and willing to turn over their self-imposed task to the profession, for they realize that only through wide medical practice and extensive research will better and simpler technics be evolved for the future.

The profession is at present in an anomalous position. Dr. J. Prentice Wilson, President of the Washington, D. C., Medical Association, points out, "At the 1933 meeting of the American Medical Association, Dr. Barton Cooke Hirst, chairman of the section on Obstetrics, Gynecology, and Abdominal Surgery, listed birth control as one of the four major problems in gynecology. At the same meeting a resolution asking that a committee be appointed to study the subject was defeated. Thus the A.M.A. placed itself on record as refusing to study one of the four major problems affecting the women of America."

A similar resolution was voted down in June of this year by the House of Delegates, despite the fact that it was favorably reported by the Committee on Public

Health and Hygiene, as well as by the Council of the Section on Obstetrics and Gynecology. At the same convention a commercial exhibitor was allowed to feature a misleading film on the "safe period," which took no account of the doubts which scientists have expressed concerning it. Such action on the part of the A.M.A. is hardly calculated to inspire confidence in its devotion to scientific ideals.

The women of the United States are waiting for the medical profession's help. All of the clinics in the country have in the past ten years taken care of probably not more than 160,000 women, while the number advised by private practitioners would hardly bring this figure up to half a million. It is quite possible that the majority of married people are using some more or less crude form of birth control. But only a small minority are instructed in reliable methods.

It is absurd that the legislators should wait for the doctors and the doctors should wait for the legislators to correct the situation. A movement is now on foot, started by Dr. Prentiss Willson, President of the District of Columbia Medical Society, to organize a National Medical Committee on State and Federal Contraceptive Legislation. It is to be hoped that the influential men on this committee will be able to break the deadlock that has so far been the fate of all contraceptive legislation.

There is no reason why the Roman Catholic Church should attempt to dictate either to the legislators or the A.M.A. Father Coughlin admitted, in testifying against the proposed Federal legislation before the House Judiciary Committee, that "63 per cent of the American population to-day profess no affiliated religion." "I recognize the fact," he went on, "that those people are favoring practical birth control. If that is their morals . . . I have no criticism to offer; that is their business."

But Father Coughlin had a criticism to offer or he would not have been testifying against the proposed bill. Amendment of the Federal law so as to admit contraceptive materials to the mails will hardly force "practical birth control" on the communicants of the Roman Catholic Church. Its priests will still be at liberty to lead their flocks as best they can. Because the Church is uncertain of its authority over its own members, it is attempting to dictate on a very vital subject to the majority of Americans, who *are not its communicants.* There could be no better proof that it is seeking to invade the domain that belongs to the State.

The only other opponents of a change in the laws are such Protestant fundamentalists as Canon William Sheafe Chase, who believe with Father Coughlin that birth control is synonymous with prostitution, and those population theorists who are alarmed by the falling birth rate. But these latter gentlemen have not proved that we should be any the worse off for having a stationary population. Over a century ago Malthus tried to alarm the world with his theory that human beings were increasing by a geometric ratio while the means of existence were increasing only by an arithmetic ratio. To-day Mgr. John A. Ryan and others argue that this country and the world at large need more and not fewer consumers. They ignore the fact that we also need fewer and not more workers.

Far more impressive—and alarming—are the Milbank Fund findings showing that the highest birth rate prevailed in 1932 (and doubtless still does) "in families which could least afford, from any point of view, to assume this added responsibility." It would be hard to deny that the drain on women's health, the broken marriages, the toll of abortions, the hardships suffered by over-large families subsisting on relief, are a medieval disgrace to a twentieth-century civilization.

4. Lydia Mendoza, the First Star of Tejano Music, Recalls Her Early Career During the Great Depression

Lydia

In 1929 when the Depression came, when a lot of people began to lose their jobs, my dad also lost his job. Finally, Papá said, "No, we're not staying here." The winter was very hard, very cold. "We're going back to Texas!"

We left right away. It must have been around 1930, because my youngest brother, Andrés, was born there in Detroit just before we left. . . .

Mamá kept on writing to our half-sister Mónica over there in Sugarland, Texas. . . .

Mamá sent a letter to Mónica . . . letting her know we were going to come. Then Mónica and José sent us some money so that we could buy them a car up there in Detroit—they were very cheap up there—and bring it down to them. They wanted a closed car, so we bought them a Chevrolet sedan. That was the car that Mamá and the youngest children rode in. Ignacio* bought a great big old Dodge—a convertible, an old used one, that was also very cheap. And finally, we sold everything we had up there, and Papá bought us a little square Model T truck which we was to drive all the way down to Houston. So we loaded everything up, and we started the journey back to Texas in a little caravan of three vehicles: the little truck and the two cars.

We left Detroit in October, and we arrived in Houston in December. We spent almost three months on the road, traveling. Because we left with so little money, we'd have to stop in the towns along the way, play some music to get some money, and then buy food and fill up the cars. We'd arrive at a town, and we would be running low on gas, so right there we would look for a place to sing. That was the way that we came, and that was how we made our trip until we arrived here in Houston.

On the road from Detroit to Houston we camped out most of the time. When we did arrive in a city—we looked for cities where we thought there might be some Mexicans—we would go and ask them for help. When they saw how we were traveling, what kind of shape we were in, that we needed help, well, they would organize *reuniones,* get-togethers, or little parties in some family's house. We would sing for them, and they would . . . help us. That's how we would get money together for traveling. We'd fill up all the cars with gasoline, and we'd hit the road, *y caminábamos.*

But since the towns were often distant from one another and sometimes pretty far from the highway as well, we would buy bread, cold meats, and we'd eat what we could on the road. At times we would have the desire for something cooked, so, well, we'd improvise a fire in the woods or fields by the side of the road, and there we would cook our little dinner, and we would eat, and then get back on the road. We didn't go to restaurants. We didn't give ourselves any luxuries. We usually contented ourselves with having a slice of bread and a piece of bologna or something—whatever we could afford. . . .

Lydia Mendoza, *Lydia Mendoza, A Family Autobiography.* Compiled and introduced by Chris Strachwitz and James Nicolopulos (Houston, TX: Arte Rublico Press, 1993).

*Ignacio was Lydia's brother-in-law.

Mónica and José helped us to move and install ourselves here in Houston in Magnolia. It seems to me that it was in Magnolia near Avenue B—that was where we lived, not right here in town. Most of the Mexicans in Houston lived in Magnolia in those days. It was the *barrio,* the Mexican neighborhood, although it no longer is today. At that time there were no Mexicans living in the central part of the city, like where I live now. The neighborhoods were separated in those days, because Mexicans couldn't live where there were Americans. We lived here in Houston during 1931 and part of 1932, almost two years.

I never thought about making a solo career for myself in those days because what I wanted was . . . for the group, to build up the group real strong, *formar aquel grupo bien formado.* At that time I was singing *la segunda* to Mamá: the harmony part. I was the second part, *yo era la segundera,* the accompanist. . . .

It was here in Houston that I taught myself to play the violin. One Cinco de Mayo we went to a *fiesta,* and I saw some musicians playing there, and one of them was playing violin. I really liked it a lot. So, just from watching him, I saw how it was played. Somehow I got a hold of a violin, and I taught myself to play by remembering what I had seen at that *fiesta.* . . .

During this time, I also helped Mamá teach my sister Panchita the guitar so that Mamá could rest sometimes. We were a group mostly of little girls—I was only fourteen or fifteen, and Panchita and María were even younger—but I think that helped. People were more likely to help us because we were children.

We sang songs like "Trigueña hermosa" ("Beautiful Brown-Skinned Girl"[)] and "El ingrato" ("Ungrateful Man"). Many of the songs that we sang were written by my mother. . . . There was another one they go around singing nowadays that was Mamá's, "Yo fui el primero" ("I Was the First"). . . .

The people would all gather around to hear the music when we would play out in front of those little stores. And then we would pass around the tambourine that Papá played, and they would throw us the money. It was a very pretty sight, and very special because we were women and very young. . . .

In Houston we continued going around singing—all of us. We would play in the little restaurants and stores, just like before. Sometimes we would also go out and sing in some of the other little towns around here, like, Richmond, Rosenburg, New Gulf. We would also go to Baytown, Texas City and, very often, down to Galveston. Especially during *las pizcas,* the harvests, when there would be a lot of Mexican workers out in the fields, we would go out and travel around to try and make a little extra money. At first, we had to go on the bus or the streetcars, because we no longer had a car of our own. Manuel was a little older now—he was now an *hombrecito*— so we gave him the triangle, and he would go along and help, too. It was still the Quinteto Carta Blanca. . . .

When we were living in Houston, times were really hard and there was very little work. Several times we couldn't pay the rent, and the landlord kicked us out. We'd try to rent a single room somewhere for the whole family until we got up enough money to rent another house. Papá didn't even go looking for a job, because he had already said that if we didn't go back to Mexico, he wouldn't work. But Ignacio would get up every morning at 4 o'clock and walk about five miles down to where the produce market used to be in those days. He would get there when the trucks arrived at 5:00 AM, and he would help unload the trucks and then do odd jobs around the market. Then in the evening he would come trudging home with his dollar that he had earned and a big sack full of potatoes, onions, chiles, tomatoes, lettuce—all kinds of produce that they would give him where he worked. Sometimes he would get mad when he got home: "Look! Look at what I've brought," he would tell Papá. "Why didn't you get up and come with me?"

"*Ay, carbón,*" Papá would say, "you go ahead, but not me, I'm not working for these damn *gringos* anymore." . . .

Both up in Michigan and back in Texas, Ignacio really helped us a lot. There in Houston, when things were really bad, it was what Ignacio brought home that kept the whole family alive. But he finally got tired of fighting it. There still weren't any jobs, so he and Beatriz and their little family went back to his *tierra:* Chihuahua. . . .

Mamá had been talking about moving to San Antonio, because she thought that it might be a little easier for us to make a living there. San Antonio had more *ambiente,* because there were a lot more Mexicans living there than in Houston. For that reason, Mamá figured there might be more interest in our music—more possibilities—in San Antonio. The one thing that was certain was that we had to do something—make some kind of change—because we couldn't go on the way we had been any longer. . . .

When we got . . . to San Antonio in 1932, the first thing we did was take part in some *concursos,* singing contests, that were going on at the Teatro Nacional. They were sort of like amateur music contests: mostly for children. The man who was in charge was a very good friend of Papá's, who he had got to know many years before. So Papá went over there when we got to town, and he told his friend, "Look, I've got this little group here, they're my children, could they possibly enter the contest?" "Sure, of course, lots of people are taking part in these contests," Papá's friend told him.

There really were quite a few people singing in those contests, and they were mostly boys: young boys who played or sang. . . .

All of the groups came out singing in turn, and then I went out with my violin, and my sister María with the mandolin and my other sister, Panchita, with our six-string guitar. Manuel and Juanita even helped out on that occasion. Manuel played the triangle and Juanita danced; she was only five years old. We won the first prize, which was a five dollar gold piece. It was a five-dollar coin, but of gold! That was the money we used to settle ourselves in San Antonio.

The first thing we did was rent a little house, and then we bought some chairs, some old chairs, . . . and we went down to the Market Plaza—where the Mercado is now. It was called the Plaza del Zacate. . . .

There were a lot of groups in the Plaza, but they were all men. We were women; we were the only women singers: my mother, my sisters and I. We were also the only group that was a family. The rest were strictly male trios or duets . . . with their guitars . . . singing . . . making their living like us. Only a lot of those groups didn't get too much business. There were . . . more than ten groups there all spread out through the open area of the Plaza. And they'd just be hanging around there playing dice at the tables; waiting for someone to turn up. There was an entrance through the middle of the Plaza where cars could come inside and stop at the edge of the tables where the hot food was sold. . . . As soon as a car would enter, everybody, all the musicians, would run and crowd around to see.

"Can I sing for you? Me? Can I sing for you? Do you want to hear "La Adelita"? Can I sing "Rancho grande" for you?"

Well, times were hard, and those musicians all made their living the same way we did: just from what people would give them. Everybody was chasing after the *centavos* in those days.

Americans and Mexicans—everybody—would come down there to eat and listen to music. As for us, well, we couldn't run after the cars like the other singers. We would just be sitting in our little corner, waiting for the people to come to us. A man who had a corner spot, a place where he put up his table and sold his food, gave us permission to sit at the edge of his stand. We had our little chairs; unlike the other groups, we played sitting down. Anyone that wanted to listen to us had to come on over to our little corner; we didn't go chasing after them like the others. The cars would arrive, and the people would get out to hear us. They would form a little knot around us and listen to us sing, while the other groups would run around as best as they could.

My sister María would stand there with her little plate that we took along, and she would take it around, and she would call out: "Échale, échale." Some of the people would throw in pennies, two pennies, a nickel. . . . We would put together fifteen, twenty, twenty-five cents a day. We played every night; that was our daily income. We would start to play as soon as it began to get dark. Summer and winter, *la familia Mendoza* sang in the Plaza every night. . . .

In those years of the Depression, there wasn't any work, and we felt the effects in every way. People didn't have money to enjoy themselves with. We were in debt. Sometimes we had to go to the Welfare where they would help you out, give you something to eat. We would go there and sing so that they would give us something to eat, and they gave us food to take home. In those days, times were very hard. There wasn't any money; there wasn't anything. All the people were suffering. Times started to get better when President Roosevelt came in and the businesses opened back up and all that.

Also, after Repeal, when they started selling alcohol legally again, there was more work for musicians. There would be dances and *cantinas* and more places to go sing.

Then, since I had already tried out signing solo by myself, when I was alone, I learned some songs that I could perform solo. So after the whole group had sung one or two or three songs—since nobody knew us there, we were just like anybody else there—I took the guitar from Mamá and I started to sing some of the songs I had learned. We still didn't have a twelve string guitar yet; I just played that same old six string that we used to have. I did this for several nights. I did this *sin darme cuenta de nada,* without noticing anything special about it. I would sing a few songs like that, just by myself, and then the group would start back up again.

And then something happened. I think that someone had heard me sing by myself once before, and then he came down to the Plaza with some of his friends one night and told us, "Well, we want the *señorita* to sing us this song."

Of course! I grabbed the guitar and sang the song he had requested, and he gave me twenty-five cents. In those days twenty-five cents was a lot of money. And the nights passed by like this. And since I saw that they were asking me for songs, and that they were paying a quarter, well then, I started to learn more songs: *tangos, boleros, rancheras,* all kinds of songs.

I learned those songs in order to at least be able to earn more money. But not thinking—God knows—not thinking that I might want to stand out, or be a . . . star. I looked at it from the point of view that they were paying more. The night finally came that the group didn't play at all. I sang by myself the whole night, because everybody paid me a quarter for each song that I sang solo. That's how I started out there, and that's how the gentleman from the radio station discovered me.

His name was Manuel J. Cortez. He was the father of the man who used to own KCOR, the big Spanish-language radio station that we have now in San Antonio. Mr. Manuel J. Cortez was the gentleman who had the "Voz Latina," a half-hour radio program that was on the air in San Antonio back in those days. The show was broadcast from above the Texas Theater. The rest of the day the station had American programs. The "Voz Latina" came on at seven o'clock at night: it was on from seven to seven-thirty every evening.

So Mr. Manuel J. Cortez came down to the Plaza with his wife to eat dinner one night and heard me sing. That was when he told my mother that I had a very pretty voice and that I would be a big star if I went over to the radio station so they could hear me.

"Well, how much will they pay if she goes there?" Mamá asked him.

"No, no, they don't pay anything," he replied.

And Mamá told him that I couldn't go, because that was our livelihood there in the Plaza. "Well, in that case, if we were to go to the radio station, we would lose out," Mamá answered. "If we were to do that, what would we eat? This is our living here, and we live from one day to the next." . . .

Then Mr. Manuel J. Cortez said, "Look, Señora Mendoza, it will be good for you to let Señorita Mendoza go to the radio station. She will gain more popularity. Moreover, for you all that sing here, well, it will be good for you, too. And I promise that it won't take very long. I'll take her over there and bring her right back. It won't take more than ten or fifteen minutes, you won't lose that much time."

And it was true, the station wasn't far away, it was just nearby. And I said to my mom, "I want to go, *Mamacita,* why don't you let me? Let's go . . . what'll we lose?"

What I wanted was to go and sing on the radio. Well, in the end my mother told him: "Well, it's all right, we'll go."

The next day Señor Cortez came very early, picked us up, and took me over to the radio station. He took Mamá and me over to KABC where I sang, and then I went back to the Plaza just as if nothing had happened. That first night I went, I only sang two songs—that was all—but I felt very happy when I finally got to the station and was able to sing on the radio. Two or three days later the gentleman came back.

"Mrs. Mendoza, I've had so many telephone calls! With just that one day on the radio"—because all of San Antonio listened to that program—"I'm getting tired of answering the phone. They're wearing me out. People are calling and saying that they want to listen to Miss Mendoza again. They want to hear that voice."

"I'm very sorry, but the day we went to the station we lost out on earning some money, and this is our living," Mamá told him.

"Well, what if I can get her an advertising sponsor that will pay her to go and sing?" he replied. "A business that will pay her for the time?"

"Well," she said, "if it's like that, yes, she can go, but no other way."

Well, he got it. He went and got me an advertisement for a tonic that was very popular in those years: Tónico Ferro-Vitamina. He got it from a Mr. García, who said that he liked my voice. Mr. García said, "I'll pay, I'll sponsor her program.

Mr. García gave me three dollars and fifty cents a week. Well, with that three-fifty, we felt like millionaires. Now at least we could be sure of paying the rent. Because to get the rent together, which was one dollar and twenty five cents a week, we had to play . . . two days. We had to play Saturday and Sunday to put together the rent. And sometimes we didn't even get it together. Now with three-fifty, we had the rent for sure.

When Mr. García started paying me that three-fifty a week, I had to sing on the "Voz Latina" for Ferro-Vitamina every night. I would only sing about two or three songs a night, though. The show was only half an hour long, and there were a lot of advertisements and announcements that took up a lot of the time, but I sang every night. And then Mr. Cortez got to thinking, and he said, "It shames me that Lydia Mendoza should be singing in the Plaza del Zacate. I'm going to take her out of there."

"Well, that's impossible. This is our living," Mamá told him.

"Well," he said, "I'm going to look for jobs for you . . . just as long as they're not here in the Plaza. I'm going to make Lydia Mendoza into a big star, and it's not right that she should be singing there in the Plaza del Zacate."

And he got us Friday, Saturday and Sunday in the restaurants . . . one hour in one, another hour in another . . . and like that until he got us out of the Plaza completely. The jobs he got were for the whole group, for all of the family. I couldn't go to the Plaza anymore because he was resolutely against my continuing there. And my fame began from there. That was in 1932.

5. Eleanor Roosevelt Urges "Better Understanding and Cooperation of Both the White and Negro Races," 1936

It is a pleasure to be with you tonight to celebrate this twenty-fifth anniversary of the Urban League, because of the purpose for which the League was founded—better understanding and cooperation of both the white and Negro races in order that they may live better together and make this country a better place to live in.

Much that I am going to say tonight would apply with equal force to any of us living in this country. But our particular concern tonight is with one of the largest race groups in the country—the Negro race.

We have a great responsibility here in the United States because we offer the best example that exists perhaps today throughout the world, of the fact that if different races know each other they may live peacefully together. On the whole, we in this country live peacefully together though we have many different races making up the citizenry of the United States. The fact that we have achieved as much as we have in understanding of each other is no reason for feeling that our situation and our relationship are so perfect that we need not concern ourselves about making them better. In fact we know that many grave injustices are done throughout our land to people who are citizens and who have an equal right under the laws of our country, but who are handicapped because of their race. I feel strongly that in order to wipe out these inequalities and injustices, we must all of us work together; but naturally those who suffer the injustices are most sensitive of them, and are therefore bearing the brunt of carrying through whatever plans are made to wipe out undesirable conditions.

Therefore in talking to you tonight, I would like to urge first of all that you concentrate your effort on obtaining better opportunities for education for the Negro

Eleanor Roosevelt, "The Negro and Social Change," a speech before the National Urban League. Published in *Opportunity,* January 1936. Reprinted by kind permission of Nancy Roosevelt Ireland.

people throughout the country. You *must* be able to understand the economic condition and the changes which are coming, not only in our own country, but throughout the world, and this, without better education than the great majority of Negro people have an *opportunity* to obtain today, is not possible. And without an improvement which will allow better work and better understanding, it will be difficult to remove the handicaps under which some of you suffer.

I marvel frequently at the patience with which those who work for the removal of bad conditions face their many disappointments. And I would like to pay tribute tonight to the many leaders amongst the colored people, whom I know and admire and respect. If they are apt at times to be discouraged and downhearted, I can only offer them as consolation, the knowledge that all of us who have worked in the past, and are still working for economic and social betterment, have been through and will continue to go through many periods of disappointment. But as we look back over the years, I have come to realize that what seemed to be slow and halting advances in the aggregate make quite a rapid march forward.

I believe, of course, that for our own good in this country, the Negro race as a whole must improve its standards of living, and become both economically and intellectually of higher calibre. The fact that the colored people, not only in the South, but in the North as well, have been economically at a low level has meant that they have also been physically and intellectually at a low level. Economic conditions are responsible for poor health in children. And the fact that tuberculosis and pneumonia and many other diseases have taken a heavier toll amongst our colored groups, can be attributed primarily to economic conditions. It is undoubtedly true that with an improvement in economic condition it will still be necessary not only to improve our educational conditions for children, but to pay special attention to adult education along the line of better living. For you cannot expect people to change overnight, when they have had poor conditions, and adjust themselves to all that we expect of people living as they *should* live today throughout our country. . . .

I think that we realize the desirability today of many social changes; but we also must realize that in making these changes and bridging the gap between the old life and the new, we have to accept the responsibility and assume the necessary burden of giving assistance to the people who have not had their fair opportunity in the past.

One thing I want to speak about tonight because I have had a number of people tell me that they felt the Government in its new efforts and programs was not always fair to the Negro race. And I want to say quite often, it is not the intention of those at the top, and as far as possible I hope that we may work together to eliminate any real injustice.

No right-thinking person in this country today who picks up a paper and reads that in some part of the country the people have not been willing to wait for the due processes of law, but have gone back to the rule of force, blind and unjust as force and fear usually are, can help but be ashamed that we have shown such a lack of faith in our own institutions. It is a horrible thing which grows out of weakness and fear, and not out of strength and courage; and the sooner we as a nation unite to stamp out any such action, the sooner and the better will we be able to face the other nations of the world and to uphold our real ideals here and abroad.

We have long held in this country that ability should be the criterion on which all people are judged. It seems to me that we must come to recognize this criterion in dealing with all human beings, and not place any limitations upon their achievements except such as may be imposed by their own character and intelligence.

This is what we work for as an ideal for the relationship that must exist between all the citizens of our country. There is no reason why all of the races in this country should not live together each of them giving from their particular gift something to the other, and contributing an example to the world of "peace on earth, good will toward men."

6. Eleanor Roosevelt Applauds the Repeal of the Married Persons Clause of the Economy Act, 1937

I am particularly happy today that the Senate has followed in the steps of the House and sent the bill repealing the so-called married persons clause of the Economy Act to the President for his signature. The bill has worked a great deal of hardship among government employees. It was probably very necessary as an emergency economy measure, but it is very satisfactory to feel Congress considers the emergency to be at an end.

The other day I received an appeal from an organization which has as its purpose the removal of any married woman whose husband earns enough to support her, from all employment. Who is to say when a man earns enough to support his family? Who is to know, except the individuals themselves what they need for daily living or what responsibilities are hidden from the public eye? There are few families indeed who do not have some members outside of their own immediate family who need assistance.

Added to this, who is to say whether a woman needs to work outside her own home for the food of her own soul? Many women can find all the work they need, all the joy they need and all the interest they need in life in their own homes and in the volunteer community activities of their environment. Because of this I have received many critical letters from women complaining that other women who did not need paid jobs were taking them. That they were working for luxuries and not for necessities, that men who had families to support were being kept out of jobs by these selfish and luxury-loving creatures.

I have investigated a good many cases and find that, on the whole, the love of work is not so great. Those who are gainfully employed are usually working because of some real need. There are a few, however, who work because something in them craves the particular kind of work which they are doing, or an inner urge drives them to work at a job. They are not entirely satisfied with work in the home.

This does not mean they are not good mothers and housekeepers. But they need some other stimulus in life. Frequently they provide work for other people. If they suddenly ceased their activities many other people might lose their jobs. As a rule, these women are the creative type.

It seems to me that the tradition of respect for work is so ingrained in this country that it is not surprising fathers have handed it down to their daughters as well as their sons. In the coming years, I wonder if we are not going to have more respect for women who work and give work to others than for women who sit at home with

---

Eleanor Roosevelt, "Married Persons Clause of the Economy Act," *My Day,* July 24, 1937. Reprinted by permission of United Features Syndicate, Inc.

many idle hours on their hands or fill their time with occupations which many indirectly provide work for others but which give them none of the satisfaction of real personal achievement.

7. P'ing Yu Publicizes a Shameful Demonstration of Racism Among White Clubwomen in California, 1937

Just when the world, the intelligent world, was getting nauseated with the patriotic purity purgings and the shameful spread of race hatred among the less democratic nations, and when we were vociferously praising the more enlightened ways of life and government in this country where we can still doff our hats to whomever we like, this had to happen to take the joy out of life. The "color line" once more became a point of issue and definitely caused a battle in the ranks of local American clubwomen when the constitution of the City and Country Federation of Women's Clubs was amended to bar non-Caucasian clubs from membership. Some of the much heated clubwomen, doing considerable chest-heaving, said that though they would be willing to work for "colored women," they wished—oh, so ardently—to reserve the right to choose their own club friends, and so on, ad nauseum.

It's just this high and mighty "holier than thou" attitude of "working for" and not "working with" people that makes this world so divided in spirit. I am sorry for the Federation. It had a wonderful chance, in this cosmopolitan San Francisco, to make world history for the cause of international peace and good will, but that's gone with the wind.

I don't like living alone, so I think I shall join the Commonwealth Club. Its members are talking of an Asia House where they can expand their inter-racial contacts—with no constitutional amendment to restrict them! I doff my bonnet to Mrs. Richard Simons, Mrs. W. F. C. Zimmerman, Mrs. Letitia Farber and Mrs. S. S. Abrams, leaders in the losing battle. Thank goodness, I can still do that.

8. Louise Mitchell Denounces the "Slave Markets" Where Domestics Are Hired in New York City, 1940

Every morning, rain or shine, groups of women with brown paper bags or cheap suitcases stand on street corners in the Bronx and Brooklyn waiting for a chance to get some work. Sometimes there are 15, sometimes 30, some are old, many are young and most of them are Negro women waiting for employers to come to the street corner auction blocks to bargain for their labor.

They come as early as 7 in the morning, wait as late as four in the afternoon with the hope that they will make enough to buy supper when they go home. Some have spent their last nickel to get to the corner and are in desperate need. When the hour grows late, they sit on boxes if any are around. In the afternoon their labor is

P'ing Yu, "Color—Chafing to Clubwomen," *Chinese Digest* (March 1937): 10.

Louise Mitchell, "Slave Markets Typify Exploitation of Domestics," *The Daily Worker,* May 5, 1940. This document can also be found in Gerda Lerner, ed. *Black Women in White America: A Documentary History* (New York: Pantheon Books, 1972), 229–231.

worth only half as much as in the morning. If they are lucky, they get about 30 cents an hour scrubbing, cleaning, laundering, washing windows, waxing floors and wood-work all day long; in the afternoon, when most have already been employed, they are only worth the degrading sum of 20 cents an hour.

Once hired on the "slave market," the women often find after a day's back-breaking toil, that they worked longer than was arranged, got less than was promised, were forced to accept clothing instead of cash and were exploited beyond human endurance. Only the urgent need for money makes them submit to this routine daily.

Throughout the country, more than two million women are engaged in domestic work, the largest occupational group for women. About half are Negro women. . . .

Though many Negro women work for as little as two dollars a week and as long as 80 hours a week . . . they have no social security, no workmen's compensation, no old age security. . . .

The Women's Bureau in Washington points out that women take domestic work only as a last resort. Largely unprotected by law they find themselves at the mercy of an individual employer. Only two states, Wisconsin and Washington, have wage or hour legislation. But enforcement is very slack. . . .

The tradition of street corner markets is no new institution in this city. As far back as 1834, the statute books show, a place was set aside on city streets where those seeking work could meet with those who wanted workers. This exchange also functions for male workers. . . . At present markets flourish in the Bronx and Brooklyn where middle-class families live. However, this method of employment is also instituted in Greenwhich Village, Richmond and Queens. . . .

The prosperity of the nation can only be judged by the living standards of its most oppressed group. State legislatures must pass laws to protect the health and work of the domestic. A world of education is still needed both for employees and employers.

Many civic and social organizations are now working toward improving conditions of domestics. Outstanding among these is the Bronx Citizens Committee for Improvement of Domestic Employees. The YWCA and many women's clubs are interested in the problem. Mayor LaGuardia . . . must be forced to end these horrible conditions of auction block hiring with the most equitable solution for the most oppressed section of the working class—Negro women.

◆ *E S S A Y S*

Elaine S. Abelson explores America's response to a sudden and sharp increase in home-lessness among women during the Great Depression. Focusing on New York City, she stresses the inability of the public to see that many women wage earners could not claim support from their families in hard times. In an era of economic crisis, women workers' relative independence from the family left them highly susceptible to homelessness; the public imagined, however, that women workers remained the lifelong dependents of men. Andrea Tone, of the Georgia Institute of Technology, explores women's role as consumers, emphasizing their vulnerability in the marketplace. Desperate to achieve some degree of reproductive control, yet unable to obtain reliable contraceptives legally, female consumers purchased unregulated commercial products that had been proven neither safe nor efficacious.

Women and Homelessness in the Great Depression, 1930–1934

ELAINE S. ABELSON

Historical memory is short and we have forgotten (if we ever knew) that homelessness has been a recurrent problem in the United States. Although both the severity and visibility of homelessness have fluctuated in the past three hundred years, only with the back-to-back depressions of the 1870s and 1890s did the modern understanding of homelessness emerge in conjunction with industrial capitalism and urban growth, economic cycles, wage dependency, immigration, and unemployment. The homeless man—the tramp, the hobo, the vagrant—became, alternately, the embodiment of rugged American individualism and a metaphor for social disorder. In the twentieth century, Skid Row, too, presented a male model; and prior to the depression of the 1930s, the Salvation Army and a few private charities combined with public sources of relief to provide whatever minimal care was necessary in Bowery districts across the country.

How do women fit into this picture? Uneasily. Poverty is gendered in specific ways at different times, and although long-term unemployment produced severe hardship for everyone, women and men have had diverse experiences. While stories of dissolute females and the unfortunate poor had wide currency in both the nineteenth and twentieth centuries, the female drifter remained an anomaly. Women, unlike men, have never been fully detached from family, domestic life, and a quasi-dependent role. Whatever the reality of their individual situations, women have been bound to the home by ideology, moral strictures, and idealized notions about motherhood and the family.

This article interrogates a new form of homelessness that appeared suddenly with the onset of the Great Depression. It examines the experience and representation of homeless urban women from the early months of 1930, when the depression began to have a visible economic and social impact in U.S. cities, through 1934 when New Deal programs and funding, particularly the Federal Emergency Relief Act (FERA) of May 1933, broke with the old tradition of poor laws and, for the first time, extended home relief to "unattached" women and men. I locate this homelessness not among the chronically dispossessed but among women who, while white and nominally middle class, lost jobs, savings, and often their homes and were cast into a particular narrative framework called the "New Poor." . . .

Women constituted more than 25 percent of the total labor force in the United States in the 1930s—over ten million women were working out of the home at the beginning of the decade, and over three million of them were married. They lost jobs at a higher rate than did men in the early years of the collapse, were often unable to find other sources of income, and were routinely discriminated against in public employment. Women's increasingly prominent yet largely unrecognized role in the workforce by 1930 is the key to understanding both their homelessness and the

Elaine S. Abelson, "'Women Who Have No Men to Work for Them': Gender and Homelessness in the Great Depression, 1930–1934," *Feminist Studies* 29, no. 1 (Spring, 2003): 105–123. © 2003 by Feminist Studies, Inc.

lack of initial concern by emergency work and relief organizations on the local and national level.

Unlike most histories of the Great Depression, which either focus primarily on Franklin D. Roosevelt and New Deal social policy or take radical politics, ethnic accommodation, and labor unrest as their lead, this article is engaged with issues raised by historians of women who have assessed the gendered character of public policy, welfare reform, and the assumptions behind the family wage. But even in this literature, homeless women have been treated only incidentally. Whether in scholarly or popular renditions of the Great Depression, homelessness has been understood narrowly as the displaced men who thronged the urban centers or the travail of the hundreds of thousands of transients—individuals and entire families—who, forced from their homes, moved restlessly across the country seeking work or relief.

This essay challenges the silences by posing three sets of questions that together suggest a different historiographic approach. First, what were the conditions that led to the surge in female homelessness between 1930 and 1934? Second, what were the factors that determined representations of the homeless population and shaped social policy? Was it the huge disparity in numbers between homeless men and women? Was it the negative social consequences of male versus female unemployment? Or was it the cultural lag between old myths and new realities—the ingrained, common understanding that defined the problem of unemployment as male? Third, how did large cities, particularly New York City, view the homeless population. What gendered decisions did officials make? How and to what extent did unconscious motivations and entrenched gender ideology work together to become crucial elements of both representation and public policy? Exploring these questions illuminates the constant intersections and crossovers between structural changes and cultural processes and underscores the interplay of forces that fed into the official silence about the homeless woman.

The situation of Belle Jones provides a typical scenario of the new dimensions and representations of female white-collar homelessness. The subject of one segment of a six-part series entitled "The Forgotten Woman," which appeared in the *New York World-Telegram* in October 1933, Belle was reported to be "one of the uncounted thousands of jobless/homeless women in New York" who came to the attention of the relief authorities only when she became severely depressed and required hospitalization. "She slipped back this week into the dream state of childhood," a psychiatrist explained to reporters, "and the amazing thing is that there are not more." This self-supporting "normal girl" had lost her white-collar job and the apartment she shared with three other young women and was unable to find any work after the Emergency Work Bureau ran out of money in the summer of 1932 and laid off thousands from made-work projects. Belle, who was described as "a proud girl who kept her chin up," lived off the charity of relatives for a while and then doubled up with a series of friends, but, with overcrowding and an exhaustion of resources, she was ultimately "tossed into the street" along with thousands of other women and men.

Writing about the dire situation of this new class of "business girls," reporters and social work professionals used similar language. As the trajectory from joblessness to homelessness became part of a familiar narrative, portrayals of women appear in starkly contradictory terms. On the one hand their positive individual, fiercely "American" qualities stand out; "their courage in the main is dauntless," read one welfare report. They are "sturdy," "proud," "plucky," "able to take it on the chin." On the other hand, they are cast as patients, traumatized by the overwhelming shock of events and primary clients for therapeutic intervention. Seemingly unwilling to ask for help even in desperate situations, many of these women "disintegrate mentally and emotionally," as did Belle Jones.

In a long article on homelessness entitled "30,000 Women Seen in Need of Winter Shelter," the *New York Herald Tribune* used the nervous breakdown of a young typist who went months without work to demonstrate the heavy toll of economic uncertainty "on the nervous systems of its victims." A study made for the Emergency Unemployment Relief Committee in New York City found that 18 percent of the women who applied to the Central Registration Bureau for the Homeless (CRB) were "near breakdown from worry." "To the woman accustomed to a home and financial security," the CRB director told relief investigators, "destitution is a serious mental hazard which is not made easier by the institutional life." Responding in fear and panic to a once-unimaginable situation, neither these women nor those who observed them could assimilate the crisis into any existing frame of reference.

Men were similarly traumatized by the economic collapse and reluctant to appear helpless, but their mental state only rarely became a public issue. Representations of the unemployed man, particularly the white-collar worker, were generally optimistic, pointing not to a state of panic or the deterioration of the human spirit, but to a strong sense of individual responsibility and determination to provide for his family, even if it ultimately meant accepting relief. Men may have been shamed by their new dependency, but for social welfare agencies homeless men were a management problem; they were numbers. Women became gender issues above all. . . .

In spite of obvious contradictions, the homeless woman was cast into a conventional narrative framework: young, single, female in peril. Her whiteness was an unquestioned category. The metaphor of the "white collar" symbolized the deserving Protestant middle class and was of overriding concern. The Salvation Army referred repeatedly to a white-collar problem and was careful to respect the privacy of the "shy, proud, new poor." So conscious was the Army about the combined impact of joblessness and homelessness on this new clientele, which was "suffering inarticulately because of unfamiliarity with their present condition," that it appointed a confidential counselor to deal with them. The Travelers' Aid Society spoke of "higher types" who needed financial aid to get them on their feet and counseling to mend their broken spirits; even the Welfare Council of New York City planned for the future needs of a "new class of impoverished women." . . .

The category "New Poor" was constructed within a context of race and gentility which conspicuously excluded the working poor and racial minorities—particularly African Americans, Puerto Ricans, and Mexicans.

Contrary to popular images of homeless women, statistical data present a more varied picture. In most northern cities, the majority of these women *were* white if not exactly middle class, but in such cities as New Orleans and Chicago, many, at times 30 to 40 percent in the early 1930s, were African American. And even in New York and other northeastern cities where the Black population hovered below 5 percent, formal if not legal racial codes governed most areas of business, social life, and the patchwork of relief and charity organizations. In the Philadelphia Public Employment Office in 1932 and 1933, 68 percent of job orders for women specified

"Whites Only," and many Black working women, particularly waitresses and domestics, found themselves replaced by desperate white women willing to take steep wage cuts in order to get or keep a job.

In New York City, the vast majority of unemployed Black women were marginalized in separate unemployment offices in Harlem and immobilized by deep-seated racial and sexual stereotyping in the labor market. They could get work only sporadically and then as domestics under the most exploitative conditions and for wages that were insufficient even to maintain a single person. Black churches and church-related institutions, traditional sources of relief and support networks in the community, were overwhelmed, and although the municipal shelter had to accept everyone, racism was the norm in shelters across the city. The Welfare Council singled out Catholic and African American women as being particularly difficult to place. Just how many homeless women in New York City were African American is not known, but the economic situation in Harlem was bleak prior to the depression, and the number of Black women lacking shelter in the early 1930s was undoubtedly substantial. If homeless women as a group were not readily visible, African American women were almost wholly invisible to the mostly white investigators.

Given the lack of data, its fragmentary and uneven character, and the different categories used from city to city, it is difficult to construct a coherent picture of the newly homeless woman during the Great Depression. As economic conditions rapidly deteriorated, a lack of knowledge and publicity about the desperate situation of a growing number of women was the norm, even as the numbers of women needing such basic necessities as food and shelter climbed from month to month. There were common elements, however, that enable us to locate these women in certain sectors of the economy. In the earliest years of the depression, 1930 and 1931, homeless women were likely to have been factory and service workers, domestics, garment workers, waitresses, and beauticians. But by the winters of 1931 and 1932, the second and third years of the depression, loss of a job was no longer a strictly blue-collar phenomenon. By 1932 white-collar and educated women—those who were accustomed "to regular employment and stable domicile"—had become the faces of the "New Poor," and a good number of them were in shelters.

More than half of the women in the various surveys had never married; the others not living with husbands were divorced, deserted, separated, or claimed to be widowed. A great many seemed to have had dependent parents and siblings, a few had children, but most were thought to be single and unattached. All the women had been unemployed for long months, some for a year or more, had used up whatever savings and insurance they may have had, and could no longer call upon their informal networks of assistance. The executive director of the Jewish Welfare Society of Philadelphia, Dorothy Kahn, testified to a Senate committee investigating unemployment relief in late 1931 that "neighborliness has been stretched not only beyond its capacity but beyond the limits of human endurance." Without resources, with eligibility for even emergency home relief restricted to families with dependent children until 1934, and racial discrimination widespread, homelessness was the inevitable outcome for many women. "Having an address is a luxury just now," an unemployed college woman told a social worker in 1932.

Even in the 1920s, when the self-supporting woman symbolized emancipation, her wages were too low in most instances to carry her over an extended period of idleness. Many of the reports on the dire economic situation in the following decade focused on the "surprising fact" that a large percentage of the women had been financially independent and living on their own prior to the depression. . . . The *Milwaukee Journal* estimated that more than 60 percent of the "non-family" women who came to the attention of relief authorities in that city had been self-supporting in 1929. In New York City, this group was said to account for over 85 percent. "Girls who usually work in the stores, offices, and factories" were out of work and increasingly without resources according to one reliable report. Unfortunately, "coming to the attention of relief authorities" did not mean that these women had recourse to welfare; on the contrary, until FERA was funded in 1934 little relief, public or private, was available to women (or men) who were located outside of recognized family units.

No one actually knew the extent of the crisis. In testimony to a Senate committee in July 1932, William Hodson, director of the Welfare Council in New York City, stated flatly that "no satisfactory estimates are available." That same year the director of the CRB conceded that "the Bureau's numbers were fragmentary, not even approximately accurate." After three winters of deepening economic crisis, private welfare agencies across the country admitted that only a small percentage of homeless women were known, although rough estimates suggest that women constituted about 10 percent of the urban homeless population. . . .

From time to time, a journalist would try to force people to "see" the new social reality. Surveying the situation in December 1932, a *New York Times* reporter moved beyond numerical abstractions and looked for "Jane Doe, Lone Woman" in a number of cities. He confirmed the paradox of her physical presence and her near invisibility. And this subjective "invisibility" was the crux of the problem. Local welfare agencies recognized something extraordinary was going on, as did the reporter, but it was easy for women to escape attention, he concluded, because "surveys revealing the plight of unemployed men have passed her by." The *Times* article estimated that in Washington, D.C., alone 10,000 women, unemployed and often homeless, were hidden "behind the ranks of hungry men." Women in the most dire straits were slow to seek assistance, city authorities claimed, preferring to "drift along" and "suffer in silence" rather than endure the public shame of asking for charity. . . . Meridel Le Sueur, . . . [w]riting for the *American Mercury* magazine in 1934, . . . described women who "starved slowly in furnished rooms. They sold their furniture, their clothes, and then their bodies." . . .

In a May 1933 article in the *New Republic,* journalist Emily Hahn attempted to historicize explanatory categories, to move beyond the limitations of a sex-gender system that began and ended with women's traditional domestic identity, and to analyze the new structure of social and family relations. "She is a new factor," Hahn explained. "In the past before she and her kind were emancipated she would have been someone's poor relation, doing the dull jobs around the house, and in hard times entitled to whatever protection her people could give. Now she is a has-been with the memory of past success to render her less malleable, less easily placed, and more alone." A month earlier, the YWCA publication, *The Woman's Press,* had echoed Hahn's theme almost word for word. "It is still difficult for the average person to comprehend how completely changed is the situation . . . [from] when the family roof tree was sufficiently spacious to accommodate those of the family who needed help and shelter. Today home is often a two or three room city apartment and the 'unattached' aunt or cousin must shift for herself." Or, as Le Sueur says simply, "Their families are gone. They are alone now." . . .

The imagined, nurturant world of pre-industrial domestic harmony was sadly out of date. In the first place, there is abundant evidence of severe pressure on families and of family breakdown. Second, unlike previous economic depressions, people this time around, with the exception of many African Americans, were often without rural roots. For some women, home protection had already failed. Often, a family connection was weak, there was no family to fall back upon, or a family could not maintain itself—over-burdened budgets and over-crowded households could not be stretched indefinitely. Many older women, women over thirty-five or forty, who were "always girls until they lost their jobs," had few options; discriminated against because of age and no longer allowed to make an economic contribution, they often had no place in the family unit and, consequently, no place to call home.

This, then, was the tension: Living outside of conventional family networks, unattached women had moved from the chimney corner to center stage, but categories of female representation remained frozen. In the face of overwhelming economic crisis, the "new woman" of the 1920s easily slipped out of sight. The new construction of reality rarely included gender as a significant factor and thus had a negligible impact on public awareness of the situation of women. Both defined and delimited by the ideology of family, home, and the private sphere, women, ironically, were ignored when that sphere was threatened or lost. . . .

Photography has been a powerful and subjective medium in our reading of this period. In the South and Midwest, Resettlement and Farm Security Administration (FSA) photographs of desperately poor families on drought-ruined farms or on the road dominate the iconography; in the North we have images of men—men selling apples, camping out in "tin cities" and Hoovervilles, working in public parks, and standing in long lines seeking work, food, shelter, or relief. Unlike the often searing FSA photographs, no one captured the trauma of urban women; their representation is almost non-existent. I found a single image of a woman selling apples in 1930, but almost no visual evidence of women in those two symbolic spatial locations of the period—breadlines and shantytowns. The twin problems of urban poverty and homelessness are framed as male; men without jobs and a regular source of income were the key factor for gauging the level of economic distress and despair in the cities. We have created our history "from visible signs whose significance is taken for granted," and families in the South and men in the North dominate both the cultural landscape of collective memory and most contemporary interpretations.

The virtual absence of homeless urban women from the photographic record and most printed primary sources says a great deal about the conditions under which meaning is produced. These women are not objectively invisible, but then as now their voices are largely silent, and most sources contain only fragments about their situation. . . .

With or without an accurate assessment of the situation, authorities in New York City and Chicago were forced by sheer numbers to acknowledge the existence of a large group of women who had lost their homes and to respond to their need for shelter. In October 1932, the Emergency Unemployment Relief Committee warned that a tragedy of major proportions was imminent in New York—demands for shelter for unattached women were estimated to be 500 percent over 1931, and, the Relief Committee predicted, the city would be called upon to house 30,000 women during the coming winter. Relief in New York, the director admitted, was on a "disaster basis."

How did the city handle the huge numbers of women needing basic shelter? The confidential *Report on the Municipal Lodging House of New York City* may be instructive here. Published by the Welfare Council in April 1932, the report documented the numbers of women and men given food and shelter by New York City at selected times during the previous year. . . .

With a capacity of 155 beds and six cribs, the women's division of the Municipal Lodging House logged over 56,000 "beds" during 1932, the third full year of the depression. And this number does not begin to reflect the need for public shelter for impoverished women in New York City. The Salvation Army recorded over 19,000 "female relief beds" at two locations during 1935—when demand had lessened to some degree. These published figures are unreliable, however, because restrictions based upon race and religion prohibited many referrals and discouraged women from seeking help. Uncounted numbers of women avoided public shelters if at all possible, sleeping in parks (which were deemed unsafe) and riding the subways at night (referred to on the street as "the old 5-cent lodging"). Not unlike the situation in the 1980s, many women patched together temporary solutions and never appeared in any census.

Beyond raw quantitative data, the report on the Municipal Lodging House concentrated on the twin issues of institutional organization and gender, particularly on the fixing of sexual boundaries. The entire second floor of the six story building was given over to women and children; they slept there and received their meals there. Deeming it "undesirable to feed women and children in public," Lodging House administrators admitted them at a separate entrance "on the far side of the building" and sent them "directly upstairs." The Salvation Army was equally concerned with gender respectability and shielded the newly-poor woman from the public gaze. At its emergency food stations and shelters, men stood on lines that stretched down the street, while women and children either waited indoors and out of sight for food and beds or were fed at separate locations.

Ironically, it was the very absence of women from the lengthy shelter and breadlines that obscured public understanding, reinforcing the assumption that women were not genuinely needy and that the economic catastrophe was a particularly male problem. Not publicly hungry, not conspicuous on the streets, and not a mainstay of the mainstream press, the destitute female was not looked for and only sporadically seen. Her invisibility was assured by a deadly combination of an entrenched ideology, public policy, and seemingly gender-based choices.

In the absence of representation to build upon, people saw only what was in front of them and what they thought it natural to see. . . . People did not see these women because they did not expect to see them; they had not learned to see them, and in complicated ways they did not want to see them. In no other period of economic crisis had so many women been marginally self-supporting and living on their own, outside the "protection" of family. Yet, the cultural expectation that women were ensconced in a stable domestic environment continued to shape perception even in the face of new realities—the loss of jobs and income and even homes. . . .

Women may have constituted more than 25 percent of the total labor force in the United States in 1930, but neither labor unions, male workers, nor any branch of government recognized women as permanent members of the labor force, and many fully employed women defined themselves as "homemakers," outside the sphere of wage work.

No matter how they interpreted their individual work lives, by 1930 the large number of women workers reflected ongoing changes in the economy and challenged entrenched gender norms. Arguments about the propriety of women, particularly married women, taking jobs away from "family men" raged during the depression. In part a reflection of the social anxieties that usually accompany perceived or actual changes in women's activities, but in part a complex mixture of legitimate fear for the security of the male breadwinners' position in a collapsing economy, these arguments created a chorus of support for what historian Lois Scharf describes as a movement to "put the women back into the home." Scharf points out that bitter rivalries between unemployed single and married women were not uncommon even though many married women workers were in fact heads of households. Some women had no man in the house, while others had disabled husbands as well as children and other family members dependent upon them. "The living depends on me," a desperate woman wrote of a sick husband and three children in August of 1933.

"The Forgotten Man" may have been a memorable image, emblematic of the devastation of the depression, but in letters to highly placed people in Washington such as Eleanor Roosevelt; Frances Perkins, the Secretary of Labor; and Harry Hopkins, director of FERA, women made it clear that they were neither passive nor victims, but they were needy. In their insistence on recognition and jobs and places to live for "The Forgotten Woman," they made tangible demands on the state. One desperate woman from Cleveland, Ohio, had been unemployed for over two years and had "no home and no friends"; she pleaded for some direction. Another described the deplorable condition of the single women of Chicago, who "are roaming the streets wondering where they are going to get the price of a meal, and how they are going to pay their room rent. . . . Do we all have to starve to death . . . in order to get a job?" the writer wondered. A Georgia woman asked, "What can be done for the woman to whom unemployment means life and necessities . . . women who have no men to work for them or [are the] sole support of others." A middle-aged widow who had been unemployed for twenty-seven weeks concluded simply, women "must live as well." Homeless or on the cusp of homelessness, the letter writers pleaded for someone to acknowledge that their needs were genuine and their losses real. . . .

Gender ideology and economic crisis went hand-in-hand. No matter the reality of women's increasing social independence, workforce participation, and prominence in political life, the assumption that women lived or should live in families as dependents of men lingered as an unacknowledged component of public discourse and revealed the gender politics embedded in social policy. Homeless women were stigmatized and often appeared immobilized by a sex-gender system that enshrined family and the male breadwinner role and rendered them publicly invisible. . . .

Although cities and states varied widely in their response to poverty, the twin problems of joblessness and providing relief had been traditionally a local and often a private responsibility in the United States. . . .

Under the Hoover administration, the federal government maintained its traditional hands-off policy with respect to most forms of social welfare, depending upon voluntary action and local communities to deal with what optimists predicted was a short-term crisis. No municipality was prepared for the magnitude of need. Although New York City was prohibited by its charter from providing general out-door relief, in 1930 the police department distributed emergency grocery orders, clothing, and even some rent vouchers to legal residents with dependent children. Private donations, including "voluntary" deductions of 1 percent from the monthly pay checks of teachers and municipal employees, were supposed to make up for inadequate city funds. When economic conditions deteriorated rapidly during what welfare agencies commonly referred to as "the disaster winter" of 1930-1931, and unemployment and real privation became a mass problem rather than an individual one, the New York State legislature, prodded by the city, passed the Wicks, or Temporary Emergency Relief Act (TERA), in late 1931. A model for the time, TERA was to provide both home relief and work projects to "eligible categories" of needy people. With funding inadequate, appropriations sporadic, and racism endemic, the categories were interpreted narrowly.

Single people were ineligible for home relief. Recognizing that "there would not be enough work for all of the persons in need," TERA administrators instituted a triage system; adults without legal dependents were placed on the bottom rungs on the "order of worker preference" and in the equation of need. One social worker explained, "the door just isn't wide enough to let in all who come to it," or, as Meridel Le Sueur commented, "it is hard for a lone woman to get much attention from the charities."

This lack of a safety net for specific groups was characteristic of welfare policy prior to 1934. Organized to aid needy families with dependent children, neither private relief organizations nor city agencies were prepared for the woman who seemed to exist outside of a normative family structure and had no one from whom she could claim support or protection. It seems as if two strands come together to structure our vision of these women. Not only are they not "publicly hungry," but there are so many impoverished groups ahead of them that they are virtually not in the queue. Public policy responds to magnitude and pressure, and in a relative sense homeless women provided neither. Prior to the Great Depression the homeless woman was not a category even recognized by social work professionals—she was no one's client. In the midst of an extended economic crisis, she was simply "a non-family woman." According to Mary Simkhovitch, director of New York City's Greenwich House, she was "a discard" whose individual needs seemed inconsequential in the face of other, more demanding priorities. . . .

The Great Depression had a profound and devastating impact on people's lives, yet throughout the decade public debate about the crisis was often treated as if it were a problem that men alone confronted. In this rendering the male body was indeed privileged. Not only were women's needs marginal to discussions of jobless-ness and lack of shelter, but the representational silence surrounding the unattached, often homeless women was marked. Women appear in fragments. . . . If seeing is the origin of knowing, women as a group were occasionally watched but not always seen in the early years of the depression. Traditionally the providers, the breadwinners, and heads of nuclear families, men were the focus.

The failure to see the homeless woman, however, rests on a more complex dynamic: expectations were inseparable from available ideologies and a sense of the social order—the certainty of how women and men should live and act, how they should be, and where they should be. This ideal social order included clear lines of racial and gender difference and enshrined the family as the quintessential social institution. Because it reinscribed more traditional social relations, in a period of crisis it was resistant to change and precluded serious consideration of the "non-family" woman. . . .

The implications of this invisibility for public policy and for feminist analysis are contradictory. In the economic devastation of the 1930s, the focus of policy was helping men get back to work. Singling out homeless women was a sympathetic but fleeting and ineffective response that ignored those who were neither white nor white collar. Today, homeless women are highly visible and often stigmatized. Women's poverty is a complex state, and although a myriad of government programs attempt to keep people housed, there are more women homeless in New York City today than there were five years ago. What feminist analysis needs to consider is just how the deconstruction of gender can work to enable policy makers to make decisions that will broaden the definition of work and create an environment in which humane political choices contribute to women's economic and social well-being.

Women, Birth Control, and the Marketplace in the 1930s

ANDREA TONE

In 1933, readers of *McCall's* probably noticed the following advertisement for Lysol feminine hygiene in the magazine's July issue:

> The most frequent eternal triangle:
> A HUSBAND . . . A WIFE . . . and her FEARS
> Fewer marriages would flounder around in a maze of misunderstanding and unhappiness if more wives knew and practiced regular marriage hygiene. Without it, some minor physical irregularity plants in a woman's mind the fear of a major crisis. Let so devastating a fear recur again and again, and the most gracious wife turns into a nerve-ridden, irritable travesty of herself.

Hope for the vexed woman was at hand, however. In fact, it was as close as the neighborhood store. Women who invested their faith and dollars in Lysol, the ad promised, would find in its use the perfect panacea for their marital woes. Feminine hygiene would contribute to "a woman's sense of fastidiousness" while freeing her from habitual fears of pregnancy. Used regularly, Lysol would ensure "health and harmony . . . throughout her married life."

The *McCall's* ad, one of hundreds of birth control ads published in women's magazines in the 1930s, reflects the rapid growth of the contraceptive industry in the United States during the Depression. Birth control has always been a matter of practical interest to women and men. By the early 1930s, despite long-standing legal restrictions and an overall decline in consumer purchasing power, it had also

Excerpted from Andrea Tone, "Contraceptive Consumers: Gender and the Political Economy of Birth Control in the 1930s," *Journal of Social History* 29, no. 3 (Spring 1996): 485–506. Reprinted by permission.

become a profitable industry. Capitalizing on Americans' desire to limit family size in an era of economic hardship, pharmaceutical firms, rubber manufacturers, mail-order houses, and fly-by-night peddlers launched a successful campaign to persuade women and men to eschew natural methods for commercial devices whose efficacy could be "scientifically proven." In 1938, with the industry's annual sales exceeding $250 million, *Fortune* pronounced birth control one of the most prosperous new businesses of the decade. . . .

It was during the Depression that the structure of the modern contraceptive market emerged. Depression-era manufacturers were the first to create a mass market for contraceptives in the United States. Through successful advertising they heightened demand for commercial birth control while building a permanent consumer base that facilitated the industry's subsequent expansion. Significantly, this consumer constituency was almost exclusively female. Condoms, the most popular commercial contraceptive before the Depression, generated record sales in the 1930s. But it was profits from female contraceptives—sales of which outnumbered those of condoms five to one by the late 1930s—that fuelled the industry's prodigious growth. Then, as now, women were the nation's leading contraceptive consumers.

An important feature distinguished the birth-control market of the 1930s from that of today, however: its illegality. Federal and state laws dating from the 1870s proscribed the inter-state distribution and sale of contraceptives. Although by the 1920s the scope of these restrictions had been modified by court interpretations permitting physicians to supply contraceptive information and devices in several states, the American Medical Association's ban on medically dispensed contraceptive advice remained intact. Neither legal restrictions nor medical disapproval thwarted the industry's ascent, however. Instead, they merely pushed the industry underground, beyond regulatory reach.

Contraceptive manufacturers in the 1930s exploited this vacuum to their advantage, retailing devices that were often useless and/or dangerous in a manner that kept the birth-control business on the right side of the law. The industry thrived within a grey market characterized by the sale of contraceptives under legal euphemisms. Manufacturers sold a wide array of items, including vaginal jellies, douche powders and liquids, suppositories, and foaming tablets as "feminine hygiene," an innocuous-sounding term coined by advertisers in the 1920s. Publicly, manufacturers claimed that feminine hygiene products were sold solely to enhance vaginal cleanliness. Consumers, literally deconstructing advertising text, knew better. Obliquely encoded in feminine hygiene ads and product packaging were indicators of the product's *real* purpose; references to "protection," "security," or "dependability" earmarked purported contraceptive properties.

Tragically, linguistic clues could not protect individuals from product adulteration or marketing fraud. Because neither the government nor the medical establishment condoned lay use of commercial contraceptives, consumers possessed no reliable information with which to evaluate the veracity of a product's claim. The bootleg status of the birth control racket left contraceptive consumers in a legal lurch. If an advertised product's implied claims to contraceptive attributes failed, they had no acceptable means of recourse. . . .

When Congress enacted the Comstock Act in 1873, a new nadir in reproductive *Lowest point* rights had arrived. The anti-obscenity law, the result of the relentless campaigning of its namesake, purity crusader Anthony Comstock, proscribed, among other things, the private or public dissemination of any

> book, pamphlet, paper, writing, advertisement, circular, print, picture, drawing, or other representation, figure, or image on or of paper or other material, or any cast, instrument, or other article of an immoral nature, or any drug or medicine, or any article whatever for the prevention of conception.

Passed after minimal debate, the Comstock Act had long-term repercussions. Following Congress's lead, most states enacted so-called "mini" Comstock acts which criminalized the circulation of contraceptive devices and information within state lines. Collectively, these restrictions demarcated the legal boundaries of permissible sexuality. Sexual intercourse rendered nonprocreative through the use of "unnatural"— that is, purchased—birth control was forbidden. Purity crusaders contended that if properly enforced, the Comstock and mini-Comstock acts would regulate birth control out of existence. Instead, they made birth control an increasingly dangerous, but no less popular, practice.

By the time state and federal legislatures had begun to abandon their laissez-faire attitude toward birth control, a fledgling contraceptive industry had already surfaced in the United States. Indeed, the two developments were integrally yoked: the initiative to regulate contraceptives arose out of the realization that there was a growing number to regulate. The nineteenth century witnessed the emergence of a contraceptive trade that sold for profit goods that had traditionally been prepared within the home. Douching powders and astringents, dissolving suppositories, and vaginal pessaries had supplemented male withdrawal and abstinence as mainstays of birth-control practice in pre-industrial America. . . . By the 1870s, condoms, douching syringes, douching solutions, vaginal sponges, and cervical caps could be purchased from mail-order houses, wholesale drug-supply houses, and pharmacies. Pessaries—traditionally used to support prolapsed uteruses but sold since the 1860s in closed-ring form as "womb veils"—could be obtained from sympathetic physicians. Thus when supporters of the Comstock Act decried the "nefarious and diabolical traffic" of "vile and immoral goods," they were identifying the inroads commercialized contraception had already made.

After the Comstock restrictions were passed, birth control continued to be sold, marketed for its therapeutic or cosmetic, rather than its contraceptive, value. Significantly, however, commercial contraceptive use became more closely associated with economic privilege. The clandestine nature of the market prompted many reputable firms—especially rubber manufacturers—to cease production altogether. Those that remained charged exorbitant prices for what was now illegal merchandise. For many wage-earning and immigrant families, the high price of contraceptives made them unaffordable. In addition, the suppression of birth-control information reduced the availability of published material on commercial and noncommercial techniques, as descriptions previously featured openly in pamphlets, books, journals, broadsides, and newspaper medical columns became harder to find. In effect, contraceptive information, like contraceptives themselves, became a privileged luxury.

Only in the 1930s were birth-control manufacturers able to create a mass market characterized by widespread access to commercial contraceptives. This market developed in response to a combination of important events. The birth-control movement of the 1910s and 1920s, spearheaded by Margaret Sanger, made birth control a household word (indeed, it was Sanger who introduced the term) and a topic of protracted debate and heated public discussion. Sanger insisted that women's sexual liberation and economic autonomy depended upon the availability of safe, inexpensive, and effective birth control. Sanger conducted speaking tours extolling the need for female contraception and published piercing indictments of "Comstockery" in her short-lived feminist newspaper *The Woman Rebel,* the *International Socialist Review,* and privately published pamphlets. In October 1916, she opened in Brooklyn the first birth-control clinic in the United States where she instructed neighborhood women on contraceptive techniques. The clinic's closure and Sanger's subsequent jail sentence only increased her notoriety. Sanger was not alone in her efforts to legitimize contraception, of course. The birth control movement was a collective struggle waged by hundreds of individuals and organizations, including IWW locals, women's Socialist groups, independent birth control leagues, and the liberal-minded National Birth Control League. But Sanger's single-minded devotion to the birth-control cause and her casual and frequent defiance of the law captured the media spotlight. In the 1910s it was Sanger, more than anyone else, who pushed contraception into the public arena and who, quite unintentionally, set the stage for the commercial exploitation that followed. . . .

By the end of the 1920s, state and federal legal restrictions on birth control remained operative and unchanged. Doctors-only bills which, had they been successful, would have permitted physicians to prescribe birth control, were introduced and defeated in New York, Connecticut, Pennsylvania, Massachusetts, New Jersey, and California. . . .

Notwithstanding these legislative setbacks, significant advances were made. Capitalizing on a 1918 New York Court of Appeals ruling that exempted physicians from prosecution for prescribing contraception necessary to "cure or prevent disease," Sanger opened the first permanent public birth-control clinic in the country in 1923. Within a year, the clinic had supplied contraceptive information to 1,208 women. By 1929, the number of medically supervised birth-control clinics across the country had increased to twenty-eight, almost all of which were affiliated with Sanger's parent organization, the American Birth Control League. Sanger was also responsible for facilitating the domestic manufacture of diaphragms and spermicidal jellies, clinics' contraception of choice. Frustrated by her inability to interest American manufacturers in the manufacture of female contraceptives, Sanger persuaded her second husband, J. Noah H. Slee, president of the Three-In-One Oil Company, to smuggle German-made Mensinga diaphragms and contraceptive jellies in oil drums across the border near the firm's Montreal plant. The smuggling system worked, but not well: the method was unreliable and legally risky, the products acquired too few in number and vastly overpriced. In 1925, with Sanger's urging, Slee financed the Holland-Rantos Company which began manufacturing spring-type diaphragms and lactic acid jelly for Sanger's clinics.

The cumulative effect of these activities—the sensationalist tactics, the organizational impetus, the failed legislative initiatives, and the expansion of public clinics—was to make Americans "birth control conscious." The popularization of the idea of birth control supplied the cultural backdrop to the economic birth-control boom of the 1930s. In the absence of government approval and regulation, the rising desire for contraceptives provided the perfect environment in which a bootleg trade could thrive. . . .

As the demand for birth control accelerated, the inability of existing institutions to satisfy it became apparent. By 1932, only 145 public clinics operated to service the contraceptive needs of the nation; twenty-seven states had no clinics at all. . . . Many women, spurred on by public attention to birth control but unable to secure the assistance needed to make informed contraception choices, took contraception—and their lives—into their own hands. . . .

That there was a commercial market to turn to was the result of liberalized legal restrictions that encouraged manufacturers to enter the birth-control trade. The structure of the birth-control industry of the early 1930s was markedly different from that which preceded it only a few years earlier. From 1925 to 1928, Holland-Rantos had enjoyed a monopoly on the manufacture of diaphragms and contraceptive jellies in the United States; other manufacturers expressed little interest in producing articles that might invoke government prosecution and whose market was confined to a handful of non-profit clinics. A 1930 decision, *Youngs Rubber Corporation, Inc., v. C.I. Lee & Co., et al*, lifted legal impediments to market entry. The *Youngs* case, in which the makers of Trojan condoms successfully sued a rival company for trademark infringement, forced the court to decide whether the contraceptive business was legal, and thus legitimately entitled to trademark protection. The court ruled that in so far as birth control had "other lawful purposes" besides contraception, it could be legally advertised, distributed, and sold as a non-contraceptive device. The outcome of a dispute between rival condom manufacturers, the *Youngs* decision left its most critical mark on the female contraceptive market. Companies that had previously avoided the birth control business quickly grasped the commercial opportunities afforded by the court's ruling. Provided that no reference to a product's contraceptive features appeared in product advertising or on product packaging, female contraceptives could now be legally sold—not only to the small number of birth control clinics in states where physician-prescribed birth control was legal, but to the consuming public nation-wide. Manufacturers realized that the court's legal latitude would not affect the diaphragm market, monopolized, as it was, by the medical profession. Because diaphragms required a physician's fitting, the number of buyers, given financial and regional obstacles to this type of medical consultation, would remain proportionately small. Jellies, suppositories, and foaming tablets, on the other hand, possessed untapped mass-market potential. They could be used without prior medical screening. And because chemical compounds were cheaper to mass produce than rubber diaphragms, they could be sold at a price more women could afford.

By 1938, only twelve years after Holland-Randos had launched the female contraceptive industry in the United States, at least four hundred other firms were competing in the lucrative market. The $212 million industry acquired most of its profits from the sale of jellies, suppositories, tablets, and antiseptic douching solutions retailed over the counter as feminine hygiene and bought principally by women. . . . The contraceptive industry thrived in the 1930s precisely because, while capitalizing on public discussions of birth control to which the medical community contributed, it operated outside customary medical channels. Manufacturers supplied women with something that clinics and private physicians did not: birth control that was conveniently located, discreetly obtained, and, most importantly, affordably priced. While the going rate for a diaphragm and a companion tube of jelly ranged from four to six dollars, a dollar purchased a dozen suppositories, ten foaming tablets, or, most alluring of all, up to three douching units, depending on the brand. Contraceptive manufacturers pledged, furthermore, that customer satisfaction would not be sacrificed on the altar of frugality. They reassured buyers that bargain-priced contraceptives were just as reliable as other methods. Without lay guides to help them identify the disjunction between advertising hyperbole and reality, women could hardly be faulted for taking the cheaper path. By the late 1930s, purchases of diaphragms accounted for less than one percent of total contraceptive sales.

Manufacturers' grandiose claims aside, not all contraceptives were created alike. The dangers and deficiencies of birth control products were well known in the health and hygiene community. Concerned pharmacists, physicians, and birth-control advocates routinely reviewed and condemned commercial preparations. Experts agreed, for instance, that vaginal suppositories, among the most frequently used contraceptives, were also among the least reliable. Suppositories typically consisted of boric acid and/or quinine, ingredients not recognized as effective spermicides. Melting point variability posed an added problem. Suppositories, usually based in cocoa butter or gelatin, were supposed to dissolve at room temperature. In practice, weather extremes and corresponding fluctuations in vaginal temperature made suppositories' diffusion, homogeneity, and contraceptive attributes unpredictable. . . .

But critics reserved their hardest comments for the most popular, affordable, and least reliable contraceptive of the day, the antiseptic douche. Noting the method's alarming failure rate—reported at the time to be as high as seventy percent—they condemned the technique as mechanically unsound and pharmacologically ineffectual. . . . Scores of douching preparations, while advertised as modern medical miracles, contained nothing more than water, cosmetic plant extracts, and table salt. On the other hand, many others, including the most popular brand, Lysol disinfectant, contained cresol (a distillate of coal and wood) or mercury chloride, either of which, when used in too high a concentration, caused severe inflammation, burning, and even death. Advertising downplayed the importance of dilution by drawing attention to antiseptics' gentleness and versatility; single ads praising Lysol's safety on "delicate female tissues" also encouraged the money-wise consumer to use the antiseptic as a gargle, nasal spray, or household cleaner. . . .

Reports on douche-related deaths and injuries and the general ineffectiveness of popular commercial contraceptive were widely discussed among concerned constituents of the health community. Sadly, however, these findings failed to prod the medical establishment as a united profession to take a resolute stand against the contraceptive scandal. Nor, regrettably, did blistering indictments of manufacturing fraud trickle down to the lay press where they might have enabled women to make informed contraceptive choices. The numerous women's magazines that published feminine hygiene ads—from *McCall's* to *Screen Romances* to the *Ladies' Home Journal*—were conspicuously silent about the safety and efficacy of the products they tacitly endorsed. The paucity of information impeded the development of informed consumerism. In advertising text and in many women's minds, the euphemism "feminine hygiene" continued to signify reliable contraception. For unscrupulous manufacturers eager to profit from this identification, feminine hygiene continued to be a convenient term invoked to sell products devoid of contraceptive value.

Manufacturers absolved themselves of responsibility by reminding critics that by the letter of the law, their products were not being sold as contraceptives. If women incurred injuries or became pregnant while using feminine hygiene for birth control, that was their fault, not manufacturers'. . . . Added to the growing list of groups unwilling to expose the hucksterism of the birth-control bonanza was the federal government. Neither the Food and Drug Administration (FDA) nor the Federal Trade Commission (FTC) was in a strong position to rally to consumers' aid. The FDA, authorized to take action only against product mislabelling, was powerless to suppress birth-control manufacturers' rhetorically veiled claims. The FTC, in turn, regulated advertising, but only when one company's claims were so egregious as to constitute an unfair business practice. The subterfuge prevalent in all feminine hygiene marketing campaigns, as well as a unanimous desire on manufacturers' part to eschew protracted scrutiny, kept the FTC at bay. Sadly for the growing pool of female contraceptive consumers, without regulation and reliable standards for discriminating among products, the only way to discern a product's safety and efficacy was through trial and error.

Clamoring for a larger share of the hygiene market, manufacturers did their utmost to ensure that their product would be one women would want to try. . . . Ads conveyed the message that ineffective contraception led not only to unwanted pregnancies, but also to illness, despair, and marital discord. Married women who ignored modern contraceptive methods were courting life-long misery. "Almost before the honeymoon ends," one ad warned, "many a young bride is plagued by foreboding. She pictures the early departure of youth and charm . . . sacrificed on the altar of marriage responsibilities." . . . "Many marriage failures," one advertisement asserted authoritatively, "can be traced directly to disquieting wifely fears." "Recurring again and again," marriage anxieties were "capable of changing the most angelic nature, of making it nervous, suspicious, irritable." "I leave it to you," the ad concluded, "is it easy for even the kindliest husband to live with a wife like that?"

Having divulged the ugly and myriad hazards of unwanted pregnancy while saddling women with the burden of its prevention, advertisements emphasized that peace of mind and marital happiness were conditions only the market could bestow. . . . As advertisements reminded prospective customers, however, not all feminine-hygiene products were the same. The contraceptive consumer had to be discriminating. Hoping both to increase general demand for hygiene products and to inculcate brand loyalty, manufacturers presented their product as the one most frequently endorsed for its efficacy and safety by medical professionals. Dispelling consumer doubts by invoking the approval of the scientific community was not an advertising technique unique to contraceptive merchandising—the same strategy was used in the 1930s to sell women laxatives, breakfast cereal, and mouth wash. What was exceptional about contraceptive advertising, however, was that the experts endorsing feminine hygiene were not men. Rather, they were female physicians whose innate understanding of the female condition permitted them to share their birth-control expertise "woman to woman."

The Lehn and Fink corporation used this technique to make Lysol disinfectant douche the leading feminine-hygiene product in the country. In a series of full-page advertisements entitled "Frank Talks by Eminent Women Physicians," stern-looking European female gynecologists urged "smart-thinking" women to entrust their health only to doctor-recommended Lysol disinfectant douches. "It amazes me," wrote Dr. Madeleine Lion, "a widely recognized gynaecologist of Paris,"

> in these modern days, to hear women confess their carelessness, their lack of positive information, in the so vital matter of feminine hygiene. They take almost anybody's word . . . a neighbor's, an afternoon bridge partner's . . . for the correct technique. . . . Surely in this question of correct marriage hygiene, the modern woman should accept only the facts of scientific research and medical experience. The woman who does demand such facts uses 'Lysol' faithfully in her ritual of personal antisepsis.

Contraceptive manufacturers' creation of a mass market in the 1930s depended not only upon effective advertising, but also on the availability of advertised goods. Prospective customers needed quick, convenient, and multiple access to contraceptives. Manufacturers made sure that they had it. . . . The department store became the leading distributor of female contraceptives in the 1930s. By the mid 1930s women could purchase feminine hygiene products at a number of national chains, including Woolworth, Kresge, McLellan, and W. T. Grant. Already fashioned as a feminized space, department stores established sequestered "personal hygiene" departments where women could shop in a dignified and discreet manner for contraceptives and other products related to female reproduction such as sanitary napkins and tampons. Stores emphasized the exclusively female environment of the personal hygiene department as the department's finest feature. The self-contained department was not only separated from the rest of the store where "uncontrollable factors . . . might make for . . . embarrassment," but it was staffed solely by saleswomen trained in the "delicate matter of giving confidential and intimate personal advice to their clients." As one store assured female readers in the local newspaper: "Our Personal Hygiene Department [Has] Lady Attendants on Duty at all Times." Female clerks, furthermore, were instructed to respect the private nature of the department's transactions; sensitive, knowledgeable, and tactful, they were "understanding wom[en] with whom you may discuss your most personal and intimate problems." . . .

Manufacturers reasoned that many prospective female customers would not buy feminine hygiene in a store. Many did not live close enough to one, while others, notwithstanding the store's discretion, might remain uncomfortable with the public nature of the exchange. To eliminate regional and psychological obstacles to birth-control buying, companies sold feminine hygiene to women directly in their homes. Selling contraceptives by mail was one such method. Mail-order catalogues, including those distributed by Sears, Roebuck and Montgomery Ward, offered a full line of female contraceptives; each catalogue contained legally-censored ads supplied by manufacturers. As a reward for bulk sales, mail-order houses received a discount from the companies whose products they sold. Other manufacturers bypassed jobbers and encouraged women to send their orders directly to the company. To eliminate the possibility of embarrassment, ads typically promised that the order would be delivered in "plain wrapper."

To create urban and working-class markets, dozens of firms hired door-to-door sales representatives to canvass urban districts. All representatives were women, a deliberate attempt on manufacturers' part to profit from the prudish marketing scheme that tried to convince women that, as one company put it, "There are some problems so intimate that it is embarrassing to talk them over with a doctor." At the

Dilex Institute of Feminine Hygiene, for example, five separate female crews, each headed by a female crew manager, combed the streets of New York. The cornerstone of the company's marketing scheme was an aggressive sales pitch delivered by saleswomen dressed as nurses. As *Fortune* discovered in an undercover investigation, however, the Dilex canvassers had no medical background. In fact, the only qualification required for employment was previous door-to-door sales experience. Despite their lack of credentials, newly hired saleswomen were instructed to assume the role of the medical professional, a tactic the Institute reasoned would gain customers' trust, respect, and dollars. "You say you're a nurse, see?" one new recruit was told, "That always gets you in." . . . The saleswoman then attempted to peddle the company's top-of-the-line contraceptive kit. For seven dollars, a woman could purchase jelly, a douching outfit, an antiseptic douche capsule, and—most alarming of all—a universal "one-size-fits-all" diaphragm. Poverty, women were told, was not an impediment to the personal happiness the company was selling: "luckily" for them, the Dilex kit was available on the installment plan.

Contraceptive companies' tactics paid off. By 1940, the size of the female contraceptive market was three times that of the 1935 market. The industry's unabated growth continued despite important changes in legal interpretation and medical attitudes in the late 1930s that might have reduced the industry's hold over American women. In 1936, the Supreme Court's *One Package* decision allowed physicians in every state to send and receive contraceptive devices and information. The following year, the American Medical Association reversed its long-standing ban on contraception, endorsing the right of a physician to prescribe birth control. The court's decision and the AMA's liberalized policy did not foster the immediate medicalization of birth control, a process that might have encouraged women to turn to the medical profession instead of the market for contraception. Indeed, in the short term, these sweeping changes proved remarkably inconsequential to the state of the industry. Many Americans could not afford the luxury of a personal physician, and only a minority lived close enough to the 357 public birth-control clinics operating in 1937 to avail themselves of clinic services. But of even more significance than medical barriers was manufacturers' enticing sales message. Companies' pledges to supply birth control that was affordable, immediate, and discreetly sold—either anonymously or in a completely feminized setting—continued to strike a responsive chord with American women. In addition, manufacturers promised what no lay guide could dispute: that what was bought from the market was as effective as doctor-prescribed methods. Out of pragmatic necessity and personal preference, most women worried about pregnancy prevention continued to obtain birth control from the contraceptive market. . . .

The commercialization of birth control in the 1930s illuminates the important but overlooked role of industry in shaping birth-control developments in the United States. Historians have typically framed birth-control history as a tale of doctors, lawmakers, and women's rights activists. The events of the 1930s suggest that we need to recast this story to include the agency of a new set of actors, birth-control manufacturers. The commercialization that manufacturers engendered at this time left an indelible imprint on the lives of ordinary women and men. It also revealed a world in which industry, gender, and reproduction were frequently and intimately intertwined.

F U R T H E R　　R E A D I N G

Blackwelder, Julia Kirk. *Women of the Depression: Caste and Culture in San Antonio, 1929–1939* (1984).

Boris, Eileen. *Home to Work: Motherhood and the Politics of Industrial Homework in the United States* (1994).

Clark, Claudia. *Radium Girls: Women and Industrial Health Reform, 1910–1935* (1997).

Cohen, Lizabeth. *Making a New Deal: Industrial Workers in Chicago, 1919–1939* (1990).

Cook, Blanche Weisen. *Eleanor Roosevelt: The Defining Years, 1933–1938* (2000).

———. *Eleanor Roosevelt, 1884–1933* (1992).

Faue, Elizabeth. *Community of Suffering and Struggle: Women, Men, and the Labor Movement in Minneapolis, 1915–1945* (1991).

Gordon, Linda. *Pitied But Not Entitled: Single Mothers and the History of Welfare* (1994).

Kessler-Harris, Alice. *In Pursuit of Equity: Women, Men, and the Quest for Economic Citizenship in 20th-Century America* (2001).

Melosh, Barbara. *Engendering Culture: Manhood and Womanhood in New Deal Public Art and Theater* (1991).

Mettler, Suzanne B. *Dividing Citizens: Gender and Federalism in New Deal Public Policy* (1998).

Mink, Gwendolyn. *The Wages of Motherhood: Inequality in the Welfare State, 1917–1942* (1995).

Orleck, Annelise. *Common Sense and a Little Fire: Women and Working-Class Politics in the United States, 1900–1965* (1995).

Roth, Darlene Rebecca. *Matronage: Patterns in Women's Organizations in Atlanta, Georgia, 1890–1940* (1994).

Ross, B. Joyce. "Mary McLeod Bethune and the National Youth Administration: A Case Study of Power Relationships," *Journal of Negro History* 60 (1975): 1–28.

Ruiz, Vicki. *From Out of the Shadows: Mexican Women in Twentieth-Century America* (1998).

———. *Cannery Women, Cannery Lives: Mexican Women, Unionization, and the California Food Processing Industry, 1930–1950* (1987).

Salmond, John A. *Miss Lucy of the CIO: The Life and Times of Lucy Randolph Mason, 1882–1959* (1988).

Santillan, Richard. "Midwestern Mexican American Women and the Struggle for Gender Equality: A Historical Overview, 1920s–1960s," *Perspectives in Mexican American Studies* 5 (1995): 79–119.

Scharf, Lois. *To Work or to Wed: Female Employment, Feminism, and the Great Depression* (1980).

Sicherman, Barbara. *Alice Hamilton: A Life in Letters* (1984).

Storrs, Landon R. Y. *Civilizing Capitalism: The National Consumers' League, Women's Activism, and Labor Standards in the New Deal Era* (2000).

Sullivan, Patricia. *Days of Hope: Race and Democracy in the New Deal Era* (1996).

Swain, Martha H. *Ellen S. Woodward: New Deal Advocate for Women* (1995).

Wandersee, Winifred. *Women's Work and Family Values, 1920–1940* (1981).

Ware, Susan. *Partner and I: Molly Dewson, Feminism, and New Deal Politics* (1987).

———. *Beyond Suffrage: Women in the New Deal* (1981).

Wolcott, Victoria W. *Remaking Respectability: African-American Women in Interwar Detroit* (2001).

CHAPTER
13

Women and the Disputed Meanings of Gender, Race, and Sexuality During World War II

Even as economic hardship continued in the United States and around the world, Americans confronted another crisis—the start of the Second World War in 1939. The war, rather than the New Deal, finally reinvigorated the industrial economy, prompted the creation of millions of new jobs, and brought an end to the Great Depression. However, the war also created new hardships and social instability for Americans, especially after the United States entered the war in response to the Japanese attack on Pearl Harbor in December 1941.

Historians have long been interested in analyzing the significance of World War II for women, noting that it opened new doors for many women, yet also aroused great anxiety and resistance to racial, gender, and sexual equality. For example, the nation's involvement in World War II produced a temporary surge in new job opportunities for women in munitions work, related war industries, government service, and the armed forces. Women's entry into fields of work previously closed to them was aided by government propaganda, which tried to convince Americans that the new jobs were a form of patriotic service and required many of the same skills used by women in their own homes and kitchens. Nevertheless, even at the height of the war, government officials, family experts, and pundits in the mass media debated the merits of women's access to nontraditional jobs, and looked forward to putting gender experimentation aside at the war's end. Often they expressed concern that women employed in positions or settings formerly reserved for men would abandon habits of nurture, modesty, and deference that were "natural" to their sex. What assumptions and fears were embedded in such concerns? What did women themselves think of wartime jobs? Did they work out of a sense of patriotism, out of a desire for the money, or for other reasons, and what did they want to do once the war ended? Were women treated fairly on the job, and did wartime employers try to comprehend or meet their needs? Did the expansion of job opportunities during the war benefit women of color as much as it did white women? These questions have been critical to the research agendas of historians.

The war also provoked a dramatic upsurge in anti-Japanese prejudice, leading the Roosevelt administration to order the removal of nearly one hundred twenty thousand Japanese Americans then living on the West Coast to hastily constructed inland concentration camps. Japanese American women who were interned in the "relocation centers" suffered a sharp loss of civil liberties and dramatic reversals in their material circumstances. They were also denied any opportunity to take high-paying jobs in the war industry. The political and material circumstances of internment have prompted historians to ask complex and probing questions with regard to Japanese American women: How did they perceive and respond to the hardships and indignities of wartime internment? Did forced relocation alter their lives and sense of self as women and Americans of Japanese heritage? Did intern-ment alter Japanese American girls' or women's status within their families?

◈ D O C U M E N T S

In 1940 Mary McLeod Bethune, a prominent black educator, civil rights activist, and director of the Negro Division of the National Youth Administration, wrote to President Roosevelt and urged him to turn to qualified black women for help in the war effort. Her letter appears as Document 1. In Document 2, a daycare worker in Utah reports on the difficulties faced by employed mothers in Utah. Document 3, drawn from an offi-cial history of the Women's Army Corp (WAC), describes women's impressive record of achievement in the Mediterranean and African theatre of war, as well as efforts to pre-vent or mitigate problems of health, discipline, and morale in the WAC. In Document 4, Jeanne Wakatsuki Houston describes (in an excerpt from her memoir) her experience as a ten-year-old schoolgirl interned in the Manzanar, California, relocation camp for Japanese Americans. Taken together, these documents show how women and the larger culture responded to the challenges and trials of the second world war.

1. Mary McLeod Bethune Urges President Roosevelt to Turn to Qualified Negro Women for Help in the War Effort, 1940

My dear Mr. President:

At a time like this, when the basic principles of democracy are being challenged at home and abroad, when racial and religious hatreds are being engendered, it is vitally important that the Negro, as a minority group in this nation, express anew his faith in your leadership and his unswerving adherence to a program of national de-fense adequate to insure the perpetuation of the principles of democracy. I approach you as one of a vast army of Negro women who recognize that we must face the dangers that confront us with a united patriotism.

We, as a race, have been fighting for a more equitable share of those opportuni-ties which are fundamental to every American citizen who would enjoy the economic

Mary McLeod Bethune, "Letter to President Franklin D. Roosevelt," June 4, 1940, in "Extension of Re-marks of Honorable Louis Ludlow of Indiana in the House of Representatives, Saturday, June 22, 1940," *Congressional Record*, Appendix, vol. 86, pt. 16, p. 4191.

and family security which a true democracy guarantees. Now we come as a group of loyal, self-sacrificing women who feel they have a right and a solemn duty to serve their nation.

In the ranks of Negro womanhood in America are to be found ability and capacity for leadership, for administrative as well as routine tasks, for the types of service so necessary in a program of national defense. These are citizens whose past records at home and in war service abroad, whose unquestioned loyalty to their country and its ideals, and whose sincere and enthusiastic desire to serve you and the nation indicate how deeply they are concerned that a more realistic American democracy, as visioned by those not blinded by racial prejudices, shall be maintained and perpetuated.

I offer my own services without reservation, and urge you, in the planning and work which lies ahead, to make such use of the services of qualified Negro women as will assure the thirteen and a half million Negroes in America that they, too, have earned the right to be numbered among the active forces who are working towards the protection of our democratic stronghold.

Faithfully yours,

Mary McLeod Bethune
President

2. Mrs. Norma Yerger Queen Reports on the Problems of Employed Mothers in Utah, 1944

My dear Mr. Hart [of the Office of War Information],

In reply to your questions about women working I should like to say that from March 1, 1943 to July 31, 1943 I was the Day Care Worker for our county and as such tried to learn the needs of day care for children of working mothers and to make possible the employment of women. Since then as child welfare worker for our county, I have continued to keep in touch with the need for women working, their problems & the attitudes of the community about it. We opened a day nursery for preschool children June 15th & closed Oct. 31st because it was never sufficiently used. It was more than well publicized but we finally decided that really not enough women with preschool children were employed to warrant keeping it open.

The people of this community all respect women who work regardless of the type of work. Women from the best families & many officers' wives work at our hospital. It is not at all uncommon to meet at evening parties in town women who work in the kitchens or offices of our hospital (Army–Bushnell–large general). The city mayor's wife too works there.

The church disapproves of women working who have small children. The church (L.D.S.) has a strong influence in our county.

For the canning season in our county men's & women's clubs & the church all recruited vigorously for women for the canneries. It was "the thing to do" to work so many hrs. a week at the canneries.

Mrs. Norma Yerger Queen to Clyde Hart, March 26, 1944, files of Correspondence Panels Division, Office of War Information, General Archives, National Archives, Washington, D.C.

I personally have encouraged officers' wives who have no children to get out and work. Those of us who have done so have been highly respected by the others and we have not lost social standing. In fact many of the social affairs are arranged at our convenience.

Some husbands do not approve of wives working & this has kept home some who do not have small children. Some of the women just do not wish to put forth the effort.

The financial incentive has been the strongest influence among most economic groups but especially among those families who were on relief for many years. Patriotic motivation is sometimes present but sometimes it really is a front for the financial one. A few women work to keep their minds from worrying about sons or husbands in the service.

In this county, the hospital is the chief employer of women. A few go to Ogden (20 miles away) to work in an arsenal, the depot, or the air field. When these Ogden plants first opened quite a few women started to work there, but the long commuting plus the labor at the plants plus their housework proved too much.

Many women thoroughly enjoy working & getting away from the home. They seem to get much more satisfaction out of it than out of housework or bringing up children. Those who quit have done so because of lack of good care for their children, or of inability to do the housework & the job.

We definitely found that having facilities for the care of children did not increase the number of women who worked. In 1942, the women kept saying they couldn't go to the canneries because they had no place to leave their children. In 1943 everyone knew we had the day nursery & private homes available & still there was difficulty in recruiting. One of the big reasons we got the nursery was to help in our canning & poultry seasons.

Most all jobs are secured thro our U.S.E.S. so I assume people know about it. It runs frequent stories in our local paper.

I am convinced that if women could work 4 days a week instead of 5½ or 6 that more could take jobs. I found it impossible to work 5½ days & do my housework but when I arranged for 4 days I could manage both. These days one has to do everything—one cannot buy services as formerly. For instance—laundry. I'm lucky. I can send out much of our laundry to the hospital but even so there is a goodly amount that must be done at home—all the ironing of summer dresses is very tiring. I even have to press my husband's trousers—a thing I never did in all my married life. The weekly housecleaning—shoe shining—all things we formerly had done by others. Now we also do home canning. I never in the 14 yrs. of my married life canned one 1 jar. Last summer I put up dozens of quarts per instructions of Uncle Sam. I'm only one among many who is now doing a lot of manual labor foreign to our usual custom. I just could not take on all that & an outside job too. It is no fun to eat out—you wait so long for service & the restaurants cannot be immaculately kept—therefore it is more pleasant & quicker to cook & eat at home even after a long day's work. I've talked with the personnel manager at the hospital & he agrees that fewer days a week would be better. The canneries finally took women for as little as 3 hrs. a day.

This is a farming area & many farm wives could not under any arrangements take a war job. They have too much to do at their farm jobs & many now have to go into the fields, run tractors & do other jobs formerly done by men. I marvel at all these women are able to do & feel very inadequate next to them. Some do work in Ogden or Brigham during the winter months.

Here is the difference between a man working & a woman as seen in our home—while I prepare the evening meal, my husband reads the evening paper. We then do the dishes together after which he reads his medical journal or cogitates over some lecture he is to give or some problem at his lab. I have to make up grocery lists, mend, straighten up a drawer, clean out the ice box, press clothes, put away anything strewn about the house, wash bric a brac, or do several of hundreds of small "woman's work is never done stuff." This consumes from 1 to 2 hrs. each evening after which I'm too weary to read any professional social work literature & think I'm lucky if I can keep up with the daily paper, Time Life or Reader's Digest. All this while my husband is relaxing & resting. When I worked full time, we tried doing the housecleaning together but it just didn't click. He is responsible for introducing penicillin into Bushnell & thus into the army & there were so many visiting brass hats & night conferences he couldn't give even one night a week to the house. Then came a mess of lectures at all kinds of medical meetings—he had to prepare those at home. I got so worn out it was either quit work or do it part time.

This has been a lot of personal experience but I'm sure we are no exception. I thought I was thro working in 1938. My husband urged me to help out for the war effort—he's all out for getting the war work done & he agreed to do his share of the housework. He is not lazy but he found we could not do it. I hope this personal experience will help to give you an idea of some of the problems.

3. The Challenges of Maintaining the Health, Discipline, and Morale of the Women's Army Corps in North Africa and the Mediterranean During World War II

Fifth Army Wacs

The [Mediterranean] theater's most unusual experiment in WAC employment was that of the Fifth Army Wacs, who claimed the honor of being the first Wacs to set foot in Italy, and in fact on the continent of Europe. Although never more than sixty women were involved, the experiment was considered to be potentially more important than its size would indicate, since it might determine the degree to which women could in future emergencies make up part of tactical units.

When the Fifth Army jumped off for Italy, the Wacs were not too far behind it, arriving in Caserta, via Naples, on 17 November 1943 under the command of 1st Lt. Cora M. Foster. The T/O called for 10 telephone operators, 7 clerks, 16 typists, 10 stenographers, 1 administrative clerk, and cooks and other cadre. In late January the unit split into forward and rear echelons, and the forward echelon, including all telephone operators and some stenographers, moved into the bivouac area near Presenzano. Here the women lived in pyramidal tents and worked chiefly in the Fifth Army's mobile switchboard trailer. By March the rear echelon was also in

Mattie E. Treadwell, *The Women's Army Corps,* Office of the Chief of Military History, Department of the Army (Washington, D.C.: GPO, 1953), 371–374.

tents near Sparanise. Unit records noted that the women "thrived on it; the sick call rate dropped way down."

For the rest of the Italian campaign, the units followed the Fifth Army up the peninsula, usually being located from twelve to thirty-five miles behind the front lines. From June to September the forward echelon's longest stay in any one place was five weeks, the average being two. The women lived in whatever billets were available—schools, factories, apartments, and chiefly tents. The forward section spent most of the winter of 1944–45 living in tents in the mountains above Florence. The women usually wore enlisted men's wool shirts, trousers, and combat boots, and carried only the few necessities that could be moved forward with them.

The unit proved unusually successful. It received Lt. Gen. Mark W. Clark's praise as well as being one of the few to receive both the Fifth Army Plaque with clasp, in 1944, and the Meritorious Service Unit Plaque in 1945. There were twenty-seven awards of the Bronze Star. The forward echelon included some of the most skilled telephone operators on the Continent, able in a matter of minutes to get through the complicated communications networks to the commanding officer of any unit sought by General Clark. The unit's morale and *esprit de corps* were perhaps the highest in the theater's WAC units. Its members wore the Fifth Army's green scarf. "They were," said Colonel Coleman, "Fifth Army first and Wacs second—perhaps the best-integrated unit in the theater."

The dangers of a combat area did not present any great problem in this case. During the last days in Anzio, air raids offered the nuisance of noise and falling shell fragments, but fortunately the area had just been vacated by a combat unit that had left adequate foxholes and dugouts. The Wacs were lucky in having no injuries, in spite of some close calls. During the advance up the peninsula, they were frequently within sound of long-range artillery, and almost always in an area of complete blackout, but required no guard except the usual one that patrolled the entire camp. Italian service troops ordinarily set up the WAC and Nurse Corps tents, and the Wacs took them down themselves, with the aid of two Italian laborers to load them on trucks.

In spite of the fatigue that developed from repeated moves, officers noted that the women "griped and complained less than soldiers in rear areas." Signal Corps units in rear areas were surprised, upon offering Wacs rotation to less exhausting conditions, to find that not one telephone operator would agree to quit the Fifth Army unit. . . .

The longer hours, the lack of privacy, the necessity for wearing clothing designed for men, all seemed to have little effect. Telephone operators seemed to be immune from the illness and tension experienced by women on identical shift work in more permanent companies a few score miles to the rear. Rude remarks from occasional unfriendly males, which caused a morale problem among Wacs elsewhere, were more or less brushed aside by women too busy to notice them and too assured of their own usefulness to doubt it. Under the circumstances, the staff director considered it a pity that all Wacs could not be employed in such units.

WAC advisers recommended that any such groups, for best success, be carefully selected. The best-suited type of woman was believed to be one whose physical stamina was average or better, who liked outdoor life, and who was well balanced mentally and emotionally. In a small isolated group, it was found fatal to include those with irritating habits and mannerisms—overtalkative, grouchy, or erratic. The ambitious or the highly qualified woman was also not a good choice, since top supervisory jobs in a tactical headquarters did not go to women, nor did they receive the high grades that those in rear areas did, many still being privates after two years. Emotional self-control was also vital, since the women were constantly surrounded by men, especially by combat troops coming back for a rest. Besides fending off advances, said the staff director, "The Wacs had to listen to the men and let them blow off steam, and this put an additional strain on the women's nerves." A mature woman was found preferable, especially one whose only interest was not the opposite sex. The lone company officer who accompanied each section had to be especially self-reliant and self-sufficient; her conduct necessarily had to be above reproach.

4. Jeanne Wakatsuki Houston, A Schoolgirl at Manzanar, 1940s

Once we settled into Block 28 that ache I'd felt since soon after we arrived at Manzanar subsided. It didn't entirely disappear, but it gradually submerged, as semblances of order returned and our pattern of life assumed its new design.

For one thing, [my older brother] Kiyo and I and all the other children finally had *a school.* During the first year, teachers had been volunteers; equipment had been makeshift; classes were scattered all over camp, in mess halls, recreation rooms, wherever we could be squeezed in. Now a teaching staff had been hired. Two blocks were turned into Manzanar High, and a third block of fifteen barracks was set up to house the elementary grades. We had blackboards, new desks, reference books, lab supplies. . . .

My days spent in classrooms are largely a blur now, as one merges into another. What I see clearly is the face of my fourth-grade teacher—a pleasant face, but completely invulnerable, it seemed to me at the time, with sharp, commanding eyes. She came from Kentucky. . . . A tall, heavyset spinster, about forty years old, she always wore a scarf on her head, tied beneath the chin, even during class, and she spoke with a slow, careful Appalachian accent. She was probably the best teacher I've ever had—strict, fair-minded, dedicated to her job. Because of her, when we finally returned to the outside world I was, academically at least, more than prepared to keep up with my peers. . . .

Outside of school we had a recreation program, with leaders hired by the War Relocation Authority. During the week they organized games and craft activities. On weekends we often took hikes beyond the fence. A series of picnic groups and camping sites had been built by internees—clearings, with tables, benches, and toilets. The first was about half a mile out, the farthest several miles into the Sierras. As restrictions gradually loosened, you could measure your liberty by how far they'd let you go—to Camp Three with a Caucasian, to Camp Three alone, to Camp Four with a Caucasian, to Camp Four alone. As fourth- and fifth-graders we usually hiked out

---

to Camp One, on the edge of Bair's Creek, where we could wade, collect rocks, and sit on the bank eating lunches the mess hall crew packed for us. . . .

In addition to the regular school sessions and the recreation program, classes of every kind were being offered all over camp: singing, acting, trumpet playing, tap-dancing, plus traditional Japanese arts like needlework, judo, and kendo. The first class I attended was in baton twirling, taught by a chubby girl about fourteen named Nancy. In the beginning I used a sawed-off broomstick with an old tennis ball stuck on one end. When it looked like I was going to keep at this, Mama ordered me one like Nancy's from the Sears, Roebuck catalogue. Nancy was a very good twirler and taught us younger kids all her tricks. For months I practiced, joined the baton club at school, and even entered contests. Since then I have often wondered what drew me to it at that age. I wonder, because of all the activities I tried out in camp, this was the one I stayed with, in fact returned to almost obsessively when I entered high school in southern California a few years later. By that time I was desperate to be "accepted," and baton twirling was one trick I could perform that was thoroughly, unmistakably American—putting on the boots and a dress crisscrossed with braid, spinning the silver stick and tossing it high to the tune of a John Philip Sousa march.

Even at ten, before I really knew what waited outside, the Japanese in me could not compete with that. It tried—in camp, and many times later, in one form or another. My visit to the old geisha who lived across the firebreak was a typical example of how those attempts turned out. She was offering lessons in the traditional dancing called *odori*. A lot of young girls studied this in order to take part in the big *obon* festival held every August, a festival honoring dead ancestors, asking them to bring good crops in the fall.

She was about seventy, a tiny, aristocratic-looking woman. She took students in her barracks cubicle, which was fitted out like a little Buddhist shrine, with tatami mats on the floor. She would kneel in her kimono and speak very softly in Japanese, while her young assistant would gracefully swing closed knees or bend her swan-like neck to the old geisha's instructions.

I sat across the room from her for an hour trying to follow what was going on. It was all a mystery. I had never learned the language. And this woman was so old, even her dialect was foreign to me. She seemed an occult figure, more spirit than human. When she bowed to me from her knees at the end of the hour, I rushed out of there, back to more familiar surroundings. . . .

Among my explorations during these months, there was one more, final venture into Catholicism. The Maryknoll chapel was just up the street now and easy to get to. I resumed my catechism. Once again I was listening with rapt terror to the lives of the saints and the martyrs, although that wasn't really what attracted me this time. I had found another kind of inspiration, had seen another way the church might make me into something quite extraordinary.

I had watched a girl my own age shining at the center of one of their elaborate ceremonies. It appealed to me tremendously. She happened to be an orphan, and I figured that if this much could befall an orphan, imagine how impressive *I* would look in such a role. . . .

This girl had already been baptized. What I witnessed was her confirmation. She was dressed like a bride, in a white gown, white lace hood, and sheer veil, walking toward the altar, down the aisle of that converted barracks. Watching her from the pew I was pierced with envy for the position she had gained. At the same time I was filled with awe and with a startled wonder at the notion that this girl, this orphan, could become such a queen.

A few days later I let it be known that I was going to be baptized into the church and confirmed as soon as the nuns thought I was ready. I announced this to the Sisters and they rejoiced. I announced it at home, and Papa exploded.

"No," he roared. "Absolutely not!"

I just stood there, stunned, too scared to speak.

"You're too young!"

I started to cry.

"How are you going to get married?" he shouted. "If you get baptized a Catholic, you have to marry a Catholic. No Japanese boys are in the Catholic church. You get baptized now, how are you going to find a good Japanese boy to marry?"

I ran to Mama, but she knew better than to argue with him about this. I ran to the chapel and told Sister Bernadette, and she came hurrying to the barracks. She and Papa had become pretty good friends over the months. Once every week or so she would visit, and while he sipped his apricot brandy they would talk about religion. But this time, when she came to the door and called *"Wakatsuki-san?"* he met her there shouting, "No! No baptism!"

She raised her eyebrows, trying to stare him down.

He rose to his full height, as if she, about the size of Mama, were the general of some invading army, and said, "Too young!"

"Old enough to know God!"

"Who knows anything of God at ten?"

This made her angry. At any other time they would have taken an hour hearing each other out. But now, when she opened her mouth to reply, his upheld flat palm stopped her. He was not going to argue. He wouldn't even let her past the door.

In exasperation she glared at him, then turned and walked away. I ran to my bunk, devastated, and wept, hating him. I was too ashamed to go back to catechism after that. I just hated Papa, for weeks, and dreamed of the white-gowned princess I might have become. Late afternoons, practicing my baton in the firebreak, angrily I would throw him into the air and watch him twirl, and catch him, and throw him high, again and again and again.

◈ *E S S A Y S*

Megan Taylor Shockley of Clemson University examines the response of working-class African American women to workplace discrimination in Detroit; she finds that they made strategic use of federal agencies and civil rights organizations to secure employment opportunities and defend new definitions of citizenship. Valerie Matsumoto of UCLA looks at the lives of Japanese American women during World War II. While the relocation camps tended to undermine family harmony, internment presented young women with new opportunities for work, travel, and education. The last essay, by Leisa D. Meyer of William and Mary College, investigates the challenges faced by Americans who supported women's inclusion in the military during World War II yet believed that female "soldiers" must uphold conventional notions of femininity and female sexual respectability.

African American Women, Citizenship, and Workplace Democracy During World War II

MEGAN TAYLOR SHOCKLEY

Historians have long noted that the context of Roosevelt's "V for Victory" campaign—victory for democracy abroad—presented new political possibilities for African Americans. Encouraged by black institutions such as the National Association for the Advancement of Colored People (NAACP) and black newspapers, African Americans fought for "Double V for Victory": victory over fascism abroad and racism at home. Although many historians have acknowledged the positive impact of World War II on the civil rights movement, they have largely ignored the effect of black women's activism on the redefinition of citizenship, focusing instead on black soldiers and workingmen. Often historians suggest that soldiers learning to understand equality in Europe, staging sit-ins on bases, and rioting against injustice in segregated camps redefined citizenship in the black community. These scholars assert that for black leaders, war duty equaled citizenship, and that returning veterans formed the vanguard of the civil rights movement as they demanded their constitutional rights in line with their obligation to defend the country.

Although these historians depict an important component of the civil rights movement, they obscure the actions of black women by equating military duty with citizenship. Clearly, African-American working women needed to use a different language in order to negotiate with local and federal governments about civil rights—and the designation of these women as potential labor for the war effort proved extremely useful in their fight for justice. In times of war, women often become vital to the operation of the home front. During World War II, African-American women became involved in gendered efforts to redefine citizenship because they had numerous chances to broaden their relationship with the government. As a result of new work opportunities, both paid and voluntary, for all women on the American home front, African-American women claimed their place at the forefront of the civil rights movement by demanding citizenship for themselves and their community based on their real and potential contributions to the war effort, which often included labor in essential industries. . . .

This study examines Detroit, a city representative of the heavily industrialized Midwest, in order to understand how northern racial structures both enhanced and inhibited African-American women's claims to citizenship. Detroit experienced a great in-migration of African Americans looking for work during World War II. Its black population grew 48 percent between 1940 and 1943, and the 1950 census reported 300,506 African Americans living in Detroit. During the war, they numbered 16 percent of the city's population. The mass mobilization for wartime industry affected the city's political and economic structures, as men were drafted and large numbers of women demanded jobs in war industries. . . .

Detroit's vibrant African-American community included women from all alks of life, and often women's attempts to reform society reflected their specific socioeconomic backgrounds. . . .

Megan Taylor Shockley, "Working for Democracy: Working Class African American Women, Citizenship, and Civil Rights in Detroit, 1940–1954." Originally published in the *Michigan Historical Review* 29:2 (Fall 2003): 125–157. Copyright © Central Michigan University. Reprinted by permission.

During the late 1920s and early 1930s many middle-class African-American women attempted to acquire jobs that would allow them to promote race-relations work and civil rights, and they attacked inequality more openly than they had during the Progressive Era. Their efforts in the 1930s contributed to the work promoted by the National Council of Negro Women (NCNW), which was formed in the mid-1920s to address African-American women's concerns, with a particular focus on employment opportunities.

Middle-class African-American women fought for the rights of all women to work in war factories in the 1940s. Often, to be sure, middle-class women failed to understand all of the issues facing women who took such jobs, but it is important to note that in Detroit clubwomen did support the labor unions, most notably the United Auto Workers (UAW). The UAW had a positive impact on hiring practices affecting black men in the 1930s; so black clubwomen understood well enough that because of its bargaining power and liberal national officers the union was one of the few institutions that could threaten to subvert the structural racism that existed within factories. . . . Perhaps because African-American clubwomen understood that black women trying to enter factories had so many more problems than black men, they became strong supporters of the union as an ally in the struggle for working-women's rights.

Although many African-American clubwomen in Detroit supported the unions and fought for the rights of factory workers, the language they used to define rights for women often suggested their lack of knowledge about job possibilities and the actual working conditions faced by working-class women. For example, the NCNW "sought the assistance" of workers in promoting responsible patriotism through maintaining standards of respectability. NCNW chapters across the country, including the one in Detroit, participated in the national "Can You Hold Your Job Campaign" in 1943. The NCNW directed this campaign at working women as an answer to employers' purported concerns about their women employees. In Detroit Jeanetta Welch Brown, executive secretary of the NCNW, informed Detroit Women's Club president Rosa Gragg that "some manufacturers have already said that they are just waiting for the time to let them [black women] go because of their conduct." The campaign, therefore, focused on making women aware of the fact that in order to keep their jobs, they must be "clean, courteous, punctual, and affable." . . .

Instead of focusing on better training, working with union representatives, and addressing other pressing issues faced by working women, . . . NCNW members wanted to teach proper dress and behavior, discourage absenteeism, and urge women to take advantage of self-improvement opportunities. To be fair, the women also tried to get employers to introduce new workers to their jobs properly so that they would do the best work possible. In order to get workers to attend the clinics, NCNW members circulated the following memo to working-class women:

> Wake Up! Your Job Is in Danger! Check up on—Your Personal Appearance: Do not offend others by being careless. Bathe frequently and insure against body odors. Dress neatly and sensibly. Be attractive! Your Behavior on the Job: Girls, be kind and not 'catty.' Lose that chip-off-of-your-shoulder. Avoid 'showing-off' and being loud and boisterous. It is better to be seen at your work station quietly doing your job than to be heard or seen all over the place. Your Attitude: It is important the way you feel about your—Employer: He has his problems, too. Be cooperative. Supervisor: He has a job to

do and you're hired to help him do it. Fellow-worker: Get along with the other workers on the job. Work with them, not against them. Your health: Eat, sleep, rest, and play sensibly. Avoid indulgence in anything. It lowers your efficiency. Your attendance: Get to work every working day and on time. Don't loaf on the job. Monday and the day after payday are not legal holidays.

Once war workers attended the clinic, NCNW sponsors required them to sign a pledge to uphold all of the tenets described in the pamphlet. Clearly, NCNW members did not have factory work experience; and in general, clubwomen's failure to understand some of the basic issues troubling working-class women led those women to being speaking for themselves during and immediately following World War II. . . .

Working-class women's demands in the 1930s and 1940s often focused on creating more opportunities in diverse occupational fields and demanding entitlements directly from government officials. . . . During the 1930s working-class African-American women formed relationships with federal government agencies to try to get both relief benefits and work. They became outspoken in their attempts to claim welfare and work rights, and they often wrote letters to President Roosevelt and Eleanor Roosevelt demanding redress for their grievances. Although direct negotiations with government agencies and unions began in the 1930s, this activity would increase tremendously in the 1940s. Women began to use unions extensively to address grievances in industries where they found employment, such as meatpacking in Chicago. Working-class African-American women showed their willingness to engage national organizations in a vocal attempt to gain equality in the job market. In addition, they proved much less likely than other women to try to conform to middle-class standards as they demanded help from federal institutions.

World War II posed specific challenges for African-American women. While white women made employment gains in industries during the war, only six hundred thousand of the seven million women in war industries were black. Only 18 percent of black women employed during the war worked in what the government considered essential wartime-production jobs. Black men gained jobs in the factories, partly because they had already established footholds in industries such as auto production prior to the war. White society's belief that black women were disreputable and oversexed created barriers in the work force when African-American women attempted to gain lucrative wartime jobs, because white women employees often refused to work in close proximity to black women. Some employers used the excuse that as long as white women could not or would not work with them, hiring black women would impede war production. Evelyn Scanlon, the representative for UAW Local 3 (Dodge Main Plant, Detroit), believed that she spoke for a majority of white women at the Women's Conference in February 1942. She objected to UAW Local 600's support of a desegregation resolution, claiming, "I don't think we should bring the problem of negro women into this meeting. I don't think we should consider bringing them into the shops—if we bring them in even in this crisis we'd always have them to contend with. And you know what that means—we'd be working right beside them, we'd be using the same rest rooms, etc. I'm against it." By mid-1943, Detroit's War Manpower Commission estimated that twenty-eight thousand black women were available for work, but most would only be hired as janitors, maids, or government inspectors. Faced with rejection by employers, many African-American women sought assistance from federal agencies and civil rights organizations in securing workplace opportunities and created a new definition of citizenship based on their potential importance as workers for victory as the basis for their claims. . . .

Fortunately, African-American women had access to new institutional structures that bolstered their negotiating power. President Franklin Roosevelt created the Fair Employment Practices Committee (FEPC) to investigate claims of unequal hiring practices after staving off a march on Washington threatened by A. Phillip Randolph, the noted leader of the Brotherhood of Sleeping Car Porters. Interestingly enough, elite black leaders denounced the idea of the march; it was a working-class group's actions that effected change, not pressure from the NAACP or other elite groups. Despite being wracked by bureaucratic problems—slow procedures and lack of enforcement power—the FEPC proved especially useful for African-American women. Although industries became increasingly willing to hire black men by 1942 as the worker shortage reached crisis levels nationwide, they remained steadfastly against employing African-American women. In fact, in 1942 the first FEPC probe in Detroit specifically addressed African-American women's complaints. According to a national newspaper, the women "were being refused employment even by those firms which employ colored men." The women pointed out the fact that these same industries sought out white women for employment, even as African-American women stood by the gates waiting to speak with employment officers. In addition to the UAW, the FEPC maintained a suboffice in Detroit, and the mayor created the Detroit Commission on Community Relations (DCCR) to investigate racial problems. Each of these institutions enabled African Americans to make claims against Detroit's white society. . . .

African-American workers in Detroit had the benefit of the UAW as well as the FEPC in their fight against discrimination. The UAW, a Congress of Industrial Organizations (CIO) affiliate, claimed to practice integration and provide representation for its black members. August Meier and Elliott Rudwick argue that the UAW worked hard to recruit African-American members, who were reluctant unionists as a result of their loyalty to the employers who hired them and because of the hostility of some union locals to integration. The UAW finally won over the black (and predominantly male) work force in the 1939–1941 period, and blacks had an ally in their fight against discrimination in hiring practices and on the factory floor. Moreover, in 1942 and 1943 Detroit's UAW officials worked with the city's NAACP chapter to recruit black factory workers. The growing presence both of African Americans and women in industry helped African-American women gain a foothold in the union; in fact, Lillian Hatcher and Gwendolyn Thomas, two African-American workers, moved up through the ranks from the factory floor to high positions within the UAW Women's Bureau. These women played important roles as investigators in many African-American women's cases.

It is important to note, however, that working-class African-American women in Detroit often had an uneasy relationship with the UAW. . . . Once they entered war factories . . . they often remained segregated from other workers and stuck in the worst jobs. African-American women had to fight to get better job assignments, but they did have the support of the UAW leadership against hate strikes that erupted when black women were upgraded. Not only were these women fighting their employers; they were also struggling against racist fellow workers. Despite union support for their claims to equal work and equal pay, however, black women still faced considerably more segregation and discrimination than did black men in the same Detroit factories.

Working-class women succeeded in gaining the attention and support of local civil rights organizations like the NAACP and the Urban League as well. During the 1930s the NAACP became a reluctant supporter of union activities, and by World War II the Detroit chapter was the largest in the country with twelve thousand members. By the 1940s the NAACP began to help African-American women in their fight for employment opportunities. In fact, many of Detroit's FEPC complaints came from the NAACP, where many African-American women went to secure help. Detroit's Urban League, which had established itself by the early 1920s as the most prominent institution for African Americans in the city, also became increasingly involved with African-American working-women's issues. The willingness of historically black institutions to help working-class women in their fight for jobs and equality suggests that the actions of these women had a significant impact on the policies of such groups. . . .

In Detroit women went to the NAACP in groups to complain about specific industries. These women must have understood that more complainants could get them more attention within the black community. They constructed legal affidavits with the help of the NAACP, which had always been active in litigation for equality and was very helpful as they filed lawsuits and filled out paperwork for the FEPC. The president of the NAACP, Gloster Current, claimed that many of the group's referrals came from women whose husbands were in the army, but who still could not secure wartime jobs. That these women were willing to call upon the government to compensate them for the sacrifices of their husbands is significant. Women used the gendered language of patriotism in order to demand that they also be allowed to show their own patriotism by working for the soldiers in the plants. . . .

After receiving complaints from numerous women about hiring practices, the NAACP determined to launch a mass protest against Detroit industries' treatment of black women. In April 1943 the NAACP led a call to action, claiming that "trained Negro women war workers are denied employment in most plants and in many where they are hired they are relegated to jobs of a status inferior to their training and skills, or given work so difficult that it was in direct violation of the labor code." The NAACP planned a mass rally that began with a parade down the main street of Detroit for several miles and ended with a demonstration in Cadillac Square. More than five thousand people demonstrated their support for working-class women's fight for jobs.

Although women complained about discrimination in many Detroit industries, a majority of the complaints cited the principal automobile manufacturers. This is not surprising, given the large number of manufacturers and suppliers in the city. Dorothy Simmons complained that she had logged 302 hours of aircraft-riveting training, but Murray Body Corporation's personnel directors turned her down because of her weight. Simmons claimed, however, that she had seen "larger" white women hired and that the firm had refused employment to countless other black women. Lillie Trim also had problems at Murray Body Corporation. She found that her 178 hours of riveting training could not secure her a job, but that white women with 64 hours of training or less had no trouble getting hired. The FEPC investigated both complaints, and Murray Body Corporation agreed to begin hiring black women in late 1942. Although there is no evidence that Simmons and Trim were among the women eventually hired at Murray, their appeals to the FEPC enabled other black women to secure jobs at the plant. . . .

African-American women did not rely solely on the federal government and the NAACP to secure employment; they also asked local unions for help. Although some UAW locals were unwilling to support employment opportunities for blacks, the national leaders were committed to integration. The UAW was most successful in fighting for the hiring of black women at Ford's River Rouge and Willow Run plants. In early 1942 the UAW supported African-American women when two hundred of their number stormed the employment offices of Ford's Willow Run plant after being refused entry at the hiring gate. This show of force and solidarity, the climax to a year of blatant employment discrimination at Ford, forced the company to start negotiating with the UAW to create some sort of program for hiring black women. . . .

In August 1942 the tension between the union and management became apparent as management . . . accused the UAW of being controlled by communists. Black women were actually beneficiaries of the power struggle between Ford and the UAW, however. The union was furious that Ford questioned its right to determine hiring practices and sponsored a massive demonstration at the River Rouge plant that jammed up the gates of the employment office. The flyer the union handed out reasserted the UAW's commitment to helping African-American women:

> We can no longer tolerate the Ford Motor Company's policy of discrimination against Negro women. We resent Harry Bennett's assertion that the Ford Motor Company is the only company giving the Negro a chance. Willis Ward, 'the Yes and No Man' of the Ford Motor Company relative to the Negro question, is a traitor to the cause of Better Labor and Race Relations among the Ford Workers. The segregated employment office set-up (all Negroes channeled through Ward's office and all white workers sent elsewhere) is a great and demoralizing factor. . . . *Mr. Ford, Negro women and men will and must play their rightful part in helping win this war.*

The UAW pressure tactics worked, and Ford started hiring a very small number of black women at the end of 1942. . . .

By 1943 working-class African-American women had managed to secure jobs in various war-production industries as well as in some nonessential businesses with the help of the FEPC and UAW. In Detroit the number of employed black women jumped from 14,451 in March 1940 to 46,750 in June 1944. In June 1942 fewer than thirty black women worked in war industries, but the Women's Bureau estimated that the number rose to fourteen thousand by November 1943. Fewer women took traditional domestic-service jobs, which is a clear indication that they received better pay in other industries. The Detroit Urban League observed that while the bulk of black women held jobs in nonessential industries, they simply refused to go back to domestic work "despite wages of $5.00 a day, carfare, meals, etc. . . . much to the consternation of former employers." As a result, the league started to look for nonservice jobs to fill its registry, which had always been inundated with requests for maids. The Women's Advisory Committee of the War Manpower Commission found that Detroit laundries suffered a 40 percent loss in their work force resulting from low wages and a 100 percent turnover every two months because their female employees found better pay elsewhere. In early 1943 the UAW conducted a survey of its plants and found that the increase in employment of black women was significant in many of Detroit's biggest war plants. Plants that hired very few black women in 1942 now employed more than one hundred. . . . Other plants, however, still refused to hire African-American women, and those plants remained a target of both the FEPC and the UAW throughout the war.

As African-American women fought to claim space on the factory floor, white women tried to maintain segregation on the assembly line and in restrooms and cafeterias. Strikes occurred when white women walked off production lines rather than share space with blacks. The UAW often found itself in a difficult position over this issue because it had to represent the interests of both its black and white employees. The union usually had to negotiate the deals that enabled black women to continue their work.

Hate strikes occurred quite frequently as white workers spontaneously walked off assembly lines when black women first entered the shop floor. In 1943 Chrysler and Packard were both wracked by a series of work stoppages until black women got the UAW to support their right to work. On February 12, Vera Sutton, Bernice Kirksey, and Pauline Johnson found themselves the victims of a spontaneous hate strike as they took their places as the first black female drill-press operators at Chrysler's Highland Park plant. When the white women walked, the company pulled the African-American women off the line and sent them back to training school. When the three women took their case to the UAW, the UAW called the FEPC, plant security, management, and an army representative to the plant. Ironically, when faced with the opposition both of the union and the government, the company that originally had shown reluctance to hire black women decided that it would support them in this instance. The FEPC reported that "management was going to stand firm on the issue of the Negro girls . . . under no circumstances would they be taken away from their machines . . . as that would be a licking for the company." With the company, the union, and the federal government on their side, the African-American women returned to their drill-press jobs. The Highland Park Packard plant erupted several weeks later when four black women joined the production line. Although the stoppages hurt plant production, the black women refused to leave. The UAW convinced Packard that the best way to solve the problem was to increase the number of black women workers so that the four original workers would not be such easy targets. Six weeks after the strike Packard had fifty black women on the assembly line, and the FEPC lauded the company's progressive policies. . . .

Although the unions and companies were supportive of the African-American women who became targets of white hatred, often the situations did not resolve themselves neatly when the protesting white women went back to work. African-American women had to remain on guard against hostile workers in one-on-one situations and in dealing with segregated facilities. Throughout their tenure in the wartime factories, African-American women fought to claim space as equal citizens and workers who had the right to fair treatment on the factory floor.

Often African-American women became involved in physical confrontations as a result of built-up tensions created by poor work environments and unfriendly coworkers. In most instances, although both black and white workers were responsible for the altercations, employers fired only the black women. The treatment of black women in these situations suggests that in confrontations with whites, blacks were labeled "provocateurs" and blamed for white retaliation. Companies tended to put the responsibility for maintaining amicable race relations on African Americans. A 1943 case illustrates the injustice many black women faced when companies accused them of causing problems. Lillian Garner found a white coworker at Murray Body Corporation eating her lunch. The woman offered her ten cents for the lunch, which offended Garner because it was worth much more than that. Garner refused the money. Georgiaphene Buford, Floysell Jones, and Effie Greer, all African-American coworkers, witnessed the exchange and returned to the assembly line with Garner. Although Garner thought that the situation had resolved itself, the white woman went to the shop steward to "straighten out" matters. She told the steward that she had offered Garner fifty cents for the lunch, at which point Garner called her a liar. Infuriated by the accusation, the white woman slapped Garner in the face. Garner did not retaliate physically. The white woman, a riveter, received only a four-day suspension because the company was short of riveters, but Garner, Buford, Jones, and Greer were fired two weeks later for "unsatisfactory work," although they had never received any unsatisfactory reports from their foremen.

These women refused to let the company treat them unfairly, however; they had fought hard for their jobs and were not willing to give them up without a pitched battle. Buford and Jones wrote to Eleanor Roosevelt, and all four women went to the NAACP, the FEPC, and UAW Local 2 to file grievances. In the subsequent investigation, the FEPC and the UAW discovered that although the women had received training as riveters, they had been dusting and painting car trunks for four and a half weeks, despite the company's riveter shortage. Often the women had nothing to do because the company refused to move them to all-white production lines. The UAW noted that Murray Body Corporation had laid off two other black women for "unsatisfactory work" before their six-week probationary period was up, ensuring the women would not have protection under seniority agreements. After the four women made their case to these powerful organizations, the groups pressured Murray Body Corporation to rehire them. All four were back at the plant by March. In this case, the women complained about their treatment after an altercation and uncovered a much deeper discrimination problem at the plant. They achieved success when the local union, the local chapter of a national civil rights group, and a federal agency joined forces and pressured the company to return their jobs.

Although tensions between black and white women gave employers an excuse to segregate bathrooms, lunchrooms, and even assembly lines, African-American women attempted to enforce the Diggs Civil Rights Law* by working hard for equal facilities in Detroit factories. Since the law banned any segregation in public areas, working-class women knew that they had a legal right to equal treatment in the factories, and they enlisted the aid of the FEPC and the UAW in order to change company segregation policies. Many women protested against segregated bathrooms. For example, while the 1943 Packard strike was in full swing, black women in the plant, with the help of the UAW, pressed the FEPC to abolish segregated

---

*The Michigan state legislature passed the Diggs Civil Rights Law in 1937, guaranteeing equal facilities to all state citizens.

bathrooms. The women were only allowed to use toilets "formerly condemned as unsanitary and fitted only for the use of males." Although local FEPC officials considered this to be a social problem and not one that they needed to investigate, the union disagreed. After negotiating with the company, the UAW managed to get separate facilities abolished. Given the fact that the FEPC's job was to examine all inequalities that affected employment, its failure to look beyond hiring practices and into the use of factory space threatened to hinder black women's opportunities to achieve equal treatment. The UAW stepped up to support black women, however, and in this case managed to help change Packard's segregation policy.

As late as 1945 African-American women workers complained about segregated facilities. An incident that year at the Chrysler-Highland Park plant changed the way both white and black inspectors ate lunch. Gladys Brown told the Detroit Commission on Community Relations that she and her friend faced continued discrimination at the plant. When the women, who were both government inspectors, tried to enter the cafeteria behind four white inspectors, the guard told all six that the cafeteria was for office workers, not inspectors, and denied all of them entry. Brown knew, however, that the four white women ate there regularly. The next day, when the four white women went alone to the cafeteria, the guard told them that they could eat after the regular lunch shift ended. When Brown and her friend asked their government representative Lieutenant Waters why they could not eat in the cafeteria, he told them that their race kept them out. They asked Waters whether he thought that was fair, especially since Brown's friend had a husband overseas. Brown stated that it hurt both of their feelings to see the white women laughing as the two had to go outside to the catering cart for lunch. Brown drew upon the discourse of gendered patriotic sacrifice—a husband given to war service—to support her right to be treated as an equal citizen. The commission notified the War Department, which told Waters to let Chrysler know that all inspectors were to be treated equally in the cafeteria, regardless of race. Rather than serve the black women, Chrysler denied service to all of the government inspectors.

Although African-American women in Detroit made significant gains in employment from 1943 to 1944, they were the first victims of industry slowdowns and demobilization. The Detroit Urban League found that three hundred thousand jobs had been eliminated from late 1944 to 1945 (production began to slow down in November 1944). As late as 1949 sixty-three thousand Detroit workers remained idle. African-American women's relatively late entry into factories placed them low on seniority lists, and they found it hard to get skilled mechanical work after they had been laid off. Moreover, all women faced layoffs before their male coworkers, and industries often overlooked seniority lists to hire men in fields that had "belonged" to male workers prior to World War II. In addition, some UAW locals failed to support women's grievances about seniority violations and unfair hiring practices, leaving African-American women with very few options when they tried to regain some of the jobs they had claimed during the wartime boom.

In addition to job displacement, working-class African-American women faced a more repressive atmosphere and restricted opportunities as a result of the government's move to the right and its subsequent red-baiting of liberal organizations. The fact that civil rights organizations and unions backpedaled on issues promoting working-class rights and racial equality hurt black women's chances of gaining institutional support for their fight to hold on to wartime gains.

African-American women nonetheless worked to retain their claims to full citizenship within the more restricted parameters of the postwar era. In addition to seeing the benefits of citizenship as access to education and the vote, decent housing, and welfare entitlements, they defined citizenship as equal access to employment and employee benefits, even as industries tried to deny black women these rights. Despite the hostility of employers and some unions, working-class African-American women in Detroit fought for seniority rights, rehires, and entry into new employment fields. They drew upon their rights as workers and contributors to industry, becoming activists for equal employment as they struggled to support themselves and their families. . . .

Often, working-class black women continued to use the same methods of activism they had relied on during wartime, as they called upon government agencies, black institutions, and unions to shore up their claims. In their fight for the rights of all citizens, they helped to form the vanguard of the civil rights movement by becoming activists for equality as they fought for jobs and dignity, demanding the same rights enjoyed by working-class white citizens.

Japanese American Women During World War II

VALERIE MATSUMOTO

The life here cannot be expressed. Sometimes, we are resigned to it, but when we see the barbed wire fences and the sentry tower with floodlights, it gives us a feeling of being prisoners in a "concentration camp." We try to be happy and yet oftentimes a gloominess does creep in. When I see the "I'm an American" editorial and write-ups, the "equality of race etc."—it seems to be mocking us in our faces. I just wonder if all the sacrifices and hard labor on [the] part of our parents has gone up to leave nothing to show for it?

—LETTER FROM SHIZUKO HORIUCHI,
POMONA ASSEMBLY CENTER, MAY 24, 1942

Thirty years after her relocation camp internment, another Nisei woman, the artist Miné Okubo, observed, "The impact of the evacuation is not on the material and the physical. It is something far deeper. It is the effect on the spirit." Describing the lives of Japanese American women during World War II and assessing the effects of the camp experience on the spirit are complex tasks: factors such as age, generation, personality, and family background interweave and preclude simple generalizations. In these relocation camps Japanese American women faced severe racism and traumatic family strain, but the experience also fostered changes in their lives: more leisure for older women, equal pay with men for working women, disintegration of traditional patterns of arranged marriages, and, ultimately, new opportunities for travel, work, and education for the younger women.

I will examine the lives of Japanese American women during the trying war years, focusing on the second generation—the Nisei—whose work and education were most affected. The Nisei women entered college and ventured into new areas

Valerie Matsumoto, "Japanese American Women During World War II," *Frontiers* 8 (1984): 6–14—with abridgements as approved by Valerie Matsumoto.

of work in unfamiliar regions of the country, sustained by fortitude, family ties, discipline, and humor. My understanding of their history derives from several collections of internees' letters, assembly center and relocation camp newspapers, census records, and taped oral history interviews that I conducted with eighty-four Nisei (second generation) and eleven Issei (first generation). Two-thirds of these interviews were with women. . . .

A century ago, male Japanese workers began to arrive on American shores, dreaming of making fortunes that would enable them to return to their homeland in triumph. For many, the fortune did not materialize and the shape of the dream changed: they developed stakes in small farms and businesses and, together with wives brought from Japan, established families and communities.

The majority of Japanese women—over 33,000 immigrants—entered the United States between 1908 and 1924. The "Gentlemen's Agreement" of 1908 restricted the entry of male Japanese laborers into the country but sanctioned the immigration of parents, wives, and children of laborers already residing in the United States. The Immigration Act of 1924 excluded Japanese immigration altogether.

Some Japanese women traveled to reunite with husbands; others journeyed to America as newlyweds with men who had returned to Japan to find wives. Still others came alone as picture brides to join Issei men who sought to avoid army conscription or excessive travel expenses; their family-arranged marriages deviated from social convention only by the absence of the groom from the *miai* (preliminary meeting of prospective spouses) and wedding ceremony. Once settled, these women confronted unfamiliar clothing, food, language, and customs as well as life with husbands who were, in many cases, strangers and often ten to fifteen years their seniors.

Most Issei women migrated to rural areas of the West. Some lived with their husbands in labor camps, which provided workers for the railroad industry, the lumber mills of the Pacific Northwest, and the Alaskan salmon canneries. They also farmed with their husbands as cash or share tenants, particularly in California where Japanese immigrant agriculture began to flourish. In urban areas, women worked as domestics or helped their husbands run small businesses such as laundries, bath houses, restaurants, pool halls, boarding houses, grocery stores, curio shops, bakeries, and plant nurseries. Except for the few who married well-to-do professionals or merchants, the majority of Issei women unceasingly toiled both inside and outside the home. They were always the first to rise in the morning and the last to go to bed at night.

The majority of the Issei's children, the Nisei, were born between 1910 and 1940. Both girls and boys were incorporated into the family economy early, especially those living on farms. They took care of their younger siblings, fed the farm animals, heated water for the *furo* (Japanese bath), and worked in the fields before and after school—hoeing weeds, irrigating, and driving tractors. Daughters helped with cooking and cleaning. In addition, all were expected to devote time to their studies: the Issei instilled in their children a deep respect for education and authority. They repeatedly admonished the Nisei not to bring disgrace upon the family or community and exhorted them to do their best in everything.

The Nisei grew up integrating both the Japanese ways of their parents and the mainstream customs of their non-Japanese friends and classmates—not always an easy process given the deeply rooted prejudice and discrimination they faced as a tiny, easily identified minority. Because of the wide age range among them and the diversity of their early experiences in various urban and rural areas, it is difficult to generalize about the Nisei. Most grew up speaking Japanese with their parents and English with their siblings, friends, and teachers. Regardless of whether they were Buddhist or Christian, they celebrated the New Year with traditional foods and visiting, as well as Christmas and Thanksgiving. Girls learned to knit, sew, and embroider, and some took lessons in *odori* (folk dancing). The Nisei, many of whom were adolescents during the 1940's, also listened to the *Hit Parade,* Jack Benny, and *Gangbusters* on the radio, learned the jitterbug, played kick-the-can and baseball, and read the same popular books and magazines as their non-Japanese peers.

The Issei were strict and not inclined to open displays of affection towards their children, but the Nisei were conscious of their parents' concern for them and for the family. This sense of family strength and responsibility helped to sustain the Issei and Nisei through years of economic hardship and discrimination: the West Coast anti-Japanese movement of the early 1920's, the Depression of the 1930's, and the most drastic ordeal—the chaotic uprooting of the World War II evacuation, internment, and resettlement. . . .

The bombing of Pearl Harbor on December 7, 1941, unleashed war between the United States and Japan and triggered a wave of hostility against Japanese Americans. On December 8, the financial resources of the Issei were frozen, and the Federal Bureau of Investigation began to seize Issei community leaders thought to be strongly pro-Japanese. Rumors spread that the Japanese in Hawaii had aided the attack on Pearl Harbor, fueling fears of "fifth column" activity on the West Coast. Politicians and the press clamored for restrictions against the Japanese Americans, and their economic competitors saw the chance to gain control of Japanese American farms and businesses.

Despite some official doubts and some differences of opinion among military heads regarding the necessity of removing Japanese Americans from the West Coast, in the end the opinions of civilian leaders and Lieutenant General John L. DeWitt—head of the Western Defense Command—of Assistant Secretary of War John McCloy and Secretary of War Henry Stimson prevailed. On February 19, 1942, President Franklin Delano Roosevelt signed Executive Order 9066, arbitrarily suspending the civil rights of American citizens by authorizing the removal of 110,000 Japanese and their American-born children from the western half of the Pacific Coastal States and the southern third of Arizona.

During the bewildering months before evacuation, the Japanese Americans were subject to curfews and to unannounced searches at all hours for "contraband" weapons, radios, and cameras; in desperation and fear, many people destroyed their belongings from Japan, including treasured heirlooms, books, and photographs. Some families moved voluntarily from the Western Defense zone, but many stayed, believing that all areas would eventually be restricted or fearing hostility in neighboring states.

Involuntary evacuation began in the spring of 1942. Families received a scant week's notice in which to "wind up their affairs, store or sell their possessions, close up their businesses and homes, and show up at an assembly point for transportation to an assembly center." Each person was allowed to bring only as many clothes and personal items as he or she could carry to the temporary assembly centers that had been hastily constructed at fairgrounds, race tracks, and Civilian Conservation Corps camps: twelve in California, one in Oregon, and one in Washington.

The rapidity of evacuation left many Japanese Americans numb; one Nisei noted that "a queer lump came to my throat. Nothing else came to my mind, it was just blank. Everything happened too soon, I guess." As the realization of leaving home, friends, and neighborhood sank in, the numbness gave way to bewilderment. A teenager at the Santa Anita Assembly Center wrote, "I felt lost after I left Mountain View [California]. I thought that we could go back but instead look where we are." . . .

Overlying the mixed feelings of anxiety, anger, shame, and confusion was resignation. As a relatively small minority caught in a storm of turbulent events that destroyed their individual and community security, there was little the Japanese Americans could do but shrug and say, *"Shikata ga nai,"* or, "It can't be helped," the implication being that the situation must be endured. The phrase lingered on many lips when the Issei, Nisei, and the young Sansei (third generation) children prepared for the move—which was completed by November 1942—to the ten permanent relocation camps organized by the War Relocation Authority: Topaz, Utah; Poston and Gila River, Arizona; Amache, Colorado; Manzanar and Tule Lake, California; Heart Mountain, Wyoming; Minidoka, Idaho; Denson and Rohwer, Arkansas. Denson and Rohwer were located in the swampy lowlands of Arkansas; the other camps were in desolate desert or semi-desert areas subject to dust storms and extreme temperatures reflected in the nicknames given to the three sections of the Poston Camp: Toaston, Roaston, and Duston.

The conditions of camp life profoundly altered family relations and affected women of all ages and backgrounds. Family unity deteriorated in the crude communal facilities and cramped barracks. The unceasing battle with the elements, the poor food, the shortages of toilet tissue and milk, coupled with wartime profiteering and mismanagement, and the sense of injustice and frustration took their toll on a people uprooted, far from home.

The standard housing in the camps was a spartan barracks, about twenty feet by one hundred feet, divided into four to six rooms furnished with steel army cots. Initially each single room or "apartment" housed an average of eight persons; individuals without kin nearby were often moved in with smaller families. Because the partitions between apartments did not reach the ceiling, even the smallest noises traveled freely from one end of the building to the other. There were usually fourteen barracks in each block, and each block had its own mess hall, laundry, latrine, shower facilities, and recreation room.

Because of the discomfort, noise, and lack of privacy, which "made a single symphony of yours and your neighbors' loves, hates, and joys," the barracks often became merely a place to "hang your hat" and sleep. As Jeanne Wakatsuki Houston records in her autobiography, *Farewell to Manzanar,* many family members began to spend less time together in the crowded barracks. The even greater lack of privacy in the latrine and shower facilities necessitated adjustments in former notions of modesty. There were no partitions in the shower room, and the latrine consisted of two rows of partitioned toilets "with nothing in front of you, just on the sides. Lots of people were not used to those kind of facilities, so [they'd] either go early in the morning when people were not around, or go real late at night. . . . It was really something until you got used to it."

The large communal mess halls also encouraged family disunity as family members gradually began to eat separately: mothers with small children, fathers with other men, and older children with their peers. "Table manners were forgotten," observed Miné Okubo. "Guzzle, guzzle, guzzle; hurry, hurry, hurry. Family life was lacking. Everyone ate wherever he or she pleased." Some strategies were developed for preserving family unity. The Amache Camp responded in part by assigning each family a particular table in the mess hall. Some families took the food back to their barracks so that they might eat together. But these measures were not always feasible in the face of varying work schedules; the odd hours of those assigned to shifts in the mess halls and infirmaries often made it impossible for the family to sit down together for meals.

Newspaper reports that Japanese Americans were living in luxurious conditions angered evacuees struggling to adjust to cramped quarters and crude communal facilities. A married woman with a family wrote from Heart Mountain:

> Last weekend, we had an awful cold wave and it was about 20° to 30° below zero. In such a weather, it's terrible to try going even to the bath and latrine house. . . . It really aggravates me to hear some politicians say we Japanese are being coddled, for *it isn't so!!* We're on ration as much as outsiders are. I'd say welcome to anyone to try living behind barbed wire and be cooped in a 20 ft. by 20 ft. room. . . . We do our sleeping, dressing, ironing, hanging up our clothes in this one room.

After the first numbness of disorientation, the evacuees set about making their situation bearable, creating as much order in their lives as possible. With blankets they partitioned their apartments into tiny rooms and created benches, tables, and shelves as piles of scrap lumber left over from barracks construction vanished; victory gardens and flower patches appeared. Evacuees also took advantage of the opportunity to taste freedom when they received temporary permits to go shopping in nearby towns. These were memorable occasions. A Heart Mountain Nisei described what such a trip meant to her in 1944:

> [F]or the first time since being behind the fences, I managed to go out shopping to Billings, Montana—a trip about 4 hours ride on train and bus. . . . It was quite a mental relief to breathe the air on the outside. . . . And was it an undescribable sensation to be able to be dressed up and walk the pavements with my high heel shoes!! You just can't imagine how full we are of pent-up emotions until we leave the camp behind us and see the highway ahead of us. A trip like that will keep us from becoming mentally narrow. And without much privacy, you can imagine how much people will become dull.

Despite the best efforts of the evacuees to restore order to their disrupted world, camp conditions prevented replication of their prewar lives. Women's work experiences, for example, changed in complex ways during the years of internment. Each camp offered a wide range of jobs, resulting from the organization of the camps as model cities administered through a series of departments headed by Caucasian administrators. The departments handled everything from accounting, agriculture, education, and medical care to mess hall service and the weekly newspaper. The scramble for jobs began early in the assembly centers and camps, and all able-bodied persons were expected to work.

Even before the war many family members had worked, but now children and parents, men and women all received the same low wages. In the relocation camps, doctors, teachers, and other professionals were at the top of the pay scale, earning $19 per month. The majority of workers received $16, and apprentices earned $12. The new equity in pay and the variety of available jobs gave many women unprecedented opportunities for experimentation, as illustrated by one woman's account of her family's work in Poston:

> First I wanted to find art work, but I didn't last too long because it wasn't very interesting . . . so I worked in the mess hall, but that wasn't for me, so I went to the accounting department—time-keeping—and I enjoyed that, so I stayed there. . . . My dad . . . went to a shoe shop . . . and then he was block gardener. . . . He got $16. . . . [My sister] was secretary for the block manager; then she went to the optometry department. She was assistant optometrist; she fixed all the glasses and fitted them. . . . That was $16.

As early as 1942, the War Relocation Authority began to release evacuees temporarily from the centers and camps to do voluntary seasonal farm work in neighboring areas hard hit by the wartime labor shortage. The work was arduous, as one young woman discovered when she left Topaz to take a job plucking turkeys:

> The smell is terrific until you get used to it. . . . We all wore gunny sacks around our waist, had a small knife and plucked off the fine feathers.
> This is about the hardest work that many of us have done—but without a murmur of complaint we worked 8 hours through the first day without a pause.
> We were all so tired that we didn't even feel like eating. . . . Our fingers and wrists were just aching, and I just dreamt of turkeys and more turkeys.

Work conditions varied from situation to situation, and some exploitative farmers refused to pay the Japanese Americans after they had finished beet topping or fruit picking. One worker noted that the degree of friendliness on the employer's part decreased as the harvest neared completion. Nonetheless, many workers, like the turkey plucker, concluded that "even if the work is hard, it is worth the freedom we are allowed."

Camp life increased the leisure of many evacuees. A good number of Issei women, accustomed to long days of work inside and outside the home, found that the communally prepared meals and limited living quarters provided them with spare time. Many availed themselves of the opportunity to attend adult classes taught by both evacuees and non-Japanese. Courses involving handcrafts and traditional Japanese arts such as flower arrangement, sewing, painting, calligraphy, and wood carving became immensely popular as an overwhelming number of people turned to art for recreation and self-expression. Some of these subjects were viewed as hobbies and leisure activities by those who taught them, but to the Issei women they represented access to new skills and a means to contribute to the material comfort of the family.

The evacuees also filled their time with Buddhist and Christian church meetings, theatrical productions, cultural programs, athletic events, and visits with friends. All family members spent more time than ever before in the company of their peers. Nisei from isolated rural areas were exposed to the ideas, styles, and pastimes of the more sophisticated urban youth; in camp they had the time and opportunity to socialize—at work, school, dances, sports events, and parties—in an almost entirely Japanese American environment. Gone were the restrictions of distance, lack of transportation, interracial uneasiness, and the dawn-to-dusk exigencies of field work.

Like their noninterned contemporaries, most young Nisei women envisioned a future of marriage and children. They—and their parents—anticipated that they would marry other Japanese Americans, but these young women also expected to choose their own husbands and to marry "for love." This mainstream American ideal of marriage differed greatly from the Issei's view of love as a bond that might evolve over the course of an arranged marriage that was firmly rooted in less romantic notions of compatibility and responsibility. The discrepancy between Issei and Nisei conceptions of love and marriage had sturdy prewar roots; internment fostered further divergence from the old customs of arranged marriage.

In the artificial hothouse of camp, Nisei romances often bloomed quickly. As Nisei men left to prove their loyalty to the United States in the 442nd Combat Team and the 100th Battalion, young Japanese Americans strove to grasp what happiness and security they could, given the uncertainties of the future. Lily Shoji, in her "Fem-a-lites" newspaper column, commented upon the "changing world" and advised Nisei women:

> This is the day of sudden dates, of blind dates on the up-and-up, so let the flash of a uniform be a signal to you to be ready for any emergency. . . . Romance is blossoming with the emotion and urgency of war.

In keeping with this atmosphere, camp newspaper columns like Shoji's in *The Mercedian, The Daily Tulean Dispatch*'s "Strictly Feminine," and the *Poston Chronicle*'s "Fashionotes" gave their Nisei readers countless suggestions on how to impress boys, care for their complexions, and choose the latest fashions. These evacuee-authored columns thus mirrored the mainstream girls' periodicals of the time. Such fashion news may seem incongruous in the context of an internment camp whose inmates had little choice in clothing beyond what they could find in the Montgomery Ward or Sears and Roebuck mail-order catalogues. These columns, however, reflect women's efforts to remain in touch with the world outside the barbed wire fence; they reflect as well women's attempt to maintain morale in a drab, depressing environment. . . .

Relocation began slowly in 1942. Among the first to venture out of the camps were college students, assisted by the National Japanese American Student Relocation Council, a nongovernmental agency that provided invaluable placement aid to 4,084 Nisei in the years 1942–46. Founded in 1942 by concerned educators, this organization persuaded institutions outside the restricted Western Defense zone to accept Nisei students and facilitated their admissions and leave clearances. A study of the first 400 students to leave camp showed that a third of them were women. Because of the cumbersome screening process, few other evacuees departed on indefinite leave before 1943. In that year, the War Relocation Authority tried to expedite the clearance procedure by broadening an army registration program aimed at Nisei males to include all adults. With this policy change, the migration from the camps steadily increased.

Many Nisei, among them a large number of women, were anxious to leave the limbo of camp and return "to normal life again." With all its work, social events, and cultural activities, camp was still an artificial, limited environment. It was stifling "to see nothing but the same barracks, mess halls, and other houses, row after row, day in and day out, it gives us the feeling that we're missing all the freedom and liberty." An aspiring teacher wrote: "Mother and father do not want me to go out. However, I want to go so very much that sometimes I feel that I'd go even if they disowned me. What shall I do? I realize the hard living conditions outside but I think I can take it." Women's developing sense of independence in the camp environment and their growing awareness of their abilities as workers contributed to their self-confidence and hence their desire to leave. Significantly, Issei parents, despite initial reluctance, were gradually beginning to sanction their daughters' departures for education and employment in the Midwest and East. One Nisei noted:

> [Father] became more broad-minded in the relocation center. He was more mellow in his ways. . . . At first he didn't want me to relocate, but he gave in. . . . I said I wanted to go [to Chicago] with my friend, so he helped me pack. He didn't say I could go . . . but he helped me pack, so I thought, "Well, he didn't say no."

The decision to relocate was a difficult one. It was compounded for some women because they felt obligated to stay and care for elderly or infirm parents, like the Heart Mountain Nisei who observed wistfully. "It's getting so more and more of the girls and boys are leaving camp, and I sure wish I could but mother's getting on and I just can't leave her." Many internees worried about their acceptance in the outside world. The Nisei considered themselves American citizens, and they had an allegiance to the land of their birth: "The teaching and love of one's own birth place, one's own country was . . . strongly impressed upon my mind as a child. So even though California may deny our rights of birth, I shall ever love her soil." But evacuation had taught the Japanese Americans that in the eyes of many of their fellow Americans, theirs was the face of the enemy. Many Nisei were torn by mixed feelings of shame, frustration, and bitterness at the denial of their civil rights. These factors created an atmosphere of anxiety that surrounded those who contemplated resettlement: "A feeling of uncertainty hung over the camp; we were worried about the future. Plans were made and remade, as we tried to decide what to do. Some were ready to risk anything to get away. Others feared to leave the protection of the camp."

Thus, those first college students were the scouts whose letters back to camp marked pathways for others to follow. May Yoshino sent a favorable report to her family in Topaz from the nearby University of Utah, indicating that there were "plenty of schoolgirl jobs for those who want to study at the University." Correspondence from other Nisei students shows that although they succeeded at making the dual transition from high school to college and from camp to the outside world, they were not without anxieties as to whether they could handle the study load and the reactions of the Caucasians around them. . . .

Several incidents of hostility did occur, but the reception of the Nisei students at colleges and universities was generally warm. Topaz readers of *Trek* magazine could draw encouragement from Lillian Ota's "Campus Report." Ota, a Wellesley student, reassured them: "During the first few days you'll be invited by the college to teas and receptions. Before long you'll lose the awkwardness you might feel at such doings after the months of abnormal life at evacuation centers." Although Ota had not noticed "that my being a 'Jap' has made much difference on the campus itself," she offered cautionary and pragmatic advice to the Nisei, suggesting the burden of responsibility these relocated students felt, as well as the problem of communicating their experiences and emotions to Caucasians.

It is scarcely necessary to point out that those who have probably never seen a nisei before will get their impression of the nisei as a whole from the relocated students. It won't do you or your family and friends much good to dwell on what you consider injustices when you are questioned about evacuation. Rather, stress the contributions of [our] people to the nation's war effort.

Given the tenor of the times and the situation of their families, the pioneers in resettlement had little choice but to repress their anger and minimize the amount of racist hostility they encountered.

In her article "a la mode," Marii Kyogoku also offered survival tips to the departing Nisei, ever conscious that they were on trial not only as individuals but as representatives of their families and their generation. She suggested criteria for choosing clothes and provided hints on adjustment to food rationing. Kyogoku especially urged the evacuees to improve their table manners, which had been adversely affected by the "unnatural food and atmosphere" of mess hall dining:

> You should start rehearsing for the great outside by bringing your own utensils to the dining hall. It's an aid to normality to be able to eat your jello with a spoon and well worth the dishwashing which it involves. All of us eat much too fast. Eat more slowly. All this practicing should be done so that proper manners will seem natural to you. If you do this, you won't get stagefright and spill your water glass, or make bread pills and hardly dare to eat when you have your first meal away from the centers and in the midst of scrutinizing caucasian eyes.

Armed with advice and drawn by encouraging reports, increasing numbers of women students left camp. A postwar study of a group of 1,000 relocated students showed that 40 percent were women. The field of nursing was particularly attractive to Nisei women; after the first few students disproved the hospital administration's fears of their patients' hostility, acceptance of Nisei into nursing schools grew. By July 1944, there were more than 300 Nisei women in over 100 nursing programs in twenty-four states. One such student wrote from the Asbury Hospital in Minneapolis: "Work here isn't too hard and I enjoy it very much. The patients are very nice people and I haven't had any trouble as yet. They do give us a funny stare at the beginning but after a day or so we receive the best compliments."

The trickle of migration from the camps grew into a steady stream by 1943, as the War Relocation Authority developed its resettlement program to aid evacuees in finding housing and employment in the East and Midwest. A resettlement bulletin published by the Advisory Committee for Evacuees described "who is relocating":

> Mostly younger men and women, in their 20s or 30s; mostly single persons or couples with one or two children, or men with larger families who come out alone first to scout opportunities and to secure a foothold, planning to call wife and children later. Most relocated evacuees have parents or relatives whom they hope and plan to bring out "when we get re-established."

In early 1945, the War Department ended the exclusion of the Japanese Americans from the West Coast, and the War Relocation Authority announced that the camps would be closed within the year. By this time, 37 percent of the evacuees of sixteen years or older had already relocated, including 63 percent of the Nisei women in that age group.

For Nisei women, like their non-Japanese sisters, the wartime labor shortage opened the door into industrial, clerical, and managerial occupations. Prior to the war, racism had excluded the Japanese Americans from most white-collar clerical and sales positions, and, according to sociologist Evelyn Nakano Glenn, "the most common form of nonagricultural employment for the immigrant women (issei) and their American-born daughters (nisei) was domestic service." The highest percentage of job offers for both men and women continued to be requests for domestic workers. . . . However, Nisei women also found jobs as secretaries, typists, file clerks, beauticians, and factory workers. By 1950, 47 percent of employed Japanese American women were clerical and sales workers and operatives; only 10 percent were in domestic service. The World War II decade, then, marked a turning point for Japanese American women in the labor force.

Whether they were students or workers, and regardless of where they went or how prepared they were to meet the outside world, Nisei women found that leaving camp meant enormous change in their lives. Even someone as confident as Marii Kyogoku, the author of much relocation advice, found that reentry into the Caucasian-dominated world beyond the barbed wire fence was not a simple matter of stepping back into old shoes. Leaving the camps—like entering them—meant major changes in psychological perspective and self-image.

> I had thought that because before evacuation I had adjusted myself rather well in a Caucasian society, I would go right back into my former frame of mind. I have found, however, that though the center became unreal and was as if it had never existed as soon as I got on the train at Delta, I was never so self-conscious in all my life.

Kyogoku was amazed to see so many men and women in uniform and, despite her "proper" dining preparation, felt strange sitting at a table set with clean linen and a full set of silverware.

> I felt a diffidence at facing all these people and things, which was most unusual. Slowly things have come to seem natural, though I am still excited by the sounds of the busy city and thrilled every time I see a street lined with trees. I no longer feel that I am the cynosure of all eyes.

Like Kyogoku, many Nisei women discovered that relocation meant adjustment to "a life different from our former as well as present way of living" and, as such, posed a challenge. Their experiences in meeting this challenge were as diverse as their jobs and living situations.

"I live at the Eleanor Club No. 5 which is located on the west side," wrote Mary Sonoda, working with the American Friends Service Committee in Chicago:

> I pay $1 per day for room and two meals a day. I also have maid service. I do not think that one can manage all this for $1 unless one lives in a place like this which houses thousands of working girls in the city. . . . I am the only Japanese here at present. . . . The residents and the staff are wonderful to me. . . . I am constantly being entertained by one person or another.
>
> The people in Chicago are extremely friendly. Even with the Tribune screaming awful headlines concerning the recent execution of American soldiers in Japan, people kept their heads. On street cars, at stores, everywhere, one finds innumerable evidence of good will.

Chicago, the location of the first War Relocation Authority field office for supervision of resettlement in the Midwest, attracted the largest number of evacuees. Not all found their working environment as congenial as Mary Sonoda did. Smoot Katow, a Nisei man in Chicago, painted "another side of the picture":

> I met one of the Edgewater Beach girls. . . . From what she said it was my impression that the girls are not very happy. The hotel work is too hard, according to this girl. In fact, they are losing weight and one girl became sick with overwork. They have to clean about fifteen suites a day, scrubbing the floors on their hands and knees. . . . It seems the management is out to use labor as labor only. . . . The outside world is just as tough as it ever was.

These variations in living and work conditions and wages encouraged and sometimes necessitated a certain amount of job experimentation among the Nisei.

Many relocating Japanese Americans received moral and material assistance from a number of service organizations and religious groups, particularly the Presbyterians, the Methodists, the Society of Friends, and the Young Women's Christian Association. . . .

The Nisei also derived support and strength from networks—formed before and during the internment—of friends and relatives. The homes of those who relocated first became way stations for others as they made the transition into new communities and jobs. In 1944, soon after she obtained a place to stay in New York City, Miné Okubo found that "many of the other evacuees relocating in New York came ringing my doorbell. They were sleeping all over the floor!" Single women often accompanied or joined sisters, brothers, and friends as many interconnecting grapevines carried news of likely jobs, housing, and friendly communities. Ayako Kanemura, for instance, found a job painting Hummel figurines in Chicago; a letter of recommendation from a friend enabled her "to get my foot into the door and then all my friends followed and joined me." Although they were farther from their families than ever before, Nisei women maintained warm ties of affection and concern, and those who had the means to do so continued to play a role in the family economy, remitting a portion of their earnings to their families in or out of camp, and to siblings in school.

Elizabeth Ogata's family exemplifies several patterns of resettlement and the maintenance of family ties within them. In October 1944, her parents were living with her brother Harry who had begun to farm in Springville, Utah; another brother and sister were attending Union College in Lincoln, Nebraska. Elizabeth herself had moved to Minneapolis to join a brother in the army, and she was working as an operative making pajamas. "Minn. is a beautiful place," she wrote, "and the people are so nice. . . . I thought I'd never find anywhere I would feel at home as I did in Mt. View [California], but I have changed my mind." Like Elizabeth, a good number of the 35,000 relocated Japanese Americans were favorably impressed by their new homes and decided to stay.

The war years had complex and profound effects upon Japanese Americans, uprooting their communities and causing severe psychological and emotional damage. The vast majority returned to the West Coast at the end of the war in 1945—a move that, like the initial evacuation, was a grueling test of flexibility and fortitude. Even with the assistance of old friends and service organizations, the transition was taxing and painful, the end of the war meant not only long-awaited freedom but more battles to be fought in social, academic, and economic arenas. The Japanese Americans faced hostility, crude living conditions, and a struggle for jobs. Few evacuees received any compensation for their financial losses, estimated conservatively at $400 million, because Congress decided to appropriate only $38 million for the settlement of claims. It is even harder to place a figure on the toll taken in emotional shock, self-blame, broken dreams, and insecurity. One Japanese American woman still sees in her nightmares the watchtower searchlights that troubled her sleep forty years ago.

The war altered Japanese American women's lives in complicated ways. In general, evacuation and relocation accelerated earlier trends that differentiated the Nisei from their parents. Although most young women, like their mothers and non-Japanese peers, anticipated a future centered around a husband and children, they had already felt the influence of mainstream middle-class values of love and marriage and quickly moved away from the pattern of arranged marriage in the camps There, increased peer group activities and the relaxation of parental authority gave them more independence. The Nisei women's expectations of marriage became more akin to the companionate ideals of their peers than to those of the Issei.

As before the war, many Nisei women worked in camp, but the new parity in wages they received altered family dynamics. And though they expected to contribute to the family economy, a large number did so in settings far from the family, availing themselves of opportunities provided by the student and worker relocation programs. In meeting the challenges facing them, Nisei women drew not only upon the disciplined strength inculcated by their Issei parents but also upon firmly rooted support networks and the greater measure of self-reliance and independence that they developed during the crucible of the war years.

The Regulation of Sexuality and Sexual Behavior in the Women's Army Corps During World War II

LEISA D. MEYER

Several years after World War II ended, a journalist summed up the difficulties the Women's Army Corps encountered in recruiting women by observing:

> Of the problems that the WAC has, the greatest one is the problem of morals . . . of convincing mothers, fathers, brothers, Congressmen, servicemen and junior officers that women really can be military without being camp followers or without being converted into rough, tough gals who can cuss out the chow as well as any dogface. . . .

The sexual stereotypes of servicewomen as "camp followers" or "mannish women," prostitutes or lesbians, had a long history both in the construction of notions of femaleness in general and in the relationship of "woman" and "soldier" in particular. Historically, women had been most visibly associated with the military as prostitutes and crossdressers. The challenge before women and men who wanted to promote "women" as "soldiers" during World War II was how to create a new category

Leisa D. Meyer, "Creating G.I. Jane: The Regulation of Sexuality and Sexual Behavior in the Women's Army Corps during World War II," *Feminist Studies* 18, no. 3 (Fall 1992): 581–601. Reprinted by permission of the publisher, Feminist Studies, Inc.

which proclaimed female soldiers as both sexually respectable and feminine. The response of Oveta Culp Hobby, the Women's Army Corps director, to this challenge was to characterize female soldiers as chaste and asexual; such a presentation would not threaten conventional sexual norms. Clashing public perceptions of service-women and internal struggles within the U.S. Army over the proper portrayal and treatment of military women were the crucibles in which this new category was created. Such struggles profoundly shaped the daily lives of women in the Women's Army Auxiliary Corps (WAAC) and the Women's Army Corps (WAC) and framed the notorious lesbian witchhunts of the mid- to late-forties.

This article focuses on the regulation and expression of women's sexuality within the army during World War II. I will examine the debates between female and male military leaders over the most appropriate methods of controlling female soldiers' sexual behavior and the actions and responses of army women themselves to the varied and often conflicting rulings emanating from WAAC/WAC Headquarters and the War Department. Framed by public concern with the possibilities of both the sexual independence and sexual victimization of servicewomen, the interactions between and among these groups illuminate the ongoing tension between the mutually exclusive, gendered categories "woman" and "soldier."

The entrance of some women into the army paralleled the movement of other women into nontraditional jobs in the civilian labor force as the need for full utilization of all resources during World War II brought large numbers of white, married women into the labor force for the first time and created opportunities for many women and people of color in jobs historically denied them. Women's service in the armed forces was especially threatening, however, because of the military's function as the ultimate test of "masculinity."

The definition of the military as a masculine institution and the definition of a soldier as a "man with a gun who engages in combat" both excluded women. Moreover, military service had historically been the obligation of men during wartime, and the presence of female soldiers in the army suggested that women were abdicating their responsibilities within the home to usurp men's duty of protecting and defending their homes and country. Thus, the establishment of the WAAC in May 1942, marking women's formal entrance into this preeminently masculine domain, generated heated public debate. It heightened the fears already generated by the entry of massive numbers of women in the civilian labor force and by the less restrictive sexual mores of a wartime environment. . . .

In a culture increasingly anxious about women's sexuality in general, and homosexuality in particular, the formation of the WAAC, a women-only environment within an otherwise wholly male institution, sparked a storm of public speculation as to the potential breakdown of heterosexual norms and sexual morality which might result. Not surprisingly, these concerns focused on the potentially "masculinizing" effect the army might have on women and especially on the disruptive influence the WAAC would have on sexual standards. Public fears were articulated in numerous editorials and stories in newspapers and journals, as well as in thousands of letters to the War Department and the newly formed WAAC Headquarters in Washington, D.C. These anxieties were expressed in accusations of heterosexual promiscuity and lesbianism and concerns over women's lack of protection within the military. Among other allegations, the public expressed fear that, in forming the WAAC, the military was trying to create an organized cadre of prostitutes to service male GI's. . . .

The sexual stereotypes of the female soldier as "loose" or "mannish" were seen both as inherent in women's military service *and* as a product of the particular kinds of women believed to be most likely to enter the WAAC. In other words, the army either attracted women who were already "sexually deviant," or the experience of military life would make them that way. In addition, the corollary to concerns with women's sexual agency [was] discussions of army women as potential sexual victims. Integral to this contention were questions of who would protect women inside the military. Removed from the control of their families, what would the state's control of servicewomen mean?

The army's response to this negative publicity was orchestrated by Col. Hobby. She organized this response around the need to assure an anxious public that servicewomen had not lost their "femininity." Hobby's definition of "femininity" was rooted in the Victorian linkage between sexual respectability and female passionlessness. As a result she characterized the woman soldier as chaste, asexual, and essentially middle-class. For example, in cooperation with the War Department she arranged public statements by a number of religious leaders who assured all concerned that the army was a safe and moral environment for young women, and further, that women who joined the WAAC/WAC were of the highest moral character and from "good family backgrounds." She characterized the WAAC/WAC as acting *in loco parentis,* as a guardian of young women's welfare and morals. And to demonstrate that the WAAC/WAC attracted "better-quality" women, Hobby emphasized the greater educational requirements mandated for women compared with their male counterparts, illustrated by the high ratio of women with college degrees. Thus, in countering allegations that to join the WAAC/WAC meant to "lower one's self," army propaganda reflected and supported contemporary definitions of respectability which explicitly connected class status and sexual morality.

These pronouncements on sexual respectability coincided with other army public relations campaigns aimed at defusing public concerns with homosexuality. In these efforts, attempts to limit the visibility of lesbians in the women's corps were linked with the implicit encouragement of heterosexuality. In responding to fears that the military would make women "mannish" or would provide a haven for women who were "naturally" that way, for instance, some army propaganda highlighted the femininity of WAAC/WAC recruits and stressed their sexual attractiveness to men. These articles assured an anxious public that "soldiering hasn't transformed these Wacs into Amazons—far from it. They have retained their femininity." Presenting women in civilian life in the period as sexually attractive to men did not necessarily imply that they were sexually available. However, public hostility toward women's entrance into the military and conjecture over the army's "real need" for Waacs/Wacs frequently focused on the potential for women's sexual exploitation and/or agency within the army. The army's policy of portraying servicewomen as feminine and sexually attractive to men worked to both contest the image of the female soldier as a "mannish" woman, or lesbian, *and* to reinforce the public characterizations of Waacs/Wacs as heterosexually available. Hobby's efforts to control the effects of these campaigns was to emphasize that Waacs/Wacs remained passionless and chaste while in the military and that their sexual behavior in the military was, and should be, profoundly different from that of men in the same institution.

The framework created by Hobby and disseminated in military propaganda efforts was occasionally undercut by the conflicting responses to the question of whether Waacs/Wacs should be treated and utilized as "soldiers" or as "women." On several occasions the male army hierarchy, much to Hobby's dismay, attempted to treat the regulation and control of women's sexuality and sexual behavior in the same manner as that of male soldiers. The army's approach to the issue of sexual regulation and control for men stressed health and combat readiness among troops, not morality. In fact, the army expected and encouraged heterosexual activity among male soldiers and controlled male sexuality with regulations prohibiting sodomy and addressing the prevention and treatment of venereal disease, as well as more informal mechanisms upholding prohibitions on interracial relationships. The male military hierarchy's desire for uniformity collided with the female WAAC director's firm belief in different moral standards for women and her insistence that this difference be reflected in army regulations. This struggle was clearly represented in the army's battle to fight the spread of venereal disease within its ranks.

Hobby believed the army's venereal disease program for men, premised on the assumption of heterosexual activity, would seriously damage the reputation of the corps if applied to women and would undermine her efforts to present Waacs as sexless, not sexual. Her strategy of moral suasion clashed with the U.S. surgeon general's efforts to institute a system of chemical prophylaxis in the women's corps. The surgeon general's plan for control of venereal disease in the WAAC included a full course of instruction in sex education and the distribution of condoms in slot machines placed in latrines so that even "modest" servicewomen might have access to them. This program was completely rejected by Hobby. She argued that even proposing such measures placed civilian and military acceptance of the WAAC in jeopardy. She pointed to public fears of women's military service and accusations of immorality already present as evidence that the course proposed by the surgeon general would result in catastrophic damage to the reputation of the WAAC and seriously hamper her efforts to recruit women to the corps.

Her concern was not with venereal disease per se, but rather with creating an aura of respectability around the WAAC. Her victory in this struggle resulted in the development of a social hygiene pamphlet and course which stressed the "high standards" of moral conduct (i.e., chastity) necessary for members of the corps and the potential damage one woman could do through her misbehavior or immoral conduct. The pamphlet, distributed to all WAAC officers, discussed venereal disease only in reference to the "frightful effects" of the disease on women and children, the difficulties in detection and treatment, and the ineffectiveness of all prophylactic methods for women. Hobby supported combining this policy with the maintenance of strict enlistment standards. She believed that if the corps accepted only "high types of women," no control measures would be necessary. . . .

Hobby's fears of the adverse public reaction that might result from the distribution of prophylactics information and equipment to Waacs were confirmed by the slander campaign against the WAAC/WAC which started in mid-1943 and continued through early 1944. This "whispering campaign" began with the publication of a nationally syndicated article which reported that in a secret agreement between the

War Department and the WAAC, contraceptives would be issued to all women in the army. This piece provoked a storm of public outcry and marked the resurgence of accusations of widespread sexual immorality in the women's corps. . . .

Public fears that the only "real uses" the army had for women were sexual were exacerbated by male officers who claimed that the most important function of the WAAC/WAC was not the soldierly duties it performed but the positive impact the women had on the "morale" of male soldiers. Although "morale boosting" did not necessarily imply prostitution or sexual service, the two were often linked in the public consciousness. For example, one army investigator reported that in Kansas City, Kansas, it was believed that "Waacs were issued condoms and enrolled solely for the soldier's entertainment, serving as 'morale builders' for the men and nothing more." Hobby worked to eliminate all references to Waacs/Wacs being used for "morale purposes," believing that these bolstered public concerns with heterosexual immorality in the corps.

In addition, the occasional use of WAAC/WAC units to control male sexuality seemed to confirm suspicions that the role the army envisioned for women was sexual. For example, African American WAAC/WAC units were in general stationed only at posts where there were Black male soldiers present. In part this was a product of the army's policy of segregating its troops by race. However, white officers, particularly at southern posts, also explicitly referred to the "beneficial" presence of African American WAAC/WAC units as a way to insure that Black male troops would not form liaisons with white women in the surrounding communities. Thus, in this instance, African American WAAC/WAC units were used by the army as a means of upholding and supporting prohibitions on interracial relationships. Similarly, in December 1944, Field Marshall Sir Bernard L. Montgomery proposed using white American WAC and British Auxiliary Territorial Service units in the Allied occupation of Germany to curb the fraternization of male GI's in the U.S. and British armies with enemy (German) women, especially prostitutes. Field Marshall Montgomery's proposal was made public in a number of articles and editorials and harshly criticized by WAC Headquarters, as well as by Wacs stationed overseas in the European theater of operations. It is clear from these examples that military policy and practice were sometimes contradictory.

This situation was made more complicated by the fact that Waacs/Wacs and male soldiers regularly dated and socialized. This was particularly true in overseas theaters of war where military women were often the only U.S. women in the area. The only army regulations dealing with the social interaction of female and male military personnel were long-standing rules against fraternization between officers and enlisted personnel. Again the question arose of whether Waacs/Wacs should be treated like all other soldiers or if allowances should be made for female/male interactions across the caste lines established by the military. No clear answer to this query developed during World War II. In practice, the regulations concerning the socializing of male officers and female enlisted personnel and vice-versa varied from post to post and over different theaters. Many Waacs/Wacs were extremely vocal in their resentment of what they perceived as army policies dictating whom they should not date. When fraternization policies were enforced between women and men, it was usually the Waac/Wac who was punished, not the male soldier or officer, if discovered in violation of these regulations. This practice made it clear that it was women's responsibility to say "no" to these encounters and reinforced the sexual double standard which excused men's heterosexual activity and punished that of women. . . .

The army's negotiation between anxieties about assertive female sexuality, whether heterosexual or homosexual, and the realities of servicewomen's sexual vulnerability to abuse by male GI's and officers can be seen by examining the army's efforts to control the sexuality of servicewomen in the Southwest Pacific Area. Upon arrival in Port Moresby, New Guinea, in May 1944, Wacs found their lives unexpectedly restricted. The theater headquarters directed that in view of the great number of white male troops in the area, "some of whom allegedly had not seen a nurse or other white woman in 18 months," Wacs should be locked within their barbed wire compound at all times except when escorted by armed guards to work or to approved group recreation. No leaves, passes, or one-couple dates were allowed at any time. Many Wacs found these restrictions unbearable and patronizing and complained that they were being treated as criminals and children. The mounting complaints from women at WAC Headquarters and rumors of plummeting morale moved Hobby to protest to the War Department and ask for a discontinuation of what many Wacs referred to as the "concentration camp system." The War Department responded that it was in no position to protest command policies, especially because the theater authorities insisted that the system was required "to prevent rape of Wacs by Negro troops in New Guinea." Societal stereotypes of African American men, in particular, as rapists, and of male sexuality, in general, as dangerous for women, were used to defend the extremely restrictive policies of the military toward Wacs in the Southwest Pacific Area. In this situation the army stepped in as the surrogate male protector defending white military women's honor and virtue by creating a repressive environment designed to insure a maximum of "protection" and supervision.

One consequence of the controls placed on women's heterosexual activities in the Southwest Pacific Area was a series of rumors in late 1944 claiming widespread homosexuality among Wacs in New Guinea. The concerns originated in letters of complaint from several Wacs stationed there who asserted that restrictive theater policies created an ideal habitat for some women to express and explore their "abnormal sexual tendencies." The War Department and Hobby sent a WAC officer to the theater to investigate the rumors. The report issued by Lt. Col. Mary Agnes Brown, the WAC staff director, noted that although homosexuality was certainly not widespread, several incidences of such behavior had occurred. Lieutenant Colonel Brown felt that the situation was accentuated by the rigid camp security system to which Wacs were subjected. She suggested increasing Wacs' opportunities for recreation "with a view of maintaining the normal relationships between men and women that exist at home and avoid the creation of abnormal conditions which otherwise are bound to arise." When faced with a choice of protecting women from men or "protecting" them from lesbian relationships which might occur in a sex-segregated and restricted compound, Lieutenant Colonel Brown's recommendation was to protect servicewomen from the possibility of homosexuality.

The more repressive framework created by Hobby to control women's sexuality in the face of public antagonism was also challenged by women, both heterosexual and lesbian, who asserted their autonomy and right to find their own means of sexual expression within the authoritarian structure of the army. Indeed, heterosexual

women sometimes manipulated fears of homosexuality in the women's corps to expand their own opportunities for heterosexual activity. They accused female officers
who enforced army regulations against fraternization of male and female officers and
enlisted personnel of being "antimale" and discouraging "normal" heterosexual
interactions. For example, in February 1944, Capt. Delores Smith was ordered to
report for duty as the commanding officer of the Army–Air Forces WAC Detachment
at Fort Worth, Texas. As a new commanding officer, Captain Smith sought the help
and advice of her officer staff in familiarizing herself with the company and environment. Receiving little support from her officers, she turned for advice to the
ranking enlisted woman, Sgt. Norma Crandall. Shortly after her arrival, Smith rep-
rimanded several of her company officers for allowing enlisted men to frequent the
WAC barracks and mess hall. In addition, she cautioned these officers on their fraternization with male enlisted personnel. Two weeks later these officers brought
charges of homosexuality against Captain Smith. They cited her restrictions on
female/male interactions on post, her "dislike" of socializing with servicemen, and
her "close association" with the enlisted woman, Sergeant Crandall, as evidence of
her "abnormal tendencies." Despite the lack of concrete documentation to support
these accusations, Hobby and the Board of Inquiry felt that to allow Captain Smith
to continue as a WAC officer would only damage the reputation of the corps, and
she was forced to resign from service.

The WAC officers at Fort Worth were angered by what they perceived as the im-
position of unfair restrictions on their social lives by Captain Smith. They responded
by invoking homophobic anxieties. In doing so they simultaneously defended their
right to choose how and with whom they would socialize and reinforced social
taboos and army proscriptions against lesbianism. The "lesbian threat" thus became
a language of protest to force authorities to broaden their heterosexual privilege.

Lesbian servicewomen, like their heterosexual counterparts, also tried to create
their own space within the WAC. In these efforts army lesbians were affected by the
contradiction between official proscriptions of homosexuality and the WAC's informal policies on female homosexuality, which were quite lenient. . . . Army regulations providing for the undesirable discharge of homosexuals were rarely used
against lesbians in the WAC, and WAC officers were warned to consider this action
only in the most extreme of situations. Hobby felt that such proceedings would only
result in more intensive public scrutiny and disapproval of the women's corps. Instead, it was suggested that WAC officers use more informal methods of control.
These including shifting personnel and room assignments, transferring individuals to
different posts, and as was exemplified in New Guinea, insuring that corps members
were provided with "opportunities for wholesome and natural companionship with
men." . . . In addition, on several posts informal WAC policy prohibited women
from dancing in couples in public and cautioned against the adoption of "mannish"
hairstyles. WAC leaders were concerned primarily with the image of the corps, and
Hobby felt that the adverse publicity generated by intense screening procedures,
investigations, and court-martials of lesbians within the WAC could only hurt the
corps. Thus, as historian Allan Bérubé has noted in his work on gay GI's during
World War II, the expanding antihomosexual apparatus of the military was focused
much more closely on regulating and screening for male homosexuals than for
their female counterparts.

Within these parameters, lesbians within the WAC developed their own culture and methods of identifying one another, although the risks of discovery and exposure remained. The court-martial of T. Sgt. Julie Farrell, stationed at an army school in Richmond, Kentucky, provides an interesting example of this developing culture and its limits. Although she was given an undesirable discharge because of "unsuitability for military service," Technical Sergeant Farrell's court-martial focused on her alleged homosexuality. According to the testimony of Lt. Rosemary O'Riley, Farrell approached her one evening, depressed at what she felt were the army's efforts to make her "suppress her individuality," including criticisms and reprimands for her "mannish hairstyle" and "masculine behavior." Receiving a sympathetic response, Farrell went on to ask the lieutenant if she understood "double talk" and if she had ever been to San Francisco. It is clear that these questions were used by Farrell to determine if it was safe to discuss issues of homosexuality with O'Riley. When the lieutenant answered in the affirmative to her queries, Farrell went on to speak more explicitly of the "natural desires" of women which the military attempted to suppress. She ended with what Lieutenant O'Riley later termed as a "humiliating suggestion." Farrell was surprised by O'Riley's insistence that she had "no interest in such things" and remarked, "Well, when you first came on this campus we thought that maybe you were one of us in the way you walked." . . .

Lieutenant O'Riley's reports of Farrell's comments and behavior resulted in a court-martial proceeding against Technical Sergeant Farrell. In the course of this proceeding it was argued that in addition to this latest breach of military regulations, Farrell had already been the subject of "malicious gossip and rumor." Most damaging, however, were love letters between Farrell and a WAAC officer, Lieutenant Pines, that were entered as evidence. The tender and explicit discussions of the women's relationship contained within these letters were crucial to the decision of the board to dismiss Farrell from service. Lieutenant Pines avoided prosecution by claiming that the interactions described in the letters occurred only in the imagination of Farrell. Pines covered herself by asserting that she had kept the letters because of her own suspicions of Farrell. Thus, in saving herself, Pines sealed the fate of her lover.

Despite the opportunities for creating and sustaining a lesbian identity or relationship within the WAAC/WAC, the process was also fraught with danger and uncertainty. Army policies provided a space in which female homosexuals could exist, recognize one another, and develop their own culture. Yet this existence was an extremely precarious one, framed by army regulations which also provided for the undesirable discharge of homosexuals, female and male. These regulations could be invoked at any time and were widely used in purges of lesbians from the military in the immediate postwar years, purges that were in part the result of the army's decreasing need for women's labor. In these efforts the army utilized the techniques illustrated in Julie Farrell's court-martial, enabling some women to protect themselves by accusing others of lesbianism. In addition, some lesbians used heterosexual privilege and respectability to obscure their sexual identity by getting married or becoming pregnant in order to leave the army and protect themselves and their lovers. Pat Bond, a lesbian ex-Wac who married a gay GI to avoid prosecution, described one of these purges at a base in Japan: "Every day you came up for a court-martial against one of your friends. They turned us against each other. . . . The only way I could figure out to save my lover was to get out. If I had been there, they could have gotten us both because other women would have testified against us."

The tensions between agency and victimization illustrated here are characteristic of women's participation within the U.S. Army during World War II. Hobby's attempts to portray Wacs as sexless and protected in response to accusations of heterosexual promiscuity were undercut by the need also to present Wacs as feminine and sexually attractive to men to ease fears that the military would attract or produce "mannish women" and lesbians. In addition, the army's occasional utilization of WAC units to control male sexuality seemed to confirm the belief that women's role within the military was sexual. Within this confusing and fluctuating environment and in negotiation with army regulations and public opinion, Wacs tried to define their own sexuality and make their own sexual choices. Their actions sometimes challenged and other times reinforced entrenched gender and sexual ideologies and were crucial to the development of a role for women within the military. The process of creating a category of "female soldier" was defined by these interactions between Wacs, the army hierarchy (which was often divided along gender lines), and public opinion. The reformulation and reconstruction of gender and sexual norms involved in this process did not end with the war but is still going on today. Women's service continues to be circumscribed by debates over the contradictory concepts of "woman" and "soldier," and servicewomen continue to grapple with the sexual images of dyke and whore framing their participation.

FURTHER READING

Anderson, Karen Tucker. *Wartime Women: Sex Roles, Family Relations, and the Status of Women During World War II* (1981).

Baker, M. Joyce. *Images of Women in Film: The War Years, 1941–1945* (1981).

Bentley, Amy. *Eating for Victory: Food Rationing and the Politics of Domesticity* (1998).

Bérubé, Allan. *Coming Out Under Fire: The History of Gay Men and Women in World War II* (1990).

Campbell, D'Ann. *Women at War with America* (1984).

Chafe, William. *The American Woman: Her Changing Social, Economic, and Political Roles, 1920–1970* (1972).

Costello, John. *Virtue Under Fire: How World War II Changed Our Social and Sexual Attitudes* (1985).

Glenn, Evelyn Nakanno. *Issei, Nisei, War Bride: Three Generations of Japanese American Women in Domestic Service* (1986).

Glensonne, Jean. *Women of the Far Right: The Mother's Movement and World War II* (1990).

Gluck, Sherna Berger, ed. *Rosie the Riveter Revisited: Women, the War, and Social Change* (1987).

Goossen, Rachel Walker. *Women Against the Good War: Conscientious Objection and Gender in the American Home Front, 1941–1947* (1997).

Hartmann, Susan. *The Home Front and Beyond* (1982).

Hoff-Wilson, Joan, and Marjorie Lightman, eds. *Without Precedent: The Life and Career of Eleanor Roosevelt* (1984).

Honey, Maureen, ed. *Bitter Fruit: African American Women in World War II* (1999).

———. *Creating Rosie the Riveter: Class, Gender, and Propaganda During World War II* (1984).

Kesselman, Amy. *Fleeting Opportunities: Women Shipyard Workers in Portland and Vancouver During World War II and Reconversion* (1990).

CHAPTER

14

Women and the Feminine Ideal in Post-War America

Throughout the 1940s and 1950s, middle-class American men and women married earlier and had larger families than their own parents, reversing a long-standing downward trend in the nation's birthrate. The parents of the baby boom generation moved by the thousands to suburban neighborhoods where childrearing became the focal point of private and public life. Meanwhile, movies and popular magazines gave generous coverage to family matters and seemed to revive, though with a modern twist, a feminine ideal based in domesticity. Writing for the lay public, many educators and mental health professionals stressed the "naturalness" of women's identification with marriage and motherhood and the critical importance of their investment in domesticity to society's well-being. So too, the nation's political leaders seemed eager to view the suburban housewife and mother as both symbol and protector of American freedom in the war against communism.

Historians have vigorously debated the significance of the so-called "revival" of domesticity in the post-war era. Why did domestic notions of womanhood suit the nation's Cold War agenda? Did the popular media offer Americans alternative images of womanhood? Can we know how women responded to representations in the popular media? Just as important, did definitions of womanhood differ for women of distinct social, sexual, or racial groups? Finally, how and under what circumstances did women ignore, subvert, or manipulate normative standards of post-war womanhood? With what gains and at what cost?

DOCUMENTS

In 1946 Louisa Church Randall wrote an article for *American Home* magazine (excerpted in Document 1) that explored the vital duties of parents who lived in a nation worried about Soviet expansionism and atomic warfare. Randall urges men and women to regard parenting as a noble duty; interestingly she also urges them to embrace gender equity. Psychiatrist Marynia Farnham and her colleague, sociologist Ferdinand Lundberg, co-authors of *The Lost Sex* (1947), have no use for gender equity; instead, as staunch anti-feminists, they offer strong praise for women who devote themselves to domesticity, and label women who tried to compete with men "neurotic" and "unfeminine." An excerpt from *The Lost Sex* appears as Document 2. Also writing in 1947, but from a decidedly feminist perspective, Pauli Murray, an African American deputy attorney general for California, describes the rebellion of educated and professional black women against racial and sexual subordination. In an article published in the *Negro Digest* (Document 3), Pauli particularly laments the tendency of black men to vent frustrations borne of racism against black women. In Document 4, Joyce Johnson, a young woman who was part of the nonconformist "Beat Generation," describes what it was like to obtain an illegal abortion in New York City in 1955. Document 5 is an anonymous letter from a black reader to *The Ladder,* America's first lesbian magazine, which began publication in 1956. In Document 6, Betty Friedan describes "the problem that has no name," trying to give voice to (white middle-class) women confined to lives of domesticity. Together, these documents point both to the varied social identities that women endorsed in the post-war decades and the obstacles they encountered in realizing their goals.

1. Louisa Randall Church Explores the Duties of Parents as Architects of Peace, 1946

On that day in August 1945, when the first atomic bomb fell on Hiroshima, new concepts of civilized living, based on the obligations of world citizenship and unselfish service to mankind, were born. Out of the smoke and smoldering ruins arose a great cry for leadership equipped to guide the stricken people of the world along the hazardous course toward peace. On that day parenthood took on added responsibilities of deep and profound significance.

Today, months later, lacking sufficient and adequate leadership the nations of the earth flounder in a perilous state of distrust, suspicion, confusion and impotency. As one historian has said, "We stand at the very door of a golden age fumbling at the lock." How right he is.

Frightened scientists warn us of dire disaster—unspeakable catastrophe—the possible atomic murder of millions of peace-loving human beings. They tell us that bombs never again will come in ones and twos; they will come in hundreds, even thousands. More frightening still, they say there is no defense. Surely, in all history, the parents of the world were never so challenged.

However, there is a defense—an impregnable bulwark—which lies in meeting the world's desperate cry for leadership. Upon the shoulders of parents, everywhere, rests the tremendous responsibility of sending forth into the next generation men and women imbued with a high resolve to work together for everlasting peace.

There is no time to lose. We must gear our thoughts and actions for this new task as we did for winning the war. The noble instincts—sacrifice, heroism, generosity, unselfishness—which stirred us to action then must stir us now.

In every American home parents ought to be thinking and talking about these questions. What has caused the scarcity of qualified leaders? What are the requirements of worthy citizenship from which leaders can be expected to emerge? What changes must be made in our concepts of family living and parenthood if our children are to become wise, co-operative, courageous world citizens? How can parents help

---

Louisa Randall Church, "Parents, Architects of Peace," *American Home* 36, no. 6 (November 1946): 18–19.

to eradicate the underlying causes of war: poverty and despair, inequality of opportunity, hatred and greed? . . .

In order to develop the qualities of leadership necessary to insure peace—vision to see the needs of all humanity, willingness to work, sacrifice and co-operate for a common goal—parents must give their children not social security but personal security.

Personal security is attained only when the individual has achieved an inner harmony of spirit, self-confidence and a sense of mastery—in short—when he has achieved complete triumph over himself and his environment. Only then can he meet the exigencies of worthy citizenship in the world of tomorrow. Personal security cannot be bought for or taught to a child. It is a by-product of harmonious family living which is based on:

(1) Love and Affection. Psychologists tell us our first duty is to surround a child, from the moment of birth, with a never-failing love, affection and the assurance of being wanted. . . . When we push a child aside as a nuisance, ignore his needs, allow ourselves to become bored with his care, or fail to accept him as a real person, is it strange that he becomes confused and troublesome? . . .

(2) Equal Rights. Parenthood is a partnership for the mutual welfare of the father and the mother, the children and the whole society and should be governed by the rules which apply to all professional partnerships. In the discipline of their children, in policies of home management or control of family finances neither father nor mother should reign supreme. There can be no harmony in a home where favoritism is shown, where the spirit of rivalry and competitive striving is encouraged or where equality of opportunity is denied. Since, more and more, women will be taking their rightful places in world affairs, girls should be provided with the same opportunities, intellectually, professionally, socially and economically as boys.

(3) Discipline. It is in the home that a child should develop his first sense of responsibility to himself and to others. From intelligent guidance in habit formation he gains self-reliance, self-control and self-direction. Such self-discipline cannot be achieved by parental tyranny which molds a child according to selfish ambitions and foolish pride. It cannot be achieved by pampering. . . .

(4) Freedom. Unless a child senses a growing inner freedom to think, act, and achieve according to his interests, his talents, his abilities and his ambitions, he cannot gain the sense of security which is his right. Parents who go through life, pruning shears in hand—clipping here, clipping there every spontaneous outburst of enthusiasm which fails to conform to their plans and desires for their children are building future robots.

(5) Enrichment. . . . A child's desire for self-expression and recognition is a basic personality need. Parents have no greater responsibility than to provide him with opportunities to develop hobbies which will open to him the world of arts, crafts and mechanical skills. Essential to his personal security, his ability to co-operate with others and to a high standard of social behavior are friendships and contacts with people from all walks of life. . . .

(6) Co-operation. Good behavior of the individual is basic to harmony in the group. Obedient, thoughtful, helpful, unselfish children are a reflection of the parent's ability to co-operate with them, and to win co-operation from them. . . . Nothing in parenthood is more important than . . . willingness to share in the dreams, ambitions and problems of their children—to share those rare, golden moments when a child bares his mind, heart and soul. At such moments parental guidance can go into action and do its best work in wise, constructive counselling. At such moments, listening with honest sincerity and understanding breeds in a child confidence, a sense of inner security and power. When he feels security in the home he will feel at home in his community, his nation and the world. . . . There is no place in today's world for the "getters"—those who seem, always, to be in trouble, who create tensions, who cause most of the problems of society. Leaders of a new stamp—the "givers" will be needed, not alone at the peace table, but in community activities, church life, education, public welfare services and youth groups.

(7) Education. . . . The time has come when potential parents should be trained for the serious business of marriage, family living, and parenthood. . . . One thing is certain: parents cannot create harmony in the home and personal security in their children if they, themselves, lack the assurance and confidence which comes from knowledge gained in advance of need. School officials, everywhere, and citizens, too, should give active support to the idea of training for parenthood. . . .

Success as a parent involves the expenditure not of money and material advantages, but of one's self; one's time, imagination, skill and effort; one's companionship and counsel; one's faith, patience and love. It involves a knowledge and an acceptance of the obligations of marriage; an understanding of the needs of children, and a willingness to co-operate with schools, churches and civic agencies for their welfare. When we build personal security not alone for our own child but for all children, everywhere, then we shall, indeed, be architects of peace!

2. Psychiatrist Marynia F. Farnham and Sociologist Ferdinand Lundberg Denounce the Modern Woman as the "Lost Sex," 1947

The woman arriving at maturity today does so with certain fixed attitudes derived from her background and training. Her home life, very often, has been distorted. She has enjoyed an education identical with that of her brother. She expects to be allowed to select any kind of work for which she has inclination and training. She also, generally, expects to marry. At any rate, she usually intends to have "a go" at it. Some women expect to stop working when they marry; many others do not. She expects to find sexual gratification and believes in her inalienable right so to do. She is legally free to live and move as she chooses. She may seek divorce if her marriage fails to gratify her. She has access to contraceptive information so that, theoretically, she may control the size and spacing of her family. In very many instances, she owns and disposes of her own property. She has, it appears, her destiny entirely in her own hands.

All of this serves less to clarify and simplify her life than to complicate it with conflict piled on conflict. These conflicts are between her basic needs as a woman and the destiny she has carved out for herself—conflicts between the head and the heart, if you will. . . .

Thus she finds herself squarely in the middle of the most serious kind of divided purpose. If she is to undertake occupation outside her home with any kind of success, it is almost certain in the present day to be time-consuming and energy-demanding. So it is also with the problems she faces in her home. Certainly the tasks of a woman in bearing and educating children as well as maintaining, as best she may, the inner integrity of her home are capable of demanding all her time and best attention. However, she cannot obtain from them, so attenuated are these tasks now, the same sort of community approval and ego-satisfaction that she can from seemingly more challenging occupations which take her outside the home. Inevitably the dilemma has led to one compromise after another which we see exemplified on every hand in the modern woman's adaptation—an uneasy patchwork. . . .

It is becoming unquestionably more and more common for the woman to attempt to combine both home and child care and an outside activity, which is either work or career. Increasing numbers train for professional careers. When these two spheres are combined it is inevitable that one or the other will become of secondary concern and, this being the case, it is certain that the home will take that position. This is true, if only for the practical reason that no one can find and hold remunerative employment where the job itself doesn't take precedence over all other concerns. All sorts of agencies and instrumentalities have therefore been established to make possible the playing of this dual role. These are all in the direction of substitutes for the attention of the mother in the home and they vary from ordinary, untrained domestic service through the more highly trained grades of such service, to the public and private agencies now designed for the care, supervision and emotional untanglement of the children. The day nursery and its more elegant counterpart, the nursery school, are outstanding as the major agencies which make it possible for women to relinquish the care of children still in their infancy.

All these services and facilities produce what appears on the surface to be a smoothly functioning arrangement and one that provides children with obviously highly trained, expert and efficient care as well as with superior training in early skills and techniques and in adaptation to social relations. This surface, however, covers a situation that is by no means so smoothly functioning nor so satisfying either to the child or the woman. She must of necessity be deeply in conflict and only partially satisfied in either direction. Her work develops aggressiveness, which is essentially a denial of her femininity. . . .

Work that entices women out of their homes and provides them with prestige only at the price of feminine relinquishment, involves a response to masculine strivings. The more importance outside work assumes, the more are the masculine components of the woman's nature enhanced and encouraged. In her home and in her relationship to her children, it is imperative that these strivings be at a minimum and that her femininity be available both for her own satisfaction and for the satisfaction of her children and husband. She is, therefore, in the dangerous position of having to live one part of her life on the masculine level, another on the feminine. It is hardly astonishing that few can do so with success. One of these tendencies must of necessity achieve dominance over the other. The plain fact is that increasingly we are observing the masculinization of women and with it enormously dangerous consequences to the home, the children (if any) dependent on it, and to the ability of the woman, as well as her husband, to obtain sexual gratification. . . .

The dominant direction of feminine training and development today . . . discourages just those traits necessary to the attainment of sexual pleasure: receptivity and passiveness, a willingness to accept dependence without fear or resentment, with a deep inwardness and readiness for the final goal of sexual life—impregnation. It doesn't admit of wishes to control or master, to rival or dominate. The woman who is to find true gratification must love and accept her own womanhood as she loves and accepts her husband's manhood. Women's rivalry with men today, and the need to "equal" their accomplishments, engenders all too often anger and resentfulness toward men. Men, challenged, frequently respond in kind. So it is that women envy and feel hostile to men for just the attributes which women themselves require for "success" in the world. The woman's unconscious wish herself to possess the organ upon which she must thus depend militates greatly against her ability to accept its vast power to satisfy her when proffered to her in love.

Many women can find no solution to their dilemma and are defeated in attempts at adaptation. These constitute the array of the sick, unhappy, neurotic, wholly or partly incapable of dealing with life. . . .

It is not only the masculine woman who has met with an unhappy fate in the present situation. There are still many women who succeed in achieving adult life with largely unimpaired feminine strivings, for which home, a husband's love and children are to them the entirely adequate answers. It is their misfortune that they must enter a society in which such attitudes are little appreciated and are attended by many concrete, external penalties. Such women cannot fail to be affected by finding that their traditional activities are held in low esteem and that the woman who voluntarily undertakes them is often deprecated by her more aggressive contemporaries. She may come to believe that her situation is difficult, entailing serious deprivations, as against the more glamorous and exciting life other women seemingly enjoy. She may be set away from the main stream of life, very much in a backwater and fearful lest she lose her ability and talents through disuse and lack of stimulation. She may become sorry for herself and somewhat angered by her situation, gradually developing feelings of discontent and pressure. As her children grow older and require less of her immediate attention, the feelings of loss increase. . . .

In this way she may easily and quickly develop attitudes of discontent and anger injurious to her life adjustment. She may begin to malfunction sexually, her libidinal depths shaken by her ego frustrations.

So it is that society today makes it difficult for a woman to avoid the path leading to discontent and frustration and resultant hostility and destructiveness. Such destructiveness is, unfortunately, not confined in its effects to the woman alone. It reaches into all her relationships and all her functions. As a wife she is not only often ungratified but ungratifying and has, as we have noted, a profoundly disturbing effect upon her husband. Not only does he find himself without the satisfactions of a home directed and cared for by a woman happy in providing affection and devotion, but he is often confronted by circumstances of even more serious import for his own emotional integrity. His wife may be his covert rival, striving to match him in every aspect of their joint undertaking. Instead of supporting and encouraging his manliness and wishes for domination and power, she may thus impose upon him feelings of insufficiency and weakness. Still worse is the effect upon his sexual satisfactions. Where the woman is unable to admit and accept dependence upon her husband as the source of gratification and must carry her rivalry even into the act of love, she will seriously damage his sexual capacity. To be unable to gratify in the sexual act is for a man an intensely humiliating experience; here it is that mastery and domination, the central capacity of the man's sexual nature, must meet acceptance or fail. So it is that by their own character disturbances these women succeed ultimately in depriving themselves of the devotion and power of their husbands and become the instruments of bringing about their own psychic catastrophe.

But no matter how great a woman's masculine strivings, her basic needs make themselves felt and she finds herself facing her fundamental role as wife and mother with a divided mind. Deprived of a rich and creative home in which to find self-expression, she tries desperately to find a compromise. On the one hand she must retain her sources of real instinctual gratification and on the other, find ways of satisfying her need for prestige and esteem. Thus she stands, Janus-faced, drawn in two directions at once, often incapable of ultimate choice and inevitably penalized whatever direction she chooses.

3. African American Pauli Murray Explains Why Negro Girls Stay Single, 1947

There exists in the United States a system of discrimination based upon sex which I call "Jane Crow" because it is so strikingly similar to "Jim Crow," or prejudice based upon race.

Women still occupy a subordinate position as citizens of the American community, even though they may represent a majority of the potential voting population. The rationalizations upon which this sex prejudice rests are often different from those supporting racial discrimination in label only.

I should like to cite two examples of this prejudice. Harvard University, for three centuries the "prestige" school of presidents, supreme court justices, ambassadors and financiers, still does not permit a woman student to darken the doors of its law school, although I am unaware of any special relation between legal acumen and sex identity. Recently, however, Harvard Law School did weaken to the degree that a Hunter College graduate, Soia Memchikoff, was appointed as a member of the law school faculty.

Secondly, I winced considerably the other day when, upon picking up a copy of Ebony Magazine, a Negro pictorial publication, and seeing a current "spread" on Negro lawyers, I saw the pictures of many personal friends and associates of mine but observed that Negro women lawyers were conspicuous by their absence. . . . I wondered what quirk of the editor's attitude had permitted him or her to ignore the contributions of women attorneys like Edith Alexander and Judge Jane Bolin, just to mention two of our outstanding lawyers who have won their spots unquestionably in the legal profession.

Pauli Murray, "Why Negro Girls Stay Single," *Negro Digest* (July 1947): 4–8.

These two "case studies" suggest that despite their numerical size, women in the United States and perhaps throughout the world, with rare exceptions, are a minority group and suffer minority status. This minority status operates independently of race, religion or politics.

Every time I begin to bemoan the submerged status of the Negro woman among my white women friends, they hastily assure me that my problems are not unique and that they suffer just as much from "Jane Crow" as I do, particularly when it comes to advancement in their professional endeavors.

Within this framework of "male supremacy" as well as "white supremacy" the Negro woman finds herself at the bottom of the economic and social scale.

She is obviously in a state of revolt. This revolt proceeds in part from the consciousness on the part of the Negro woman that she has been compelled to act as breadwinner and cementer of family relationships in the Negro community since its inception. Historically, few Negro women have belonged to the leisure class, and what few social privileges they now enjoy have very often come "the hard way."

The rebellion against racial and sexual status is felt most keenly among Negro college-trained and professional women. With reference to my own generation, people now in their thirties, it is a matter of history that more Negro women proportionately have availed themselves of higher education than Negro men.

The complete hopelessness and dejection which led Negro boys of my age group to abandon their studies in droves before they completed a high school education or a trade, and to flounder about for years without vocational direction, is one of the tragic sources of frustration to the Negro woman of marriageable age. If professionally trained, she finds a shortage of her educational peers among men in Negro circles. She very often cannot find a mate with whom she can share all the richness of her life in addition to its functional aspects.

Having stayed in school far beyond the period of the average Negro boy, she now emerges with certain educational skills and often has a potential earning power far beyond the range of the majority of available single males—a social handicap if she wants marriage. Men usually shy away from women more highly trained than they are when the question of marriage is involved. It is too great a threat to their security.

Since the chances of the Negro trained woman for economic security are necessarily precarious because of the general underprivileged economic status of the Negro minority, in her relationship to the Negro male she can hope for little beyond emotional security.

But here again she is defeated. Emotional security arises from mature relationships among free and uninhibited individuals. The American Negro male is not prepared to offer emotional security because he has rarely, if ever, known it himself. His own emotional balance is that of a blindfolded tightrope walker before a jeering crowd. His submerged status in American life places unnatural stresses and strains upon his already inadequate equipment inherited from an immature democracy.

Our general mis-education of the sexes and our outmoded social tabus have helped to form rigid moulds into which the sexes are poured and which determine in advance the role men and women are to play in community life. Men are expected to act as if they are the lords of creation, the breadwinners and the warriors of our time and of all time. They play the role with varying degrees of ham-acting and success. . . .

The discerning eye soon discovers that many Negro men are well marked products of this sex mis-education. Charming individual exceptions appear here and there, but they are few. The Negro man who attempts to play the role of the dominant sex in a setting where the Negro woman has partially emancipated herself by dint of hard labor is face to face with emotional disaster. Particularly is this true in the case of the trained Negro woman who has become perhaps the most aggressive of the human species.

This impending emotional disaster is born of the contradictions in the life of the Negro male. He is the victim of constant frustration in his role as a male because socially he is subordinate to the white woman although he is trained to act as a member of the dominant sex. He is required to fit his human emotions into a racially determined pattern which may have nothing to do with his desires.

There is no earthly reason why a Negro man should not admire in a clean and healthy sort of way physical beauty, whether the bearer of the beauty be a Nordic Blonde or a West Indian Bronze. There is no reason why the Negro man today should find the white woman less attractive than did his white slave-owning ancestor find the African slavewoman desirable. Yet what sister of a Negro boy or man today does not know the family terror at the thought that some unguarded and unconscious look or gesture, though completely spontaneous and meaningless, may lead straight to ostracism, the faggot or the lynchman's noose!

The frustrations implicit in being a Negro are not only catastrophic to the Negro male's emotions, but lead him often to vent his resentments upon the Negro woman who may become his sex partner. The situation may be described in the homely saying, "Pa beats Ma, Ma beats me, and I beat hell out of the cat." Here, the Negro woman is without doubt "the cat."

On top of these difficulties, census figures suggest an unbalance between the sexes within racial groupings. Negro females far outnumber Negro males.

If the emotional security of the Negro woman depends upon proper mating and marriage, she is confronted with the inexorable logic of numbers which demands that she find a mate elsewhere than among Negro males, unless the American society which enforces bi-racialism also permits legal racial polygamy. From a biological and functional point of view, the logical solution to a shortage of available Negro males would be that Negro women find their mates in other ethnic groups.

This alternative faces the practical difficulty that there is a shortage of available males of marriageable age today in all groups. Secondly, to consciously seek interracial marriage would be denounced as sheer "treason" in the eyes of the "no social equality" advocates throughout the country. Yet, what other alternatives are open?

On the other hand, our racial stockades being what they are, Negro men who are in the market for Negro wives are not required to face honest and above-board competition from white members of their sex. Few white men are either mature or courageous enough to lift their emotional attractions for Negro women outside of the red light districts within the ghetto or the sub-rosa arrangements outside the ghetto into the clean light of healthy sex relationships looking toward legal marriage.

The Negro male, therefore, not only has no outside stimulus which operates to force him to improve his relationships with the Negro woman, but more damning, he stores up huge resentments against his rival, the white male who "slinks across the line" after dark, and very often turns this resentment upon himself and the Negro woman.

All of this contributes to a Jungle of human relationships, aggravates among Negroes the alienation of the sexes, intensifies homosexuality and often results in a rising incidence of crimes of passion, broken homes and divorces.

The problem of the Negro male cannot be solved within the Negro group unless it is being resolved simultaneously in the larger society. Readers of Negro periodicals will recall that Miss Almena Davis, editor of the Los Angeles Tribune, attempted more than a year ago to articulate the resentment of the Negro woman against the exposed position in which she finds herself by directing a critical editorial toward the sex habits of the Negro male. She won the Willkie Award in Journalism for her pains but incurred the wrath of almost every Negro male journalist in the country. Ann Petry added another fragment to the growing literature of revolt "from way down under," with her recent article, "What's Wrong With Negro Men," in NEGRO DIGEST. I have now jumped into the arena with both feet. What I think Almena Davis, Ann Petry and Pauli Murray are trying to say from their varied approaches is this:

We desire that the Negro male accept the Negro female as his equal and treat her accordingly and that he cease his ruthless aggression upon her and his emotional exploitation of her made possible by her admittedly inferior position as a social human being in the United States. That he strive for emotional maturity himself and see the Negro woman as a personality, an individual with infinite potentialities, and that in turn he require from the Negro woman an equal maturity and acceptance of responsibility in human relationships. That he maintain the dignity and respect for human personality with relation to the Negro woman in the sanctity of the marital chamber which he is expected to show in the law office or other professional set-up.

Despite the numerous limitations forced upon Negro men and women by our society, nevertheless certain improvements between the sexes are desirable and can be achieved.

4. Nonconformist Joyce Johnson Recounts Her Experience in Obtaining an Illegal Abortion in New York City, 1955

In June I didn't get my period. First it was a little late, and then a lot, but I still thought it would come anyway, and I waited, thinking I felt it sometimes. But finally it didn't come. A tangible, unbelievable fact, like sealed doom.

I was going to have a baby. But it was impossible for me to have a baby. . . .

The father was a child of my own age—a wrecked boy I'd known from Columbia who already had a drinking problem and lived, doing nothing, with his parents in Connecticut. I didn't love this boy. Sometimes you went to bed with people almost by mistake, at the end of late, shapeless nights when you'd stayed up so long it almost didn't matter—the thing was, not to go home. Such nights lacked premeditation, so you couldn't be very careful; you counted on a stranger's carefulness. The boy promised to pull out before the danger—but he didn't. And although I could have reminded him of his promise in time, I didn't do that either, remembering too late it was the middle of the month in a bedroom on East Ninety-sixth Street that smelled of smoke and soiled clothing, with leftover voices from that night's party outside the closed door.

I'd gotten a therapist by then—a $7.50 man, a rejected boyfriend of the woman whose apartment I was living in. I told him my problem. "I see," he said, rubbing his large chin, staring out over Central Park West.

There was a box of Kleenex on the small Danish-modern table near my head. He had pointedly placed boxes of tissues in several locations in his office. But I never cried.

I explained to this therapist why I didn't see how I could become a mother. Aside from being twenty years old, I lived on fifty dollars a week and had cut myself off from my family. I said I would rather die. And then I asked him what Elise had told me to: "Could you get me a therapeutic abortion?" (I'd never heard the term before she explained what it meant.)

"Oh, I wouldn't even try," he said.

I hadn't thought he wouldn't try.

Life was considered sacred. But independence could be punishable by death. The punishment for sex was, appropriately, sexual.

There were women in those days who kept slips of paper, like talismans to ward off disaster, on which were written the names of doctors who would perform illegal abortions. Neither Elise nor I knew any of these women. You had to ask around. You asked friends and they asked friends, and the ripples of asking people widened until some person whose face you might never see gave over the secret information that could save you. This could take time, and you only had two months, they said, and you'd lost one month anyway, through not being sure.

The therapist called my roommate, got from her the name of the boy who had made me pregnant. He called the boy and threatened to disclose the whole matter to his parents unless the boy came up with the money for an illegal abortion. The boy called me, drunk and wild with fear. I hadn't expected anything of this boy except one thing—that when I had an abortion he'd go there with me; there had to be someone with you, I felt, that you knew. But as for blaming this boy—I didn't. I knew I had somehow let this happen to me. There had been a moment in that bedroom on Ninety-sixth Street, a moment of blank suspension, of not caring whether I lived or died. It seemed important to continue to see this moment very clearly. I knew the boy wouldn't come with me now.

I went to see the therapist one last time to tell him he had done something terribly wrong.

"Yes," he admitted, looking sheepish. "I've probably made a mistake."

I said, "I'm never coming back. I owe you thirty-seven fifty. Try and get it."

Someone finally came up with a person who knew a certain doctor in Canarsie. If you called this person at the advertising agency where he worked, he wouldn't give you the doctor's name—he'd ask you if you wanted to have a drink with him in the Rainbow Room, and over martinis he might agree to escort you out to see the doctor. This person wasn't a great humanitarian; he was a young man who had a weird hobby—taking girls to get abortions. He'd ask you if you wanted to recuperate afterward at his house on Fire Island. You were advised to say no.

Blind dates were a popular social form of the fifties. As I sat in the cocktail lounge of the Rainbow Room, staring through the glass doors at crew-cutted young men in seersucker suits who came off the elevator lacking the red bow tie I'd been told to watch out for, I realized that despite the moment in the bedroom, I probably didn't want to die, since I seemed to be going to an enormous amount of effort to remain living. If it happened that I died after all, it would be an accident.

He turned up a half-hour late in his blue and white stripes. "Why, you're pretty," he said, pleased. He told me he liked blondes. He made a phone call after we had our drinks, and came back to the table to say the doctor would see us that night. "I hope you don't have anything lined up," he said.

He offered me sticks of Wrigley spearmint chewing gum on the BMT to Canarsie. People in jokes sometimes came from there, but I'd never been to that part of Brooklyn in my life.

Canarsie was rows of small brick houses with cement stoops and yards filled with wash and plaster saints. Boys were playing stickball in the dusk. You could disappear into Canarsie.

The doctor seemed angry that we had come, but he led us into his house after we rang the bell, and switched on a light in his waiting room. He was fat, with a lot of wiry grey hair on his forearms; a white shirt wet and rumpled with perspiration stretched over his belly. The room looked like a room in which only the very poor would ever wait. There were diplomas on the walls, framed behind dusty glass; I tried to read the Latin. He glared at me and said he wanted me to know he did tonsillectomies. To do "the other"—he didn't say *abortions*—disgusted him. I made efforts to nod politely.

My escort spoke up and said, "How about next week?"

"All right. Wednesday."

I felt panic at the thought of Wednesday. What if my mother called the office and found out I was sick, and came running over to the apartment? "No," I said, "Friday. It has to be Friday."

"Friday will cost you extra," the doctor said. . . .

I'd managed to borrow the five hundred dollars from a friend in her late twenties, who'd borrowed it from a wealthy married man who was her lover. With the cash in a sealed envelope in my purse. I stood for an hour that Friday morning in front of a cigar store on Fourteenth Street, waiting for the young advertising executive. I got awfully scared that he wouldn't come. Could I find the doctor's house myself in those rows of nearly identical houses?

There was a haze over Fourteenth Street that made even the heat seem grey. I stared across the street at Klein's Department Store, where my mother had taken me shopping for bargains, and imagined myself dying a few hours later with the sign KLEIN's the last thing that flashed through my consciousness.

But finally the young man did materialize out of a cab. "Sorry to have kept you waiting." He'd brought some back issues of *The New Yorker,* and planned to catch up on his reading during the operation.

Upstairs in Canarsie, the doctor who did tonsillectomies had a room where he only did abortions. A freshly painted room where every surface was covered with white towels. He himself put on a mask and a white surgeon's gown. It was as if all that white was the color of his fear.

"Leave on the shoes!" he barked as I climbed up on his table almost fully clothed. Was I expected to make a run for it if the police rang his doorbell in the middle of the operation? He yelled at me to do this and do that, and it sent him into a rage that my legs were shaking, so how could he do what he had to do? But if I didn't want him to do it, that was all right with him. I said I wanted him to do it. I was crying. But he wouldn't take the money until after he'd given me the local anesthetic. He gave me one minute to change my mind before he handed me my purse.

The whole thing took two hours, but it seemed much longer through the pain. I had the impression that this doctor in all his fear was being extremely careful, that I was even lucky to have found him. He gave me pills when it was over, and told me I could call him only if anything went wrong. "But don't ever let me catch you back here again, young lady!"

I staggered down the cement steps of his house with my life. It was noon in Canarsie, an ordinary day in July. My escort was saying he thought it would be hard to find a cab, we should walk in the direction of the subway. On a street full of shops, I leaned against the window of a supermarket until he flagged one down. Color seemed to have come back into the world. Housewives passed in floral nylon dresses; diamonds of sunlight glinted off the windshields of cars.

On the cab ride across the Manhattan Bridge, the young man from the ad agency placed his hand on my shoulder. "I have this house out on Fire Island," he began. "I thought that this weekend—"

"No thanks," I said. "I'll be okay in the city."

He removed his hand, and asked if I'd drop him off at his office—"unless you mind going home alone."

I said I'd get there by myself.

5. A Letter to the Editor of *The Ladder* from an African American Lesbian, 1957

Please find enclosed a money order for $2.00. I should like to receive as many of your back issues as that amount will cover. In the event $2.00 is in excess of the cost of six issues—well, fine. Those few cents may stand as a mere downpayment toward sizeable (for me, that is) donations I know already that I shall be sending to you.

I hope you are somewhat interested in off-the-top-of-the-head reactions from across the country because I would like to offer a few by way of the following:

(1) I'm glad as heck that you exist. You are obviously serious people and I feel that women, without wishing to foster any strict *separatist* notions, homo or hetero, indeed have a need for their own publications and organizations. Our problems, our experiences as women are profoundly unique as compared to the other half of the human race. Women, like other oppressed groups of one kind or another, have partic-ularly had to pay a price for the intellectual impoverishment that the second class status imposed on us for centuries created and sustained. Thus, I feel that THE LADDER is a fine, elementary step in a rewarding direction.

(2) Rightly or wrongly (in view of some of the thought provoking discussions I have seen elsewhere in a homosexual publication) I could not help but be encouraged and relieved by one of the almost subsidiary points under Point I of your declaration of purpose, "(to advocate) a mode of behaviour and dress acceptable to society." As

L. H. N., *The Ladder* 1, no. 8 (May 1957): 26.

one raised in a cultural experience (I am a Negro) where those within were and are forever lecturing to their fellows about how to appear acceptable to the dominant social group, I know something about the shallowness of such a view as an end in itself.

The most splendid argument is simple and to the point, Ralph Bunche, with all his clean fingernails, degrees, and, of course, undeniable service to the human race, could still be insulted, denied a hotel room or meal in many parts of our country. (Not to mention the possibility of being lynched on a lonely Georgia road for perhaps having demanded a glass of water in the wrong place.)

What ought to be clear is that one is oppressed or discriminated against because one is different, not "wrong" or "bad" somehow. This is perhaps the bitterest of the entire pill. HOWEVER, as a matter of facility, of expediency, one has to take a critical view of revolutionary attitudes which in spite of the BASIC truth I have mentioned above, may tend to aggravate the problems of a group.

I have long since passed that period when I felt personal discomfort at the sight of an ill-dressed or illiterate Negro. Social awareness has taught me where to lay the blame. Someday, I expect, the "discreet" Lesbian will not turn her head on the streets at the sight of the "butch" strolling hand in hand with her friend in their trousers and definitive haircuts. But for the moment, it still disturbs. It creates an impossible area for discussion with one's most enlightened (to use a hopeful term) heterosexual friends. Thus, I agree with the inclusion of that point in your declaration to the degree of wanting to comment on it.

(3) I am impressed by the general tone of your articles. The most serious fault being at this juncture that there simply is too little.

(4) Would it be presumptuous or far-fetched to suggest that you try for some overseas communications? One hears so much of publications and organizations devoted to homosexuality and homosexuals in Europe; but as far as I can gather these seem to lean heavily toward male questions and interests.

Just a little afterthought: considering Mattachine; Bilitis, ONE; all seem to be cropping up on the West Coast rather than here where a vigorous and active gay set almost bump one another off the streets—what is it in the air out there? Pioneers still? Or a tougher circumstance which inspires battle? Would like to hear speculation, light-hearted or otherwise.

L. H. N.
New York, N.Y.

6. Betty Friedan Reveals the "Problem That Has No Name," 1963

The problem lay buried, unspoken, for many years in the minds of American women. It was a strange stirring, a sense of dissatisfaction, a yearning that women suffered in the middle of the twentieth century in the United States. Each suburban wife struggled with it alone. As she made the beds, shopped for groceries, matched slip-cover material, ate peanut butter sandwiches with her children, chauffeured Cub

Scouts and Brownies, lay beside her husband at night—she was afraid to ask even of herself the silent question—"Is this all?"

For over fifteen years there was no word of this yearning in the millions of words written about women, for women, in all the columns, books and articles by experts telling women their role was to seek fulfillment as wives and mothers. Over and over women heard in voices of tradition and of Freudian sophistication that they could desire no greater destiny than to glory in their own femininity. Experts told them how to catch a man and keep him, how to breastfeed children and handle their toilet training, how to cope with sibling rivalry and adolescent rebellion; how to buy a dishwasher, bake bread, cook gourmet snails, and build a swimming pool with their own hands; how to dress, look, and act more feminine and make marriage more exciting; how to keep their husbands from dying young and their sons from growing into delinquents. They were taught to pity the neurotic, unfeminine, unhappy women who wanted to be poets or physicists or presidents. They learned that truly feminine women do not want careers, higher education, political rights— the independence and the opportunities that the old-fashioned feminists fought for. Some women, in their forties and fifties, still remembered painfully giving up those dreams, but most of the younger women no longer even thought about them. A thousand expert voices applauded their femininity, their adjustment, their new maturity. All they had to do was devote their lives from earliest girlhood to finding a husband and bearing children. . . .

The suburban housewife—she was the dream image of the young American women and the envy, it was said, of women all over the world. The American housewife—freed by science and labor-saving appliances from the drudgery, the dangers of childbirth and the illnesses of her grandmother. She was healthy, beautiful, educated, concerned only about her husband, her children, her home. She had found true feminine fulfillment. As a housewife and mother, she was respected as a full and equal partner to man in his world. She was free to choose automobiles, clothes, appliances, supermarkets; she had everything that women ever dreamed of.

In the fifteen years after World War II, this mystique of feminine fulfillment became the cherished and self-perpetuating core of contemporary American culture. Millions of women lived their lives in the image of those pretty pictures of the American suburban housewife, kissing their husbands goodbye in front of the picture window, depositing their stationwagonsful of children at school, and smiling as they ran the new electric waxer over the spotless kitchen floor. They baked their own bread, sewed their own and their children's clothes, kept their new washing machines and dryers running all day. They changed the sheets on the beds twice a week instead of once, took the rug-hooking class in adult education, and pitied their poor frustrated mothers, who had dreamed of having a career. Their only dream was to be perfect wives and mothers; their highest ambition to have five children and a beautiful house, their only fight to get and keep their husbands. They had no thought for the unfeminine problems of the world outside the home; they wanted the men to make the major decisions. They gloried in their role as women, and wrote proudly on the census blank: "Occupation: housewife."

For over fifteen years, the words written for women, and the words women used when they talked to each other, while their husbands sat on the other side of the room and talked shop or politics or septic tanks, were about problems with their children, or how to keep their husbands happy, or improve their children's school, or cook chicken or make slipcovers. Nobody argued whether women were inferior or superior to men; they were simply different. Words like "emancipation" and "career" sounded strange and embarrassing; no one had used them for years. When a Frenchwoman named Simone de Beauvoir wrote a book called *The Second Sex,* an American critic commented that she obviously "didn't know what life was all about," and besides, she was talking about French women. The "woman problem" in America no longer existed.

If a woman had a problem in the 1950's and 1960's, she knew that something must be wrong with her marriage, or with herself. Other women were satisfied with their lives, she thought. What kind of a woman was she if she did not feel this mysterious fulfillment waxing the kitchen floor? She was so ashamed to admit her dissatisfaction that she never knew how many other women shared it. If she tried to tell her husband, he didn't understand what she was talking about. She did not really understand it herself. For over fifteen years women in America found it harder to talk about this problem than about sex. Even the psychoanalysts had no name for it. When a woman went to a psychiatrist for help, as many women did, she would say, "I'm so ashamed," or "I must be hopelessly neurotic." "I don't know what's wrong with women today," a suburban psychiatrist said uneasily. "I only know something is wrong because most of my patients happen to be women. And their problem isn't sexual." Most women with this problem did not go to see a psychoanalyst, however. "There's nothing wrong really," they kept telling themselves. "There isn't any problem."

But on an April morning in 1959, I heard a mother of four, having coffee with four other mothers in a suburban development fifteen miles from New York, say in a tone of quiet desperation, "the problem." And the others knew, without words, that she was not talking about a problem with her husband, or her children, or her home. Suddenly they realized they all shared the same problem, the problem that has no name. They began, hesitantly, to talk about it. Later, after they had picked up their children at nursery school and taken them home to nap, two of the women cried, in sheer relief, just to know they were not alone.

Gradually I came to realize that the problem that has no name was shared by countless women in America. As a magazine writer I often interviewed women about problems with their children, or their marriages, or their houses, or their communities. But after a while I began to recognize the telltale signs of this other problem. I saw the same signs in suburban ranch houses and split-levels on Long Island and in New Jersey and Westchester County; in colonial houses in a small Massachusetts town; on patios in Memphis; in suburban and city apartments; in living rooms in the Midwest. Sometimes I sensed the problem, not as a reporter, but as a suburban housewife, for during this time I was also bringing up my own three children in Rockland County, New York. I heard echoes of the problem in college dormitories and semi-private maternity wards, at PTA meetings and luncheons of the League of Women Voters, at suburban cocktail parties, in station wagons waiting for trains, and in snatches of conversation overheard at Schrafft's. The groping words I heard from other women, on quiet afternoons when children were at school or on quiet evenings when husbands worked late, I think I understood first as a woman long before I understood their larger social and psychological implications.

Just what was this problem that has no name? What were the words women used when they tried to express it? Sometimes a woman would say "I feel empty somehow . . . incomplete." Or she would say, "I feel as if I don't exist." Sometimes she blotted out the feeling with a tranquilizer. Sometimes she thought the problem was with her husband, or her children, or that what she really needed was to redecorate her house, or move to a better neighborhood, or have an affair, or another baby. Sometimes, she went to a doctor with symptoms she could hardly describe: "A tired feeling . . . I get so angry with the children it scares me . . . I feel like crying without any reason." (A Cleveland doctor called it "the housewife's syndrome.") . . .

Most men, and some women, still did not know that this problem was real. But those who had faced it honestly knew that all the superficial remedies, the sympathetic advice, the scolding words and the cheering words were somehow drowning the problem in unreality. A bitter laugh was beginning to be heard from American women. They were admired, envied, pitied, theorized over until they were sick of it, offered drastic solutions or silly choices that no one could take seriously. They got all kinds of advice from the growing armies of marriage and child-guidance counselors, psychotherapists, and armchair psychologists, on how to adjust to their role as housewives. No other road to fulfillment was offered to American women in the middle of the twentieth century. Most adjusted to their role and suffered or ignored the problem that has no name. It can be less painful for a woman, not to hear the strange, dissatisfied voice stirring within her.

It is no longer possible to ignore that voice, to dismiss the desperation of so many American women. This is not what being a woman means, no matter what the experts say. For human suffering there is a reason; perhaps the reason has not been found because the right questions have not been asked, or pressed far enough. I do not accept the answer that there is no problem because American women have luxuries that women in other times and lands never dreamed of; part of the strange newness of the problem is that it cannot be understood in terms of the age-old material problems of man: poverty, sickness, hunger, cold. The women who suffer this problem have a hunger that food cannot fill. It persists in women whose husbands are struggling internes and law clerks, or prosperous doctors and lawyers; in wives of workers and executives who make $5,000 a year or $50,000. It is not caused by lack of material advantages; it may not even be felt by women preoccupied with desperate problems of hunger, poverty or illness. And women who think it will be solved by more money, a bigger house, a second car, moving to a better suburb, often discover it gets worse.

It is no longer possible today to blame the problem on loss of femininity: to say that education and independence and equality with men have made American women unfeminine. I have heard so many women try to deny this dissatisfied voice within themselves because it does not fit the pretty picture of femininity the experts have given them. I think, in fact, that this is the first clue to the mystery: the problem cannot be understood in the generally accepted terms by which scientists have studied women, doctors have treated them, counselors have advised them, and writers have written about them. Women who suffer this problem, in whom this voice is stirring, have lived their whole lives in the pursuit of feminine fulfillment. They are not career women (although career women may have other problems); they are women whose greatest ambition has been marriage and children. For the oldest of these women, these daughters of the American middle class, no other dream was possible. The ones in their forties and fifties who once had other dreams gave them up and threw themselves joyously into life as housewives. For the youngest, the new wives and mothers, this was the only dream. They are the ones who quit high school and college to marry, or marked time in some job in which they had no real interest until they married. These women are very "feminine" in the usual sense, and yet they still suffer the problem. . . .

If I am right, the problem that has no name stirring in the minds of so many American women today is not a matter of loss of femininity or too much education, or the demands of domesticity. It is far more important than anyone recognizes. It is the key to these other new and old problems which have been torturing women and their husbands and children, and puzzling their doctors and educators for years. It may well be the key to our future as a nation and a culture. We can no longer ignore that voice within women that says: "I want something more than my husband and my children and my home."

⬦ E S S A Y S

In the first essay, Joanne Meyerowitz of Yale University contends that America's post-war popular media "delivered multiple messages" to women, simultaneously glorifying and subverting domesticity. Meyerowitz's claim that the post-war discourse offered women some opportunity to construct individual identities that resisted domesticity is contested by Rickie Solinger, at least with regard to reproduction and abortion. Solinger, an independent scholar, examines the politics of abortion in America from 1950 to 1970, arguing that post-war turmoil among medical doctors over the issue of abortion produced hospital policies that curtailed women's already limited ability to end unwanted pregnancies safely and legally. These essays differ greatly in their approach to the construction of female identity in the post-war era.

Competing Images of Women in Postwar Mass Culture

JOANNE MEYEROWITZ

In 1963 Betty Friedan published *The Feminine Mystique,* an instant best seller. Friedan argued, often brilliantly, that American women, especially suburban women, suffered from deep discontent. In the postwar era, she wrote, journalists, educators, advertisers, and social scientists had pulled women into the home with an ideological stranglehold, the "feminine mystique." This repressive "image" held that women could "find fulfillment only in sexual passivity, male domination, and nurturing maternal love." It denied "women careers or any commitment outside the home" and "narrowed woman's world down to the home, cut her role back to housewife." In Friedan's formulation, the writers and editors of mass-circulation magazines, especially women's magazines, were the "Frankensteins" who had created this "feminine monster." In her defense of women, Friedan did not choose a typical liberal feminist language of rights, equality, or even justice. Influenced by the new human potential

Joanne Meyerowitz, "Beyond the Feminine Mystique: A Reassessment of Postwar Mass Culture, 1946–1958," *Journal of American History* 79, no. 4 (March 1993): 1455–1482. Reprinted by permission of the Organization of American Historians.

psychology, she argued instead that full-time domesticity stunted women and denied their "basic human need to grow." For Friedan, women and men found personal identity and fulfillment through individual achievement, most notably through careers. Without such growth, she claimed, women would remain unfulfilled and unhappy, and children would suffer at the hands of neurotic mothers.

The Feminine Mystique had an indisputable impact. Hundreds of women have testified that the book changed their lives, and historical accounts often credit it with launching the recent feminist movement. But the book has also had other kinds of historical impact. For a journalistic exposé, Friedan's work has had a surprisingly strong influence on historiography. In fact, since Friedan published *The Feminine Mystique,* historians of American women have adopted wholesale her version of the postwar ideology. While many historians question Friedan's homogenized account of women's actual experience, virtually all accept her version of the dominant ideology, the conservative promotion of domesticity.

According to this now-standard historical account, postwar authors urged women to return to the home while only a handful of social scientists, trade unionists, and feminists protested. As one recent rendition states: "In the wake of World War II . . . the short-lived affirmation of women's independence gave way to a pervasive endorsement of female subordination and domesticity." Much of this secondary literature relies on a handful of conservative postwar writings, the same writings cited liberally by Friedan. In particular, the work of Dr. Marynia F. Farnham, a viciously antifeminist psychiatrist, and her sidekick, sociologist Ferdinand Lundberg, is invoked repeatedly as typical of the postwar era. In this standard account, the domestic ideology prevailed until such feminists as Friedan triumphed in the 1960s.

When I first began research on the postwar era, I accepted this version of history. But as I investigated the public culture, I encountered what I then considered exceptional evidence—books, articles, and films that contradicted the domestic ideology. I decided to conduct a more systematic investigation. This essay reexamines the middle-class popular discourse on women by surveying mass-circulation monthly magazines of the postwar era (1946–1958). The systematic sample includes nonfiction articles on women in "middlebrow" magazines (*Reader's Digest* and *Coronet*), "highbrow" magazines (*Harper's* and *Atlantic Monthly*), magazines aimed at African Americans (*Ebony* and *Negro Digest*), and those aimed at women (*Ladies' Home Journal* and *Woman's Home Companion*). The sample includes 489 nonfiction articles, ranging from Hollywood gossip to serious considerations of gender. In 1955 these magazines had a combined circulation of over 22 million. Taken together, the magazines reached readers from all classes, races, and genders, but the articles seem to represent the work of middle-class journalists, and articles written by women seem to outnumber ones by men.

My goal in constructing this sample was not to replicate Friedan's magazine research, which focused primarily on short story fiction in four women's magazines. Rather my goal was to test generalizations about postwar mass culture (that is, commodified forms of popular culture) by surveying another side of it. To this end, I chose nonfiction articles in a larger sample of popular magazines. Some of the magazines of smaller circulation, such as *Harper's* and *Negro Digest,* were perhaps outside the "mainstream." But including them in the sample enabled me to incorporate more of the diversity in American society, to investigate the contours of a broader bourgeois culture and some variations within it. Since my conclusions rest on a sample of nonfiction articles in eight popular magazines, they can provide only a tentative portrait of postwar culture. Future studies based on different magazines or on fiction, advertisements, films, television, or radio will no doubt suggest additional layers of complexity in mass culture and different readings of it. . . .

For Betty Friedan and for some historians, popular magazines represented a repressive force, imposing damaging images on vulnerable American women. Many historians today adopt a different approach in which mass culture is neither monolithic nor unrelentingly repressive. In this view, mass culture is rife with contradictions, ambivalence, and competing voices. We no longer assume that any text has a single, fixed meaning for all readers, and we sometimes find within the mass media subversive, as well as repressive, potential.

With a somewhat different sample and a somewhat different interpretive approach, I come to different conclusions about postwar mass culture than did Friedan and her followers. Friedan's widely accepted version of the "feminine mystique," I suggest, is only one piece of the postwar cultural puzzle. The popular literature I sampled did not simply glorify domesticity or demand that women return to or stay at home. All of the magazines sampled advocated both the domestic and the nondomestic, sometimes in the same sentence. In this literature, domestic ideals coexisted in ongoing tension with an ethos of individual achievement that celebrated nondomestic activity, individual striving, public service, and public success. . . .

In popular magazines, the theme of individual achievement rang most clearly in the numerous articles on individual women. These articles appeared with frequency throughout the postwar era: they comprised over 60 percent, or 300, of the 489 nonfiction articles sampled. These articles usually recounted a story of a woman's life or a particularly telling episode in her life. In formulaic accounts, they often constructed what one such article labeled "this Horatio Alger success story—feminine version." Of these articles, 33 percent spotlighted women with unusual talents, jobs, or careers, and another 29 percent focused on prominent entertainers. Typically they related a rise to public success punctuated by a lucky break, a dramatic comeback, a selfless sacrifice, or a persistent struggle to overcome adversity. Such stories appeared in all of the magazines sampled, but they appeared most frequently in the African-American magazines, *Ebony* and *Negro Digest,* and the white "middlebrow" magazines, *Coronet* and *Reader's Digest.* Journalists reworked the formula for different readers: In *Negro Digest,* for example, articles returned repeatedly to black performers who defied racism; in *Reader's Digest* they more often addressed white leaders in community service. In general, though, the articles suggested that the noteworthy woman rose above and beyond ordinary domesticity. Or, as one story stated, "This is the real-life fairy tale of a girl who hurtled from drab obscurity to sudden, startling fame."

At the heart of many such articles lay a bifocal vision of women both as feminine and domestic and as public achievers. In one article, "The Lady Who Licked Crime in Portland," the author, Richard L. Neuberger, juxtaposed domestic stereotypes and newsworthy nondomestic achievement. The woman in question, Dorothy McCullough Lee, was, the article stated, an "ethereally pale housewife" who tipped "the scales at 110 pounds." But more to the point, she was also the mayor of Portland, Oregon, who had defeated, single-handedly it seems, the heavyweights of organized crime. Before winning the mayoral election in 1948, this housewife had opened a law firm and served in the state legislature, both House and Senate, and as Portland's commissioner of public utilities. Despite her "frail, willowy" appearance, the fearless mayor had withstood ridicule, recall petitions, and threatening mail in her "relentless drive" against gambling and prostitution. She was, the article related without further critique, a "violent feminist" who had "intense concern with the status of women." And, according to all, she was "headed for national distinction." The article concluded with an admiring quotation describing Mayor Lee's fancy hats as the plumes of a crusading knight in armor. Here the feminine imagery blended with a metaphor of masculine public service. . . .

While feminine stereotypes sometimes provided convenient foils that enhanced by contrast a woman's atypical public accomplishment, they also served as conservative reminders that all women, even publicly successful women, were to maintain traditional gender distinctions. In their opening paragraphs, numerous authors described their successful subjects as pretty, motherly, shapely, happily married, petite, charming, or soft voiced. This emphasis on femininity and domesticity (and the two were often conflated) seems to have cloaked a submerged fear of lesbian, mannish, or man-hating women. This fear surfaced in an unusual article on athlete Babe Didrikson Zaharias. In her early years, the article stated, the Babe's "boyish bob and freakish clothes . . . [her] dislike of femininity" had led observers to dismiss her as an "Amazon." But after her marriage, she "became a woman," a transformation signaled, according to the approving author, by lipstick, polished nails, and "loose, flowing" hair as well as by an interest in the domestic arts of cooking, sewing, and entertaining. In this article, as in others, allusions to femininity and domesticity probably helped legitimate women's public achievements. Authors attempted to reassure readers that conventional gender distinctions and heterosexuality remained intact even as women competed successfully in work, politics, or sports. . . .

Nonetheless, the emphasis on the domestic and feminine should not be overstated; these articles on women's achievement did not serve solely or even primarily as lessons in traditional gender roles. The theme of nondomestic success was no hidden subtext in these stories. In most articles, the rise to public achievement was the first, and sometimes the only, narrative concern. When addressing both the domestic and the nondomestic, these articles placed public success at center stage: they tended to glorify frenetic activity, with domesticity at best a sideshow in a woman's three-ring circus. . . .

Marriage and domesticity were not prerequisites for star status in magazine stories. Over one-third of the articles on individual women featured unmarried women, divorced women, or women of unmentioned marital status. The African-American magazines seemed least concerned with marital status, but all of the magazines included articles that did not conjoin public success with connubial harmony. While a few such articles advocated marriage, others discounted it directly. Still other articles related the public achievements of divorced women, with consistent sympathy for the women involved. . . .

Magazines articles, of course, do not reveal the responses of readers. Formulaic stories of success do not seem to have provoked controversy: those magazines that published readers' responses rarely included letters regarding these stories. Some supplementary evidence, however, suggests that the language used in success stories also appeared in the language of at least some readers. The *Woman's Home Companion* conducted opinion polls in 1947 and 1949 in which readers named the women they most admired. In both years the top four women were Eleanor Roosevelt, Helen Keller, Sister Elizabeth Kenny (who worked with polio victims), and Clare Boothe Luce (author and congresswoman), all distinctly nondomestic women. Why did readers select these particular women? They seemed to offer the same answers as the success stories: "courage, spirit, and conviction," "devotion to the public good," and "success in overcoming obstacles." While a feminine version of selfless sacrifice seems to have won kudos, individual striving and public service superseded devotion to home and family.

On the one hand, one might see these success stories as pernicious. They applied to women a traditionally male, middle-class discourse of individual achievement that glorified a version of success, honor, and fulfillment that was difficult enough for middle-class white men, highly unlikely for able-bodied women of any class and race, and nearly impossible for the ill, disabled, and disfigured. As fantasies of unlikely success, they offered false promises that hard work brought women public reward. They probably gave women readers vicarious pleasure or compensatory esteem, but they provided no real alternatives to most women's workaday lives. They usually downplayed the obstacles that women faced in the public arena, and they implicitly dismissed the need for collective protest. Further, they did not overtly challenge traditional gender roles. With frequent references to domesticity and femininity, narrowly defined, they reinforced rigid definitions of appropriate female behavior and sexual expression, and they neglected the conflicts between domestic and nondomestic demands that many women undoubtedly encountered.

On the other hand, these articles subverted the notion that women belonged at home. They presented a wide variety of options open to women and praised the women who had chosen to assert themselves as public figures. They helped readers, male and female, envision women in positions of public achievement. They tried openly to inspire women to pursue unusual goals, domestic or not, and they sometimes suggested that public service brought more obvious rewards than devotion to family. By applauding the public possibilities open to women, including married women, they may have validated some readers' nondomestic behavior and sharpened some readers' discontent with the constraints they experienced in their domestic lives. At least one contemporary observer noticed this subversive side to stories of individual success. Dr. Marynia Farnham, the antifeminist, railed not only against the "propaganda of the feminists'" but also against "stories about famous career women," which, she claimed, undermined the prestige of motherhood. . . .

The postwar popular discourse on women, then, did not simply exhort women to stay at home. Its complexity is also seen in . . . articles that addressed questions of gender directly. The topics of those articles ranged from women in India to premenstrual tension, but most fell into four broad categories: women's paid work, women's political activism, marriage and domesticity, and glamour and sexuality. . . .

On the issue of paid employment, there was rough consensus. Despite concerns for the postwar economy, journalists in this sample consistently defended wage work for women. Articles insisted that women, including married women, worked for wages because they needed money. . . . Articles praised women workers in specific occupations, from secretaries to doctors. These articles related exciting, stimulating, or rewarding job possibilities or the "practically unlimited" opportunities allegedly available to women. Like the success stories, these articles sometimes encouraged individual striving. "Advancement," one such article claimed, "will be limited only by [a woman's] intelligence, application, and education." The African-American magazines, *Ebony* and *Negro Digest,* alert to racism, showed more explicit aware- ness of institutional barriers to individual effort and sometimes noted discrimination based not only on race but also on gender. One article, for example, not only praised black women doctors but also denounced the "stubborn male prejudice" faced by "petticoat medics." In general, though, the articles on specific occupations did not attack sexism or the sexual division of labor directly; they simply encouraged women to pursue white-collar jobs in business and the professions.

Beneath the consensus, though, a quiet debate exposed the tensions between the ideals of nondomestic achievement and of domestic duty. Echoing earlier debates of the 1920s, some authors advised women to subordinate careers to home and mother- hood while others invited women to pursue public success. The question of careers was rarely discussed at any length, and the relative silence itself underscores how postwar popular magazines often avoided contended issues. But throwaway lines in various articles sometimes landed on one side of the debate or the other. In a single article in *Ebony,* for example, one unmarried career woman warned readers, "Don't sacrifice marriage for career," while another stated, "I like my life just as it is." . . .

The postwar popular magazines were more unequivocally positive on increased participation of women in politics. The *Ladies' Home Journal,* not known for its feminist sympathies, led the way with numerous articles that supported women as political and community leaders. In 1947, lawyer and longtime activist Margaret Hickey, former president of the National Federation of Business and Professional Women's Clubs, launched the *Journal*'s monthly "Public Affairs Department," which encouraged women's participation in mainstream politics and reform. In one article, Hickey stated bluntly, "Make politics your business. Voting, office holding, raising your voice for new and better laws are just as important to your home and your family as the evening meal or spring house cleaning." Like earlier Progressive reformers, Hickey sometimes justified nondomestic political action by its benefits to home and family, but her overall message was clear: women should participate outside the home, and not just by voting. . . .

Reports on women politicians stressed the series' recurring motif, "They Do It . . . You Can Too." This article presented women politicians as exemplars. With direct appeals to housewives, it praised women who ran for office, even mothers of "babies or small children" who could "find time and ways to campaign and to win elections." It presented political activism not only as a public service but also as a source of personal fulfillment. For women who held political office, it claimed, "there is great pride of accomplishment and the satisfaction of 'doing a job.'" . . .

Historians sometimes contend that the Cold War mentality encouraged domes- ticity, that it envisioned family life and especially mothers as buffers against the al- leged Communist threat. But Cold War rhetoric had other possible meanings for women. In the *Ladies' Home Journal,* authors often used the Cold War to promote women's political participation. One such approach contrasted "free society" of the United States with Soviet oppression, including oppression of women. . . . Other articles stressed that Soviet citizens, male and female, did not participate in a democratic process. American women could prove the strength of democracy by avoiding "citizen apathy," by "giving the world a lively demonstration of how a free society can serve its citizens," by making "free government work well as an example for the undecided and unsatisfied millions elsewhere in the world." . . .

The role of the housewife and mother was problematic in the postwar popular discourse. On the one hand, all of the magazines assumed that women wanted to marry, that women found being wives and mothers rewarding, and that women would and should be the primary parents and housekeepers. In the midst of the baby boom, some articles glorified the housewife, sometimes in conscious attempts to bolster her self-esteem. On the other hand, throughout the postwar era, numerous articles portrayed domesticity itself as exhausting and isolating, and frustrated mothers as overdoing and smothering. Such articles hardly glorified domesticity. They provided their postwar readers with ample references to housewife's discontent. . . .

In the postwar magazines, marriage also presented problems. . . . An article in *Ebony* stated, "Most women would rather be married than single but there are many who would rather remain single than be tied to the wrong man." The magazines gave readers contrasting advice on how to find a good husband. One article told women, "Don't fear being aggressive!," while another considered "aggressive traits" as "handicaps . . . in attracting a husband." Within marriage as well, journalists seemed to anticipate constant problems, including immaturity, incompatibility, and infidelity. They saw divorce as a difficult last resort and often advised both husbands and wives to communicate and adjust. . . .

Postwar authors did not, as Friedan's *Feminine Mystique* would have it, side automatically with "sexual passivity, male domination, and nurturing maternal love." They portrayed the ideal marriage as an equal partnership, with each partner intermingling traditional masculine and feminine roles. One article insisted: "The healthy, emotionally well-balanced male . . . isn't alarmed by the fact that women are human, too, and have an aggressive as well as a passive side. . . . He takes women seriously as individuals." This article and others condemned men who assumed an attitude of superiority. . . . Yet, to many it seemed that "individualism" could go too far and upset modern marriage. While husbands might do more housework and wives might pursue nondomestic activities, men remained the primary breadwinners and women the keepers of the home. . . .

The postwar magazines seemed least willing to entertain alternatives in the area of sexuality. As Friedan argued, popular magazines emphasized glamour and allure, at least for young women, and as Elaine Tyler May has elaborated, they tried to domesticate sexual intercourse by containing it within marriage. Magazines presented carefully framed articles with explicit directives about appropriate behavior. Young women were to make themselves attractive to men, and married women were to engage in mutually pleasing sexual intercourse with their mates. Articles presented "normal" sex through voyeuristic discussion of sexual problems, such as pregnancy before marriage and frigidity after. Other forms of sexual expression were rarely broached, although one article in *Ebony* did condemn "lesbians and nymphomaniacs" in the Women's Army Corps.

While all of the magazines endorsed a manicured version of heterosexual appeal, the African-American magazines displayed it most heartily. This may have reflected African-American vernacular traditions, such as the blues, that rejected white middle-class injunctions against public sexual expression. But it also reflected an editorial decision to construct glamour and beauty as political issues in the fight against racism. Articles admired black women's sex appeal in a self-conscious defiance of racist white standards of beauty. In this context what some feminists today might read as sexual "objectification" presented itself as racial advancement, according black womanhood equal treatment with white. Thus, *Ebony,* which in most respects resembled a white family magazine like *Life,* also included some of the mildly risqué cheesecake seen in white men's magazines like *Esquire.* One editorial explained: "Because we live in a society in which standards of physical beauty are most often circumscribed by a static concept of whiteness of skin and blondeness of hair, there is an aching need for someone to shout from the housetops that black women are beautiful." . . .

Still, despite the magazines' endorsement of feminine beauty and heterosexual allure, Friedan's polemical claim that "American women have been successfully reduced to sex creatures" seems unabashedly hyperbolic. Try as they might, popular magazines could not entirely dictate the responses of readers. In most cases, we have little way of knowing how readers responded to magazine articles, but in the case of sex appeal we have explicit letters of dissent. In the African-American magazines, some readers, women and men both, objected to the photos of semiclad women. One woman complained that the "so-called beauties" were "really a disgrace to all women." And another protested "those girl covers and the . . . so-called realism (just a cover up name for cheapness, coarseness, lewdness, profanity and irreverence)." . . .

In his ground-breaking 1972 book, *The American Woman,* William Henry Chafe offers what still stands as the best summary of the debates on womanhood in the postwar era. In Chafe's reconstruction, a popular "antifeminist" position, promoted by such authors as Farnham and Lundberg, stood opposed to a more feminist "sociological" perspective, promoted primarily by social scientists such as Mirra Komarovsky and Margaret Mead. While the antifeminists insisted on marriage and domesticity, the social scientists called for new gender roles to match modern conditions. In the popular magazines sampled for this essay, this debate rarely surfaced. Articles sometimes drew on one position or even both, but the vast majority did not fall clearly into either camp. Still, the antifeminist position did appear occasionally as did an opposing "women's rights" stance. These positions emerged in various magazines, but they both appeared most unequivocally in the highbrow magazines, the *Atlantic Monthly* and *Harper's,* which did not avoid controversy as assiduously as did others.

The antifeminist authors promoted domesticity as a woman's only road to fulfillment. Women should not compete with men, they argued; instead, they should defer to, depend on, and even wait on men, especially their husbands. According to these conservatives, women and men differed fundamentally, and attempts to diminish sexual difference would lead only to unhappiness. Often invoking a version of Freudian thought, these authors sometimes engaged in psychological name-calling in which they labeled modern woman neurotic, narcissistic, unfeminine, domineering, nagging, lazy, materialistic, and spoiled. These conservative arguments and the attendant name-calling were by no means typical of popular discourse. Of the 489 articles sampled, only 9, or less than 2 percent, even approached such starkly conservative claims.

This is where the oft-cited Dr. Marynia Farnham stood in the postwar discourse, at the conservative margin rather than at the center. For Farnham, modern women who attempted to compete with men or expressed discontent with their natural career as mothers suffered from mental instability, bitterness, and worse. Industrialization, Farnham claimed, had undermined women's productive functions in the home. Women, "frustrated at the inmost core of their beings," attempted tragically to emulate men in the world of work, led "aimlessly idle," "parasitic" lives as frigid housewives, or indulged in "overdoting, overstrict or rejecting" mothering, with a cumulative outcome of neurotic children, including future Adolph Hitlers. Farnham called for a renewed commitment to motherhood, dependence on men, and "natural" sexual passivity. She spelled out these arguments in ceaseless detail in her 1947 book, *Modern Woman: The Lost Sex,* coauthored with Ferdinand Lundberg.

Although Farnham's position had some influence, especially among psychologists, it did not represent the mainstream in the mass culture; rather, it generated "a storm of controversy." Book reviews, some of them scathing, called *Modern Woman* "neither socially nor medically credible," "dogmatic and sensational," "intensely disturbing," "unfair," and "fundamentally untrue." And Farnham's articles in *Coronet* provoked enough letters that the editors promised to include opposing viewpoints in future issues, this in a magazine that generally avoided any inkling of debate. While bits and pieces of Farnham's arguments appeared in other popular magazines, the antifeminist position was rejected more often than embraced. In the era of positive thinking, magazines tended toward more upbeat and celebratory representations of women.

Also at the boundaries of the discourse, a few "women's rights" articles counterbalanced the conservative extreme. . . . While conservatives insisted on domestic ideals, women's rights advocates insisted on women's right to nondomestic pursuits. Like the antifeminists, the authors of these articles often argued that women's functions in the home had declined, and they, too, often found the modern housewife restless and discontented. These authors, however, condemned isolation in the home and subordination to men. They admired women who pursued positions of public responsibility and leadership, and they identified and opposed discrimination in the workplace and in politics. They insisted that women were individuals of infinite variety. In *Harper's,* Agnes Rogers wrote, "[T]here would be a healthier distribution of civic energy if more attention were paid to individuals as such and if it were not assumed that men hold the executive jobs and women do what they are told." In contrast with antifeminist writings, these articles either downplayed sex differences or derogated men for their militaristic aggression of "masculine self-inflation." The women's rights articles were only slightly less common than the antifeminist attacks. (With a conservative count, there were five, about 1 percent of the sample.) Like the antifeminist articles, they sometimes generated controversy, especially when readers read them as frontal attacks on the full-time housewife.

The antifeminists and the women's rights advocates competed for mainstream attention. Both tempered their arguments in seeming attempts to broaden appeal: antifeminists sometimes disavowed reactionary intention and denied that married women had to stay in the home, and women's rights advocates sometimes dis-avowed feminist militance and denied that married women had to have careers. Through the 1950s, though, neither position in any way controlled or dominated the public discourse, at least as seen in nonfiction articles in popular magazines. Both antifeminists and women's rights advocates clearly represented controversial minority positions. . . .

Why does my version of history differ from Betty Friedan's? The most obvious, and the most gracious, explanation is that we used different, though overlapping, sources. The nonfiction articles I read may well have included more contradictions and more ambivalence than the fiction on which Friedan focused. But there are, I think, additional differences in approach. Friedan did not read the popular magazines incorrectly, but she did, it seems, cite them reductively. . . . For the postwar era, she cited both fiction and nonfiction stories on domesticity. But she downplayed the articles on domestic problems (belittling one by saying "the bored editors . . . ran a little article"), ignored the articles on individual achievement, and dismissed the articles on political participation with a one-sentence caricature. Her forceful protest against a restrictive domestic ideal neglected the extent to which that ideal was already undermined.

My reassessment of the "feminine mystique" is part of a larger revisionist project. For the past few years, historians have questioned the stereotype of postwar women as quiescent, docile, and domestic. Despite the baby boom and despite discrimina-tion in employment, education, and public office, married women, black and white, joined the labor force in increasing numbers, and both married and unmarried women participated actively in politics and reform. Just as women's activities were more varied and more complex than is often acknowledged, so, I argue, was the postwar popular ideology. Postwar magazines, like their prewar and wartime predecessors, rarely presented direct challenges to the conventions of marriage or motherhood, but they only rarely told women to return to or stay at home. They included stories that glorified domesticity, but they also expressed ambivalence about domesticity, en-dorsed women's nondomestic activity, and celebrated women's public success. They delivered multiple messages, which women could read as sometimes supporting and sometimes subverting the "feminine mystique."

Women and the Politics of Hospital Abortion Committees, 1950–1970

RICKIE SOLINGER

This essay reviews discussion within the medical community in the postwar years concerning contraindications to pregnancy and the circumstances, if any, justifying therapeutic abortion. Such discussions reflect broader cultural attitudes toward women, mothers, babies, and pregnancy in the postwar era. They also illuminate the

Rickie Solinger, "'A Complete Disaster': Abortion and the Politics of Hospital Abortion Committees, 1950–1970," *Feminist Studies* 19, no. 2 (Summer 1993): 241–268. Reprinted by permission of the pub-lisher, Feminist Studies, Inc.

turmoil within the profession over these issues and the uneasy, insecure, but some-times enduring, resolutions physicians devised to quell internal dissension and rein-force medical authority in the two decades immediately preceding *Roe v. Wade.* . . .

Dissension over abortion within the medical community was not a long-standing . . . problem. The post–Civil War state laws against abortion, which turned back the traditional right of girls and women to abort in the first trimester of pregnancy, stipu-lated that abortions were permissible only in cases where, due to a medical condition, the pregnant woman's life was in danger. These new, late-nineteenth-century laws granted the determination to licensed physicians only. Through the late 1940s, legal abortions were performed often and routinely in most hospitals across the country. Medically approved contraindications to pregnancy included cardiovascular condi-tions . . . ; kidney dysfunction . . . ; neurologic diseases . . . ; toxemia; respiratory disease . . . ; uterine disease . . . ; orthopedic problems; and blood diseases such as leukemia, ulcerative colitis, diabetes, premature separation of the placenta, otoscle-rosis, bowel obstruction, lupus, and thyrotoxicosis. Physicians occasionally per-formed abortions on women suffering from severe psychiatric disorders.

With such an extensive list of contraindications to pregnancy, abortion ratios at some hospitals were high in various decades before 1950, especially in comparison to what they would soon be, for example: 1 abortion to every 76 live births at Belle-vue Hospital in New York; 1 to every 167 at New York Lying-In; and 1 to every 169 deliveries at Iowa University Hospital. Given the state of medical knowledge and the range of medical options, as well as prevailing ideas about the physical toll pregnancy took on women, non-Catholic physicians were often willing to sacrifice the pregnancy in favor of the well-being of the woman. Medical decisions concern-ing these matters were often predicated upon an assumption that pregnancy itself was a physical event or a medical condition which happened to girls and women, sometimes under conditions that were not physically or medically favorable. In these cases, it could be assumed that pregnancy could interact with and worsen a preexisting condition. . . . This perspective assumed that the woman's body was an integrated system which the pregnancy *could* undermine or disintegrate. The preg-nancy itself might well take precedence over disease as the more destructive agent. Where contraindications existed, pregnancy—or the "unborn child"—was not granted precedence, or healing power, or constructed as a special condition virtually separate from the biological body or psychological mind of the impregnated female. The pregnancy was an additive, not an autonomous factor. . . . In short, abortion served a function when pregnancy invaded and threatened a woman's body.

By the early postwar years, the medical consensus about the indications for abortion had fractured, and therapeutic abortion rates were plummeting in hospitals across the country. One authoritative study reported that the therapeutic abortion rate per 1,000 live births in the United States declined from 5.1 in 1943 to 2.9 in 1953, a 43 percent decline. . . .

The sharp decline in legal, therapeutic abortions performed in hospitals re-flected the fact that by mid-century, mainstream medical opinion held that medical-technological and obstetrical advances obviated the need to interrupt pregnancy for most of the medical conditions previously considered incompatible with preg-nancy. . . . Shared access to new technologies and treatments, however, did not mean that physicians shared a professional opinion about when and how these innovations should be applied. In fact, the new medical developments gave rise to a very complicated situation for physicians; the situation could be called a *crisis* which extended over a twenty-year period, at least.

The crisis derived, in part, from a profoundly paradoxical relationship between medical progress, the law, and politics. On the one hand, physicians were scientific and humanitarian heroes for subduing the role of pregnancy as an "added burden" and for devising methodologies to conquer diseases threatening to pregnancy and the pregnant female. On the other hand, state laws still required that the life of the pregnant women must be medically endangered to permit abortion. The legal system persisted in requiring a condition that the medical system said rarely existed. Consequently, legal demands were at odds with medical advances which claimed to have virtually removed the basis for medical judgments concerning indications for abortions.

Given their continuing legal relationship to abortion, however, and their interest in sustaining medical authority over pregnant women, physicians struggled to establish new bases for medical decision making. By the early 1950s, a number of physicians were airing these struggles before the medical community in the pages of the most prestigious medical journals in the United States. They described a bitterly contentious intraprofessional situation. The reports indicated that any sense of common purpose among physicians considering abortion had been severely underminded in the aftermath of medical advances. . . . Two Chicago physicians asserted that no agreement among medical doctors can "be achieved regarding either individual indications [for abortions] or general principles." Another physician called his attempt to study the therapeutic abortion situation "a complete disaster" because "the categories of opinion were almost equal in number to the men concerned." . . .

[M]any felt that the new disunity over the abortion issue hurt the standing of physicians as expert, objective practitioners of medical science. Dissension also raised questions about the source and scope of medical authority. One physician observed, unhappily, that "if interruption of a pre-viable pregnancy is requested, the law at present dictates what medical opinion should be." . . . Others expressed deep uneasiness that they were facing pressures to look beyond their traditional subject—the physical condition of the individual pregnant woman. They were being urged, inappropriately, to include social factors in their medical diagnoses.

The rise of psychiatric indications as grounds for abortion solved the issue of medical authority for many practitioners but deepened the uneasiness of many others not convinced in the 1950s that psychiatry belonged within the ranks of medical science. A Cleveland obstetrician identified his hospital's biggest abortion problem as "those cases done for psychiatric indications, many times questionable psychiatric reasons." Another obstetrician wrote that "medical men . . . have been able to markedly reduce the therapeutic abortion rate throughout the country only to find that this least justifiable of all indications, psychiatric reasons, has been allowed to run rampant." . . . Psychiatrists were portrayed in this way as pawns of importuning women, unlike real medical doctors who initiated any abortion decision in the interest of their passive, pregnant patients. . . .

By the mid-1950s, most non-Catholic hospitals had begun to address their vulnerability in relation to abortion by finding ways to reassert medical authority over the issue and to sustain physicians' control over pregnant girls and women. Two strategies governed this process in a great many hospitals across the country. First, physicians recognized that they had to reassemble themselves as a collectivity from which professional expert diagnoses and decisions regarding individual women could be issued in one voice. In this setting, psychiatrists could be team players. They could bring their special perspective on the individual into the arena of experts and thus come to the aid of the profession while validating their own standing. Second, physicians redefined pregnancy in relation to women's bodies in such a way as to efface the woman herself while giving precedence to the law and the fetus. Again, psychiatrists played a pivotal role in accomplishing the redefinition.

By the mid-1950s, in many hospitals, physicians assembled themselves collectively into abortion boards or committees. As a group, obstetricians, cardiologists, psychiatrists, and others considered abortion recommendations and requests and issued definitive decisions on each case. The chief of a department of obstetrics and gynecology in a large northeastern hospital described the way decisionmaking processes changed in many hospitals in the early 1950s.

> At Mount Sinai Hospital [in New York], before [Alan Guttmacher's innovations], a request for therapeutic abortion merely had to be signed by two senior staff members. Guttmacher established the abortion committee of five members: the chief in medicine, representatives of pediatrics and of surgery, the chief of psychiatry, and the chief of obstetrics and gynecology who acts as chairman. Requests to the committee must be supported by two consultants recommending the procedure and outlining the indications for it. One of the consultants must appear before the committee to answer additional questions. The committee must be unanimous in its approval of any request.

These committees protected physicians, individually and as a profession, in a number of ways. Of paramount importance to many was the legal protection the boards provided. . . . Rudolph W. Holmes insisted that because the law drew such a "tenuous" line of demarcation between legal and illegal abortions, "it behooves medical staffs of all reputable hospitals to institute [abortion boards]. It would be a great protection to the operator as well as a deterrent to dangerous aspersions by outsiders." For many concerned physicians, insiders could be as dangerous as outsiders. These medical doctors felt that committees functioned best to mute, neutralize, or "curb liberal obstetricians" favoring too many abortions or abortions on questionable grounds. . . .

These interests in reputation and control were undoubtedly central concerns of many physicians in part because so many of them spoke and behaved one way publicly and another way privately. For example, a number of professional, illegal abortionists who conducted thriving businesses in this era have reported that hundreds of medical doctors—surely among them, those who publicly claimed medical, hospital control over abortion decisions—routinely referred clients for illegal abortions. By insisting on the righteousness of the mechanisms of hospital abortion committees, physicians could disassociate themselves from professional and public concerns about widespread illegal abortions, thus diminishing personal vulnerability and, perhaps, individual crises of conscience. . . .

Many contemporary commentators referred to the actual legal vulnerability of physicians who performed abortions as a "phantom," and many pointed out that "no reputable physician has ever been convicted for performing an abortion in a reputable hospital." This was the case both before and after abortion committees began to operate. It seems probable, then, that the most valuable service the boards actually performed was to bolster the image of physicians as members of a highly functioning professional body guided by scientific expertise and collective wisdom. The committee could transform public dissension within the medical community into public harmony, and at the same time, reduce the incidence of abortion. . . .

Moreover, physicians could more confidently assert their right and duty to retain medical control over the abortion decision once they established the committee as a respectable forum dedicated to processing individual women in an orderly fashion. In short order, the committee became a vehicle for bringing professional wisdom to bear on the issue, in part as a way to forestall the situation "where the decision for abortion may be made by legal, social or welfare groups outside of the profession." . . .

As physicians assumed a judicial role regarding individual requests for abortion—whether the requests originated with the obstetrician, another medical specialist, or the pregnant woman herself—inevitably, committee physicians, donning their robes in earnest, perceived the individual woman as "on trial." Unfortunately, however, in many cases, the cardinal principle of the U.S. legal system seems to have been inoperative. Physicians warned each other not to assume the woman's innocence. A New York medical doctor put it this way: "The physician must have a high index of suspicion for the patient who tries to pull a fast one." The source of danger was the "individual [woman] seeking to satisfy selfish needs." . . . One physician spoke for many of his colleagues when he warned of the "clever, scheming women, simply trying to hoodwink the psychiatrist and obstetrician," when they asked permission to abort. Another identified "woman's main role here on earth as conceiving, delivering and raising children." Thus, he concluded, any woman who claims not to want a certain pregnancy, must not be believed. In this environment, it is not surprising that, as one physician put it, "we have had a great many less requests for abortion [in his California hospital] since the patient and the doctor know that the patient must . . . have her case become an open trial so to speak to be decided on its merits." . . .

[A]lthough the psychiatric perspective had been initially problematic for many medical doctors involved in abortion determinations, by the late 1950s, the situation had changed. By this time, the abortion committees had provided psychiatrists with a rich proving ground for their specialty. According to a number of essayists, psychiatrists did rise to the aid of their colleagues by providing the expert basis for medical decisionmaking and medical control that would have otherwise been lacking. As the biology of both disease pathology and pregnancy became less mystified and less remote because of medical-technological advances, psychiatrists stepped in, forestalling the possible empowerment of the pregnant patient. Psychiatrists constructed and drew on the unconscious as an entity which was only accessible to, and could only be decoded by, the expert. One physician observed, "If we have learned anything in psychiatry, we have learned to respect the unconscious far more than the conscious and we have learned not to take [abortion requests] at face value." Another demonstrated how this observation worked in practice. "An example is a woman who comes in seemingly with an unambivalent wish to be aborted which, upon interview, turns out to be an unconscious attempt on her part to punish her husband." Such a discovery, as the basis of diagnosis, could only be available to the physician.

This physician and many of his colleagues were, in part, responding to the new pressure from many women in their offices initiating requests for legal, therapeutic abortions. They were also responding from a new definition of pregnancy itself which emerged following the decline of medical indications for the interruption of pregnancy and alongside the validation of the psychiatric perspective.

Pregnancy became, at this time, a state inhering to the woman-as-custodian, but the pregnant woman and fetus no longer presented an integrated system. . . . After medical doctors determined that there were no longer any medical contraindications to pregnancy, pregnancy ceased to be a physical issue. Physicians now argued that "for most conditions, the natural history of the disease is not influenced deleteriously by an intercurrent pregnancy. Convertly, neither is the course of pregnancy seriously affected by a complicating medical condition."

Neither did physicians consider pregnancy a psychological issue. One argued: "Statistical analysis shows that childbearing has only a small influence on the mental disorders of women and that the majority of individuals predisposed to mental disorder go through childbirth unscathed." . . . In essence, pregnancy was most centrally a *moral* issue, but the moral ground had shifted. As the fetus was constructed as a little person, medical doctors constructed the pregnant woman's body as a safe reproductive container. The woman, along with her physician, had the moral duty, to sustain the container as fit. One obstetrician explained the suitability of women for this role. "Woman is a uterus surrounded by a supporting organism and a directing personality." Completely effaced, the woman-as-uterus simply housed the child. . . .

Drawing on the innovative notions of pregnancy and pregnant women, psychiatrists were prepared to explain the behavior of the growing number of women asking medical doctors for abortions in the postwar years. Their explanations created a broad category of women who were, by definition, in the absence of traditional medical problems, *morally* and psychologically unsuited for childbearing and certainly for motherhood because they were unwilling to serve as pregnancy vessels. Where there was an unhappily pregnant woman, there was a defective vessel. Many medical doctors agreed that an abortion *could* be performed on such a woman, but the procedure would not help as the problem was not the pregnancy. The problem was called a "psychiatric disorder" involving the woman's denial of her destiny and "amendable to treatment" as such. But the tone of the diagnosis, like the tone so often used to judge women on one grounds or another in these years, dripped with moral rectitude and condemnation. One psychiatrist identified the request for abortion "as proof [of the petitioner's] inability and failure to live through the destiny of being a woman." . . .

A physician who responded to such a woman's expressed desire to violate her destiny was, according to many, in serious error. One highly experienced author-psychiatrist placed women who chose abortion on a sullied moral plane when he asserted that he had "never seen a patient who has not had guilt feelings about a previous . . . abortion." Others felt that because the pregnancy itself was not the source of difficulty, an abortion did not solve a woman's problems but could create serious problems for her. For example,

> [Abortion] coupled with ideas of guilt, self-deprecation, some recurrent preoccupation centering around the abortion and the general theme of "I let them kill my baby" might well disturb a poorly integrated personality even to psychotic proportions. Feelings of love, admiration and respect for the male partner . . . may well be distorted in the aborted

woman to ideas of disgust, hate, and disrespect; "He gave me a baby then took it away." The unconscious motivation and even the flow of emotions during the readjustments to a normal sexual nonpregnancy cycle may result in deeply engrained feelings of hostility toward the husband. Abortions we may say can produce psychotic cicatrix.

Well-known to unhappily pregnant women in the postwar era, however, was one method of resistance that sometimes cut through the language of morality; the threat of suicide. This condition alone raised the specter for medical doctors of a reintegrated mind, body, and pregnancy. A pregnant woman's threat of suicide suggested that the woman might destroy the reproductive container which gave definition to her very existence. Women recognized early that they could get their medical doctors' attention by making such a threat, but many physicians found it easier to believe that a woman was using her pregnancy rather than throwing away her destiny. Thus, physicians proceeded very cautiously in this area. One wrote that "a mere threat of suicide or even an abortive attempt at suicide is not in itself regarded as a medical indication for therapeutic abortion; it may be nothing more than an effort to blackmail the surgeon into performing the operation." . . .

[A] survey reported in the *Stanford Law Review* provides an excellent example of a suicidal pregnant woman who physicians were willing to believe deserved an abortion. An unprecedented 80 percent of reporting hospitals agreed to sanction abortion in this hypothetical case.

> Mrs. C. is 32 years old and is the mother of children, aged 7, 4, and 3. Following the birth of her last child, she had what was diagnosed as a postpartum depression in which she became completely withdrawn. She was hospitalized in a state hospital for 6 months during which time she had electroshock therapy with some improvement. She has remained under psychiatric care since then but she still becomes depressed very easily and talks freely about committing suicide, saying that her family will be better off without the burden of her care.
>
> Four weeks ago it was diagnosed that she was approximately 4 weeks' pregnant. The news of this precipitated a severe emotional crisis. This has been manifested by vomiting, spells of uncontrollable crying lasting for hours at a time, at which time the patient locked herself in her room. She threatened suicide several times in the last four weeks, saying that she could never be a "good mother" and that she was a "useless member of society."
>
> Last night Mrs. C. was found unconscious on the floor of her living room. There was an empty bottle, which should have contained approximately eighteen sleeping pills, in her bedroom. She was taken to the hospital and has apparently responded to vigorous therapy for her barbiturate overdose.

Mrs. C.'s case evoked near-consensus because this woman demonstrated her commitment to destroy the reproductive container she had become. Only in the case of such a demonstration could the moral dimension be eclipsed and the condition of pregnancy assume its previous status as an "added burden" or a destructive agent.

The other way that physicians frequently revealed their commitment to the new construction of women's bodies as reproductive containers was in their association of therapeutic abortion with simultaneous sterilization. . . . The prevalence of sterilization was widely featured in the obstetrical and psychiatric literature of the day, specifically in cases involving what one prominent expert called the "tainted individual." One group of obstetricians found that "some women desiring an abortion were required to have a simultaneous sterilization operation as a condition of approval of the abortion in from one-third to two-thirds of [those] teaching hospitals [studied] in different regions of the country. In all, 53.6 percent of teaching hospitals made this a requirement for some of their patients." Another physician reported his finding of a 40 percent concomitant sterilization rate in all U.S. hospitals in the 1940s and 1950s. . . .

Some physicians justified simultaneous sterilization on the grounds that any woman ill enough to warrant abortion should never again be pregnant. Others shared this position but shifted the emphasis on to the medical doctor's dilemma: "A serious effort is made to control [by sterilization] the need for dealing with the same problem in the same patient twice." A California psychiatrist described what he felt was a strong trend among medical doctors, "penalizing" by sterilization the patient who "needs" a therapeutic abortion. He explained the practice this way: "Often, the surgeon's stipulation for sterilization may reflect his reluctance to perform the abortion, his misunderstanding of its necessity, and his resentment of the psychiatric indications." Another commentator felt that some physicians in this era resented sexual women more than they resented psychiatry: "The abortion committee [at one hospital] evaluated all patients in terms of recommendations for sterilization. Medical grounds for this 'final solution' to 'promiscuous' abortions were forcefully debated by individual members and typically included the physician's evaluation of the woman's condition and moral character." The widespread use of sterilization, whatever the expressed justification, seems to suggest that many physicians in the postwar era were willing to use the sterilization option to cap the defective reproductive container. . . .

One physician, unhappy about the coupling of sterilization and therapeutic abortion in U.S. hospitals, observed that this practice actually drove women to illegal abortionists to escape the likelihood that a legal abortion would entail the permanent loss of their fertility. He added, "I would like to point that out, because the package [therapeutic abortion–sterilization] is so frequent I therefore consider them fortunate to have been illegally rather than therapeutically aborted, and thus spared sterilization." This aspect of the discussion foreshadowed, of course, the legal institutionalization, in our time, of the link between abortion and sterilization, via the Hyde Amendment.

The literature reviewed in this essay makes it clear that some influential medical doctors in the postwar era derived professional strength and ideological coherence from abortion committees and from a new, disembodied definition of pregnancy. But by the middle of the 1960s, it was also clear that the same factors which had pushed physicians into a defensive posture in the early postwar years continued to exert considerable pressures on the profession. These and additional factors combined to facilitate the eclipse of medical authority over the abortion decision much sooner than many practitioners had predicted.

Over time, the committees themselves could not sustain the image of professional unity and scientific purpose, even if an individual hospital could issue abortion decisions with one voice. Harold Rosen, a prominent medical doctor interested in abortion reform, noted widespread inconsistencies between hospital abortion committees in the mid-1960s which hurt the credibility of the profession.

Not infrequently, for instance, the abortion board of one hospital, but not another, may refuse to accept a recommendation for interruption; on nine separate occasions during the past seven years, patients who have been seen in consultation in one hospital have afterwards been therapeutically aborted at adjacent hospitals with, at times, almost the same visiting staff.

At the heart of this apparent capriciousness was a continuing inability among physicians to agree on indications, even medical indications.

If physicians do not wish to force a specific woman to carry a specific pregnancy to term, and if that woman is actually suffering from some severe physical disease then, but only then, the pathological process, provided it falls within certain categories, is in certain hospitals and by certain physicians and hospital boards considered sufficient indication for interruption. In others, it is not. . . .

Other factors which exerted increasing pressure in the abortion arena include first, of course, women's growing insistence on breaking the link between law and medicine, so that women themselves could take the power to decide who was a mother and to decide when a woman was a mother. After the rubella epidemic and the thalidomide episode of the early 1960s, women also began to insist on a legal, publicly sanctioned right to decide who was a child. The sensationally and intrusively reported plight of Sherri Finkbine in 1962 raised, above all, the specter of the pregnant woman's right to reject a fetus deeply damaged by thalidomide.

Additional pressures which struck at medical authority came from the flowering of the quality of life (or "life-style") ethic among the middle-class in the United States which undermined the acceptability of the simple life/death dichotomy that the law mandated must govern abortion decisions. Also, in the 1960s as social criticism seeped back into mainstream public discourse, some physicians began to accept and use a definition of the purpose of medicine—in this case, of indications for abortion, which placed unhappily pregnant women in desperate social and economic contexts. . . .

Of equal or greater importance to all these pressures undermining medical authority in the abortion arena by the mid-1960s was widespread concern and fear among whites in the United States about the "population explosion," rising welfare costs, the civil rights movement, and the "sexual revolution." Critics of these social, political, and cultural phenomena tended to target women's bodies and their reproductive capacity as a source of danger to the fabric of U.S. society. Demedicalizing and decriminalizing the abortion decision became one way to diminish the damage women's bodies could do.

This essay leaves unexplored many issues that would shed additional light on the concerns and strategies of medical doctors sitting on hospital abortion committees in the postwar era. These include physicians' attitudes toward abortion and women of various races, ethnicities, and classes. Much research is needed in this area. The essay does not explore medical doctors' attitudes toward and relationships with illegal abortionists, a subject well worth pursuing. Also left unexplored are the sources and complex nature of physicians' changing attitudes toward abortion in the 1960s and 1970s. Pregnant women themselves have not been given voice in this essay.

But the subjects of this study, a highly visible segment of the medical community, have been given voice here in order to allow us to consider what was at issue for many physicians in the immediate pre–*Roe v. Wade* decades. What is most striking in the literature reviewed for this essay is that, with the exception of the few articles prepared by Catholic medical doctors, the physicians who wrote on the abortion issue were not primarily concerned with the issue of when life begins. They were, however, very concerned with what they took to be their role in the postwar cultural mandate to protect and preserve the links between sexuality, femininity, marriage, and maternity. They were also deeply concerned about their professional dignity and about devising strategies to protect and preserve the power, the prerogatives, and the legal standing of the medical profession.

An important strategy of many physicians in this era was to draw on the vulnerability of pregnant women to construct a definition of pregnancy that effaced the personhood of the individual pregnant woman. This definition created a safe place for the fetus and also for the physician forced by law to adjudicate the extremely personal decisions of women, many of whom were resisting effacement. The subordination of the pregnant woman to the fetus revitalized medical participation in the abortion decision because the medical doctor was now required to make sure that the woman stayed moral, that is, served her fetus correctly. These postwar ideas demonstrate the relationship between scientific advances and ideological positions regarding women, pregnant women, pregnancy, and fetuses.

FURTHER READING

Black, Allida M. *Casting Her Own Shadow: Eleanor Roosevelt and the Shaping of Postwar Liberalism* (1996).

Chafe, William. *The Paradox of Change: American Women in the 20th Century* (1991).

Cohen, Lizabeth. *A Consumer's Republic: The Politics of Mass Consumption in Postwar America* (2003).

Coontz, Stephanie. *The Way We Never Were: American Families and the Nostalgia Trap* (1992).

Faderman, Lillian. *Odd Girls and Twilight Lovers: A History of Lesbian Life in Twentieth-Century America* (1991).

Feldstein, Ruth. *Motherhood in Black and White: Race and Sex in American Liberalism, 1930–1965* (2000).

Gans, Herbert. *The Levittowners: Ways of Life and Politics in a New Suburban Community* (1967).

Glendon, Mary Ann. *A World Made New: Eleanor Roosevelt and the Universal Declaration of Human Rights* (2001).

Harrison, Cynthia. *On Account of Sex: The Politics of Women's Issues, 1945–1968* (1988).

Horowitz, Daniel. *Betty Friedan and the Making of the Feminine Mystique: The American Left, the Cold War, and American Feminism* (1998).

Jackson, Kenneth T. *Crabgrass Frontier: The Suburbanization of the United States* (1985).

Jones, Jacqueline. *Labor of Love, Labor of Sorrow: Black Women, Work, and the Family from Slavery to the Present* (1985).

Kaledin, Eugenia. *Mothers and More: American Women in the 1950s* (1984).

Kennedy, Elizabeth Lapovsky, and Madeline D. Davis. *Boots of Leather, Slippers of Gold: The History of a Lesbian Community* (1993).

Komarovsky, Mirra. *Blue Collar Marriage* (1964).

Laughlin, Kathleen A. *Women's Work and Public Policy: A History of the U.S. Department of Labor, 1945–1970* (2000).

Luibheid, Eithne. "'Looking Like a Lesbian': The Organization of Sexual Monitoring at the United States–Mexican Border," *Journal of the History of Sexuality* 8 (1998): 477–505.

Luker, Kristin. *Dubious Conceptions: The Politics of Teenage Pregnancy* (1996).

Lynn, Susan. *Progressive Women in Conservative Times: Racial Justice, Peace, and Feminism, 1945 to the 1960s* (1992).

Marsh, Margaret. *Suburban Lives* (1990).

McEnaney, Laura. *Civil Defense Begins at Home: Militarization Meets Everyday Life in the Fifties* (2000).

Meyerowitz, Joanne. *How Sex Changed: A History of Transsexuality in the United States* (2002).

———, ed. *Not June Cleaver: Women and Gender in Postwar America, 1945–1960* (1994).

Reagan, Leslie. *When Abortion Was a Crime: Women, Medicine, and Law in the United States, 1867–1973* (1997).

Richards, Yevette. *Maida Springer, Pan-Africanist and International Labor Leader* (2000).

Rossiter, Margaret W. *Women Scientists in America: Before Affirmative Action, 1940–1972* (1995).

Rupp, Leila J., and Verta Taylor. *Surviving the Doldrums: The American Women's Rights Movement, 1945 to the 1960s* (1987).

Schmidt, Patricia L. *Margaret Chase Smith: Beyond Convention* (1996).

Sherman, Janann. *No Place for a Woman: A Life of Senator Margaret Chase Smith* (2000).

Solinger, Rickie. *Wake Up Little Susie: Single Pregnancy and Race Before* Roe v. Wade (1992).

Weigand, Kathleen Anne. *Red Feminism: American Communism and the Making of Women's Liberation* (2000).

Weiss, Jessica. *To Have and to Hold: Marriage, the Baby Boom, and Social Change* (2000).

Weiss, Nancy Pottishman. "The Invention of Necessity: Dr. Benjamin Spock's 'Baby and Child Care,'" *American Quarterly* 29 (Winter 1977): 519–546.

CHAPTER
15

Second-Wave Feminism
in America, 1960–1990

The years from 1960 to 1990 witnessed an extraordinary cycle of liberal/radical rebellion and conservative reaction in the United States. Second-wave feminism played a central role in the rebellion of the era and was also a major impetus for the conservative reaction that followed. During the 1960s, young adults, members of the "baby boom" generation, participated in a frontal attack on American society and its institutions, condemning the nation's misuse of military power around the globe, especially in Vietnam, and its indifference to oppression and inequality at home. Women of diverse class, race, and ethnic backgrounds devoted tremendous energy to the political movements of the era, including the civil rights and Black Power struggles and the anti-war, anti-poverty, and labor movements. In the late sixties, some women—many of them former members of the Student Non-Violent Coordinating Committee (SNNC) and Students for a Democratic Society (SDS), and nearly all of them white and middle-class—launched a new radical feminist movement. Radical feminists organized small "consciousness raising" groups that combined investigations of gender discrimination in employment, education, and politics with analyses of gender oppression in private, familial, and sexual contexts. Like Black Power activists, they were often frankly separatist, doubting the dominant society's willingness to grant women (or blacks) true equality. Meanwhile, older and more moderate women (mostly white and middle-class) formed the National Organization for Women (NOW) in 1966, adopting integrationist goals that paralleled those of the National Association for the Advancement of Colored People (NAACP) and the Southern Christian Leadership Conference. The two branches of "second-wave" feminism often argued over goals and tactics, but together they helped to bring about massive changes in attitudes toward the role of women in American society.

By the early seventies African American women and Chicanas had also begun to form organizations that explicitly addressed the intersections of racial, ethnic, and gender oppression, and they challenged white feminists to broaden the agenda of the women's movement. Simultaneously, working-class and professional women began to organize across racial and ethnic lines to demand access to fields of employment still closed to women. Women of varied class, racial, and ethnic backgrounds also participated in the feminist health revolution of the era, trying to enhance women's *power with the medical community. Lesbian feminists claimed the right to free themselves from the bonds of heterosexuality. Straight and lesbian women demanded that Americans acknowledge rape as a crime of violence against women; so too, women of varied backgrounds demanded an end to the criminalization of abortion, arguing that prohibitions against abortion unjustly limited women's reproductive and sexual freedom and forced them to seek abortions from illegal and unsafe practitioners. Responding to feminists and their allies, Congress passed an Equal Rights Amendment (ERA) in 1972 and sent it to the states for ratification. The next year, the Supreme Court struck down existing state laws against abortion in* Roe v. Wade *(1973) and ruled in favor of women's unrestricted right to abortion in the first trimester of pregnancy. These two important victories for feminists provoked a backlash from social conservatives, who began to organize in opposition to feminists. Antifeminists with ties to fundamentalist Protestant churches, the Catholic Church, and the Republican Party mounted a political campaign that obstructed the ratification of the ERA. The women and men of the so-called New Right also pressured presidents Ronald Reagan and George H. Bush to appoint conservative justices to the Supreme Court in hopes of overturning* Roe v. Wade. *Emboldened social conservatives created a myriad of organizations devoted to advancing "family values" and embedding the moral precepts of evangelical Christianity in governmental policy. They condemned feminists for promoting immorality and selfish individualism, thereby undermining the cohesiveness of families and the well-being of the nation.*

Historians are engaged in vigorous efforts to explain the circumstances that provoked feminist activism in the 1960s and 1970s, the place of class, race, and ethnicity in the women's movement, and the impact of "second-wave" feminism on American women and the larger society, even in the wake of a conservative reaction. What prompted American women to develop feminist groups and organizations in the 1960s? To what extent were feminists of different class and ethnic or racial backgrounds able to forge common agendas, and to what extent did their agendas remain distinctive or at odds? What were the values and backgrounds of those who organized against feminists? What have been the lasting effects of "second-wave" feminism on American society? The documents and essays in this chapter offer partial answers to these and other questions.

◈ D O C U M E N T S

In 1965 Casey Hayden and Mary King, white activists in SNCC and SDS, wrote "a kind of memo" (Document 1) to others in the peace and freedom movements, trying to draw attention to the issue of gender oppression. In 1966, the founding statement of NOW (extracted in Document 2) laid out the organization's central premises. In Document 3, Frances Beale describes the "double jeopardy" of being both black and female; Beale condemned the sexism of the Black Power movement and the racism of the women's movement. Mirta Vidal wrote an essay on the critical importance of feminism for Chicanas, which appears here as Document 4. Document 5 offers the text of the Equal Rights Amendment (1972). Document 6 provides an excerpt from *Our Bodies, Ourselves* (1973) in which the Boston Women's Health Book Collective describes feminist goals with regard to childbirth. The Supreme Court's ruling in *Roe v. Wade* is excerpted in Document 7. In Document 8, Lindsy Van Gelder reports on an unusually important sex-discrimination lawsuit against the *New York Times*. Connaught C. Marshner explains the concerns and goals of social conservatives in Document 9.

1. Casey Hayden and Mary King, "A Kind of Memo" to Women in the Peace and Freedom Movements, 1965

We've talked a lot, to each other and to some of you, about our own and other women's problems in trying to live in our personal lives and in our work as independent and creative people. In these conversations we've found what seem to be recurrent ideas or themes. Maybe we can look at these things many of us perceive, often as a result of insights learned from the movement:

•   Sex and caste: There seem to be many parallels that can be drawn between treatment of Negroes and treatment of women in our society as a whole. But in particular, women we've talked to who work in the movement seem to be caught up in a common-law caste system that operates, sometimes subtly, forcing them to work around or outside hierarchical structures of power which may exclude them. . . . It is a . . . system which, at its worst, uses and exploits women.

This is complicated by several facts, among them: 1) The caste system is not institutionalized by law (women have the right to vote, to sue for divorce, etc.); 2) Women can't withdraw from the situation (a la nationalism) or overthrow it; 3) There are biological differences (even though those biological differences are usually discussed or accepted without taking present and future technology into account so we probably can't be sure what these differences mean). Many people who are very hip to the implications of the racial caste system, even people in the movement, don't seem to be able to see the sexual-caste system and if the question is raised they respond with: "That's the way it's supposed to be. There are biological differences." Or with other statements which recall a white segregationist confronted with integration.

•   Women and problems of work: The caste-system perspective dictates the roles assigned to women in the movement, and certainly even more to women outside the movement. Within the movement, questions arise in situations ranging from relationships of women organizers to men in the community, to who cleans the freedom house, to who holds leadership positions, to who does secretarial work, and to who acts as spokesman for groups. Other problems arise between women with varying degrees of awareness of themselves as being as capable as men but held back from full participation, or between women who see themselves as needing more control of their work than other women demand. And there are problems with relationships between white women and black women.

•   Women and personal relations with men: Having learned from the movement to think radically about the personal worth and abilities of people whose role in society had gone unchallenged before, a lot of women in the movement have begun trying to apply those lessons to their own relations with men. Each of us probably has her own story of the various results, and of the internal struggle occasioned by trying

Casey Hayden and Mary Elizabeth King, *Freedom Song: A Personal Story of the 1960s Civil Rights Movement* (New York: William Morrow, 1987), appendix 3, 571–574. Reprinted by permission of Gerard McCauley Agency, Inc.

to break out of very deeply learned fears, needs, and self-perceptions, and of what happens when we try to replace them with concepts of people and freedom learned from the movement and organizing.

• Institutions: Nearly everyone has real questions about those institutions which shape perspectives on men and women: marriage, childrearing patterns, women's (and men's) magazines, etc. People are beginning to think about and even to experiment with new forms in these areas.

• Men's reactions to the questions raised here: A very few men seem to feel, when they hear conversations involving these problems, that they have a right to be present and participate in them, since they are so deeply involved. At the same time, very few men can respond nondefensively, since the whole idea is either beyond their comprehension or threatens and exposes them. The usual response is laughter. That inability to see the whole issue as serious, as the straitjacketing of both sexes, and as societally determined often shapes our own response so that we learn to think in their terms about ourselves and to feel silly rather than trust our inner feelings. The problems we're listing here, and what others have said about them, are therefore largely drawn from conversations among women only—and that difficulty in establishing dialogue with men is a recurring theme among people we've talked to.

• Lack of community for discussion: Nobody is writing, or organizing or talking publicly about women in any way that reflects the problems that various women in the movement come across and which we've tried to touch above. . . .

The reason we want to try to open up dialogue is mostly subjective. Working in the movement often intensifies personal problems, especially if we start trying to apply things we're learning there to our personal lives. Perhaps we can start to talk with each other more openly than in the past and create a community of support for each other so we can deal with ourselves and others with integrity and can therefore keep working.

Objectively, the chances seem nil that we could start a movement based on anything as distant to general American thought as a sex-caste system. Therefore, most of us will probably want to work full time on problems such as war, poverty, race. The very fact that the country can't face, much less deal with, the questions we're raising means that the movement is one place to look for some relief. Real efforts at dialogue within the movement and with whatever liberal groups, community women, or students might listen are justified. That is, all the problems between men and women and all the problems of women functioning in society as equal human beings are among the most basic that people face. We've talked in the movement about trying to build a society which would see basic human problems (which are now seen as private troubles), as public problems and would try to shape institutions to meet human needs rather than shaping people to meet the needs of those with power. To raise questions like those above illustrates very directly that society hasn't dealt with some of its deepest problems and opens discussion of why that is so. (In one sense, it is a radicalizing question that can take people beyond legalistic solutions into areas of personal and institutional change.) The second objective reason we'd like to see discussion begin is that we've learned a great deal in the movement and perhaps this is one area where a determined attempt to apply ideas we've learned there can produce some new alternatives.

2. NOW Issues Its Statement of Purpose, 1966

We, men and women who hereby constitute ourselves as the National Organization for Women, believe that the time has come for a new movement toward true equality for all women in America, and toward a fully equal partnership of the sexes, as part of the world-wide revolution of human rights now taking place within and beyond our national borders.

The purpose of NOW is to take action to bring women into full participation in the mainstream of American society now, exercising all the privileges and responsibilities thereof in truly equal partnership with men.

We believe the time has come to move beyond the abstract argument, discussion and symposia over the status and special nature of women which has raged in America in recent years; the time has come to confront, with concrete action, the conditions that now prevent women from enjoying the equality of opportunity and freedom of choice which is their right as individual Americans, and as human beings.

NOW is dedicated to the proposition that women first and foremost are human beings, who, like all other people in our society, must have the chance to develop their fullest human potential. We believe that women can achieve such equality only by accepting to the full the challenges and responsibilities they share with all other people in our society, as part of the decision-making mainstream of American political, economic and social life.

We organize to initiate or support action, nationally or in any part of this nation, by individuals or organizations, to break through the silken curtain of prejudice and discrimination against women in government, industry, the professions, the churches, the political parties, the judiciary, the labor unions, in education, science, medicine, law, religion and every other field of importance in American society. . . .

There is no civil rights movement to speak for women, as there has been for Negroes and other victims of discrimination. The National Organization for Women must therefore begin to speak.

WE BELIEVE that the power of American law, and the protection guaranteed by the U.S. Constitution to the civil rights of all individuals, must be effectively applied and enforced to isolate and remove patterns of sex discrimination, to ensure equality of opportunity in employment and education, and equality of civil and political rights and responsibilities on behalf of women, as well as for Negroes and other deprived groups.

We realize that women's problems are linked to many broader questions of social justice; their solution will require concerted action by many groups. Therefore, convinced that human rights for all are indivisible, we expect to give active support to the common cause of equal rights for all those who suffer discrimination and deprivation, and we call upon other organizations committed to such goals to support our efforts toward equality for women.

WE DO NOT ACCEPT the token appointment of a few women to high-level positions in government and industry as a substitute for a serious continuing effort to recruit and advance women according to their individual abilities. To this end, we

National Organization for Women, Statement of Purpose, 1966.

urge American government and industry to mobilize the same resources of ingenuity and command with which they have solved problems of far greater difficulty than those now impeding the progress of women.

WE BELIEVE that this nation has a capacity at least as great as other nations, to innovate new social institutions which will enable women to enjoy true equality of opportunity and responsibility in society, without conflict with their responsibilities as mothers and homemakers. In such innovations, America does not lead the Western world, but lags by decades behind many European countries. We do not accept the traditional assumption that a woman has to choose between marriage and mother-hood, on the one hand, and serious participation in industry or the professions on the other. We question the present expectation that all normal women will retire from job or profession for ten or fifteen years, to devote their full time to raising children, only to reenter the job market at a relatively minor level. This in itself is a deterrent to the aspirations of women, to their acceptance into management or professional training courses, and to the very possibility of equality of opportunity or real choice, for all but a few women. Above all, we reject the assumption that these problems are the unique responsibility of each individual woman, rather than a basic social dilemma which society must solve. True equality of opportunity and freedom of choice for women requires such practical and possible innovations as a nationwide network of child-care centers, which will make it unnecessary for women to retire completely from society until their children are grown, and national programs to provide retrain-ing for women who have chosen to care for their own children full time.

WE BELIEVE that it is as essential for every girl to be educated to her full potential of human ability as it is for every boy—with the knowledge that such edu-cation is the key to effective participation in today's economy and that, for a girl as for a boy, education can only be serious where there is expectation that it will be used in society. We believe that American educators are capable of devising means of imparting such expectations to girl students. Moreover, we consider the decline in the proportion of women receiving higher and professional education to be evi-dence of discrimination. This discrimination may take the form of quotas against the admission of women to colleges and professional schools; lack of encouragement by parents, counselors and educators; denial of loans or fellowships; or the traditional or arbitrary procedures in graduate and professional training geared in terms of men, which inadvertently discriminate against women. We believe that the same serious attention must be given to high school dropouts who are girls as to boys.

WE REJECT the current assumptions that a man must carry the sole burden of supporting himself, his wife, and family, and that a woman is automatically entitled to lifelong support by a man upon her marriage, or that marriage, home and family are primarily woman's world and responsibility—hers, to dominate, his to support. We believe that a true partnership between the sexes demands a different concept of marriage, an equitable sharing of the responsibilities of home and children and of the economic burdens of their support. We believe that proper recognition should be given to the economic and social value of homemaking and child care. To these ends, we will seek to open a reexamination of laws and mores governing marriage and divorce, for we believe that the current state of "half-equality" between the sexes discriminates against both men and women, and is the cause of much unnecessary hostility between the sexes.

WE BELIEVE that women must now exercise their political rights and responsibilities as American citizens. They must refuse to be segregated on the basis of sex into separate-and-not-equal ladies' auxiliaries in the political parties, and they must demand representation according to their numbers in the regularly constituted party committees—at local, state, and national levels—and in the informal power structure, participating fully in the selection of candidates and political decision-making, and running for office themselves.

IN THE INTERESTS OF THE HUMAN DIGNITY OF WOMEN, we will protest and endeavor to change the false image of women now prevalent in the mass media, and in the texts, ceremonies, laws, and practices of our major social institutions. Such images perpetuate contempt for women by society and by women for themselves. We are similarly opposed to all policies and practices—in church, state, college, factory, or office—which, in the guise of protectiveness, not only deny opportunities but also foster in women self-denigration, dependence, and evasion of responsibility, undermine their confidence in their own abilities and foster contempt for women.

NOW WILL HOLD ITSELF INDEPENDENT OF ANY POLITICAL PARTY in order to mobilize the political power of all women and men intent on our goals. We will strive to ensure that no party, candidate, President, senator, governor, congressman, or any public official who betrays or ignores the principle of full equality between the sexes is elected or appointed to office. If it is necessary to mobilize the votes of men and women who believe in our cause, in order to win for women the final right to be fully free and equal human beings, we so commit ourselves.

WE BELIEVE THAT women will do most to create a new image of women by *acting* now, and by speaking out in behalf of their own equality, freedom, and human dignity—not in pleas for special privilege, nor in enmity toward men, who are also victims of the current half-equality between the sexes—but in an active, self-respecting partnership with men. By so doing, women will develop confidence in their own ability to determine actively, in partnership with men, the conditions of their life, their choices, their future and their society.

3. Frances Beale, "Double Jeopardy: To Be Black and Female," 1970

In attempting to analyze the situation of the Black woman in America, one crashes abruptly into a solid wall of grave misconceptions, outright distortions of fact, and defensive attitudes on the part of many. The system of capitalism (and its afterbirth—racism) under which we all live has attempted by many devious ways and means to destroy the humanity of all people, and particularly the humanity of Black people. This has meant an outrageous assault on every Black man, woman, and child who reside in the United States.

In keeping with its goal of destroying the Black race's will to resist its subjugation, capitalism found it necessary to create a situation where the Black man found

From Frances Beale, "Double Jeopardy: To Be Black and Female," in Toni Cade, ed., *The Black Woman: An Anthology,* 1970. Reprinted by arrangement with Toni Cade, c/o Joan Daves Agency as agent for the proprietor. Copyright 1970 by Toni Cade.

it impossible to find meaningful or productive employment. More often than not, he couldn't find work of any kind. And the Black woman likewise was manipulated by the system, economically exploited and physically assaulted. She could often find work in the white man's kitchen, however, and sometimes became the sole bread-winner of the family. This predicament has led to many psychological problems on the part of both man and woman and has contributed to the turmoil that we find in the Black family structure.

Unfortunately, neither the Black man nor the Black woman understood the true nature of the forces working upon them. Many Black women tended to accept the capitalist evaluation of manhood and womanhood and believed, in fact, that Black men were shiftless and lazy, otherwise they would get a job and support their fami-lies as they ought to. Personal relationships between Black men and women were thus torn asunder and one result has been the separation of man from wife, mother from child, etc.

America has defined the roles to which each individual should subscribe. It has defined "manhood" in terms of its own interests and "femininity" likewise. There-fore, an individual who has a good job, makes a lot of money, and drives a Cadillac is a real "man," and conversely, an individual who is lacking in these "qualities" is less of a man. . . .

The ideal model that is projected for a woman is to be surrounded by hypocriti-cal homage and estranged from all real work, spending idle hours primping and preening, obsessed with conspicuous consumption, and limiting life's functions to simply a sex role. We unqualitatively reject these respective models. A woman who stays at home caring for children and the house often leads an extremely sterile exis-tence. She must lead her entire life as a satellite to her mate. He goes out into society and brings back a little piece of the world for her. His interests and his understand-ing of the world become her own and she cannot develop herself as an individual having been reduced to only a biological function. This kind of woman leads a para-sitic existence that can aptly be described as legalized prostitution.

Furthermore it is idle dreaming to think of Black women simply caring for their homes and children like the middle-class white model. Most Black women have to work to help house, feed, and clothe their families. Black women make up a substan-tial percentage of the Black working force, and this is true for the poorest Black family as well as the so-called "middle-class" family. . . .

Unfortunately, there seems to be some confusion in the Movement today as to who has been oppressing whom. Since the advent of Black power, the Black male has exerted a more prominent leadership role in our struggle for justice in this country. He sees the system for what it really is for the most part, but where he rejects its values and mores on many issues, when it comes to women, he seems to take his guidelines from the pages of the *Ladies' Home Journal.* Certain Black men are main-taining that they have been castrated by society but that Black women somehow escaped this persecution and even contributed to this emasculation.

Let me state here and now that the Black woman in America can justly be de-scribed as a "slave of a slave." By reducing the Black man in America to such abject oppression, the Black woman had no protector and was used, and is still being used in some cases, as the scapegoat for the evils that this horrendous system has per-petrated on Black men. Her physical image has been maliciously maligned; she has been sexually molested and abused by the white colonizer; she has suffered the worse kind of economic exploitation, having been forced to serve as the white woman's maid and wet nurse for white offspring while her own children were more often than not starving and neglected. It is the depth of degradation to be socially manipulated, physically raped, used to undermine your own household, and to be powerless to reverse this syndrome.

It is true that our husbands, fathers, brothers, and sons have been emasculated, lynched, and brutalized. They have suffered from the cruelest assault on mankind that the world has ever known. However, it is a gross distortion of fact to state that Black women have oppressed Black men. The capitalist system found it expedient to enslave and oppress them and proceeded to do so without consultation or the signing of any agreements with Black women.

It must also be pointed out at this time that Black women are not resentful of the rise to power of Black men. We welcome it. We see in it the eventual liberation of all Black people from this corrupt system of capitalism. Nevertheless, this does not mean that you have to negate one for the other. This kind of thinking is a product of miseducation; that it's either X or it's Y. It is fallacious reasoning that in order for the Black man to be strong, the Black woman has to be weak.

Those who are exerting their "manhood" by telling Black women to step back into a domestic, submissive role are assuming a counter-revolutionary position. Black women likewise have been abused by the system and we must begin talking about the elimination of all kinds of oppression. If we are talking about building a strong nation, capable of throwing off the yoke of capitalist oppression, then we are talking about the total involvement of every man, woman, and child, each with a highly developed political consciousness. We need our whole army out there dealing with the enemy and not half an army.

There are also some Black women who feel that there is no more productive role in life than having and raising children. This attitude often reflects the conditioning of the society in which we live and is adopted from a bourgeois white model. Some young sisters who have never had to maintain a household and accept the confining role which this entails tend to romanticize (along with the help of a few brothers) this role of housewife and mother. Black women who have had to endure this kind of function are less apt to have these utopian visions. . . .

Much has been written recently about the white women's liberation movement in the United States, and the question arises whether there are any parallels between this struggle and the movement on the part of Black women for total emancipation. . . .

Any white group that does not have an anti-imperialist and anti-racist ideology has absolutely nothing in common with the Black woman's struggle. In fact, some groups come to the incorrect conclusion that their oppression is due simply to male chauvinism. . . .

If white groups do not realize that they are in fact fighting capitalism and racism, we do not have common bonds. If they do not realize that the reasons for their condition lie in the system and not simply that men get a vicarious pleasure out of "consuming their bodies for exploitative reasons" (this kind of reasoning seems to be quite prevalent in certain white women's groups), then we cannot unite with them around common grievances or even discuss these groups in a serious manner because they're completely irrelevant to the Black struggle.

4. Mirta Vidal Reports on the Rising Consciousness of the Chicana About Her Special Oppression, 1971

At the end of May 1971, more than 600 Chicanas met in Houston, Texas, to hold the first national conference of Raza women. For those of us who were there it was clear that this conference was not just another national gathering of the Chicano movement.

Chicanas came from all parts of the country inspired by the prospect of discussing issues that have long been on their minds and which they now see not as individual problems but as an important and integral part of a movement for liberation.

The resolutions coming out of the two largest workshops, "Sex and the Chicana" and "Marriage—Chicana Style," called for "free, legal abortions and birth control for the Chicano community, controlled by *Chicanas*." As Chicanas, the resolution stated, "we have a right to control our own bodies." The resolutions also called for "24-hour child-care centers in Chicano communities" and explained that there is a critical need for these since "Chicana motherhood should not preclude educational, political, social and economic advancement."

While these resolutions articulated the most pressing needs of Chicanas today, the conference as a whole reflected a rising consciousness of the Chicana about her special oppression in this society.

With their growing involvement in the struggle for Chicano liberation and the emergence of the feminist movement, Chicanas are beginning to challenge every social institution which contributes to and is responsible for their oppression, from inequality on the job to their role in the home. They are questioning "machismo," discrimination in education, the double standard, the role of the Catholic Church, and all the backward ideology designed to keep women subjugated. . . .

The oppression suffered by Chicanas is different from that suffered by most women in this country. Because Chicanas are part of an oppressed nationality, they are subjected to the racism practiced against La Raza. Since the overwhelming majority of Chicanos are workers, Chicanas are also victims of the exploitation of the working class. But in addition, Chicanas, along with the rest of women, are relegated to an inferior position because of their sex. Thus, Raza women suffer a triple form of oppression: as members of an oppressed nationality, as workers, *and* as women. Chicanas have no trouble understanding this. At the Houston conference 84 percent of the women surveyed felt that "there is a distinction between the problems of the Chicana and those of other women."

On the other hand, they also understand that the struggle now unfolding against the oppression of women is not only relevant to them, but *is* their struggle.

Because sexism and male chauvinism are so deeply rooted in this society, there is a strong tendency, even within the Chicano movement, to deny the basic right of Chicanas to organize around their own concrete issues. Instead they are told to stay away from the women's liberation movement because it is an "Anglo thing."

We need only analyze the origin of male supremacy to expose this false position. The inferior role of women in society does not date back to the beginning of time. In fact, before the Europeans came to this part of the world women enjoyed a position of equality with men. The submission of women, along with institutions such as the church and the patriarchy, was imported by the European colonizers, and remains to this day part of Anglo society. Machismo—in English, "male chauvinism"—is the one thing, if any, that should be labeled an "Anglo thing."

When Chicano men oppose the efforts of women to move against their oppression, they are actually opposing the struggle of every woman in this country aimed at changing a society in which Chicanos themselves are oppressed. They are saying to 51 percent of this country's population that they have no right to fight for their liberation.

Moreover, they are denying one half of La Raza this basic right. They are denying Raza women, who are triply oppressed, the right to struggle around their specific, real, and immediate needs.

In essence, they are doing just what the white male rulers of this country have done. The white male rulers want Chicanas to accept their oppression because they understand that when Chicanas begin a movement demanding legal abortions, child care, and equal pay for equal work, this movement will pose a real threat to their ability to rule. . . .

All other arguments aside, the fact is that Chicanas *are* oppressed and that the battles they are now waging and will wage in the future, are for things they need: the right to legal abortions, the right to adequate child care, the right to contraceptive information and devices, the right to decide how many children they do or do not want to have. In short, the right to control their own bodies. . . .

Coupled with this campaign to repeal all abortion laws, women are fighting to end all forced sterilizations, a campaign in which Chicanas will play a central role. This demand is of key importance to Chicanas who are the victims of forced sterilizations justified by the viciously racist ideology that the problems of La Raza are caused by Raza women having too many babies.

In line with other brutal abuses of women, Chicanas have been used as guinea pigs for experimentation with contraception. This was done recently in San Antonio by a doctor who wanted to test the reaction of women to birth control pills. Without informing them or asking their opinion, he gave some of the women dummy pills (placebos) that would not prevent conception, and as a result some of the women became pregnant. When questioned about his action, his reply was: "If you think you can explain a placebo test to women like these you never met Mrs. Gomez from the West Side."

The feminist movement today provides a vehicle for organizing against and putting an end to such racist, sexist practices. And that is what women are talking about when they talk about women's liberation.

Another essential fight that Chicanas have begun is around the need for adequate child care. While billions of dollars are spent yearly by this government on war, no money can be found to alleviate the plight of millions of women who, in addition to being forced to work, have families to care for. . . .

An important aspect of the struggles of Chicanas is the demand that the gains made through their campaigns be *controlled by Chicanas*. The demand for community control is a central axis of the Chicana liberation struggle as a whole. Thus, when Chicanas, as Chicanas, raise demands for child-care facilities, abortion clinics, etc., controlled by Chicanas, their fight is an integral part of the Chicana liberation struggle.

When Chicanas choose to organize into their own separate organizations, they are not turning away from La Causa or waging a campaign against men. They are saying to Chicanos: "We are oppressed as Chicanas and we are moving against our oppression. Support our struggles." The sooner that Chicanos understand the need for women to struggle around their own special demands, through their own organizations, the further La Raza as a whole will be on the road toward liberation.

5. The Equal Rights Amendment, 1972

[Sent to the states, 1972]

Section 1   Equality of rights under the law shall not be denied or abridged by the United States or by any State on account of sex.

Section 2   The Congress shall have the power to enforce, by appropriate legislation, the provisions of this article.

Section 3   This amendment shall take effect two years after the date of ratification.

6. "We Are Trying to Find a Way to Have Our Babies Safely and with Dignity," The Boston Women's Health Book Collective, 1973

Childbirth preparation means educating ourselves about what is likely to happen to our bodies, our minds, and our lives during the childbirth experience. It also means finding someone—husband, friend, or relative—to share this period with us. It is certainly not impossible to go through pregnancy, childbirth, and motherhood alone and unprepared, but it is difficult and unnecessary.

Above all, we must try not to be alone during labor. The companion we choose (early in our pregnancy) should be reading the same books, attending the same classes, and learning the same exercises and breathing techniques as we are. This person will serve as our coach during labor, and will stay with us throughout the entire birth process. Often the baby's father will be our coach. Sharing the labor experience and witnessing the birth with him is an important beginning to sharing the responsibilities and joys of parenthood. Some of us want to be with another woman during labor. We will find it most helpful to have as coach a woman who has already given birth. She will be able to support us with her firsthand knowledge, and her presence is a witness to the fact that it can be done. . . .

However, there are hospitals that will allow only a registered nurse to be with you during labor, and many hospitals will not allow any outsider into the delivery room. We must work to change these rules, but until they are eliminated, search around until you find a doctor and a hospital that meet your requirements. Be particular, and make all the demands you feel are necessary to your best interests and your baby's security.

Ninety-second Congress, 1972, Vol. 86 *U. S. Statutes at Large,* 1523–1524.

Prepared childbirth is often called natural childbirth. The only thing natural is that a woman's body is biologically equipped to bear and give birth to children. This doesn't mean that we have to have children or that we shouldn't be able to choose when we want to have children. It also doesn't mean that we should go through childbirth without preparation. Although much of our society considers it normal for us to have our babies while heavily drugged, in helpless ignorance and pain, and totally dependent on the medical profession, we believe it is much more natural for us to want to know what is happening to our bodies during labor. We want to give birth to our babies with confidence.

We are trying to find a way to have our babies safely and with dignity. The concept of dignity in labor was made popular in the West by two obstetricians. In 1932 Dr. Grantly Dick-Read, an Englishman, first introduced a method of concentrated relaxation during labor with the publication of his book *Childbirth Without Fear.* He understood that fear causes tension, and tension causes pain. Thus his approach was to try to eliminate the fear of labor through education and exercise. A French doctor, Fernand Lamaze, offered a different idea, called the psychoprophylactic method for childbirth. Lamaze asked that women respond actively to labor contractions with a set of prelearned, controlled breathing techniques. As the intensity of the contraction increased, so would the woman's rate of breathing. As a result, the laboring woman's posture and attitude changed. She was no longer flat on her back, to be pitied by all onlookers; now she was active, changing positions and breathing patterns as she knew she must. The onlookers cheered.

Marjorie Karmel introduced the Lamaze method of childbirth to the United States with her book *Thank You, Dr. Lamaze,* published in 1959. She had had her first child delivered in Paris by Dr. Lamaze, and when she returned to the States and tried to have her second child delivered by the same method, she ran into tremendous opposition and a great deal of ignorance on the part of the doctors here. Mrs. Karmel finally joined with Elisabeth Bing, a physical therapist from Berlin, and founded the American Society for Psychoprophylaxis in Obstetrics (ASPO). The purpose of this society was to train doctors, nurses, and expectant parents in prepared childbirth techniques.

Now there are childbirth-preparation classes in every major city in the United States. . . . There are also many books, articles, and films on the subject. . . . Yet, as with everything else in our impersonal society, neither the classes nor the books will meet our very individual needs unless we demand that they do. Many of the classes are too large, sometimes with ten to twenty couples attending at a time. So it's often difficult to learn more than just the fundamentals, such as basic anatomy and routine breathing techniques. These are essential to a prepared delivery, but they are sometimes not enough. If you look for them, you can usually find smaller, more personal classes, and the fee is generally the same as the fee for the larger, group classes. However, in either case the fee is higher than many women or couples can afford.

Furthermore, although physical preparation is necessary, psychological and emotional preparation can sometimes be more important. Often large classes are not conducive to discussions of personal problems. People should have the opportunity to talk to each other about all phases of childbearing, from the original decisions to conceive a child to the all-too-neglected fears and feelings about child raising. Ideally there should be voluntary, free classes open to anyone who feels the need to talk to other people about any aspect of pregnancy and parenthood. Since these classes are nonexistent in most communities, we must organize ourselves to get them started if we want them.

It's up to us to seek the support we need. Until the time when we can persuade the medical profession to give us less mechanized care, we will have to find all the help we need from each other. But it's often hard to find each other! One way is to ask doctors and hospitals to provide us with the names of the pregnant women they are seeing. They cooperate with diaper services, so why shouldn't they cooperate with us? A way to find the names of women in your area who have just delivered babies to check the town and state registries of births.

Once we have the people, we must have a place to meet. Hospitals and community centers can provide us with meeting rooms. As for books and teachers, one source is the department of public education. Information about pregnancy and childbirth is so vitally important to so many of us that we have the right to ask that it be supported by public funds. Surely if the state department of education can pay the salary of a person who teaches cake decorating in an adult education class, we might expect it to pay a teacher to prepare us for childbirth.

Home or Hospital?

So far we haven't said anything about avoiding the hospital altogether by having our babies at home. Whereas in England over 50 percent of the women have their babies at home, in the United States almost all of us are hospitalized for delivery. In England there is an extensive system of midwives and traveling emergency units which makes home delivery routine, and it is often only the special case that is delivered in a hospital with an attending obstetrician. In the United States we have no such system, and thus home delivery can indeed be very risky. We feel that one of our demands must be to make home delivery feasible here in America. Many women have already experienced successful home deliveries, some with their doctor's help, and many without it. In northern California there is apparently a movement afoot to convince doctors to participate in deliveries at home. Some doctors themselves are behind this movement. However, until our society is willing to break up the hospital's monopoly on safe deliveries by financing small traveling oxygen and emergency-equipment units for use at home, every woman must decide between hospital and home with their eyes wide open to the dangers as well as the joys. . . .

7. The Supreme Court Legalizes
Abortion in *Roe v. Wade,* 1973

Mr. Justice Blackmun delivered the opinion of the Court.

This Texas federal appeal and its Georgia companion. *Doe v. Bolton,* present constitutional challenges to state criminal abortion legislation. The Texas statutes under attack here are typical of those that have been in effect in many States for approximately a century. The Georgia statutes, in contrast, have a modern cast and are a

---

Roe v. Wade, 410 U.S. 113 (1973).

legislative product that, to an extent at least, obviously reflects the influences of recent attitudinal change, of advancing medical knowledge and techniques, and of new thinking about an old issue.

We forthwith acknowledge our awareness of the sensitive and emotional nature of the abortion controversy, of the vigorous opposing views, even among physicians, and of the deep and seemingly absolute convictions that the subject inspires. One's philosophy, one's experiences, one's exposure to the raw edges of human existence, one's religious training, one's attitudes toward life and family and their values, and the moral standards one establishes and seeks to observe, are all likely to influence and to color one's thinking and conclusions about abortion.

In addition, population growth, pollution, poverty, and racial overtones tend to complicate and not to simplify the problem.

Our task, of course, is to resolve the issue by constitutional measurement, free of emotion and of predilection. We seek earnestly to do this, and, because we do, we have inquired into, and in this opinion place some emphasis upon, medical and medical-legal history and what that history reveals about man's attitudes toward the abortion procedure over the centuries. . . .

It perhaps is not generally appreciated that the restrictive criminal abortion laws in effect in a majority of States today are of relatively recent vintage. Those laws, generally proscribing abortion or its attempt at any time during pregnancy except when necessary to preserve the pregnant woman's life, are not of ancient or even of common-law origin. Instead, they derive from statutory changes effected, for the most part, in the latter half of the 19th century. . . .

Three reasons have been advanced to explain historically the enactment of criminal abortion laws in the 19th century and to justify their continued existence.

It has been argued occasionally that these laws were the product of a Victorian social concern to discourage illicit sexual conduct. Texas, however, does not advance this justification in the present case, and it appears that no court or commentator has taken the argument seriously. . . .

A second reason is concerned with abortion as a medical procedure. When most criminal abortion laws were first enacted, the procedure was a hazardous one for the woman. . . . Thus, it has been argued that a State's real concern in enacting a criminal abortion law was to protect the pregnant woman, that is, to restrain her from submitting to a procedure that placed her life in serious jeopardy.

Modern medical techniques have altered this situation. Appellants and various amici refer to medical data indicating that abortion in early pregnancy, this is, prior to the end of the first trimester, although not without its risk, is now relatively safe. Mortality rates for women undergoing early abortions, where the procedure is legal, appear to be as low as or lower than the rates for normal childbirth. Consequently, any interest of the State in protecting the woman from an inherently hazardous pro-cedure, except when it would be equally dangerous for her to forgo it, has largely disappeared. Of course, important state interests in the area of health and medical standards do remain. . . .

The third reason is the State's interest—some phrase it in terms of duty—in protecting prenatal life. Some of the argument for this justification rests on the theory that a new human life is present from the moment of conception. The State's interest and general obligation to protect life then extends, it is argued, to prenatal life. Only when the life of the pregnant mother herself is at stake, balanced against the life she carries within her, should the interest of the embryo or fetus not prevail. Logically, of course, a legitimate state interest in this area need not stand or fall on acceptance of the belief that life begins at conception or at some other point prior to live birth. In assessing the State's interest, recognition may be given to the less rigid claim that as long as at least *potential* life is involved, the State may assert interests beyond the protection of the pregnant woman alone. . . .

The Constitution does not explicitly mention any right of privacy. In a line of decisions, however, the Court has recognized that a right of personal privacy, or a guarantee of certain areas or zones of privacy, does exist under the Constitution. . . .

This right of privacy, whether it be founded in the Fourteenth Amendment's concept of personal liberty and restrictions upon state action, as we feel it is, or, as the District Court determined, in the Ninth Amendment's reservation of rights to the people, is broad enough to encompass a woman's decision whether or not to terminate her pregnancy. The detriment that the State would impose upon the pregnant woman by denying this choice altogether is apparent. Specific and direct harm medically diagnosable even in early pregnancy may be involved. Maternity, or additional offspring, may force upon the woman a distressful life and future. Psychological harm may be imminent. Mental and physical health may be taxed by child care. There is also the distress, for all concerned, associated with the unwanted child, and there is the problem of bringing a child into a family already unable, psychologically and otherwise, to care for it. In other cases, as in this one, the additional difficulties and continuing stigma of unwed motherhood may be involved. All these are factors the woman and her responsible physician necessarily will consider in consultation.

On the basis of elements such as these, appellant and some amici argue that the woman's right is absolute and that she is entitled to terminate her pregnancy at whatever time, in whatever way, and for whatever reason she alone chooses. With this we do not agree. Appellant's arguments that Texas either has no valid interest at all in regulating the abortion decision, or no interest strong enough to support any limitation upon the woman's sole determination, is unpersuasive. The Court's decisions recognizing a right of privacy also acknowledge that some state regulation in areas protected by that right is appropriate. As noted above, a State may properly assert important interests in safeguarding health, in maintaining medical standards, and in protecting potential life. At some point in pregnancy, these respective interests become sufficiently compelling to sustain regulation of the factors that govern the abortion decision. The privacy right involved, therefore, cannot be said to be absolute. . . .

We, therefore, conclude that the right of personal privacy includes the abortion decision, but that this right is not unqualified and must be considered against important state interests in regulation. . . .

The appellee and certain amici argue that the fetus is a "person" within the language and meaning of the Fourteenth Amendment. In support of this, they outline at length and in detail the well-known facts of fetal development. If this suggestion of personhood is established, the appellant's case, of course, collapses, for the fetus' right to life is then guaranteed specifically by the Amendment. The appellant conceded as much on reargument. On the other hand, the appellee conceded on reargument that no case could be cited that holds that a fetus is a person within the meaning of the Fourteenth Amendment.

The Constitution does not define "person" in so many words. Section 1 of the Fourteenth Amendment contains three references to "person." The first, in defining "citizens," speaks of "persons born or naturalized in the United States." The word also appears both in the Due Process Clause and in the Equal Protection Clause. "Person" is used in other places in the Constitution. . . . But in nearly all these instances, the use of the word is such that it has application only postnatally. None indicates, with any assurance, that it has any possible prenatal application.

All this, together with our observation, supra, that throughout the major portion of the 19th century prevailing legal abortion practices were far freer than they are today, persuades us that the word "person" as used in the Fourteenth Amendment, does not include the unborn. . . .

Texas urges that, apart from the Fourteenth Amendment, life begins at conception and is present throughout pregnancy, and that, therefore, the State has a compelling interest in protecting that life from and after conception. We need not resolve the difficult question of when life begins. When those trained in the respective disciplines of medicine, philosophy, and theology are unable to arrive at any consensus, the judiciary, at this point in the development of man's knowledge, is not in a position to speculate as to the answer. . . .

With respect to the State's important and legitimate interest in the health of the mother, the "compelling" point, in the light of present medical knowledge, is at approximately the end of the first trimester. This is so because of the now-established medical fact that until the end of the first trimester mortality in abortion may be less than mortality in normal childbirth. It follows that, from and after this point, a State may regulate the abortion procedure to the extent that the regulation reasonably relates to the preservation and protection of maternal health. . . .

With respect to the State's important and legitimate interest in potential life, the "compelling" point is at viability. This is so because the fetus then presumably has the capability of meaningful life outside the mother's womb. State regulation protective of fetal life after viability thus has both logical and biological justifications. If the State is interested in protecting fetal life after viability, it may go so far as to proscribe abortion during that period, except when it is necessary to preserve the life or health of the mother. . . .

To summarize and to repeat:

1. A state criminal abortion statute of the current Texas type, that excepts from criminality only a *life-saving* procedure on behalf of the mother, without regard to pregnancy stage and without recognition of the other interests involved, is violative of the Due Process Clause of the Fourteenth Amendment.
   a. For the stage prior to approximately the end of the first trimester, the abortion decision and its effectuation must be left to the medical judgment of the pregnant woman's attending physician.
   b. For the stage subsequent to approximately the end of the first trimester, the State, in promoting its interest in the health of the mother, may, if it chooses, regulate the abortion procedure in ways that are reasonably related to maternal health.
   c. For the stage subsequent to viability, the State in promoting its interest in the potentiality of human life may, if it chooses, regulate, and even proscribe,

abortion except where it is necessary, in appropriate medical judgment, for the preservation of the life or health of the mother. . . .

Mr. Justice White, with whom Mr. Justice Rehnquist joins, dissenting.

At the heart of the controversy in these cases are those recurring pregnancies that pose no danger whatsoever to the life or health of the mother but are, nevertheless, unwanted for any one or more of a variety of reasons—convenience, family planning, economics, dislike of children, the embarrassment of illegitimacy, etc. The common claim before us is that for any one of such reasons, or for no reason at all, and without asserting or claiming any threat to life or health, any woman is entitled to an abortion at her request if she is able to find a medical advisor willing to undertake the procedure.

The Court for the most part sustains this position: During the period prior to the time the fetus becomes viable, the Constitution of the United States values the convenience, whim, or caprice of the putative mother more than the life or potential life of the fetus; the Constitution, therefore, guarantees the right to an abortion as against any state law or policy seeking to protect the fetus from an abortion not prompted by more compelling reasons of the mother.

With all due respect, I dissent. I find nothing in the language or history of the Constitution to support the Court's judgment. The Court simply fashions and announces a new constitutional right for pregnant mothers and, with scarcely any reason or authority for its action, invests that right with sufficient substance to override most existing state abortion statutes. The upshot is that the people and the legislatures of the 50 States are constitutionally disentitled to weigh the relative importance of the continued existence and development of the fetus, on the one hand, against a spectrum of possible impacts on the mother, on the other hand. As an exercise of raw judicial power, the Court perhaps has authority to do what it does today; but in my view its judgment is an improvident and extravagant exercise of the power of judicial review that the Constitution extends to this Court.

8. Lindsy Van Gelder Reports on the "World Series of Sex-Discrimination Suits," 1978

The *New York Times* has long been known to the press corps and media buffs as "the Good Gray Lady." The term is not without endearment, but it refers only to the *Times'* somber (some would say stuffy) sense of itself as both the Number One newspaper of record and the influential editorialist of liberal Establishment values. The far livelier tabloid *Daily News* is read by many more New Yorkers, but the *Times* is the Bible of the upwardly mobile and professional classes—and its editors fancy the Good Gray Lady the collective information font . . . for the cultural, financial, educational, and political elite.

"Ladies" and other females, however, are in comparatively scant supply at the *Times,* and the prevailing pigmentation is white.

Lindsy Van Gelder, "Women vs. The New York 'Times': The World Series of Sex-Discrimination Suits," *Ms. Magazine* 7, no. 3 (September 1978): 66–68, 104. Reprinted by permission of the author.

The *Times* itself conceded this point last November in an editorial entitled "The Complaints of White Men," its response to charges that affirmative action programs for women and minorities constitute "reverse discrimination" against white males. "As the list of our company officers testify each day on this page," the editorial began, "we are an institution run mostly by white men. As in most other institutions, women and non-whites came later than white men into the hierarchies from which our managers have been chosen. Recognizing the inadequacy of the result, and faced with social and legal pressures that we ourselves helped to generate, we have undertaken corrective measures, affirmative action, to expand opportunity in our company." . . .

It is thus somewhat of a blow to the Gray Lady's image of fairness and rectitude that the newspaper is currently the target of employment discrimination suits brought under Title VII of the Civil Rights Act by both female and minority personnel. . . . Although most sex-discrimination cases that go as far through the federal machinery as the *Times* suit has are settled out of court, the paper's management, insisting they have not discriminated, is determined to see this one through the courts, and the case is scheduled to go to trial this fall. (The separate minority suit is at an earlier legal stage.) Given the cast of characters and the issues being raised, the women's day in court already promises to be the Title VII World Series.

It all began five years ago when a group of *Times* women—including reporters, clerks, telephone solicitors, and other non-newsroom personnel—began meeting among themselves and later with publisher Arthur O. (Punch) Sulzberger to discuss their grievances. It was only after they became convinced that they would find no redress through informal "gentlemanly" channels that they contacted attorneys Harriet Rabb and Howard Rubin, co-directors of Columbia Law School's Employment Rights Project. A by-now almost legendary Title VII specialist, Rabb is an outspoken feminist who has chalked up victories for women employees at *Reader's Digest, Newsweek,* New York Telephone, and a dozen Wall Street law firms.

Several women formally filed charges with the Equal Employment Opportunity Commission in the spring of 1973. It was difficult for the *Times* to dismiss the original group as a band of no-talent radical malcontents since they included several of the paper's most respected female staff members. One was star political reporter Eileen Shanahan (now with the Department of Health, Education, and Welfare), whose annual salary was $2,500 less than that of the average male in the *Times'* Washington bureau. Another was Elizabeth Boylan, known professionally as Betsy Wade, then chief of the paper's foreign copydesk, and once glowingly described in an in-house *Times* publication as being able to do "a man's work with a woman's delicacy." Wade, who earns more than her average male colleague, charged that for 10 years she had coveted the post of assistant news editor and had been passed over in favor of at least nine men.

The women won a significant point when the federal court ruled that theirs was a class action suit, which meant that they could act on behalf of all female *Times* employees. A cohesive women's caucus now exists at the paper.

"There's a real feeling of camaraderie among us," according to one member—perhaps all the more surprising since journalists tend traditionally to be apolitical loners, and the *Times* in particular is known for its Byzantine newsroom competitiveness. . . .

According to one male former *Times* executive, sexism does indeed exist there, but in a genteel form in keeping with the overall tone of the paper: "The editors look around furtively before they make their tits-and-ass cracks." . . .

The ex-*Times*man recalled being introduced to Betsy Wade by managing editor Seymour Topping in 1969 and later being told by Topping that Wade was "a really fine newspaperwoman. If she weren't a woman, she'd be in the bullpen [the main news desk] right now!" Since the initiation of the women's suit, he added, *Times* executives have given a great deal of lip service to hiring and promoting women. But he's skeptical: "Abe Rosenthal [executive editor] would get up at meetings, roll his eyes heavenward, and moan about 'our problem' and how he wanted to see some blacks and women around the place. Then last year he personally hired three people—all white, middle-class men."

The rumor in the city room is that Rosenthal and publisher Sulzberger made the decision not to settle out of court with the women's caucus, although it is also said that some other top executives were dismayed by this decision. By many accounts, however, women have no special monopoly on generally rough treatment at the hands of management. "Listen," said one reporter. "Blacks are oppressed at the *Times*. Gays are oppressed. But even white Jewish males feel oppressed. They're an equal opportunity oppressor." Since a great many journalists feel that the *Times* is the pinnacle of the profession, they are apparently willing to endure a fair amount of psychic scarring in exchange for a *Times* byline.

The upcoming trial will at least in part be a war of numbers. Harriet Rabb and her colleagues have amassed a staggering array of statistics purporting to show that the *Times* discriminates against women at all levels, from editors to cleaning women, in hiring, promotions, pay, assignments, among other areas. For example:

• Scores of positions at the *Times* have never been held by women.

• A 1977 government report based on personnel information supplied by the *Times* concluded that women were "underutilized" in 27 out of 37 divisions.

• According to Rabb's proposed pretrial order, the number of men employed by the *Times* in "craft union" jobs (*i.e.,* printers, newspaper deliverers, press workers, et cetera) in 1976 was 5,760. The number of women in such jobs was 19. Among white-collar workers and professionals, as of January, 1976, 26.2 percent were women—at a time when fully 40 percent of the U.S. and New York labor force as a whole was female.

• As of January, 1976, males averaged higher salaries in 73.4 percent of all jobs than women. The difference between the average male and female salary was $5,159 a year. Even when length of service, total work experience, and education are factored in, the *Times* pays men an average $3,735 more a year than women are paid.

• In 1976, when the *Times* conducted a performance evaluation of its reporters, 18 men who were ranked "OK But Needs Improvement To Meet Normal Requirements" or "Satisfactory," earned more than women receiving the highest rating of "Better than Most."

Rabb's research also turned up a number of less-than-enlightened interoffice memos. One evaluated the "work" of a woman in the circulation and promotion department this way: "Very pleasant. Good at shorthand and typing. Her chief ambition is probably to get married. Has a good figure and is not restrained about dressing it to advantage." Another was a response from the Sunday editor to a *Times* employee who had recommended a female job applicant: "What does she look like? Twiggy? Lynn Redgrave? Perhaps you ought to send over her vital statistics, or a picture in a bikini." A third memo praised a female mail clerk, adding "I would make her my first assistant if she were a man." Another goodie brought forth in a proposed pretrial order was the fact that a female foreign correspondent—one of the few ever for the *Times*—was once ordered out of Vietnam to cover the Paris fashion collections, something no male war correspondent was ever assigned to do. . . .

The *Times* . . . answers charges of discrimination in promotion, salary, and assignment, at least in the newsroom, by noting that the deployment of reporters and editors is a fairly subjective process, in which people are judged by intangibles such as "news judgment" rather than by what graduate degrees they have or how long they've been on the job. Executive vice-president James Goodale added that "women, for reasons I don't think are our fault, don't constitute a large talent pool in the thirty to forty-five age group, where you would find people for middle-management jobs." . . .

While Harriet Rabb will attempt to prove a pattern of discrimination at the *Times*, the paper's attorneys will in many cases be countering that a specific woman didn't get a specific job, raise, or assignment because she just plain wasn't good enough—a prospect that both sides view as regrettable, but unavoidable. "The idea of going to trial doesn't fill me with radical fervor," admitted one *Times* woman. "Everybody's going to be spattered with mud, and it won't do any of our careers any good. But at this point our basic contention is so clear-cut that there's just no question of turning back."

9. Connaught C. Marshner Explains What Social Conservatives Really Want, 1988

By now everyone knows that pro-family conservatives are a powerful political force. . . . What follows are the presumptions of the moral traditionalists.

The family is the fundamental institution of society; in the traditional society, it was your main source of comfort and strength. When you were a child, your father geared his life to providing shelter for your mother and you. As you grew, your family imparted the skills of survival, and gave you your religion and your politics. In your old age, someone with a blood connection would offer you a bed and a seat by the fire.

Today, these functions have atrophied. Your existence needn't cause your father to change his lifestyle, and in many circles it changes your mother's as little as she can possibly arrange. It is no reason for your father to stay with your mother; in the modern myth, she may even be more "fulfilled" without him around. If they do stay together, they play an increasingly small role in your upbringing: the public-education system, backed by the courts, positively puts obstacles in the path of parents wishing to exercise control over what their children read and study, while

"What Social Conservatives Really Want" by Connaught C. Marshner, from *National Review*, September 2, 1988, 38–41. Copyright © 1988 by *National Review*, Inc., 150 East 35th Street, New York, NY 10016. Reprinted by permission.

government-sponsored clinics are permitted to dispense contraceptives and perform abortions on teenagers without their parents' even being told. In your old age, Medicare will pay the costs of your medical treatment if you are put into an institution, but not if your relatives care for you at home. It's likely that your children and their spouses will all have careers anyhow, which means they can hire someone to look after you but can't spend time with you themselves.

In one area after another, functions once performed by the family are now provided by the government or government-style agencies and institutions. The goal of the pro-family movement is not to destroy these institutions but to restore to the family its proper functions, and to restore to the institutions an understanding of the proper proportion of their role.

The family fulfills many functions—social, psychological, and even economic— but these are *not* the reason for its existence. The family has one overriding task: raising children. It is each individual's entry point into society and the staging area of his personality.

Children are thus a gift and a responsibility, a long-term duty that arises from the nature of marriage. Marriage is not a contract, balancing conflicting interests, measuring competing obligations, forcing compliance with fear of consequences; it is a covenant, a permanent and exclusive union that sets no limits on what is to be given or forgiven by either party. The purposes of this covenant are the mutual support of the partners and the procreation, education, and rearing of children. Human nature being what it is, in practice many marriages are more reminiscent of contract than of covenant. But public policy should not seek the lowest common denominator and proclaim it as the model.

Modern society has, admittedly, lost sight of marriage in covenant terms. Fifty per cent of marriages in the U.S. today are second marriages for at least one of the partners. In 1984, over one million children were involved in the divorce of their parents; we can expect that over 11 million children—about one-fifth of the nation's total—will experience the misery of divorce over the next decade.

That trauma is rarely studied. In the famous California Children of Divorce Project, Dr. Judith Wallerstein of UC Berkeley followed children over a period of years after their parents divorced. Ten years after a divorce, 42 per cent of children were functioning poorly (exhibiting consistent depression, drug or alcohol abuse, sexual promiscuity, and/or poor performance in school); 15 per cent were functioning unevenly; and only 43 per cent were doing well most of the time. And the decline in upward mobility is just beginning to be noted: Dr. Wallerstein found in one study that, although 41 per cent of their divorced fathers were professionals, only 27 per cent of the children had professional aspirations.

A further result of the contract approach is no-fault divorce, which regards children as options that can be adjudicated like cars and stereos, with no long-term consequence to anyone. Some women may feel their "sense of self-worth" enhanced by bearing the costs of child-rearing alone, but their babies have no such illusions of self-reliance. Thanks to divorce and illegitimacy, children are the poorest class in America today: 20.5 per cent of all children were below the poverty line in 1986.

Nor are children the only victims. Stanford professor Lenore Weitzman, in her landmark study, *The Divorce Revolution,* found that in the year after a divorce, women experience a 73 per cent decline in their standard of living, while their former husbands experience a 42 per cent increase. The typical liberal response to this is to lament the feminization of poverty and wonder what the Federal Government is going to do to force fathers to pay child support. But even if every father met every child payment, 97 per cent of divorced women with children would still be in poverty. The real problem, again, is state laws and judges that adhere to no-fault divorce, expecting divorced mothers to function like young professional men. Despite what many would like to believe, traits of gender and the condition of motherhood make a tremendous difference in the way people can and will act. Any world view that pretends otherwise is either dishonestly or maliciously inviting human misery. . . .

It should be an achievable goal that every baby born have an adult male responsible for it, that the norm be children nurtured by their own, married parents. But support for the traditional family flies in the face of the reigning orthodoxy by hinting that there is something inherently superior in children's being raised by their own parents in an intact family. Many professional women, single parents, and human-services personnel seem to take this praise of the ideal as an insult to the good they do. Many single parents *are* doing an excellent job of raising their children. But should we pretend that divorce and unwed motherhood are symptoms of social *strength?*

Liberalism since the Sixties has repudiated the validity of the ideal, anxious to placate feminism and the demand for instant pleasure without negative consequences. The facts of human nature do not change, however: to develop into stable, virtuous men and women, children need the constant, loving, particular attention of one or two consistent adults.

If we are to reassert the ideal, we must re-examine employment policies that lure mothers into the workforce, change tax policies that favor working mothers over full-time homemakers, and create tax oases for families of young children. Technology can come to our aid here, if it is not trammeled by politics as it has been in previous opportunities. Thirteen million new jobs could be created at home (presumably mostly for women) if government resists pressure from organized labor to outlaw home employment. Local laws restricting businesses operated out of the home—including computer work—must be corrected. . . .

It all comes down to values. Traditional values work because they are the guidelines most consistent with human nature for producing happiness and achievement. Children who are not trained to traditional values are deprived of the best opportunity to understand their own nature and achieve that happiness. Children who *are* trained to these values are nonetheless free, upon maturity, to reject them: that is why, contrary to what the relativists insist, instilling them is not oppressive. But if these values are at least transmitted to all members of society, the possibility for a fundamental consensus on behavior exists.

Ronald Reagan got elected and reelected in large part because enough people agreed that the policies of the welfare state had failed, and enough wanted to hear more about traditional values. The public wanted government to shrink its role in their lives. That basic impulse has been developed for eight years now. In the meantime, we still have a welfare state that shows no signs of curing a single social ill, let alone withering away—it is, of course, intrinsically incapable of doing either. . . . This system perpetuates itself and the problems it pretends to solve; and yet we cannot follow the vision on which Ronald Reagan was elected until the way society organizes its approach to problems is changed—until people are again in charge of their own affairs, and those of their local community. . . .

Liberal solutions don't work because institutions cannot change hearts or minds. *People* do that. That's why the family must hold onto as many functions as it can, and reclaim those that have been taken from it: because the consolidation of tasks in the family intensifies the interaction among members, and heightens awareness of and commitment to one another's welfare. That gives the long-range focus to our lives that connects us to society and enables us to extend our concern to our fellow citizens.

E S S A Y S

In the first essay Alicia Chávez explores the life of Dolores Huerta, a Mexican American union organizer, civil rights activist, and feminist. Huerta's first political commitments were to union organizing for Mexican American farm workers, but by the 1970s she had begun to incorporate feminist views into her politics. Nancy MacLean explores in the second essay the history of women and affirmative action in the 1970s, arguing that through their use of affirmative action laws, working-class women made long-lasting contributions to modern feminism. In the last essay, Wendy Kline examines the feminist health movement of the 1970s and 1980s, highlighting the critical importance of the book, *Our Bodies, Ourselves* to American women's empowerment as medical patients and healthcare consumers.

Dolores Huerta and The United Farm Workers

ALICIA CHÁVEZ

While she appears mild-mannered and even soft-spoken, Dolores Huerta has been a fearless warrior in her career as an activist. Unflappable as a union organizer, uncompromising as a contract negotiator, unapologetic as she lived against the grain of the social and political norms of her era, she leaves an indelible legacy of labor-organizing in U.S. history. In 1962, after almost a decade of activism in the Stockton, California, chapter of the Community Service Organization, a self-help Mexican American civil rights organization, Huerta joined fellow activist César Chávez in co-founding the National Farm Workers Association (NFWA) to address the issues of migrant farm workers in California. In September 1965, the NFWA joined the Agricultural Workers Organizing Committee, an affiliate of the AFL-CIO, for the famous Delano Grape Strike, and a year later the two groups merged to form the United Farm Workers Organizing Committee, also an affiliate of the AFL-CIO. Later, the new union shortened its name to the United Farm Workers of America (UFW).

With her children in the backseat of her barely operable car, and living on only $5 per week, Huerta embarked on an exhausting and dangerous journey of speaking engagements and door-to-door canvassing, activities that established the UFW's membership base. She also did strategic planning for the Grape Strike of 1965, and in 1968 and 1969, she directed the table grape boycott in New York City. In her un-yielding style, Huerta became the first woman and the first Mexican American to negotiate a union contract with California growers in 1970. As the UFW extended its reach to the lettuce and strawberry fields, Huerta continued her unflagging organ-izing while lobbying legislators in both Sacramento and Washington, D.C., for laws that would aid farm workers. Her work as a persuasive lobbyist facilitated the passage of the Agricultural Labor Relations Act of 1975, which for the first time recognized and protected the collective bargaining rights of agricultural laborers in California.

Huerta's work seems all the more extraordinary when combined with her rearing eleven children. In addition, she carried her messages and life lessons to the wider political world around her, speaking out, for example, on women's rights. Her work illuminated how women's activism could be an essential ingredient to a successful Mexican American political movement, and how political engagement could be a path to women's self-determination.

Huerta's activism was sparked by the deleterious impact that transformations in California agriculture had on Mexican communities there. Once marked by indi-vidual relationships to the land, agricultural production became a very impersonal agribusiness, with an increasing demand for inexpensive wage labor, on land where there had formerly been tenant farmers. These changes began at the turn of the twen-tieth century with the technological improvements in farming during the advance of industrialization; by World War II, a lot of agricultural land was owned in large tracts by corporations who sought low-wage workers to perform farm labor. The U.S. government permitted labor contracting in Mexico and other places to meet the increased demand for wartime foodstuffs. The most physically arduous jobs were regarded as menial and reserved for these nonwhite laborers. In this economic milieu, wages and working conditions declined substantially. Life expectancy for California farm workers by the 1960s was only approximately forty-nine years. Exposed to dangerous pesticide chemicals, entire families often had to work and continually migrate with the growing seasons, keeping their children out of school. While Dolores Huerta did not grow up in a migrant family, her evolution as an or-ganizer stemmed from lessons she learned from her parents and her own youthful experiences in a Mexican agricultural community.

Dolores Huerta was born Dolores Fernández on April 10, 1930, to Juan and Alicia Fernández, in the small coal-mining town of Dawson, New Mexico. Huerta's father was a coal miner, but like many of his peers, he supplemented his income with farm labor, traveling to Colorado, Nebraska, and Wyoming for the beet harvests. Fernández also developed a strong interest in labor issues and used his predomi-nantly Latino local union as a base upon which to win election to the New Mexico state legislature in 1938.

When her parents divorced in 1935, five-year-old Dolores and her brothers, John and Marshall, moved with their mother to the central San Joaquin Valley agricultural community of Stockton. Alicia Fernández found it very difficult to support her young family as a single parent in this Depression-era town. Dolores described her mother as "a very genteel woman, very quiet but very hardworking," yet also "a very ambitious woman." Her mother saved the wages she earned at her nighttime cannery shift (a common occupation for Mexican-origin women) and as a waitress during the day in order to buy her own business. First she bought a lunch counter, then a bigger restaurant, and finally, during World War II, a seventy-room hotel. She often offered free lodging to farm worker families and thus modeled for Huerta the value of acquiring resources and knowledge that could meet community needs. Both her parents demonstrated to Dolores the value of leadership and service.

Another crucial lesson Huerta learned from her mother was the value of self-sufficiency for both men and women. With five children in the house, there was plenty of domestic work to be done, but it was divided fairly between the boys and the girls. . . . Dolores and her brothers labored in their mother's restaurant in the summers, and though it went against her mother's wishes, Dolores also went to work in the fields and the packing sheds in order to experience the work lives of her friends. According to Huerta, her mother's entrepreneurial successes and business acumen enabled her to go to school and enjoy "a more affluent background than the other kids." Dolores Huerta learned from her mother to chart her own course in life, to work with determination, and to take action for those in need.

In recalling her early life, Huerta fondly described the vibrant diversity of her neighborhood in Stockton, with Japanese, Chinese, Jewish, Filipino, and Mexican folks of the working class—all intermingling. She participated in a wide range of youth activities, which, years later, she indicated had taught her to organize people and to deal with them democratically. A Girl Scout until the age of eighteen, she also took piano and violin lessons, studied dance, sang in the church choir, and participated in Catholic youth organizations. She knew she was more fortunate than most of her Mexican American peers. Her class status protected her from the stings of discrimination, particularly in Lafayette grammar school and Jackson Junior High, where she studied in her early adolescence. . . . This all changed when she got to Stockton High School in 1944. For the first time, Huerta felt discriminated against in a segregated environment. A straight "A" student, Huerta experienced memorable disappointment when a teacher told her that she could not receive an "A" grade because the teacher did not believe that Dolores had submitted her own original work. This experience marked the beginning of her political awakening.

As was common for women of her generation, Dolores Huerta married her high school sweetheart, Ralph Head, after graduation in 1948. He was an Irish American with whom she had the first two of her eleven children, Celeste and Lori. Though she described him in a later interview as "a very nice man, very responsible," they divorced after three years. Huerta then began studying, first at Stockton Junior College and then at the College of the Pacific in Stockton, where she earned an associate's degree and provisional teaching credentials. Afterward, she taught English to rural children for one year. Working with the children of farm workers gave Huerta a very intimate perspective on their lives. She decided thereafter that she could do far more for farm workers by organizing them around labor issues than by teaching basic lessons to their barefoot, hungry children.

She found a venue to begin community service work when she met organizer Fred Ross in 1955. . . . Ross traveled around California, organizing Mexican Americans into chapters of the Community Service Organization (CSO), a statewide confederation that mobilized Mexican American communities for voter registration campaigns and improved public services. Upon his arrival in Stockton, Ross assured Huerta and others that they could "turn everything around" by registering Mexican-origin voters and electing Spanish-speaking representatives. Huerta, however, was not immediately or easily convinced. She recalled with some embarrassment: "I thought he was a communist, so I went to the FBI and had him checked out. I really did that. . . . See how middle class I was. In fact, I was a registered Republican at the time." Before long, however, Huerta concluded that Ross's organization had potential, as she had "always hated injustice" and "always wanted to do something to change things." "Fred opened a door for me," Huerta declared. "Without him," she insisted, "I'd probably just be in some stupid suburb somewhere." Huerta worked with the CSO to register Mexican-origin voters, to keep the police department from "searching and harassing people arbitrarily," and to get equitable access to the county hospital. Huerta continued her work with the CSO, and through the organization, she met César Chávez in the late 1950s. After a very successful voter registration drive in 1960, Chávez, then executive director of the CSO, decided that Huerta would make a talented lobbyist; in 1961, he sent her to Sacramento where she headed the legislative program of the CSO. . . . One of Huerta's primary concerns was that many farm workers, as Mexican citizens, were excluded from the social service benefits that had been established in the New Deal era, like social security, disability insurance, and retirement pensions. Huerta pushed for legislation that would ease the burdens that workers experienced trying to navigate their way through life in the United States, regardless of citizenship status or language skills. At the California state capitol, Huerta, with her small children at her side, lobbied successfully with her team for an old-age pension, a welfare bill, the right to register voters door to door, and the right to take the driver's license exam in Spanish.

During her CSO years, Huerta met and married her second husband, Ventura Huerta, also a community organizer. Together they had five children: Fidel, Emilio, Vincent, Alicia, and Angela. Huerta described it as "a terrible marriage," which deteriorated due to incompatible temperaments and disagreements about the manner in which Huerta balanced her public commitments with her private, domestic ones. Huerta later said of the marriage: "I knew I wasn't comfortable in a wife's role, but I wasn't clearly facing the issue. . . . I didn't come out and tell my husband that I cared more about helping other people than cleaning our house and doing my hair." Her second marriage ended in 1961; after it dissolved, she stated, "I put everything into my relationships," but "I have to do what I have to do." Huerta thus alluded to the fact that despite her own personal commitment to her spouse, she refused to let their conflicting visions of her responsibilities prevent her from working as an activist in the Mexican American community, as she felt compelled to do.

Meanwhile, Huerta and César Chávez were becoming more interested in rural labor issues than urban ones. . . . In 1962, they co-founded the National Farm Workers Association in Chávez's hometown of Delano, California, and began down the long road of forging an agricultural labor union in California's San Joaquin Valley. Chávez was elected the first president, and Dolores Huerta and their colleague Gilbert Padilla were elected the first vice presidents. . . .

Huerta and Chávez relied on a method they had learned from Fred Ross, called the "house meeting," to earn the trust of individual farm workers and persuade them to join the NFWA. They tried to persuade groups of workers in the neutral, safe space of someone's home, where they could talk to them freely and at length about issues that farm workers faced, knowing that the workers were extremely vulnerable to dismissal and violent reprisals from growers. . . .

Huerta . . . often lacked a working automobile, gas money, and a babysitter for her children, and she identified these things to Chávez as the "handicaps" of her organizing. With her children in tow, she canvassed the fields, struggling to garner support for the union and to provide for the needs of her kids at the same time. She told Chávez: "You can only imagine how rough my financial situation is. Any help I get from my two ex-es has to go for grub for my seven little hungry mouths, and I am keeping one jump ahead of PG and E [Pacific Gas and Electric] and the Water Dragons who close off water for non-payment." . . . Working for no regular income, Huerta and Chávez were also anxious in those early years over raising sufficient dues to cover the costs of organizing. . . .

However, she ultimately decided to work for the NFWA full-time, giving up gainful employment and everything that goes with it. . . .

Dolores Huerta's advocacy for farm workers took many forms. In 1965, she contacted the Department of Motor Vehicles to get revoked licenses reinstated and persuaded insurance companies to write automobile policies for union members. She also pressured the Welfare Department of Kern County to set clear policies regarding patient access to the county hospital so the Mexicanos seeking medical attention would not be humiliated by hospital social workers.

Dolores Huerta's busy schedule was complicated even further by her continued political lobbying in both Sacramento and Washington, D.C. She began to develop a substantial rapport with legislators who were sympathetic to the union's objectives. One of these was Congressman Phillip Burton of California, who in 1967 introduced a bill to extend the National Labor Relations Act (NLRA) to include agricultural workers—a bill that, despite Huerta's efforts, did not pass. . . . Although César Chávez recognized that support from politicians could clearly help the union, he began to question the amount of time Huerta spent lobbying. She defended her support of the Aid to Dependent Children Bill in the late 1960s by saying, "Let me remind you that at least the workers we are trying to represent will have bread in the winter months." Even as the demands of the NFWA work increased, Huerta continued to see certain legislative victories as paramount to securing true economic justice for farm workers.

One of Huerta's most important goals was the demise of the Bracero program. Begun in 1942 as a wartime emergency measure between the United States and Mexican governments, the program had provided for the legal contracting of large numbers of Mexican nationals to work in the agricultural fields of the Southwest. The program was renewed after the war as growers insisted the *bracero* (worker) migration was still necessary due to continued labor shortages, but these Mexicanos were often ill-paid and ill-treated and had little recourse. Huerta and Chávez knew that as long as these workers were available to growers as "scab" labor (replacement during union strikes), strikers would never be able to force growers to negotiate with the their union.

When Congress abolished the Bracero program in 1964, farm labor activists in California were encouraged by this victory. . . .

In September 1965, Mexican and Filipino workers in Delano, California, walked off the fields, refusing to pick grapes. Three weeks after the initial walkout, the strike had spread, and almost three thousand workers had left the fields. Growers used legal injunctions to stop picketing and resorted to violence to subdue demonstrations and protect their scab replacement workers. In contrast, nonviolent protest to effect social change marked union organizing from the beginning. Both César Chávez and Huerta adhered to the principles of Mahatma Gandhi and Dr. Martin Luther King Jr. Public pilgrimages, growing support from Catholic and Protestant church groups and clerics, and significant financial contributions by the AFL-CIO helped build and sustain the new union—the United Farm Workers Organizing Committee. The 1966 march (known as the *peregrinación,* or Easter pilgrimage) to the state capitol in Sacramento increased the visibility of the union and made the workers' struggle more than a labor issue—it became symbolic of a national civil rights movement among Mexican Americans. Built out of the Filipino AWOC* and the Mexican NFWA, the new union, which would soon be known as the UFW, would change the course of American labor history.

Realizing that the battle would not be won in the fields of California, union leaders decided that they would have to carry their message to the marketplace, boycotting table grapes and other produce in supermarkets. Their objective was to force growers to negotiate contracts with the UFW that established increased benefits and improved conditions for union members; while they were successful in securing a few contracts by 1967, dozens of growers, including the powerful John Giumarra Corporation, would not budge. Although the boycott initially targeted only a few labels, Dolores Huerta ultimately moved to New York City, the center of grape distribution, to coordinate the industry-wide boycott in 1968 and 1969. The commercial boycott received tremendous public support and proved very effective, with polls showing that an estimated 17 million consumers supported the boycott by the early 1970s. In the fourth year of the boycott, growers found a powerful ally in the newly elected California Republican governor, Ronald Reagan, who ate grapes at several photo opportunities. In response, the UFW stepped up the boycott aspect of union activities, and by 1970 shipments to the top grape-consuming cities were down by 22 percent.

Finally, on April 1, 1970, after five long years, one grower came through: Lionel Steinberg of the Freedman Ranches signed a contract with the UFW. Shipments of grapes produced on its land were now stamped with the UFW label, signaling the union's approval to consumers. In the economic climate of the boycott, "union" grapes could now be sold for a premium price, and the price of nonunion grapes sunk. As a result, growers began to clamor for the UFW union label on their product, and at that point Dolores Huerta and her colleagues could hardly negotiate the contracts fast enough. Finally, on July 29, 1970, John Giumarra Jr. and the rest of the growers in the Delano area met to sign contracts with the UFW at the union hall in Delano. Dolores Huerta handled the negotiations, and years later, as she reflected on the experience, she insisted, "It never, ever, ever, ever crossed my mind that it

---

*Agricultural Workers Organizing Committee

couldn't happen. Not once. I always knew that we would be able to do it." Huerta possessed the tenacity and faith that enable one to carry on for years working toward a seemingly impossible goal.

In negotiating these historic contracts, Dolores Huerta earned a nickname among the growers—"dragon lady"—referring to her ability to speak "with fire" as she held fast to the terms and conditions that UFW members demanded. At that time, twenty-six Delano-area growers signed contracts, raising wages to $1.80 per hour plus $.20 per box, as well as establishing provisions for hiring workers directly from the UFW hiring hall, hiring by seniority, and placing strict controls on the use of pesticides. . . .

As one might expect in a movement with two determined visionaries, the relationship between Huerta and Chávez could be tense at times. Both believed passionately in their cause and committed their lives to overcoming seemingly insurmountable obstacles to realize its goals. Both raised families while living, working, and organizing in the fields. Both did these things for a sum of money so small, it can hardly be called an "income." It is no surprise that facing such challenges day in and day out would raise tensions. The president of the UFW until his death in 1993, Chávez had become the national symbol of the farm worker movement, and even though he and Huerta did not favor celebrity, they both knew the support it brought to their cause had some positive consequences. Wholly committed to the realization of UFW goals, Huerta often deferred to Chávez's final authority on issues, especially in the beginning. Sometimes she did so calmly, as when she states, "I bow to your better judgment and experience and will do as you say." Other times, she did so with sarcasm, as when she retorted, "But then again, I am not getting paid to ask questions, right?" On other occasions, and particularly later, she did exactly as she thought best. Whatever the case, she respected Chávez tremendously: "César Chávez is an extremely creative person," she declared; "He is a genius." Huerta knew that they were on the same page about things, and she exercised diplomacy in order to deal with him effectively *and* act upon her own views. For the most part, Chávez and Huerta managed to work together in a manner that enabled the best qualities of each to be put to work toward achieving union objectives.

One of their most important victories came in 1975 with the passage of the Agricultural Labor Relations Act (ALRA) in California. It was modeled after the National Labor Relations Act of 1935 (also known as the Wagner Act), part of Franklin Delano Roosevelt's New Deal. . . . Dolores Huerta was a major force in lobbying legislators to support the ALRA, which provided the right to boycott, voting rights for migrant seasonal workers, and secret ballot elections and control over the timing of these elections. Also, the ALRA, like the NLRA, established an enforcement board, the Agricultural Labor Relations Board (ALRB), for the redress of grievances and the certification of union elections. . . .

Huerta continued her lobbying efforts throughout the 1980s. In 1985, she lobbied to outlaw a federal "guest worker program" (a new incarnation of the bracero program), which would once again enable growers to legally bring Mexican nationals into the fields to work for below minimum wages in substandard conditions. When it was introduced, U.S. congressman from southern California Howard Berman, a longtime ally of Huerta and the UFW, successfully led the opposition to the program.

Huerta's primary concern in this period, however, was lobbying to outlaw the use of harmful pesticides. On September 14, 1988, in the course of a peaceful political rally where she spoke on that issue, San Francisco police severely beat Dolores Huerta. She suffered six broken ribs and the removal of her spleen in emergency surgery; she ultimately received an unprecedented monetary settlement from a lawsuit she brought against the offending law enforcement agency.

The longevity of Dolores Huerta's political career is particularly remarkable considering that at its height she embarked on her third marriage and reared another four children. She and Richard Chávez (brother of César) were the parents of Juanita, María Elena, Ricky, and Camilla. Speaking of the demands that her many duties placed on her, Huerta confessed: "I don't feel proud of the suffering that my kids went through . . . but by the same token I know that they learned a lot in the process." Managing this guilt [w]as one of the biggest challenges in her life; she recalls "driving around Stockton with all these little babies in the car, the different diaper changes for each one." Huerta spoke forthrightly about the tremendous pressure she felt to be a conventional mother while she worked as a major American labor leader. Lori De León, her daughter, revealed, "She was always on the road, and we were left to take care of ourselves." Huerta noted that, as in other poor people's movements, farm workers of the UFW were very willing to care for one another's children while other adults performed the work necessary to effect economic justice. Huerta has often insisted that she could only truly improve the conditions of farm workers' lives by living in the same circumstances as the workers. As a result, she could not realistically shelter her children from that reality. "Although criticized for putting *la causa* first, Dolores Huerta has had few regrets. As she informed [historian Margaret] Rose, 'But now that I've seen how good they [my children] turned out, I don't feel so guilty.'" She is filled with parental pride at the course of her children's lives; many of her children now have careers rooted in community service and activism, with some holding advanced professional degrees.

Huerta's own experience as an activist and a mother has given her very particular views about the roles of women in unions and in public life in general. Her first engagement with mainstream U.S. feminism came in the late 1960s, when Huerta's own place in the national spotlight gave her occasion to become acquainted with noted feminist Gloria Steinem. Huerta slowly began to incorporate woman-centered views into her own politics, calling herself a "born-again feminist." As a co-founder of the Coalition of Labor Union Women in 1974, Huerta has lobbied for countless female candidates for political office, addressed the National Organization of Women, and served on the board of the Feminist Majority Foundation. Her work has demonstrated her resolve that the public political agenda should embrace women's issues, and that women should be the ones to bring such issues to the table of political negotiations. She cites her experience in the UFW as an eye-opener on this point: "My mission has crept into my life. I want to see women treated equally in the union. After we fought hard, I found some women were discriminated against. I realized, in about 1978, it was almost like a conspiracy." Huerta is convinced that "the women decided the fate of the union," with the determination that they brought as they struggled to ensure the survival of families during the years of strikes in the fields. Huerta believes her mission is to encourage women to fight on the public side of battles they are often fighting privately—for themselves and for others.

Uncovering the History of Working Women and Affirmative Action in the 1970s

NANCY MACLEAN

In 1993, the New York City Fire Department issued a curious order: no pictures could be taken of Brenda Berkman, on or off duty, inside or outside of a firehouse. Berkman was a firefighter, a fifteen-year veteran of the force. The order was the latest shot in a protracted battle against Berkman and others like her: women claiming the ability to do a job that had been a men's preserve for all the New York City Fire Department's 117-year, tradition-conscious history. The struggle began in 1977, when the city first allowed women to take the Firefighter Exam—and then promptly changed the rules on the physical agility section when 400 women passed the written portion of the test. Five years and a victorious class-action suit for sex discrimination later, forty-two women passed the new, court-supervised tests and training and went on to become the first female firefighters in New York's history. Among them was Berkman, founding president of the United Women Firefighters, and the most visible and outspoken of the group.

Their struggle dramatizes many elements in the larger story of women and affirmative action, which involved remaking "women's jobs" as well as braving male bastions. What Berkman and her colleagues encountered when they crossed those once-undisputed gender boundaries was not simply reasoned, judicious skepticism from people who doubted the capacity of newcomers to do the job. Repeatedly, what they met was elemental anger that they would even dare to try. Hostile male coworkers used many tactics to try to drive the women out, including hate mail, telephoned death threats, sexual harassment, refusing to speak to them for months on end, scrawling obscene antifemale graffiti in firehouses, and organizing public demonstrations against them. Male firefighters also slashed the tires of women's cars, urinated in their boots, and, in one instance, tried to lock a woman in a kitchen that they had filled with tear gas. Sometimes, the men resorted to violence: one woman was raped, and a few others endured less grave sexual assaults. Some men even carried out potentially deadly sabotage—as when one newcomer found herself deserted by her company in a burning building and left to put out a four-room fire on her own.

Frozen out by white male coworkers and betrayed by the firefighters union, the women found their only dependable internal allies in the Vulcan Society, the organization of Black male firefighters, who had themselves fought a long battle against discrimination in the department. They now stood by the women, even to the point of testifying in support of their class-action suit, despite "enormous pressure to remain silent." The tensions surrounding the entrance of women into the fire department were explosive although women constituted a mere 0.3 percent of the city's 13,000-member uniformed fire force. The no-photographs order from the top, the uncoordinated acts of hostility from would-be peers, as well as the support of the Vulcan Society, signal us that a great deal was at stake. Even in cases less

Nancy MacLean, "The Hidden History of Affirmative Action: Working Women's Struggles in the 1970s and the Gender of Class," *Feminist Studies* 25, no. 1 (Spring 1999): 43–78. Reprinted by permission of the publisher, Feminist Studies, Inc.

egregious than the New York firefighters, boundary crossing backed by affirmative action affected something that mattered deeply to many men, especially many white men, in a way that often transcended logic.

Yet, historians of the modern United States have only begun to examine workplace-based sex discrimination and affirmative action struggles such as those of the United Women Firefighters. More attention is in order. On the one hand, disgust with discrimination and low-paying, dead-end jobs moved large numbers of working women to collective action in the last quarter-century. On the other hand, these struggles produced an unprecedented assault not just on previously unyielding patterns of occupational sex and race segregation and the economic inequality stemming from them but also on the gender system that sustained men's power and women's disadvantage and marked some women as more appropriate for certain types of work than others. "*Work* is," after all, "*a gendering process*," as the scholar of technology Cynthia Cockburn has observed—and, one might add, a race-making process as well. "While people are working, they are not just producing goods and services," Cockburn argues, "they are also producing *culture*." . . .

In challenging discrimination and demanding affirmative action, . . . the struggles described here redefined gender, race, and class by undermining associations built up over more than a century. . . . These associations led women and men to have some sharply different experiences of what it meant to be working class. And although my focus here is on the transformation in class and gender specifically, race is deeply embedded in both of these categories and in the associations they carry, if not always accessible in the extant sources. Wage-earning women in 1965, for example, could not expect that the jobs available to them would pay enough to live in modest comfort, certainly not with children; they *could* expect to have to provide personal services to the men in their work places, to clean up after them, and to endure demeaning familiarities from them as a condition of employment. Working-class white men, by contrast, had their own indignities to endure. But they might at least hope for a job that would provide a "family wage," and they could expect that no boss or co-worker would ask them to do domestic chores or grope them on the job.

Anti-discrimination and affirmative action struggles challenged this system of expectations and the patterns of inequality it perpetuated. Time and again, the system-recasting properties of affirmative action proved necessary to ensure equal treatment. Breaking down job ghettos and the habits that kept them in place required new practices such as wider advertising of job openings, recruitment from new sources, the analysis of jobs to determine skill requirements, the setting up of training programs to teach those skills, and in some cases the setting of specific numerical goals and timetables for recruiting and promoting women (impugned misleadingly by critics as "quotas"). By performing old work in new ways and by breaking into jobs formerly closed to them, the women involved in these efforts began, in effect, to reconstitute gender, and with it class, permanently destabilizing the once-hegemonic distinction between "women's work" and "men's work." To reconstitute is not to root out, of course: class inequality is if anything more shamelessly robust today than it was a quarter-century ago. Yet the *meaning* of particular class positions and experiences has shifted with the entrance of minority men and women of all groups in ways that demand attention. That we have forgotten how dramatic and radical a departure this was is a tribute to the success of their efforts.

Concentrating so heavily on gender and class in a discussion of affirmative action will strike many readers as odd and with good reason. Black civil rights organizations struggled for generations against employment discrimination, and it was their organizing that secured the most significant reforms to combat it. African Americans have also borne the brunt of recent attacks on affirmative action and the larger project of white racial revanchism that drives them. Indeed, so single-mindedly do contemporary critics of affirmative action focus on Blacks that one would never know from their arguments that the policy has served other groups. This sleight of hand has left both affirmative action and African Americans more vulnerable than they would be if the policy's other beneficiaries were acknowledged. Rather than accept the terms of debate used by affirmative action critics, then, this work seeks to bring into discussion another key group involved in the modern struggle against employment discrimination and the responses its members encountered. Recovering women's relationship to affirmative action also seems important in its own right, because women—especially white women—are so often cast as "free riders" in the discourse, as passive beneficiaries living off the labors of others. This article aims to combat the historical amnesia which makes that image possible and to recognize in the process the cross-racial coalitions built among working-class women at a time when few of their more affluent counterparts yet saw this as a priority. . . .

In what follows, I will sketch out a preliminary reading of the story of women and affirmative action, focusing on three types of collective action that became widespread in the 1970s. In the first type, a decentralized mass movement arose as working women across the country took hold of the new ideas in circulation about gender, applied them to their own situations, and agitated for change, typically through the vehicle of ad hoc women's caucuses that involved women in a range of job categories. In the second type, full-time organizers sought to expand these caucus efforts into citywide organizations for working women in clerical jobs. And in the third variant, individual low-income women and advocates for them turned to affirmative action as an antipoverty strategy for women, particularly female household heads, and began a concerted push for access to "nontraditional" blue-collar jobs for women. Those involved in all three efforts worked to mobilize working women across racial and ethnic lines. Although smaller numbers of women of color became involved in the first two forms of collection action, they became especially visible in campaigns for "nontraditional" employment. . . .

[T]he first big challenges to sex discrimination in the 1960s . . . came from wage-earning women in factory jobs, who discovered a new resource in legislation won by the civil rights movement in 1964. "Although rarely discussed in class terms," the Civil Rights Act's prohibition on race and sex discrimination in employment (Title VII), as the legal scholar Cynthia Deitch has pointed out, "had an unprecedented impact on class relations." . . . When the Equal Employment Opportunities Commission (EEOC) opened for business in the summer of 1965, all observers were stunned at the number of women's complaints, which made up more than one-fourth of the total. Some 2,500 women in the initial year alone, overwhelmingly working-class and often trade union members, challenged unequal wages, sex-segregated seniority lists, unequal health and pension coverage, and male-biased job recruitment and promotion policies—among other things. Alice Peurala, for example, who had been stymied each time she tried for promotion since she was first hired at U.S. Steel Corporation in 1953, said that when the Civil Rights Act came along "I thought, here's my chance." The protests of women such as Peurala, we can see now, prompted the development of an organized feminist movement. It was, after all, the EEOC's negligence in handling these charges of sex discrimination that led to the formation of NOW, whose founders included labor organizers and women of color as well as their better-known, affluent, white counterparts. . . .

Such efforts were brought to the attention of a broad audience by the mass media. By the early 1970s, television news, magazines, and newspapers all carried stories about sex discrimination in employment and women's struggles against it, as well as reports of the wider women's movement. Whether the reporters were sympathetic, hostile, or patronizing, their coverage . . . stimulated women to look at their jobs afresh and to imagine class itself in new ways. By 1970, large numbers of American women began to act on this new thinking at work. Borrowing a tactic from mostly male, blue-collar African Americans, and taking strength from the general ferment among rank-and-file workers in the early 1970s symbolized by the famed Lordstown wildcat strike, these women joined together with like-minded co-workers to organize women's caucuses as their characteristic vehicle of struggle. The caucuses embodied, in effect, a new social theory: Blacks of both sexes and women of all races who joined together implicitly announced that traditional class tools—such as unions—were ill suited to the issues that concerned them. In form, the caucuses crossed divisions of occupation in order to overcome the isolation and competition that allowed their members to be pitted against one another. Using separate structures, they fought not simply to achieve racial and gender integration at work but also to redefine it.

Having first appeared about 1970, the caucuses spread rapidly within a few years, one sparking the next like firecrackers on a string. . . . Women were organizing in steel plants and auto factories, in banks and large corporations, in federal and university employment, in trade unions and professional associations, and in newspaper offices and television networks. Few sites remained undisturbed. . . . Caucuses not only developed a critical consciousness among working women but they also won tangible improvements. Without their efforts, Title VII would have been a dead letter for women.

These early women's caucuses nearly always came about because a few women suddenly rejected some expectation arising from contemporary constructions of gender and class. . . . Time after time, the fresh recognition of some longstanding practice as sexist—a practice usually first identified as such in the course of casual lunchtime conversation among female coworkers—impelled women to organize. Often a small slight triggered a sense that a broader pattern of discrimination had just been revealed. For example, . . . the refusal of editors at the *New York Times* to allow the title "Ms." in the paper led several women on staff to wonder whether "this style rigidity was symptomatic of more basic problems." . . .

[T]he resulting *New York Times* Women's Caucus . . . challenged the newspaper to practice the fairness it preached to its readers. Prompted by the editors' curious resistance to nonsexist language, nine female employees in the news department began to compare experiences in 1972. Ironically, the *New York Times* had once boasted in an advertisement that one of the leaders, then a copy editor, had a "passion for facts." Now, however, the facts so carefully assembled by Betsy Wade, the self-proclaimed "Mother Bloor" of this particular struggle, brought less pride to management. The investigation and organizing continued until eighty women drew up a petition that complained of sex-based salary inequities; the confinement of women to poorer-paying jobs; the failure to promote female employees even after years of exemplary service; and their total exclusion from nonclassified advertising sales, management, and policy-making positions. The more women came to understand and label discrimination, the more of it they discovered. When "nothing happened" to address their complaints, the women secured a lawyer and filed charges with the EEOC. In turning to the state, they found they had to broaden their ranks beyond the original group to include secretarial staff and classified ad workers. . . . Ultimately, in 1974, the enlarged group filed a class-action suit for sex discrimination on behalf of more than 550 women in all job categories at the *New York Times,* including reporters, clerks, researchers, classified salespeople, and data processors. For the next four years, as the suit wound its way through the courts, the caucus held meetings, put out newsletters, and continued to agitate. By 1978, management was willing to concede. Settling out of court, the *New York Times* compensated female employees for past discrimination and agreed to a precedent-setting affirmative action plan. "Considering where we were in 1972," said one of the original plaintiffs, the settlement was "the sun and the moon and the stars."

That settlement highlights a more common pattern: in virtually every case where women's caucuses came together, demands for affirmative action emerged logically out of the struggle against discrimination. So striking is this pattern that I have yet to come across a case in which participants did *not* see affirmative action as critical to the solution. Examples are legion: they range from the *New York Times* group, to steel workers, telephone operators, and NBC female employees, of whom two-thirds (600 of 900) were secretaries when they began organizing in 1971. Even the Coalition of Labor Union Women (CLUW), loyal to a trade union officialdom skeptical about affirmative action, came out strongly in its favor. Prioritizing seniority over diversity where the two came in conflict, CLUW nonetheless fought to establish affirmative action for women—and to keep it in place. The logic appeared inescapable: if male managers had for so many years proven oblivious to women's abilities and accomplishments and unwilling to stop preferring men when they hired and promoted, and if women themselves could have been unaware of or resigned to the discrimination taking place, then something was needed to counterbalance that inertia. Successful efforts by African American men to wield affirmative action as a battering ram against discrimination only reinforced women's resolve. Time and again, it was affirmative action that women embraced to open advertising of jobs, broaden outreach for recruitment, introduce job analysis and training, set specific numerical goals for recruiting and promoting women, and mandate timetables for achieving these changes, all commitments for which management would be held accountable. . . .

Yet, the largest single number of wage-earning women—one in three—remained in clerical jobs, and they became the target of the second kind of organizing initiative. These jobs were among the most sex segregated: in 1976, for example, women made up 91.1 percent of bank tellers and 98.5 percent of secretaries and typists. The income of clerical workers fell below that of male wage earners in every category except farming. Seeking to make the women's movement more relevant to working-class women, some feminists set out in 1973 to develop an organizing strategy geared to women office workers and to build a network that could spread the new consciousness. "The women's movement was not speaking to large numbers of working women," remembered Karen Nussbaum, one of the national leaders of the effort, "we narrowed the focus of our concerns, in order to broaden our base." Among the groups thus created were 9 to 5 (Boston), Women Employed (Chicago), Women Office Workers (New York), Cleveland Women Working, Women Organized for Employment (San Francisco), and Baltimore Working Women. By the end of the 1970s, a dozen such groups existed and had affiliated with an umbrella network called Working Women; together, they claimed a membership of eight thousand. The racial composition of the groups varied by locality, but Black women appeared to participate in larger numbers in these than in the women's caucuses, sometimes making up as much as one-third of the membership.

What linked all the members together was a categorical rejection of the peculiar gender burdens of their work: above all, the low pay and demands for personal service. Of these expectations, making and fetching coffee for men quickly emerged as the most resented emblem of women's status. Of the low pay, one contemporary said: "As long as women accepted the division of work into men's and women's jobs—as long as they *expected* to earn less because women *deserved* less—the employers of clerical workers had it easy." Now, however, the women active in these groups insisted on their standing as full-fledged workers who deserved, in what came to be the mantra of the movement, both "rights and respect." Appropriating National Secretaries' Day for their own purposes, the groups demonstrated for "Raises, Not Roses!" and a "Bill of Rights" for office workers. "What we're saying," as one 9 to 5 speaker explained in 1974, "is that an office worker is not a personal servant, and she deserves to be treated with respect and to be compensated adequately for her work." . . .

Neither professional associations nor unions, office worker organizations constituted a new model, one that used research, creative publicity, and media-savvy direct action to develop a mass membership and power base. Increasing wages and respect for office workers were their top concerns, but not far behind was securing and monitoring affirmative action programs. From the beginning, organizers understood the problems of women office workers in terms of discrimination: poor pay, blocked mobility, and gender-specific personal affronts—or, one might say, economics, social structure, and culture. They therefore turned to the legal tools provided by Title VII of the Civil Rights Act and Revised Order No. 4 (the federal regulation stipulating that federal contractors must practice affirmative action for women). In the late 1970s, for example, sometimes working with local NOW chapters, all the Working Women affiliates took up a campaign targeting sex discrimination in banks. After distributing job surveys to female bank employees, the chapters held public hearings and demonstrations to publicize the results and prodded government antidiscrimination agencies to take action. Ultimately, these investigations resulted in several major settlements featuring novel affirmative action plans. . . .

As women's caucuses and office worker groups continued into the late 1970s, a new form of organizing for affirmative action spread: training and placement of women in "nontraditional" blue-collar jobs, particularly in construction. Here, advocates of gender equity came up more directly against sex-typed class consciousness among craftsmen who by long tradition equated working-class pride and "defiant egali- tarianism" vis-à-vis bosses with, as the labor historian David Montgomery once ob- served, "patriarchal male supremacy." Feminists turned to the nontraditional work strategy in the belief that as women got access to these jobs and the higher wages they offered, their movement out of the female job ghetto would also relieve the overcrowding that pulled down women's wages. Men without college educations had long found in these jobs both good wages and personal pride; that women were steered away from even considering them was itself a mark of gender discrimination. Building on the reforms wrested by civil rights workers and women's caucuses, the new initiatives marked both a more self-conscious attempt to relieve female poverty and a more frontal challenge to the sexual division of labor in working-class jobs. . . .

One of the pioneer organizations was Advocates for Women, founded in San Francisco in 1972. Its founders self-consciously broke ranks with women's move- ment organizations such as NOW that seemed ever more single-mindedly focused on the Equal Rights Amendment and the concerns of better-off women. Taking ad- vantage of newly available federal funds, Advocates for Women began recruiting and training women for nontraditional jobs. Directed by a Latina, Dorothea Hernandez, the organization aimed to reach "women of all races and cultures with emphasis on low-income women who must support themselves and their families." The rationale for the effort was to the point: "Poverty is a woman's problem"; hence, "women need money." The best way to ensure their access to it was through their own earnings. This strategy seemed more reliable than indirect claims on men's paychecks and more generous and empowering than Aid to Families with Dependent Children (AFDC). But the low-paying occupations into which most women were shunted wouldn't provide enough money to escape poverty, particularly to those with limited educations and work experiences. Advocates for Women reasoned that government- mandated affirmative action could be made to work for women in the construction industry. Because the skilled trades had long enabled men with only high school educations to secure good incomes, these jobs ought to be able to do the same for women—if they had the needed advocacy, training, and support services. . . .

Over the next few years, variations on the basic nontraditional jobs model sprang up in locations across the country. By mid-decade, 140 women's employment programs were in operation, from San Francisco, New York, Chicago, and Wash- ington, D.C., to Atlanta, Dayton, Louisville, Raleigh, San Antonio, and Wichita. In an initiative launched in 1979, over ninety of them, from twenty-seven states, joined together to form the Women's Work Force Network, which soon created a Construction Compliance Task Force to facilitate women's entrance into the build- ing trades. Women of color tended to be prominently involved, both as workers and as leaders. . . .

Even in the Appalachian South, often thought of as a bulwark of tradition, women began to organize for access to the better-paying work long monopolized by men. In 1977, several women who had grown up in the region's coal fields set up the Coal Employment Project "to help women get and keep mining jobs." Within a year, working with regional NOW chapters, they had filed complaints against 153 leading coal companies for practicing blatant sex discrimination in all areas: men comprised 99.8 percent of all coal miners and 98.6 percent of all persons employed in *any* capacity in the coal industry. Women's interest in this work expanded in tandem with their access. The number of female underground coal miners grew from zero in 1973, to over 3,500 by the end of 1981, when they comprised 2 percent of the work force. Often widowed or divorced and raising children on their own, coal-mining women took these jobs for the same reasons that led other women to construction sites: the work paid more than three times as much as they could get elsewhere. To the extent that working-class women could get jobs in Appalachia, after all, it was nearly always as waitresses, store clerks, or unskilled operatives in factories that came to the region for its low wages. More challenging than these "women's jobs," mining also held more interest and prestige. To women who had grown up in the area, coal was, as one put it, "part of our heritage," it was "part of who we are." "Women go into mining for the money," summed up one reporter: "They stay, they say, because they like it."

These endeavors marked an explicit feminist challenge not only to prevailing ideas of employment as something that fitted men for self-reliance and women for dependence on and service to men but also to the public policy model enshrined in the War on Poverty. Constructed on the premises set forth in the Moynihan Report, which explicitly argued that the problem for poor Black families was that so many were female-headed, this approach assumed that the key task was to generate jobs for poor men, particularly Black men, that would enable them to support families. Women's employment at best signaled family pathology; at worst, it created it, by depriving men of rightful dominance. Disparaged today, this thinking exerted a powerful influence through the 1970s, not just in government but in civil rights and Black nationalist circles as well. Participants in women's nontraditional employment programs, Black and white, argued a very different case. Not only were large numbers of women likely to continue heading families: they had a right to do so in comfort and dignity. Poor men needed good jobs, to be sure, but so did poor women. Society should not expect gains for one to come at the expense of the other. This position had far-reaching ramifications. Saying good riddance to both the old family-wage system and the privations and humiliations of AFDC, it aimed at a new model, a model in which women could build families from positions of autonomy and power, heading or coheading households while being recognized as full citizens at the same time. "Money meant independence," a divorced electrician explained, "a trade meant . . . being able to support my family without having a man around, if I couldn't find a decent man to relate to the family."

If we look at these initiatives in light of theories that gender is constituted through performance and see these women as engaged in performances that revised existing notions of womanhood and manhood alike, richer, subtler meanings emerge. Performing nontraditional work changed many of the women who did it, as did receiving the higher wages once reserved for men. . . . Coal mining, for example, was one of the most dangerous, demanding occupations in the United States; doing it well changed women's sense of themselves. "As I grow stronger," wrote one woman miner, "as I learn to read the roof [of the mine] like the palm of a hand, the confidence grows that I can do this work. . . . To survive, you learn to stand up for yourself. And that is a lesson worth the effort to learn." . . . And for men, too, the entrance of women into these jobs led to adjustments in identity and social understanding. "Some of the men would take the tools out of my hands," a pipefitter recalled. "When a woman comes on a job that can work, get something done as fast and efficiently, as well as they can, it really affects them. Somehow if a woman can do it, it ain't that masculine, not that tough." . . .

As women in these struggles remade class and gender, they often found themselves tackling race as well: struggle led to deeper learning. Even when women's caucuses arose in predominantly white offices, for example, at least one, and sometimes a few, Black women were usually actively involved. Inquiries into sex discrimination uncovered racial discrimination as well, as in a landmark suit by Women Employed against the Harris Trust and Savings Bank in Chicago. Many women's groups thus quickly realized the need to establish ties with Black workers' caucuses or informal groups. . . . The resulting coalitions were rarely tension-free—particularly for Black women, who likely felt keenly the need for both groups and the limitations of each—but they were certainly educational and often effective at bringing greater rewards to the partners than they could have achieved alone. When full-time organizations developed, white women initially occupied all or most of the staff positions. This became a particular problem in the construction industry drive, because women of color made up a large proportion of the low-income constituency the organizations aimed to serve. Recognizing this, some of these groups consciously set out to reconstruct themselves by applying affirmative action internally.

At the same time, the nontraditional jobs effort enabled even predominantly white women's groups to develop alliances with Black and Chicano rights organizations fighting for fair employment. One case in point is the United Women Firefighters with whom this story began, who won support from the Black male firefighters of the Vulcan Society. Another example is the *New York Times* Women's Caucus, which coordinated its efforts with those of the Black workers' caucus throughout the struggle. . . . Alliances such as this could alter both parties, making the women's groups more antiracist and making the civil rights groups more feminist in their thinking and programs. . . .

I do not want to overstate the changes that occurred. If women tried to rewrite the script, so could men. Resistance was common, and sometimes fierce, as the example of the New York City firefighters illustrates. To take one obvious case: as if to certify their own now-uncertain masculinity and remind women of their place, some men turned to sexual harassment. Although hardly new, this tactic seemed to be used more aggressively and self-consciously where men found treasured gender privileges and practices in question—as in the case of the New York firefighters. . . .

By and large, working women still face serious obstacles in trying to support themselves and their families. As much as occupational sex and race segregation have diminished, they have hardly disappeared, as any glance at a busy office or construction site will show. For women and men to be equally represented throughout all occupations in the economy today, 53 out of every 100 workers would have to change jobs. The absolute number of women in the skilled trades has grown, but they hold only 2 percent of the well-paying skilled jobs. In any case, these good jobs for people without higher education, as each day's newspaper seems to announce, are themselves an endangered species. In fact, although the wage gap between the sexes has narrowed, only about 40 percent of the change is due to improvement in women's earnings; 60 percent results from the decline in men's real wages. The persistent disadvantage in jobs and incomes contributes to another problem that has grown more apparent over the last two decades: the impoverishment of large numbers of women and their children, particularly women of color. Many of these poor women, moreover, are already employed. In 1988, more than two in five women in the work force held jobs that paid wages below the federal poverty level. So I am not arguing that some kind of linear progress has occurred and all is well.

Still, affirmative action was never intended as a stand-alone measure or panacea. From the outset, advocates were nearly unanimous in their insistence that it would work best in conjunction with full employment above all but also with such measures as pay equity, unionization, and improvements in education and training. Affirmative action's mission was not to end poverty, in any case, but to fight occupational segregation. And there it has enjoyed unprecedented, if modest, success. The best indicator is the index of occupational segregation by sex: it declined more in the decade from 1970 to 1980, the peak years of affirmative action enforcement, than in any other comparable period in U.S. history. As of 1994, women made up over 47 percent of bus drivers, 34 percent of mail carriers, and 16 percent of police—all jobs with better pay and benefits than most "women's work." This lags slightly behind nontraditional jobs requiring postsecondary training: women now account for nearly 40 percent of medical school students (20 percent of practicing physicians), nearly 50 percent of law school students (24 percent of practicing lawyers), and almost one-half of all professionals and managers. The ways that white women and women of color fit into these patterns complicate analyses based on sex alone. Yet whether in blue-collar, pink-collar, or professional jobs, white and Black women have gained benefits from breaking down sex barriers.

It would be absurd, of course, to give affirmative action exclusive credit for these changes. The policies described here came to life as the result of a broader history involving women's own determination to close the gap between the sexes in education and labor force participation, institutional fears of lawsuits for discrimination, new developments in technology and labor demand, and changes that feminism and civil rights brought about in U.S. culture. The mass entry of women into hitherto "men's work" in particular is deeply rooted in the breakdown of the family wage-based gender system. It is both result and reinforcement of a host of other changes: new expectations of lifelong labor force participation among a majority of women, the spread of birth control, the growing unreliability of marriage, the convergence in women's and men's patterns of education, the demise of associational patterns and sensibilities based on stark divisions between the sexes—even the growing participation of women in sports. But if it would be foolish to exaggerate the causative role of affirmative action, it would also be sophistry to deny or underrate that role. It has furthered as well as been fostered by these other developments. Women simply could not have effected the changes described here without its tools and the legal framework that sustained them. There are sound reasons why by 1975 virtually every national women's organization from the Girl Scouts to the Gray Panthers supported affirmative action, and why today that support persists from the African American Women's Clergy Association at one end of the alphabet to the YWCA at the other.

Yet there is a curious disjuncture between these organizations and the female constituency they claim to represent: repeated polls have found that white women in particular oppose affirmative action by margins nearly matching those among white men (which vary depending on how the questions are worded). No doubt several factors help to explain this paradox, not least of them the racial framing of the issue, which encourages white women to identify with white men against a supposed threat from nonwhites. The preference for personal politics over political economy at the grassroots has also led many women to interpret feminism in terms of lifestyle choices rather than active engagement in public life. Struggles for the ERA and reproductive rights ultimately eclipsed employment issues on the agenda of the women's movement in the 1970s. And most major women's organizations have come to emphasize service or electoral politics over grassroots organizing, and staff work over participation of active members. All these developments help to explain why today there is so little in the way of a well-informed, mobilized, grassroots female constituency for affirmative action—a vacuum that, in turn, has made the whole policy more vulnerable to attack.

Surely another reason, however, for the paradoxical gulf between national feminist organizations and grassroots sentiment on this issue is the historical amnesia that has obliterated the workplace-based struggles of the modern era from the collective memory of modern feminism—whether women's caucuses, clerical worker organizing, the fight for access to nontraditional jobs, or union-based struggles. If not entirely forgotten, these efforts on the part of working women are so taken for granted that they rarely figure prominently in narratives—much less interpretations—of the resurgence of women's activism. This disregard is especially ironic in that such struggles likely contributed more than we realize to our own era's heightened consciousness concerning the social construction and instability of the categories of gender, race, and class. Activists, that is, had begun the task of denaturalizing these categories and their associated hierarchies well before academics took up the challenge. If historians have now begun excavating the buried traditions of working-class women that can help us rethink the trajectories of modern feminism, there are still many, many more stories to be uncovered.

Women Readers and the Feminist Health Movement in the 1970s and 1980s

WENDY KLINE

"*We are saying this: Knowledge is power,*" declared the members of the Boston Women's Health Book Collective (BWHBC) in the first comprehensive book on women's health, *Our Bodies, Ourselves: A Book By and For Women.* Utilizing a familiar phrase from 1960s activism, the authors suggested that it pertained directly to women's health. "To get control of your own life and your own destiny is the first and most important task," they announced to women readers, "[b]ut it begins with getting control of your own body everywhere in your life. Demand answers and explanations from the people you come in contact with for medical care . . . and insist on enough information to negotiate the system instead of allowing the system to negotiate you."

Wendy Kline, "Readers Respond to *Our Bodies, Ourselves*," *Bulletin of the History of Medicine* 79, no. 1 (2005), 81–110. Copyright © The Johns Hopkins University Press. Reprinted with permission of The Johns Hopkins University Press.

The response to this challenge was enormous. *Our Bodies, Ourselves* created a spark that ignited the grass-roots-based women's health movement beginning in the 1970s. Education and self-help were central strategies of the movement, and manuals such as *Our Bodies, Ourselves* became the organizing tools that allowed women to translate personal health concerns into political ones. In the process, ordinary women transformed themselves from passive patients to active consumers, building feminist coalitions centered on patients' rights, disability rights, and reproductive rights.

The resulting women's health movement had an enormous impact on the so-called Second Wave of feminism. Incorporating that movement into the history of feminism forces us to reconsider the legacies of the Second Wave. The women's health movement did not follow—and thus challenges—the typical trajectory of fragmentation and declension that characterizes the history of Second Wave feminism. Fraught with internal conflict, plagued by the contradictory goals of universal sisterhood and individualism, many feminist organizations and networks failed to survive the 1970s. Yet though the women's health movement suffered its share of tensions, contradictions, charges of racism and exclusion, it prospered, along with its popular texts, throughout the rest of the century and into the next.

The movement also affected health care. Between 1970 and 1990, the number of women physicians in the workforce quadrupled to more than 100,000. In addition to increasing specialized care for women, these doctors have also stressed that research and funding must consider women's health needs. Many view the changes in women's health services and policy as "nothing short of stunning," yet few recognize the origins of these changes. The key to understanding these developments lies in the ideas and actions of a loose network of women who collectively created a new approach to knowledge and teaching about women's bodies and women's health.

In this paper I focus on those ordinary women who responded to editions of *Our Bodies, Ourselves* in the 1970s and 1980s, illustrating how readers played a crucial role in the development and articulation of health feminism. By analyzing the exchange between writers and readers of the most popular and influential women's health text of this era, I reveal the process by which feminists translated and interpreted medical information about women's bodies. To understand the nature and impact of the women's health movement on feminism and health, scholars need to look beyond the feminist literature and feminist organizations of the 1970s. Everyday women readers, whose voices inform this study, actively redefined women's health from a feminist perspective.

The 1960s

Women's health emerged as a major social and political issue in a turbulent decade. A new generation of Americans expressed dismay that the wealthiest, most powerful nation in the world could neither adequately provide for nor protect those at home, and they sought alternative solutions. Two best-sellers published in 1962, Rachel Carson's *Silent Spring* and Michael Harrington's *The Other America,* drew attention to the destruction and poverty on American soil that were largely invisible to most middle-class Americans. . . . Students for a Democratic Society (SDS) issued their manifesto of New Left activism, the Port Huron Statement, in 1962. The following summer, more than 250,000 civil rights protestors marched on Washington for freedom and jobs in the largest political demonstration in U.S. history. In 1968, radical feminists staged a series of dramatic protests, such as crowning a sheep at the Miss America pageant to protest the sexual objectification of women. The final year of the decade brought about five days of rioting in Greenwich Village, fueling the gay liberation movement. In this unsettled period no social issue was left unexplored, no political structure unchallenged. By its end, a postwar climate of confidence had been replaced by cynicism and doubt—which included disillusionment with the medical profession.

Science and medicine had enjoyed unprecedented authority and power in post–World War II America, when medical care became one of the nation's largest industries. But by 1970, medicine, along with other social institutions, had suffered a "stunning loss of confidence." Beginning in the mid-1960s, according to David Rothman, the practice of medicine became thoroughly transformed, a process completed within just a decade. An intrusion of outsiders, including academic scholars, government officials, lawyers, and judges, completely altered the doctor-patient relationship and brought "new rules to medicine." Exposés on patient experimentation and unethical treatment challenged the notion that the doctor had the patient's best interest in mind. In this social climate, only outsiders, presumed to be objective, could effectively regulate and monitor a doctor's decisions. As they brought these concerns to light, popular agitation ensured that patients' rights would join the broader spectrum of civil rights. Patients, like African Americans, gays and lesbians, and women, were easily exploited as human subjects and therefore required a language of rights. The doctor had become a stranger and a potential enemy, and patient trust virtually disappeared along with house calls by the 1960s. Empowered by a new language of bioethics to replace bedside ethics, patients became wary consumers who sought protection *from* doctors rather than *by* doctors.

A number of new health programs emerged in the 1960s to address what many were pronouncing a national health-care crisis. Congress approved Medicare and Medicaid programs in 1965, and President Lyndon Johnson's Office of Economic Opportunity legislation included funding for neighborhood health centers by the following year. These were designed to improve access to health care, particularly for the poor. Johnson became the first president to establish federal funding of family planning (excluding abortion) and maternal health programs. In addition, hundreds of free clinics opened in the late 1960s providing treatment that was less expensive or hierarchical than traditional services. For some, however, these measures did not begin to scrape the surface of a more fundamental problem in American society: sexism.

Of all social movements, the women's health movement had its most direct roots in women's liberation. By the late 1960s, women inspired by the civil rights movement and the demand for equal citizenship created a new wave of feminist activism. Though a fragmented movement (historians refer to several branches of feminism, including liberal, socialist, radical, cultural, and multiracial), its unifying characteristic has been the claim that the personal is political. By challenging the divide between the two, feminists asserted that the most private aspects of their identity— relationships, sexuality, health, and family life—were indeed political issues. . . .

Thus, at a time when medical authority was already undermined, when activists sought protection for human rights, and when feminists argued that deeply personal issues had political consequences, renewed activism in women's health appears almost inevitable. Female bodies, argued health feminists, had been subjected to male medical authority; women could not achieve full equality without the right to reclaim their bodies. Doctors were overwhelmingly male (in 1970, only 7.6 percent of physicians and 7.2 percent of obstetrician-gynecologists were female) and, according to critics, paternalistic, condescending, and judgmental. In addition, they had medicalized reproductive issues and turned women into human guinea pigs, argued activists at hearings on abortion, the birth control pill, DES (diethylstilbestrol), and the Dalkon Shield IUD.

The women's health movement was a grass-roots campaign that used a wide range of strategies to increase women's power over their own bodies, including alternative health-care organizations, advocacy, and education. It was enormously successful. By 1974, there were more than twelve hundred women's groups providing health services in the United States, according to a nationwide survey. Other groups worked through legislative channels to ensure protection and services, from abortion to FDA regulation of contraception. As more and more women became active consumers in the health-care industry, they sought out accurate, easy-to-understand information on women's health.

Such information became available from women's health literature. The first and most comprehensive book to provide information about women's health and sexuality was *Our Bodies, Ourselves.* Beginning as a 130-page newsprint manual in 1971, the comprehensive book on women's health was by 1998 a 780-page treatise that had sold four million copies and had been translated into nearly twenty foreign languages.

Our Bodies, Ourselves: **A Collective Story**

In May 1969, Emmanuel College in Boston hosted a female liberation conference. This in and of itself was not so unusual; "women's liberation" had erupted in major cities beginning in 1967, and had introduced consciousness-raising as a formative process by which women could explore the political aspects of personal life. But what made this particular weekend conference significant was a two-hour workshop on Sunday afternoon, called "women and their bodies." The participants, some of whom had never before been in any kind of women's group, spent their time sharing stories of frustration and anger about experiences at the doctor's office. They resolved to continue meeting after the conference, calling themselves the "doctor's group," with the idea that they would create a list of "reasonable" obstetrician-gynecologists in the Boston area. (By reasonable, they meant doctors who listened to the patient, respected her opinions, and explained procedures and medications.) They quickly discovered, however, that they were unable to put together such a list—and, more importantly, that they shared a desire to learn as much as possible about their bodies and their health. So they decided on a summer project: Each member would research a topic of personal importance about women's bodies and bring the information back to the group. Group members would then share personal experiences related to this topic. "In this way," they later explained, "the textbook view of childbirth or miscarriage or menstruation or lovemaking, nearly always written by men, would become expanded and enriched by the truth of our actual experiences. It was an exciting process."

From the beginning, then, personal stories were at the heart of this project. The stories did more than illustrate medical viewpoints on health and sexuality: they expanded, enriched, and challenged them. In this context, consciousness-raising transformed medical knowledge by suggesting that personal experience offered a "truth" just as valid as textbook views. In doing so, it reduced the "knowledge differential between patient and practitioner" and thereby challenged medical hierarchy.

By 1970, the summer project had turned into a 130-page newsprint manual, *Women and Their Bodies* (published by the New England Free Press), and three years later, a best-selling 276-page Simon & Schuster paperback (*Our Bodies, Ourselves*). All writing was under the direction of the twelve-person Boston Women's Health Book Collective, but it included many voices. "Many, many other women have worked with us on the book," they explained in the 1973 preface:

> A group of gay women got together specifically to do the chapter on lesbianism. Other papers were done still differently. . . . Other women contributed thoughts, feelings and comments as they passed through town or passed through our kitchens or workrooms. There are still other voices from letters, phone conversations, a variety of discussions, etc., that are included in the chapters as excerpts of personal experiences.

This inclusion of as many voices and stories as possible turned out to be crucial. One of the authors, Susan Bell, recalls the challenge of translating medical information for nonspecialists. The authors themselves were outsiders, whose role was to understand and interpret medical information in a way that would speak to as many women as possible. When revising the chapter on birth control in 1984, Bell had to attempt "to see from and speak to the perspectives of teenagers, single women, women of color, poor women, women with disabilities, and women without health insurance (and so forth) without falling into the trap of believing I could 'be' simultaneously in all, or wholly in any, of these subjugated positions." How, then, could she attempt to speak for such a broad spectrum of women? "One way out of this trap lies in positioning, opening up the process of knowledge construction to diverse perspectives by being attentive and responsible to other people," she acknowledged. The Collective could not claim to represent all women, but by including their stories, it could speak to a more diverse body of women. In her study of the impact of *Our Bodies, Ourselves* on global feminism, Kathy Davis notes that "it was the method of knowledge sharing and not a shared identity as women which appeared to have a global appeal."

Indeed, letters from American readers suggest that while not all women identified with the tone or content of every chapter of the book, it still had enormous appeal. . . .

Reader Responses

Our Bodies, Ourselves offered a level of intimacy that encouraged readers to respond to its text. At the suggestion of the authors (who solicited feedback for book revisions in magazines such as *Ms.*) or on their own accord, more than two hundred women wrote to the Collective in the 1970s and 1980s to share stories, seek advice, chastise, or praise. They commented on what was helpful, what was vague, what made sense, and what was missing, on subjects ranging from dental care to diaphragms. These letters, currently housed at the Radcliffe Institute's Schlesinger Library, leave many questions unanswered: names and addresses have been blacked out, and most do not reveal the writer's economic, racial, or educational background. Viewed as a whole, however, they suggest both the appeal of the book and the expectations it engendered. Because readers strongly identified with the book (or at least the idea behind it), they believed that their own experiences should be represented or accounted for in the text. The emotional expressiveness of the letters reveals readers' desire to be part of a virtual community of health feminists, from locations all over the United States.

The responses from readers also tells us something more broadly about the development of feminist ideas and communities. Women did not have to be actively involved in an organized group of feminists, or even in a consciousness-raising group, to participate in the movement. Since many women did not have access to these groups (demand far outstripped the resources), they turned to reading as a consciousness-raising resource. . . .

Certainly that was the case with *Our Bodies, Ourselves,* where reading was often described as a revelatory experience . . . that drew a woman out of isolation and into a widespread dialogue about feminism and health. "When I realize how similar my feelings are to some of the letters in your book, it is indeed reassuring," one reader confided. Establishing connections by reading personal accounts enabled readers to experience consciousness-raising at their own kitchen tables. They did not have to join a feminist organization or a self-help group to recognize their oppression in the stories of others. "I was overwhelmed by the support I felt in all the information you gave me," another reader wrote; "What I felt then as skepticism about the women's movement vanished and my lonely farm-housewife lifestyle became a step in a steady progression of changes." . . .

By its very formation, then, *Our Bodies, Ourselves* encouraged readers to respond. It provoked passionate letters filled with heartfelt personal accounts of infections, miscarriages, depression, and disability. Some were humorous, while some were angry. Some readers wrote in the name of sisterhood, while others were simply scared. Together, their responses reveal that readers were active agents who identified women's health as a crucial component of feminism. . . .

A series of letters exchanged between Sarah and author Norma Swenson in 1979 demonstrates the Collective authors' struggle to effectively translate medical knowledge to their readership. It began in February, when Sarah wrote: "I have trusted you and learned much from your book in the past. But having spent the last year trying to conceive a child, and coming up with nothing, and then a Class 3 pap smear, the cause of which has not been terribly easy to find out, the last thing I need is a statement like the one I tripped over on page 147." She was referring to the discussion of D&C in a chapter on medial health problems. Sarah's abnormal pap smear had suggested the possibility of cervical cancer, and her doctors recommended a D&C and possibly conization (removing a cone of tissue from the cervix during the procedure). She returned home and immediately picked up her copy of *Our Bodies, Ourselves* to learn more about it. The 1979 edition of the book concluded the discussion of D&C by stating that conization "may lead to complications in future pregnancies." Her reaction to that sentence was so powerful that she later described it to the Collective in two different letters. Already feeling cheated, she

> got to the line that said conizations might lead to complications in pregnancy. New paragraph. You didn't tell me *what* complications. *The* book didn't tell me; it just added another layer of mystery and innuendo. I hate veiled warnings, vague threats—just tell me what the options are, or the facts. I know enough to worry, but not enough to answer my own questions. . . . Before you and your book there was nothing, but still. . . .

Angrily, she had ended her first letter by stating "your part in the trauma of the last few days will long be remembered. . . .

Sarah's letter reveals her expectation that Collective authors should shore up the boundaries between feminist women's health and a misogynist medical establishment, rather than blur those boundaries.

Coauthor Norma Swenson responded carefully, sensitive to the charge: "We are really sorry that you found our section on conization in relating to pregnancy upsetting and unhelpful." She admitted that there was no way of knowing who had written the passage, but accepted full responsibility; without knowledge of authorship, culpability had to be shared by all members of the Collective. Swenson made it clear that the authors faced quite a challenge when discussing and analyzing medical treatment. "One of the problems we constantly stumble over as we try to research medical practice," she explained, "is that habits of treatment and prognosis get established with very little real evidence. . . . In sharing this kind of information with women, we want to be sure to include as much as we can of what is known, while at the same time leaving women some room to question and challenge the dogma about themselves and their conditions." This process of translation, author Susan Bell later pointed out, complicates rather than simplifies medical procedure. By 1994, she had learned that "the trick is to provide access to scientific uncertainty, and to contested knowledge, without simply leading to confusion and paralysis." But in 1979, when Swenson corresponded with Sarah, authors were still very much on a learning curve. "I wouldn't have sensed how unhelpful our sentence was if you hadn't shown us," Swenson acknowledged; "I'm not sure how to fix it, but you can be sure we'll make some modification next time around. We'll also try to do more research." Indeed, the statement was omitted in the next edition and replaced by a more specific description of what the potential complications are and why they happen.

Sarah was clearly moved by Swenson's response, calling it a "generous" letter. In the "relative calm of early summer," she was able to reflect upon her experience: "I don't blame anyone for that open-ended response; I just wish it hadn't been written," she noted, and then added, "(except that there are definitely good points to this correspondence)." The dialogue, which Sarah now cast in a positive light, had begun directly from the text (because Sarah believed it did not speak adequately to her), and had expanded into a warm exchange of ideas and explanations. "I probably wrote initially partly because it matters to me what your book says," Sarah explained. "By writing it you stuck your and our necks out, and I want us to look good, since efforts like these are still scrutinized so closely." Like other readers, Sarah perceived *Our Bodies, Ourselves* as a broader collective in which the readers as well as the writers all shared responsibility for the outcome.

It may seem surprising that feminist readers would direct their hostility toward the Boston Women's Health Book Collective rather than at misogynist medicine. Yet Amy Farrell locates a similar trend in the relationship between the readers and editors of *Ms.* Magazine during this time. As Farrell argues, readers "forged strong yet volatile ties" with the magazine: they identified with it, but also insisted that it "live up to its promise as a resource for the women's movement." Feminist scholar Phyllis Chesler spent years researching the more general question of why women turn against each other, especially feminists of her generation who referred to each other as "sisters": "I expected so much of other feminists—we all did—that the most ordinary disappointments were often experienced as major betrayals," she recollects:

> Like most women, feminists expected less of men and forgave them, more than once, when they failed them. Feminists expected far more of other women, who paradoxically had less (power) to share than men had. We held grudges against other women in ways we dared not do against men. We were not always aware of this.

In the case of women's health, an erosion of trust in the medical establishment created critical consumers. These consumers were all the more willing to critique those feminist texts that claimed to speak for all women; they saw it as crucial that their particular perspective or experience was included in such a text. Indeed, the most common complaint of readers who wrote to the Collective had to do with their sense of exclusion. Readers expected to find themselves described within the pages, and expressed confusion, disappointment, frustration, or anger if they did not. Though the women's health movement had the potential to cut across racial and class boundaries, argued feminist scholars Barbara Ehrenreich and Deirdre English in 1973, it would become only "'some women's health movement' unless the diversity of women's priorities were taken into account." Over time, readers ensured that such diversity was reflected in *Our Bodies, Ourselves.*

Surprisingly, one of the most fundamental categories of exclusion—namely, race—does not emerge from the letters. Yet many women have voiced their concern in other venues about the book's limited treatment of race, and more generally, the ways in which white women had paid scant attention to the specific health needs and perspectives of women of color. Sheryl Ruzek noted in 1978 that the women's health movement remained "largely white and middle class—especially in leadership and in focus." Byllye Avery, director of the National Black Women's Health Project, recalled: "white women had no idea about certain issues affecting black women." This problem continued into the 1990s; in 1997, four BWHBC staff members resigned, arguing that the organization refused to "grapple honestly with racism and issues of power with respect to the women of color within the organization."

The Collective did not specifically address this problem until the 1998 edition, writing:

> While it is exciting that this book stays alive, growing and changing, the process of becoming more inclusive has been difficult and painful at times. For example, like many groups initially formed by white women, we have struggled against society's, and our own, internalized presumption that middle-class white women are representative of all women and thus have the right to define women's health issues and set priorities. This assumption does a great injustice by ignoring and silencing the voices of women of color, depriving us all of hard-won wisdom and crucial, life-saving information. This

time around, many more women of color have been involved in creating the book, writing some of the chapters, and editing and critically reading every chapter. During this process, tensions sometimes arose about what to include or leave out and how to frame certain issues. The resulting vigorous discussions have greatly enriched the book's content. But as in any organic process, some conflicts still remain to be resolved.

Though readers did not address race directly in their letters to the Collective, they touched on issues that had certainly affected, and been affected by women of color, namely, reproductive rights and sexuality. Readers adamantly expressed their views as to how these particular issues should be portrayed in the book. Their concerns challenged some basic assumptions about feminism and health, forcing the authors to reconsider their stance on a number of issues.

Greta wrote the authors to critique their portrayal of sterilization. . . . "The one section which I continually skipped over was entitled 'When you are through with having children—sterilization.' I glanced at the pictures of tubal ligation and thought, 'That's not for me.'" But then she recalled the experience of a single, childless female friend who had expressed relief and satisfaction with a tubal ligation. "It struck me that the title of this section in your book suggests that married or single women who have never had children don't, shouldn't, or mustn't have tubal ligations."

In the 1970s, voluntary sterilization was the most popular form of birth control for white women and men. But it was also a controversial procedure, one that proved to be a divisive issue between white feminists and feminists of color. Beginning in the late 1960s, Black Nationalist groups drew attention to the problem of sterilization abuse. Some organizations, including the Black Panther Party and the Nation of Islam, believed that any type of fertility control among black Americans equaled genocide. This issue made feminists of color uncomfortable with the reproductive rights agenda of white feminists. Some mainstream white feminists wanted to include access to sterilization as part of the reproductive rights platform, because many doctors refused to perform the operation on young white middle-class women; they were therefore not supportive of black feminists' demand for stricter regulation of the procedure. As Rebecca Kluchin argues, restrictive hospital policies "prevented 'fit' women from choosing voluntary sterilization," while federal family planning programs "forced 'unfit' women to 'consent' to the same procedure."

While the BWHBC included a discussion of sterilization in their birth control chapter as early as their first edition, they were aware that it was a complex issue. "Black women in the South are all too familiar with the 'Mississippi Appendectomy' in which their fallopian tubes were tied or their uterus removed without their knowing it," they wrote. But for women like Greta, sterilization was a safe and effective method of birth control for women of any age, and thus an important aspect of reproductive choice. She suggested that in the next edition, "tubal ligation might be referred to as an alternative method of birth control rather than a step to be taken presumably after having had children already." In the 1984 edition, the authors completely rewrote the section on sterilization (no longer entitled "when you are through having children"). They warned younger women that "nearly one-third of the women who were sterilized at one point in their lives regretted this decision later on, particularly if they were under thirty years old when sterilized. Some women turn to sterilization in desperation because there is no suitable form of contraception for them"— but they also took into consideration the opinions of women like Greta: "For some women, however, the choice to be sterilized is a positive wish to avoid pregnancy forever. Some have already had children; others decide they never want children." Significantly, they also included a separate section on sterilization abuse in a new chapter on violence against women, and listed the addresses of anti-sterilization-abuse organizations. . . .

"Only about 1/3 of the Book Applies to Me"

The most divisive issue that the Collective struggled with in reader correspondence and revisions during this time period was lesbianism, an issue that divided many women's liberationists in the 1970s. So many women wrote letters in response to the lesbian chapter that *The New Our Bodies, Ourselves* gave special thanks to the hundreds of women "all over the country telling about their experiences and asking for advice, news, contacts, support." Though many were enthusiastic, they also pushed for more material. "What I most wanted to comment on was the assumption of heterosexuality throughout the book," wrote Barbara: "There is a way that even though lesbianism is acknowledged as an option for women, it is still ghettoized in the one chapter and male-female relationships become the norm throughout."

In the 1971 New England Free Press edition, the sixteen-page chapter on sexuality had just over one page on homosexuality. By the 1973 Simon & Schuster edition, it was the subject of an entire eighteen-page chapter, entitled "In Amerika They Call us Dykes" and written by women involved in gay liberation. Conflict between the Collective and the lesbian authors of "In Amerika" was apparent in the published introduction to the chapter. "We had no connection with the group that was writing the rest of the book . . . and in fact we disagreed, and still do, with many of their opinions," wrote the lesbian authors. The Collective clarified its position with a footnote linked to the chapter's title: "Since the gay collective insisted on complete control over the style and content of this chapter, the Health Book Collective has not edited it. Because of length limitations, however, the gay collective has had to leave out much material that they feel is important." In meeting minutes and memos of the mid-to-late 1970s, the Collective authors made it clear that they were not happy with some of the content of the article: based on reader feedback "from both gay and straight women," they recognized that the chapter "gives only part of a picture," and that it needed to be "balanced out in some way (with input from older women, poor women, women with a longer experience of living a gay life, etc.)." The title was also problematic; Sanford argued that "someone who isn't a lesbian and who is fearful might feel pushed away by [it]," and she suggested alternatives, including "Loving Women: Lesbian Life" (which eventually became part of the title in a later edition with different authors), but the gay collective insisted on keeping the original title.

Internal meeting notes reveal that by 1978 there was a great deal of frustration over how to integrate material on lesbianism into the next edition. When the Collective attempted to revise the chapter, the gay women rejected the changes, instead asking for more space (sixty manuscript pages instead of thirty-five). After a divisive meeting with them, one Collective member proposed stopping the writing process entirely until the disputes were resolved, despite the upcoming revisions deadline imposed by Simon & Schuster. Some resented the fact that though "the gay women haven't been part of our process, we spend our precious hours talking about the gay chapter." Finally, at midnight, the Collective resolved to limit the gay paper to fifty manuscript pages and to explain in the revised edition that "they weren't with us writing other chapters and they feel other chapters don't reflect them."

But readers continued to complain. "I'm a Lesbian, which means that only about 1/3 of the book applies to me," wrote Maggie in 1982. "Now I'm sure you've had it suggested many times before that the rest of the book should integrate lesbianism more thoroughly," she chided. "These things should be obvious in 1982—every section except 'In Amerika' assumes the heterosexuality of the reader." And even "In Amerika" had problems: though it had been "very influential" in her coming out, and was "probably the most well read piece of Lesbian literature in the English language," it was "completely out of date now." She was sorry to see it go (note her assumption that it would not make it into the next edition), because it exuded the excitement of the beginnings of an important movement. "It would be hard to find someone to write a new one who would seem, like these Lesbians did, to be sharing something new which they were just putting together themselves for the first time."

Maggie's assumption was correct: "In Amerika" did not survive the next edition. It was replaced by "Loving Women: Lesbian Life and Relationships," written by the "Lesbian Revisions Group." None of the authors had worked on the original piece; in fact, it had "provided crucial support and inspiration for several of us when we first came out as lesbians." They had written a chapter "quite different in focus and tone from the original one, using briefer stories so as to make room for more topics." This time around, the Collective authors' footnote linked to the chapter title was more conciliatory: "Although this edition of *Our Bodies, Ourselves* includes lesbian voices throughout, the Collective decided also to have a separate chapter for a more careful focus on issues and information which specifically affect lesbians." *The New Our Bodies, Ourselves* thus incorporated the suggestions and concerns of lesbian readers. But it and later editions also revealed tensions within the text, underscoring the most basic challenge to the movement: there simply was no universally shared perspective on women's health.

Conclusion

When the Boston Women's Health Book Collective announced in 1973 that "knowledge is power" and urged women to gain control of their bodies, they were also, in the words of feminist scholar Catharine Stimpson, assigning "extraordinary moral weight to the body." Women readers from Maine to Montana contributed to that assignment by articulating very specific ways to reclaim their bodies. They became part of a widespread network of women determined to rethink the relationship between gender and medicine. And their stories challenge us, as historians, to consider how ordinary women helped to shape the development of the women's health movement. They did so in three important ways: First, their letters demonstrate that consciousness-raising and the sharing of personal stories were a crucial aspect not just of women's liberation, but also of health education in the 1970s and 1980s. In other words, their stories influenced the way people learned about and understood a topic previously relegated to the medical profession.

Second, by challenging the writers of *Our Bodies, Ourselves* on a number of points—from remedies for vaginitis to cervical conization—readers influenced the way in which Collective authors, in the words of one of them, "translated science to the people." They also helped to determine the topics covered in the text, by demanding and sharing information on topics from vaginitis to hypoglycemia. Confrontational letters to the Collective reveal readers' expectations and assumptions about how women's health should be portrayed, as well as their desire to have their perspectives included.

Finally, by demanding greater inclusion and diversity within the text, these readers ensured that *Our Bodies, Ourselves* would continue to be read by generations of women. The conflicts expressed in letters—over how to define women's health, the inclusion of lesbians, the portrayal of disability, and other issues—were experienced by many Second Wave feminist organizations. And yet these tensions, and the fact that they made their way into revisions of the text, allowed *Our Bodies, Ourselves* to prosper decades after the Second Wave.

◈ *F U R T H E R   R E A D I N G*

Bailey, Beth. *Sex in the Heartland* (1999).

Banner, Lois W. *Women in Modern America* (1984).

Berry, Mary Frances. *Why ERA Failed* (1986).

Blee, Kathleen. *Inside Organized Racism: Women in the Hate Movement* (2002).

Boles, Janet. *The Politics of the Equal Rights Amendment* (1979).

Carden, Maren Lockwood. *The New Feminist Movement* (1974).

Caron, Simone M. "Birth Control and the Black Community in the 1960s: Genocide or Power Politics?" *Journal of Social History* (1998): 545–570.

Chafe, William. *Women and Equality* (1977).

Collins, Patricia. *Black Feminist Thought: Knowledge, Consciousness, and the Politics of Empowerment* (1990).

Crawford, Vicki, Jacqueline Ann Rouse, and Barbara Woods, eds. *Women in the Civil Rights Movement: Trailblazers and Torchbearers, 1941–1965* (1990).

Daniel, Robert. *American Women in the Twentieth Century* (1987).

Davis, Flora. *Moving the Mountain: The Women's Movement in America Since 1960* (1991).

Davis, Martha. "Welfare Rights and Women's Rights in the 1960s," *Journal of Policy History* 8 (1996): 144–165.

Deckard, Barbara. *The Women's Movement* (1983).

DeHart-Matthews, Jane and Donald Mathews. *The Equal Rights Amendment and the Politics of Cultural Conflict* (1988).

D'Emilio, John. *Sexual Politics, Sexual Communities: The Making of a Homosexual Minority in the United States, 1940–1970* (1998).

Dewey, Scott Hamilton. "'Is This What We Came to Florida For?': Florida Women and the Fight Against Air Pollution in the 1960s," *Florida Historical Quarterly* 77 (1999): 503–531.

Dill, Bonnie Thorton. "Race, Class, and Gender: Prospects for an All-Inclusive Sisterhood," *Feminist Studies* 9, no. 1 (1983): 131–150.

———. "The Dialectics of Black Womanhood," *Signs* 4 (Spring 1979): 543–555.

Douglas, Susan J. *Where the Girls Are: Growing Up Female with the Mass Media* (1994).

Echols, Alice. *Shaky Ground: The Sixties and Its Aftershocks* (2002).

———. *Daring to Be Bad: Radical Feminism in America, 1967–1975* (1989).

Ehrenreich, Barbara. *Hearts of Men* (1983).

Eisenstein, Zillah. *The Radical Future of Liberal Feminism* (1981).

Evans, Sara. *Personal Politics: The Roots of Women's Liberation in the Civil Rights Movement and the New Left* (1979).

Evans, Sara, and Barbara J. Nelson. *Wage Justice: Comparable Worth and the Paradox of Technocratic Reform* (1989).

Farrell, Amy Erdman. *Yours in Sisterhood:* Ms. *Magazine and the Promise of Popular Feminism* (1998).

Felsenthal, Carol. *Sweetheart of the Silent Majority: The Biography of Phyllis Schlafly* (1981).

Fleming, Cynthia Griggs. *Soon We Will Not Cry: The Liberation of Ruby Doris Smith Robinson* (1998).

Garcia, Alma M. *Chicana Feminist Thought: The Basic Historical Writings* (1997).

Garrow, David. *Liberty and Sexuality: The Right to Privacy and the Making of Roe v. Wade* (1994).

Giele, Janet. *Woman and the Future* (1978).

Harrison, Cynthia. *On Account of Sex: The Politics of Women's Issues, 1945–1968* (1988).

———. "A 'New Frontier' for Women: The Public Policy of the Kennedy Administration," *Journal of American History* 68 (1981): 630–646.

Hartmann, Susan M. *The Other Feminists: Activists in the Liberal Establishment* (1998).

———. *From Margin to Mainstream: American Women and Politics Since 1960* (1989).

Hochschild, Arlie. *The Second Shift: Working Parents and the Revolution at Home* (1989).

Hoff-Wilson, Joan, ed. *Rites of Passage: The Past and Future of the ERA* (1986).

Hoikkala, Paivi. "Feminists or Reformers? American Indian Women and Political Activism in Phoenix, 1965–1980," *American Indian Culture and Research Journal* 22 (1998): 163–186.

Hole, Judith, and Ellen Levine. *Rebirth of Feminism* (1971).

hooks, bell. *Talking Back: Thinking Feminist, Thinking Black* (1989).

———. *Ain't I a Woman? Black Women and Feminism* (1981).

Honig, Emily. "Women at Farah Revisited: Political Mobilization and Its Aftermath Among Chicana Workers in El Paso, Texas, 1972–1992," *Feminist Studies* 22 (1996): 425–452.

Horn, Miriam. *Rebels in White Gloves: Coming of Age with Hillary's Class—Wellesley '69* (1999).

Horne, Gerald. *Race Woman: The Lives of Shirley Graham Du Bois* (2000).

Horowitz, Daniel. *Betty Friedan and the Making of the Feminine Mystique: The American Left, the Cold War, and American Feminism* (1998).

Klatch, Rebecca E. *Women of the New Right* (1987).

Klein, Ethel. *Gender Politics* (1984).

James, Joy. *Race, Women, and Revolution: Ella Baker and Black Female Radicalism* (1999).

Joseph, Gloria, and Jill Lewis. *Common Differences: Conflicts in Black and White Feminist Perspectives* (1981).

Lederer, Lauren, ed. *Take Back the Night: Women on Pornography* (1980).

Lees, Chna Kai. *For Freedom's Sake: The Life of Fannie Lou Hamer* (1999).

Linden-Ward, Blanche, and Carol Hurd Green. *Changing the Future: American Women in the 1960s* (1993).

Luker, Kristin. *Abortion and the Politics of Motherhood* (1984).

Mansbridge, Jane. *Why We Lost the ERA* (1986).

McGlen, Nancy and Karen O'Connor. *Women's Rights* (1983).

Mohr, James. *Abortion in America* (1980).

Morgen, Sandra. *Into Our Own Hands: The Women's Health Movement in the United States, 1969–1990* (2002).

Murphy, Michelle. "Toxicity in the Details: The History of the Women's Office Worker Movement and Occupational Health in the Late-Capitalist Office," *Labor History* 41 (2000): 189–213.

Okin, Susan Moller. *Justice, Gender and the Family* (1989).

Petchesky, Rosalind Pollack. *Abortion and Woman's Choice: The State, Sexuality and Reproductive Freedom* (1990).

Polatnik, M. Rivka. "Diversity in Women's Liberation Ideology: How a Black and White Group of the 1960s Viewed Motherhood," *Signs* 21 (1996): 679–706.

Rosen, Ruth. *The World Split Open: How the Modern Women's Movement Changed America* (2000).

Rothschild, Mary. "White Women Volunteers in the Freedom Summers: Their Life and Work in a Movement for Social Change," *Feminist Studies* 5 (1979): 466–495.

Rupp, Leila J., and Verta Taylor. *Survival in the Doldrums: The American Women's Rights Movement, 1945 to the 1960s* (1987).

Santillan, Richard. "Midwestern Mexican American Women and the Struggle for Gender Equality: A Historical Overview, 1920s–1960s," *Perspectives in Mexican American Studies* 5 (1995): 79–119.

Smith, Merril D. *Sex Without Consent: Rape and Sexual Coercion in America* (2002).

Snitow, Ann et al., eds. *Powers of Desire: The Politics of Sexuality* (1983).

Swerdlow, Amy. *Strike for Peace: Traditional Motherhood and Radical Politics in the 1960s* (1993).

Vance, Carol, ed. *Pleasure and Danger: Exploring Female Sexuality* (1984).

Wandersee, Winifred D. *On the Move: American Women in the 1970s* (1988).

Watkins, Elizabeth Siegel. *On the Pill: A Social History of Contraception, 1950–1970* (1998).

Weiss, Jessica. *To Have and to Hold: Marriage, the Baby Boom, and Social Change* (2000).

Weitzman, Leonore J. *The Divorce Revolution: The Unexpected Social and Economic Consequences for Women and Children in America* (1985).

Yates, Gayle Graham. *What Women Want: The Ideas of the Movement* (1975).

C H A P T E R
16

Women, Social Change, and Reaction from the 1990s to the New Millennium

Vigorous debate about the meaning of gender and its relationship to race, class, and ethnicity is commonplace in contemporary America. Women and men have expressed a great range of opinions about change in gender relations. Conservatives are adamant about their opposition to specific feminist priorities such as legal abortion, but they, along with liberals, have become generally accepting of women's presence in politics and elite professions such as law, medicine, and science. At the same time, Americans have been reluctant to support policies that overtly acknowledge gender discrimination or ease the social and economic burdens of women who work while caring for families. In the face of conservative organizing, feminists of varied backgrounds have tried to prevent the dismantling of affirmative action programs and the loss of women's right to reproductive privacy. On other issues feminists continue to express divergent viewpoints and priorities. For example, in the mid-1990s, when conservative Republicans and so-called "new" Democrats worked on legislation to put an end to "welfare as we know it," many white feminists lent their support, even though women of color argued that the new legislation attacked the interests of poor and non-white women. Feminists of color and immigrant women from nations around the world continue to challenge white Americans, male and female, to understand what it means to live between two cultures. A new generation of "third-wave" feminists has begun to articulate and promote the distinctive interests of young women. And within the past several years, the United States' military intervention in Iraq has provoked a new wave of feminist peace activism.

Historians and other scholars have reached no consensus as to whether women in contemporary America are making gains or losing ground. What has become of their quest for freedom? Are they better able than women of previous generations to comprehend both their commonalities and differences? The documents and essays in this chapter offer multiple responses to these questions. They attest to the varied viewpoints and interests of women in America, whether they are

self-proclaimed feminists or not, and explore key issues in women's lives, includ-
ing their relationship to the welfare state, reproductive freedom, immigration
and the "borderland" experience, and third-wave feminism. While this chapter
explores divisions and differences between women in the United States, it looks
as well at American women's relationship to women in other nations around
the globe.

◈ D O C U M E N T S

Document 1 is an excerpt of Anita Hill's 1991 testimony before the Senate Judiciary
Committee on the nomination of Clarence Thomas to the Supreme Court. In 1992 a
divided Supreme Court reaffirmed the central holding of *Roe v. Wade* in *Planned
Parenthood v. Casey* (Document 2), but it gave states permission to enact rules and
regulations that, short of imposing an "undue burden," encouraged women to seek
options to abortion. In Document 3, feminist writer Gloria Anzaldua, a seventh-
generation American, speaks about her life in the "borderland" between Chicano and
Anglo cultures. In Document 4, first- and second-generation immigrant women also
speak of living between American culture and the cultures of their countries of origin:
Pakistan and Japan. Document 5 presents the "personal story," published online in 2002,
of Jamala McFadden, a welfare recipient of the early 1990s who opposes the changes in
welfare law that were implemented in 1996. Rebecca Walker, in Document 6, describes
the interests and goals of young "third-wave" feminists. In Document 7, *Ms. Magazine*
list the rights of American women that could be threatened by the appointment of conservative justices to the Supreme Court.

1. Anita Hill's Testimony Before the Senate Judiciary Committee, 1991

Mr. Chairman, Senator Thurmond, members of the committee, my name is Anita F.
Hill, and I am a professor of law at the University of Oklahoma.

I was born on a farm in Okmulgee County, OK, in 1956. I am the youngest of
13 children. I had my early education in Okmulgee County. My father, Albert Hill,
is a farmer in that area. My mother's name is Erma Hill. She is also a farmer and a
housewife.

My childhood was one of a lot of hard work and not much money, but it was
one of solid family affection as represented by my parents. I was reared in a religious atmosphere in the Baptist faith, and I have been a member of the Antioch
Baptist Church, in Tulsa, OK, since 1983. It is a very warm part of my life at the
present time.

For my undergraduate work, I went to Oklahoma State University, and graduated from there in 1977. . . .

Testimony of Anita F. Hill, Professor of Law, University of Oklahoma, Norman, Okla., in *Hearing Before
the Committee on the Judiciary, United States Senate, One Hundred Second Congress, First Session on
the Nomination of Clarence Thomas to be Associate Justice of the Supreme Court of the United States,
Oct. 11, 12, 13, and 14, 1991,* part 4 of 4, 36–40.

I graduated from the university with academic honors and proceeded to the Yale Law School, where I received my J.D. degree in 1980.

Upon graduation from law school, I became a practicing lawyer with the Washington, DC, firm of Wald, Harkrader & Ross. In 1981, I was introduced to now Judge Thomas by a mutual friend. Judge Thomas told me that he was anticipating a political appointment and asked if I would be interested in working with him. He was, in fact, appointed as Assistant Secretary of Education for Civil Rights. After he had taken that post, he asked if I would become his assistant, and I accepted that position. . . .

During this period at the Department of Education, my working relationship with Judge Thomas was positive. I had a good deal of responsibility and independence. I thought he respected my work and that he trusted my judgment.

After approximately 3 months of working there, he asked me to go out socially with him. What happened next and telling the world about it are the two most difficult things, experiences of my life. It is only after a great deal of agonizing consideration and a number of sleepless nights that I am able to talk of these unpleasant matters to anyone but my close friends.

I declined the invitation to go out socially with him, and explained to him that I thought it would jeopardize what at the time I considered to be a very good working relationship. I had a normal social life with other men outside of the office. I believed then, as now, that having a social relationship with a person who was supervising my work would be ill advised. I was very uncomfortable with the idea and told him so.

I thought that by saying "no" and explaining my reasons, my employer would abandon his social suggestions. However, to my regret, in the following few weeks he continued to ask me out on several occasions. He pressed me to justify my reasons for saying "no" to him. These incidents took place in his office or mine. They were in the form of private conversations which would not have been overheard by anyone else.

My working relationship became even more strained when Judge Thomas began to use work situations to discuss sex. On these occasions, he would call me into his office for reports on education issues and projects or he might suggest that because of the time pressures of his schedule, we go to lunch to a government cafeteria. After a brief discussion of work, he would turn the conversation to a discussion of sexual matters. His conversations were very vivid.

He spoke about acts that he had seen in pornographic films involving such matters as women having sex with animals, and films showing group sex or rape scenes. He talked about pornographic materials depicting individuals with large penises, or large breasts involved in various sex acts.

On several occasions Thomas told me graphically of his own sexual prowess. Because I was extremely uncomfortable talking about sex with him at all, and particularly in such a graphic way, I told him that I did not want to talk about these subjects. I would also try to change the subject to education matters or to nonsexual personal matters, such as his background or his beliefs. My efforts to change the subject were rarely successful.

Throughout the period of these conversations, he also from time to time asked me for social engagements. My reactions to these conversations was to avoid them by limiting opportunities for us to engage in extended conversations. This was difficult because at the time, I was his only assistant at the Office of Education or Office for Civil Rights.

During the latter part of my time at the Department of Education, the social pressures and any conversation of his offensive behavior ended. I began both to believe and hope that our working relationship could be a proper, cordial, and professional one.

When Judge Thomas was made chair of the EEOC, I needed to face the question of whether to go with him. I was asked to do so and I did. The work, itself, was interesting, and at that time, it appeared that the sexual overtures, which had so troubled me, had ended.

I also faced the realistic fact that I had no alternative job. While I might have gone back to private practice, perhaps in my old firm, or at another, I was dedicated to civil rights work and my first choice was to be in that field. Moreover, at that time the Department of Education, itself, was a dubious venture. President Reagan was seeking to abolish the entire department.

For my first months at the EEOC, where I continued to be an assistant to Judge Thomas, there were no sexual conversations or overtures. However, during the fall and winter of 1982, these began again. The comments were random, and ranged from pressing me about why I didn't go out with him, to remarks about my personal appearance. I remember him saying that "some day I would have to tell him the real reason that I wouldn't go out with him."

He began to show displeasure in his tone and voice and his demeanor in his continued pressure for an explanation. He commented on what I was wearing in terms of whether it made me more or less sexually attractive. The incidents occurred in his inner office at the EEOC.

One of the oddest episodes I remember was an occasion in which Thomas was drinking a Coke in his office, he got up from the table, at which we were working, went over to his desk to get the Coke, looked at the can and asked, "Who has put pubic hair on my Coke?"

On other occasions he referred to the size of his own penis as being larger than normal and he also spoke on some occasions of the pleasures he had given to women with oral sex. At this point, late 1982, I began to feel severe stress on the job. I began to be concerned that Clarence Thomas might take out his anger with me by degrading me or not giving me important assignments. I also thought that he might find an excuse for dismissing me.

In January 1983, I began looking for another job. I was handicapped because I feared that if he found out he might make it difficult for me to find other employment, and I might be dismissed from the job I had.

Another factor that made my search more difficult was that this was during a period of a hiring freeze in the Government. In February 1983, I was hospitalized for 5 days on an emergency basis for acute stomach pain which I attributed to stress on the job. Once out of the hospital, I became more committed to find other employment and sought further to minimize my contact with Thomas.

This became easier when Allyson Duncan became office director because most of my work was then funneled through her and I had contact with Clarence Thomas mostly in staff meetings.

In the spring of 1983, an opportunity to teach at Oral Roberts University opened up. I participated in a seminar, taught an afternoon session in a seminar at Oral Roberts University. The dean of the university saw me teaching and inquired as to whether I would be interested in pursuing a career in teaching, beginning at Oral Roberts University. I agreed to take the job, in large part, because of my desire to escape the pressures I felt at the EEOC due to Judge Thomas.

When I informed him that I was leaving in July, I recall that his response was that now, I would no longer have an excuse for not going out with him. I told him that I still preferred not to do so. At some time after that meeting, he asked if he could take me to dinner at the end of the term. When I declined, he assured me that the dinner was a professional courtesy only and not a social invitation. I reluctantly agreed to accept that invitation but only if it was at the very end of a working day.

On, as I recall, the last day of my employment at the EEOC in the summer of 1983, I did have dinner with Clarence Thomas. We went directly from work to a restaurant near the office. We talked about the work that I had done both at Education and at the EEOC. He told me that he was pleased with all of it except for an article and speech that I had done for him while we were at the Office for Civil Rights. Finally he made a comment that I will vividly remember. He said, that if I ever told anyone of his behavior that it would ruin his career. This was not an apology, nor was it an explanation. That was his last remark about the possibility of our going out, or reference to his behavior.

In July 1983, I left the Washington, DC, area and have had minimal contacts with Judge Clarence Thomas since. I am, of course, aware from the press that some questions have been raised about conversations I had with Judge Clarence Thomas after I left the EEOC.

From 1983 until today I have seen Judge Thomas only twice. On one occasion I needed to get a reference from him and on another, he made a public appearance at Tulsa. On one occasion he called me at home and we had an inconsequential conversation. On one occasion he called me without reaching me and I returned the call without reaching him and nothing came of it. I have, at least on three occasions been asked to act as a conduit to him for others. . . .

It is only after a great deal of agonizing consideration that I am able to talk of these unpleasant matters to anyone, except my closest friends as I have said before. . . . Telling the world is the most difficult experience of my life, but it is very close to having to live through the experience that occasioned this meeting. I may have used poor judgment early on in my relationship with this issue. I was aware, however, that telling at any point in my career could adversely affect my future career. . . .

Perhaps I should have taken angry or even militant steps, both when I was in the agency or after I had left it, but I must confess to the world that the course that I took seemed the better, as well as the easier approach.

I declined any comment to newspapers, but later when Senate staff asked me about these matters, I felt that I had a duty to report. I have no personal vendetta against Clarence Thomas. I seek only to provide the committee with information which it may regard as relevant.

It would have been more comfortable to remain silent. . . . I took no initiative to inform anyone. But when I was asked by a representative of this committee to report my experience I felt that I had to tell the truth. I could not keep silent.

2. The Supreme Court Rules on Abortion Rights and State Regulation in *Planned Parenthood v. Casey*, 1992

Justice O'Connor, Justice Kennedy, and Justice Souter announced the judgment of the Court. . . .

Liberty finds no refuge in a jurisprudence of doubt. Yet 19 years after our holding that the Constitution protects a woman's right to terminate her pregnancy in its early stages, *Row v. Wade*, that definition of liberty is still questioned. Joining the respondents as *amicus curiae*, the United States, as it has done in five other cases in the last decade, again asks us to overrule *Roe*.

At issue in these cases are five provisions of the Pennsylvania Abortion Control Act of 1982 as amended in 1988 and 1989. . . .

After considering the fundamental constitutional questions resolved by *Roe*, principles of institutional integrity, and the rule of *stare decisis*, we are led to conclude this: the essential holding of *Roe v. Wade* should be retained and once again reaffirmed.

It is . . . tempting . . . to suppose that the Due Process Clause protects only those practices, defined at the most specific level, that were protected against government interference by other rules of law when the Fourteenth Amendment was ratified. . . . But such a view would be inconsistent with our law. It is a promise of the Constitution that there is a realm of personal liberty which the government may not enter. . . . Our law affords constitutional protection to personal decisions relating to marriage, procreation, contraception, family relationships, child rearing, and education. . . . Beliefs about these matters could not define the attributes of personhood were they formed under compulsion of the State.

These considerations begin our analysis of the woman's interest in terminating her pregnancy but cannot end it, for this reason: though the abortion decision may originate within the zone of conscience and belief, it is more than a philosophic exercise. Abortion is a unique act. It is an act fraught with consequences for others: for the women who must live with the implications of her decision; for the persons who perform and assist in the procedure; for the spouse, family, and society which must confront the knowledge that these procedures exist, procedures some deem nothing short of an act of violence against innocent human life; and, depending on one's beliefs, for the life or potential life that is aborted. Though abortion is conduct, it does not follow that the State is entitled to proscribe it in all instances. That is because the liberty of the woman is at stake in a sense unique to the human condition and so unique to the law. The mother who carries a child to full term is subject to anxieties, to physical constraints, to pain that only she must bear. That these sacrifices have from the beginning of the human race been endured by woman with a pride that ennobles her in the eyes of others and gives to the infant a bond of love cannot alone be grounds for the State to insist she make the sacrifice. Her suffering is too intimate and personal for the State to insist, without more, upon its own vision

---

Planned Parenthood v. Casey, 1992, in Leslie Friedman Goldstein, *Contemporary Cases in Women's Rights* (Madison: University of Wisconsin Press, 1994), 99–151.

of the woman's role, however dominant that vision has been in the course of our history and our culture. The destiny of the woman must be shaped to a large extent on her own conception of her spiritual imperatives and her place in society. . . .

The woman's right to terminate her pregnancy before viability is the most central principle of *Roe v. Wade*. It is a rule of law and a component of liberty we cannot renounce.

On the other side of the equation is the interest of the State in the protection of potential life. . . .

Though the woman has a right to choose to terminate or continue her pregnancy before viability, it does not at all follow that the State is prohibited from taking steps to ensure that this choice is thoughtful and informed. Even in the earliest stages of pregnancy, the State may enact rules and regulations designed to encourage her to know that there are philosophic and social arguments of great weight that can be brought to bear in favor of continuing the pregnancy to full term and that there are procedures and institutions to allow adoption of unwanted children as well as a certain degree of state assistance if the mother chooses to raise the child herself. . . . It follows that States are free to enact laws to provide a reasonable framework for a woman to make a decision that has such profound and lasting meaning. This, too, we find consistent with *Roe's* central premises, and indeed the inevitable consequence of our holding that the State has an interest in protecting the life of the unborn.

We reject the trimester framework, which we do not consider to be part of the essential holding of *Roe*. . . . The trimester framework suffers from these basic flaws: in its formulation it misconceives the nature of the pregnant woman's interest; and in practice it undervalues the State's interest in potential life, as recognized in *Roe*. . . .

Numerous forms of state regulation might have the incidental effect of increasing the cost or decreasing the availability of medical care, whether for abortion or any other medical procedure. The fact that a law which serves a valid purpose, one not designed to strike at the right itself, has the incidental effect of making it more difficult or more expensive to procure an abortion cannot be enough to invalidate it. Only where state regulation imposes an undue burden on a woman's ability to make this decision does the power of the State reach into the heart of the liberty protected by the Due Process Clause. . . . In our view, the undue burden standard is the appropriate means of reconciling the State's interest with the woman's constitutionally protected liberty. . . .

We permit a State to further its legitimate goal of protecting the life of the unborn by enacting legislation aimed at ensuring a decision that is mature and informed, even when in so doing the State expresses a preference for childbirth over abortion. . . . Requiring that the woman be informed of the availability of information relating to fetal development and the assistance available should she decide to carry the pregnancy to full term is a reasonable measure to insure an informed choice, one which might cause the woman to choose childbirth over abortion. This requirement cannot be considered a substantial obstacle to obtaining an abortion, and, it follows, there is no undue burden. . . .

The Pennsylvania statute also requires us to reconsider the holding in *Akron I* that the State may not require that a physician, as opposed to a qualified assistant, provide information relevant to a woman's informed consent. Since there is no evidence on this record that requiring a doctor to give the information as provided by the statute would amount in practical terms to a substantial obstacle to a woman seeking an abortion, we conclude that it is not an undue burden. . . .

Whether the mandatory 24-hour waiting period is . . . invalid because in practice it is a substantial obstacle to a woman's choice to terminate her pregnancy is a closer question. The findings of fact by the District Court indicate that because of the distances many women must travel to reach an abortion provider, the practical effect will often be a delay of much more than a day because the waiting period requires that a woman seeking an abortion make at least two visits to the doctor. The District Court also found that in many instances this will increase the exposure of women seeking abortions to "the harassment and hostility of antiabortion protestors demonstrating outside a clinic." . . .

These findings are troubling in some respects, but they do not demonstrate that the waiting period constitutes an undue burden. . . .

Section 3209 of Pennsylvania's abortion law provides, except in cases of medical emergency, that no physician shall perform an abortion on a married woman without receiving a signed statement from the woman that she has notified her spouse that she is about to undergo an abortion [or that she fit into one of the statute's exceptions]. . . .

In well-functioning marriages, spouses discuss important intimate decisions such as whether to bear a child. But there are millions of women in this country who are the victims of regular physical and psychological abuse at the hands of their husbands. Should these women become pregnant, they may have very good reasons for not wishing to inform their husbands of their decision to obtain an abortion. . . .

The spousal notification requirement is thus likely to prevent a significant number of women from obtaining an abortion. It does not merely make abortions a little more difficult or expensive to obtain; for many women, it will impose a substantial obstacle. . . . It is an undue burden, and therefore invalid. . . .

[As to parental consent w]e have been over most of this ground before. Our cases establish, and we reaffirm today, that a State may require a minor seeking an abortion to obtain the consent of a parent or guardian, provided that there is an adequate judicial bypass procedure. . . .

The judgment [of the Circuit Court] is affirmed. . . .

Justice Blackmun, concurring in part, concurring in the judgment in part, and dissenting in part. . . .

Three years ago, in *Webster v. Reproductive Health Serv.,* four Members of this Court appeared poised to "cas[t] into darkness the hopes and visions of every woman in this country" who had come to believe that the Constitution guaranteed her the right to reproductive choice. . . . All that remained between the promise of *Roe* and the darkness of the plurality was a single, flickering flame. Decisions since *Webster* gave little reason to hope that this flame would cast much light. . . . But now, just when so many expected the darkness to fall, the flame has grown bright.

I do not underestimate the significance of today's joint opinion. Yet I remain steadfast in my belief that the right to reproductive choice is entitled to the full protection afforded by this Court before *Webster.* And I fear for the darkness as four Justices anxiously await the single vote necessary to extinguish the light. . . .

Roe's requirement of strict scrutiny as implemented through a trimester framework should not be disturbed. No other approach has gained a majority, and no other is more protective of the woman's fundamental right. Lastly, no other approach properly accommodates the woman's constitutional right with the State's legitimate interests. . . .

Chief Justice Rehnquist, with whom Justice White, Justice Scalia, and Justice Thomas join, concurring in the judgment in part and dissenting in part.

The joint opinion, following its newly-minted variation on *stare decisis,* retains the outer shell of *Roe v. Wade,* but beats a wholesale retreat from the substance of that case. We believe that *Roe* was wrongly decided, and that it can and should be overruled consistently with our traditional approach to *stare decisis* in constitutional cases. We would adopt the approach of the plurality in *Webster v. Reproductive Health Services* and uphold the challenged provisions of the Pennsylvania statute in their entirety. . . .

In *Roe v. Wade,* the Court recognized a "guarantee of personal privacy" which "is broad enough to encompass a woman's decision whether or not to terminate her pregnancy." We are now of the view that, in terming this right fundamental, the Court in *Roe* read the earlier opinions upon which it based its decision much too broadly. Unlike marriage, procreation and contraception, abortion "involves the purposeful termination of potential life." *Harris v. McRae* (1980). . . . One cannot ignore the fact that a woman is not isolated in her pregnancy, and that the decision to abort necessarily involves the destruction of a fetus. . . .

We think, therefore, both in view of this history and of our decided cases dealing with substantive liberty under the Due Process Clause, that the Court was mistaken in *Roe* when it classified a woman's decision to terminate her pregnancy as a "fundamental right" that could be abridged only in a manner which withstood "strict scrutiny." . . . The Court in *Roe* reached too far when it . . . deemed the right to abortion fundamental.

3. Gloria Anzaldúa Speaks About Her Identity as a Borderland Chicana, 1999

Karin Ikas: In your life, particularly in your personal life but also in your writing career, you had to struggle a lot, as there was a lot of hardship and oppression to overcome right from the beginning. Can you tell us a bit more about that, about your childhood and how you were raised?

Gloria Anzaldúa: I grew up on a ranch settlement called Jesus María in the Valley of South Texas. At that time there were four or five of these ranches in that area. And on each of these ranch settlements there lived between two and four families. My mother and my father, who each lived on one of these adjoining ranches, met there and married while they were quite young. My mother had just turned 16 when I was born. Both of my parents had no high school education. Until I was eleven years old we lived in a ranching environment, and all of us had to participate in farm work like, for example, working in the fields, raising animals—cows and chickens, et cetera. Then we moved closer to a little town called Hargill, Texas. We had a little house and continued ranching there. However, until I turned ten we were continually changing places as we were working on different ranches and in different places as migrant workers. We had started out as migrant workers when I was about seven or eight. But I had missed so much school in the first years at elementary school that after a year my father decided he would just migrate by himself and leave us at home so that all of us children could go to school regularly. I first went to school permanently in Hargill, and I graduated there after eighth grade. Then we, my sister and I, were bussed to school in Edinburgh, Texas. Although I stopped being a migrant laborer while I was still very young, I continued working in the fields of my home valley until I earned my B.A. from Pan American University in 1969. So I had learned the hardships of working in the fields and of being a migrant laborer myself, and that experience formed me. I have a very deep respect for all the migrant laborers, the so-called *campesinos.* That experience also reinforced me in my work with migrant kids. After I got my M.A. in English and Education from University of Texas, Austin in 1972 I became a high school teacher and I taught a lot of migrant kids. For one summer I even traveled with the migrant families who were on their way from Texas to the Midwest. By doing so, I became a liaison between the migrant camps and the regular school teachers for one year. Later they hired me to be the bilingual and migrant director of the full state of Indiana. At that time I was already teaching. But I was mostly working with kids in South Texas—migrant kids, emotionally disturbed and mentally retarded kids.

K.I.: Were these kids of different ethnic or racial background or were they mainly Chicano/as?

G.A.: Not all were Chicano/as. It depended on the kind of class I was teaching. The migrant kids' classes were all one hundred percent Mexican. But I was also teaching the so-called genius classes, ninth, tenth, eleventh and twelfth grade. And these genius classes were about fifty percent white. The Chicano/a enrollment in the schools of south Texas is, all together, about eighty percent. Then I started teaching bilingual five-year-olds. And I also taught emotionally disturbed and mentally re-tarded students who were ages seven to thirteen. Later I moved on to high school, where I taught English and literature at ninth, tenth, eleventh and twelfth grade. After-wards I lived in Indiana for a while. After Indiana I became a Ph.D. candidate at the University of Texas at Austin. While I was in Austin I was also a lecturer in Chicano studies. So I was teaching while I was going to school myself. . . .

K.I.: Did you also participate in the Chicano Movement then?

G.A.: Yes, I did. Actually, I started out with MECHA, a Mexican American youth organization. Also I was involved with different farm worker activities in South Texas and later in Indiana. When I became more recognized as a writer, I started articu-lating a lot of these feminist ideas that were a kind of continuation of the Chicano Movement. But I call it *"El Movimiento Macha."* A *marimacha* is a woman who is very assertive. That is what they used to call dykes, *marimachas,* half-and-halfs. You were different, you were queer, not normal, you were *marimacha.* I had been witnessing all these Chicana writers, activists, artists and professors who were very strong and therefore very *marimacha.* So I named it *"El Movimiento Macha"* as the Chicano Civil Rights Movement kind of petered out. And there were women like my-self, many Chicanas, who were already questioning, having problems with the guys who were ignoring women's issues. Therefore, in the eighties and nineties, there are all these women—Chicana activists, writers and artists—around, and I listen to them, read them and reflect their influence on my life as well. What you could say is that in the sixties and the early seventies the Chicanos were at the controls. They were the ones who were visible, the Chicano leaders. Then in the eighties and nineties, the women have become visible. I see a lot of Chicanas when I travel. They come up to me, and while we are talking I ask them about their role models. They mention names like Cherríe Moraga, Gloria Anzaldúa and other Chicana authors. It is, and will continue to be, women that they are reading, that they respect. Not the guys. So it—the Chicano Movement—has shifted into the *Movimiento Macha.*

K.I.: What motivated you in particular to edit *This Bridge Called My Back?*

G.A.: One motivation for doing *This Bridge Called My Back* was that when I was at UT I wanted to focus my dissertation on feminist studies and Chicana literature and soon realized that this seemed to be an impossible project. The advisor told me that Chicana literature was not a legitimate discipline, that it didn't exist, and that women's studies was not something that I should do. You know, this was back then in 1976–77. If you were a Chicana at a university, all you were taught were these red, white and blue American philosophies, systems, disciplines, ways of knowledge. They didn't consider ethnic cultural studies as having the impact or weight needed to enter the academy. And so in a lot of these classes I felt silenced, like I had no voice. Finally I quit the Ph.D. program at UT and left Texas for California in 1977. When I moved to San Francisco, I participated in the Women's Writers' Union, where I got to know Susan Griffin, Karen Brodine, Nellie Wong and Merle Woo, among others. Also I joined the Feminist Writers' Guild, which was a little bit less radical. This is where I met Cherríe Moraga, whom I asked a few months later to become my co-editor for *This Bridge Called My Back.* Anyway, I found that this little community of feminist writers in San Francisco, Oakland and Berkeley, this Feminist Writers' Guild, was very much excluding women of color. Most of the white women I knew were part of that organization. I did meet Luisah Teish there, though. She is an Afro-American woman from Louisiana who has all those books on spirituality and practices all that in her own life, so you can call her a *santería.* Every two weeks we would have our meetings and everybody would talk about the white problems and their white experiences. When it was my turn to talk, it was almost like they were putting words into my mouth. They interrupted me while I was still talking or, after I had finished, they interpreted what I just said according to their thoughts and ideas. They thought that all women were oppressed in the same way, and they tried to force me to accept their image of me and my experiences. They were not willing to be open to my own presentation of myself and to accept that I might be different from what they had thought of me so far. Therefore one of the messages of *This Bridge Called My Back* is that gender is not the only oppression. There is race, class, religious orientation; there are generational and age kinds of things, all the physical stuff et cetera. I mean, somehow these women were great. They were white and a lot of them were dykes and very supportive. But they were also blacked out and blinded out about our multiple oppressions. They didn't understand what we were going through. They wanted to speak for us because they had an idea of what feminism was, and they wanted to apply their notion of feminism across all cultures. *This Bridge Called My Back,* therefore, was my sweeping back against that kind of "All of us are women so you are all included and we were all equal." Their idea was that we all were culture-less because we were feminists; we didn't have any other culture. But they never left their whiteness at home. Their whiteness covered everything they said. However, they wanted me to give up my Chicananess and become part of them; I was asked to leave my race at the door.

K.I.: So *This Bridge Called My Back* was your response to all that?

G.A.: Yes, exactly. . . . However, after several months of struggling with *This Bridge* on my own, and trying to convince other women of color that they really have a voice worth being listened to and being published, I asked Cherríe Moraga to become a co-editor and support me with this project that had become too over-whelming for me alone.

K.I.: How did Chicanas then receive your next book, *Borderlands / La Frontera?*

G.A.: Well, when Chicanas read *Borderlands,* when it was read by little Chicanas in particular, it somehow legitimated them. They saw that I was code-switching, which is what a lot of Chicanas were doing in real life as well, and for the first time after reading that book they seemed to realize, "Oh, my way of writing and speaking is okay" and, "Oh, she is writing about *La Virgen de Guadalupe,* about *la Llorona,* about the *corridos,* the gringos, the abusive, et cetera. So if she [Gloria Anzaldúa] does it, why not me as well?" The book gave them permission to do the same thing. So they started using code-switching and writing about all the issues they have to deal with in daily life. To them, it was like somebody was saying: You are just as important as a woman as anybody from another race. And the experiences that you have are worth being told and written about.

K.I.: How do you feel about the critical reception of *Borderlands?*

G.A.: Critics are more open towards it right now. For some reason or other I got lucky in that they still teach my book at school and university. They teach it as a way of introducing students to cultural diversity. However, some of the writing is glossed over as, particularly, white critics and teachers often pick just some parts of *Borderlands.* For example, they take the passages in which I talk about *mestizaje* and borderlands because they can more easily apply them to their own experiences. The angrier parts of *Borderlands,* however, are often ignored as they seem to be too threatening and too confrontational. In some way, I think you could call this selective critical interpretation a kind of racism. On the other hand, I am happy that the book is read at all. For us, it is not always easy to have people read our work or deal with our art. If the work is not interesting or entertaining enough, forget it. So I have to keep all these different issues regarding the reception of my work in mind and try to compromise. For example, if I had made *Borderlands* too inaccessible to you by putting in too many Chicano terms, too many Spanish words, or if I had been more fragmented in the text than I am right now, you would have been very frustrated. So there are certain traditions in all the different genres—like autobiography, fiction, poetry, theory, criticism—and certain standards that you have to follow. Otherwise you are almost naked. It is like when you write a dissertation: there are certain rules you have to apply; otherwise they won't pass you. . . .

K.I.: So do you think intercultural understanding is possible and can be enhanced by writing?

G.A.: I do. I believe that both inter- and intracultural understanding can be enhanced. "Intracultural" means within the Chicano culture and Mexican culture.

"Intercultural" is about how we are related with other cultures like the Black culture, the Native American cultures, the white culture and the international cultures in general. I am operating on both perspectives as I am trying to write for different audiences. On the one hand, I write for more of an international audience that came across from one world to the other and that has border people. Actually, more and more people today become border people because the pace of society has increased. Just think about multi-media, computers and World Wide Web, for example. By the Internet you can communicate instantly with someone in India or somewhere else in the world, like Australia, Hungary or China. We are all living in a society where these borders are transgressed constantly.

K.I.: How do you see this intercultural situation with regard to the Chicano culture and the Anglo-American influence?

G.A.: In that context, one particular image comes into my mind: the Banyan Tree. It is a tree that is originally from India but which I saw in Hawaii first. It looks like a solid wall. When the seeds from the tree fall, they don't take root in the ground. They take root in the branches. So the seeds fall in the branches, and it is there, above the earth, where the tree blooms and forms its fruits. And I thought, that is where *we* are getting it. Instead of going to the roots of our Hispanic or Chicano culture we are getting it from the branches, from white dominant culture. I mean, it is not that I reject everything that has to do with white culture. I like the English language, for example, and there is a lot of Anglo ideology that I like as well. But not all of it fits with our experiences and cultural roots. And that is why it is dangerous not to know about your own cultural heritage at all, because then you don't have the chance to choose and select.

4. First- and Second-Generation Immigrant Women Speak of Living Between Cultures, 2000

Asma Gull Hasan, Pakistani-American

American Muslim women are really between two worlds: the old world of traditions, preserved and passed down by immigrant parents or older members of the indigenous community, and the new world, as presented to us by the feminist movement, American emphasis on gender equality and by the Qur'an, in a sense, too.

The idea of a Muslim feminist also strikes Americans as odd. American Muslim women are in the unique and paradoxical position of living in a society where they are free to explore their religion but are stereotyped by the greater population of their country as oppressed women. The West cites its perceptions of arranged marriages, polygamy (actually polygyny, meaning a plurality of wives), veiling and other aspects of Islamic life that are perceived to degrade women as evidence of Islam's cultural inferiority.

At the same time as they encounter this criticism, American Muslim women are re-discovering the freedoms Islam gives them. Muslims believe that God revealed to Prophet Muhammad several provisions emphasizing a woman's independence, provisions which are recorded in the Qur'an. Of particular note is that in the Qur'an, Eve is created independently of Adam, providing no Qur'anic basis for women's existence as the result of the creation of men.

In the Qur'an, men and women are fully equal before God. Marriage is a contract to be negotiated, even to the woman's benefit, and, women have the right to divorce, one of many Qur'anic "innovations" that ". . . brought legal advantages for women quite unknown in corresponding areas of the Western Christian world," says Jane Smith. Other innovations include the right to property and the right to inherit money. According to Islamic law, a woman can keep her maiden name and her personal income. Islam also grants women the right to participate in political affairs (imagine, if we had all followed the Qur'an, there would have been no need for the suffragette movement), to stand equally with men in the eyes of the law, to receive child support in the event of a divorce, to seek employment and education, to take or turn down a marriage proposal and to live free from spousal abuse. Islam also gives women high status as mothers, to be respected and admired by their children. On two occasions the Prophet highlighted the mother's role, telling one follower to stay with his mother rather than join the military, ". . . for Paradise is at her feet." Muslim women also can draw on a history of strong women, particularly those women who lived in Muhammad's time. Some Muslims even support a woman's right to abortion because the procedure is believed to have been performed in the Prophet's time without his dissent.

However, along with Qur'anic tradition, one is also subject to other traditions that, over centuries of time, have come to be associated with being Muslim, though they may have nothing to do with Islam, like female circumcision (an African tribal custom) and an emphasis on marriage. Furthermore, women bear the brunt of traditional aspects of cultures associated with Islam—like wearing *hijab*. Algerian lawyer and specialist in Muslim women's rights for UNESCO, Wassyla Tamzali, told *The New York Times*, ". . . [W]omen symbolize tradition and cultural identity. It is as if the whole burden of the Islamic tradition rests on their shoulders." Rifaat Hassan, an American Muslim scholar, writes, "Even when a Muslim woman is able to acquire an education and secure a job, she is seldom able to free herself from the burden of traditionalism that confronts her on all sides."

This coercive nature of traditional aspects of Islam manifests itself in America with an emphasis on marriage, in my opinion. Young Muslim women are bombarded with messages of not only the importance of marriage but marriage *at a young age.* Even with parents and families like mine, who show hardly any vestiges of traditionalism or conservatism . . . , the pressure for daughters to marry young is strong. That is a part of American-Muslim culture, for better or for worse. . . . There doesn't seem to be a really good reason to, other than marriage in our culture is a preferred alternative to dating, as sex outside of marriage is *haram* (unlawful). Marriage at a young age or marriage at all is not a religious obligation, but the centrality of family in Islamic culture makes marriage very important. In addition, marriage means acceptance into the Muslim social community. . . .

The importance of marriage in the American Muslim community is exemplified by the myriad ways the community has developed for finding a spouse: personal advertisements in Islamic publications, matrimonial booths at Islamic conferences, enlisting peers in a search or through "word of mouth" and mosque-arranged singles gatherings. American Islamic publications run how-to articles on finding a spouse. Marriage is so important that immigrant parents worry about a scarcity of young Muslim men for their daughters; some even wonder if the Islamic law allowing Muslim men to marry Christian or Jewish women should be rescinded in America.

However, today's Muslim woman is not necessarily doomed to failure because she marries young, according to traditional values. In many ways, it's good that the community is taking an active role in pairing off the young ones. As a result of parental flexibility and the perception of a scarcity of Muslims of similar ages, inter-ethnic marriages have become more popular, particularly intermarriage between racial backgrounds. That sounds like the American dream to me: young married people, sometimes of diverse backgrounds, with a stable financial footing and strong family setting.

A more subtle form of oppression against American Muslim women is carried out by American Muslim men who feel threatened by modern American culture. Rifaat Hassan writes, "Nothing perhaps illustrates men's deep insecurities . . . so well as the sternness and strictness with which they compel their women to cover themselves from head to foot and keep them confined to their houses." Kathleen Gough's essay, "The Origin of the Family," says that one of the characteristics of male power is physical confinement and prevention of movement of women; this characteristic is manifested by *purdah* (the separation of men and women at all gatherings especially during prayer, which has no solid Qur'anic basis but is practiced by most Muslims) and *hijab*. Muslim men, and eventually the females in their community, force *hijab* and severe forms of modesty on women that result in gender segregation. Such behavior is sometimes coerced through community attitudes onto Muslim women and chalked up to the noble purpose of protecting women. These attitudes are reminiscent of how the Christian male group, the Promisekeepers, allegedly protect their women. With both groups, a fine line exists between protection and encouragement versus oppression and suppression. . . .

Though the problems Muslim women face seem insurmountable, women can improve their situation by taking advantage of the opportunities a Muslim woman has in America. Living in the US is positively affecting the lives of American Muslim women in two ways: (1) American culture encourages female participation in religious activities and (2) Muslim women are readily able to learn Arabic, read the Qur'an and analyze the Qur'an for themselves.

One of the greatest phenomena occurring in the Muslim world today is Qur'anic exegesis by Muslim feminists. The Qur'an, a book regarded as the divine work for over 1400 years, is being interpreted from a non-male perspective on a large scale for *the first time ever.* A diverse group of the world's female Muslims are ". . . fundamentally rework[ing Islam] . . . from a feminist and egalitarian point of view." Their work is controversial because they are trying to prove that the Qur'an does not support oppression of women undermining or questioning the validity of the Qur'an itself, only certain interpretations. Some credit the Beijing United Nations Conference on women as bringing this intellectual, yet politically charged, dialogue to the surface, and now, the Ford Foundation, the National Endowment for Democracy and the Council on Foreign Relations are funding projects in this area.

I say it's about time. For 1400 years, men like my grandfather have told women like me what the Qur'an says. I'm not saying all those men are wrong. And frankly, the only interpretations I'm really interested in challenging are the ones regarding women's so-called inferiority. I'm just saying that now that women have an opportunity to be literate, to read the Qur'an in Arabic and tell us if they think God made men superior, let's have a listen!

The core complaint of these feminist Muslim theologians is that though the Qur'an is clear in its support of women's rights, men have been interpreting the Qur'an to their own advantage since its revelation. Amina Wadud-Muhsin, Philosophy and Religion Professor at Virginia Commonwealth University in Richmond, says, "[N]ow . . . many women are making the point that . . . men's interpretation of our religion . . . has limited women's progress, not our religion itself." For example, the gender segregation during prayer now suggests inferiority on women's part when, in actuality, the Prophet initiated the practice so that women would not have to prostrate in front of men. Realizing that a male perception of Islam has been used and accepted for centuries, Muslim women are taking back their right to Qur'anic education and interpretation.

Kyoko Mori, Japanese-American

Getting on the plane to leave Japan at the end of my trip is like boarding a time machine. The moment I take my seat, everything that happened in the last week falls into the distant past. From the small window of the plane, the observation decks and the gates of the airport look far away, as though I were seeing them through binoculars. That's how the whole trip strikes me as soon as I'm on the plane: small, far away, detailed. Like the migratory birds I watch through my binoculars, Japan becomes something for me to observe, study, recall.

I am jolted by the sudden shift of perspective. During my stay in Kobe, I feel as though I had never really left my childhood home. "I'll be here again soon," I say to my relatives and friends. "We'll always be in touch." Vaguely I imagine myself spending more time in Kobe in the future, by teaching a semester at a Japanese university or applying for a grant, and seeing my uncles, aunts, and cousins regularly for a while. If I had a teaching job, I reason, maybe living in Japan would not make me feel so helpless and scared: a job would remind me that I am a full, functioning adult; it would give me a chance to know Japan from a different perspective, and I could finally become more than an occasional visitor to my family.

Sitting on the plane and remembering these thoughts, I wonder, *What was I thinking? There's no way I could stay there for more than a couple of weeks. Who was I trying to fool?* As the plane begins to taxi and then to life off into the sky, I am relieved. *I got out of there in time,* I think, *Thank goodness.* Up in the air, it's easy to admit the truth: it will be a long time before I am in Japan again, on another short visit; until then, I will think of my family and friends often, but they won't know because I won't write or call. This truth fills me with regret. I wish things had turned out a different way—it would be so nice if I could live my adult life without leaving behind my past in a foreign country—but a wish is only a wish: a strong feeling that does not affect the course of my life or the choices I make. . . .

The contradictory emotions I feel are nothing unusual. Most of my friends experience the same feelings when they visit their parents' home in another city or another state. During the visit, they feel as though they had never left home, but as soon as they drive away or board the plane, the week they just spent "back home" seems more a part of their lives from twenty years ago than a recent event in their present life. "Was I really helping my father with his lawn this morning, or was it twenty years ago before I went to college?" they wonder as they travel back to their present homes—already making plans for the classes they will teach on Monday or reminding themselves that tomorrow is their daughter's first soccer game of the season. The week "back home" with their parents seems oddly out of place and time. The visit is a trip across time as well as distance.

When people ask me how I could leave my "home" at twenty and never go back, I remind them that there is nothing unusual about my choice. Many people leave home at eighteen to go to college and end up settling in another state, perhaps across the continent. They don't write, call, or visit their original families much more than I do. Or else people move to the next suburb only three miles away and yet feel a dissonance when they go "home" on holidays, because they have traveled a long distance from their parents' politics or religion. It's not so difficult to leave your "home" at eighteen or twenty, when you think of it as a place you were born to, not a place you have chosen. It didn't require any special courage for me to leave behind everything I loved about my home at twenty. There was very little I loved about Kobe back then. I was eager to leave the house where I never felt safe, much less "at home," and the culture that did not value intelligent and independent women—the kind of woman I wanted to become.

When I miss home now, it is the place itself I miss more than anything. At least once every month in my dreams, I stand on a seashore looking at a blue stretch of salt water, knowing that I am home. The dream may start out in another part of my home town: the busy downtown shopping district, my grade school up on the hill. Or it may begin some place far away. I am driving across the bridge on a country road in Wisconsin. Below me, there is an ice-covered river, and ahead, another long expanse of bare, brown fields. I turn the next corner, and suddenly, I am face to face with the salt water of my childhood. . . .

But the familiarity with childhood landscapes is only one way to feel at home. Happy as I am too see the mountains and the sea on my trips back "home," I begin to feel restless after only a few hours there. As I gaze at the mountains and the sea or sit down to dinner with my family and friends, time goes into slow motion. Moments seem like lifetimes, and I want to live them as though nothing else mattered, but deep down I know this is not my life, that my real life happens far away from my childhood landscape.

We mean so many things by *home*. Kobe would still be my home if *home* simply meant the place where we grew up, a place that is special to us because of our memories. But *home* also means a place where we have made a life for ourselves, where we feel a sense of purpose. I have never held a full-time job, voted, or paid taxes in Kobe, never supported a political cause or donated money or volunteered my time to help other people there. I could never call a place home without doing some of these things—without feeling that I have a part to play in the community. I left Japan because there was nothing for me to do there. I could get married and try to become an exemplary mother and wife, or live alone to pursue a career in isolation.

Neither of these choices offers the kind of community involvement I find fulfilling: to have my own life and yet to be part of a larger life, a web of friends and like-minded people.

I don't regret leaving, but as a result, I have two halves of the whole when it comes to *home*—home as a special place of childhood, home as a place where I can live, work, be part of the community, and feel happy. The two halves don't make a smooth whole. Driving through the endlessly flat landscapes of the Midwest, I long for the mountains and the sea, the dramatic rise and fall of land and water around me. Like most people who grew up near any sea, I stare at Midwesterners with polite disbelief when they tell me that the Great Lakes are like the ocean. Nobody who grew up near salt water would say that. I am always lonely for a home where I can have everything: the past, the present, the future. . . .

Living in and between two cultures, I am often more confused than helped by the lessons I learned or rebelled against in both places. The question of home will always make me feel a little anxious and edgy. Often, when I meet people at academic conferences and tell them where I live, they laugh a little and say, "Really?" as though there was something incongruous about me—a Japanese woman from Kobe—making my home in Green Bay, Wisconsin. Perhaps these people are right. If I could move my job and my close friends, my whole adult life, somewhere else, I would choose to live in Milwaukee or Chicago. Ten years ago, if someone had asked me to name my ideal city, I would have said New York or San Francisco, or even Albuquerque. I've settled into a life in the Midwest. I love the easy pace of life, even the all-pervasive "niceness" I used to make fun of a long time ago: a place like Green Bay allows my friends and me to put together a living without much effort, to do whatever we want among people who are too nice not to let us be. So I don't long for the coasts or even for better weather. Some days I still miss a childhood place where everything seemed clear and simple—north meant the mountains and south meant the sea—but I know that this place is more mythical than actual. The past doesn't have all the answers.

In spite of my mother's love, my childhood home was a place of sadness, secrets, and lies. My mother's unhappiness with her life, a life that included me, is one of the hard truths I have to face. Love isn't always enough to keep someone alive or to pull her out of unhappiness. My mother chose to die rather than to practice the Japanese virtue of *gaman* in hopes of a better future with me. I know she would be pleased with my attempt to be honest about that. My mother spent most of her adult life trying to live a polite lie of a stable and harmonious marriage, trying, day after day, to make the lie become the truth somehow; her death meant a final rejection of that lie. If there was one thing she wanted me to do, it was to resist the polite lies and the silences of my childhood, to speak the truth.

The last conversation my mother and I had, when I was twelve, was over the phone. Somehow, that has made it easier for me to imagine her voice even after her death, even in a foreign country. I picture invisible telephone wires stretching over the ocean, across that immense gap of time I travel into my childhood on my visits to Japan. My mother's voice continues to reach me across that distance and time. The summer I left home, I stood looking at the waves coming in to San Francisco Bay and knew that in a roundabout way, the same water moved back and forth across the world—it didn't matter where I was. I had left home, I was sure, not to forget about my mother but to be closer to her memory. All these years later, my conviction remains the same: I speak her words though I speak them in another language.

5. Jamala McFadden Tells Her Story of Welfare Assistance in the 1990s, 2002

In 1991, at the age of fifteen, I had a child. My mother had five children and already received aid from the state of Illinois. My son was simply added to our family allotment. Even with the monthly cash, food stamps, and minimal child care subsidies, the amount was simply inadequate to support our family. I eventually supplemented the assistance by working and had enough money to buy, at most, diapers, milk, and other basic necessities for my child.

After two years, I completed high school and was fortunate enough to be able to go away to college. For four years (1994–98) I attended the University of Illinois at Urbana-Champaign. My son, two at the time, went along with me. Because my mother needed to provide for herself and my siblings, she was unable to provide financial support for my son and I. It was my responsibility to single-handedly supply all of our basic needs, including housing. As a full-time college student caring for a child alone, my needs were definitely not the needs of a traditional college student who had the financial support of her family. In Urbana, I was able to receive government assistance in my name for my child and myself. I was a full-time student caring for my child alone.

Welfare definitely made it easier for me to get through the critical transition period between high school and college and sustained me through undergraduate school. In my first year of college, there was no work prerequisite to receive aid. However, I worked anyway. During my second and third years, welfare recipients who were students were required to work a minimum of eight hours per week. That I did. However, by my last year, 1997–98, the state required that students work twenty hours per week. Fortunately for me, I was "grandfathered in" and wasn't forced to work the additional hours to receive assistance. I was told that "times are changing" and that "welfare as we know it was over." Indeed, college students were a very low priority for childcare subsidies. The perception was that "we didn't need it. . . . Getting a college degree was a personal decision—of no concern to the state." For the government at least, it was time to prioritize securing and maintaining a job over getting a good education.

Fortunately, I was successful. I finished college in four years. I finished before many of my peers who had little or no responsibilities and were completely supported by their families. Not only did I earn my college degree, I was active in several school organizations, co-founding a single-parent support group on campus. I graduated with high distinction in political science, achieving a 3.7 G.P.A. I went on to law school at the University of Michigan—one of the top ten law schools in the country. If I had to work twenty hours per week, be a successful full-time student, and be a good mother to a small child, I doubt that I would have been as successful as I have been thus far.

"Jamala McFadden's Story of Welfare Assistance in the 1990s" from "Personal Stories, Welfare Made a Difference," National Campaign, 2002. Reprinted with permission of Jamala McFadden.

Contrary to popular stereotype, welfare in no way held me back. I was fortunate and indeed blessed. Welfare made a difference in my life. Welfare made it easier for me to succeed and concentrate on what was important—my child and my education. For those who believe in the theory that welfare is cyclical and repeats throughout generations—for this family, the cycle is broken. Welfare helped me show my son, younger siblings, my community, and particularly other teenage mothers that anything is possible. For mothers, if it is necessary, welfare can be a stepping stone to great things in their lives.

6. Rebecca Walker Offers an Interview About "Riding the Third Wave," 2005

[*Sangamithra Iyer:*] Can you describe the Third Wave of feminism and how it addresses the shortcomings of the movements that came before, specifically with respect to race?

[*Rebecca Walker:*] Third Wave was founded in response to the idea that young people were apathetic and too busy trying to get their MBAs to be concerned with social change; that feminism, or what I would call "the movement for the eradication of discrimination based on gender difference," was dead; and the idea that men had no place in such a movement. Third Wave was also a response to critiques of the Second Wave. It was important to us (the founders) that Third Wave be, at its very core, multiracial, multi-ethnic, multi-issue, pan-sexual orientation, with people and issues from all socio-economic backgrounds represented. We built an organization with certain infrastructural mandates, so that it will never be run by people who are not of color, or who are over 30, or who are not at least somewhat cognizant of the needs of GLBT and underprivileged and underserved communities. There are many different ways to address race and racism within organizations and movements, but the key is to make sure that true diversity is at the very core. This takes some effort in terms of finding commonality and developing strategies for negotiating profound differences in outlook and belief, but those are two goals we envisioned for Third Wave. We [also] decided that social change agents (us) needed to be paid for our labor. After watching a generation burn itself out with little or no remuneration, we thought there must be a way to financially survive an attempt to change the world. Hence our original name: Third Wave Direct Action Corporation. We had the idea that we could capitalize social change work, which is really what the entire nonprofit youth movement (which didn't exist then in the way we know it now) is about. When the founders of Third Wave Foundation came together (Caterine Gund, Dawn Lundy Martin, Amy Richards, and myself) in 1996 we were also responding to the political climate of the moment and worrisome projections about the future. Our concern was that young women were not a) recipients of a large slice of the philanthropic pie (at the time something like two percent of all philanthropic dollars went toward women 15 to 30), and b) were not being cultivated to be philanthropists themselves, having no understanding of the importance of contributing resources to help others as a way of redistributing wealth.

Sangamithra Iyer, "Riding the Third Wave, The *Satya* Interview with Rebecca Walker," *Satya Magazine* (January, 2005). Reprinted with permission, www. satyamag.com.

[*S.I.:*] You describe yourself as a feminist but not a Feminist, can you elaborate on that distinction?

[*R.W.:*] This is a very important point, and one that has put me in a fairly controversial position within what is popularly called the women's movement. I felt strongly when we were founding Third Wave that the word feminist had become too divisive and culturally loaded, and that it had inherent problems in that it was a label that encouraged people who did not consider themselves feminists to make baseless assumptions about those who did, and encouraged people who did consider themselves feminists to cultivate and codify a kind of morally superior, Us vs. Them, Superwoman vs. the patriarchy kind of identity. Neither, in my opinion, seemed to serve the ultimate goals of gender equality and world peace. Because I was very invested in building a bridge between Second and Third Wave, I had no problem dropping "feminist" from our in-house lexicon and culture. It seemed clear to me that the term had more of a repellent effect than a magnetizing one within my generation, and I did not feel the need to prove my allegiance and gratitude to the women that came before me by holding on to something that had meant so very much to them, but did not mean that much to me. Of course, this position also had racial ramifications, in that many women of color do not feel an affinity with the term because, among other things, we know firsthand that people who call themselves feminists are not always our friends. They have not de facto done their work around race, the way we may not have de facto done our work around class, for example, though would become appalled if we suggested that some "feminists" were also racist. In any case, this was a struggle that I lost within the organization. Many of my colleagues, in addition to droves of Second Wavers, found this to be a capitulation to mass media's negative stereotyping of feminists. I believed it was a smart organizing tool. The goal after all was for young women and men to get involved in social change work, not to become so attached to a word that we would spend a lot of valuable energy trying to reclaim. I continue to feel strongly that the left is getting our collective ass kicked because of just this kind of romantic, naïve attachment to movement narratives and aesthetics of 20 and 30 years ago. The right moves fast, changing rhetoric at will, lying if they have to, having no allegiance to the past, doing whatever is necessary to win the battle. We, on the other hand, are still taking the "moral high ground" which is a) culturally constructed like any other moral high ground, and b) not facilitating many victories. My belief was and still is that if we could attract young people by being in confluence with rather than opposition to their resistance to the term, we could have real intergenerational continuity and thus greater impact. I mean really, do you think Christian fundamentalists are upset that George Bush is calling their Christian crusade the War on Terror instead of Contract with America or some other such? I don't think so. The key is addressing social ills with rhetoric that is effective on an intuitive as well as political level. I still do not believe that the use of the term Feminist galvanizes, unifies, or inspires at the moment. I think it did at one time and that was fantastic. But not now.

[*S.I.:*] Can you tell us a bit about your book *What Makes a Man: 22 Writers Imagine the Future?* How do you feel feminism has shaped/can shape the other gender?

[*R.W.:*] WMAM is a collection of essays about the changing face of masculinity. Most of the writers are men, all challenging traditional ideas of what it means to be a man and sharing their own more humane and psychologically integrated hopes and dreams for manhood. I decided to do the book after a discussion one night with my son. He had come home from school and told me that he wanted to play sports so that girls would like him. I was shocked and appalled. He is so bright and at the time had so many other interests. It was as if I had a daughter and she had said she was going to pretend to be dumb so that boys would like her. It occurred to me that while many of us who grew up conscious of the ways in which women and girls are forced into limiting social scripts, we were not yet, as a culture, giving boys the same kind of consideration. And while we are busy looking the other way, the culture is seducing them with a kind of hyper-violent masculinity in the form of video games, advertising, movies, sporting events and comic books. Once I began to really think about the programming slated for boys, the more I realized that our beautiful sons are being primed to go to war, to fight in battles not of their own making, on behalf of people and interests who care very little about them. I did the book so that I could hand my son something to support him on the perilous journey of becoming his own man. I never want him to equate domination, killing, and control of others with being a real man, and if he does, I don't want it to be because I was asleep on the job and didn't try to provide options. I think the women's movement has been key in making space for a book like this, and for the men who are stepping out of the shadows with their strength and vulnerability. If species survival calls for men to be whatever women need in order to ensure procreation, I think the women's movement has made it possible for us to articulate a different set of needs. Because we have laws, we no longer need the same kind of physical protection from men, and because we work, we no longer need them to provide the means for our survival. What we need now are life partners, people with whom we can share the trials and tribulations of life on a deep and profound level, with whom we can strategize and make effectual decisions on behalf of ourselves and our children. I think many men are rising to this challenge. More encouraging perhaps is that some women are letting them!

7. *Ms. Magazine* Reports on the Five Rights Women Could Lose, 2005

While many of us like to assume that our rights will always be secure, the stark reality is that many hard-won protections hang by a thread—and that thread, metaphorically, is attached to the robe of a Supreme Court justice. Here are five rights that, with an ultraconservative Supreme Court, we could stand to lose:

1. Reproductive Privacy

The constitutional right to reproductive privacy, embodied in *Griswold v. Connecticut* . . . and then expanded in *Roe v. Wade,* has withstood 30-plus years of attack. By a narrow majority, the Court has upheld this fundamental right and rebuffed numerous efforts to overturn its decisions.

National Partnership for Women and Families (2005). Reprinted with permission.

Most recently, in *Stenberg v. Carhart* (2000), the Court invalidated a state law that criminalized late-term abortion procedures, even when necessary for preserving the health of pregnant women. The state law could also have outlawed the most common abortion procedures used during second-trimester pregnancies.

With the addition of just one anti-choice justice, the Court could overturn not only this decision but *Roe v. Wade,* and even possibly *Griswold.*

2. Affirmative Action

Affirmative-action programs have been invaluable tools for expanding opportunities for women and minorities, remedying discrimination and bringing much-needed diversity to America's institutions.

In a series of 5-4 decisions, the most recent being *Grutter v. Bollinger* (2003), the Court has upheld the use of affirmative action to achieve these goals. The replacement of one justice could effectively bring affirmative-action measures to an end.

3. Protection Against Gender-Based Discrimination

Since the 1970s, the Court has made clear that we should look closely at laws treating women and men differently, or excluding women from opportunities and benefits.

In recent years, the Court has teetered between supporting and discouraging gender-based protections. In *United States v. Virginia* (1996), it struck down a males-only admissions policy that discriminated against women, but in *Nguyen v. INS* (2001), the Court reinforced gender-based stereotypes by allowing different rules for fathers and mothers when establishing citizenship for children born abroad. The change of one or two justices could resurrect and solidify the Court's acceptance of harmful gender stereotypes.

4. Family and Medical Leave

More than 50 million Americans have used the federally mandated unpaid leave granted by the Family and Medical Leave Act (FMLA) to care for a seriously ill family member or spend time with a new baby.

But a crucial 2003 case in which the Court ruled that state employees could challenge their employers for violating their right to FMLA (*Nevada Dept. of Human Resources v. Hibbs*) was decided by just a 6-3 margin. A change of two justices could undermine FMLA protections in the future.

5. Quality Health-Care Services

By a slim 5-4 margin in the 2002 case *Rush Prudential HMO Inc. v. Moran,* the Court upheld an Illinois law permitting independent review of and HMO's decision to deny a treatment it didn't consider "medically necessary."

The Court agreed that patients have the right to have an independent panel of doctors review an HMO's decision about medical necessity. Just one other dissenting opinion would cost millions of Americans a key patient protection that helps ensure good medical care.

◈ *E S S A Y S*

In the first essay, Gwendolyn Mink, of Smith College, investigates why many white middle-class feminists supported the Personal Responsibility Act of 1996. She deplores the limited understanding of those feminists who favored the new welfare legislation, noting that it denies critical freedoms to poor women and women of color. In the second essay, Barbara Epstein, of the University of California at Santa Cruz, examines how and why a feminist consciousness has spread in recent decades, despite the decline of a mass women's movement in America. She argues that the women's movement of the 1960s, 1970s, and 1980s helped women in the United States understand and critique gender equality; since that time, women's persistence in the work force and public life, and their continued experience of inequality, have made it impossible for them to dispense with a feminist consciousness. Nonetheless, in becoming separated from a mass movement, feminist consciousness may have lost its critical edge and capacity to provoke meaningful change.

Feminists and the Politics of Welfare Reform in the 1990s

GWENDOLYN MINK

When the Personal Responsibility Act of 1996 transformed welfare, it also transformed citizenship. Flouting the ideal of universal citizenship, the act distinguishes poor single mothers from other citizens and subjects them to a separate system of law. Under this system of law, poor single mothers forfeit rights the rest of us enjoy as fundamental to our citizenship—family rights, reproductive rights, and vocational liberty—just because they need welfare. The law continues to injure poor single mothers' rights even after time limits end their access to benefits, for it directs them to forsake child raising for full-time wage earning. Both while they receive benefits and after they lose them, the Personal Responsibility Act (PRA) taxes poor women who have chosen motherhood and endangers their care and custody of children.

The PRA was the most aggressive assault on women's rights in this century. Yet it provoked only scanty protest from the millions of women who call themselves feminists. In fact, during three years of concerted debate leading up to enactment of the new welfare law, most feminists actually supported many of the restrictions contemplated by both the Clinton and the Republican versions of welfare reform. In their various roles as constituents, members of movement organizations, and even elected officials, they endorsed the core principles of welfare reform: child support rules that require welfare mothers to identify and associate with biological fathers even when they do not want to and work requirements that mandate work outside the home even at the expense of children.

The PRA's child support provisions exchange poor single mothers' income support from government with income support from individual men. Forwarding its statutory purpose of "encourag[ing] the formation and maintenance of two-parent families," the provisions compel each mother to associate not just with any man, but with *the* man the government tells her to: the biological father of her children. In addition to imposing potentially unwanted associations on mothers who need welfare, mandatory sperm-based paternal family headship impairs their sexual and family privacy. Under the PRA's child support provisions, mothers must help government identify biological fathers and locate their whereabouts so that government can collect child support from them. Where a mother is married, the establishment of paternity does not involve too much: paternity is a matter of public record, because the law assumes that a mother's husband at the time of her child's birth is the father, whether or not he is biologically related to the child. Where a mother has not been married, though, it means having to tell a welfare official or a judge about her sex life. It also means that government decides who belongs to welfare mothers' families and what those families should look like.

The PRA's work requirements further injure poor mothers' rights. For one thing, they deny poor mothers' parental choices about whether and how much outside employment is compatible with the needs of children. Further, like the child support provisions, the PRA's work requirements promote mothers' economic dependence on men, not independence through their own income. Sanctioning extramarital child raising, the act provides that where there are *two* parents, one may stay at home to care for children. Where there is only *one* parent, in contrast, the act says she *must* leave her home and children to work for wages. This means that if a poor single mother can't find reliable child care, or wants to raise her own children—if she needs or wants to work *inside* the home—she would be well-advised to get married.

What the new law means by "personal responsibility," then, is not personal responsibility at all. The Personal Responsibility Act makes *government* responsible for how poor mothers lead their lives. . . . Association, vocation, privacy, and parenting are basic constitutional rights—rights that are strictly guarded for everyone except mothers who need welfare.

The Personal Responsibility Act contradicts basic feminist axioms about the conditions for women's equality. Feminists long have argued that women's equality pivots on our ability to make independent choices. Constitutionally anchored liberties protect our choices, but we often cannot make them without having the means to do so. For thirty years, welfare was the currency for poor single mothers' choices, however constrained those choices may have been. Once the Supreme Court recognized welfare as an entitlement—a guarantee—to mothers and children based on economic need, poor mothers had the means to decide to not be dependent on particular men or to not risk their own or their children's safety. For these reasons, during the late 1960s and early 1970s, some feminists hailed welfare rights as part of their agenda for women's equality.

The connections between welfare rights and women's rights were never widely appreciated, however. Hence, when the Personal Responsibility Act directly invaded poor single mothers' rights, few feminists regarded that invasion as a problem for *women*. . . . Punitive welfare reform was not accomplished by one political party or by one side of the ideological spectrum. Republicans and Democrats, conservatives and liberals, patriarchalists *and feminists* were in consensus about basic elements of reform, including measures that interfere with the decisional liberties of poor women. Moreover, many feminists agreed with welfare reformers in both parties that welfare isn't "good for" women.

Not all feminists joined the welfare reform consensus, of course. Leaders of many national women's and feminist organizations—groups ranging from the American Association for University Women to the National Organization for Women—loudly and unwaveringly opposed the Personal Responsibility Act. They called press conferences, participated in vigils, appealed to their memberships, and lobbied Congress. Some leaders—like Patricia Ireland—even engaged in dramatic acts of civil disobedience. Other nationally visible feminists—including Gloria Steinem and Betty Friedan—joined the Women's Committee of One Hundred, a feminist mobilization against punitive welfare reform that was organized by feminist scholars and activists. As the cochair of the Women's Committee of One Hundred, I know firsthand that some feminists raised their voices in defense of poor single mothers' rights, including their entitlement to welfare. But I also know that feminist voices were relatively few. . . .

Sometimes by their silence and sometimes in their deeds, many feminists actually collaborated with punitive welfare reformers. The feminists I'm talking about form the movement's mainstream. Most are middle-class and white. Many have ties to formal organizations, contributing to NARAL or to Emily's List and participating in local NOW chapters. Others march for abortion rights, work for feminist candidates, or simply vote feminist. Some have high political positions—one is a cabinet secretary, several are members of Congress. Although feminism has many iterations, these feminists often speak for all of feminism. When mobilized, they can wield impressive political clout—creating gender gaps in elections and saving abortion rights, for example. Yet when it came to welfare, for the most part they sat on their hands. Ignoring appeals from sister feminists and welfare rights activists to defend "welfare as a women's issue" and to oppose "the war against poor women" as if it were "a war against *all* women," many even entered the war on the antiwelfare/antiwoman side.

Some examples: on Capitol Hill, all white women in the U.S. Senate—including four Democratic women who call themselves feminists—voted *for* the new welfare law when it first came to the Senate floor in the summer of 1995. In the House of Representatives in 1996, twenty-six of thirty-one Democratic women, all of whom call themselves feminists, voted *for* a Democratic welfare bill that would have stripped recipients of their entitlement to welfare. Meanwhile, across the country, a NOW–Legal Defense and Education Fund appeal for contributions to support an economic justice litigator aroused so much hate mail that NOW–LDEF stopped doing direct mail on the welfare issue.

Feminist members of Congress did not write the Personal Responsibility Act, of course. Nor did members of the National Organization for Women or contributors to Emily's List compose the driving force behind the most brutal provisions of the new welfare law. My claim is not that feminists were uniquely responsible for how welfare has been reformed. My point is that they were uniquely positioned to make a difference. They have made a difference in many arenas across the years, even during inauspicious Republican presidencies. They undid damaging Supreme Court decisions, for example, by helping to win the Civil Rights Restoration Act of 1988 after the Court gutted Title IX in *Grove City College v. Bell*. They even expanded women's rights while George Bush was president: in the Civil Rights Act of 1991, they won women's right to economic and punitive damages in sex discrimination cases. So they certainly could have made a difference under a friendly Democratic president who both needs and enjoys the support of women. Indeed, such feminists as were opposed to welfare reform did make a difference initially, in concert with antipoverty groups and children's advocates: President Clinton vetoed the first Republican version of the Personal Responsibility Act in November 1995. Had greater numbers of feminists cared that welfare reform harms poor mothers, we could have pressured the president to repeat his veto when a second bill crossed his desk in August 1996.

But welfare reform did not directly bear on the lives of most feminists and did not directly implicate their rights. The new welfare law did not threaten middle-class women's reproductive choices, or their sexual privacy, or their right to raise their own children, or their occupational freedom. So middle-class feminists did not raise their voices as they would have if, say, abortion rights had been at stake. This gave the green light to feminists in Congress to treat welfare reform as if it didn't affect women. . . .

Silence among feminists was not the only problem. At the same time feminists were generally silent about the effects of new welfare provisions on poor women's rights, some were quite outspoken about the need to reform welfare so as to improve the personal and family choices poor single mothers make. When feminists did talk about welfare as a women's issue, it often seemed that they were more concerned with reconciling welfare with feminism than with defending poor single mothers' right to receive it. Feminists I've talked to in communities and feminists I've listened to in Congress often reiterated the assumptions of welfare reformers: that welfare has promoted single mothers' dependency on government rather than independence in the labor market; that it has discouraged poor women from practicing fertility control; and that it has compensated for the sexual and paternal irresponsibility of individual men. . . .

The welfare debate focused on the deficiencies of welfare mothers, rather than on the deficiencies of the welfare system. It trafficked in the tropes of "illegitimacy," and "pathology," and "dependency," and "irresponsibility," to deepen disdain toward mothers who need welfare. Feminists did not dispute the terms of the debate, although many tried to soften it. In Congress, feminists called for more generous funding for child care, for example. This would ease the effects of mothers' wage work on many poor families; but it did not contest the premise that poor single mothers should be forced to work outside the home. Hence, feminists did not fight for a policy that would enable poor mothers to make independent and honorable choices about what kind of work they will do and how many children they will have and whether they will marry. If anything, many feminists agreed with conservatives that welfare mothers do not make good choices.

Feminist reservations about welfare mothers' choices strengthened the bipartisan consensus that there's something wrong with mothers who need welfare and that cash assistance should require their reform. The two pillars of the new welfare law—work and paternal family headship—were born from this consensus. The harshness of the law's work requirements and the brutality of its sanctions against nonmarital child rearing by mothers may be Republican and patriarchal in execution. But the law's emphasis on women's labor market participation and on men's participation in families were Democratic and feminist in inspiration.

Feminists left their boldest imprint on the paternity establishment and child support provisions of the Personal Responsibility Act. For quite some time, feminists in Congress, like feminists across the country, have been emphatic about "making fathers pay" for children through increased federal involvement in the establishment and enforcement of child support orders. When Republicans presented a welfare bill without child support provisions, several feminist congresswomen embarrassed Republicans into adopting them.

The child support provisions impose stringent national conditions on nonmarital child rearing by poor women. The first condition is the mandatory establishment of paternity. Welfare law stipulates that a mother's eligibility for welfare depends on her willingness to reveal the identity of her child's father. Since the purpose of paternity establishment is to assign child support obligations to biological fathers, the second condition is that mothers who need welfare must cooperate in establishing, modifying, and enforcing the support orders for their children. The law requires states to reduce a family's welfare grant by at least 25 percent when a mother fails to comply with these rules and permits states to deny the family's grant altogether.

The "deadbeat dad" thesis—the argument that mothers are poor because fathers are derelict—is quite popular among middle-class feminists, as it is among the general public. Finding the costs of child bearing that fall disproportionately on women a wellspring of gender inequality, many feminists want men to provide for their biological children. Incautious pursuit of this objective aligned middle-class feminists behind a policy that endangers the rights of poor single mothers. . . .

When middle-class women think of the circumstances that might lead them to welfare, they think of divorce—from middle-class men who might have considerable financial resources to share with their children. . . . The compulsory features of paternity establishment and child support enforcement may be unremarkable to a divorced mother with a support order: she escapes compulsion by choosing to pursue child support, and what matters to her is that the support order be enforced. But some mothers do not have support orders because they do not want them. A mother may not want to identify her child's father because she may fear abuse for herself or her child. She may not want to seek child support because she has chosen to parent alone—or with someone else. She may know her child's father is poor and may fear exposing him to harsh penalties when he cannot pay what a court tells him he owes. She may consider his emotional support for his child to be worth more than the $100 the state might collect and that she will never see.

"Making fathers pay" may promote the economic and justice interests of many custodial mothers. But *making mothers* make fathers pay means making mothers pay for subsistence with their own rights—and safety. The issue is not whether government should assist mothers in collecting payments from fathers. Of course it should. Neither is the issue whether child support enforcement provisions in welfare policy help mothers who have or desire child support awards. Of course they do. Nor is the issue whether it is a good thing for children to have active fathers—of course it can be. The issue is coercion, coercion directed toward the mother who doesn't conform to patriarchal conventions—whether by choice or from necessity. It is also coercion directed toward the mother whose deviation from patriarchal norms has been linked to her racial and cultural standing. . . .

The mandatory maternal cooperation rule targets mothers who are not and have not been married, as well as mothers who do not have and do not want child support. Nonmarital mothers are the bull's-eye, and among nonmarital mothers receiving welfare, only 28.4 percent are white. This means that the new welfare law's invasions of associational and privacy rights will disproportionately harm mothers of color. Inspired by white feminist outrage against middle-class ex-husbands, the paternity establishment and child support provisions both reflect and entrench inequalities among women.

Feminists' general support for the claim that poor mothers need "work, not welfare" proceeded more from the internal logics of the late-twentieth-century women's movement than from specific policy goals. Feminists have long fought for women's right to work outside the home, and to do so on terms equal to men. Rather than demand honor and equity for all forms and venues of work, our bias has been toward work performed in the labor market. We've even been a little suspicious of the woman who doesn't work in the labor market—as if by working inside the home full-time she somehow undermines feminism. Often, we have demeaned her as "just a housewife."

The feminist work ethic made sense for the white and middle-class women who rekindled feminism in the 1960s. . . . Middle-class feminists understandably keyed on work outside the home as the alternative to domesticity—and therefore as the defining element of women's full and equal citizenship. . . .

Feminists of color have struggled alongside white feminists for equality in the workplace—for better pay, improved benefits, and due recognition of our merit. However, the idea that liberation hinges on work outside the home historically has divided feminists along class and race lines. Women of color and poor, white women have not usually found work outside the home to be a source of equality. To the contrary, especially for women of color, such work has been a site of oppression and a mark of inequality. Outside work has been required or expected of women of color by white society, though white society does not require or expect outside work of its own women. It also has been necessary for women of color because often their male kin cannot find jobs at living wages, if they can find jobs at all. And it has been exploitative because women of color earn disproportionately low wages. Since women of color have always worked outside their own homes—often raising other people's children—the right to care for their own children (to work inside their own homes) has been a touchstone goal of women of color struggles for equality.

For their part, white, middle-class feminists have been reluctant to make equality claims for women as family care givers. Still, they have never denied that women's family work has social value. During the early 1970s, for example, some feminists argued that the gross national product should include the value of women's work in the home. Many radical and socialist feminists challenged the sexual division of labor, illuminating connections between women's unpaid labor in the home and their gender-based inequality. Some on the feminist left drew the conclusion that "women's work" should be remunerated—that women should be paid "wages for housework." But across ideological divisions, most white, middle class feminists found the home to be the prime site of women's oppression and accordingly stressed the liberating potential of leaving it—for the labor market. . . .

Although feminism is fundamentally about winning women choices, our labor market bias has put much of feminism not on the side of vocational choice—the choice to work inside or outside the home—but on the side of wage earning for all women. In the Personal Responsibility Act, the feminist *right* to work outside the home has become poor single mothers' *obligation* to do so. . . .

To be sure, many feminists have fought ardently to attenuate the PRA's harshest provisions. For example, the NOW–Legal Defense and Education Fund has been working hard to get states to adopt the Family Violence Option, which exempts battered women from some of the most stringent welfare rules. Lucille Roybal-Allard in the U.S. House and Patty Murray in the U.S. Senate have fought hard to broaden the domestic violence exemption to include exemption from the PRA's strict time limit for welfare eligibility. Patsy Mink in the U.S. House has battled to secure vocational education funds for single mothers. At the local level, grassroots feminists and welfare rights activists have been struggling to enforce fair labor standards in welfare mothers' jobs.

If successful, all of these efforts could improve some women's fate in the new welfare system. But they do not disturb the principles behind the welfare law: they do not refute the idea that poor single mothers *should* seek work outside the home. . . . Nor has anyone paid serious attention to the racial effects of welfare principles. Although work requirements aim indiscriminately at all poor single mothers, it is mothers of color who bear their heaviest weight. African American and Latina mothers are disproportionately poor and, accordingly, are disproportionately enrolled on welfare. In 1994, adult recipients in AFDC families were almost two-thirds women of color: 37.4 percent white, 36.4 percent Black, 19.9 percent Latina, 2.9 percent Asian, and 1.3 percent Native American.

So when welfare rules indenture poor mothers as unpaid servants of local governments (in workfare programs), it is mothers of color who are disproportionately harmed. And when time limits require poor mothers to forsake their children for the labor market, it is mothers of color who are disproportionately deprived of their right to manage their family's lives, and it is children of color who are disproportionately deprived of their mothers' care.

What can we do now for poor mothers who need welfare? . . . [W]e need to defend the right to have children as a basic reproductive right; and we need to defend the right to raise one's own children as basic to family privacy as well as to associational and vocational freedom. But we also must argue further, that women's basic constitutional rights depend on a right to welfare—that a right to welfare is a condition of women's equality. . . .

We all know that care giving work—household management and parenting—takes skill, energy, time, and responsibility. We know this because people who can afford it *pay* other people to do it. Many wage earning mothers pay for child care; upper-class mothers who work outside the home pay for nannies; very wealthy mothers who don't even work outside the home pay household workers to assist them with their various tasks. Moreover, even when we are not paying surrogates to do our family care giving, we pay people to perform activities in the labor market that care givers also do in the home. We pay drivers to take us places; we pay nurses to make us feel better and help us get well; we pay psychologists to help us with our troubles; we pay teachers to explain our lessons; we pay cooks and waitresses to prepare and serve our food.

If economists can measure the value of this work when it is performed for other people's families, why can't we impute value to it when it is performed for one's own? In 1972, economists at the Chase Manhattan Bank did just that, translating family care giving work into its labor market components—nursemaid, dietitian, laundress, maintenance man, chauffeur, food buyer, cook, dishwasher, seamstress, practical nurse, gardener. The economists concluded that the value of family care givers' work was at least $13,391.56 a year (1972 dollars)—an amount well above the poverty line!

Once we establish that *all* care giving is work and that it has economic value—whatever the racial, marital, or class status of the care giver and whether or not it is performed in the labor market—we can build a case for economic arrangements that enable poor single mothers to do their jobs. In place of stingy benefits doled out begrudgingly to needy mothers, welfare would become an income owed to nonmarket, care giving workers—owed as a matter of right to anyone who bears sole responsibility for children (or for other dependent family members).

This would not require a radical restructuring of social policy, or an unprecedented departure from past practice. The survivors' insurance system—which has been around since 1939—does for widowed parents and their minor children exactly what I'm advocating for poor single mothers. Survivors' insurance is an entitlement and does not involve stigma and social control. Mothers who are eligible for survivors' insurance do not have to submit to governmental scrutiny to receive benefits and do not have to live by government's moral and cultural rules. Benefits are nationally uniform and are paid out automatically—much like social security benefits are paid out to the elderly. . . .

In my view, if widowed mothers are entitled to public benefits, poor single mothers should be, too. In fact, all family care givers are owed an income in theory, for all care giving is work. . . . A care giver's income would relieve the disproportionate burdens that fall on single mothers and in so doing would lessen inequalities among women based on class and marital status and between male and female parents based on default social roles. But although paid to single care givers only, this income support should be universally guaranteed, assuring a safety net to all care givers if ever they need or choose to parent—or to care for other family members—alone. The extension of the safety net to care givers as independent citizens would promote equality, as it would enable adults to exit untenable—often violent—relationships of economic dependency and to retain reproductive and vocational choices when they do. . . . It might even undermine the sexual division of labor, for some men will be enticed to do family care giving work once they understand it to have economic value. Offering an income to all solo care givers in a unitary system—to nonmarital mothers as well as to widowed ones—would erase invidious moral distinctions among mothers and eliminate their racial effects. Further, universal income support for single parents would restore mothers' constitutional rights—to not marry, to bear children, and to parent them, even if they are poor. It would promote occupational freedom, by rewarding work even when work cannot be exchanged for wages. So redefined, welfare would become a sign not of dependency but of independence, a means not to moral regulation but to social and political equality. . . .

Middle-class feminists were right to reject *ascribed* domesticity, and they have taught us well that fully independent and equal citizenship for women entails having the right *not* to care. So we must also win labor market reforms to make outside work feasible even for mothers who are parenting alone. Unless we make outside work affordable for solo care givers, a care givers' income would constrain choice by favoring care giving over wage earning.

The end of welfare, then, includes "making work pay," not only by remunerating care giving work but also by making participation in the labor market equitable and rewarding for women, especially mothers. Thus, for example, we need a minimum wage that provides a sustaining income—so that poor mothers can afford to work outside the home if they want to. We need comparable worth policies that correct the low economic value assigned to women's jobs. We need unemployment insurance reforms covering women's gendered reasons for losing or leaving jobs—such as pregnancy or sexual harassment. We need paid family leave so that the lowest paid workers can take time off to care for sick kids or new babies just as better paid workers do. We need guaranteed child care so that a parent's decision to work inside the home is truly a decision—not something forced on her because she can't find affordable and nurturing supervision for her children. We also need universal health care; full employment policy; a massive investment in education and vocational training; and aggressive enforcement of antidiscrimination laws.

This end to welfare will take us down many paths, in recognition of women's diverse experiences of gender and diverse prerequisites for equality.

Feminist Consciousness After the Women's Movement

BARBARA EPSTEIN

There is no longer an organized feminist movement in the United States that influences the lives and actions of millions of women and engages their political support. There are many organizations, ranging from the National Organization for Women to women's caucuses in labor unions and professional groups, which fight for women's rights, and there are many more organizations, many of them including men as well as women, whose priorities include women's issues. But the mass women's movement of the late sixties, seventies, and early eighties no longer exists. Few, among the many women who regard themselves as feminists, have anything to do with feminist organizations other than reading about them in the newspapers. Young women who are drawn to political activism do not, for the most part, join women's groups. They are much more likely to join anticorporate, antiglobalization, or social justice groups. These young women are likely to regard themselves as feminists, and in the groups that they join a feminist perspective is likely to affect the way in which issues are defined and addressed. But this is not the same thing as a mass movement of women for gender equality. A similar dynamic has taken place in other

Barbara Epstein, "Feminist Consciousness After the Women's Movement," *Monthly Review* 54, no. 4 (2002), 31–37. Copyright © 2002 by Monthly Review Press. Reprinted by permission of the Monthly Review Foundation.

circles as well. There are now very large numbers of women who identify with feminism, or, if they are reluctant to adopt that label, nevertheless expect to be treated as the equals of men. And there are large numbers of men who support this view.

The extent of feminist or protofeminist consciousness, by which I mean an awareness of the inequality of women and a determination to resist it, that now exists in the United States, is an accomplishment of the women's movement. But it is also something of an anomaly, since it is no longer linked to the movement that produced it. When the first wave of the women's movement in the United States went into decline, after woman suffrage was won in 1921, feminism went into decline with it. By the 1950s, feminism had almost entirely disappeared, not only as an organized movement, but also as an ideology and a political and social sensibility. Even in the early sixties, in the New Left, to describe oneself as a feminist was to invite raised eyebrows and probably more extreme reactions. Now, for a second time in U.S. history, the memory of a movement that engages the energy of very large numbers of women is receding into the past. But this time feminist consciousness has if anything become more widespread. This raises the question: what accounts for this difference? How and what does feminism change when it becomes a cultural current rather than a movement for social change?

In part this different history may have to do with the disparities between the first and second waves of feminism. The first wave of feminism began, in the 1840s, as a demand for women's equality generally. The women's movement emerged out of the abolitionist movement, and at first feminism was part of an egalitarian worldview, closely connected to antislavery and antiracism. But in the last decade of the nineteenth century, and to an even greater degree over the first two decades of the twentieth, mainstream feminism narrowed to the demand for woman suffrage. Leading feminists, mostly middle- and upper-middle-class, native-born white women, even made racist and anti-immigrant arguments for woman suffrage. Though the women's movement also included working-class women, many of them socialists, for whom feminism remained a part of a broader commitment to social equality, by the second decade of the twentieth century, radicalism was a minor current within the women's movement. Emma Goldman, who combined determination to resist the oppression of women with anticapitalist politics, was not typical of feminists of the first two decades of the century. For most feminists, and for the public, feminism had come to mean the vote for women and little more. Once suffrage was won, feminism lost its *raison d'etre* and so had little future either as a movement or as consciousness.

The second wave of the women's movement turned out differently. It did not narrow ideologically, nor did it run into any dead end, as its predecessor had. If anything over time the radical currents within the movement gained influence; women who had entered the movement thinking that women's equality would not require major social changes tended to become convinced that gender inequality was linked to other dimensions of inequality, especially class and race. The women's movement declined, in the eighties and nineties, mostly because the constituency on which it had been largely based, young, mostly white, middle-class women, gradually put political activity behind them. These women were beneficiaries of, what John Kenneth Galbraith has called, the "culture of contentment" of the eighties and nineties.

They benefited, along with the rest of the class, from the prosperity of the time; they also benefited from affirmative action. Even as they left political activity, few feminists thought that the aims of the women's movement had been accomplished. Many thought that they could continue to work towards these aims in the arenas, mostly professional, that they were entering. Feminist consciousness was sustained in part, no doubt, because it was widely understood that its aims had not been achieved, and because many women who left the movement remained committed to its goals.

This in itself would not have led to the widespread acceptance of feminism that has taken place over the last twenty years. In the wake of the September 11 attacks, some commentators have argued that the inequality of women in the Arab world is a sign of the deep cultural gap involved: to reject feminism is to reject modernity and the West. For instance, Laura Bush, speaking on the weekly presidential radio address, on November 17, 2001, supported the Bush administration's attack on Afghanistan on grounds of the denial of women's rights by the Taliban. In the sixties, probably even in the seventies, such an argument would have been unthinkable. Many feminists, especially radical feminists, thought that their challenge to male supremacy was also a challenge to the existing social order. Many, who regarded themselves as guardians of that social order, agreed. How has feminism become an accepted part of modern, Western society rather than an enemy of it?

The emergence of the second wave of feminism in the United States, was connected to a transformation of the economy that was drawing women into the labor force on a permanent basis. Before the Second World War few women worked outside the home after marrying and having children; most of the few who did were blacks or immigrants. The middle class set the cultural standard: marriage meant domesticity for women. Working-class people, including immigrant groups, strove to attain this idea. Even the depression of the 1930s did not put much of a dent in it; many women supported their families after their husbands lost their jobs, but often by taking work into the home. During the Second World War many women worked outside the home, but that was understood as a temporary, wartime necessity, and most women who worked in industry lost their jobs when the war ended.

The postwar United States was suddenly prosperous. The struggles of the thirties (and the fear that those struggles might continue once the war was over) helped to prompt the creation of a large welfare state bureaucracy and a wide array of social services. This brought new jobs, mostly white-collar jobs. Prosperity also led to a massive economic expansion and to the creation of many white-collar jobs in the private sector as well. Many of these jobs required some higher education. By the late fifties many women—mostly white middle-class women with some college education—were taking such jobs, partly because there were not enough men to take them, partly because many families and women needed more income, and partly because some women were tired of domesticity and wanted jobs. In the sixties, these trends accelerated. By the seventies it became clear that it was not only middle-class but also working-class women who were in the labor force for good. Meanwhile, during the fifties and sixties, higher education had expanded dramatically, and women, mostly white middle-class women, had begun attending colleges and universities in large numbers. College and university degrees gave expanding numbers of young women the credentials they needed in order to get the jobs that were becoming available. Colleges and universities also provided the arenas that young women needed to form bonds with each other, to develop a new female consciousness and a feminist movement. The movements of the sixties, despite their problems of sexism, provided a supportive environment for the development of a radical women's consciousness and a movement that demanded women's equality and linked it to demands for class and racial equality. Women civil rights activists, prompted by the parallel between the oppression of blacks and that of women, were the first to develop a feminist perspective. The antiwar movement on northern campuses provided a supportive environment for the growth of a large and radical feminist movement.

The women's movement thus emerged in the contradiction between an economy that not only invited but required the participation of women, and a culture that continued to define femininity in terms of passivity and subservience to men. This contradiction still exists. Feminism quickly became a mass movement because young women needed a new set of values, and each other's support, in making the transition between the domestic world that most of their mothers had inhabited and the world of work that they were entering. The demand for women's labor, and the strength of the radical movements of the time, also gave young women the leverage to challenge the culture and structures of gender inequality, and to confront the men who expected women to abide by these rules. Other than the antiwar movement, the women's movement was, by the early seventies, the largest of the radical movements of the time. It was certainly the most lasting of the movements of the sixties, expanding and becoming stronger through the seventies. The size and strength of the women's movement had to do with the fact that it was challenging a dying institution, the patriarchal nuclear family, revolving around women's domesticity.

Despite the media's portrayal of the family, in the fifties, as utterly stable, in fact divorce rates were already rising. With or without the women's movement, women would have moved into the labor force in huge numbers over the following decades, further destabilizing the form of family life anchored by women's domesticity. But neither the destabilization of the traditional nuclear family nor the massive entry of women into the labor force guaranteed any overall improvement in women's status. Rising divorce rates meant, among other things, a loss of security for women. The ability to work, to hold a job, does not guarantee equality or even, necessarily, hold out the promise of it. The women's movement took the opportunity presented by women's entry into the labor force to demand better terms for women, in the workplace, the public arena, and the family.

For women, working for wages outside the home has become the norm. This, in combination with feminist pressure for greater gender equality on all levels of society, has transformed the lives of U.S. women as well as the very structure of U.S. society. The feminist goal of gender equality has not been achieved; not only do women still earn less than men, but in the ranks of the poor, single women and their children have come to predominate. The prejudices that discourage women from entering traditionally male fields remain and violence against women persists. Though the nuclear family of the forties and fifties was based on male supremacy, the increasing instability of family life has hardly been a blessing for women. But women's equality has become a publicly accepted principle. Glaring deviations from this principle are open to challenge, and very large numbers of women are ready to make such challenges when necessary. This in itself is an enormous and transforming advance.

So, over the last two decades feminist consciousness has spread even as the organized women's movement has contracted. This is partly because of the increasing numbers of women in the labor force, and in other areas of public life, who, in talking to each other and giving each other support, spread and redefined feminism, even if they do not call themselves feminists or use the word. It was possible for the first wave of feminism to disappear because the women's movement that it was associated with had come to an end without the majority of American women having gained access to arenas outside the home. The fact that women are now in the labor force and the public arena to stay makes it hard to imagine that feminism and what it stands for could disappear again. This is a measure of progress. Probably feminism will continue to be a major political current in the United States, though perhaps not based in any movement, and in that sense a cultural as well as a political phenomenon.

One danger posed by the attenuating connection between feminist consciousness and the movement from which it emerged is that feminist consciousness is losing its radical edge. This has happened to some degree: in the professions, feminism has tended to absorb the obsession with individual success that prevails in that arena. A large, actively engaged movement does not necessarily prevent such developments; first wave feminism, in its suffragist phase, absorbed the perspective of the upper-middle class of that time. But a movement can make it possible for movement activists to look critically at their own class, and develop an independent perspective. This is what happened in the sixties and early seventies, making radical feminism, and radicalisms of other varieties, possible.

It does not seem likely that another mass women's movement will emerge any time soon. But feminism is being given new vitality by its association with the range of activist groups that make up the antiglobalization and anticorporate movements. Young women in these movements are very likely to describe themselves as feminists; feminism is accepted as one of the ideological currents that shape these movements, along with anarchism, environmentalism, and the struggle against white supremacy. Inside these groups, women tend to take for granted the equality that women of the movements of the sixties and seventies fought for. If the labor movement makes headway in its effort to organize the unorganized, feminism will inevitably become part of the culture that develops within it, because so many of the unorganized are women. Such movement-based versions of feminism could introduce radicalism into wider feminist discussions.

Over the last two decades other movements have followed the same trajectory as the women's movement. The environmental movement is a clear case: once consisting of large numbers of people engaged in political activity, it now consists on the one hand of a series of staff-driven organizations, and on the other, of a large sector of people who consider themselves environmentalist, or who have an environmental consciousness, but who take action on environmental issues largely in individual ways, such as in their shopping habits and in recycling. A similar argument could be made about the African-American movement, whose organizations have shriveled while militant forms of racial and ethnic consciousness have expanded, at least culturally, among young people. To some degree this expansion of various forms of consciousness going way beyond the borders of the movements in which they first emerged shows the lasting influence of those movements. But it also has to do with what appears to be the decline of political and protest movements, and the difficulty of finding compelling forms of political engagement. The tendency of the political to collapse into the cultural, even as it connotes a measure of triumph, weakens the left.

◈ *F U R T H E R   R E A D I N G*

Ahmed, Leila. *A Border Passage: From Cairo to America—A Woman's Journey* (2000).

Bendroth, Margaret Lamberts. "Fundamentalism and the Family," *Journal of Women's History* 10 (1999): 35–54.

Buhle, Mary Jo. *Feminism and its Discontents* (1998).

Chun, Gloria Heyung. *Of Orphans and Warriors: Inventing Chinese American Culture and Identity* (2000).

Criag, Maxine Leeds. *Ain't I a Beauty Queen? Black Women, Beauty, and the Politics of Race* (2003).

D'Amico, Francine, and Laurie Weinstein, eds. *Gender Camouflage: Women and the U.S. Military* (1999).

Enloe, Cynthia. *Maneuvers: The International Politics of Miltarizing Women's Lives* (2000).

Evans, Sara M. *Tidal Wave: How Women Changed America at Century's End* (2003).

Faludi, Susan. *Backlash: The Undeclared War Against American Women* (1992).

Garcia, Alma M. *Chicana Feminist Thought: The Basic Historical Writings* (1997).

Hoff, Joan. *Law, Gender, and Injustice: A Legal History of U.S. Women* (1991).

Hull, N. E. H., and Peter Charles Hoffer. *Roe v. Wade: The Abortion Rights Controversy in American History* (2001).

Kenny, Lorraine Delia. *Daughters of Suburbia: Growing Up White, Middle Class, and Female* (2000).

Leidholdt, Dorchen, and Janice G. Raymond, eds. *The Sexual Liberals and the Attack on Feminism* (1990).

Lerner, Barron H. *The Breast Cancer Wars: Hope, Fear, and the Pursuit of a Cure in Twentieth-Century America* (2001).

Maciel, David R., and Isidro D. Ortiz, eds. *Chicanas/Chicanos at the Crossroads: Social, Economic, and Political Change* (1996).

Mezey, Susan Gluck. *In Pursuit of Equality: Women, Policy, and the Federal Courts* (1992).

Mink, Gwendolyn. *Hostile Environment: The Political Betrayal of Sexually Harassed Women* (2000).

———. *Welfare's End* (1998).

Rodriguez, Felix V. Matos, and Linda C. Delgado, eds. *Puerto Rican Women's History: New Perspectives* (1998).

Rosenberg, Harriet G. "From Trash to Treasure: Housewife Activists and the Environmental Justice Movement," in Jane Schneider and Rayna Rapp, eds. *Articulating Hidden Histories: Exploring the Influence of Eric R. Wolf* (1995).

Rosenberg, Rosalind. *Divided Lives: American Women in the 20th Century* (1992).

Ruiz, Vicki L. *From Out of the Shadows: Mexican Women in Twentieth-Century America* (1998).

Shakir, Evelyn. *Bint Arab: Arab and Arab American Women in the United States* (1997).

Schneider, Elizabeth M. *Battered Women and Feminist Lawmaking* (2000).

Shalit, Wendy. *A Return to Modesty: Discovering the Lost Virtue* (2000).

Sidel, Ruth. *Women and Children Last: The Plight of Poor Women in Affluent America* (1986).

Silverberg, Helene. "State Building, Health Policy, and the Persistence of the Abortion Debate," *Journal of Policy History* 9 (1997).

Smith, Barbara. *Home Girls: A Black Feminist Anthology* (1983, 2000).

Smith, Barbara Ellen. "Crossing the Great Divides: Race, Class, and Gender in Southern Women's Organizing, 1979–1992," *Gender and Society* 9 (1995).

Smith, Jane I. *Islam in America* (1999).

Solinger, Rickie. *Beggars and Choosers: How the Politics of Choice Shapes Adoption, Abortion, and Welfare in the United States* (2001).

Tuan, Mia. *Forever Foreigners or Honorary Whites?: The Asian Ethnic Experience Today* (1998).

Vogel, Lise. *Mothers on the Job* (1993).